MW01050426

SALTWATER FOODWAYS

SALTWATER FOODWAYS

New Englanders and their food, at sea and ashore, in the nineteenth century

Sandra L. Oliver

MYSTIC SEAPORT MUSEUM, INC.
Mystic, Connecticut

This book is printed in China
ISBN 0-913372-72-2

Designed by Trish Sinsigalli LaPointe, Old Mystic, Connecticut
Layout Production by Joel Bergeron
First Edition
Color photographs by Mary Anne Stets, Mystic Seaport Museum
Color photographs on pages 51, 69, 212, 219, 280, 292, 297, 310, 313, 316, 318
by Jamie MacMillan, Isleboro, Maine

Other images: pages x and 23: The Society for the Preservation of New England Antiquities; 2: Sandra L. Oliver; 7: The Connecticut Historical Society; 11: MSM 94-6-52; 18: The Spectre Collection; 37: MSM 92-9-5; 38: MSM 92.18; 39: MSM 81.98.12; 64: MSM 94-4-5; 16, 63, 68, 154, 238, 243, 320: The Spectre Agricultural Collection; 237: The Connecticut State Library—photo by Mary Anne Stets; 93: MSM 93-11-37; 130: MSM 94-3-13; 258 and 263; The Yuletide Archive; 284 and 288: The Spectre Collection; 287: courtesy of William H. Ewen; 309: MSM 85-115; 365: MSM 85-10-29; 371: MSM 81.98.14; 383: MSM 85.111; 387: New Haven County Historical Society; 388: MSM 80.107.16

Cataloging-in-publication data:

Oliver, Sandra Louise, 1947—
Saltwater foodways

Bibliography: p.
Includes indexes.

1. Cooking, American - History - 19th century.
2. Cookery, American - New England. 3. Dinners and dining - New England - History - 19th century. 4. New England - Social life and customs - 19th century.
5. Seafaring life - 19th century. 6. Mystic Seaport Museum.
TX645.O54

MYSTIC SEAPORT MUSEUM
75 Greenmanville Avenue
Mystic, Connecticut 06355

Dedicated to my father
Charles M. Oliver

XXX
ALE

SALTWATER FOODWAYS

Acknowledgements	VIII
Introduction	X
CHAPTER I The Buckinghams: Saltwater Farming	4
CHAPTER II The Greenmans: Prosperity and Plenty	30
CHAPTER III The Burrows Household: Risk and Uncertainty	60
CHAPTER IV Eating Forward and Dining Aft	82
CHAPTER V Fishermen's Fare	122
CHAPTER VI The Life-Saving Service: Messroom Meals	148
CHAPTER VII Fresh and Exotic Provisions	166
CHAPTER VIII Meals Ashore for All Hands	190
CHAPTER IX Fourth of July: America's Day of Days	212
CHAPTER X Thanksgiving: New England's Premier Holiday	234
CHAPTER XI Christmas at Sea and Ashore	254
CHAPTER XII Clambakes and Shore Dinners	280
CHAPTER XIII Chowder and Chowder Parties	292
CHAPTER XIV And Refreshments Were Served	310
CHAPTER XV Not as Nutritious as Flesh: Fish-Eating in New England	330
CHAPTER XVI Cooking and Eating Seafood	362
Notes	402
Bibliography	422
Cook's Index	430
General Index	434

Acknowledgements

Everyone knows by now that authors, despite appearances, do not work alone, especially on a book like this—one that has been in the works for a long time. I am no exception. Over the years, I have accumulated a very long list of helpful friends and colleagues.

Most authors thank their editor even though I hear a fair amount of grumbling about what the editor has done. So one might think that two editors is twice as much aggravation. But my experience with Andy German and Joe Gribbins has been extraordinary—actually a lot of fun for me. Two more calm, supportive, and intelligent people could not be found.

Considerable extra appreciation is due Andy. Ever since then-Director of Publications Gerry Morris said that he thought Mystic Seaport Museum would be interested in a book like this, roughly 1985, it was Andy who consistently affirmed the Seaport's desire to have me finish the project. And it was Andy who finessed the material support that made it possible for me to dedicate my time to the book for the past and final year. Plus it was Andy who kept me from foundering too badly with anything to do with the fisheries, an area of New England's history he knows thoroughly.

Joe has done a tremendous amount to make this book look gorgeous. He threw open the door for the color photography and artful design. I certainly never conceived of anything like this when I began; that has been Joe's vision.

Certain people deserve particular thanks for their roles in helping me think about food, history, and food in history. They are, in alphabetical order: Dr. Joanne Bowen, L. Maria Child, Andy German, Rabbit Goody, Glenn Gordinier, Karen Hess, Dr. William Koelsch at Clark University, Paula Marcoux, and Barbara Ketcham Wheaton. Joanne and Rabbit have helped me speak food history with an anthropological accent. Andy's early discussion of the role of filletting in popularizing fish-eating first revealed to me the whole range of "problems" with fish which enabled me to view past and present fish-eating differently.

Because this is a cookbook, too, I owe a deal of thanks to anyone who lifted spoon or pan to try a recipe. And there were many—practically anyone in my acquaintaince for the past fifteen years and far too many to list them all here, although I think of them with gratitude. There were some who did more testing than most others and they deserve particular thanks: Juanita Chester, Baily Crichton, and Ruth Stetson.

Librarians always astound me. I have been so lucky to have in my corner some really wonderful ones. At Mystic Seaport Museum, a succession of librarians have dug, shuffled, strained themselves on my behalf. Pam McNulty and Paul O'Pecko, research librarians; curator of manuscripts Doug Stein and a succession of his marvelous assistants: Lydia Frank, Dottie Thomas, and Leah Prescott, who have even made and maintained a subject heading "Food at Sea!" No researcher could ask for more (except for stack privileges, for which I owe thanks to the G.W. Blunt White Library at the Seaport). Paula Pintaro at North Stonington Public Library acquired many, many books on inter-library loan for me in the early stages of this project. Paige Lilly at Penobscot Marine Museum, Searsport, Maine, and Ellen Nelson at Cape Ann Historical Association in Gloucester, Massachusetts, have both helped me very much. The exceptional collection in the Schlesinger Library at Radcliffe, Cambridge, Massachusetts, and Barbara Wheaton and Patricia Kelly's extraordinary bibliography, have helped me answer countless food questions. Very early—more than twenty years ago—the Research Library and librarian at Old Sturbridge Village, Sturbridge, Massachusetts, got me off to a terrific start in culinary history, with access to manuscript materials and their generosity with inter-library loans of many early imprints.

The Curatorial Department at the Seaport, especially the Registrar's Office, has been very kind to me, answering all kinds of questions over the years: Francis Bowker, Phil Budlong, Jennifer Johnson, Marifrances Trivelli, and Rodi York. Most recently, the Registrar's Office folks have found photographs and artwork in the collection to bring my words to life and to enhance these pages.

Other folks have been generous with their research material and perspectives: Mystic Seaport Museum curator Bill Peterson knows *so* much about southeastern Connecticut, and he has patiently answered my questions for years and read much of this manuscript. Virginia Coope shared her work on Charles W. Morgan; Beverly Gregg, who has a real instinct for revealing details, is responsible for most of the Mystic *Press* and *Pioneer* quotes. Richard Boonisar, Robert Downey, and Wick York shared information on the Life-Saving Service; Nancy d'Estang, historian for the Shipyard at Mystic Seaport, provided details on the museum's vessels; Nancy Piianaia shared her knowledge of food in foreign ports; Mary Hughes helped with the house and holiday chapters and ship launchings; Sarah Ostlund shared a great deal on the fisheries; Holly Malloy and Donna Bellantone contributed to the house chapters; and Glenn Gordinier on historic food vending. Mystic Seaport Museum's Interpretation Division, of which I used to be part, has always been an enthusiastic supporter of this project. Florence Button, Frances Jaixen Dodge, Fred and Katie Hermes, Virginia Leavitt, and Marjorie Vignot have all been generous with their personal recollections. I have been incredibly lucky to know such people.

Anna North Coit, besides being a beloved friend, has been a valuable link to the past via her own considerable knowledge of local history, and particularly her extensive family archive. Her wonderful, wry sense of humor and her own clear writing style have been an inspiration to me.

Ginny Hall wrestled a heap of inventories to the ground for me and read pieces of the manuscript. Sharon Daley, Joanne Bowen, and Paula Marcoux all made time in their busy lives to read and criticize various chapters.

Doing the food photography was a totally new undertaking for me and I had some wonderful help with it. First, gratitude to my husband, Jamie MacMillan, and to Mary Anne Stets, star photographer at Mystic Seaport, who took the pictures, for their professionalism and patience with all my food twinking.

On Islesboro, the island in Maine I call home, thanks to my patient helpers Bonnie Bacon, Ruth Hatch, John Phelan and stepdaughter, Sara Giles, who cooked and/or carried food from kitchen to field. When Jamie put his camera down, it must be said he washed many, many dishes. Thanks to Lynn and Ginny Hall, William Warren and Jean Anderson, and the Society for the Preservation of the Free Will Baptist Church who let us use their beaches and yards.

In Mystic many thanks to the Photo Lab crew, particularly Judy Beisler, Mary Anne's steady assistant, and to Sarah Ostlund and Linda Pryor who tirelessly cooked, washed dishes, and carted stuff around. Thanks to Jane Keener, Robert and Ruth Stetson, and the Gordiniers, Pam and Glenn, who gave me places to stay and let me make messes in their kitchens. Special thanks to Dr. Jim Carlton who let me turn his Kemble Basement office and lab at Mystic Seaport into a working kitchen for three weeks while we took pictures on the museum grounds. Anna North Coit allowed us to use Pachunganuc Farm, North Stonington, and its extraordinary collection of ceramics and flatware, as a site for many of the photos. Anna also advised me on period table arrangement and appropriate use of the dishes. Joel Bergeron of Ironwood Antiques in Mystic loaned a good many objects for us to use, too. Many thanks to all.

Certain people deserve thanks for deep and distant—in time—support for this work. Michael Sturgis and Jane Keener gave me the chance to work with historical food; Percy and Behri Knauth, and Tom Aageson, encouraged my fledgling efforts at a cookbook; Gerald Morris encouraged what became the larger and the latter effort. My parents, Charles and Louise Oliver, fostered an early interest in history by taking my sister and me to museums—including, when I was eight, Mystic Seaport. Plus, my mother gave me the idea that writing was a good way of life, and my father encouraged me to be myself.

Some very dear friends went out of their way to help me with "life" while "the book" was in progress. Special blessings on Jean Anderson, who did laundry for three of my more horrendous weeks; on Nancy Wuori, who picked strawberries for the freezer; on Maggy Aston, who kept *Food History News* afloat; on Ruthie Hatch, who did fall cleaning; on Jamie, a good cook in his own right, and a cook who, for the past five months especially, has developed a much more personal relationship with a dishpan and vacuum cleaner than he may have *ever* wanted.

Introduction

"But I believe that if there is nothing in one's circumstances to make one peculiarly happy or unhappy, his state will depend on so material & vulgar a thing as his stomach."

Richard Henry Dana, well-known to maritime cognoscenti for his *Two Years Before the Mast,* wrote those words in his journal as a mature traveler at sea aboard the bark *Early Bird* between San Francisco and China in 1860, some thirty years after his adventures in the fo'c'sles of the *Pilgrim* and *Alert.* Although he was considering the state of so vulgar as thing as his stomach at sea, he could easily have written the words ashore as well.

All human beings consider their stomachs at least daily—in our culture thrice daily. Religion, politics, philosophy, economics, war, peace, art, science—all acknowledge the power of the stomach. All human endeavor depends on a supply of sufficiently nourishing food to sustain life. In spite of this, the study of the history of food has seldom been more than a footnote to the rest of history. In the twenty or so years that some form of this book has been in progress, that has changed.

How This Book Came to Be Written

My interest in food history began in 1971 when I was given the job of developing a fireplace-cooking demonstration at Mystic Seaport Museum's Buckingham House. At that time food history was fairly amorphous. Other living history museums were demonstrating fireplace cookery. A handful of books had been written by historians about the history of food in America—but most were very general in their scope and largely descriptive. An even smaller handful of historic cookery books had been reprinted. Besides that, the topic was considered so unimportant that I, a college drop-out in 1971 and former English major, could be asked to develop interpretive materials, select utensils and train fellow interpreters in the art and history of fireplace cooking for a major American outdoor history museum! As it was I could barely cook: a child of the twentieth century, I had only passing knowledge of cookery from scratch—a few experiences with bread-making, some blue ribbons won at 4-H fairs for gingerbread and brownies—that was about it. I did not know enough to disqualify myself; and besides I, a clerk typist in the museum's subterranean Photo Lab, was so grateful to be let out into the sunshine of the museum grounds, and to be in contact with visitors and members, that once offered the chance I never looked back.

It was a lucky move for me. I fell in love with food history. Fortunately, having no direction to do otherwise, I turned to every possible source for information. I learned hands-on fireplace cookery at Old Sturbridge Village. I read anthropology, folklore, agricultural studies, literature, historical geography, music, and the new social history: all grist for the mill. I read cookbooks, diaries, newspapers, seafarers' journals: I didn't care what the source was—food was everywhere—usually not indexed, either. Part way through the process I left the Buckingham House kitchen long enough to go back to college at Clark University to get a degree in History, where I learned that the approach I had unknowingly used all along had a name: interdisciplinary studies. After graduation in 1977, I was back at the museum and held a succession of jobs in the Interpretation Division, some of which took me away from food history.

Still the topic never left my mind. I continued to collect references and train the new Buckingham-House cooks. Gradually, elsewhere, other people were beginning to work in food history, too, and some really wonderful and scholarly books were published by culinary historians, social historians, and students of material culture. Historical archaeologists, anthropologists, and nutritionists published work that shed light on food and eating in past times. Period cookbooks and annotated versions of facsimilie reprints were increasingly available. All kinds of stuff I would have died for in the early 1970s was finally appearing.

I left Mystic Seaport Museum in 1985 after sixteen years, intending to write and work in food history. Ever since the Buckingham House demonstration began, there was tremendous interest, naturally, in a cookbook, one of which I actually had begun, focusing on fireplace cookery techniques and incorporating the recipes we used in the demonstration. This project, one which had the patient assistance of everyone I knew for testing recipes, was the one generally known as "Sandy's cookbook." That cookbook was pushed to the back burner (actually, right off the top of the stove) when I took on the responsibilities of Supervisor of Interpretation in 1978. Suddenly with eighty to one hundred employees to keep track of I had no time or energy in my spare time to finish it.

In 1985 after leaving the museum staff, I rethought the whole project, this time conceiving of a cookbook that integrated as many of Mystic Seaport Museum's exhibits as possible under the heading of food history. After all, wherever human beings lived or worked or played, they ate food, and the museum was full of such places. Add to that the small-craft fleet, much of which was built to gather food from the sea, and you have a very broad table on which to spread the story of New England foodways at sea and ashore in the nineteenth century.

But by that time more than a cookbook seemed appropriate. More was—and is—expected of food historians and rightly so. Food history is social history. We can learn much about human behavior and choices from a study of food. My job was to write a collection of historical essays illustrated with period recipes. I hoped then, and do now, that this book will travel between the livingroom and the kitchen. I hope people who do not care to cook will find fascinating the ideas, attitudes, likes, dislikes and customs about food in past times. I hope people who like to cook will want to try the recipes for a taste of history in their own homes.

Thinking About Food History

This book was written for and about Mystic Seaport Museum and its exhibits. Despite the focus on the museum's vessels and buildings, I have made every effort to take the reader beyond the museum's story to that of a region, essentially southern New England, and occasionally to the nation as well. But beyond the information about the place where this food history was enacted, I am also offering ideas about how to think about food and human activity: the role that food plays in human interactions; how it reveals distinctions among classes and between genders; how it is used as a symbol of identity or celebration; how it responds to technological or social change; how it changes over time, as New England's foodways changed in the nineteenth century.

Part of a publication program's responsibility is to bring to the public the parts of the collection they never see on exhibit: the words and images filed away in the library and archives. In the spirit of that purpose, I used almost exclusively the manuscript collection at Mystic Seaport Museum's G. W. Blunt White Library even though there are fine collections elsewhere of seafarers' journals, narratives, and papers and letters of coastal people ashore. I think the cast of characters represented by the museum's collection is sufficiently typical and varied to represent their time and region.

About This Word "Foodways"

The word "foodways" makes some people's skin crawl. But a better term to describe the study of food in history and culture—the wide-ranging, interdisciplinary study of food—hasn't been developed yet. Culinary history describes the development of cuisine. Food history leaves out folklore and anthropology. Historical gastronomy has elitist tones.

The term foodways seems to encompass all the approaches that are needed to complete the picture of food in the past. Until there is a better word, that's the one we'll use.

Continuing My Education

A respected colleague and friend tells me that to write and publish a book is to continue your education in the public view, a thoroughly daunting prospect. Nevertheless, I offer this book to you in all sincerity, expecting that I shall make my share of mistakes where you all can see them. I hope this opens an exchange—a conversation—with you.

I have tried to reveal my sources as I went along, to show my evidence and the influences on my thinking. I imagine it is a common experience among historians and others that one's interpretation of the past constantly shifts around, adjusting to each new piece of information. The very act of writing changes one's perspective of a topic as it did mine in the course of writing this. Another few years from now, no doubt I will heartily disagree with myself on some points.

I learned a great deal from my visitors in the Buckingham House where sharing what I knew constantly enriched and challenged me as visitors told me about their lives, memories of food, and all the many other things they knew. I expect this will be a similar experience, and invite you to participate.

Using the Recipes in this Book

How the recipes were chosen: The recipes in this book were selected primarily because they are good examples of their type; by good, I mean as clear and as typical as I could find. I have chosen them to illustrate the text, so that when you read a diary or journal entry and the historic person reports that they ate a certain thing, I wanted you to be able to read a recipe for that thing, and even make it yourself. There are obviously some twentieth-century influences on my choices. I have not included things which I have learned by trial and error on friends and acquaintances that modern people dislike. If you are curious about those dishes, there is a culinary bibliography at the back and you may find there some dishes that intrigue you.

In the interest of typicality, I did not pick only the most delicious recipes. However, many of these dishes are very delicious indeed, and have supplanted modern ones in my personal repertoire. Nor were they selected for how well they matched up with modern nutritional considerations. As you will read in the text, the nineteenth-century metabolism was different from the one that most of us know in the late twentieth century, and people tolerated larger quantities of butter, salt pork, and eggs. If you substitute other ingredients for these, please understand that you won't get the right taste of the past. You might make something just as good, but it will be different from the historic dish. I really do believe you could try, at least once, a salt-pork-laden dish and not drop dead in your tracks tomorrow. If you really want to know what food was like in the 1800s, do try the recipes as written.

What I mean by "an interpretation follows:" I feel very strongly that the original recipe should be presented as it was written in its source, and each of these is given that way. But I understand that many modern cooks feel uncomfortable with nineteenth-century terminology. I have interpreted the recipes as directly as I could into familiar modern cookery terms, and in the recipe sections of the book this process is indicated by the phrase, "an interpretation follows." I have tried not to alter the recipes from the original in order to make them more suitable to the modern palate. I have suggested ways which you, in the freedom of your kitchen, can make something taste more familiar or modern, which I in the interest of historical accuracy would not do. *But* those suggestions are not usually incorporated into the recipe.

Not for beginners: Most of the recipes assume that you have some familiarity with cooking. If you don't, take heart. I was pretty much of a novice when I started to do historic cooking, and I learned a great deal by trial and error. No great harm is done by just giving it a try. Just loosen up your expectations a little. Experienced cooks have a lot to gain by letting go, if they haven't already, the idea of absolute precision on every little thing.

New England cuisine: Over and over when I cook these things for my friends and family, I am struck by how delighted people are with these simple foods. In the tradition of foods that taste of themselves, it is startling sometimes to discover how a mere handful of ingredients simply prepared can be so very, very good.

It seems to be the trendy thing to disdain the Anglo-American tradition as being awful. This is a judgment on the past I am not willing to level because I believe that people historically made choices based on their values and priorities, just as we do today. Viewing their choices without prejudice helps us to understand them, and gives us a new perspective on *our* choices.

Sandra L. Oliver
Isleboro, Maine
May 25, 1994

SALTWATER FOODWAYS

New England Foodways at Sea and Ashore

Between 1800 and the 1930s, coastal New Englanders lived their daily lives, including three meals a day, in six of Mystic Seaport Museum's exhibits. Three of these domestic settings—the Buckingham, Greenman, and Burrows houses—look exactly as we expect homes to look. Three others, the working vessels *Charles W. Morgan* and *L.A. Dunton*, and the New Shoreham Life-Saving Station, don't look very homey. Nevertheless, these places devoted to other pursuits were home to hard-working men—and, at least occasionally on the *Morgan*, women and children—often for extended periods of time.

When "at home" people do what they must to sustain themselves physically for the vocations and avocations that most of history is written about—farming, fishing, commerce, art, literature, politics, religion, invention. The sleeping, eating, procreating, child-rearing, housekeeping, and health maintenance which make possible all the other endeavors have been much neglected by historians until fairly recently. Unlike the public evidence of lives and livelihoods, these private activities are tremendously under-documented, especially those of ordinary people like the Buckinghams and Burrowses, and of the hundreds of men who lived aboard the *Morgan*, the *Dunton*, and in the life-saving station. It is far easier to learn the domestic arrangements of Presidents and Kings than of farmers and tradesmen, but it is not impossible to discover the everyday habits of everyday people.

The next six chapters describe the foods and foodways of the people who lived in each of the six "homes" restored and interpreted at the Seaport. The first three descriptions—of the

Buckinghams, Greenmans, and Burrowses and their peers—form a base line on which we can build our understanding of what happened when people like them went to sea, visited in foreign places, and celebrated holidays and special occasions. At the same time, we will see how certain habits and food preferences changed or stayed the same over time in coastal New England.

In these descriptions you will see that kitchen arrangements and furnishings, cooking equipment, water and food supplies, dining-room furnishings, and who cooked the food and who sat down to eat it, all determined what and how various foods were selected and served. Some foods were more important than others, symbolizing sometimes much more than sustenance, and you will hear about them. Some foods are important to us today that weren't important in the nineteenth century, and you will learn how they were regarded in past times.

The Buckinghams begin the century for us, living their later years in the kind of home that the Greenman brothers and Wint Burrows grew up in. We will see how life was lived before the many refinements of the later 1800s, a kind of life that seems even more remote to twentieth-century people than the lives of late-Victorian New Englanders.

The Greenmans, reaping the profits of shipyard and factory, did not live as grandly as some in their class, but their life gives us a glimpse of prosperity and gentility in contrast to the marginal and scapegrace life lived by Wint Burrows and his family.

The *Charles W. Morgan* discussion shows us how aboard virtually any ship in the nineteenth century there were two distinct foodways—one for the fo'c'sle crew and another for the cabin. Shipboard food reflected and reinforced ship's discipline and hierarchy. By contrast, the fishing fleet's highly democratic and generous foodways, exemplified by the *L. A. Dunton*, underlines how much the divided foodways of the deepwater vessels were a matter of choice, not circumstance or technology.

Occasionally fishermen came ashore to work, and some turned to the Life-Saving Service where, at least at first, they were supposed to do their own cooking. How the life-saving crew did their grocery shopping and resolved cooking duties within the confines of governmental regulation and their own social expectations clarifies our view of gender roles in the last quarter of the 1800s.

The Buckinghams: Saltwater Farming

Born in 1747, Lydia Watrous Buckingham learned cooking and other women's work as soon as she was old enough to observe her mother in the kitchen. She formed her habits and tastes during the 1750s and 1760s. She married Samuel Buckingham in 1768, and for the next forty-seven years of married life, if she was a typical eighteenth-century woman, she spent her time raising her five children, cooking, cleaning, sewing, mending, gardening, taking care of the cows and poultry, and observing life in the Ferry District of Saybrook (now Old Saybrook), Connecticut, during the American Revolution and the early years of the republic.

Above is the Buckingham House at Mystic Seaport, a center-chimney I-house with an attached ell. At left, a New England boiled dinner—the corned-beef version—with potatoes, cabbage, and beans boiled with the meat, the beans having been tied up in a cloth and sunk in the pot during cooking. [MSM 82-10-2118]

Lydia's home is the oldest dwelling on exhibit at Mystic Seaport Museum, and it describes a way of life from which we can observe the changes that occurred in nineteenth-century southern New England—including people's eating habits. The house was built in the middle of the 1700s, and its ell—moved and added to it—dates to the end of the 1600s. The period of time the Seaport's restoration of the house represents, roughly the 1830s, is familiar to students of American history as a time of transition that followed the colonial period and began the many changes that make the middle and late nineteenth century seem more similar to our time than the decades before the 1830s or the previous century.

Lydia Buckingham saw many changes in her years, but over the course of her life she experienced less transition in many important aspects of day-to-day living than did Charlotte Greenman, born in 1820, whose home we will visit in the next chapter. Lydia's girlhood corresponded with gradually developing Yankee foodways that were distinct from traditional English cookery. New England's gentry and people in some of the southern colonies continued the old ways longer, but rural families, coastwise and inland, were settling on the dishes we think of today as typically New England. Cooking habits are part of an evolution, and Lydia Buckingham participated in the process.

Her kitchen, old-fashioned at the time her husband Samuel died in 1815, was much like the one she learned to cook in. At sixty-eight then, she was probably set in her ways, and Samuel's probate inventory tells us that the house furnishings, at least those recorded, were conservative. The unmarried Buckingham daughter, Mehetebel, who was in her early forties when her father died, lived with Lydia; perhaps the younger woman added a few newer tools and procedures to housekeeping before and after Samuel's death.

The Buckinghams and Saybrook in the Early Nineteenth Century

The family that lived in this house were descendents of one of the town's earliest settlers and of one of the Puritan founders of the school that became Yale University. Samuel, born in 1740, was in the fifth generation, not quite as distinguished in life as some of his predecessors, nor as one of his descendents, a grandson who became Governor of Connecticut in 1858. Samuel, a veteran of the French and Indian War, farmed, as many did even if they had a trade or other occupation. Samuel was moderately prosperous. His saltwater farm included nearly three acres of salt meadow, and he owned land around his home that he acquired gradually during the last part of the eighteenth century. A seaport town in peacetime was a good place to live.

The Ferry District of Saybrook, on the west bank of the Connecticut River where it narrows above Saybrook proper, was its own discrete settlement and saw the river traffic of a prosperous agricultural valley and the land traffic that moved along the old Boston Post Road, the coastal post road that became U.S. Route 1. A ferry crossed between Lyme on the east side of the river and Saybrook, the charter for which was held by Whittleseys and Dudleys, relatives of the Buckinghams.[1]

The Ferry District contained several shipyards when Samuel was a child, and vessels sailed from Lyme and Saybrook in the West Indies trade—carrying barrel staves, apples, cedar shingles, even horses to work the sugar-cane mills—but there is no evidence that Samuel ever went to sea. By the time we catch up with the Buckinghams they are in their old age, and their children are grown. Samuel's son Samuel had purchased land for farming in Lebanon in 1803[2] and started his own family. A year later he brought his son William (the governor-to-be) to be baptized at his parents' home. Twelve years later, at age seventy-five, the elder Samuel Buckingham died.

In Governor William Buckingham's biography, his father, the younger Samuel, is described as a thrifty and enterprising farmer, known for his fruit-growing.[3] From his temperance leanings, we may guess at the younger Buckingham's openness to reform, and more progressive farming methods than those he learned at home. Before young Samuel left the elder Buckinghams' home in Saybrook "he and two or three others built the first two fishing piers at the mouth of the Connecticut to take shad, and retained all his life his interest in these fisheries which were worth as much to him as his farm."[4] We don't know whether the older Samuel Buckingham took a financial interest in the shad fishery his son helped develop. Other probate inventories from early-nineteenth-century Saybrook reflect the fisheries by listing boats and nets. If Samuel ever had any, he may have turned them over to his son by 1815.

We do know that both Samuels were farmers in Saybrook, the father since perhaps 1760 and the son for at least the last decade of the eighteenth century, helping his father. Even though the Buckingham House's exhibit period reflects its inhabitants' declining years, we know something of how they, and probably their neighbors, lived in the early years of the nineteenth century, enough at least to shed light on their foodways and social life.

The Ferry District's location just outside a port town like Saybrook meant that farmers, besides supplying themselves, had a market for produce. The Buckinghams, with so many family members in the area, may have had exchange networks for perishables like fresh meat, and may have raised animals for professional or merchant cousins, or sold their produce in town. We know that old Samuel had a salt-hay meadow. Salt hay was particularly valued as bedding hay, allowing farmers to reserve upland hay for feed. Samuel may have sold his for cash or credit, or perhaps used it for his dairy animals.[5]

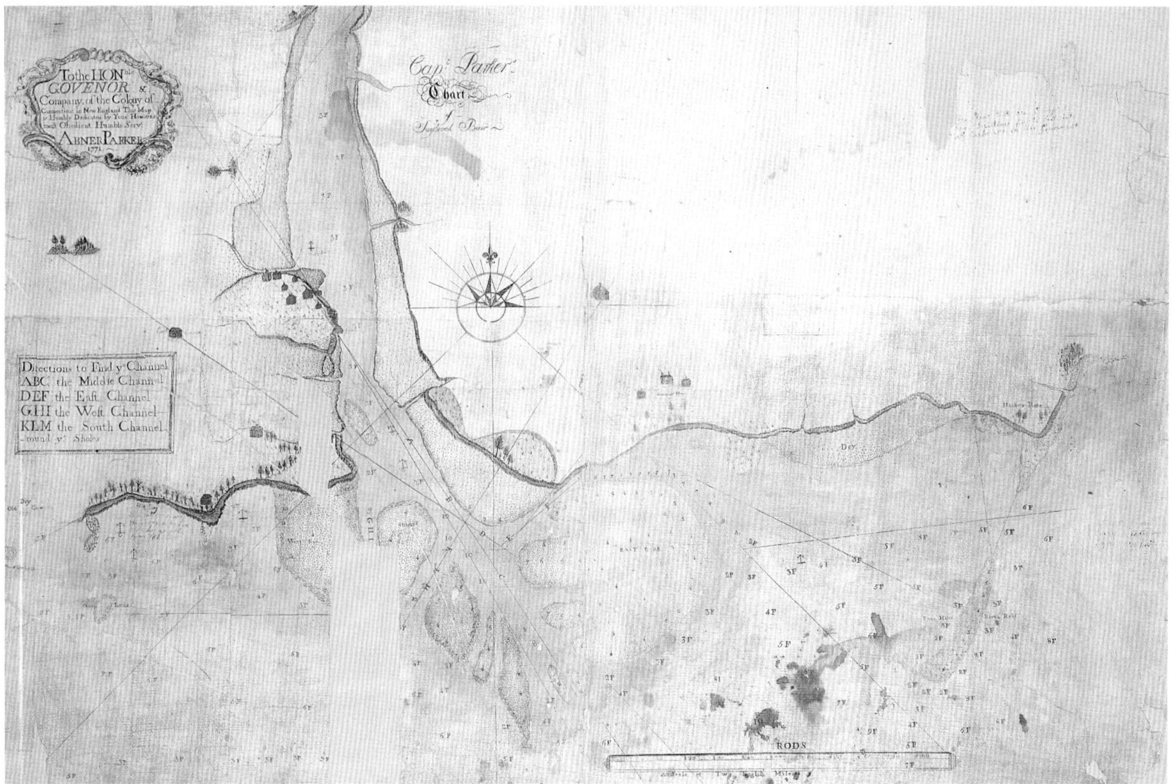

This chart, drawn by Captain Abner Parker and engraved by Abel Buel around 1783, shows the mouth of the Connecticut River at Saybrook in Samuel and Lydia Buckingham's time. Because of the shoals shown here, neither Saybrook or Lyme (now Old Saybrook and Old Lyme) developed into major seaports. [Courtesy Connecticut Historical Society]

Port towns were exposed to a world rarely glimpsed by inlanders, and even a small port like Saybrook was in touch with Boston, New York, the southern colonies, the West Indies, even Africa and Asia. Saybrook's shipping activity was, by the early 1800s, slipping compared to other New England port cities and towns; but the Buckingham children and grandchildren may have shared some portion of Lucy Larcom's experience. In the 1820s when she was a child, Larcom lived in Beverly, Massachusetts, where, she said, "We were accustomed to seeing barrels full of cocoa-nuts rolled about and there were jars of preserved tropical fruits, tamarinds, ginger-root, and other spicy appetizers, almost as common as barberries and cranberries, in the cupboards of most housekeepers."[6] Larcom also reported that "every third man you meet in the street, you might safely hail as 'Shipmate,' or 'Skipper,' or 'Captain'....It was hard to keep the boys from going off to sea before they were grown."[7] Saybrook may not have had so many captains, but it trafficked with the world in the same way.

Lydia's Kitchen

The Buckingham House kitchen ell is the older of the two parts of the house; it was moved from another site and attached when the front portion was built in 1768.[8] The central chimney and the large stone fireplace with the beehive oven on the right side of the back were constructed when the main part of the house was built. The Buckingham fireplace is an old type, the mouth of the chimney wide enough that three people can stand next to each other inside it, and daylight is clearly visible at the top of the chimney. The oven uses the chimney as its flue. Lucy Larcom described a similar big fireplace around 1825 in her Beverly, Massachusetts, childhood home: "The fireplace was deep, and there was a 'settle' in the chimney corner, where three of us youngest girls could sit together and toast our toes on the andirons...while we looked up the chimney into a square of blue sky, and sometimes caught a snowflake on our foreheads."[9]

The amount of wood burned on these old wide hearths helps explain why by the nineteenth century so much of southern New England was deforested. Saybrook had been settled for a little over a hundred years by the time the Buckinghams built their home. Although the shallower and narrower fireplaces with separately flued side-ovens were known when this fireplace was built, and were known to consume less wood for heat provided, they were not as common as they would be in another thirty years. In some cases, people modernized the old-style fireplace later in the 1700s or earlier in the 1800s by bricking-in the space and angling the sides better to reflect heat; but it appears that the Buckinghams never did this.

Large old fireplaces of this type often were fitted with lugpoles set up inside the mouth of the chimney. These required the housewife to step inside the fireplace to shift her trammels or pot hooks up and down; but apparently Lydia had a crane, a back-saving device that allowed her to swing kettles out toward the room to move them on or off

Mrs. Farnsworth's annual social tea featured "a la mode beef," cold chicken, tongue or ham, fruit cake and preserves.

their hooks. Much cooking was also done directly on the hearth. When we examine the Buckinghams' cooking utensils we can see how they were used on an open fire.

Lydia's generation of New Englanders was in some households the last, more often the next-to-the-last, generation to use open fires and fireplaces for daily cooking. As the nineteenth century progressed and people settled in the West, the change to stove technology followed, moving from urban to rural and east to west. At mid-century, it would have been possible for a traveler from coastal New England, full of cookstoves and other improvements to civilization, to find in the hinterlands people living much as most Americans had fifty or more years before. Poor or backwoods or conservative folks changed slowly, the poor and the frontier people because they could not afford the change, the conservative because they did not want to change. Considering that the old open-hearth technology had been successful for much of human history, the change to cookstoves was dramatic, a very new experience for a cook.

With open hearths, cooks could tell immediately the condition of a fire; later, when fires were enclosed in a stove's firebox, cooks had to learn new ways of handling heat and in some cases a new kind of fuel—coal. Wide hearths allowed for several simultaneous culinary operations: lively boiling in kettles hung low and directly over the fire; a steady simmer in a pot hung higher; roasting before the fire; and, down hearth or to the sides of the main fire, grilling or more gentle heats on piles of coals. There could be as many of these little "burners" as a meal required and the cook's skill in fire-handling could allow—even bake-kettle baking on the side. In many respects, the hearth was more flexible and capacious than stoves would be later. An appreciation of fireplace cooking—and fireplace cooks—seems appropriate here. It is tempting to equate the relatively primitive nature of an open fire on a New England hearth to simplicity in cooking; this would be a modern conceit. Sophisticated and complex cookery was entirely possible in these old fireplaces; one-pot meals were not the only technical possibility.

The heavily beamed kitchen of the Buckingham House had a cellar beneath and an attic above, both of which could be used for storage. An unheated room above the kitchen could also have been used for storage, although during the lives of Lydia and Samuel Buckingham it may have served as a work space or sleeping chamber as well. Evidence of a pantry or dairy room, if it ever existed, is missing. Unlike modern homes, a house like the Buckinghams', and even those of the Burrows and Greenman families later in the century, was ideally suited to a variety of food-storage environments, and these changed seasonally. When there is no central heating or air conditioning, spaces in a house assume a climate: upstairs spaces that are seldom heated in winter stay cool and dry, sometimes dropping to freezing or below; cellars remain cool and humid. In summer, rooms on the north sides of houses, catching less sunlight, remain cool if the kitchen heat is excluded. Cellars remain cool—but not cool enough for fresh meat.

Housewives matched up food storage with these in-house climates: root vegetables, fruits, and salted or brined meats went into cellars. Fresh meats were hung in places where they would freeze in winter. Pumpkins and squashes needed cool and dry places that would not freeze. Cabbages which gave off a strong odor were stored separately from other foods. Parsnips were stored over the winter in the ground where they grew, and were dug in the spring for fresh eating. Grains and beans were stored where they would stay free of mold. Anything that could not keep had to be eaten right away, or pickled or preserved. We are so accustomed to such things as a cucumber pickle or strawberry jam being a condiment that it is easy to forget that these were processed for preservation, not just for flavor and variety. Many early descriptions of kitchens mention crocks of pickles, smoked meats hung from hooks in beams overhead, cheeses lining pantry shelves. Food was stored all over the house, in a way we would find almost casual but which was deliberate and customary.

Lydia Buckingham, if she was a careful housewife, monitored her stored food to be sure it was in good condition and to remove spoiled items. Cookbooks and household-advice books often discussed the care of stored foods. When Amelia Simmons in *American Cookery*, 1796, described the potato, fairly recently introduced, she also advised on storage: "All potatoes should be dug before the rainy seasons in the fall, well dryed in the sun, kept from frost and dampness during the winter, in the spring removed from the cellar to a dry loft, and spread thin, and frequently stirred and dryed, or they will grow and be thereby injured for cookery."[10] Mrs. Child added to this advice in the 1830s, advising to snap the sprouts off potatoes: "They never sprout but three times; therefore, after you have sprouted them three times, they will trouble you no more."[11]

Mrs. Child had some other cautions: "See that the beef and pork are always under brine; and that the brine is sweet and clean." "Indian meal and rye meal are in danger of fermenting in summer; particularly Indian. They should be kept in a cool place, and stirred open to the air, once in a while. A large stone put in the middle of a barrel of meal, is a good thing to keep it cool." "Examine preserves, to see that they are not contracting mould; and your pickles, to see that they are not growing soft and tasteless."[12] All this was in Lydia Buckingham's purview.

Water supply: The Buckinghams drew their water from a well a few yards from the kitchen door. This was a common way to supply household water; but there were other ways, including constantly flowing gravity-fed water piped directly into a house, with overflow piped outside for animals. Sometimes part of a New England home was built directly over a well; water could be drawn right up into the living quarters and no one was obliged to step outdoors to carry heavy pails of water into the house.

Lydia's Cooking Utensils and Dinnerware

When Samuel died in 1815 at age 75, the usual inventory was made of his estate,[13] and this gives us a snapshot of some of the household goods the Buckinghams acquired over the years. The most valuable items were enumerated, including an array of dinnerware and some basic kitchen utensils. From the inventory we can conclude some things about their cooking, eating, and drinking habits. While the inventory is not room-specific, there is a progression as if the appraisers, Augustus Bushnell and Elisha Dudley, moved from room to room. The cooking utensils are clumped together, and they include basic fireplace furnishings—two trammels, two pairs of andirons, shovels and tongs.

Trammels, hung from the crane or lug pole, had a hook at the bottom from which a pot or other hooks could be hung, and usually had some feature that allowed the pots and kettles to be raised and lowered, either a ratchet with teeth, or holes punched in the strap through which a hook was put. The andirons were two of three pairs that appeared in the inventory. Obviously in a house with five fireplaces not all rooms had andirons or ones worth mentioning. Lydia could have cooked nicely with no andirons at all, as some families did. Her andirons may have had hooks on them for holding a roasting spit, although a spit and skewers are not listed.

If Lydia was lucky, the tea kettle listed on the inventory was equipped with a tipping device so she need not lift it off the trammel or hooks each time she wanted to pour out hot water. She had "two iron pots" and "one iron kettle" which probably had bails and three little feet so they could be set on a nest of coals as well as hung. These cooking vessels probably varied in size, and Lydia probably used them for her basic boiling, stewing, and simmering.

The inventory lists a brass kettle which was probably large, with a bail to hang it and possibly a tin lining. She may have used it for making preserves. Her bake kettle was a shallower, straight-sided cast-iron kettle with feet, which Lydia could set on a bed of coals on the hearth. Its lipped lid was covered with hot coals to create an oven quickly without the trouble of building a big fire in the beehive oven. A bake kettle was just right for making a single pan of Indian cake, warming a pie, or creating a hot baked dish for dinner.

Mrs. Buckingham had one gridiron and a skillet. The gridiron was useful for broiling; usually made of wrought iron, it had feet and a handle. A piece of meat or a fish, like one of the shad that son William caught, could be laid right on it and the whole business set over coals. A skillet was often cast iron, and it looked like a saucepan with legs. The skillet was also used on the hearth, set over a pile of coals.

Lydia may have used the "two dish kettles" noted in the inventory to heat water for dishwashing, for she had

Lydia Buckingham's cooking fireplace had a crane from which she hung pots and kettles while, at the same time, she could use her bake kettle, left, and gridiron, over coals at left front. She could also use a tin oven, or "tin kitchen," shown here pulled slightly away from the fire at right. The oven is at upper right, in which a fire was built and baking was done a few hours later with retained heat. [MSM 94-6-49]

neither running water nor a sink. Recent research into the dishwashing methods of the early 1800s has been prompted by archaeological evidence of generous scatterings of ceramic shards outside doors and windows of sitting rooms and parlors as well as kitchens.[14] Mrs. Buckingham probably had the habit of washing her nicer dishes in the place where they were used and stored in her home, probably the front room to the right of the entry way. This kept them separate from greasier pots, kettles and cooking utensils in the kitchen. When dishwashing was over, Mrs. Buckingham opened a window or stepped to a door and heaved out the dishwater. Any cup or saucer or plate that was broken went out the same way. Outside the kitchen door she tossed cooking refuse, including bones, garbage, egg shells, and the greasier water from washing kettles and pots. It would take the passage of time and the work of reformers like the Beecher sisters, and the writers of popular agricultural publications, to break the ages-old habit of discarding garbage immediately outside dwellings.

Mrs. Buckingham kept "ten pounds of pewter" in the kitchen, while she kept her nicer china in another room. Pewter had so declined in value by the nineteenth century that individual pieces were no longer enumerated, but the whole lumped together and weighed. The old stuff must have come in handy for kitchen and everyday use, saving the china for serving and dining. It may have included spoons, a large platter or two, bowls or a pitcher.

A "pair steelyards" was a hanging beam scale used for weighing. It is probable that these had a largely seasonal use—for example, at butchering time for weighing out quantities of salt, sugar, and meat to ensure the best proportion of brine to meat.

Kitchen furniture included "one chest, one table, six old chairs." The chest may have been a large wooden box in which Lydia stored her rye and Indian meals, or other dry staples. Was the one table her only work surface, or did Mrs. Buckingham have other unlisted furniture, such as a trestle with boards? Perhaps she had a shelf hinged beneath a window, sometimes depicted in paintings of kitchen interiors. The inventory listed a total of twenty-two Windsor chairs throughout the house. In addition to these there were six "old" chairs that seem to have been in the same place as the cooking utensils—the place I interpret as the kitchen. It is appropriate that old chairs would be shifted to a utilitarian space, reserving the better furniture for other rooms.

Some other things found their way into the kitchen space that caught the appraisers' eyes: a pair of silver knee buckles and a warming pan were worth listing, as were a pair of sadirons for ironing day.

Listed together in proximity to miscellaneous farm tools and other implements—including spinning wheels— were some items that speak to Mrs. Buckingham's other responsibilities—laundry, dairying, and pickling and preserving. There were one tin pail, three wooden pails, two wash tubs, a churn, five earthen milk pans, and four stone pots. Mr. Buckingham left three cows, so a modest amount of dairying activity must have continued—perhaps mostly the single daughter Mehetebel's job. The five milk pans were to allow the cream to rise and later be churned into butter. No cheese-making equipment was listed; either it was not considered valuable or it simply was not there. Other farm households made cheese, and the Buckinghams could have purchased their supply, if they chose. The stone pots saw a variety of uses—butter storage, or pickle-making, for example.

What is missing? No griddle or spider for frying was listed. Nor were other small utensils listed, although they were part of other inventories of the period—things like dippers, ladles, skimmers, forks, knives, spoons, chopping tools, toasting devices, and waffle or wafer irons. Not all these items were universally owned, but the Buckinghams surely had some of them. Other Saybrook probate inventories omitted many small utensils; details in inventories of this period were often uneven or missing, according to scholars who have assessed the value of probate inventories in historical research.[15]

Other kinds of earthenware, especially redware so commonly used in New England for storage or mixing and even baking, is not listed. Did Mrs. Buckingham have some pie plates? Some mixing bowls? A canister or jar or two? No glass bottles are included.

Wooden ware of various sorts—chopping bowls, bread bowls, mortar and pestle, dough trough, rolling pin, spoons, and the like—are not listed. Wooden barrels for general storage are not listed, but in most households there were variously sized casks and barrels for storing molasses, meat, meal, and flour. Many of these small items have survived as artifacts, can be seen in paintings and drawings from the period, and their use is described in cookbooks. It is reasonable to expect that some were used in the Buckingham House.

How would Lydia roast? Roasting devices—a spit and skewers, or a tin kitchen, by that name—do not appear in Samuel's inventory, although a "tin oven" does. Mrs. Buckingham could have suspended her roasts before the fire from a string, as was often done at this time, twisting the string so the roast would turn and rewind itself for a while. Had small utensils been enumerated, we might have found a spit and skewer. Andirons fitted with hooks held the ends of spits with meat skewered in place; a drippping pan below caught the gravy, and the cook turned the spit by hand or assigned the job to a child.

The cook in a wealthy household or a tavern might use a clock jack, a geared roasting device connected to weights similar to those in a clock, that turned the meat continuously. Sometimes a vane installed in the chimney turned with rising heat and drove a geared device connected to a spit. But these sophisticated mechanical spits were rarely found in ordinary homes like the Buckinghams'.

In the late 1700s and early 1800s, a roasting device called a "tin kitchen" was introduced in America from England. Sarah Anna Smith Emery, the daughter of a moderately prosperous farm family living in West Newbury, Massachusetts, in the late eighteenth and early nineteenth century, first saw a "tin kitchen" when she visited with relatives in nearby Newburyport. She said "Aunt Betsy displayed [it] as a rare implement of the culinary art."[16] Because the tin kitchen enclosed the side of the meat away from the fire, it was a far more efficient roasting device. It both shortened the cooking time and made the process neater by collecting the drippings in the curved bottom. In addition, a prong on the spit was aligned with a pattern of holes in one end of the tin kitchen. The cook periodically rotated the roast part way, then stuck the prong in one of the holes. Freed from continuous attention to the roast, the cook was able to do something else.

But tin kitchens were not universally adopted—not everyone could afford them, and some people may have been satisfied with their old methods. Since it is likely that some Saybrook people had tin kitchens, and since other Saybrook inventories from the period do not list "tin kitchens" by that name, the frequently mentioned "tin ovens" were probably the local term for the device. A tin oven was listed in the Buckingham inventory, and it was almost certainly what other people called a tin kitchen.

Archaeological evidence: Mystic Seaport Museum acquired the Buckingham House in 1951 just before a major highway was put through the site and, unfortunately, an archaeological dig was not performed, so we will never have the little chips and pieces of redware, stoneware, iron, glass, and bones that would shed light on Lydia's kitchen and its food.

Dining at the Buckingham House

Listed all together in the inventory, and separately from the kitchen stuff, was the nicer dinnerware. This was a mixture of china and earthenware, with various sizes of service pieces, silver, and other flatware.

It included twenty-two pieces of china, two servers, two fruit dishes, one large oval platter, three quart bowls, twenty-three green-edged plates, milk cup, butter boat, and pepper box. Mrs. Buckingham could set a full table with all this at her disposal. Was the "large cherry table" listed the one used for meals? The china was not described in detail so we have no idea what it looked like, and whether it included matched pieces, as we expect a set of china to do today. The green-edged plates were listed as "10 Green edged plates $1- 13 do.[ditto] $2," so there may have been two different sizes. Green-edged plates were very similar to the familiar blue-edged, or feather-edged, dinnerware so common in early-nineteenth-century New England.

While matched sets of dishes were becoming popular at the time this inventory was taken, it would have seemed less important to Mrs. Buckingham that each person have a matched place setting than that each have their own plate. She was probably only the third or fourth generation in her family to put any importance on individual plates. Communal eating habits were not that far in the past.

There was a set of knives plus forks, and seven more knives and forks. The number of knives and forks in the "set" was not specified, but it was valued at $1.50, compared to seven knives and forks at $1.26, so perhaps there were six in better condition, or else more of a poorer quality. In any event, the knives probably had enlarged and rounded ends and the forks were two-tined. Samuel and Lydia probably ate with their knives as most people did at that time, especially in rural areas.[17] A knife used this way worked very much as a flattened spoon would and was fine for such fare as fricasees, hashes, mashed potatoes, squash, or turnips. With practice, diners could even balance peas and beans on a knife and convey them to their mouths. Forks were fine for spearing larger pieces of meat or firm pieces of boiled vegetables or pudding, but they were inadequate for the soft food that knives handled well. Spoons for soups and soft fare may have been found among the pewter.

The Buckinghams drank both tea and coffee. Although no teapot was listed in the inventory, there were a tea canister, earthen cups and saucers, coffee pot, twelve silver teaspoons and sugar tongs, sugar box, and two sugar bowls. The earthenware cups might have been the softer ceramic pearl or creamware, which would suffice for serving either beverage. Silver sugar tongs meant Mrs. Buckingham could serve the broken loaf sugar from the sugar bowl in a genteel manner; in fact, at this time taking tea was a sociable activity and done with some ceremony. Perhaps she used the cherry tea table listed elsewhere in the inventory.

The inventory showed two wine servers, two quart decanters, one pint decanter, one quart tumbler, and four "tumblers." Like most people of their time, the Buckinghams apparently drank wine and probably other spirits as well—perhaps especially the rum that was a staple of New England's West Indies trade. Though it would be another decade or so before New England saw intemperance peak, the amount of rum, madeira, beer, cider, and gin tossed back would astonish most modern people.[18]

Immediately following the chinaware—and preceding a foot stove, case with drawers, looking glass, old desk, and the third of three pairs of andirons, shovel and tongs—are six tin pans and the tin oven. It is as if a certain amount of food preparation was done in or near the room where the china was kept; in fact, the smaller fireplaces in many houses of this period were fitted with a crane suitable for suspending a tea kettle or small pot. George J. Cummings, recalling his childhood in a New Hampshire farmhouse, described how a "tin oven" might have been used. "Biscuits were cooked in tin ovens placed before a bright fire. The oven was made of shining metal so the heat could be reflected on all sides of the dough which rested on a tin plate in the center of the oven."[19]

Eighteen fifteen is little too early in the century for us to designate this room as the dining room. The gentry at this time had rooms set aside strictly for dining, but most people in the early nineteenth century did not—especially if, like the Buckinghams, they were accustomed to older fashions. While one room might be reserved for best occasions, other rooms were multi-purpose: for work, entertaining, or eating, with one project cleared away to make room for the next.

So the room where the china was kept may have seen Samuel at work on his farm or business accounts at the old desk (there is no other desk listed), and Lydia attending to sewing projects between meals and possibly visits from neighbors for tea.

The Food Supply

Samuel's inventory included three cows, five sheep, two hogs, ten bushels of corn, and eight bushels of rye. All this represents food raised domestically; cows for beef and veal, milk, butter, and perhaps cheese; hogs for fresh pork, lard, salt pork, ham, and sausage; sheep for lamb, mutton, and of course wool to spin on the wheels listed in the inventory. Considering that the inventory was taken in March, and that farmers often chose not to keep many animals over winter, two hogs may not be entirely representative of how many Samuel raised annually once the sow had piglets. Perhaps even as the inventory was taken, the sheep and cows were ready to drop their young.

Samuel raised corn and rye, the two staple grains, for family use in breads and puddings. This inventory just precedes the time in New England that wheat flour came back into common use after a long absence. The earliest settlers attempted to grow wheat in New England, but found it susceptible to disease. Rye succeeded, as did maize—called "Indian"—and those two were commonly used for bread, producing loaves called brown bread. Some parts of New England were able to grow wheat, but not in a sufficient quantity for everyday use in bread-making. Wheat had to be imported from the Middle Atlantic and southern parts of the country until the Erie Canal was completed in 1825. Thereafter greater quantities than ever were brought eastward. But wheat was costly before the canal brought supplies of it from new farmlands in the West, and families like the Buckinghams usually reserved it for nice baking—cake and pastry or bread for special occasions. Or they extended it with rye for pie crusts or puddings. New England's gentry could afford to have white bread and do fancy baking with wheat flour, but the middle classes did as the Buckinghams did—raised corn and rye, and purchased wheat in small quantities.

Fish-eating: Most New Englanders, particularly coastal people, had fish once a week in the early decades of the 1800s. As Puritan descendants, they were not required by a church to observe a fast day on Friday but the once-a-week habit from a much earlier time lingered in the diet, shifted to a different day of the week, sometimes Saturday. Caroline "Kiddy" King in Salem, Massachusetts, wrote that, "On Saturdays, we always had salt fish."[20] In *New England Economical Housekeeper*, Mrs. Howland suggested "A Course of Dinners for a Week," and Saturday's dinner was "Salt cod-fish boiled, with apple pie."[21] This was the fish equivalent of a boiled corned beef or ham dinner, accompanied by vegetables. If Saturday was baking day, and a pot of beans was put in to bake at the low, gradually declining temperature of a brick oven—whose higher heat had been spent on bread, cakes, and pies—then Saturday night supper was beans. The leftovers of both meals might then have met each other at Sunday breakfast, with salt-fish hash and beans on the side. As Kiddy King reported, "On Sunday we had the inevitable New England fish balls for breakfast, with baked beans,"[22]—a combination that endured through the nineteenth century, appearing in the 1896 edition of Fanny Merritt Farmer's *Boston Cooking School Cookbook*.[23] Fish cakes and beans for Sunday breakfast can still be found occasionally.[24]

Fresh fish was a seasonal treat for many of those who lived close to

Described by Sarah Anna Emery as a "rare implement of the culinary art" when first brought here from England in the late 1700s, the tin kitchen was in use throughout New England by the early 1830s in households that could afford one. Cooks put meat on the spit seen in the center, and placed the open side just in front of the fire. The meat could be rotated and held in place by inserting the pin on the handle in one of the holes on the end. The drippings were caught in the bottom. [MSM 94-6-47]

Bread and milk with its variations—brewis, cream toast, milk toast—made simple suppers or breakfasts.

rivers that saw the spawning runs of alewives, shad, and salmon. Certainly the Buckinghams and their neighbors ate these fish from the Connecticut River. Coastal families who could get other fish and shellfish in season were likely to add the most popular—haddock, tautog, cod, mackerel, bass, eels—to their weekly bill of fare. And, like inlanders, they ate salted fish—cod and mackerel—year round. Shad was also salted for consumption year round. Communities up the Connecticut River from Saybrook also benefited from the spring shad run. In Southington, for example, in the first third of the nineteenth century, the Stephen Walkleys, a farm family of modest means, had neighbors who would go down to the river and "bring up a load of shad," from which, son Stephen recalled, "Father would buy two or three dozen and salt them down."[25] In Suffield, some members of the community owned "fish places" along the river, where they went to gather shad or salmon,[26] a situation probably common wherever there was a fishery worth exploiting.

What about fresh meat? Quite a lot of attention has been paid over the years to the quantities of salted meat consumed in the eighteenth and early nineteenth centuries. Perhaps our perceptions are skewed because stored food is recorded in surviving documentation: probate inventories, household or diary records of quantities stored, and in recipes used for brines recorded in manuscript notebooks. Family butchering was a significant annual event, and the resulting salted and smoked meat, laid away in barrels or emerging from murky smoke chambers, was particularly memorable for people recalling their life histories and relating them to younger generations. The boiled dinner now designated "New England" is symbolic of the region and its people, and its importance as a way of identifying regionality stresses the dish beyond its probable prominence in the diet.

The fresh meat exchanged among households was considerably more ephemeral, both in fact and in memory. Moderately prosperous farmers like the Buckinghams exchanged, or bought and sold, fresh meat among their peers, recording kinds and quantities in their account books.[27] This made fresh meat available year round, varying in kind season to season: veal in the late spring and summer, mutton in the late summer and early fall, and pork and beef in the late fall. Urban butchers dealt mostly in fresh meat without regard to the calendar, selling it to in-town people who could have more frequent access to fresh meat than country people.

Much pork was, of course, salted and smoked, supplying the table year round. But it was often used in small quantities to add relish to bland food, like beans or peas. Some beef was also salted, or pickled and smoked, to insure both a steady supply and variety. Because large animals like hogs and beef animals were slaughtered at winter's onset, some meat was frozen.

Corning beef yielded a range of products, from lightly to heavily salted. At the lightest end of the scale, beef was rubbed over well with salt and put in the cellar. In *The American Frugal Housewife*, Mrs. Child recommended, "If you have provided more meat than you can use while it is good, it is well to corn it in season [i.e. in time] to save it." She cautioned against keeping it longer than a day and a half in summer, but said it would keep a fortnight in winter.[28] Corning was the ideal treatment for the seasonal transitions, when freezing was unreliable. For a higher degree of preservation, beef was pickled in a brine. The most reliable long-term storage—for example, for use aboard ship—was salting which took the process a step further, nearly drying the meat.

With an exchange of beef, farmers like the Buckinghams might obtain several meals of fresh meat, steaks, small roasts, stewed pieces, or beef *à la mode*. Some of it they would lightly corn, put in the cellar, tend carefully, and eat when the fresh was gone. Mutton received similar treatment, some eaten fresh, some lightly corned. Smaller animals, lamb and veal, often exchanged by the quarter, were easier to use up quickly, a concern from late spring to early fall, although these meats could also be corned if it seemed necessary.

The Suffield study, as well as faunal remains (bones) from archaeological digs in New England, indicates that beef was the preferred meat. Many more pounds of beef were consumed than any other kind of meat; pork, particularly salt pork, cropped up frequently in cookery and narrative texts, but it was used often in small quantities, and the total pounds consumed never matched that of beef. Nor, by the late 1700s, did many coastal New England people eat wild meat, except as a seasonal specialty, greatly preferring domestic.

The urban and rural well-to-do had more extensive networks of exchange and purchase to maintain both fresh and preserved meat supplies. In some cases, tenant farmers or farm-dwelling relatives tended the cattle and hogs owned by the wealthy. Samuel Rodman, one of New Bedford's whaling gentry, recorded in his diary how he obtained animals and saw to the preservation of beef and ham. He methodically noted the quantities and procedures he used, possibly to remind him what worked so it could be repeated. On 14 December 1821, he wrote: "This day had Freeman to salt my beef. It was a young creature bought of Thos. Almy...."[29] In February 1822 he reported he had his two oldest hogs killed and the next day "Attended to the cutting and salting of my pork,"[30] particularly the shoulders and hams, which he smoked after sufficient pickling. In July, he wrote, "Had what remains of my hams and shoulders taken from the smoke house and sewed in crash [coarse cloth] preparatory to putting them in ashes to preserve them from flies."[31] Another year, he hired a man named Reuben Sharpe to dress his hogs,[32] and in 1830 he reported that he "Rode out to my brother B's farm to see a cow. Exchanged my Normandy for a heifer (with a calf) 2 to 3 years old."[33] Rodman clearly had several ways to supply his table with meat. Samuel Buckingham likely became involved in arrangements like these with family or members of Saybrook's gentry.

Among the less well off, there were few such arrangements. Fresh meat did not come their way often, and they ate cheese or the salted meat given them as pay for their labor. In urban settings, they were the people who purchased the less-meaty pieces, like neck bones and hocks. Sarah Emery was married to David Emery, a butcher near Newburyport, Massachusetts. She reported in her memoirs that during the hard times of the War of 1812, "Mr. Emery was in the habit of giving away livers, heads and the cheaper pieces. Young lads out of our most respectable families...were glad to give an helping hand at the slaughter house, receiving in pay a liver, sweetbread, or bones for soup."[34]

Grain predominated in the diet of the poor, and sometimes there was little enough of that. Mary Emma Weaver Farnsworth, growing up in the 1830s in New London, Connecticut, recalled that one family sat down to a meager breakfast of johnnycake, and a feeble-minded son said, as a kind of blessing, "One little johnnycake for the four of us. Thank the Lord there aren't any more of us."[35]

People like the Walkleys, Buckinghams, and Sarah Emery's family probably participated in food exchanges to add variety to their diet. The technological changes of the later nineteenth century would support and maintain these patterns and preferences: people *liked* fresh meat, and refrigeration made transporting it easier. People *liked* beef, and moving great quantities of it to eastern cities became the goal of western cattle raisers, with railroads and refrigeration easing the process. The technological changes did not create the preferences in the diet. Rather the preferences pointed the way for technological change.

Dairying and Garden Produce

While men tended field crops and animals, dairying and vegetable gardening were largely women's work. We do not know for certain what the Buckinghams did with their milk; certainly some of it was consumed at home. With their proximity to the town of Saybrook, they could have carried some down to sell. Emma Farnsworth reported that family friends, the Congdons in Quaker Hill, a little north of New London, had a dairy herd and twice a day sent milk to town.[36]

Perhaps the Buckinghams did not produce cheese, or perhaps they did at one time, but no longer owned the equipment at the time of Samuel's death. They may have already passed it along to one of their grown children. Cheese- and butter-making were seasonal activities, dependent upon great enough quantities of milk twice daily to work with. As with meat exchanges, milk exchanges were made, especially among families with just a few milking cows.[37] These exchanges made possible sufficient milk for one household to make a substantial cheese. If the Buckinghams did not make their own cheese, they surely could have purchased it or exchanged something of like value for it.

"In hot weather we usually had boiled salted meat and vegatables," reported Sarah Anna Emery.

Cheese, like much southern New England produce, particularly beef and pork, was traded coastwise and to the West Indies. A Stonington, Connecticut, diary from 1809 tells us about such traffic. Ethan Denison, a farmer, school teacher, and surveyor, reported in July that he delivered four oxen and eight sheep to go to Bermuda in the sloop *Revenue*.[38] Later that month he took a load of cheese to New York and Baltimore, returning late in August.[39] If the Buckinghams themselves never engaged in such ventures, surely they witnessed other Saybrook people shipping cheeses to a distant market.

Farm wives often grew potatoes, peas, beans, onions, cabbages, turnips, squash, and pumpkins on a large scale. This depended a great deal on a family's labor resources and on their taste for vegetables. Although period gardening manuals, almanacs, cookbooks, and seed catalogs dutifully listed all the different vegetable varieties available, with explanations of how to grow and cook them, numerous vegetables we enjoy today were likely neglected by people like the Buckinghams. American food historians do not agree on the popularity of many vegetables. Nevertheless, the more substantial vegetables—cabbages, squashes, beans, peas, and cucumbers; root vegetables like carrots, beets, and parsnips; and some kinds of salad stuff such as lettuce and spinach were popularly grown and eaten.

People like the Buckinghams wanted a vegetable that could be planted and forgotten, or, at the most, needed minimal attention for the quantity produced. Ideally, after harvest it could be stored and would keep well, again with minimal attention.

Small fruits were a welcome addition to the diet. In fact, they occasioned special parties for sharing. Joseph Anthony, another member of New Bedford's gentry, recorded: "Moses received some cherries and sent them up to our house and in the evening we had a party to partake of them."[40] Up in Salem, Kiddy King reported that her family, too, had cherry parties and gatherings to eat strawberries.[41] Ethan Denison noted in his diary that he "set out gooseberries & currents & rose bushes in the dooryard."[42] People gathered wild fruit as well: raspberries, blackberries, huckleberries, and beach plums in coastal areas. Mrs. Child suggested that "it is a great deal better for the boys and girls on a farm to be picking blackberries at six cents a quart, than to be wearing out their clothes in useless play." Since they will tear their clothes anyway, she reasoned, they might as well earn something to offset the cost of new clothes by selling blackberries in town.[43]

The Meals of the Day

The Buckinghams ate at least three, and possibly four, meals a day. First came breakfast, the second-largest meal of the day, which families ate after morning chores. The largest meal was dinner, usually served at noon. Gathering at midday was entirely possible for a family who all worked at home. In late afternoon the family had tea or supper, the lightest meal of the day. Variations on the order and content of teas and suppers depended on whether the meal was for family or company.

Breakfast: Timothy Dwight described the New England breakfast: "A breakfast in the large towns is chiefly bread and butter, the bread in the cool season generally toasted. In the country almost universally this is accompanied with smoke-dried beef, cheese, or some species of fish or flesh broiled or otherwise fitted to the taste of the family."[44] Sarah Anna Emery lived on a farm in "the country" outside the seaport town of Newburyport. After milking her family had "the fires built, and breakfast prepared. Many families had milk for this meal, but we always had coffee or chocolate, with meat and potatoes."[45] Dwight observed that New Englanders were likely to have meat—"flesh or fish"—two or three times a day, and "so universal is this custom that a breakfast without such an addition is considered as scarcely worth eating."[46]

John Perkins, before embarking on the *Tiger* in Stonington, Connecticut, for a whaling voyage in 1846, accompanied a friend to his grandfather's house, "a farmer of the true old fashioned stamp. We got there a little after their breakfast was over, still they insisted upon our taking something to eat. The table was soon set & I never eat such a meal that I relished better in my life; it was a true farmers meal. We had both coffee & a bowl of bread & milk, the true home made brown bread, 'punkin' pie, honey, pancakes & cider, excelent butter & cheese. They would make us fill everything capable of holding them, that we had, ful of excelent apples."[47]

For breakfast Stephen Walkley said that he and his family in Southington had "usually some fried meat (ham or sausage) or fresh meat of some kind when we had it. The morning after we had pot-luck [Walkley's family's name for a boiled dinner of salt beef and potatoes] it was corned beef hash." His mother fried a tin pan full of doughnuts made of wheat flour, and "We made our breakfast of these crumbled in tea, which for us boys was hot water and milk."[48]

Dinner: The noon meal, the most substantial of the day, featured a piece of boiled or roasted meat, accompanied by vegetables. The quantity and variety of vegetables depended on family preferences, but the quantities were less than common today. When people in the early nineteenth century stretched a meal, they did it with grains in the form of bread, brown bread, made of rye and Indian meal,[49] or Indian cakes, breads, and biscuits, or a boiled pudding.

Joseph Anthony reported in 1823 on some of the dinners he ate: on 30 January, "Dined at N. Hathaway—had an excellent haunch of mutton, cooked venison style"; on 30 March he "Had a fine leg of roast mutton"; on 1 June, "roast beef (a great rarity this season of the year)"; on 12 June, "Dined at Cornelius on roast pig"; in October, "We had a grand dinner of stall fed wild pigeons roasted and a partridge pie."[50] Of course, perhaps the reason he recorded these dinners was that they were unusually sumptuous. New Englanders were not famous at the beginning of the 1800s (or after, for that matter) for haute cuisine, even among the wealthier classes. A "good dinner" was synonymous with a large joint of fresh meat, a standard that lasted through the whole century. All classes aspired to this standard and, when possible, imitated it, if only once a year at Thanksgiving.

Even when wealthier people ate simpler dinners, some of their dishes required quite a bit of culinary attention. Kiddy King reported: "We had no clear soups, but often a very rich calf's head soup with balls of forced meat, and a beef soup, thick with good things, like a stew, only it was served in a tureen, and always a chowder once a week. And these were not the prefix to a dinner, but the piece de resistance itself."[51]

Calf's head soup with forced meat balls was quite a production and required access to fresh meat. (One calf's head, after all, had many pounds of calf attached to it, which also had to be cooked or distributed for fresh eating. Such soup was much easier to manage in an urban setting with a head purchased from a butcher's shop. Rural people would have made this dish less frequently.) Forced meat balls were fresh chopped meat, with bread, egg, and seasonings, browned like meatballs, and then added to the soup. A plain boiled dinner was a snap compared to calf's head soup.

The stew and chowder Caroline described were considerably simpler, and we can imagine meals like these being enjoyed up and down the social scale.

Menus from the Middle Classes

"In hot weather," said Sarah Emery, "we usually had boiled salted meat and vegetables, and if it was baking day, a custard or pudding."[52] The meat would have been presented on a platter, as a centerpiece surrounded by the vegetables. Stephen Walkley recalled that his family, too, ate dinners of salt beef and pork, and that he did not like them. "We rarely had side dishes, unless it was a dish of sauce or pickles, and when we had meat, had just meat and potatoes or sometimes turnips. When we had boiled corned beef, which was frequently, we had a vinegar pot or mustard pot on the table, which was passed to those who used those relishes. Sometimes an Indian pudding was put into the pot [of boiling meat and vegetables] in a tin case and the whole boiled together. A sauce for the pudding, a bowl of pure cream sweetened with molasses was set on, to which each helped himself. If we had company, the cream was sweetened with brown sugar instead of molasses."[53]

It is important to keep in mind that the simplicity of these dinners was not the result of a limited fireplace technology, but rather the function of the Walkleys' social and economic situation. Another Walkley child, Mary Angelina, reported that her "Father was poor in worldly goods, his father having had a seafaring life and enfeebled his constitution by exposure."[54] As a small-scale farmer with minimal cash flow, Walkley could provide his family with much of their own food, so the salted meats that lent themselves so well to the boiled dinners that son Stephen disliked would have been Walkley's own product. Because he would butcher his stock only occasionally, fresh meat, which was better suited for roasting or broiling, was obtained through food exchanges among the neighbors.

The wife's workload also helped determine the menu. Mrs. Walkley had nine children between 1812 and 1832. Besides caring for a continuous procession of infants, she did the milking; made cheese, butter, bread, candles, soap, and preserves; wove some of the family's textiles; sewed; and, of course, did the laundry, ironing, and cleaning. She had help from her husband's two sisters, who also lived with them, but she also had to care for the enfeebled elder Walkley. As the children grew older, she certainly put them to work assisting her. Nevertheless, she had a *tremendous* amount of work to do in this household. When it came to food preparation, the main purpose of meals was to nourish and fill the family. More prosperous families with hired help could prepare more elaborate dishes, like the saddle of mutton, venison style, that Joseph Anthony reported eating.

On a scale of prosperity and stylishness between wealthy Joseph Anthony and subsistence-level Stephen Walkley, the Buckinghams probably fell closer to the Walkleys and Sarah Emery's family than to Joseph Anthony of New Bedford. They may very well have sat down to the kind of dinners suggested by Mrs. E.A. Howland in her *New England Economical Housekeeper*. Reflecting the modest menus common in the early 1800s, "A Course of Dinners for a Week" was consciously varied. Except for baked beans oddly placed on Friday, rather than Saturday night, it rings true:

"MONDAY. Tea, coffee, and cocoa, with mince meat, and bread and butter, in winter; bread and milk in summer.

TUESDAY. Boiled dish, with apple dumplings.

WEDNESDAY. Roasted or baked meat, with bread pudding.

THURSDAY. Broiled steak, or fresh fish, with baked rice pudding.

FRIDAY. Baked beans, with baked Indian pudding.

SATURDAY. Salt cod-fish, with apple pie.

SUNDAY. Morning, hashed fish and coffee. Noon, bread and butter—cheese—pie—doughnuts."[55]

Keep in mind that Monday was wash day. In the early 1800s, the enormity of that task diverted all the housewife's attention. A small meal requiring very little effort was in order for the day. The "mince meat" mentioned here is meat minced up with vegetables and gravy,[56] not the preserve put into pie. Tuesday's boiled dinner was followed by apple dumplings, which at this time was also a boiled dish. The two may have been cooked together in one pot.

Wednesday and Saturday were baking days for many households. Emma Farnsworth recalled the beehive oven in her childhood home. "Oh what things came out of that oven semi-weekly. Bread, cake and pies were made on Wednesday but on Saturday there was a greater variety in cold weather baked beans and brown bread with Indian pudding," she wrote.[57] Mrs. Howland's suggestion for Wednesday—of baked meat followed by a baked pudding—would have been appropriate for those who heated their ovens mid-week, and the Friday combination is similar to the one Farnsworth described occurring on Saturday.

By the early 1800s, most people in New England were gently bending the strict Sabbath rule about not building cooking fires and making large meals, but Mrs. Howland's suggestion for a simple hash breakfast and cold baked goods all the rest of the day meant a day of rest for the women in the house.

Supper or tea: Later in the day, most people had a small meal, often a sociable one, which went by the nearly interchangeable names of tea or supper; supper was more likely to have warm food or meat, though a tea at which men were expected was likely to have meat. In some cases, people had both: tea earlier to tide them over, then supper later.

For example, Joseph Anthony reported in January 1823: "Took tea at Nat's in the evening—had an oyster supper"[58] (another possible interpretation of this is that tea *was* a supper of oysters); And "Took tea at father's...[socialized with several friends]...returned home about ten. They accompanied us. We had a little supper and a real good time."[59] A warm, late evening supper like Anthony's was more likely among the well-to-do, and people like the Buckinghams probably had theirs earlier in the evening.

"Supper...is like breakfast," said Timothy Dwight in describing New England habits, "except that it is made up partially of preserved fruits, different kinds of cake, pies, tarts, etc. The meats used at breakfast and supper are generally intended to be dainties."[60] By "dainties" he meant small portions, not like substantial pieces seen at dinner.

A tea menu, like the supper Dwight described, tended to feature bread and butter, perhaps some preserves, apple or pear sauce, and short cake. Mary Angelina Walkley reported that her family had pie instead of cake for tea.[61]

One of Saybrook's daughters became known for a "light supper" she served. The oldest of Captain Elisha Hart's daughters married the Reverend Samuel Jarvis, the rector of St. Paul's Church in Boston, who once desired to bring some fellow rectors home for tea, so the story goes. "'But don't let it make you trouble, just serve a light supper'...'Very well I will do so' replied Mrs. Jarvis." But when the Reverend and his colleagues were ushered into the dining room the table bore nothing but lighted candles. This marriage apparently ended unhappily.[62]

A good many suppers were truly "light," very often consisting of leftovers. The more substantial ones were similar to a modern lunch; the lighter ones resembled our breakfasts. A bowl of hasty pudding would be adequate for some. Stephen Walkley said, "For supper we had bread and butter or bread and milk with cheese, dried beef, or some kind of sauce, usually apple or pear."[63] Sarah Emery wrote of bread and milk suppers, and Kiddy King described "Brewis, which was little crusty bits of brown bread stewed in cream."[64] One of Emma Farnsworth's earliest childhood memories was of a family friend preparing to feed her: "She went to the pantry and bringing out a tin cup of milk crumbled bread in it and drawing out ashes, placed it to warm."[65]

The Buckinghams' vegetable garden, along with poultry and dairying work, were in Lydia's charge if the Buckinghams were like other Yankee farmers in the early 1800s. Samuel's probate inventory, taken in 1815, shows butter-making equipment, but no equipment for cheese-making, nor any stored vegetables. It is likely that the Buckinghams grew root vegetables and hearty varieties of other vegetables such as cabbages and beans. With all their other farm work, they needed a kitchen garden that was long on vittles and short on fuss. [MSM 78-10-96]

This combination of bread and milk, either informally mixed or more carefully prepared as cream toast or brewis, is the precedent for twentieth-century cereal and milk. Bread soaked in either milk, water, the boiling water for meat, or even beer or cider, was commonly eaten at this time. Yet the documentary record does not accurately represent how frequently it was eaten. Some older people today recall a cracker and milk supper, especially during the Great Depression, or being given cream toast when they were sick. These are venerable dishes, and when Stephen Walkley reported that "Sometimes, too, we were permitted to soak our bread in the pot liquor in which the meat had been boiled," he was speaking of an ongoing practice many centuries old.[66]

Social teas: One tea attended by a twenty-two-year-old Charles Morgan elicited this crabby response: "I sit down to write on my return from a little tea party at which I was I must

A well-developed sponge made with the yeast recipe to be found on page 25.

confess a rather unwilling guest this evening at my sister's [in Philadelphia] it has passed all those kinds of meetings usually do—and no pleasant impression remains—all was light, all airy nothings, no substantial food—if my friends knew how disadvantageous these kinds of parties were for me, I think they would let me rest in peace and quiet at home."[67] It is hard to know if it was the insubstantial conversation or the insubstantial food that irritated Morgan the most, or whether it was that he was obliged to attend.

Mrs. Farnsworth, the daughter of a successful storekeeper, recalled the annual social tea her mother gave. "Once a year generally after the earlier fruits were preserved 'pound for pound' mother made a practice of inviting all the cousins living in the city to a social tea. There being too many to accommodate all at once, the older ones [those who were Lydia Buckingham's age, for example] were invited the first day, the younger ones the day following."

Emma was fascinated by the preparations, "seeding raisins and cutting citron for cake." The children did not attend the party but were given little bits of loaf sugar and were encouraged to go out and play. "I cared less for play and remained to see...the pretty china white with a gold band, the bright silver reserved for extra occasions, the sunny cloth. Then the dishes of a-la-mode beef, cold chicken, tongues or ham, a variety of cake always rich fruit cake (made once a year) two or three kinds of sweetmeats, jellies, pickles, cheese; light flaky short-biscuit with tea and coffee were the usual refreshments served."[68]

And to wash it all down: Cider was the common beverage of New Englanders, rich and poor alike, according to Timothy Dwight, describing the region in the early part of the nineteenth century. Made from the apples that, he said, "abound more in New England, it is believed, than any other country....The cider when well made and well preserved is generally thought more finely flavored than any other drink."[69] This was not the sweet cider we think of drinking fresh in the fall, but deliberately fermented cider, with alcohol content to preserve it. Emma Farnsworth recalled: "Father also put in [the cellar] two or three barrels of cider as that was a common beverage then, and we needed it for mince pies. One barrel was allowed to get hard, when it was bottled for medicinal purposes."[70] Mrs. Farnsworth, writing her memoirs in the later nineteenth century, by that time sensitized to temperance issues, may have embroidered the Weaver household cider use. Though she described her mother making bitters with some of the hard cider, it seems unlikely a family would need a whole barrel full. And using two barrels of cider before it had time to ferment, even if a lot was drawn off for mincemeat, would have required concerted effort, besides wreaking havoc on the family's digestive systems.

Home brewing of beer was a housewifely practice centuries old. Lydia Maria Child in her 1833 *American Frugal Housewife* declared "Beer is a good family drink," provided instructions for making it, and advised "If your family be large, and the beer will be drunk rapidly, it may as well remain in the barrel; but if your family be small, fill what bottles you have with it; it keeps better bottled."[71] And was easier to share that way: Ann Hathaway Burgess in Fairhaven, Massachusetts, writing to her husband Paul at sea in 1829, said of a family member: "George brew'd yesterday and Elvira came down just now and brought me a bottle of beer very nice. I wish you could have it."[72]

Mrs. Child also gave instructions for ginger beer and for currant wine, about which she observed in her frugal way, "Those who have more currants than they have money, will do well to use no wine but of their own manufacture."[73] One cheap substitute for wine was nonalcoholic "shrub" made from raspberries, which eventually developed into a preferred temperance drink, although it was originally developed simply as an economical substitute for the usual brandy and rum-based raspberry shrub.

Joseph Anthony, at age twenty-six, employed at Rotch's New Bedford countinghouse, wrote in his diary on 13 January 1824 that he had gone with various family members to his father's home "to eat oysters with 'Neal, Betsy, Warren, Wm. T. and the girls. We had a grand time. Father brought out a bottle of the 'June Wine' left by cousin Fanny which put us all in high glee. 'Neal had his new suit...which he got pretty well torn. After Catherine and Betsy went home, we adjourned over the Doctor's and drank a bottle of his 'York Wine.' For my own part I was pretty well cut and the others not much better off. We did not get home till one." The next day he wrote "Felt shocking bad all the morning from last night's frolic."[74]

Wine was served even at parties for young people. Elizabeth Buffam Chace, who grew up in Smithfield, Rhode Island, in the first quarter of the nineteenth century, remembered: "At our evening parties...we had for refreshments fruits or nuts or both, and often cake and light wine."[75] Sarah Anna Emery also recalled that cake and wine were a favorite refreshment to offer guests.

In addition to home-brewed beers, wines, and cider, there was a variety of imported beverages: in 1809 Ethan Denison of Stonington recorded in his diary that he had fetched home from Mystic's Pistol Point "3 bbls flour 1 bbl peach brandy & 16 1/4 gls of Cogniack brandy & 2 bbls of sugar," some of which he may have distributed among neighbors. Another time he brought "three barrels of flour & nine gallons Peach Brandy" from Packer's Ferry.[76] Joseph Anthony reported: "Devoted the day [18 July 1823] to bottling port wine, rec'd by the [ship] Parthian. I filled 300 bottles and stowed them in the wine cellar."[77] Another day he "Bought a quarter cask [24 gals] Maderia wine of Capt. Lumbard and put it to settle."[78]

Not many people in the Buckinghams' time were concerned about Yankee drinking habits. As Elizabeth Chace recalled, "Total abstinence had not been thought of at that time but I remember when I was fourteen years old, I found that [wine] made me dizzy and I renounced it without ever thinking or hearing that there was any moral harm in it. Cider was the family dinner drink and I renounced that for the same reasons."[79] Writing her memoirs late in the nineteenth century, Sarah Emery observed that in the 1870s "many of the every-day customs of our fathers would not be tolerated for a moment. Our young ladies would not so smilingly receive a band of young men reeling from the dining to the drawing room with the lightly deprecating remark that 'they were only a little over-dinnerish, and not to be minded.'"[80]

Gradually temperance societies were formed in response to what was truly heavy and widespread alcohol use. Lydia and Samuel Buckingham's oldest son was known as a temperance supporter, providing neither rum nor cider for his haying crew at a time when it was customary.[81] In all likelihood his father had done so in *his* time.

Special-Occasion Foods

Salt-haying: Wherever meadows lay close to tidal waterways, New England's coastal farmers harvested salt hay. At Saybrook, there were meadows along the Connecticut River, and opposite the Ferry District in Lyme the Lieutentant River was lined with salt meadows. Farmers owned salt meadowland outright, as did Samuel Buckingham, or had the rights to harvest hay. Teams of oxen and workers went out to these meadows by scow, if the tide was high enough to follow up the creeks or rivers, or by wagon if there was access by road. As with other haying, farmers worked together and had a sociable time, including time "to relax and consume a substantial lunch."[82]

Sarah Emery's father had a salt meadow, and she recalled that the haying season in late August and early September "brought a dog-days Thanksgiving baking. Mince pies, plum cake, rich doughnuts, nice meats, baked beans and other tempting viands were packed in a wooden chest, along with a small keg of cider and a bottle of 'santa cruz' or 'jamaica' rum."[83] There is no question that it was hot, hard work for everyone: the men in the meadows and the women at home fixing meals.

Election Day's election cake and Training Day's training cake: Two holidays now gone from the New England calendar, although widely observed in the early 1800s, were days of civic obligation: Election Day, or in some places Election Week, in March or May,[84] and Training Days in May and September on which the militia gathered and drilled. On both days, people from outlying districts came into town; a great deal of socializing among family and friends accompanied the more serious duties of voting or drilling.

Election cake: There are several variations on what is called election cake in New England. In their early manifestations, they were sweet yeasted cakes, a richer version of modern yeasted coffee cake. Election cake represents an enduring tradition of yeasted sweet baking that was giving way to the use of chemical leavenings during this period as the nineteenth century progressed.

John Howard Redfield, who grew up in Cromwell, Connecticut, between 1815 and 1825, apparently paid very close attention to election cake, leaving us this description:

"In preparation for [Election Week] every family baked ovenfuls of what was called "election cake," which was a delicious loaf cake, too sacred to be used for anything but weddings, high teas, and Election week. [For weddings] it was usually made extra rich, and covered with very ornate and appropriate frostings. [For Election week] it was prepared as a somewhat more plain and digestible compound, but the supply had to be abundant, for the whole juvenile population expected to feast upon it through the week. And what feasts! Was every cake so delicious? The delicate frostings of white of egg and sugar, the rich, sweet, and spicy substance of the cake itself, and the raisins which were embedded in the toothsome compound were joys which no Connecticut boy could ever forgo or forget."[85]

Besides baking cake for company, a good many households prepared other special foods for the many balls and parties also held at election time. Large banquets and dinner parties were given for the clergy, political leaders, and state officials.

Training cake: In Connecticut, local militia companies gathered in May, and companies from a whole district convened in September.[86] The September Training Day meant huge crowds of people gathering in large, central towns. An event that size drew vendors selling food and drink to the militiamen and their families. Redfield and other little boys were so busy mimicking the uniformed men that he did not pay as close attention to the cookies and cakes being sold as he had to election cake, and he left us no description of training cake at all.

Training cake in its varieties was similar to modern cookies or cookie bars. Some were made with molasses as a cheap sweetening, others with sugar. They were variously spiced—ginger, cinnamon, nutmeg appear in recipes. Training cakes stiff enough to roll and cut were sometimes decorated by being stamped with a wooden mold, often in some patriotic motif.[87]

Cookies and cakes: During Mrs. Buckingham's youth, small sweet baked items that we would call cookies were called "cakes" plural. Recipe books from the eighteenth and early nineteenth centuries are full of references to cake and cakes. Usually, but not always, the word "cake" meant a single, large baked item. In the earlier days it was most often raised with eggs or with yeast, and it was something that we would recognize as a cake. There were also small baked sweets, some of which had their own distinct names, like cracknells, jumbals, naples biscuits, whigs. There were other small baked sweets, like Shrewsbury cakes, seed cakes, almond cakes, ratafia cakes, or "small cakes," which were understood at the time to be baked in small individual portions, just as we would make a cookie. Over Lydia Buckingham's lifetime, the word cookie, an Anglo corruption of the Dutch "koekje," came into usage in New England, and recipes merely named "cookie" appeared in some of the early American cookbooks, most notably *American Cookery* by Amelia Simmons, published in 1796. The words "cookie" and "cakes" were used in parallel for most of the nineteenth century, until the word cookie won out in the late 1800s with descriptive adjectives added to distinguish one kind of cookie from another.

Small cakes and cookies were labor-intensive. Lydia Buckingham may have seldom, if ever, made any of this group of baked goods, perhaps preferring to bake whole pans full of gingerbread, or sponge, pound, cup, or composition cake, or to fry a large batch of doughnuts to satisfy the family sweet tooth.

Some Things Change, Some Things Stay the Same

Lydia Buckingham died in 1833; Mehetebel, by then in her late fifties, went to live with her brother Samuel in Lebanon, where in her declining years she could observe the great changes under way as America's Federal period ended and the Victorian age began. Meanwhile, in Waterford, Connecticut, Charlotte Rogers was born in 1820—about the same year as Emma Weaver Farnsworth—and in this transitional period learned a great many skills she would end up never needing. Unlike Mehetebel Buckingham, who learned in her girlhood skills she continued to use as a woman in her mother's home—hearth cooking and baking, yeast- and bread-making, dairying and the care of dairy animals, spinning and weaving—Charlotte Rogers would learn many of these skills, only to have change overtake her and require new learning, new skills.

But while technology, transportation, fashions, political ideas, and even the view of the past itself changed, the idea of what made a good breakfast, dinner, and supper in New England did not, at least not substantially. People eagerly embraced the fashionable new furniture of the Empire period—when Emma Farnsworth's family moved to a new house in 1839 they bought "new furniture in latest style"—marble-topped tables and sofas and chairs stuffed with horsehair.[88] But New Englanders went on eating pork and beans on Saturday night, enjoying boiled dinners of beef, ham, or salt fish, serving Indian pudding, and making pies and doughnuts. New Englanders stayed with the foods and foodways they had created in the eighteenth century.

Lydia Buckingham could have sat down at Charlotte Greenman's dinner table and found virtually everything familiar, although she might have been amazed at how it got there or had been prepared. She might have been disappointed at having to drink tea instead of cider, but that would have happened at her son's house, too.

In the coming chapters we will see how the basic New England diet was refined by the Greenmans; maintained by the Burrows family under financial stress; taken to sea on distance-voyaging ships like the *Charles W. Morgan* and fishing vessels like the *L. A. Dunton*, and served up by men in the U.S. Life-Saving Service.

The Recipes

The recipes included here were, of course, all cooked in a fireplace in the era of the Buckingham House. You won't need a fireplace to use these recipes at home, but if you have one equipped for cooking you should give it a try. The beef soup and salt pork and apples are main dishes, the kind of food Lydia Buckingham and her neighbors prepared for themselves. The recipes for grilled shad, mackerel, and salmon that follow tell how to prepare some of the fish to which Mrs. Buckingham had access.

While Mrs. Buckingham probably made brown bread of the rye and cornmeal grown by her husband, it is a difficult bread to master for those of us accustomed to working with wheat flour. The recipe for a bread made of one third each rye, Indian, and wheat flour is a compromise loaf, with historic precedents, challenging for experienced bakers but well worth the effort. "Indian," in these recipes and in the text, refers to corn meal, preferably a finely ground white meal, commonly known as jonnycake meal in southeastern New England. I have greatly increased the amount of yeast to be used in bread recipes because I understand that the slow progress of rising with the smaller amounts of historic yeast is unnerving to modern cooks. I would like you to consider using the homemade yeast recipe that follows, and using it in all the historic yeasted recipes in this book. It is a slow-acting, but competent, yeast, and you simply cannot expect the kind of response from it we are accustomed to with the dry yeasts now available.

Some desserts and tea fare follow: pound cake, apple dumplings, caraway cakes, and finally election cake, so much admired by John Redfield.

SALT PORK FRIED WITH APPLES OR POTATOES

Fried salt pork and apples is a favorite dish in the country; but it is seldom seen in the city. After the pork is fried, some of the fat should be taken out, lest the apples should be oily. Acid apples should be chosen, because they cook more easily; they should be cut in slices across the whole apple, about twice or three times as thick as a new dollar. Fried till tender, and brown on both sides—laid around the pork. If you have cold potatoes slice them and brown them in the same way.

From *American Frugal Housewife,* by Lydia Maria Child, 1833, page 60

This would have been a good, quick dish for an early-nineteenth-century breakfast or supper for rural coastal people like the Buckinghams, who probably put down their own salt pork, and probably had an apple tree. It is delicious, but most modern people will shy away from the salt pork.

If you decide to try it, select lean salt pork, slice it as thick as slab bacon is usually sliced and fry it. As Mrs. Child suggests, drain off most of the fat, and lay your sliced apples on the pan around the pork. The apples should be a tart, cooking apple, sliced a quarter of an inch or so thick. Since Mrs. Child does not specify coring the apples, I assume she intended the diner to eat around it at table.

Cold, boiled potatoes are also good fried up this way.

BEEF SOUP

Beef soup should be stewed four hours over a slow fire. Just enough water to keep the meat covered. If you have any bones left of roast meat, &c. it is a good plan to boil them with the meat, and take them out half an hour before the soup is done. A pint of flour and water, with salt, pepper, twelve or sixteen onions, should be put in twenty minutes before the soup is done. Be careful and not throw in salt and pepper too plentifully; it is easy to add to it, and not easy to diminish. A lemon, cut up and put in half an hour before it is done, adds to the flavor. If you have tomato catsup in the house, a cupful will make soup rich. Some people put in crackers; some thin slices of crust, made nearly as short as common shortcake; and some stir up two or three eggs with milk and flour, and drop it in with a spoon.

From *American Frugal Housewife,* by Lydia Maria Child, 1833, page 48

Here is one way to prepare fresh beef in a way that Lydia and Mehetebel Buckingham may have done. In her usual fashion, Mrs. Child offered two or three variations on a recipe within a single set of instructions: in this case, there are varying ways to thicken the soup, including flour and water to make a gravy; crackers; "the thin slices of crust" being, apparently, baked shortcake, which was similar to modern-day biscuits; and the last a rich dumpling made with eggs.

The only vegetables in this soup are onions. They are there for flavor, and the resulting beef soup looks more to the modern eye like stewed beef in a thick gravy. A dish like this is ideally suited to fireplace cookery. Even a novice can have stunning success, and the flavor of this dish cooked over fire is outstanding.

The catsup Mrs. Child called for was considerably different from modern catsup; early catsup was not sweet, and the recipe she gave uses salt, cloves, allspice, pepper, mace, garlic, and mustard seeds for the spices. If you want the flavor Mrs. Child intended for this dish, unless you make homemade catsup, your best bet is to eschew commercial catsup and look in a specialty or health-food store for a low or no-sugar catsup; or substitute tomato paste thinned with water, to which you add some of the spices listed above.

The following interpretation of Mrs. Child's recipe suggests a procedure to use.

stewing beef, cubed, one-third to half a pound per serving
soup bones, or bones left over from roasts, steaks, ribs
water to cover the above
2 cups water

1 cup flour
a dozen small onions, peeled
salt and pepper
catsup, optional
lemon, optional, quartered
your choice of thickener:
plain crackers
biscuit dough, rolled thin, baked and cut into strips
dumplings (recipe below)

1. Put the meat and bones in a deep heavy pot (a cast-iron pot with a tight-fitting lid would be ideal) and just cover them with water. Put the lid on and stew gently for three and a half hours.
2. Half an hour before serving time, remove the soup bones. Add the onions, salt and pepper. Shake the flour and water together in a jar till it looks milky, and add gradually to the stew, stirring all the time.
3. If you choose, add lemon and catsup at this time.
4. If thickening with the crackers or biscuit, plan to add them five minutes or so before serving. If you wish dumplings, have them ready to drop in twenty minutes before serving.

DUMPLINGS FOR BEEF SOUP

A proportion of one egg to one cup of flour and about half a cup of milk will give you about two cups of dumplings; if you wish more, double the recipe.

1 egg
1/2 cup milk
1 scant cup flour

1. Beat the egg lightly in the milk.
2. Add the egg and milk mixture to the flour, stirring gently till blended.
3. Drop by small spoonfuls into the stew, cover with the lid and cook for twenty minutes.

TO MAKE YEAST

Put 2 quarts of water and 2 tablespoonfuls of hops on to boil. Pare and grate 6 large potatoes. When the hops and water boil, strain the water on the grated potatoes, and stir well. Place on the stove and boil up once. Add half a cup of sugar and one fourth of a cupful of salt. Let the mixture get blood warm; then add one cupful of yeast, or one cake of compressed yeast, and let it rise in a warm place five or six hours. When well risen, turn into a stone jug. Cork this tightly and set in a cool place.

From *Miss Parloa's New Cookbook and Marketing Guide*, by Maria Parloa, 1880, page 381-82

Although this recipe is dated later than the period we have been discussing in this chapter, I include it because it tells how to use a modern yeast product to make the old-style liquid yeast. This is the yeast to use in all the period recipes in this book that call for "a cup full of yeast." Making it is not as difficult as it sounds. It is pictured on page 47 with rolls in the chapter about the Greenmans.

Potato-based yeast seems to have been popular in the nineteenth century; many of the manuscript cookbooks I have seen have potato-yeast recipes in them, although Mrs. Child and others also have recipes which use bran, Indian meal, rye, and other grains and use molasses instead of sugar. This is not a sourdough. It does not have to be fed, and should be stored tightly covered, as recommended, and unlike sourdough.

"Those who make their own bread, should make their own yeast, too. When bread is nearly out, always think whether yeast is in readiness; for it takes a day and a night to prepare it."[89] Such was the yeast counsel of Mrs. Child. Of course, not everyone made their own yeast; it could be purchased from a baker or brewer. Claude Chester, as a boy in Noank, Connecticut, in the late nineteenth century, remembered being sent with a pitcher and a penny to a neighbor who made potato yeast and sold it to people in town. This recipe is clear enough that an interpretation is not necessary. I have a a few observations, however. Hops may be difficult to get locally, but stores for beer and wine hobbyists usually have it. Be sure to strain the hops out of the hop water when adding it to the potatoes. Cake yeast is, unfortunately, harder to find in the stores than dry; it keeps less well and is less popular than dried yeast. You can use one package of dried yeast in this recipe even though it is a slightly different yeast. I found this yeast very active when it had its first rising.

This recipe produces quite a lot of yeast, about three quarts, but it keeps well (I had no trouble keeping it for more than a month) and if you bake frequently you could easily use it up. Be sure to keep a cupful to start the next batch.

THIRDED BREAD

Some people like one third Indian in their flour. Others like one third rye; and some think the nicest of all bread is one third Indian, one third rye, and one third flour, made according to the directions for flour bread. When Indian is used, it should be salted, and scalded, before the other meal is put in. A mixture of other grains is economical when flour is high.

Flour bread should have a sponge set the night before. The sponge should be soft enough to pour; mixed with water, warm or cold, according to the temperature of the weather. One gill of lively yeast is enough to put into sponge for two loaves....About an hour before your oven is ready, stir in flour into your sponge till it is stiff enough to lay on a well floured board or table. Knead it up pretty stiff, and put it into well greased pans...Common sized loaves will bake in three quarters of an hour. If they slip easily in the pans it is a sign they are done.

From *American Frugal Housewife*, by Lydia Maria Child, 1833, page 78

Making bread was so commonly done that recipes were, for most nineteenth-century cooks, superfluous. Most cookbook writers described variations on familiar breads and provided practical hints for performing a familiar process. As Mrs. Child observed, "It is more difficult to give rules for making bread than anything else; it depends so much on judgment and experience."

Thirded bread is heavy, crusty, and flavorful, best eaten as an accompaniment to soups, stews, chowders, and even baked beans. The following interpretation is an attempt to provide rules for what I agree is the "nicest of all bread."

To set the sponge:
3 cups lukewarm water
1/2 cup molasses
1 tablespoon or 1 package dry yeast
3 cups whole wheat flour

1. Mix the water, molasses, and yeast in a warm bowl and let stand until the yeast begins to foam.
2. Stir in the flour, and beat until the batter is smooth, about 100 strokes.
3. Cover with a damp towel and set in a warm place; allow to rise till the batter is doubled, about an hour.

To scald the Indian meal:
3 cups stone-ground white cornmeal (Indian)
2-3 cups boiling water
1 tablespoon salt

1. Mix the cornmeal and salt together in a large bowl.
2. Add the boiling water and stir to prevent lumps, until you have a fairly loose mixture.
3. Let stand until mixture cools, about twenty minutes, or until the sponge is ready.

To make the bread:

3-4 cups rye
1-2 cups whole wheat flour

1. When the sponge is ready, fold the rye flour in one cup at a time, using the back of a spoon.
2. Spoon the scalded meal onto the rye and sponge mixture, using the back of a spoon to work the Indian meal into the dough, until the Indian is mixed evenly throughout. The dough will be very sticky, moist, and grainy in texture.
3. Dust a board with wheat flour, turn dough out onto it, and sprinkle more flour on the top. Knead, adding more flour as needed (it may take up to 2 1/2 cups of flour) until the dough is semielastic. It will still be sticky and grainy: expect the dough to cling to your hands. Set to rise, covered, in a warm place.
4. When doubled in bulk, after about an hour, punch it down. Divide dough into two portions, knead, and shape into loaves. Put into greased loaf pans (or on a baking sheet or baking stone sprinkled with cornmeal). Set to rise. Preheat oven to 375°.
5. When doubled, bake at 375° for ten minutes, reduce oven to 325° and bake for another forty to fifty minutes, or until the loaves come out of the pans easily, or sound hollow when tapped.

Yields two loaves.

POUND CAKE

Take 1 lb. butter, 1 lb. sugar, beat them together, 10 eggs, 1 lb. flour, and a little spice.

From the manuscript recipe notebook of Caroline Hastings, ca. 1820, in the collection of Old Sturbridge Village

Modern recipes for pound cake measure the ingredients in cups, obscuring the reason for the name "pound" cake (ten medium eggs weigh about one pound). For spice in pound cake, I like nutmeg. Your choice of spice, or none at all, is fine.

This recipe will yield two standard-sized loaves of cake. Or bake it in a bundt or tube pan. The following interpretation could easily be cut to create a "half-pound" cake.

2 cups butter
2 cups sugar
10 eggs
4 1/2 cups flour
Preheat oven to 325°

1. Cream together butter and sugar, then beat in the eggs until all is well blended and frothy.
2. Mix in the flour and spice, sifted together. Stir to make a smooth batter.
3. Pour into two greased loaf pans. Bake one hour or until a knife inserted comes out clean.

Yields two loaves.

FISH GRILLED ON A GRIDIRON

To Broil Shad, Mackerel, and Salmon.
Have the bars of the gridiron well greased with lard; lay your fish on, flesh side down; when half done, turn it and finish, skin down; when done, pour over sweet cream, if you have it, or spread over a little butter.

From *New England Economical Housekeeper*, by Mrs. E.A. Howland, 1845, page 62

In 1845, many people were still cooking in open fireplaces, and broiling fish on gridirons. No matter how carefully I have done it, I have always found grilling fish tricky and now own a wonderful grilling device that clasps shut so you can turn the fish at will without prying it off the bars of a gridiron.

Shad, mackerel, and salmon, oilier fish than many, are enhanced tremendously by being cooked over a wood fire or charcoal. The instructions above are perfectly useful for outdoor grilling. If you are doing it in a standard oven, reverse the process: skin side up for a few moments, turn, and finish with the flesh down. To serve, turn it on the platter skin down. Sweet cream *is* good poured over it, but you could get away with plain melted butter, too. Plan on one-third to one-half pound of fish per person. Allow about eight to twelve minutes per side, depending on the size of the fish.

ELECTION CAKE

Four pounds of flour, three quarters of a pound of butter, four eggs, one pound of sugar, half a pint of good yeast, wet with milk as stiff as can be molded on a board. Set to rise overnight in winter; in warm weather three hours is usually enough to rise. Bake about three quarters of an hour.

From *New England Economical Housekeeper,* by Mrs. E.A. Howland, 1845, page 21

This sweetened bread sometimes had spices and fruit added. The *New Family Receipt Book,* published in Hartford in 1829, recommended nutmeg, mace, wine, brandy, and raisins.[90] The modern Fanny Farmer cookbook declares that election cake is an old Connecticut specialty (though I don't think it was always associated with the state) and calls for lemon rind, cloves, mace, nutmeg, raisins, and whiskey. Adding these makes the cake like a yeasted coffee cake.

The interpretation that follows includes spices, raisins, and brandy.

Preheat oven to 350°.

1 package yeast dissolved in 1 cup of lukewarm milk
1 cup sugar
1/3 cup butter
2 eggs
4 1/2 cups flour
2 teaspoons nutmeg and/or cinnamon
1 cup raisins
1/2 cup brandy

1. Dissolve the yeast in the milk and set aside. Rub together the butter and sugar.
2. Beat the eggs and add to the butter and sugar. Then add the yeast and milk. Add the brandy.
3. Sift together the flour and spices. Gradually add the raisins. If necessary, knead in the remaining flour. Then on a floured board knead an additional fifteen or twenty times.
4. Butter a tube pan, or two small loaf pans. Put the dough in and allow to rise till double in size.
5. Bake for 35 to 45 minutes. Turn out on a rack to cool.

If you wish, you can make a drizzle icing of confectioners sugar and milk.

CARAWAY CAKES

Take one pound of flour, three quarters of a pound of sugar, half a pound of butter, a glass of rosewater, four eggs, a half a teacup caraway seed—the materials well rubbed together and beat up. Drop them from a spoon on tin sheets and bake twenty or thirty minutes in rather a slow oven.

From *New England Economical Housekeeper,* by Mrs. E.A. Howland, 1844, page 20

This recipe is identical to the one for caraway cakes in *American Frugal Housewife* written by Mrs. Child several years earlier. In the tradition of early-nineteenth-century cookies, it is not as sweet as modern cookies. Rosewater was a fairly frequent ingredient in many early recipes and can still be obtained if you would like to try it. You can use either brown or white sugar. When made with brown sugar, the cookies take a bit longer to bake.

The interpretation which follows cuts the original old recipe in half.

2 cups flour
3/4 cup sugar
1 cup butter
2 eggs
1/2 cup caraway seeds
1 1/2 teaspoons rosewater or milk
Preheat the oven to 325°

1. Rub flour, sugar, butter together till it looks like crumbs.
2. Beat the eggs and stir into the rubbed mixture. Then beat all together, adding the milk or rosewater.
3. The dough should be stiff. Drop on greased cookie sheets in walnut-sized pieces, or larger, if you prefer.
4. Bake for 20 minutes until golden.

Yields 48 small cookies.

APPLE DUMPLINGS

Apple Dumpling, No. 2.
Select large, fair, pleasant sour, and mellow apples; pare them, and take out the core with a small knife, and fill up the place with sugar; prepare some pie-crust, roll it out quite thick, and cut it into pieces just large enough to cover one apple. Lay an apple on each piece, and enclose them entirely; tie them up in a thick piece of cloth that has been well floured, put them in a pot of boiling water, and boil them one hour; if the boiling should stop they will be heavy. Serve them up with sweet sauce, or butter and sugar.

From *New England Economical Housekeeper*, by Mrs. E.A. Howland, 1845, page 36

Most modern recipes for apple dumplings call for the crust-encased apples to be baked. The truth of the matter is that to twentieth-century people boiled apple dumplings are heavy even if they *don't* stop boiling. They are good-tasting either boiled or baked: if you want an authentic apple dumpling, boil it; if you don't care, bake it.

Use your favorite pie-crust recipe (or the one on pages 252-253), and a cooking apple like a Cortland or a Baldwin. Serve with the traditional butter and sugar, or a sweet sauce, or just heavy cream. An interpretation follows.

apples (as many as there are to be servings)
brown sugar
pie crust (a two-crust recipe will wrap up 6 medium apples)
Preheat oven to 350° or set a large kettleful of water to boil.

1. Core and, if you wish, pare your apples. Fill the centers with brown sugar.
2. Divide the pie dough into as many equal-sized pieces as needed for the number of apples you have. Roll the crust out a quarter of an inch thick. Set the apple into the center and wrap the crust up around it.

If boiling apples:

3. Smooth the dough all around the apples. Make sure your boiling cloth or bag is thoroughly wet in hot water, and flour it generously. Tie up the apples in the cloth separately and tightly. Put into the pot.
4. Boil for an hour, making sure they are floating and boiling the whole time. Add water, if necessary, from a hot teakettle full.
5. When done, cut through the ties, and put the dumplings into individual serving dishes. Cut them open and put butter and sugar on to serve.

If baking apples:

3. Pinch the dough shut around each apple, making the crust a bit decorative if you wish.
4. Set in a baking pan and bake for about an hour, or until the crust is golden. Serve warm.

The Greenmans: Prosperity and Plenty

Charlotte Rogers Greenman was born in 1820, and grew up in Waterford, Connecticut. She learned to cook, we suppose, from her mother, during a time of many changes in the housekeeping and cooking habits of New England. She went to live in the Greenmanville District of Stonington, Connecticut, in 1842 when she married the youngest of the three Greenman brothers who had a shipyard where Mystic Seaport Museum stands today.

Above, Thomas Greenman is shown with his grand-daughter Charlotte Stillman, circa 1885, next to his Greenmanville home. Opposite, a supper of tea, toast, and pear sauce similar to suppers enjoyed by Arthur Story's family. [MSM 81-11-130]

The United States Census records give us four snapshots of Charlotte's household over thirty years, and of those of many of her family and neighbors. Her husband's business records have survived. The Greenmanville Seventh Day Baptist Church records exist, and there are letters and diaries of the Greenmans' peers in Mystic, with details of home and social life. All taken, a portrait of a comfortable, upper-middle-class life emerges. With Charlotte, and with her sisters-in-law, Harriet and Abby, we can sense the texture of daily life, so much harder to discern with Lydia Buckingham.

Unlike Lydia's, Charlotte's kitchen no longer exists. Her home was altered many times after Thomas's death, including a conversion into apartments, and the rooms that probably were kitchens and supporting pantries and workrooms now hold desks and filing cabinets for a busy museum. The three brothers' homes were much the same, and Abby Greenman's kitchen, despite some modernization, is still whole enough for us to envision Charlotte's, which probably resembled it.

Charlotte Rogers Greenman, shown here as a mature woman, meets our ideal of the prosperous Victorian Yankee. [Carte de visite, MSM 76.41.15]

Although the Museum intends in the future to restore and exhibit George Greenman's house, Charlotte's is the only Greenman home open to the public. The first-floor exhibit as it appears to visitors today is furnished to the 1870s, the last nine years of Charlotte's life. By the 1870s the Greenmans were prosperous, and they made improvements in all three houses, redecorating in Victorian fashion. Thomas and Charlotte's only surviving child—a daughter—had grown up; after Thomas was widowed she, her husband, and their children, spent the summer months in Mystic.

In the thirty-seven years of her married life, Charlotte's household changed several times, as we will see—changes that surely had an impact on the food cooked and eaten by this family.

The Greenmans and Greenmanville Between 1840 and 1880

Charlotte's husband, Thomas, was the youngest of three brothers who operated the shipbuilding business of George Greenman & Co., along with the Greenmanville Manufacturing Co. textile mill, on several acres along the east shore of the Mystic River. The yard, mill, church, and homes for the Greenmans and workers formed a community named for the family. Charlotte's sisters-in-law, Harriet Almy, married to Clark, and Abby Chipman, married to George, lived in the two houses to the south of Charlotte's. Another sister-in-law, Catherine Edmondson, Thomas's sister, lived in a small house kitty corner from Charlotte, down a lane that led to the water. Other neighbors included many relatives by marriage and friends who had relocated to Greenmanville from the Westerly area to work in the shipyard or the mill. Many of these people—anyone who was important to the operation of the shipyard or mill—were Seventh Day Baptists.

Shared Seventh Day Baptist beliefs united the Greenmanville community even before they formed their own congregation in 1850. They were Sabbatarians, observing Saturday as the day of rest, but otherwise they held basic Baptist doctrines.[1] Many New England Protestants, in the Calvinist tradition, generally avoided ostentatious display in personal style and daily life, including their foodways, and as Seventh Day Baptists the Greenmans seem to have done so, too, living well within their means for many years.

The Greenmans were also abolitionists, temperance supporters, and anti-Masons. Political or religious beliefs do not always affect foodways directly, but they can influence what are now popularly called "lifestyle" choices. Since the Greenmans were temperance supporters—later actually prohibitionists—we can be sure they did not drink alcoholic beverages as the Buckinghams apparently did. It was one thing to drink a glass of wine, and another to use it in a recipe, but because Thomas was so strict on this point, Charlotte probably held to an absolute "no-alcohol" rule. Others felt there was room for flexibility with recipes calling for wine, brandy, or Madeira. Mrs. Charles Henry Mallory, for example, wife of the wealthy maritime entrepreneur, who grew up in Mystic and later lived in New York City, conventionally preferred temperance politics, but made brandied peaches and tolerated liquor in plum puddings and mince pies.[2] Some temperance people also adopted some early health-food principles, particularly those promoted by Sylvester Graham, even if this went no further than using the whole-wheat flour bearing his name.

Far more influential in Charlotte and Thomas Greenman's eating habits was what they were used to from their childhood, particularly Thomas's preferences, and the variations on those early habits played over time by food transportation and industry. Also influential was the size of the household, who was available to do the cooking, and the nature of the food supply.[3]

Besides the shipyard, the Greenman enterprise included two farms that produced meat and dairy products for the families. In the middle of the century, they operated a small general store for the convenience of the Greenmanville neighborhood. The brothers hired out their oxen to anyone who needed a garden plowed or manure hauled. Mystic—at that time two villages, Mystic River, on the west side, and Mystic Bridge, on the east—was a comfortable fifteen-minute walk from Greenmanville and had grocery stores, butcher shops, bakeries, and confectioners, many of which delivered goods to the customer.[4]

Thomas Greenman, youngest of the three Greenmanville shipbuilding brothers, was locally famous for his temperance work. [Carte de visite, MSM 76.41.16]

Charlotte's and Abby's Kitchens

The two-story Greek Revival houses the brothers built between 1839 and 1842 each had ells, originally one-story, containing the kitchen and probably pantries or additional storage or work spaces. Abby's and Harriet's ells extended south from the main house, and Charlotte's extended north. It appears that the kitchens were built to accommodate cookstoves.[5] Each kitchen had an entry facing the street and another at the back of the house on the river and shipyard side; each kitchen was next to its respective dining room, and had direct access to the cellar. In Charlotte's house the back stairway leads directly off the kitchen; in Abby's, it leads from the front entryway. Abby's kitchen pantry still exists; Charlotte's and Harriet's, which do not, were probably very much like it.

We can discern some of the kitchen arrangements from architectural evidence. The chimney placement in Abby's and Charlotte's kitchens meant their stoves were against inside walls. In Abby's kitchen, the sink was probably by the south window under which a cistern is located. In the room that was Charlotte's kitchen, a cupboard and shelves, which may have survived from her occupancy, are set into the space beneath the back stairs. Charlotte's kitchen wasn't the bright and sunny room that Abby's was—a disadvantage in winter—but it was cooler in summer.

Abby's pantry was a small rectangular room, with a window toward the river. Shelves and cupboards once lined three of the walls. On the north end of the pantry, the lower cupboard could accommodate two barrels side by side. Three shelves line three sides of the room above the cupboard top, deep enough to provide a table-height work surface. The placement and arrangement of Charlotte's pantry has been obscured by alterations but was probably not very different.

All three houses had full cellars. In Abby's house the brick cellar floor, laid in a herringbone pattern, is still in place undisturbed, and traces of the floor in Charlotte's house are still visible. Easy to sweep and keep clean, the brick floors ensured that anyone going down cellar for potatoes or salted meat did not track dirt back up into the kitchen. The houses' stone foundations are deep and the cellars roomy. The portion of cellar under the main part of Abby's house contains several crude coal bins, and the ell's section, just below the kitchen, was separated from the rest by a simple board wall with a door in it. Though evidence of coal bins or any kind of sectioning is missing in Charlotte's cellar, one can imagine that she, too, similarly protected her vegetables, meats, and preserves from coal dust. In Abby's cellar, a large rough cupboard and several shelves handily contained canned vegetables and jars of preserves.

The pantries and cellars were obvious storage facilities. Mrs. Abell, in the mid-century *The Mother's Book of Daily Duties*, helps us envision how the Greenman women may have used their storage spaces: "It is best to have the store closet open from the kitchen, but it should not be kept warm by the door left open. A window for light and fresh air is important, and it should be dry."[6]

Certain goods kept better if cool in summer, especially grains, which would become rancid. With the kitchen stove heated daily, a pantry with an open door could warm up. "Indian Meal should be kept in a small keg, and not more than half a bushel purchased at a time in summer....Stir it occasionally, or keep a cold stone in the centre." Similarly rye, buckwheat, and rice "should be got in small quantities." "Flour may as well be kept in the barrel, with a cover made larger than the barrel to keep it perfectly clean and nice, with a flour scoop to dip with." Flour was bolted at this time; thus it was less liable to become rancid. Mrs. Abell cautioned that in warm weather fermenting molasses could burst the demijohn in which it was stored, and she recommended purchasing it by the gallon, which the Greenmans did. She said cake and bread could be kept in boxes in the pantry. Mrs. Abell cautioned housekeepers to keep nearly all kinds of stores including coffee, tea, raisins, tapioca, salt, and pepper in closely covered containers.[7]

Hams "must be put in bags of paper or cloth, and packed in oats, bran or ashes, to keep them from flies, bugs, &c....Dried beef should be kept in the same way, and when cut, hung in the cellar passage, to keep moist and cool." Ham, once cut, could also be hung in the cellar way. Codfish was hung there, too, "by a string around the small end."[8]

The Greenman houses were at that time without central heating, and their cellar ways hung with hams, beef, and codfish were cool and moist. Root vegetables in bins or barrels would have kept well from autumn into the following summer. Mrs. Abell's warnings about spoilage were well taken. A good housewife checked her food regularly and watched out for signs of insects or vermin, discarding damaged food when necessary. Even under these ideal home conditions, food went bad; and, as we shall see, the spoilage problem was even more acute for seafarers.

The water supply: Architectural or archaeological evidence is missing for the water supply of the Thomas Greenman house. In the George Greenman house, there is evidence of a cistern in the ground just south of the kitchen ell. A large half circle of stone rests below the southwest kitchen window. Perhaps Thomas and Clark had similar cisterns.

At that time, cisterns both collected water from the roofs of houses and served as storage tanks for water pumped into them from wells. Hand pumps at kitchen sinks drew water up from below, although some houses had a cistern in the attic, from which gravity moved the water down to a sink. Cistern water was not always ideal for drinking, and period housekeeping manuals contained advice on monitoring it. A well just outside the east entry at Abby's house probably predated the cistern, but may have provided drinking water. In 1879, the year of Charlotte's death, Thomas installed a water sytem fed by gravity, unbelievably enough through a pipe from the west side of the river.[9] This fresh gravity-driven running water from a source on the hillside overlooking the river could have supplied water for both drinking and washing.

All three houses had generous backyards, and each family had a barn. The photograph on a previous page of Thomas standing by the southwest corner of his home shows clothes-line poles set up immediately to the west of the walkway that connected Charlotte's back door with those of her sisters-in-law, along which they could walk to one another's houses.

In Clark and Harriet's backyard, a generous-sized vegetable garden grew immediately behind the ell and south of a small building identified variously as a tool shed and a wash house. Two small buildings stood at the back of George and Abby's house. The southernmost one was for a long time a single room—a workroom—with a chimney in the south wall. A smoke chamber on the west side of the chimney, still rich with the odor of slowly smoldering chips, has hooks for hanging sausage, hams of beef or pork, or

One of several Greenman gardens, this was at the rear of Clark's house. The many poles and stakes seem to point to pole beans, which with fresh corn and peas were favorites in the late 1800s. [Edward Scholfield photo, MSM 80.26.39]

Snow pudding, an elegant nineteenth-century molded dessert, more easily made when mechanical egg beaters appeared. The recipe is on page 58.

bacon. A space like this–sometimes connected to a house and sometimes separate–was a general work space for large messy tasks—like lard, soap-making, or butchering operations. A pair of doors opposite one another provided fresh air; proximity to the cistern eased water hauling. All three families may have used this little outbuilding. Even though the Greenmans' store accounts show they purchased soap by the bar, they may also have made general-purpose soap for laundry and household use. They may have made their own lard, and pickled and smoked their own meat, or they may have hired the work out.[10]

The Greenman families could choose to do whatever part of the butchering process they wished; they could have the work done at the farms they owned or, in later years, they could use the pig-slaughtering-and-scalding service D. Dunn advertised in the 19 October 1876 Mystic *Press*: "The subscriber is now fully prepared to DRESS HOGS in the very best manner. Will take to the Slaughter House, Dress by Scalding, and return, price $1.50". A similar announcement appeared in the Stonington *Mirror* of 19 November 1874, by Thomas H. Hinckley, who told "Public Houses, Steamers, Ships, & Families" to "bring on your hogs," to be slaughtered at reasonable rates.

What the Greenmans chose to do probably varied over time, as their family's size changed, or as they grew older and more prosperous and could afford to buy finished products, or pay someone to do the work for them. Much depended on personal preference. Shipbuilder William Ellery Maxson, co-owner of the Maxson & Fish shipyard, a Seventh Day Baptist, and Thomas and Charlotte's friend, recorded in his diary that he had salted his beef, pork, and hams, as any one of the Greenmans may also have done.[11]

Cooking Utensils and Dinnerware

Although we do not have a list of the pots and pans, griddles, skillets, bowls, and pie plates that she had on hand, Charlotte probably equipped her kitchen gradually over time, adding utensils as they came on the market or family need required, and replacing others as they broke.

A plain family dinner at noon in homes like those of the Greenman brothers might begin with a soup course, here tomato soup, recipe page 51, fried beef steaks, mashed potatoes, Graham bread, recipe page 56, and pickles. Snow pudding follows for dessert. Table linens and individual place settings were signs of gentility.

An era of specialization: As the nineteenth century progressed, highly specialized cooking utensils, chinaware and silverware were developed by manufacturers, so that items like "vegetable cutters," glass dishes to serve bananas, or a spoon for eating sectioned oranges, were available for people who wished and could afford to be up-to-the-minute. Specialized utensils and service pieces were not, of course, new: the wealthy in the time of the Buckinghams, and before, certainly could have owned single-use items such as chocolate pots, sugar nippers, and fancy little pans for baking. Anyone else wishing to make and serve chocolate would be obliged to adapt another container, perhaps a tea pot; they would use a mallet to break up the loaf sugar; they would settle for less-ornate baked goods. In the nineteenth century, mass manufacturing lowered the costs of specialized items so that more households could be equipped with them. Specialized cooking utensils simplified some fancy cookery, and when the middle classes had access to the utensils (and sufficient time or help to use them), certain stylish dishes moved down from the kitchens of the wealthy and stylish to the homes of the prosperous middle classes, certainly losing some of their cachet enroute. This, of course, moved the very wealthy to create other ways to distinguish themselves.

A good example of this was molded desserts. Since medieval times, ornate presentations of highly formed food were a standard feature of elegant occasions. The upper classes in colonial America used elaborate molds for making blanc mange and jellies, even ice cream, in a variety of shapes from a stately obelisk to a fish or half moon. In the early nineteenth century, cooks poured jelly or blanc mange into ceramic and tin molds, or dishes shaped with pressed designs in the bottom—clusters of grapes or flowers, for example—then let the concoction set up, then turned it out for garnishing. Plus, earlier jellies needed isinglass, usually imported, or jelly made at home from calves' feet, a task requiring time and skill. In ordinary households, this fuss if braved at all would be reserved for best occasions.

Over the course of the 1800s, fancy molds proliferated, and by the last half of the century, when gelatin was a *manufactured* and widely distributed product, relatively cheap and easy to use, the long-stylish molded jellies came to the kitchen of virtually any middle-class family, to be served at any nice dinner. In our time, even with its long and elegant history, Jello salad seems ordinary, and trendy people today distinguish themselves by *not* serving it.

Gadgets and processed foods: Another dynamic at work in the nineteenth century, which we have just seen in the de-gentrification of jellies, was how much industry peered over the shoulders of homemakers, observing which processes lent themselves to the development of a gadget or a shortcut of processed food. In some cases the result was a boon: egg beaters, meat grinders, mechanical churns. Other gadgets never caught on and can be found virtually unused in antique shops, suffering the fate of the electric carving knives and vegetable slicing machines so common in today's yard sales.

Similarly, certain processed foods were great labor

savers: seedless raisins, granulated sugar, fancy condiments and sauces. Self-rising flours presaged packaged cake, biscuit, and muffin mixes. Canned foods extended vegetable and fruit seasons and the distribution of seafood and meat, improving the diet of seafarers, soldiers, miners, and anyone in a remote area unable to raise food for themselves. Some canned foods, like baked beans, were of dubious value to many housewives, a problem industry solved later with advertising; others, like canned tomatoes, were widely accepted, recommended by cookbook writers to keep among groceries always on hand.[12]

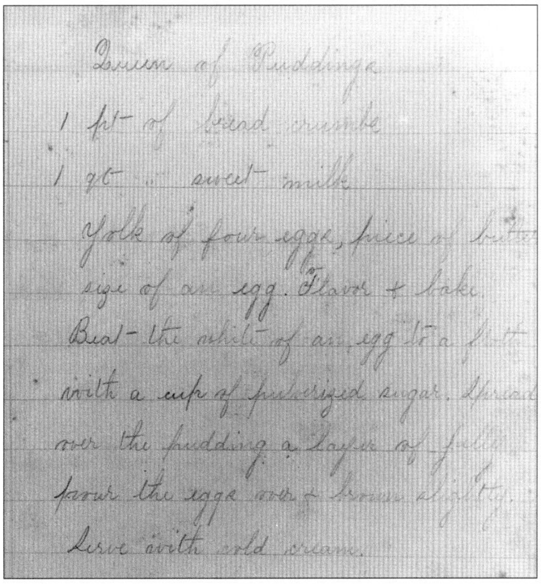
Queen of Puddings
1 pt of bread crumbs
1 qt sweet milk
Yolk of four eggs, piece of butt
size of an egg. Flavor & bake.
Beat the white of an egg to a fr
with a cup of pulverized sugar. Spread
over the pudding a layer of jelly
pour the eggs over & brown slightly.
Serve with cold cream.

These changes were occurring in Charlotte, Harriet, and Abby's time. With the evidence we have, it is very hard to know with certainty which tools they decided were worth having, or which processed foods seemed like good additions to the larder. Abby, with a houseful of children, had very different needs in food preparation than Charlotte and Harriet, who had smaller families. Early in their marriages the three women did the work themselves, with help from children, but later had live-in servants; how much labor went into food preparation affected their home food production and meal planning. Most indications for this group of people, though, show a fairly conservative set of preferences. Charlotte probably bought an egg beater, offered molded jellies to guests, but served pudding and pie to her family for dessert and canned her own tomatoes, probably with help from her domestic, Sarah Mundy.

Equipping Charlotte's kitchen: We have to extrapolate about Charlotte's and Thomas's kitchen furnishings because specific evidence is slender for the Greenmans when we collect all the usual documents and sources. A longstanding belief about the Greenman brothers was that they purchased household goods in triplicate, and that may have been true for certain items. But even the most unanimous families will have personal preferences, one household from another.

On 11 May 1877, about two weeks after Clark died at age 69, a probate inventory of the house was made. It appears that in the kitchen only items considered valuable were listed—mainly furniture and silverware. The room contained at least two tables, seven chairs, and one rocking chair. A carpet was on the floor. Harriet's cooking utensils were lumped under "tin and stove furniture," her mixing bowls, pie plates, and tumblers under "glass, crockery and lamps." Six flat irons were enumerated. Her kitchen knives were called "common cutlery," and a dozen teaspoons, six dessert spoons, and three tablespoons, all described as "silver," probably sterling, were listed. But she and Clark also had silver-plated ware: a tea set, a dozen knives, and a dozen and a half forks. An ice pitcher was listed, too. Charlotte may have had a similar array, at least of types.[13]

Several kitchen items have come to Mystic Seaport from the descendants of George Greenmans', and may have been used by Abby and her daughters: an apple parer, butter mold, and butter knife. More elegant items—a tureen, plates, and a large table, quite possibly a dining table—help us visualize Abby's taste in furnishing her dining room.

George's and Clark's inventories both listed a "refrigerator." Clark's was in the kitchen; George's was listed as appearing in the dining room. It is likely that Thomas and Charlotte had one as well by the 1870s, perhaps one of the items they all purchased together. Coal and ice were both vended in the village, and in winter ice was harvested off many area ponds.[14]

Another source for determining kitchen furnishings is household advice books like *American Woman's Home* by Charlotte Beecher and Harriet Beecher Stowe, published in 1869. Charlotte and her sisters-in-law probably were aware of these Connecticut natives' reputations, and the Greenmans shared Mrs. Stowe's famous abolitionist views. *American Woman's Home*, however, reflected ideal homemaking methods and was written by reformers; their recommended kitchen outfit ran heavily toward specialized storage containers and small utensils. Comparisons among similar advice books show general agreement on a basic set of tools. Some books advocated higher-style cooking techniques, and recommended equipment needed to accomplish it.[15]

The Beecher sisters' list of "Kitchen Furniture" assumed fireplace use, which was still true for a great many homes at the time. In fact, people in rural areas around Mystic and Stonington were still making the shift from fireplace to stove at the time the Beechers' book was printed. Various sheet-iron or cast-iron stoves were developed in the early 1800s, and were adopted first in urban homes, where issues of space and cost of fuel eased their acceptance. Gradually rural people in New England closed up their fireplaces and installed the new cookstoves. Like most new technology, cookstoves varied at first in quality, design, and ease of use, improving and becoming more standardized through the middle of the century. Stove technology required cooks to learn different ways of managing fire and cookery, a thing not all housewives were pleased to do. Many households clung to older ways, especially if the cooks were older people. Younger homemakers like Charlotte gave the cookstove a try. Even though she probably learned to cook on an open hearth as she grew up, Charlotte started with a stove in the Mystic house. Stoves at that time commonly came with a set of basic pots and pans—"stove furniture"—so she probably had a variety of sizes in cast iron, with lids, a tea kettle, iron frying pan—also called a skillet or spider—and saucepans of different sizes, in iron or tin. When she first began housekeeping she may have chosen a well-tinned brass kettle for preserving, but by mid-century porcelained iron pots were made, and she may have chosen one of those for preserve-making. She may have had a gridiron for broiling. For roasting, she could have used either a tin kitchen, which many people continued to use, or she may have roasted in the oven.[16]

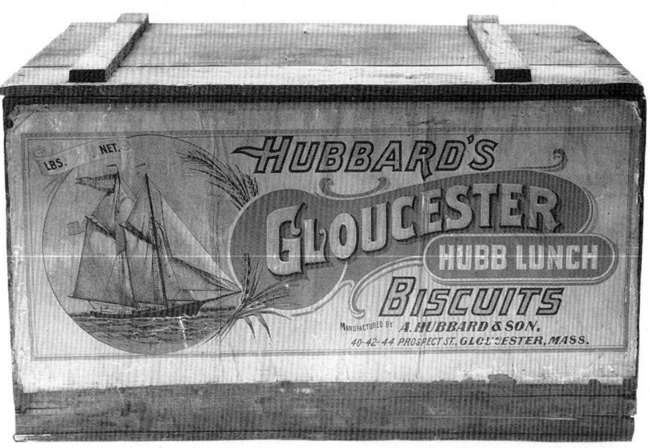

A comparison of household advice-book furnishing suggestions with lists of ships' outfits and recommended furnishings for the life-saving stations clarifies what was considered absolutely necessary for accomplishing basic cookery and what was a refinement appropriate for a home kitchen. The following list of items which Charlotte Greenman probably owned was drawn from these sources.

Lists in advice books, vessel-outfitting lists, and casual inventories suggest that the basic kitchen utensils of the period were an iron fork, spoon—sometimes specified as a basting spoon—dipper, ladle, skimmer, butcher or meat knife with a steel for sharpening it, chopping knife, often with a chopping bowl or tray, and skewers. Among other common kitchen utensils were a colander; a grater, small and large (used both for grating potatoes for laundry starch and for grating food items like cheese or bread); a pepper box—actually a can-shaped tin with perforated lid for shaking pepper out; in coffee-drinking households, a coffee mill and pot; a pudding bag, which could have been made of fabric or tin, because when the material changed the name change lagged behind. For measuring, mixing, and baking, there were earthenware bowls of various sizes, either redware or, at mid-century, yelloware; for mixing bread, bread pans, which often looked like dish pans; tin measures in pint or quart sizes; tin cups; nutmeg grater; tin and earthenware baking dishes; sieves; bread pans for baking loaves; pie plates; and scoops. Crocks and tea canisters were two of the most frequently mentioned storage containers; and by mid-century the modern style of dish washing was common enough that dishpans, so called, appeared on lists of recommended household equipment.[17]

These items, about 40 in all, are the ones that seemed to be considered essential: they appear in advice books, were part of ships' outfits, and were used in the U.S. Life-Saving Service. A well-equipped home kitchen might have, as well, especially after mid-century, some further refinements seen less often at sea or in the life-saving stations: a rolling pin, egg beater, apple corer, potato masher, cleaver, toasting iron, waffle iron, strainer, and a few more specialized items like jelly molds, patty pans, jelly-cake pans, bread board, bread box, cake box, and biscuit cutter.

As tidy as these lists appear, however, they do not always match up with historic reality. For example, among items which appear less frequently are some that have survived from the era, like cookie cutters, muffin pans, and bean pots. Cooks subverted an object's use: an inverted tumbler worked well for cutting cookies or biscuits. An empty bottle could be used for mashing potatoes, tenderizing meat, or rolling dough. Tableware like cups, spoons, and glasses were substituted for measuring tools.

When Charlotte's Mystic contemporary Julia Gates wrote down her recipes she usually listed ingredients without specifying procedures. But she did mention some cooking utensils by name or implication. Measuring devices: pint and quart measures; a tea cup, coffee cup, and plain "cup"; teaspoon, tablespoon, and plain "spoon"; glass, wineglass, and tumbler. Scales are implied because she measured things in pounds and ounces, though once she wrote a "bowl" full of raisins. She must have had a grater for grating lemon, coconut, and nutmeg. She put a pudding in a "deep dish," but another time baked it in a "pudding dish." She mentioned "moulds" often in snow custard recipes and for Spanish cream. She whipped cream and egg whites with an egg beater, chopped raisins and suet perhaps with a chopping knife and tray, and used a "skimmer"; she also used "jelly tins," and "tin" for "cakes," which were probably small and cookie-like. Her steamed brown bread recipe called for a "3 quart pudding mould or pail," tomato catsup needed a "fine colander," green tomato sauce was cooked in a "kettle," and she drained mixed pickles in a "basket." She had a "jumble cutter" for jumbles—a cookie—that she baked on "tin sheets."

Julia apparently did not have a double boiler, because she gave directions to cook custard over a "pot" of boiling water, to pour a white wine sauce into a pail and set it on boiling water, and another time to put lemon sauce into a pail "set on top tea kettle until sauce is hot." An omelet required a "frying pan" and a "broad knife"; and while some people had muffin pans, her muffin recipes called for "muffin rings." Pie recipes imply pie plates, sponge cakes imply tube pans.[18]

Had a recipe book survived from Charlotte, or Abby, or Harriet Greenman, it might reveal a similar collection.

Dining

On board the ship *Comet* between San Francisco and Manila in 1857, Sarah Hix Todd wrote a poignant letter that reveals some interesting details about the importance of tableware and good table manners among the middle class in the middle of the nineteenth century. At sea with her captain husband and a new baby named Ida Reveley, Mrs. Todd was dying. She wrote to her parents requesting them to raise the child, and outlined some particulars: she asked them to raise the little girl gently, and to take her to Church and Sabbath School and learn to love her Maker. Mrs. Todd provided for the disposal of some of her household possessions to her child and her parents: "I want her to have all my bedding, my dishes, my castor, and my plated ware to use; my silver when she gets older. I want her to have such things, and I know you cannot get them any other way. Use them the same as if you bought them yourself....

"Make her loving and lovable. Mother, I would have her learn to use a napkin. I have enough, and when they are gone, she can have more. Let her eat with a clean knife neatly; never mind if yours wear out, there are mine, use them."[19] That one of a dying mother's last wishes involved the use of table napkins and flatware underlines how important refined dining habits were as the mark of civilized people in the nineteenth century, especially to those new to the middle class, as Mrs. Todd seems to have been.

The knife-eating that the Buckinghams employed was being phased out gradually, though it sounds as if Mrs. Todd intended at mid-century that little Ida learn how to use one. An article headlined "Hyper-Gentility" in *Scribner's Magazine* in 1873 described the process of change from knife to fork eating, and the manners that accompanied it. Three "very high toned" city ladies sat down to dinner in the house of a country friend and found there were fresh peas on the table: "'Peas,' wrote one of the immaculate trio, 'such as we never see in town—fresh, green, plump, and luscious, and so delightfully hot and tempting! But as the forks had only two prongs, making it quite useless to try to eat peas with them, we were obliged to leave the delicious things on our plates. The family ate their peas with their knives but of course we could not do that.'" The *Scribner's* editor commented that a true lady would have eaten the peas with her knife, remarking that what is genteel in one place is boorish in another.[20]

Both Charlotte and Thomas would have grown up at a time when country people like themselves ate with knives. We have no way of knowing for sure when they acquired modern-style three- or four-tined forks and made the switch, or even whether they ever did change completely. Like the country friends above, they may have continued to use a knife at least sometimes. Clark's inventory in 1877 listed plated knives and forks; this standard manufactured flatware included, by that time, the familiar modern-style fork. Perhaps this is a clue to when the brothers acquired modern-style flatware.

None of the Greenman families seem to have owned such specialized pieces as asparagus tongs, oyster forks, or ice cream spoons, which were available for the fashionable consumer. Even specialized serving pieces are missing from Clark's inventory, such as a soup ladle or pie knife. Clark and Harriet could, however, set the table with at least a

Another Greenmanville garden, located in the late 1800s near the George Greenman and Company shipyard, stands in the midst of what is now Mystic Seaport Museum. Here it appears that the Greenmans grew large quantities of potatoes, corn, and squashes. In the background, right to left, are George Greenman's barn; the little house occupied by the Greenmans' sister Katherine Greenman Edmondson and her husband, John, employed at the mill; the blacksmith shop for the shipyard; and the Mystic Manufacturing Company, a textile mill. Outside Greenmanville, the family owned farms that supplied fruits, vegetables, and dairy products. [E. A. Scholfield photograph, MSM 80.26.25]

dozen place settings of knife, fork, and spoon, or entertain eighteen if forks alone were used—as they might have been for cake and tea.[21]

The dinnerware carried aboard ship for the cabin clarifies what the middle class considered essential for civilized dining. When we discuss the *Charles W. Morgan*, it will be apparent that individual place settings of plate, soup bowl, cup, saucer, knife, fork, teaspoon, and soup spoons were expected. A castor and castor bottles for condiments, a tureen, salt cellars, platter, pitchers and serving dishes of various sizes and purposes, gravy boats, carving sets, teapots, and bread trays commonly went to sea, while for the U.S. Life-Saving Service the service pieces only seldom exceeded a platter, pitcher, and a couple of serving dishes. The Greenmans probably set their table as well as, or better than, a captain's table would be set at sea and, except for perhaps the simplest family meals, better than the Life-Saving Service.

Clark's and George's inventories mentioned napkins and table cloths, and the three families surely used them, and taught their children to use them, just as Mrs. Todd wished her daughter to learn.

Though Clark's inventory does not mention a set of china, it is very likely that all three Greenman families had basic place settings in some matched set. The process, already underway in the period of the Buckinghams, of individual place settings, reached its modern standard by the middle of the nineteenth century.

None of the Greenmans would have dreamed of using their fingers for eating at the table, except for bread or obvious finger food, like doughnuts and cookies. They would have been displeased at having to share a plate or bowl. So ingrained was the notion of individual service that when people of this class encountered the communal eating habits of people in other lands, and saw no flatware or even spoons, they sometimes concluded they could not eat. We will see examples of this in a chapter coming up—"Meals Ashore For All Hands."

The Food Supply

More about the store: The surviving Greenmanville Store daybooks from the early 1850s indicate that the store carried a few basic food items, with a handful of other products available on occasion. Molasses, vinegar, two grades of sugar—white and brown—cream of tartar, baking soda, coffee, tea, crackers, rice, salt, and "meal"—probably corn—appear frequently. Raisins, currants, and dried apples were available. There was a selection of spices—cinnamon, cassia, (a spice similar to cinnamon, but less expensive), ginger, allspice, nutmeg, cloves, and pepper. Cheese was regularly offered, and butter and eggs occasionally. Meat was limited to hams—both beef and pork—and codfish, probably the dried product. Other useful household necessities like matches, soap by the bar, starch, and brooms were in stock. There was a limited selection of dry goods, but almost anything needed for a mending job, and occasional items such as hymn books, paper, lumber, and coal.[23]

A Greenmanville housewife out of almost any commonly needed item could run down to the store to pick it up. An advertisement for the store in 1864 candidly described it: "Choice Family Groceries. We can sell cheap for the times, but not at very low prices. CALL AND EXAMINE."[23]

Some goods were rarely stocked: wheat flour, for example; other grains like rye or oats, dried peas or beans; virtually all other meats and fish; and other fruits and vegetables. At the Burrows Store and Park Central Market in Mystic Bridge, in contrast, consumers could purchase beef, pork, mutton, lamb, veal, game in season, fish, lobsters, clams, salt fish of all kinds, and fruits and vegetables.[24] The Greenmanville Store was clearly meant to be a service to the neighborhood, not a full-scale grocery store.

An examination of the daybook shows, too, that while some Greenmanvillagers shopped there often, others were infrequent customers. Mystic Bridge stores were not very far away—in fact, some offered free delivery—and many vendors took their carts door to door offering milk, meat, and fish, so there were several alternatives to the Greenmanville Store for supplying pantry and kitchen.

The store also had a financial function in the community. George Greenman & Co. extended credit to employees, which was paid off in cash or hours worked. The store provided cash to account holders. Some people sold goods to the store, and in exchange received credit or cash, or credit to a third party. Services were charged through the store; for example, when Eb Denison plowed Thomas Greenman's garden, he was paid by the store.

The Farm and Gardens

The Greenmans' enterprises included a farm. As we saw in the chapter about Mrs. Buckingham, it was not unusual to find fresh-food exchanges among relatives, particularly meat. Or those who could afford it hired someone to produce food, as Joseph Anthony and Samuel Rodman did with relatives outside of town. The Greenmans owned two farms, one of which yielded income from the sale of agricultural products. An inventory of the company's taxable property maintained over several years shows a slightly fluctuating population of oxen, cows, calves, swine, sheep, and poultry. The three brothers may have kept their own animals at the farm, or perhaps nearer to home in their barns.[25]

It seems that the arrangement was flexible. In 1867, for example, among George Greenman's personal taxable property was ownership of half a cow. If we had a glimpse into the early 1850s, when George's family were younger, we might find him requiring sole use of a cow, as his son did in 1883 with a household of nine. In 1883, George and Clark's widow shared a cow between them.[26]

Across the river, Julia Gates also kept a cow, on which she reported to her shipmaster husband George, in March 1871: "I shall feel glad when our cow again furnishes us with milk. It has been a scarce article this winter....I suppose the calf will come along the last of April. [Son] Georgie takes care of the cow and I think he must do the milking this summer." Two years later, in April 1873, she reported to George: "I miss my cow this spring very much. It was a luxury to have plenty of milk. But I still think it best not to buy one. The children seem to miss milk very much. Georgie says he could live on it." At that point, Mrs. Gates may have purchased just enough milk for general cooking purposes, but not enough for the children to drink.[27]

To handle the milk from the Greenmans' four cows, listed in 1868 with the taxable farm equipment, were nearly four dozen milk pans, wooden pails, milk pails, a cream pail, and a strainer. Butter boxes, a butter bowl and butter press, and a churn were listed. There was no mention of cheese-making equipment.[28]

When the farms were sold in 1888, the Lower Farm, located a half mile above Mystic Bridge, was described as having "Two Orchards of best of Fruit." Both it and the "Upper Farm," a mile north and about half a mile below Mystic (what today is called Old Mystic), were considered "well situated for Market Gardening, Fancy Stock, as well as ordinary farm purposes." So, within a short distance of Greenmanville were supplies of milk, cream, butter, eggs, beef, pork, possibly lamb and mutton, and poultry from the farm. Greenmanvillagers may have kept their own chickens, for a backyard supply of eggs and poultry. In her March 1871 letter Julia Gates described her flock: "We have a nice flock of hens 14 in all. They furnish us well with eggs and shall have some to spare; we get 9 or 10 eggs per day most of the time."[29]

Photographs of the Greenman backyards and shipyard, most from the latter part of the nineteenth century, show gardens and large patches for items like corn, potatoes, squashes, or pumpkins. One winter or fall view across George Greenman's yard shows cornstalks, and an 1882 newspaper article commented on his strawberry bed, "a sight of which is a rare show. By actual test of tapemeasure, some of the berries measure five inches in circumference, and it is a small berry that does not go three inches." George Greenman's apple trees were the object of another recollection. A photograph of Clark's garden shows many stakes, possibly for beans and tomatoes, in a garden that seems very large for a family of four. We do not know, however, if the Greenman families exchanged foods. Perhaps the Greenmans did with excess produce as fellow Mystic shipyard owner Nathan Fish did, since he described some of his potatoes as "merchantable." Mr. Fish's diary entry for 31 October 1868, sums up his growing year, describing in detail the kinds of produce he grew: "We had an abundance of green corn, new potatoes, peas, bush and pole beans, cucumbers, etc and we have dug some 250 bush[els] potatoes, 5 bush beans, 8 bush corn, 10 bush turnips a good lot of cabbage etc so that we feel quite satisfied with our farming this season." Such produce would have been perfectly appropriate—and likely—for the Greenmans to have grown.[30]

The local newspapers reported on the gardening prowess of community members, many of whom were the Greenman brothers' social peers—sea captains and businessmen: "Capt. Thomas Miner is high hoe on squashes this year. ["High hoe" was the editors' humorous take-off on the phrase "high line" which referred to the fisherman with the largest catch] John Forsyth [a ship designer and, for a while, storeowner] has one from his grounds which weighs just 100 pounds, and I.W. Denison [a merchant] another which turns the scale at 115 pounds." "The biggest potato yet is an early rose weighing a pound and a quarter, from the garden of Capt. Wm. Morgan."[31]

Greenman Grocery Lists

We cannot reconstruct a complete picture of the Greenmans' foodways for any particular period in their lives. Instead we have fragmentary information from scattered years and diverse sources, one of which is the Greenmanville Store daybook, which lists items each brother's household purchased. Rarely were more than three or four items purchased at one time, and hardly ever do the groupings suggest a particular culinary effort, though large amounts of sugar in the fall seem to point to preserve making. Nor is it obvious that any one Greenman household obtained their entire supply of any single commodity at the company's store. Nevertheless, some patterns emerge.

A comparison of just tea, coffee, sugar, and molasses purchases made by the three households between May 1853 and May 1854 shows that Thomas and Charlotte were tea drinkers, while Clark and George bought both tea and coffee. George bought substantially more coffee than tea. Thomas's household used close to a third of a gallon of molasses a week, as did Clark's; George and Abby sweetened with sugar, though both Thomas and Clark used it, too. Without knowing, of course, if George and Abby bought molasses elsewhere, or if Thomas purchased coffee downtown, we can't be absolutely sure if this information reflects family preferences or is lopsided because the brothers had access to other supplies.[32]

At the store, Charlotte bought crackers, vinegar by the gallon, made periodic purchases of codfish, cheese, both brown and white sugar, and occasional purchases of ham and beef. She bought Indian meal more often than rye, at least some dried corn—apparently unground—and barely any rice—just six pounds in one year. She used baking soda and cream of tartar for leavening, and allspice, cassia, cinnamon, and nutmeg in her baking. She also bought raisins and currants.

Unfortunately, incomplete information allows us only

Behind George and Abby Greenman's house stood this little two-room building. At the near end, which in the photo is the room with two windows and a door, was a space appropriate for large messy tasks, like butchering, which any family would choose to keep out of the kitchen of the house. Built into the chimney was a chamber fitted with hooks ideal for smoking home-produced bacons and hams. [MSM 83.8.45]

A lettuce salad dressed with sugar and vinegar and garnished with hard-boiled egg, instructions on page 54.

the equivalent of a peek into Charlotte's pantry through a door opened only a crack, with many items hidden from view. At least among this selection there is nothing startling, just plain New England fare.

Who Cooked?

All three brothers, at some stage in their married lives, had households extended beyond a nuclear family by boarders and servants—either people who were relatives or were associated through shipyard and mill. When George came to Mystic and started his family in the 1830s, both Thomas and Clark lived with him and Abby and their children. Later, in their own homes, with their young families, Clark and Thomas each housed extra people. In 1850 Thomas's home accommodated Charlotte and their daughter Charlotte Elizabeth plus a whole other household—the Haines family—and still another, a single ship carpenter, Horace Champlin. Ship carpenter William Haines would become a key member of the George Greenman & Co. shipyard operation, and when he and his wife Sally and their young son came to Greenmanville they lived with the Thomas Greenmans until Haines built his own home. Thomas and Charlotte's household then shrank down to a genteel nuclear family, with Sarah Mundy, a 24-year-old domestic described as mulatto. When daughter Charlotte married and left home, the older Greenmans continued on with Sarah there to help.[33]

We don't know just what the domestic arrangement was while the Haines and Greenman families shared the house, but the Haineses had their own account at the store, and they did not necessarily board with the Greenmans. The two women may have shared the kitchen, or perhaps Sally had a stove in another part of the house. It was not uncommon at this time for living accommodations to be shared, especially for young families getting started in life or in a new location.

While in 1850 the census described Thomas as a shipwright and listed his personal worth at $3,500, ten years later he was a "Master Ship Carpenter" with a combined personal and real-estate value of $40,000. The shipyard and their textile mill and investments had prospered in the 1850s, so it was appropriate for Thomas and Charlotte to occupy their home without boarders, although some other Greenmanvillagers continued to take in boarders for many years. It was also expected that, even with a smaller household, they have a domestic servant, as others in their class did. George and Abby's household, consisting of five, also had a servant—a young Irish woman—even though they had two daughters old enough to help around the house.

None of this tells us who actually did the cooking, but

Chicken salad, à la Julia Gates, circa 1870, garnished exactly as she specified with celery and "curlied" parsley.

letters from Julia Gates to her husband indicate that she did quite a bit of the cooking, and that the hired girl helped out with the more tiresome work of laundry, ironing, and cleaning.[34] Perhaps Charlotte Greenman cooked, too, with Sarah pitching in, possibly serving dinners and cleaning up after. A woman in her forties and fifties in the 1860s and 1870s, Charlotte was young enough to see to her housekeeping, but Sarah's help gave her an amount of leisure to be envied by someone like Mrs. Burrows, whom we meet in the next chapter. She was certainly more privileged than most of the other Greenmanville women, especially those who worked in the textile mill and did all their housework as well.

Charlotte's leisure could be absorbed somewhat by her work for the Seventh Day Baptist Church, for which she was remembered at her death: organizing ice cream festivals or donation suppers to raise money for missionary, temperance, or Sunday-school work. Perhaps she and her sisters-in-law visited with one another once the noon dinner dishes were done, looked at one another's gardens, or walked to the shipyard to see the progress of new vessels.

Meals of the Day

"The substantial and hearty meal partaken of by Americans [breakfast], is the bone of a very great contention. On the one hand it is maintained as the ruin of digestions and the most prolific source of dyspepsia, etc. On the other it is shown that, for a busy active people, and also for a people who generally have only two meals a day—breakfast and dinner—the meal is none too substantial. However, what is right and wrong must be a matter of individual opinion and experience. The difficulty lies in what is eaten at breakfast," claimed *Goodholme's Domestic Cyclopedia* in the 1880s.[35]

The real difficulty was that the American metabolism was changing. A larger urban population of professional and business people—including many who moved from small coastal towns like Mystic to New York City—grew up in a time when Americans walked nearly everywhere, began and ended their day with farm chores, hauled wood to keep warm, carried water, and lived in homes that were uninsulated. Their eating habits developed in a time when a high-calorie diet was desirable or even necessary; when people sat at desks and rode trains or trolleys the old diet created health problems. Even those who worked in factories, like the textile mill in Greenmanville, found their work was less vigorous than their farm or trade work had been; tending machinery was often dangerous, noisy, and required concentration, but it was not aerobic.

But as we can see in our own time, eating habits are slow to change. The population of a town like Mystic had a variety of dietary needs: the shipyard workers, fishermen, laborers, and farmers needed quite a bit more to eat than the merchants, bankers, and shipyard owners.

The Goodholme article also commented on the matter of two meals a day. Along with the sedentary life, which changed the caloric needs of many, came a change in the pattern of daily meals that resulted from a standardized work week. With the Buckinghams we saw that the main meal came at noon, on the assumption that everyone could gather for it. This was no longer true when people left home to work all day in jobs or professions. Families gathered for breakfast; increasingly the noon meal was a lunch hastily eaten away from home; and dinner was shifted to late in the day when a family could be together again. Some families switched their "dinner" to a more or less ceremonial spot at mid-day Sunday, continuing weekday suppers. Late-day dinners compounded nineteenth-century digestion problems—people went to bed with full stomachs, perhaps a satisfying sensation but not conducive to burning calories.

In Greenmanville, a traditional early nineteenth-century daily meal pattern could continue because home and work were so close. The brothers could eat dinner at noon with their families—as could many key shipyard workers—return to the yard and work till quite late in the day by our standards, then eat a small supper or tea-like meal after work. Dana Story's shipyard-owner father, in Essex, Massachusetts, early in the twentieth century followed a pattern of meals through the day typical of the nineteenth century: "It was father's custom to go to the shipyard at seven o'clock and start the gang off. Then, after a little while, he would come home for breakfast, do a little bookkeeping...then go back for the rest of the forenoon. Dinner-time came at twelve o'clock on the dot. After enjoying a leisurely meal it was father's invariable custom to stretch out on the living room sofa for a half-hour nap....Six o'clock was supper time. Please note that in Essex, the evening meal is and always was supper. None of this dinner business at night. Our big meal came at noon. Supper was of a rather light nature and usually included something in the order of toast and pear sauce."[36] The Greenmans' routine was probably similar.

What the Greenmans Ate

So far, we have seen what foods were available to the Greenman families and neighbors, and we have had a glimpse into their way of life. By the mid-to-late 1800s, a recognizably modern diet had been established—a diet elaborated upon in the twentieth century by the addition of ethnic foods and diminished seasonal differentiation.

There are no Greenman family letters or diaries that record meals eaten in the three brothers' homes. We know they went on chowder parties, attended clambakes, and sponsored church festivities featuring ice cream and cake. Their peers recorded special-occasion meals—Fourth of July, weddings—and only once in a while mention routine menus. A smattering of manuscript recipe books record what someone wished to remember how to make. And there was for this era a great plenty of cookbooks and magazine articles advising on menus and how to serve them fashionably and correctly. Let's sort through all this to decide what Charlotte and Thomas, and their Greenman relations, put on the table three times a day.

Breakfast: It is reasonable to assume that Thomas as a young man ate a hearty breakfast of meat—such as sausage or ham—and/or eggs with the buckwheat cakes that were so popular at this time—or bread, jonnycakes, or biscuits. When he grew older, he may have found a porridge such as hasty pudding, or a bowl of bread and milk, satisfying enough. Since he and Charlotte were tea drinkers, we can suppose a full teapot was on the table as well.

The Goodholme article recommended variety in the day's first meal, that one not eat hot bread, and that fruits and salads be eaten at breakfast. And it provided many seasonal menus, all starting with a cereal course, fruit, a bread course with butter, coffee, etc., meat dishes with eggs or potatoes, toasts, then cakes and muffins. Since they were prescribing this, I think it is safe to assume that the Greenmans, like most people, did not do as the book said. Breakfast is one meal where even modern people have the highest tolerance for repetition; no one even today eats salad at breakfast, and for most people the fruit course is a glass of orange juice. Americans love hot bread at breakfast, especially hot biscuits, muffins, and pancakes, and not many people in the nineteenth or the present century make time for as large a breakfast as *Goodholme's Domestic Cyclopedia* suggested.

About jonnycakes: Among the hot breads the Greenmans probably ate at breakfast were jonnycakes. Thomas, Clark, and George (and other Westerly-dwelling siblings) were, in all likelihood, jonnycake-eating Rhode Islanders. Jonnycakes without an "h" were in this region a distinct food item, an unleavened mixture of white flint corn meal, salt, hot water, and perhaps a dash of milk to thin it, fried on a griddle in lard, or preferably salt-pork or sausage fat. Earlier in the century, when the brothers were children, their mother may have baked the jonnycake on a board tipped up in front of the open fire, in which case it was one large jonnycake, baked by reflected heat. Because of Rhode Island's proximity, and because many in the area, particularly Baptists, had settled there from Rhode Island, a number of people in southeastern Connecticut were also jonnycake eaters.

The Mystic *Press* observed in October 1878, "The sound of grinding has been low at the grist mills of the vicinity, but the rainfall of Saturday has made it possible for Messrs. Bindloss and Manning to get out a little of the needful for 'Rhode Island johnnycakes.'" Grace Denison Wheeler recalled from her childhood her grandmother's open fireplace and the jonnycakes, also called bannocks, baked there. Grace's grandmother used her fireplace in the 1850s at the very same time Charlotte made her jonnycakes on the top of the stove. Even at the very end of the century, jonnycakes were made daily along with biscuits to accompany most meals, from breakfast to tea.[37]

We saw from the store accounts that the Greenmans purchased cornmeal, and a good amount probably found its way into jonnycakes, the rest being used to make Boston brown bread, Indian puddings, and, for variety, leavened forms of cornbread.

Dinner: The noon meal, the largest, was certainly a family meal, quite possibly a social one as well. "There is no pleasanter way of passing time among friends when you [wish] to be easy & sociable. The occupation of attending to something on your plate relieves awkwardness & excuses occasional silence. The course of dinner also makes breaks wh. are pleasant," wrote Richard Henry Dana, Jr.[38] How many courses might the Greenmans have eaten for a daily dinner? One job of cookbooks was to provide menu suggestions, although, of course, we don't know how many and which suggestions someone like Charlotte may have taken. Certainly meal planning in her household depended on the season, who was at home for dinner, and what other chores she had that day. It also depended on how much help she had in the kitchen, and how skilled the help was. As we saw, Charlotte had Sarah Mundy's help in the 1860s and 1870s.

Dinner in the nineteenth century required meat—beef, pork, mutton, lamb, chicken, or turkey—either a large piece roasted or boiled, or chops and cutlets broiled or fried, or an entree made up substantially with meat in a pie, ragout, fricassee, hash, or stew. Organ and specialty meats—tripe, liver, tongue, kidneys, hearts, heads—which have virtually disappeared from modern markets, were fixed in a variety of ways. A family like the Greenmans may have relished the infrequent servings of the specialty meats from their own butchered animals, but if they liked them well enough they could probably obtain them more often from local butchers.

Meat-eating and fish-eating: Mid-nineteenth-century New Englanders—in fact, most Americans—were meat eaters and, as we saw in the chapter about the Buckinghams, had been for quite some time. Eating meat, and not having to rely heavily on grains or legumes and vegetables, was for Europeans a sign of prosperity and well-being. When Europe's economy worsened after the sixteenth century—a decline that lasted into the nineteenth century—meat-eating declined, too, especially in the lower classes. But the culture's memory of meat's value and status persisted. Coming to America meant aspiring to more meat, an aspiration so resolutely gratified that most Americans equated well-being and satisfying food with meat. They regarded vegetarianism with puzzlement at best and suspicion at worst.[39] As we shall see, they ate vegetables more to provide variety than substance. And they found fish and meatless foreign foods insufficient.

People living in coastal towns had access to fish, enviably fresh compared to the hinterlands where fish was peddled perhaps only once a week. As we shall see, of the many kinds caught, the preferred fish for dinner were haddock, cod, salmon, shad, and halibut, with mackerel, trout, herrings, eels, and the like preferred as supper or breakfast fish. Oysters were enormously popular, and other shellfish like crabs and lobsters were made up into salad or croquettes. But menu suggestions in cookbooks from the mid- to late-1800s often pair seafood entrees with meat or poultry, as if to make sure there would be substantial enough food on the table.

For example, C.I. Hood and Company's *Combined Cookbooks* contained "Plain Family Dinners" for a week in the winter—day-to-day menus for the main meal. Wednesday featured boiled haddock with plain melted butter, roast chickens, potato balls, stewed apples, boiled onions, squash, and cottage pudding. On Friday, broiled halibut was paired with chicken pie, preceded by oyster soup, and accompanied by French peas, lettuce, shredded potatoes and steamed apple pudding. Marion Harland's *Dinner Year Book*, which offered 364 dinner menus, similarly paired fish and meat entrees; one example, the dinner menu for Friday in the Fourth Week of April, called for salmon croquettes and mutton chops, broiled. Miss Parloa recommended broiled halibut and braised tongue on the same menu, boiled bluefish and veal cutlets, and boiled haddock and lobster sauce with chicken croquettes, although she did propose a salmon dinner accompanied only by green peas, potatoes, rice croquettes, and lettuce salad.[40]

The courses at dinner: All these menus were recommended for family dinners, in contrast to much more elaborate company dinners. Most family dinner menus began with a soup course, followed by the main course with the meat or poultry or fish dish; potatoes; often a second starch such as rice, macaroni, or sweet potatoes; one or two vegetables; sometimes a salad; and finally a dessert, often a pudding, custard, ice cream or a bavarian, and cake. These books were suggesting top-of-the-line family fare, while other books, which told the reader that their menus were intentionally economical, simplified things to one entree, one vegetable or potato dish, and dessert no more luxurious than pudding or pie.[41]

But cookbook writers proposed and homemakers disposed. And diary-keepers and letter-writers recorded the main features of meals, omitting some details, such as how many of which vegetable. At mid-century, for example, R.H. Dana, visiting his Aunt Martha and Uncle Allston, the painter, "Found Mr. A. dining at 7 upon roast beef & boiled rice." Writing to her husband James, master of a whaleship in 1873, Phebe Sherman said, "We had one of mother's hens stewed for dinner."[42]

Julia Gates informed her husband Captain George, in June 1873: "It is Saturday and I have been busy in the kitchen cooking. I suppose if you were here to spend Sunday you would wish 10 lbs. of lobsters. The quantity I get is 4 lbs. and it is plenty. But tomorrow [Sunday] we shall dine on boiled ham. I should like to have some of the good vegetables that you speak of. But our garden is growing finely."[43] While it is hard to be certain what Julia was planning, it sounds as if lobster in some form, perhaps in a salad, was to be served together with boiled ham, just as

Mrs. Gates's French rolls, recipe on page 55, and the potato yeast they are made from, recipe on page 25.

some of the books suggest. Or perhaps the lobster was destined for supper. It was a little too early in June for Julia to have much, if anything, in her garden except spinach, radishes, or lettuce.

Salad and vegetable eating: Many of the cookbooks and advice books of the period promote lettuce as a salad, and it is apparent that people grew and ate it, but salad eating as we know it now does not seem to have been common in the Greenmans' time. Salads had been known for centuries. Raw greens and vegetables like onions and radishes, with salad herbs and dressed with oil and vinegar, were described in medieval cookery books, and in seventeenth-century English sources as well. But among late-eighteenth and early-nineteenth-century New Englanders there seems to have been relatively little interest in salad. For example, Amelia Simmons, in her 1796 *American Cookery*, discussed parsley (for garnishing), lettuce, cucumbers (mostly for pickling), garlic (for medicinal purposes), and radishes, but she gave no instructions for salad. In 1833, Mrs. Child's *American Frugal Housewife* similarly listed vegetables and ways to serve them, virtually all cooked. Of the vegetables mentioned, we might consider only two for salad: lettuce and cucumbers. The only recipe named "salad" is for lobster salad. By mid-century, salad vegetables were mentioned a little more frequently, but were often only a raw vegetable dipped in salt.[44]

Aside from the proof of vegetable eating in the sale of seeds, the mention of vegetables in gardening handbooks, almanacs, and garden record books, and instructions for preparing vegetables in cookbooks, we would hardly know from letters, diaries, or period narratives that anyone ever ate them. Since reformers like the Beecher sisters felt obliged in the 1860s to point out that "in America, far too large a proportion of the diet consists of animal food," and to urge Americans to eat more vegetables, we may be reasonably sure that vegetables, raw or cooked, were regarded with mild interest.[45]

Later in the 1800s changes in salad-eating habits reveal the most about what may have happened at mid-century. In the 1852 *Skillful Housewife's Book*, Mrs. Abell described one of three ways of preparing lettuce as a salad: "If you choose, it may be dressed with sugar and vinegar, with a little salt before it goes to the table." This way of fixing lettuce apparently endured. Recalling her childhood in the late 1890s, Florence Button remembered eating wilted lettuce, made by pouring hot vinegar over lettuce, and sprinkling it with sugar. Anna North Coit remembered eating sugared lettuce in her girlhood in the first two decades of this century. She also reported that her mother, born in 1873, loved pickled vegetables, or fresh ones vinegared: sliced cucumbers or onions sprinkled with vinegar and salt and pepper. In her childhood, her mother "didn't make salads," though Anna remembered as a child eating a slice of pineapple with raisins in the center of it, laid on a leaf of lettuce, dressed with mayonnaise. Similarly, the author's mother remembers, in the 1920s, having a leaf of lettuce, a slice of tomato, and a slice of cucumber dressed with mayonnaise that went by the name of "combination salad," considered in her family to be quite an up-to-date item, even though her grandfather often ate a salted cucumber for breakfast.[46]

Salad dressing recipes do appear in both manuscript and

E. A. Scholfield, Mystic's photographer in the late 1800s, took this picture of Harriet Almy Greenman, Clark's widow, sitting—comfortably, we hope—in her rocker just off the porch with a couple of younger companions. When her husband died, the first of the three Greenman brothers to do so, a probate inventory was made of the furnishings of this house, and this gives us a peek into Harriet's kitchen and dining room. [E. A. Scholfield, MSM 80.26.23]

printed recipe books, but they were as likely to be used for chicken or seafood salads as with greens, except for "cabbage salad." Recipes for this dish—shredded cabbage with a boiled dressing—appear in local community cookbooks from the turn of the twentieth century through the first decade and a half. This was clearly a kind of cole slaw.[47]

At the back of Charles Chace's journal from voyages on the *Charles W. Morgan* are some pages filled when he came ashore, and titled: "On Account of Produce Sold Commencing January 1st 1875, Produce of the Farm." Chace kept his record through 23 September 1875, and though we cannot know from this account if Chace was attempting a market-gardening operation or merely selling off surplus, the selection of vegetables does tell us about preferences. Chace grew potatoes, turnips, carrots, beets, and cabbage, which he sold not only in the winter but also in summer. In July he sold peas, lettuce, and cucumbers, and in August beans, tomatoes, corn, and pumpkins. In September he sold onions as well as tomatoes, corn, pumpkins, potatoes, turnips, beets, and carrots. Chace also had rhubarb, "berries," and grapes for sale.[48]

You will recall Nathan Fish summing up his garden produce in 1868, listing green corn, new potatoes, peas, bush and pole beans, and cucumbers. Both Chace's and Fish's accounts list the heartier summer vegetables preferred by them, their families and neighbors—and probably by the Greenmans. The peas, shelled beans, green beans, and corn were well-cooked, a New England habit that survived into the twentieth century. Root and winter-keeping vegetables like carrots, beets, turnips, cabbage, parsnips, and squash were similarly well-boiled. Lettuce and cucumbers were eaten raw, and cucumbers, onions, and beets were often pickled.

Charlotte may have served fresh cucumbers and tomatoes sliced and salted or vinegared, and lettuce with boiled dressing or hot or cold vinegar and sugar. She may have also pickled cucumbers. Tomatoes were eaten stewed, and, in many households, canned, as they were in Nathan Fish's household. "Susan has been canning tomatoes and getting ready for winter," he wrote in 1868—so we may imagine Charlotte Greenman and Sarah Mundy canning tomatoes, as well as making other pickles and fruit preserves.[49]

Tomato canning was described in the 22 September 1866 *Harper's Weekly* as "a very simple matter....They should merely be cooked, without seasoning, and while hot put into wide-mouthed jugs or cans. The jugs or cans should be entirely filled, and securely corked and covered. Preserved in this manner, they keep almost as fresh as when first picked from the vine." By this time, canning jars were available for home canning, with screw-on lids–usually called "fruit jars"–and a domestic version of a boiling-water bath process had been understood for a number of years. Tomato canning was one of the earliest vegetable-preservation processes to become an industry, and even Mystic had a tomato-canning factory for a while in the 1870s, spurring tremendous interest among local farmers in raising tomatoes for the plant.

Canned food, however, needs to be kept in perspective. In her history of food in America, Kathleen Smallzreid pointed out that in 1870 less than a hundred canners were in business in the United States, and at the close of the century there were eighteen hundred preserving and selling food. But since in 1856 the population was 35 million, and that year 5 million cans were marketed, each American ate one-seventh of a can of commercially prepared food; in 1870, with the population at 38 1/2 million, and 30 million cans marketed, each American ate fifteen-sixteenths of a can. Smallzreid believes that much canned food went to cities, restaurants, and homes unable to afford home canning.[50] We will soon see that some went to sea.

In the 1860s and 1870s, people like Julia Gates and Charlotte Greenman, in the midst of garden surplus, were certainly able to do some home canning and were less likely to buy vegetables canned, except perhaps for special items like canned shellfish or sardines. Canning companies had to overcome resistance to canned products; in the next quarter of a century they made some progress. In 1900, Smallzreid says, Van Camps prepared an advertisement for the *Ladies Home Journal* in which they stated that a million women had given up making their own baked beans in favor of the canned variety.

By mid-century, the boiled pudding that had often accompanied the main course earlier in the century was shifted to the end of the meal for a dessert. With stove ovens, freshly baked rice, bread, and Indian puddings were easier to have daily than in the brick-oven days, as were cake and pie. For company or special occasions, a fancy or molded dessert would be in order, like a floating island, snow pudding, queen of puddings, or rice meringue. Cookbooks included recipes for bavarian creams, charlotte russe, and other elaborate desserts, but these crop up only occasionally in manuscript sources and early community cookbooks, which makes me wonder how often they were served by the middle class.

Julia Gates included 25 pudding recipes in her manuscript recipe notebook, 61 cake recipes, and 18 for pie and pie fillings. She collected three for floating island, a meringue set on a custard, and five for "snow" pudding. This was a beaten mixture of gelatine and egg white, flavored with lemon and poured into a mold, and when turned out surrounded with a custard. These beautiful desserts were more easily made with an egg beater—a relatively new device at mid-century—and the almost-instant gelatin being manufactured by Coxe, primarily, and Cooper. Maria Parloa, in her *New Cook Book and Marketing Guide*, told her readers that an egg beater "will do in five minutes the work that in former years required half an hour." Gelatine displaced domestic use of isinglass, which "was formerly used for jellies, blancmange, &c., but Coxe's gelatine and Cooper's gelatine and isinglass, are found so excellent and are so much cheaper, that it is now but rarely used for these purposes." By the 1880s even middle-class people without much household help could afford to serve meringues and snows, and beat egg whites for cakes and frostings.[51]

Supper: Supper was a small meal. If it was a cold meal, it would resemble the early nineteenth-century tea: leftover meat from dinner, bread, perhaps toasted, and butter, apple or pear sauce in winter, fresh fruit or berry pie in summer, or cake. If it was a warm meal, soups and stews were served. William Ellery Maxson, a close Greenman friend and co-owner of a shipyard with Nathan Fish, recorded in his diary on 14 October 1862 that he had had an oyster stew that evening. A chowder with lots of crackers could be quickly prepared for a cold-weather supper. Mrs. Gates wrote to George on a stormy New Year's Eve, 1864, that if he had been there she would have served him pork and beans. As we will soon see, George, aboard his ship, probably had pork and beans sometime that week. Jonnycakes were used as toast or potatoes would be, over which dried beef, or salt pork, or salt codfish, in milk gravy, would be served, making ideal supper dishes. Tag-ends and leftovers were the stuff of supper.[52]

Landsmen like the Greenmans made a concerted effort at sea to maintain the eating habits they had ashore. When we look at the cabin fare of vessels like the *Charles W. Morgan*, we will see many of the menu patterns that we saw here, repeated as closely as possible within the limits of shipboard life.

The Greenmans and Nineteenth-Century Standards for Food

Charlotte and Thomas Greenman's foodways were a gentrified version of Lydia and Samuel Buckingham's, but not nearly as gentrified as they could have been. The Greenmans' general lack of ostentation precluded many of the extraordinary lengths to which some Victorian New Englanders went in dining habits and style. Their close connection to a rural way of life meant that they still actively participated in growing and preserving their food, and it insulated them from the fads and vanities of the cities.

Charlotte and Thomas, both born early in the nineteenth century, probably laid over their early habits a veneer of new food choices and styles: jonnycakes and cole slaw, Indian pudding plus snow custard, biscuits and Graham bread. White flour dropped in price and became more common in Charlotte's mature years, so white bread, always favored, became standard. But Charlotte's and Thomas's generation, remembering, perhaps fondly, the old brown bread, transformed it into a steamed pudding.

Those changes that would really make a difference in modern New England's eating habits—more processed foods, more food traveling across the country to markets in towns like Mystic, strange new cuisines from parts of the world Charlotte may only have read about, scientific cooking, and the absorption with a healthy diet to match the modern metabolism—those changes were just beginning in her time.

The Recipes

Recipes enough for a couple of nineteenth-century dinners follow; surely the Greenmans ate each of these dishes, except for the brandied peaches, at least once. To start the dinners with a soup course, here are oyster stew and tomato soup; though, of course, as we heard from Mr. Maxson, oyster stew could be supper. Instructions for broiling beefsteak and boiling mutton follow for entrees. "Cold" slaw–in Charlotte's lifetime a new way to prepare cabbage, along with lettuce salad and stewed tomatoes, provide vegetable dishes, though if you wish to replicate a Victorian Yankee's meal, then you must serve potatoes as well. The French rolls recipe comes from Julia Gates. The Graham gems and Graham bread were named for a whole-wheat flour promoted by Sylvester Graham, whose followers believed, as many do today, that a whole-food diet helps break addiction to alcohol. In honor of Mrs. Mallory, a recipe for brandied peaches and pears follows. There are two company desserts, a meringue-topped bread pudding named queen of pudding, and the elegant snow pudding, also from Mrs. Gates. The simpler steamed pudding with lemon dip, also with a temperance slant, was suitable for family dessert.

OYSTER STEW

Put a quart of oysters on the fire in their own liquor. The moment they begin to boil, skim them out, and add to the liquor a half pint of hot cream, salt and cayenne pepper to taste. Skim it well, take it off the fire, add to the oysters an ounce and a half of butter broken into small pieces. Serve immediately.

From *Practical Cooking and Dinner Giving*, by Mrs. Mary F. Henderson, 1882, page 115

Many nineteenth-century oyster stew recipes call for a thickening of roux, and this recipe from Mrs. Henderson is unique because it does not. It is, however, fairly typical of most modern oyster stews. For comparison, see the roux-thickened oyster stew recipe in chapter fifteen, page 357, which you may find that you like as well.

The recipe is clear enough that an interpretation is not necessary.
Yields 4 servings.

Tomato soup was one way to use canned tomatoes in the last half of the 1800s. Recipe below.

TOMATO SOUP

TOMATO SOUP. Put three pints of tomatoes, stewed, strained, and sweetened, to two quarts of beef stock; add an onion, salt and pepper. Hood's Sarsaparilla vitalizes the blood.
BEEF SOUP STOCK. Take a shank of beef and cut the meat in fine pieces; take out the marrow and with a piece of butter put into a kettle; put over the fire, and when hot add the meat and cook till brown; then add the bones and sufficient hot water to cover; boil four hours; strain and set away to cool. Try Hood's Sarsaparilla this season.

From *Hood's Combined Cook Books*, by C.I. Hood & Co., 1875-1885, Hood's #1, page 3

Here was one thing Mr. Fish's family could make with their canned tomatoes. In the last quarter of the nineteenth century, the three favorite ways of preparing tomatoes seem to have been making soup, making ketchup, or stewing them (recipe on page 54). Some recipes also appear for scalloping tomatoes in a casserole with macaroni, though sometimes that dish is identified as baked macaroni.

This is a nicely flavored, light soup, which tastes better the second day. The recipe above is clear enough that an interpretation is not needed. Modern cooks may want to use prepared beef boullion or canned stock, in which case add salt cautiously. Canned tomatoes are fine; run them through a food mill or chop them coarsely in a food processor.
Yields 10 servings.

BEEFSTEAK

The first requirement is not so much a tender and juicy steak, though this is always desirable, but a glowing bed of coals, a wire gridiron—a stout one with good sized wires, and double so that you can turn the steak without touching it. The steak should be pounded only in extreme cases, when it is cut too thick and is "stringy." Attempt nothing else when cooking the steak; have everything else ready for the table; the potatoes and vegetables dished and in the warming-closet. From 4 minutes onward is needed to cook the steak. The time must depend on the size, and you can easily tell by the color of the gravy which runs from the steak, when gently pressed with a knife, as to its condition. If the master of the house likes "rare done," it will be safe to infer that it is done enough for him, when there is a suspicion of brown gravy with the red; if, as is generally the case, the next stage is the favorite one, remove the steak from the gridiron the instant the gravy is of a light brown. Remove it to a platter, pepper and salt to suit your taste, put on small lumps of butter, and then for two brief moments, cover it with a hot plate, the two moments being sufficient to carry it to the table. One absolutely essential factor in the preparation of good beefsteak is that it must be served at once.

From *Hood's Combined Cook Books,* by C.I. Hood & Co., 1875-1885, Hood's #2, page 6

A "good meal" and "beefsteak" was, and is, synonymous for many Americans. The Greenmans and their neighbors in Mystic, like the residents of most towns in coastal New England, were able to buy fresh meat, certainly steak, almost anytime they wanted it. Local farmers raised cattle for market, and a steady supply came from the West to eastern cities. While a roast may have been considered the best thing for a Sunday or company dinner, beefsteaks were perfectly suitable for family weekday dinners.

The detail to which the Hood's cookbook writer went to describe the proper method of grilling a steak may tell us more about how people really did cook it than how they ought to have done. Most cookbooks of the period emphasized the need for good judgment in preparing steak—from selecting the best one in the first place to the best length of time for grilling. Steak was often buttered, salted, and peppered before being served, and was not generally served with gravy. Mrs. Henderson said "there should be no gravy. The juice of a properly cooked steak should be in the inside of the steak, and not swimming in the dish."[53]

I offer this recipe for your interest; the old recipe is clear enough that an interpretation is not needed.

BOILED MUTTON

LEG OF MUTTON—BOILED.

Do not have the mutton too fat or too large. Cut off the shank, which the butcher will have nicked for you, leaving about two inches beyond the ham. Wash and wipe carefully and boil in hot water, with a little salt, until a fork will readily pierce the thickest part. About ten or twelve minutes to the pound is a good rule in boiling fresh meat. Serve with caper sauce. Since you intend to use the liquor in which the meat is boiled for to-morrow's soup, do not over salt it. But sprinkle, instead, salt over the leg of mutton after it is dished; rub it all over with butter and set in a hot oven for a single minute.

From *The Dinner Year Book,* by Marion Harland, 1878, pages 23-24

Boiling fresh meat is seldom done today but was fairly common in the nineteenth century. Larger cuts of many sorts of meat, like the leg of mutton above, as well as poultry, like turkeys and chickens, were boiled. In the cooler seasons of the year, with the kitchen stove going all the time, a cook would have a nice steady heat for boiling just about all the time.

Mutton is hard to find these days, unless one has sheep-raising friends. Once a sheep is over a year old, it should be considered mutton. In her 1860 *Practical American Cookery and Domestic Economy*, Miss Hall said this about mutton: "This is a delicate and favorite meat; it is susceptible of many modes of cooking...[and] requires care in the cooking for which it will amply repay. The roasting parts are the better for hanging some time, especially the haunch or saddle; but not for boiling, as the color is apt to be injured....If boiled, serve drawn butter, parsley, or mock caper sauce, with tomatoes stewed, and plain boiled potatoes."[54]

In this recipe, Mrs. Harland says that "you intend to use the liquor...for to-morrow's soup." That is because this cookbook, *The Dinner Year Book*, was designed to provide a menu for every dinner, for each day for one whole year. She built in uses for leftovers like the mutton broth, which was used to make Vermicelli Soup, and the leftover boiled mutton, which made a reappearance as "Mince of Mutton with Potato Frill" (simply, warmed-up chopped mutton in a nice gravy surrounded decoratively with browned mashed potatoes.) I offer this recipe for your interest, so no interpretation will follow.

CHICKEN SALAD

The meat of five chickens. Same quantity of celery cut small with knife. The yolks of 7 eggs.

Tablespoons powdered sugar, 3 large teaspoons of Taylors Mustard after it is made, 1/2 pint vinegar, 2 gills sweet oil, 1 quart thick cream, salt to suit the taste.

Boil three eggs very hard, use the yolks, rubbing them smooth with oil, dropping the latter very slowly. Then add the rest of the yolks raw, adding one at a time with the cream mixing slowly. Then add the vinegar & sugar in the cream mixing slowly. Then add the vinegar & sugar in the same way.

This will make enough for 30 or 40 people. For this take the yolks of 2 eggs and so on.

The dressing should not be mixed with the chicken till just before going to the table.

Mix thoroughly in an ordinary dish, then place it nicely in the Salad dish for the table. Decorate with hard boiled eggs cut in quarters like an orange and put them upright around the edge of the salad with small sprigs of celery or curlied parsley. Cabbage can be used sparingly, if celery cannot be obtained, cut up in fine shreds with a sharp knife.

From the manuscript recipe notebook of Julia Gates, 1857-1930, Mystic River Historical Society

As we know from her letters, and as discussed in chapter four, Mrs. Gates helped prepare food for weddings and special occasions for friends and relatives, and that accounts for this recipe for a large quantity of chicken salad. It is interesting that this main-dish recipe appears in her handwritten recipe notebook at all. Most manuscript recipe notebooks contain cake, pastry, pickle, and preserve recipes—dishes infrequently prepared enough that the cook never memorized the procedure.

The dressing appears to be modified mayonnaise. A true mayonnaise would have had only uncooked yolks and oil, and certainly would have no cream, which stretched the dressing and perhaps made it more economical for large amounts.

Her instructions for garnishing are unusually complete. Unlike a roast, which can come to the table in solitary splendor, a chicken salad probably seemed a little messy to the Victorian eye. In her *Practical Cooking and Dinner Giving*, Mrs. Henderson provided a similarly detailed recipe with instructions for rows of capers, slices or "little cut diamonds" of hard-boiled egg and celery tufts stuck in the top.

Here is an interpretation of Mrs. Gates's recipe for chicken salad for five or six, in which we will define the "and so on."

meat of 1 cooked chicken, diced
an equal quantity of celery, diced
1 hard boiled egg yolk
5 tablespoons olive oil
1 raw egg yolk
1 1/3 cup heavy cream
1/4 cup cider vinegar
1/2 teaspoon sugar
1 teaspoon dry mustard mixed to a paste with a little water and salt and pepper to taste

1. Rub finely the hard-boiled egg yolk, gradually adding olive oil.
2. Beat in the raw egg yolk adding cream gradually.
3. Beat in the vinegar, sugar, and mustard. Add salt and pepper to taste.

4. Mix the dressing, chicken, and celery all together coating the meat and celery well. Taste again and adjust for salt and pepper.
5. If you wish, put the salad in its own dish, garnish with the hard-boiled egg whites, celery tops, curly parsley.

Yields 5-6 servings.

BOILED TONGUE

to dress beef tongue
To dress them, boil the tongue tender; it will take five hours; always dress them as they come out of the pickle, unless they have been very long there; then they may be soaked three or four hours in cold water; or if they have been smoked, and hung long, they should be softened by lying in water five or six hours; they should be brought to a boil gently, and then simmer until tender.

From *Practical American Cookery and Domestic Economy* by Miss Hall, 1855

Cold tongue was a standard offering for teas and suppers in nineteenth-century New England, served by itself or in sandwiches. It could be cooked and eaten fresh shortly after slaughtering, or it could be pickled as beef was in salt, brown sugar, and saltpetre. As the recipe above says, it was sometimes smoked as well. Today smoked tongue is the rule and you may have to order fresh tongue.

Beef tongue was not the only tongue eaten; veal, sheep, and lambs tongues also appear in period recipes. Animal "spare parts" like heart, kidney, liver, tripe, lights (lungs), heads, and feet were all commonly used but are hard to find on meat counters today.

LETTUCE SALAD

LETTUCE. Strip off the outside leaves, split it and lay in cold water awhile. Drain and lay in a salad dish. Have ready two hardboiled eggs, cut in two, and lay on the leaves. If you choose, it may be dressed with sugar and vinegar, with a little salt, before it goes to the table. Some prefer a dressing of salt, mustard, loaf sugar, and vinegar, sweet oil, and a mashed hard boiled egg. With the salad cut fine, and this over it.

From *The Complete Domestic Guide*, by Mrs. L.G. Abell, 1853, page 109

This set of instructions actually contains several ways of preparing a lettuce salad; the simplest is vinegar, sugar, and salt sprinkled over the lettuce and eggs, the amounts determined clearly by personal taste.

The second is a more elaborate dressing, similar to a vinaigrette with additional sugar and the mashed boiled egg. Also, the lettuce in this variation should be shredded. "Sweet oil" was the name for olive oil. "Loaf sugar" was white sugar.

STEWING TOMATOES

In stewing tomatoes, pour away the surplus water, so soon as they begin to boil, and add a small piece of butter, a very little sugar, pepper, and salt; cook about 15 minutes, then stir in bread crumbs, if you like them. Hood's Vegetable Pills cure constipation.

From *Hood's Combined Cook Books*, by C.I. Hood & Co., 1875-1885, Hood's #3, page 31

Tomatoes took to canning well, both domestically and industrially. Mrs. Harland in *The Dinner Year Book* wrote in her stewed-tomato recipe: "Open a can of tomatoes an hour before cooking them." She also recommended that the cook "Leave out the cores and unripe parts. Cook them always in tin or porcelain saucepans. Iron injures color and flavor."[55]

Modern people like raw tomatoes so much, and make every effort to have them fresh year round, that cooked tomatoes now seem relegated to spaghetti sauces and casseroles. Nineteenth-century New Englanders certainly did eat tomatoes raw in season, but preferred them cooked.

The recipe above is clear enough that an interpretation is not needed. Dry bread crumbs work best because they do not get as mushy as fresh ones do. If you use canned tomatoes, read the label to see if sugar has already been added. If you use fresh tomatoes, taste before you add the sugar. Modern tomato breeding has created sweeter tomatoes than were available a hundred years ago.

COLD SLAW

Shred a white cabbage and pour over it the following.

Dressing

2 beaten eggs; 2 teaspoonfuls of sugar; 6 tablespoonfuls of vinegar; 1/2 teaspoon of made mustard and same of pepper and salt; 1/2 teaspoonful of celery essence; 1 tablespoonful of butter.

Mix well, stir over the fire until scalding hot. When cold add the cabbage. Toss and stir, and set in a cold place until wanted.

From *Practical Cooking and Dinner* Giving, by Marion Harland, 1882, page 599

Many old slaw recipes are called "cold" slaw. Hot or cold, this is a good recipe, and the dressing is peppery and tangy.

The recipe is clear enough not to require an interpretation. Note that made mustard means what we call prepared mustard. I use cider vinegar; 3 ounces is equivalent to 6 tablespoons. I have not located celery essence, but a tablespoonful of celery seeds would be good.

Combine everything in a double boiler and cook over a low heat for five minutes. Once it begins to thicken, it goes very quickly.

Yields 2/3-cup dressing.

FRENCH ROLLS

Take two quarts of flour before it is sifted, two tablespoonsful of lard, not quite 1/2 cup sugar, little salt, mix this together. Then take 1 cup of yeast & a pint of milk, and make a sponge—let this stand until morning—then mix in a stiff dough. Let this rise until about 1/2 past three—then knead and cut into cakes about 1/2 inch thick. Spread a thin coating of butter on 1/2 the circle & fold it over—let them rise until tea time, then bake in a quick oven 1/2 hour.

From the manuscript recipe notebook of Julia Gates, 1857-1930

French rolls or buns are a pleasant light roll suitable for breakfast, dinner, or tea. If made overnight with a sponge, and finished up the next morning, these rolls, as Mrs. Gates noted, would be ready freshly baked at teatime, which would have been late in the afternoon or early evening. That timing depended on the ambient temperature and the use of the slower-working liquid yeast. They would, of course, rise more quickly in summer than winter.

Some of the other French roll or bun recipes of the period called for spice to be added, which makes them seem more suitable as a breakfast roll to eat with jam. You could certainly add spice to this recipe if you wished. Use the liquid yeast made from the recipe on page 25, and to hurry the dough along set it to rise in a warm place like an oven with a pilot light or on top of a radiator.

Sponge:
2 cups milk
2 cups flour
1 cup yeast or 1 package dry yeast

1. Make a sponge as follows: scald the milk, cool to lukewarm, then mix together with the flour and yeast. Beat it till smooth.
2. Set aside to work. (If overnight, let stand at room temperature. If in the morning, put in a warm place.) It is ready when it has a foamy, light appearance (about 4 hours in a warm place).

Dough:
4-6 cups flour
2 tablespoons melted shortening or lard
1 teaspoon salt
softened butter

3. When sponge is ready, add flour, shortening, and salt. Knead, adding flour as necessary, until the dough is smooth and elastic. Let rise again until doubled, about 2 hours if in a warm place.
4. Punch down, knead, and shape into rolls by rolling or patting out to 1/2-inch thick; cut into 2-to 3-inch rounds. Spread softened butter on half the rounds and fold over. Place on greased sheets. Let rise again till doubled, about an hour, if in a warm place.
5. Bake in a 400° oven for 10 minutes, reduce the heat to 375° and bake for another 15 minutes.

Yields 24 rolls.

GRAHAM BREAD

Two cups Graham flour, two tablespoons molasses, one teaspoon salt, one coffee cup of scalded milk, one coffee cup of water, one-half yeast cake, enough entire wheat to thicken. Mix over night, knead in the morning, then put into pans and raise an hour. This makes two loaves.

From *Rhode Island WCTU Recipe Book,* recipe by Mrs. Henry Bates, 1905, page 10

This makes a very flavorful, substantial bread. "Entire wheat" is what we call whole wheat. It is slow-rising, so mixing it and allowing it to rise overnight is not a bad idea. You could also mix it in the morning to bake later in the afternoon to serve with supper.

2 cups Graham flour
2 tablespoons molasses
1 teaspoon salt
1 cup scalded milk
1 cup water
1/2 yeast cake
1 1/2 - 2 cups whole wheat flour

1. Scald milk and add the cold water. When just warm to the touch, dissolve yeast cake in the mixture. Add molasses.
2. Mix Graham flour and salt in a large bowl, add milk mixture, and beat for several strokes.
3. Add whole wheat flour, about half a cup at a time, and continue to mix, using the back of the spoon, until the flour is all mixed in and dough is stiff. Don't knead.
4. Let rise overnight or several hours if in a cool place, less time if in a warm place.
5. When risen, punch down, and knead, adding as little flour as you can, until the dough is smooth and elastic. Put into one large or two small greased loaf pans.
6. Let rise one to two hours. Preheat oven to 425°.
7. Bake for ten minutes at 425° then reduce oven to 350° for forty-five minutes, or until the bread is golden and sounds hollow when you tap it.

Yields one large or two small loaves.

GRAHAM GEMS

One quart composed of two-thirds graham and one-third wheat flour, half a teaspoon of salt, a dessertspoonful of sugar, one teaspoon of soda in a pint of sour milk and beat to a foam; stir this into the meal and bake in hot gem-irons. Hood's Sarsaparilla purifies the blood.

From *Hood's Combined Cook Books,* by C.I. Hood & Co., 1875-1885, High Street, page 4

These Graham gems, a variation on muffins, come out of the oven with crisp exteriors. They are not too sweet so can be served with jam or jelly and, of course, butter. Like most muffins, they are best eaten hot.

Gem pans are basically muffin pans, but in the late nineteenth century some had rectangular shapes instead of the more familiar round shapes and were most often made of cast iron. If you have an iron gem or muffin pan, by all means use it for this recipe.

1 1/3 cups unbleached flour
2 2/3 cups Graham flour
1 scant tablespoon salt
2 cup sour milk
1 teaspoon baking soda
Heat oven to 400°

1. If you are using an iron pan, put the pan in the oven to preheat; when it is hot, remove and grease it.
2. Mix together flours, sugar, and salt in a mixing bowl.
3. Add soda to sour milk and stir quickly to mix.
4. Add to flour mixture immediately and mix. Avoid over-mixing.
5. Pour batter into hot, greased pan.
6. Bake for 20 minutes.

Yields a dozen and a half gems (will vary depending on your gem pans).

BRANDIED PEACHES OR PEARS

Preserved Peaches

Give them a scald but not boil them. Put them into cold water then dry in a stove & put in a wide mouthed bottle. To half a dozen peaches put a quarter of a lb. clarified Sugar, fill the bottles with brandy & stop close

From the manuscript recipe notebook of Mary Miller, 1850-1896, in a private collection

Four pounds sugar, four pounds fruit, one pint best white brandy. Make a syrup of the sugar, with water enough to dissolve it. When this boils, put in the fruit peeled, and let boil five minutes. Remove the fruit carefully; boil the syrup well until it thickens; then add the brandy, take the kettle from the fire immediately, and pour the hot syrup over the fruit previously put into jars.

From *Mrs.Winslow's Domestic Receipt Book for 1876,* page 31

Here are two recipes for preserved peaches. Mary Miller's recipe refers to a time when a housewife often had to refine sugar at home. Clarifying meant dissolving loaf sugar in water beaten up with egg white, boiling the mixture until a scum rose to be skimmed off, then straining the whole through a jelly bag or cloth. In some cases it was allowed to recrystalize, and was powdered up when needed.[56] This recipe is a bit ambiguous, but because it was weighed the sugar seems to have been dry and the brandy predominated as the liquid in the preserve.

Mrs. Winslow makes a preserving syrup out of the sugar with brandy as a flavoring and the product is peaches to process in canning jars.

Mrs. Mallory probably did her peaches *à la* Mrs. Winslow. I offer this recipe for your interest, so no interpretation will follow. There are a number of brandied-peach recipes in modern sources very similar to Mrs. Winslow's. Remember that the amount of brandy can be adjusted to taste.

QUEEN OF PUDDING

One pint of nice bread crumbs, one quart of milk, one cup of sugar, the yolks of four eggs, the grated rind of one lemon, a piece of butter the size of an egg. Bake like a custard. When baked spread over the top slices of jelly of any kind, and cover the whole with the whites of the eggs beaten to a stiff froth, with one cup of sugar and the juice of the lemon. Brown slightly in the oven. Hood's Sarsaparilla makes the weak strong.

From *Hood's Combined Cookbooks* by C.I. Hood and Co., 1885-1895, Hood's #1, page 14

It is a shame that this elegant and delicious pudding should have virtually disappeared after its popularity late in the nineteenth century, although modern variations can be found occasionally. Revived during Victoria's reign, and named for her, it is a variation on an earlier bread pudding. People who do not usually enjoy bread pudding like the custard-like quality of this one. The colorful jelly layer and meringue top make it very dressy.

One period recipe for queen of pudding suggests using currant jelly. Testing shows that a tart jelly is better than sweet jelly or jam.

For the crumbs use a slightly stale solid-style white bread. Five slices will give you the pint required when grated in a food processor or blender.

The recipe list above is clear. I recommend the following procedure.

Preheat oven to 350°

1. Set the crumbs to soak in the milk.
2. Cream together butter and sugar and beat in the yolks. Add the lemon rind.
3. Add the milk-soaked crumbs to the mixture above, and stir to blend. Pour into a greased baking dish and bake for about 30 minutes or until set in the middle.
4. Take out of the oven and put as much jelly as you like over the whole top of the pudding. You will not be able to spread it, so the recipe's instructions for "slices" is appropriate.
5. Beat the whites of the four eggs, gradually adding the sugar and lemon juice. Spread this over the jelly-topped pudding and run it back into the oven till slightly browned on top.
6. Serve cold with cream.

Yields 8-12 servings.

SNOW PUDDING

1/2 package gelatin
3 eggs—1 pint milk
1 cup sugar. 1 lemon

Soak gelatin one hour in a teacup of cold water—Then add 1 pint boiling water—when dissolved add sugar & lemon juice. Beat the whites to a stiff froth & when gelatin is quite cold whip it into the whites a spoonful at a time for an hour—whip steadily and evenly—& when all is stiff pour into a mould—turn into a glass dish. Make a custard of milk, eggs, pour around the base.

From the manuscript recipe notebook of Julia Gates, 1857-1930

The most striking thing about this recipe is the instruction to beat the mixture steadily for an hour. Writing about snow pudding in *The Dinner Year Book* Mrs. Harland said: "whip...for half an hour, if you use the Dover egg-beater (at least one hour with any other.)"[57]

In testing the recipe, I found that with a rotary hand beater, like the famed Dover, it does take half an hour to whip. But modern people have electric beaters, which means making this pudding today is a great deal easier for us than for Mrs. Gates. This recipe makes a lovely-looking pudding, especially if you chill it in a mold. It has a light texture and refreshing flavor, a nice light dessert after a heavy meal.

The instructions on packages of modern gelatine say that one envelope will gel two cups of liquid, but this recipe really requires a higher gelatine-to-liquid ratio to work properly. Mrs. Gates did not specify any garnishes for this dessert, but in her floating island and quaking custard recipes she recommended dotting the desserts with bits of jelly, which you could do, too. A modern interpretation follows.

Snow
2 1/2 tablespoons gelatine dissolved in 1 cup cold water
1 pint boiling water
juice of one lemon
3 egg whites

1. Soak gelatine in cold water. When dissolved, add the boiling water and lemon juice. Chill till it begins to set up.
2. Beat the whites of the eggs till stiff, and gradually add the chilled gelatine mixture. Beat constantly till all the gelatine mixture is added and the whole is fluffy. Pour into a two-quart mold (or two smaller molds) and chill.

Custard
1 pint milk
3 egg yolks
sugar to taste

1. Beat together the yolks and sugar and stir into the milk.
2. Cook in a double boiler till thickened. Set aside to cool.

To serve
1. Unmold the snow by holding the mold in hot water a moment, or wrapping in a hot towel, turn it out on a platter, and pour the custard over and/or around the pudding.
2. You may wish to garnish it with dots of jelly or, in a more modern vein, with fruit or flowers.

Yields a two-quart pudding.

STEAMED PUDDING
with lemon dip

Steam Pudding — *Three cups flour; one cup of suet; one cup of raisins; one cup of molasses; two cups of milk; one teaspoonful of bicarbonate of soda. Chop the suet very fine, put it in the flour with the other ingredients, and steam it two hours. To be eaten with lemon dip.*

Lemon Dip — *Thin two tablespoonsful of flour with water; stir it into a pint of boiling water; let it boil once; take it up and stir in four tablespoonsful of sugar, a little butter, and the juice of one lemon. Some prefer wine or brandy dip, but teetotalers prefer the aforesaid lemon dip.*

From the Mystic *Pioneer*, 2 April 1859

Reformers often recognized the importance of offering alternatives to prevalent usage and, as a result, countless lemons gave up their juice to battle rum or—in the case of pudding sauce—wine. This recipe is a standard suet-pudding recipe, suitable for everyday use, and just as likely to be served, despite the editor's special comment to teetotalers, with either a lemon or wine sauce. It would have been steamed in a pudding pan, bowl, or mold. The lemon dip is a flour-thickened sauce.

I offer this recipe mainly for your interest, so an interpretation will not follow. It would not be difficult to make. Be sure to grease your pudding mold well. In the sauce, you may wish to substitute cornstarch for flour: use three teaspoons of cornstarch for the two tablespoons of flour.

The Burrows Household: Risk and Uncertainty

While the Greenmans lived their comfortable, temperate, religious, middle-class life, the Burrows family got into debt, scraped along in storekeeping, saw Seth Winthrop "Winty" Burrows arrested and tried for selling liquor after it had been prohibited, and came to depend, at least in part, on Mrs. Burrows's millinery shop for income. How might this family's foodways reflect their circumstances? A family's choices derive in part from their financial condition, time in life, family size, and personal preferences. As we saw with the Greenmans, much of this can depend on confidence, character, and aspiration, what we in the twentieth century might call "self-image."

At the time Winty and Jane lived here, the Burrows house was the second story of a building which housed a street-level grocery store. But the back of the second story opened onto a small patch of land where the family could have had a garden if they wished. Opposite, a winter breakfast of herring, fried potatoes, biscuits, pancakes with molasses, and apple pie left over from supper. Recipes are at the end of the chapter. [MSM 76.8.97]

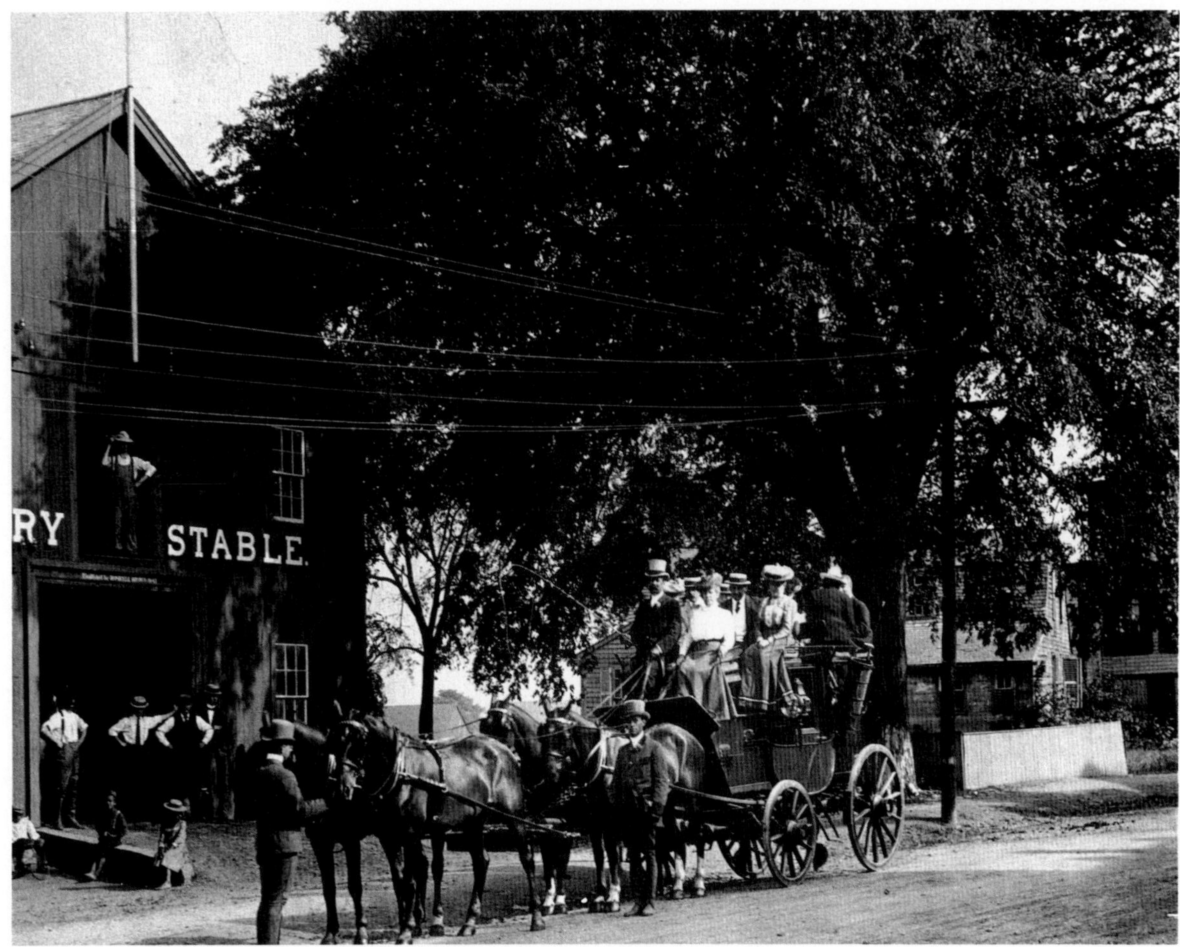

Right across the street from the Burrows house and store was Brown's Livery Stable. Wint was an admirer of horseflesh, and for a time owned a race horse named Fun. Gambling on horse racing compounded his financial difficulties and was only one of his risk-taking activities. His principal risky activity was the sale of liquor from the store—prohibited by law in Mystic River and Mystic Bridge in 1869. Thus, S. Winthrop Burrows found himself in court from time to time. [MSM 91-12-117]

Winty Burrows went to storekeeping in Mystic when times were reasonably good, but the cyclical nature of the nation's economy caught up with him and many others, forcing him into bankruptcy. Combine this bad timing with some poor political and personal choices, and there you have a recipe for financial insecurity and distress. S. W. Burrows was only five years younger than Charlotte Greenman, and his children were the same age as various Greenman progeny, but where George's son George H. could look forward to a life in business after his father, Seth's son Ambrose became a sailor; Greenman daughters married lawyers, doctors, and professional men, while Lizzie Burrows worked as a mill girl before marrying a man whose occupations included boatman and watchman.

Much of what we know about the Burrows family comes from accounts of Seth's brushes with the law, and what can be gleaned from the census and various town records. His was not a stable life, compared to the Greenman family's great and long career. He lived in Mystic for a relatively short period of time, and for work he kept a store, although he apparently had learned carpentry when young. His first wife died and left him with three youngsters, and he remarried, to a woman younger than himself. His life certainly reminds us that not everyone in small coastal towns enjoyed a consistently comfortable livelihood, and that entrepreneurial activity in the nineteenth century was risky indeed. His experience gives us a perspective on some people who lived even more marginally.

The house the Burrows family lived in was built around 1815 on the Groton side of Mystic, a bit north of the Mystic River ferry and the business district. By the time Burrows bought the house in 1860, the business district had moved north along the street leading to the bridge that now connected the two sides of the river. Other stores and businesses were in the neighborhood, including a livery stable right across the street. After he purchased the building, Burrows raised the house one story against a hillside, and put a grocery and dry goods store in the street-level portion. He also added an ell at ground level on the back, presumably for an updated kitchen.[1]

When the building was moved to Mystic Seaport Museum, the ell was removed, and the building was returned to a two-story structure as it appeared before it became the Burrows home and store. The Museum plans to add an ell in order to interpret the building to the 1870s, but while there are exterior photographs of the house before it was moved, the interior arrangement and furnishings of the kitchen ell is for now a matter of educated speculation.

Two Mrs. Burrows lived in this house, but we know little about them. Seth's first wife, Ann Catherine Park, five years younger than Winty, and three children–Ambrose, nine, Annie Elizabeth, five, and Mabel, three—moved to Mystic with him from Groton, near Burnett's Corner, shortly after he successfully survived two brushes with the law. (He had been awarded damages in an assault and battery case, and although he had been arrested for selling liquor, the charges were dropped because of insufficient evidence.) Ann died about a year later, the day after their fourth child, a premature baby, died.[2]

Wint waited two years, then in New London on 17 July, 1864, he married Jane L. Thompson, who at age twenty-four was fifteen years his junior.[3] Jane and Burrows did not have children of their own, but Jane had her hands full with Ambrose, at thirteen, and Annie and Mabel, eight and six, respectively. It was this Mrs. Burrows who ended up sharing the difficulties of her husband's Mystic years.

We can imagine that Jane Burrows was as busy as other women were at that time cooking, cleaning, and caring for children—probably even busier because she could not afford the help that the Greenman or Gates families enjoyed. We do not know how she interacted with her community and how Mr. Burrows's successes and failures affected her place in Mystic River society. Future research may reveal more of these details.

The Burrows House Kitchen

When the house was built early in the century, it was constructed around a central chimney, similar to the one in the Buckingham house. The cooking fireplace was put in the room at the end of the front hall; on the original site it was the southwest corner. Reflecting changes in fireplace design since the eighteenth century it was a shallow fireplace, considerably more heat-reflective than the Buckingham fireplace. The oven was on the right side, with an independent flue and the door flush with the chimney face. This arrangement was much more convenient for the cook, who did not have to bend over and step into the fireplace to use the oven.

Visitors to Mystic Seaport today see this fireplace boarded up, with a cookstove on the hearth. This was the fate of many such fireplaces by the middle of the nineteenth century in homes where the room continued as a kitchen. The fireplace might have been left open, if the kitchen was located elsewhere and if the occupants were sentimental about the traditional hearth around which a family could gather. Or it might have been closed up to make a place for a parlor stove; in some cases, so the author has been told, the old cooking fireplaces were closed up with the crane, trammels, and obsolete cooking pots hung in place, since cookstoves came with their own sets of pots and kettles. Women accustomed or desiring to do large bakings could continue to use fireplace side ovens, even when the fireplace was boarded up, though it is hard to tell from the record how often this was done.

The ell Seth Burrows added to the southwest back corner of the house presumably contained a new kitchen. A door on the south side of the ell led into the room, and a smaller chimney provided a place for a stove. The old kitchen probably became a family sitting room, possibly also the room for dining.

Many Mystic River homes had running water by this time. As a newspaper article noted, "After one has become accustomed to draw water from a faucet, the pump is a very tame institution."[4] Considering its in-town location, perhaps the Burrows house was on the system. Any evidence of a well that supplied the house when it was first built (plus other archaeological information) was destroyed when the site was excavated to make room for the present Chelsea Groton Savings Bank building and parking lot which occasioned the house's removal to the Museum in 1953.

The lot included a sufficient backyard to accommodate a few chickens, and possibly a small garden patch, but the Burrows property did not have adjacent land suitable for the extensive gardening operations that the Greenmans enjoyed. There is, however, no question where Mrs. Burrows got some of her groceries—at least as long as Seth Burrows had a thriving business.

Guessing About Mrs. Burrows

We know that at least some of the time this family lived on the edge financially, and that Mr. Burrows was willing to test the boundaries of middle-class propriety. How might that affect his wife's choice of kitchen furnishings and, ultimately, food choices as well? When they were enjoying palmy times, did Jane and Seth Burrows indulge in purchases of silver-plated flatware, or did they reinvest in store merchandise? Had Mrs. Burrows acquired some silver teaspoons by inheritance or as a wedding gift? Did she keep them, or did they have to be sold to settle a debt? Did Mrs. Burrows do as some women did, and some still do, scrimp along, managing as best she could, while Mr. Burrows put bets on horses—for a while, Wint had a race horse named "Fun"—and risked his livelihood by selling liquor? Or was Mrs. Burrows profligate, spending money when she had it, furnishing her kitchen and table handsomely while the family slipped deeper in debt? Did she approve of his selling liquor illegally? Did she try to influence his choices? Did she share with Seth an occasional glass of gin or rum?

GROCERIES.

I have on hand and offer for sale the following articles:—

FLOUR, BUTTER, LARD, BEANS, PEAS, POTATOES, INDIAN MEAL, WHORTLEBERRIES, ONIONS, SQUASHES, CONFECTIONERY, CROCKERY, OIL CLOTHS, FLUID, DRY GOODS, FANCY ARTICLES, UMBRELLAS, NAILS, &c. &c.

Please call and examine my stock. Everything is offered cheap for cash.

S. W. BURROWS.

Mystic River, Conn., Aug. 9th.

Not everyone, male or female, marched in lockstep with the middle-class standards of the nineteenth century. The feminine ideal of spiritual goodness, loving motherhood, and devoted wifery could be put to a severe test when a family was distressed. We do not know where along this continuum Mrs. Burrows came to rest. We do not know what her character was like. We have to guess, then, at her choices.

Here is my guess about Mr. and Mrs. Burrows, which, until we have a bit more hard evidence, will form the basis of my scenario about how they lived and what they ate. I believe that they were pragmatic Yankee people who ricocheted between moderate prosperity and disaster and were not particularly troubled by being in debt, especially if it seemed necessary to stay in business. Their rejection of a temperance movement, which was moving toward prohibition, was, I believe, based on a feeling that a drink or two did no one great harm; probably Seth, and Jane as well, enjoyed a drink themselves. In this they were more conservative than the Greenmans, who were zealous about prohibition; when the Greenman brothers and wives were children, after all, hard cider and small beer were considered family beverages, and the Burrowses simply did not change in their attitude towards liquor, even though some of society was changing around them. They had no particular scruples about selling spirits; in fact, when they moved back to New London Jane apparently owned and operated a saloon.[6]

In the political discussion over prohibiting liquor sales, the towns of Mystic and Stonington were not unanimous; both towns had prohibition enthusiasts, but the Mystic people were aided by the anti-drink sentiments of the Mystic *Pioneer*, while the Stonington *Mirror* advocated a temperate approach to the temperance movement and mocked the self-righteous tone of the Mystic paper. A month after the prohibition law took effect in the two Mystics—Mystic River (Groton) and Mystic Bridge (Stonington)—the *Mirror* had this to say about the wisdom of the ban: "To argue that rum in itself is an evil, shows about as much common sense as it would to maintain that 'pork and beans' are an evil, because several thousand New England families persist in gourmandizing it every Sunday morning, and washing it down with a decoction of coffee, strong enough to paralyze the brain, and insure indigestion and misery for a week, and then go to church and get to sleep over a dull sermon." It was, the *Mirror* pointed out, abuse, not use, that constituted evil, and to inconvenience many moderate people for the sake of the very few immoderates was "trespassing upon individuals rights and abridging the sensible use of liquor, or pork and beans."[7] I can imagine, on a winter evening, Wintyreading this aloud to Jane while she darned socks—and their hearty agreement.

The Burrowses were obviously reluctant to give up the profitable liquor sales, especially on the stock in the store. In 1869, when store- and saloon-keepers in Mystic were interviewed by a visiting committee of prohibition workers, Burrows said he would be the first to stop selling if the committee would buy his stock—a pragmatic, perhaps cynical, reply.[8] As a matter of fact, they did buy his and others' supplies, emptying it all out on the eve of a town ban on selling liquor. But in the future Wint Burrows merely restocked, setting himself up for arrest.

Mrs. Burrows may have attended church occasionally, perhaps more for the social contact than spiritual support, but it does not seem likely. There is a bit of tangential evidence that she could act crudely. A newspaper account about a horse trade that went bad featured a pair of pseudonymed characters who probably were the Burrowses. The female was described as telling the third party, in so many words, where to stuff it, hardly a sign of gentility. Her step-daughter Annie Elizabeth may have attended public school but, at age sixteen, pitched in by working in a woolen mill until she married at the young age of seventeen.[9]

Within six years of Jane's marriage to him, Winty Burrows was less of a grocery and dry goods seller than a "liquor dealer," according to the 1870 census taker's description of his occupation. And a couple of years later another businessman, Mr. J.G. Lowe, began keeping store in Burrows's building. Jane herself advertised in 1874 that she had opened a millinery store.[10] At least two of her step-children were grown up and out of the house by that time, and the bank foreclosure that would end their stay in

Mystic was still two years away. Having endured with him his protracted legal battles, some of the costs for which were borne by a liquor dealers' association, Jane Burrows may have seen that the only way out was for her to help support them. When things were going well for this family, financially and legally, I imagine them living comfortably but not expansively, choosing traditional foods, enjoying beef steak served on a plainly laid table. If there was spare cash, I'll bet Wint spent it on horse racing, or speculating on real estate.

When their finances contracted, Jane Burrows made do, skimping on costly ingredients—using more brown sugar than white, for example—and buying fresh meat less often. She and her step-daughters would turn and mend dresses, and freshen them with new ribbons. The Burrowses would have their tin pots repaired, glue broken plates, and make a handful of kitchen utensils serve many purposes. In Jane Burrows's life, there was little time for fussy foods; except on the special occasions that came into everyone's life, rich or poor, she made do with plain fare, and plenty of it. Wint Burrows never went hungry; a news article reported after one arrest: "The law took a fresh grip on S. Winthrop Burrows last Saturday. It has took hold of him so many times before that it was rather difficult for deputy Sheriff Brown to remember how many times he had arrested the *corpulent corporosity* [emphasis added] of the aforesaid S.W.B." [11]

Shown here is the fireplace wall closed up with a cook stove installed in place of an open hearth. The exhibit kitchen at Mystic Seaport is arranged to show a modest household's furnishings. In the pantry just out of sight is a pump for water. [MSM 94-4-10]

Furnishing the Burrows Kitchen

The first Mrs. Burrows, born in 1830, may have learned to cook in a fireplace and switched to a stove later. Jane Burrows, born in 1840, was just enough younger to belong to the generation that learned first to cook at a stove, and that is what she had in her Mystic River house. Jane, of course, moved into an already furnished house and kitchen and took up use of her predecessor's possessions.

If Jane Burrows wanted to avoid spending money, she could eschew specialized cooking utensils: who needed an apple parer and apple corer when one sharp knife would answer for both? A biscuit cutter could be replaced by an inverted tumbler. In the unlikely case that there was no rolling pin, one of Wint's empty wine bottles would do very nicely. But an egg beater would have been hard to resist.

For general cooking purposes, Jane's kitchen may have been simply furnished with the most basic tools. One square tin pan could double for baking and roasting; instead of pie

plates and iron cooking spoons in multiples, she may have had just one or two of each. Where the Beecher sisters recommend fry pans, gridirons, saucepans, ladles, and teakettles of different sizes, we can imagine Mrs. Burrows with just one size of each. Jane may not have even owned tin measures, but instead relied on a coffee or tea cup to scoop flour from the barrel and measure it.

Imagine your own kitchen and its tools. Picture yourself selecting out only those items that you use daily, or at the very least weekly, and discarding the rest. This then is how we may envision Jane Burrows's kitchen to have been equipped: not much stuff, but all of it used often.

Dining with the Burrows Family

Almost everybody has a few prized possessions, and Jane Burrows was probably no different. Among her nicest things may have been a teapot, sugar and creamer, and a few nice tea cups, a few silver teaspoons, perhaps a small selection of heirloom wine glasses. For everyday use, the Burrowses likely had an older style of chinaware, perhaps what was called blue-edged or feather-edged ware, or old Staffordshire plates and bowls, or the simplest plain white and very durable stoneware, of the sort with which the life-saving station was furnished. Stoneware mugs or tin cups were serviceable for coffee and tea. If the Burrows household ever saw a nice matching set of plates, sauce dishes, soup bowls, and cups and saucers with serving pieces it would have been reserved for very special occasions, unless Jane wished to make an everyday brave show of prosperity and comfort.

The simplest kind of steel case knives and forks, two- or three-pronged, with iron spoons for soup, seem the most likely choice here, or possibly iron flatware; but if there was silver-plate flatware it, like the matching dishes, would have been for special use.

In the summer of 1861 Burrows was selling oil cloth, the ideal table covering for everyday.[13] Perhaps the Burrowses had a piece for their own table. Otherwise, a household like this may have converted flour or sugar bags into household linens: dish towels, table cloths, or napkins, which may have shared space with better-quality but older and worn linens left from more prosperous days. The nice linen or damask tablecloths, if any, were reserved for special times.

The Burrows House Food Supply

The first advertisement for Wint Burrows's new store appeared in the 10 August 1861 issue of the Mystic *Pioneer*.

"GROCERIES. I have on hand and offer for sale the following articles: Flour, Butter, Lard, Beans, Peas, Potatoes, Indian Meal, Whortleberries, Onions, Squashes, Confectionery, Crockery, Oil Cloths, Fluid, Dry Goods, Fancy Articles, Umbrellas, Nails etc., etc. Please call and examine my stock. Everything is offered cheap for cash. S. W. Burrows."

Right downstairs the first Mrs. Burrows had quite a number of items from which several different dishes could be made. If we added the ever-present molasses, some salt pork, eggs, and milk, here is what she could have made from the food items in the list above:

- flour and lard for pie crust with either whortleberry or squash filling
- Indian pudding
- Boston brown bread with Indian meal and flour
- biscuits
- jonnycakes
- griddle cakes
- gems
- corn bread
- pork and beans, with or without onion
- pea soup
- bean soup
- side dish of boiled squash
- plain batter pudding with whortleberries
- potatoes boiled, fried, mashed, roasted
- salt pork and potatoes fried or boiled together
- salt pork and milk gravy, served on biscuits or jonnycakes or potatoes

It could have been the menu for a week or more.

The Burrows family, like most southern New Englanders at this time—even the Greenmans—shared a basic group of favorite dishes. The Greenmans would have been happy to dine on any of the above, to which they could have more frequently added meat—whole joints that may have just been beyond the reach of Seth and Jane Burrows—perhaps a greater variety of fruits and vegetables, and more plentiful supplies of eggs, milk, butter, cheese, and cream when they were available.

We have no clear picture of what Wint continued to carry in his store—except, of course, the rum, gin, brandy, and wine that got him in so much trouble—so what Jane Burrows could run downstairs for, or ask Wint to bring up for dinner, is left, like so much else, to educated guesswork.

Mystic newspapers from the Burrows family's years there give a glimpse of what food arrived in town and how it was distributed. Here are some examples:

An article deploring the state of the economy listed food and household goods bought in the village of Mystic in 1860 and 1861. It included beef by the pound and quarter, veal, pork by the hog, butter, quinces, apples, cider, vinegar, potatoes, eggs, cheese, lard, smoked hams, buckwheat, turkeys, chickens, cabbage, turnips, flour, crackers, sugar, raisins, molasses, coffee, codfish, and tea.[14]

October 20, 1866: Oysters sold "in any quantity from a pint to a cargo" or served on the half shell, fried, stewed, or roasted by Capt. Jo. Freeman.

August 29, 1873: Spark's Bakery advertises: "...prepared to furnish families good bread, pies, cakes, crackers, family yeast, always on hand...confectionery, nuts, fruits, etc.,"

A winter succotash made with dried beans and corn, recipe on page 76.

while John Forsyth's store lists "Groceries, Provisions, flour, meal, feed,...TEA, COFFEE, SPICES, BUTTER, AND CHEESE made a specialty. All kinds of canned fruit, preserves, jellies, &c. Borden's Condensed Milk."

May 1, 1874: "The season for buckwheat cakes is nearly past, but maple syrup is always in season, and goes nicely with wheat griddles and other like articles. L.A. Morgan & Co. have a supply from headquarters."

June 12, 1874: "If you don't know the difference between piccalilli and chow-chow go to Denison's and buy a bottle of each and try it; then if you can't tell the difference, it don't make much difference."

January 28, 1875: "Mystic eels are said to be the best in the world...And yet we have wretches that complain of hard times."

May 28, 1875: "Shad. Pineapples."

June 18, 1875: "Mrs. Hammond brings the first Ledyard strawberries of the season, for which she gets the handsome price of forty cents a box."

July 16, 1875: "Peas....Watermelons. Peddlers increase....Garden vegetables coming in."

September 10, 1875: "Pears for canning....Pie Apples scarce and high. Peaches plenty and very good.

September 17, 1875: "The diminutive blue fish which have been numerous in the Thames for a season or two—and for aught we know may always have been—are quite plenty in the Mystic just now, and furnish fine sport for fishermen of every grade and age, messes of a dozen to a hundred being taken daily."

October 1, 1875: "Mackerel have been plenty for a week past at the mouth of river, and everyone who makes any pretense as a fisherman has been out to try them, bringing in strings ranging from a dozen to a hundred."

January 6, 1976: "The eeling is fair and long rows of them threaded on sticks adorn the sides of the houses."

June 29, 1876: "A fair crop of cherries; strawberries on the wane."

July 6, 1876: "Fine fish....An active ice cream market....Long Bar is still fertile and daily beseiged by assiduous clam diggers."

July 13, 1876: "Fresh tomatoes. Cherries falling."

September 21, 1876: "Farmers complain of the very low prices of beef this fall. We haven't heard any housekeepers complaining the same way." "Among the arrivals at the port of Mystic last week were, Capt. Nickerson's schooner with salt fish; the sloop *Live Yankee*, Capt Tingley, with apples and melons from the Connecticut River;...the *Spray* from Sag Harbor [Long Island] with onions, etc. etc."

November 16, 1876: "Turnip vendors abound. Smelt fishermen are on the alert, but only the knowing ones fill their bags...Another load of northern potatoes arrived at the depot last week. They sold off like hot cakes, which tells the story as to their quality and price."

August 16, 1877: "Delaw-a-r-e p-e-a-c-h-e-s! Three q-u-a-r-t-s f'ra q-u-a-r-t-e-r!!" Probably a quote from a street hawker; "O, give us a rest," is the editorial comment.[15]

Fresh fruits and vegetables grown both nearby and at a distance were arriving in Mystic, and other coastal towns as well, wherever train and water eased transportation. The salt water yielded up various fish and shellfish for variety from the monotony of domestic beef and pork or, for those less well off, provided a source of protein. The quantities of fish taken—hundreds of mackerel, strings of eels—lead us to believe that families might have done some home salting and smoking. Similar reports in other area papers include blackberries, codfish, news about milk peddlers, and lobstering.

Not much on this list would be unfamiliar to modern people. It is, in fact, a modern diet, one that remained basically unchanged up into the twentieth century, and then changed largely in its quality and availability when the seasons of food were extended, by transportation and refrigeration improvements, and by many items being made ready-to-eat.

Meals of the Day

How did Jane Burrows translate this supply into meals for her family? Considering that she probably did not have household help, except from her step-daughters, and that money was periodically in short supply, Jane probably kept it simple. The Burrowses shared a way of life with other working people: laborers, fishermen, craftsmen, a group whose foodways are very poorly documented.

The Burrows family's pattern of meals through the day probably resembled that of the Greenmans—largely unchanged from the era of the Buckinghams, at least until Lizzie went to work in the mill. A breakfast and supper of similar size and content flanked the largest meal of the day at noon.

Breakfast: The nineteenth-century breakfast varied from very small and simple—hasty pudding or bread and milk—to a warm meal with a piece of meat, such as ham or sausage, or fish, eggs, a hot bread of some sort—like the buckwheat cakes mentioned above—and coffee or tea. We can imagine the Burrows family's breakfasts varying along with their economic status. For breakfast, fish was a likely choice: "Salt mackerel for breakfast at this season of the year clears the complexion, invigorates the intellect, and imparts a flavor to the mustache that will vanquish the most obstinate odor of hair dye," reported the Mystic *Press* on 5 May 1876. And "No. 1 Extra Mackerel" was considered a good winter breakfast, according to the Mystic *Press* of 30 October 1874.

Two New England breakfasts recorded ten to twenty years before the Burrows family lived in Mystic show how little things changed over two decades. Richard Henry Dana, Jr., during a fishing vacation in 1843 on the Isles of Shoals, stayed at the home of the fisherman-pilot Joseph C. Swell, and wrote: "Breakfasted with great relish & appetite at seven. Ate hot bread, fish, pie & everything, with coffee." Interestingly, the supper menu the day before had been virtually identical: "apple pie, fried fish, cake, hot bread, &c."[16] This was a meal for guests, and whether the Swells ate the same fare without company we do not know.

Henry Thoreau recorded the breakfast he ate on Cape Cod at the home of a Wellfleet oysterman in October 1849: "At breakfast we had eels, buttermilk cake, cold bread, green beans, doughnuts, and tea...I ate of the applesauce and doughnuts."[17] If Dana or Thoreau had breakfasted at the Burrows home in Mystic River they might have received similar fare.

At the bottom of the molasses barrels in Wint's store there may have been an especially memorable commodity that Edward Knapp, recalling his childhood in the 1860s and 1870s, saw at Uncle Cephas Fitch's store down the river in Noank: "In the cellar were barrels of salt pork and beef, and those great sticky barrels of gen*uine* New Orleans molasses; the kind that was so rich and strong in sugar, it must be wet down with cold water, or lowered in the tide to keep it from working and mayhap bursting the barrel and when the barrel was empty (?) there still remained from twenty to fifty pounds of the most delicious Molasses sugar, sold at about two cents a pound, and nothing better has been devised to make Pancakes go down sweetly, than that molasses barrel sugar."[18] Molasses and cheap brown sugar of this sort probably sweetened many Burrows family dishes.

Dinner: The noon meal would combine meat and potatoes, bread, and a vegetable dish: sometimes no more than a pickle, sometimes substantial cooked vegetables like beans, corn, green beans, or root vegetables. It seems unlikely that the Burrowses were salad eaters. A sweet followed for dessert, probably pudding or pie. The pie-eating habit was thoroughly entrenched by this time in New England. Edward Knapp wrote, "Pies, 'fit to kill,' because you could not avoid eating twice too much, if the chance offered getting up in the middle of the night, for just one more piece: 'and for luck, let's make it a quarter pie each.' "[19]

Americans have usually preferred beef, when they could afford it, with pork a close second, so Jane would have given Wint a beefsteak-and-potato meal whenever it was possible. Boiled dinners of corned beef or ham provided an ample family dinner without a great deal of minute-to-minute attention. Chowders with lots of crackers in them, and soups with bread or biscuits, would have made a good weekday dinner or supper. For special occasions, a roasted chicken would have seemed right.

Edward Knapp described both how to get a chicken for dinner and how to serve another dish the Burrowses may have had: "It never occurred to anyone then to take a hen or Rooster off the roost at night for a meal; but some boy was engaged to run one down; thru Gardens, over fences, etc....I ran one down for Mrs. Jerusha Brown, and she treated me to Succotash with brown sugar in it—that spoiled me I must have sugar in Beans and succotash to this day."[20]

Supper: Supper was another small meal of quick breads, perhaps with some preserves, baked goods, maybe a small piece of fried meat, or warmed-up leftovers. All classes of New England people ate pork and beans, if not Sunday morning before church, then Saturday night. By this time, pork and beans, besides being a dish that people enjoyed eating, had become a symbol of old New England. During the Centenary year of 1876, the Mystic Methodist Church women held a "Centennial Tea Party or Supper of ye Antient Times." On the menu were their interpretation of colonial foods: "Pork and Benes [*sic*], Boiled Vittles, Punkin Pies, Dough Nuts, etc."[21]

Captain Samuel Samuels went to sea at age eleven as cook on a coasting vessel. He learned some of his cooking from the captain's sister in Newport: "She was adept at shortcake and corn-bread, knew how to fry fish and ham, and at baking beans had no superior."[22] Quick breads, like biscuits and the cornbread mentioned here, raised with chemical leavenings like baking soda—sometimes called saleratus—and cream of tartar, were very popular among New Englanders and other busy Americans who were concerned more with saving time and money than having good flavor.

What the Reformers Were Fixing

When Catherine Beecher and Harriet Beecher Stowe described the Christian home in *American Woman's Home*, it was people like the Greenmans they had in mind, and with the additional hope of reforming people like the Burrowses.[23] To understand better how Mrs. Burrows may have conducted her household, perhaps we can read the advice books of the period—inside out: if *Godey's Lady's Book* and the Beecher sisters say "do not..." we might surmise that Jane, like many people, *did*.

In November 1859, *Godey's* ran an article on the importance of learning good housekeeping habits. "Let it be observed that it is the *middle and working classes* [emphasis added] on whom we wish to urge the study. A gentleman's daughter can afford to be so ignorant of common things..." The article went on to urge "the art of making a little go a great way."[24] Surely there were times when Jane Burrows would have heartily agreed. So how

A New England apple pie, recipe on page 73.

The Burrows' home and store stood at the corner of Water and West Main Streets in Mystic River, the village on the west side of the river. This picture of West Main Street shows Central Hall on the right and some of the businesses that lined the street in 1869. Some of them were Winty's competition in grocery, and, until the temperance movement overtook the town, liquor sales. [Collodion stereo glass-plate negative, MSM 65.959.24]

might she have accomplished this?

Beginning in the early nineteenth century New Englanders' cookbooks acknowledged that the economical could cut corners on virtually any recipe. The *American Frugal Housewife* was based entirely on that premise. Books entitled *How to do Things Well and Cheap, for Domestic Use, by One Who Knows*, and *New England Economical Housekeeper*, appealed to housewives, as did books containing "practical," "simple," "family," or "domestic economy," in titles or descriptions.[25] The same appeal works today.

Costly ingredients—particularly butter, sugar, and eggs—were called for in smaller quantities or substituted with cheaper ones: lard, molasses, soda, and cream of tartar. Labor- or attention-intensive procedures—raising baked goods with yeast or beaten egg whites, or carefully roasting meat—were dropped in favor of chemical leavenings and frying or boiling, or were saved for very special occasions. Any recipe calling for both costly ingredients and time and attention did not have a chance; for example, sauces thickened with egg yolks were readily replaced by gravies thickened with flour.

At the same time that New Englanders simplified and speeded up their cookery, the wheat from the newly opened West dropped flour prices, putting flour in the reach of most. The germ, which caused flour to become rancid, was routinely removed, and improved bolting meant more people had access to white flour as whole-wheat flour became a thing of the past, except in its form as Graham flour.[26] Sugar became a less-expensive commodity, and stove ovens made it so much easier to make a batch of biscuits, cake, or cookies than ever before.

When some of these trends were taken to extremes, compounded by some of the general slowing of the American metabolism, there was fertile ground for reform. In an 1859 article, "Letter to a Dyspeptic" in the *Atlantic Monthly*, we can read a satirical account of a day's meals for the American middle class:

"Breakfast: The breakfast table was amply covered for you were always what was termed by judicious housewives, 'a good provider.' I remember how the beef-steaks (for the sausages were destined for your two youngest Dolorosi, who were recovering from the measles, and needed something light and palateable) vanished in huge rectangular masses down your throat, drawn downward in a maelstrom of coffee;...the resources of the house also afforded certain very hot biscuits or breadcakes in a high state of saleratus;...also fried potatoes, baked beans, mince-pie, and pickles. The children partook of these dainties largely but without undue waste of time. They lingered at the table precisely eight minutes, before setting out to school.

"Dinner: Two of the children took luncheon baskets with them, with the 'cold remains of breakfast' in them. Another child skipped lunch because he snacked on 'cold baked beans and vinegar.' Dinner consisted of 'fried pork,' ditto roasted, strong coffee, turnips, potatoes, and a good deal of gravy. For dessert...we had mince-pie, apple-pie, and lemon pie....We lingered long at that noon meal—fifteen minutes at the very least."

Later that day at tea: "We partook of pound-cake (or pound-and-a-half, I should say) and sundry hot cups of tea."[27] Here then was summed up the American proclivity for meat—beef and pork—fried, for fatty food of all kinds, hot quickbreads, vinegar or pickles for sharpness, pastry, and hot beverages. And, if you carefully consider it, you see that these are all elements of fast-food restaurant fare today.

Richard Henry Dana, while visiting in China and observing the Eastern diet, wrote in his journal: "Think of our grease & fat, & tough meat, bad bread, & worse hot cakes. I have seen something of the cooking of England, France, Sp. America & China,—& believe the worse cooking in the world is that of the middle & poorer classes in America....Think too of the great junks & slices of heavy meat we all eat at home! Think of the head of the family, up to his elbows in blood, distributing half raw meat among his children, from fork & knife reeking with blood! Then a few waxy potatoes, clammy bread & hard thick pie crust."[28]

With the same food-reforming spirit, and with none of Dana's sanguinary examples, the Beecher sisters wrote that "a debilitated constitution from the misuse of food" was caused by: "Eating *too much*, eating *too often*, eating *too fast*, eating food and condiments that are *too stimulating*, eating food that is *too warm* or *too cold*, eating food that is *highly concentrated*, with a proper admixture of less nourishing matter, and eating hot food that is *difficult of digestion*." They were taking aim at grease, sugar, hot beverages, iced beverages, candies and cakes for children between meals, hot biscuits, and too much meat. They advocated more vegetables, grains, leaner meat, and whole wheat.[29] This message will be familiar to modern people.

What did this have to do with Jane Burrows? The Beechers said that "The most unhealthful kinds of food are those which are made so by *bad cooking* [emphasis added]; such as heavy and sour bread, cakes, pie-crust, and other dishes consisting of fat mixed and cooked with flour. Rancid butter and high seasoned foods are equally unwholesome."[30] Jane was clearly responsible for whatever came out of her kitchen to be ingested by the "corpulent corporosity" of Wint Burrows. That she cooked what he probably liked, and what was considered pretty regular victuals for her time and place, did not make much difference to the reformers. But the fact that many of these new ideas did not make cultural headway until fairly recent times demonstrates how very persistent foodways are. If Jane Burrows ever heard any of the ideas of the Beecher sisters, she probably ignored or dismissed them as most people of her class did.

If Jane Burrows ever got stuck on the question of "what to cook for dinner," and if she was the sort to turn to recipe books, it would not be the French Soyer, the English Mrs. Beeton, or even New England's Miss Parloa. She might pick up a little advertising receipt book like *Mrs. Winslow's Domestic Receipt Book for 1868*, published by Jeremiah Curtis and John I. Brown, manufacturers of Brown's Bronchial Troches and Mrs. Winslow's Soothing Syrup, or *Hood's Cookbook*, published by C.I. Hood, maker of Hood's Sarsaparilla. These little books included sensible recipes for Imitation Apple Pie (using raw sliced pumpkin in place of apples), Fruit Cake and Cheap Fruit Cake, Chicken Pie, and occasional oddities like Podovies (odd in Mystic, but not in the manufacturing cities where the patent medicines originated). These were interleaved with letters of endorsement and claims of success with all the diseases curable by their products, which a storekeeper like Wint Burrows might have carried.

Working-Class Diet

We will see evidence of the Burrows family's foodways again in the foodways of the New Shoreham Life-Saving Station; it was from working people that the Life-Saving Service recruited its surfmen and keepers. A simplified version of the Burrows family's diet was served to the men in the forecastles of whalers and merchant vessels of the time. And a generous version of it was cooked up for the men of the fishing fleets. We will investigate these seafaring diets in the next two chapters.

This way of choosing, preparing, and serving food—a foodway—could be termed vernacular, but was it shared up and down the social scale. Women like Jane Burrows, Charlotte Greenman, and Julia Gates learned how to make these dishes from their mothers and neighbors, by asking how it was done, seeing the finished product, and tasting it. They taught their daughters how to cook by showing them. The only reminder was a jotted list of ingredients, the most common form of recipe in nineteenth-century manuscript sources.

The decision of what to cook rested on examining the food supply and seeing what suggested itself from the cook's own repertoire of experience and knowledge. It was a foodway that planned for certain quantities of preferred supplies; it determined how many bushels of potatoes, barrels of salt pork, sides of beef, and what staples seemed "right" or "enough." When necessary it was an opportunistic foodway, capitalizing on leftovers, luck in fishing, gardening, gathering, and shared surplus. And because it did not depend on books or cooking schools, this foodway could be prepared by anyone regardless of their education or social class. It could even be prepared by men not trained to cook. It went to sea and made a home out of fishing camps and life-saving stations.

This foodway was largely immune to high-style influences; when a new dish or ingredient was introduced it had to fit the established diet like an interlocking piece of a puzzle, or else the new food, or new mode of preparing or using a familiar food, was treated somehow as a special item.

From this selection of recipes you could make three meals for one day of the type the Burrows family might have eaten. Have salt mackerel and apple pie (preferably leftover) for breakfast, and don't forget the fried potatoes. Plan on boiled ham and vegetables for dinner, with a little pickled cabbage on the side, with sponge cake for dessert. Save the ham bone, boiling water, and scraps for the pea soup that follows. For supper revel in cornmeal and molasses and have baked beans, brown bread, and Indian pudding. Make a batch of gingerbread in case you have someone stop in for tea, or feel a little peckish yourself. For a night-cap or any time, a whiskey punch recipe follows in honor of the anti-temperance sentiments of Seth and Jane.

There are some surprises here, both in the foods these recipes produce and in the sources. The soft gingerbread recipe comes from the logbook of the schooner *William B. Herrick*, author unknown, clearly intended for use at sea but an odd place to find a recipe.[31] You will discover that the brown bread was a descendant of the thirds recipe in the previous chapter about Lydia Buckingham; that apples in apple pie were often stewed before being put into pie; that baked beans were not sweet.

FRIED SALT MACKEREL

Soak them two days, inside down, in cold water, changing the water once or twice; when fresh enough, clean thoroughly, and wipe dry. It may then be fried or broiled, or boil in a little water. Serve the fish with bits of butter over it.

From *Practical American Cookery and Domestic Economy,* by Miss Hall, 1855, page 111

A good breakfast dish, fried mackerel would probably have been fried up in salt-pork fat or butter. A two-day soaking sounds a bit long; Mrs. Beecher says overnight is sufficient and explains that "In soaking all kinds of salt fish, put it into a large pan or dish, with the *skin up*; else the salt, which of its own weight naturally sinks to the bottom, will settle in the skin, and the fish will not be freshened at all."[32]

Plain salted mackerel like the ones commonly available in the nineteenth century are hard to find today. You can find mackerel that is salted and spiced or smoked, and these are certainly suitable for breakfast, which you could prepare as Miss Hall suggests. You could, if you were feeling adventurous, consider buying mackerel in the round in the spring, then splitting and salting it yourself. I offer this recipe for your interest, so no interpretation will follow.

APPLE PIE

When you make apple pies, stew your apples very little indeed; just strike them through, to make them tender. Some people do not stew them at all, but cut them up in very thin slices, and lay them in the crust. Pies made in this way may retain more of the spirit of the apple; but I do not think the seasoning mixes in as well. Put in sugar to your taste; it is impossible to make a precise rule, because apples vary so much in acidity. A very little salt, and a small piece of butter in each pie, makes them richer. Cloves and cinnamon are both suitable spice. Lemon brandy and rose-water are both excellent. A wineglassful of each is sufficient for three or four pies. If your apples lack spirit, grate in a whole lemon.

From *The American Frugal Housewife,* by Mrs. Child, 1833, pages 67-68

This recipe from the earlier part of the century sums up just about everything that could be said about apple pies, and *was* subsequently said as well. There is a great tradition of apple-pie eating in this country and there are many references to the frequency of it being served and eaten. Yet not one of the dozen or so manuscript recipe notebooks I own contains an apple pie recipe; period apple pie recipes are found almost exclusively in *printed* cookbooks. That makes me believe that it was one of many dishes that was commonly prepared without benefit of a strict recipe. When apple pie recipes do occur in cookbooks, they either have some special little fillip (like adding a few spoonfuls of cream to the filling), or describe the process painstakingly for the uninitiated cook, or they say basically what Mrs. Child did in the recipe above.

There are several things of interest to note in Mrs. Child's recipe. First, she recommended stewing the apples before putting them in a pie, apparently more usual in the nineteenth century. Today we almost always make them from raw apples, which Mrs. Child acknowledged "some people" did then.

Second, she noted that "apples vary so much in acidity," which was certainly much more true in the nineteenth century, when there were many more varieties of apples available than today. Apples varied in keeping qualities, ripening times, acidity, value for cooking or cider-making, and, of course, flavor. So the addition of sugar was a subjective decision, not quantifiable for a recipe.

Third, she commented on lemon brandy and rosewater "sufficient for three or four pies," which underlines the nineteenth-century habit of making pies in large batches, which you will read more about in the chapter on Thanksgiving.

Other recipes, both from Mrs. Child's time and later, recommended lemon juice or peel for apple pie, and added nutmeg to the list of suggested spices. Rosewater is still available today, and you may like to try a bit sometime. Remember that a wine-glassful is about a quarter cup, and if that is sufficient for three or four pies then a tablespoonfull should be sufficient for one pie.

If you have not yet had the experience of cooking without a precise, scientific recipe, then making an apple pie under Mrs. Child's tutelage is a good way to start. To put you in the place of Mrs. Burrows no modern interpretation will be provided. Just don't worry about it; taste as you go, and remember that if you use raw apples they will shrink, so you will want to pile them high.

CURING HAMS

Dr. McKnight's Receipt for putting down Hams

7 lbs. Coarse salt, 5 lbs. brown sugar, 2 oz. Saltpetre, 1/2 an oz. pearlash, 4 gallons water. Boil all together & skim the pickle well & when cold pour it on the meat. Pork Hams to remain in eight weeks. Beef 3 weeks. The above is for 100 lbs.

From an anonymous manuscript recipe notebook from Essex, Connecticut, 1848-57, Essex Historical Society

A good many families put down their own beef and pork hams to cure, some in preparation for smoking later. Pickle recipes like the one above are to be found in manuscript sources because meat curing was for many people an annual activity and, unless written down, the recipe might be forgotten from one year to another.

The process of curing pork for storage varied then as now depending on the size and fattiness of the cut, and on its intended use. There seems to have been more variety than today in the kinds of cuts that were salted or pickled, as we will see in recipes like the one for pork and beans (page 79).

I offer this recipe for your interest, but it is similar to modern pickle recipes for ham, and you could give it a try. Be sure you read up in a reliable modern source on the process of packing and storing the meat while it is curing so that you know how to do it safely.

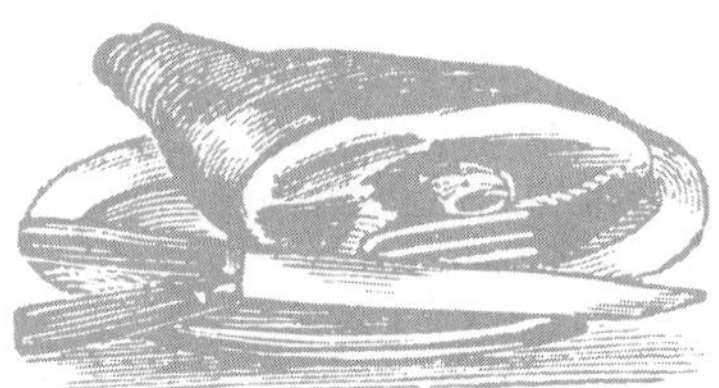

BOILED HAM

To boil hams it should be boiled in large quantity of water-in that for a long time-one quarter of an hour for each pound: the ham is most palatable when cold-and should be sent to the table with eggs-horseradish and mustard.

From the manuscript recipe notebook of Julia Palmer, ca. 1840-60, Anna North Coit, North Stonington, Connecticut

It is fairly unusual to find a recipe for preparing a meat or main dish like this in a manuscript source. Most manuscript cookbooks contain recipes less frequently used for such things as cakes, cookies, pickles and preserves, which required many ingredients mixed in certain proportions. Printed cookbooks tend to be written for the inexperienced or those seeking variety or style. And diaries and letters seldom describe the specifics of how something was prepared and served, especially if it was an everyday item.

Despite the fact that Miss Palmer recorded the opinion that ham was "more palatable" when cold, a good many New Englanders ate it boiled hot for dinner, which was the way Palmer family descendants frequently ate it. Period cookbooks give similar instructions for boiling, sometimes recommending an overnight soak to freshen it, then advising the cook to remove the skin, sprinkle the ham with cracker or bread crumbs, dot it with cloves, and put it before a fire to brown.[33] Some describe how to trim the protruding bone with a frill of paper before serving, all of which seems to be advice for a special occasion. Today hams come in many degrees of cure and moisture. Traditional hams, like a Smithfield or one prepared according to Dr. McKnight's recipe above, would need to be soaked overnight to reduce the saltiness, while soaking and boiling a commercially prepared picnic shoulder, for example, could leave it almost insipid.You will have to use your own taste and judgment after tasting a slice. A ham can be used in a boiled dinner just as you would use corned beef (pages 161 and 228). A garnish of eggs with cold leftover ham, and horseradish and mustard on the side, still seems like a good idea.

PICKLED CABBAGE

CABBAGE, WHITE, PICKLED.

Slice your cabbage thin; then lay it in salt for twenty-four hours, strain it very dry, then put it in a stone jar with allspice, mace, and vinegar, and pour it on boiling hot; tie it very close, repeat the vinegar three times, and it will be fit for use.

From *Practical American Cookery and Domestic Economy*, by Miss Hall, 1855, page 253

Red cabbage seems to have been slightly more popular for pickling than green or, as Miss Hall described it, white. But the instructions for white and red pickled cabbage are similar and seem to have no counterpart in modern cookbooks. Do not confuse pickled cabbage with sauerkraut, which is a fermented product created by salting cabbage and letting nature have her way. Sauerkraut was not typically a New England dish and does not commonly appear in manuscript sources or imprints.[34]

Miss Hall was very modest in her choice of spices; in other sources, ginger, cloves, and black peppercorns were also listed as spices suitable for pickled cabbage. Most recipes recommend pouring on hot vinegar, repeating that operation on subsequent days till the cabbage is tender. Most agree that salting for at least a day improves the pickle. Mrs. Child said to let the cabbage remain in pickle "eight to ten days before you eat them."[35]

Modern distilled vinegar is probably sharper than it was in the nineteenth century; you can approximate the earlier type by adding water to your vinegar until it is still sharp but palatable. Although most modern instructions for pickling emphasize the need for sufficient acidity to preserve vegetables safely, keep in mind that Miss Hall did not intend anyone to keep this cabbage for a long time. You may want to store the pickled cabbage in the refrigerator if you don't intend to eat it right away. Serve this in small portions or as a salad.

1 pound cabbage or 4-6 cups shredded
1/2 cup pickling salt
1 cup vinegar mixed into 3 cups water
1 teaspoon each your choice of whole allspice, blade mace, cloves, black peppercorns, whole dried ginger root

1. Shred cabbage, and toss it with the pickling salt. Let it stand overnight. Next day, drain it and turn onto a towel to take up excess moisture.
2. Heat the vinegar and water in an enameled saucepan with the spices in it. When boiling hot, remove from fire.
3. Put the shredded cabbage in large sterilized glass jar(s) and pour the hot vinegar over it, dividing the spices among the jars.
4. Close the jar tightly. In two or three days, open the jar, drain off the vinegar, reheat and put back over the cabbage.
5. In another two or three days, repeat this. At the end of the next two days, taste the cabbage and, if you wish, repeat heating the vinegar again.
6. Store the finished cabbage in the refrigerator or, if you wish, process and seal it in canning jars according to the usual canning procedure for pickles.

Yields about 3 cups pickled cabbage.

PEA SOUP

Take one quart of split peas. Put them to soak in a large quantity of water over night. In the morning pour off the water; put them on to boil in a gallon of water. Have a teakettle of boiling water to add, in case it becomes too thick. When the peas are very soft, pour them into a cullender, and rub them with a wooden spoon. Wash the pot that they were boiled in thoroughly, because if any of the peas adhere, they will be apt to burn. Then put them back, and let them boil slowly, over a gentle fire, till they are sufficiently thick. Take a pound of nice salt pork; boil it in a separate kettle for an hour; then put it in with the peas, and let it boil another hour, to season them. Serve the soup in a tureen, and the pork on a dish. Have toasted bread, cut in small pieces, to eat with it.

From *Practical American Cookery and Domestic Economy*, by Miss Hall, 1855, pages 45-46

This is a very economical soup. Nineteenth-century New Englanders used ham bones for pea soup as well as salt pork; Mrs. Bliss said to boil the peas with a "knuckle of boiled ham," and this was the ideal thing to do with that bit of leftover.[36] But a nice piece of lean salt pork served the same purpose here as it did in the baked beans.

An elderly friend once recited to me a little verse she remembered hearing as a child: "Pea soup and jonnycakes, gives a Yankee belly aches." The combination of the legumes in the soup and the grain in the jonnycakes would have created a completed protein. The familiar side effects of dried pea and bean eating can be mitigated somewhat by following Miss Hall's suggestion of draining away the first cooking water. The "toasted bread cut in small pieces" was croutons, a common garnish for pea soup then as now. Your family may not enjoy eating slices of boiled salt pork, even if it is lean; you may prefer to discard it, though the first boiling will reduce the fattiness somewhat. The old recipe is clear enough that a modern interpretation is not needed. Since it will yield close to a gallon of soup, you may wish to halve the recipe and start with two cups of split peas. Season to your taste.
Yields 1 gallon soup.

SUCCOTASH

Take one pint of shelled green lima beans, wash, cover with hot water, let stand for five minutes, pour off water, and place beans in hot water over fire; boil fifteen minutes. Prepare six good sized ears of corn, by cutting down carefully, add to beans; boil half an hour, add pepper, salt, and two tablespoonfuls of butter. Watch that it does not scorch. Or, to cook with meat, boil one pint of salt pork two hours, add beans, cook fifteen minutes, then add corn, omitting butter.

From *Food for the Hungry: A Complete Manual...*, compiled by Julia Wright, 1896, page 81

Cut hot boiled corn from cob, add equal quantity of hot boiled shelled beans; season with butter and salt; reheat before serving.

From *The Boston Cooking School Cookbook*, by Fannie Merritt Farmer, 1896, page 260

These two succotash recipes, only two of many published in the late 1800s, show how many variations could be played on the theme of beans and corn. Marion Harland even wrote a succotash recipe that called for "one can of sweet corn," and "one can of string beans."[37] These recipes all assume the use of fresh corn off the cob or canned sweet corn. Most succotash recipes call for stewing the corn with shelled horticultural or lima beans. Strictly speaking this version of succotash would be a summer-only dish, unless canned corn and beans were used. The woman Edward Knapp remembered may very well have done this. Brown sugar is good on it, but modern sweet corn is even sweeter than the corn Knapp would have known. A winter version of succotash made from dried, hulled corn and dried beans was another possibility.

There is no mystery to succotash. Equal quantities of corn and beans is the usual, but if you prefer one over the other use more of your favorite. For a meaty dish, you certainly can use lean salt pork as you might for baked beans. Some recipes recommend cooking the cobs sans kernels in with the corn and beans, which is nice and intensifies the flavor; remember to take them out before serving. I personally like onion in mine, but that is a modern touch. Some specifics follow.

3 ears fresh corn on the cob
1 cup fresh shell beans (or canned or frozen shell beans or limas)
water
1 tablespoon butter
salt and pepper
small piece of salt pork, optional

1. Cut the corn from the cobs, scraping the cob with the back of your knife to get all the little bits of kernel.
2. Put corn and beans into a heavy saucepan and add enough water that you can barely see them through the mixture. If you use salt pork, add it now. Simmer the mixture for a half hour, or, if you used fresh beans, until the shell beans are tender.
3. Add butter, and salt, and pepper to taste. Succotash is often better the second day.

Yields four servings.

SPONGE CAKE

Eight eggs balance 6 with sugar four with flour: half a glass of brandy-one nutmeg.

Sponge Cake Superior

One pound of sugar : half a pound of flour : one pound of eggs : the rind grated and juice of one lemon : beat the yolks very light-and mix them well with the sugar
then add the lemon : beat these well together-then add the [whites] beaten stiff : lastly shake the flour in very gently : it should not be stirred after the flour is well mixed : if baked in two pans one hour and a quarter is sufficient-

From the manuscript recipe notebook of Julia Palmer, ca. 1840-60

Sponge cake recipes usually outnumber all other cake recipes in manuscript sources. Mrs. Gates, for example, had no fewer than a dozen recipes for it, compared to five for White Mountain cake, which is the next most frequent. Sponge cake, besides being a very nice cake to serve at tea, formed the basis for the popular desserts charlotte russe and trifle. To serve sponge cake Fannie Card said "cut in squares and sprinkle with sugar."[38]

The classic sponge cake recipe was written with ingredients measured by their weight in eggs, as is the first of Miss Palmer's recipes above. As the nineteenth century passed, sponge cake recipes were increasingly written down in measures, as the second of Miss Palmer's recipes is. In some manuscript sources, these later recipes are even described as "measured sponge cake" to distinguish them from the old style.

The number of eggs varies in the old recipes—eight to ten was an average—but the amount of sugar and flour did not change much from recipe to recipe, averaging about two cups of each. In the middle of the nineteenth century, cooks began to use cream of tartar (added while beating the whites) and soda to help with rising. Recipes with those ingredients in them usually halved or even quartered the number of eggs, which meant cooks who had to buy their eggs could make this favorite cake cheaply.

Miss Palmer offered two sorts of flavorings for sponge cake. Brandy, more common in pre-temperance New England and in households like the Burrowses, was edged out by lemon flavoring in the last half of the century. Lemon is still a popular addition today; do use the rind as well as the juice in the interpretation below. Remember, eggs will beat up more successfully if they are at room temperature. This recipe makes a beautiful, nicely textured, classic sponge cake.

2 cups sugar
8 eggs
1 lemon, rind and juice
2 cups flour
Preheat oven to 350°

1. Separate the eggs, and beat the yolks till light and lemon-colored. Add the sugar and continue to beat well, till the mixture will hold its shape briefly when dropped from a spoon. Add lemon juice and rind.
2. In separate bowl, beat the whites till stiff, but not dry. Fold into the yolks and sugar.
3. Last, sprinkle the flour a little at a time onto the batter and fold gently and lightly into the mixture. Spoon into a greased 8-inch tube pan or two 8-inch pans.
4. Bake for one hour. Shake confectioner's sugar over the top of the cake, or over squares of cake.

Yields one 8-inch tube cake or two 8-inch layers.

BROWN BREAD

2 cups Indian meal
1 1/2 cups of rye meal
1/2 cup flour
1 cup molasses
2 cup sweet milk
1 cup warm water
1 teaspoonful saleratus

From the manuscript recipe notebook of Mary Miller, ca. 1850

Sometime around the middle of the nineteenth century the old recipe for brown bread—"rye and indian," "brown bread," and the thirded bread discussed in the Buckingham House chapter—became what we now know as steamed brown bread. Molasses and milk were added to the familiar combination of Indian and rye meals, and a quick-rising agent replaced the yeast. When steamed, this bread was almost pudding-like and was a common accompaniment to baked beans.

Period recipes for brown bread vary in the flours and meals used. Some are made only with rye and wheat flour, or only with cornmeal and flour, reminiscent of the combinations Mrs. Child recommended for bread (see page 26). Cookbooks require steaming the bread for an average of four hours, and suggest putting it in an oven "if a crust is wanted."

You must use rye *meal*, as rye flour is much too sticky. Steam the bread in one-pound coffee cans, all-metal shortening containers, pudding molds, or greased pans. Aluminum foil tied over the container makes a good lid. Set the cans in a larger pot with an inch or two of hot water. The whole recipe produces a two-quart-plus-sized bread, so I have halved the recipe in the interpretation which follows.

1 cup Indian meal
3/4 cup rye meal
1/2 cup flour
1/2 teaspoon baking soda
1 teaspoon salt
1/2 cup molasses
1 cup milk

1. Grease the coffee cans, and get the pot of water boiling hot.
2. Mix together the meals, flour, and baking soda.
3. Add the milk and molasses and blend well. Pour into the cans, filling each half full. Cover with foil, and set into the large pot.
4. Steam 4 hours.

Yields two loaves.

BAKED BEANS

The species of bean used for baking is called the white field bean. There are two varieties,—the large and the small, or pea-bean,—the last is considered the best.

Soak one quart in cold, soft water over night; the next morning remove the water in which the beans have soaked, and wash the beans in fresh water; then put them into a pot with two quarts of cold water, set the pot over a slow fire, and let simmer two hours, then score one and a half pounds of fat salt pork, and put it into the pot, concealing it, except the rind, in the middle of the beans; pour in a tea-spoonful of salt, and water enough to cover the pork and beans, set the pot in a hot oven and bake six hours; if the water wastes so that the beans become too dry, add a little more.

Baked beans, after having stood a day or two, are very good warmed over. In some parts of New England they are considered indispensable at a Sunday breakfast.

Lima and kidney beans, and other varieties, are sometimes dried and baked as above; they cook in a shorter time than the white field bean.

From *The Practical Cookbook*, by Mrs. Bliss, 1864, page 89

There are few recipes for baked beans in nineteenth-century cookbooks, but there is considerable anecdotal evidence of people eating them. They seem to have been one of the foods people made all the time by eye, though when instructions are written down there is a generally accepted ratio of one quart of beans to one pound of salt pork. Pepper is almost always added. Molasses as a sweetener seldom appears until the last quarter of the century, and when it does it is limited to a tablespoonful per quart of beans. This is less sweetening than we have now in allegedly old-fashioned beans.

The salt pork used would have been a leaner product than salt pork is today. Mrs. Child said "Pieces of pork alternately fat and lean are the most suitable; the cheeks are the best."[39] Once in a while a recipe will recommend corned beef to be cooked with beans. When served, the dish would have been presented with the meat on a platter of its own or in a dish with the beans all around.

Modern people would probably find nineteenth-century-style pork and beans pretty bland. We have gotten used to molasses and/or brown sugar, onion, and mustard. Prepared the old way, it is a simple and economical dish. The period recipe is clear enough that an interpretation is not needed. A quart of soaked and boiled navy beans will yield a half-gallon of baked beans.

INDIAN PUDDING

Scald the milk, and stir in the sifted meal to make a batter not very thick. Then add two spoonsful of flour, molasses to your taste, a little salt, lemon, nutmeg, or cinnamon, and bake two hours and a half. Made in this way, it is quite as good as when made with eggs

From *The Complete Domestic Guide*, by Mrs. L.G. Abell, 1853, page 143

Indian pudding is a much-neglected dessert nowadays, even in New England where it was long a traditional dish. One secret to a really good Indian pudding is using corn ground from flint corn, available in southeastern New England, which produces a smoother pudding.

There is considerable variation in early recipes for Indian pudding, even in the ratio of cornmeal to milk. Some recipes call for "seven spoonfuls" while others call for an even cupful. Some recipes call for eggs, while others are made only with milk, molasses, and meal; some have water instead of milk. Some puddings are baked, some steamed or boiled.

Today we seem to prefer a softer Indian pudding than many of the older recipes will produce. Mrs. Child's recipe in *American Frugal Housewife*, which will make a soft pudding, and the classic one in the modern Fannie Farmer cookbook, are actually very similar. Mrs. Abell's recipe above seems to leave much to the judgment of the cook. The interpretation that follows is based closely on Mrs. Child's, but includes Mrs. Abell's suggestion to substitute flour for eggs. Also, this recipe makes a pudding that, in the cooking process, separates slightly, or produces whey, something often mentioned by nineteenth-century cookbooks as desirable.[40]

1 quart plus 1/2 cup milk
1/2 cup cornmeal
3/4 cup molasses
1 teaspoon salt
2 tablespoons flour
1 tablespoon cinnamon or ginger
Preheat oven to 300°

1. Scald the quart of milk in a double boiler. Add the cornmeal mixed up with just enough cold milk to make a thin batter, and pour into the scalded milk, then cook this mixture for twenty minutes.
2. Take off the heat and add the molasses. Sift together the salt, flour, and spice and stir gradually into the scalded milk and cornmeal. Mix together well.
3. Pour into a greased quart-and-a-half or two-quart baking dish.
4. Pour the 1/2 cup of cold milk over the top without mixing.
5. Bake for 2 1/2 to 3 hours. Serve with cream.

Yields a one-quart pudding.

SOFT GINGERBREAD

One cup of molasses, one cup of warm water, one teaspoon of ginger, one teaspoon saleratus, four tablespoons of melted butter Stir flour in very thin. Use top of the pot or pork fat for shortening.

From logbook of schooner *William B. Herrick*, 1874-76, Log 713, G.W. Blunt White Library, Mystic Seaport Museum

There were two basic types of gingerbread in the nineteenth century: one was a soft cake-like gingerbread made with molasses, and called either soft or molasses gingerbread, and the other was a hard, cookie-like gingerbread made with sugar and called hard or sugar gingerbread. This soft gingerbread from the logbook of the *Herrick* is typical of the soft gingerbreads, made with water (instead of milk) and without eggs.

This recipe is particularly interesting because of the note about alternative shortenings. Ashore, butter was easy to come by. At sea, a ready and cheap source of shortening could be lard, pork fat (from fried pork or even bacon), or fat from boiled meat, which would rise to the top of the pot, congeal when cold, and could be skimmed off. The molasses would overwhelm the stronger flavor of the meat fats.

This gingerbread is a nice moist one with a rich flavor and a crusty top when fresh out of the oven. An interpretation follows.

2 cups flour
1 teaspoon of ginger
1 teaspoon baking soda
4 tablespoons of melted butter
1 cup molasses
1 cup of warm water
Preheat oven to 350°

1. Sift together the dry ingredients.
2. Melt the butter, add the molasses and warm water (from the tap), and mix well.
3. Stir gradually into the dry ingredients, blending well but not over-mixing.
4. Pour into a greased 8 x 8-inch pan and bake for 30 minutes, or until the top cracks slightly and a skewer inserted comes out clean.

Yields one 8 x 8-inch gingerbread.

The three-masted schooner *William B. Herrick* shown here was engaged in coastwise and trans-Atlantic trade for about 40 years. Built in 1874 by the G. E. Currier yard at Newburyport, she was owned by Captain E. K. Crowell for her entire career. [Photo from Captain W. J. L. Parker]

WHISKEY PUNCH

Whiskey's the fellah,—said the young man John.—Make it into a punch, cold at dinner-time, 'n' hot at bed-time. I'll come up and show you how to mix it....real Burbon's (sic) the stuff. Hot water, sugar, 'n' jest a little shavin' of lemon-skin in it,—skin, mind you, none o' your juice; take it off thin,—shape of one of them flat curls the factory-girls wear on the sides of their foreheads.

From "The Professor at the Breakfast-Table. What He Said, What He Heard, and What He Saw," *Atlantic Monthly* (June 1859)

This recipe for whiskey punch comes from a regular *Atlantic Monthly* column written tongue-in-cheek about what the "Professor" hears discussed at his boardinghouse breakfast table. The topic *du jour* happened to be a cough plaguing one of the boarders, for which a whiskey punch was the recommended medication.

Many will agree with the young man John who says that "real Burbon's the stuff"—though, of course, a very good whiskey punch can be made from Irish and Scotch whiskies. This is a very agreeable drink whether you have a cough or not. It may be that Winty and Jane Burrows would agree.

When you make a whiskey punch, plan to mix the drink in a heatproof mug or glass. The amount of water and sugar are really a matter of opinion and taste; mix in the same proportion you like whiskey and water. Nowadays you will want to wash the lemon before skinning off a curl of peel, and put it into the glass or mug before you add the hot water.

Eating Forward and Dining Aft

At sea, says Ishmael in Moby Dick, *you "are never troubled with the thought of what you shall have for dinner—for all your meals for three years and more are snugly stowed in casks, and your bill of fare is immutable."*[1] *Immutable—with a few exceptions—but not out of mind. For at sea, where the days pass in alternating four-hour, round-the-clock work periods called watches, food was one of the few ways to punctuate the routine of ship's duty and make-work projects.*

In this small galley located at the starboard-side stern quarter of the *Charles W. Morgan*, the whaleship's cooks prepared three meals a day. One of the meals might have been lobscouce, opposite, a salt-meat stew thickened with pounded hardtack. The cabin scouce, top, served in a stoneware bowl, had in it "everything edible in the ship," including carrots, cabbage, and onions. The fo'c'sle scouce, bottom, was meat and potatoes. [MSM 55-1-14]

Dinner in the cabin resembled a home meal with a soup course, a roasted or boiled piece of meat, vegetables and dessert—here a whortleberry pie, recipe on page 120. Cabin perks included fresh bread, butter, milk and sugar.

Thousands of American ships sailed the oceans in the nineteenth century. Whaleships like Mystic Seaport's *Charles W. Morgan* wandered the seas in search of whales; in the 1840s and 1850s, clipper ships rushed goods and gold-seekers to California or tea home from China. Through the 1860s, packet ships made regular transatlantic passages, and traders like the down-easter *Benjamin F. Packard* trundled cargo along well-defined routes. Others, tramps, sailed at the whim of the market, carrying cargoes wherever a profit might be made. They varied in size, shape, speed, and destination, but these ships all resembled one another in the human conditions on board. A sailing ship was a tight, regimented little world, with a clearly defined hierarchy. Officers lived aft at the more comfortable end near the ship's steering mechanism. Sailors lived foreward near their work, in the grandly named but humble forecastle (fo'c'sle). The afterguard included the captain, the two mates, who commanded the two watches, and aboard a whaleship a mix of lesser officers who had duties in the capture and processing of whales. The sailors, or foremast hands as they were sometimes called, included the most experienced able-bodied seamen, less-skilled ordinary seamen, and novice greenhands. The crew was divided into two watches at the beginning of the voyage by the two mates who chose the men.

Next to sleeping and smoking, eating was one of the few pleasures regularly available to the foremast hands in their constricted environment. And food was their only source of energy when work was constant and sleep impossible. However, since Richard Henry Dana, Jr. could write after his two years before the mast that "provisions are not good enough to make a meal anything more than a necessary part of a day's duty," it is clear that the crew's food was neither as plentiful nor as palatable as they might have desired.[2] Simply, the crew ate a limited diet in a rough, communal fashion: they were fed and they ate.

By contrast, in the after cabin, the officers, passengers, and often the captain's wife considered food and mealtime their chief source of amusement. Sallie Smith, the seagoing wife of a whaleship master, wrote that she had "nothing to do but read and eat bananas." She later observed she had "grown so fleshy...hardly got a dress I can wear."[3] Compared with the crew, the cabin had better food, both in quality and quantity, and it was presented in a formal manner: they were served and they dined.

The foodways of seafarers are merely landsmen's foodways taken to sea, adapted for use aboard ship. What they kept and what they changed tell us a great about the social structure of a vessel's population and about seafarers' value systems. Following the pattern of previous chapters, we will take a close look at the cooking facilities aboard ship, the food supply, the cooks who prepared the food, and the comparative and contrasting foodways of the fo'c'sle and the cabin.

However much American sailors might disparage their fare, American ships generally fed crews better than foreign vessels did. Aboard a down-easter at the end of the nineteenth century, Felix Riesenberg described the crew of a British vessel next to theirs in Honolulu, which was "in no way representative of the best traditions of the English service." "These poor devils talked of food, thought of food, and dreamt of food; they did everything but eat it in satisfying quantities." Compared to what was provided aboard British and Scandinavian vessels, the quantity of food on American ships was usually good, even if the quality was variable, and the American reputation for better food gave foreign sailors cause to desert to Yankee ships.[4] Changes in seafaring diet occurred as the nineteenth century progressed. Before the middle of the century, sailors ate the plainest fare imaginable. General concern for sailors' welfare at about mid-century resulted in slightly improved food. After the Civil War, canned goods and a revised scale of victuals considerably benefited sailors. At the same time, steamships began competing with sailing vessels in cargo-carrying, and besides, they provided their crews better fare, partly because steamers were more efficient and the owners could afford better food, but also because fresh food depended on how often a vessel came into port. Steamers (and some coasting vessels under sail), in port more often than deepwater ships, were able to feed fairly well, a substantial contrast to the distance-voyaging vessels of the same era.[5] The focus here, however, will be on sailing ships.

Galleys and Pantries

On the *Charles W. Morgan*'s starboard side near the stern, a small space was partitioned off to be the galley. The forwardmost one-third of this space was occupied by the stove, and the after third was filled by a storage chest, the top of which made a work surface for the cook. In this five-by-ten-foot space, three square meals a day were cooked for a crew of thirty-three people.

Through the middle of the nineteenth century, the galley of a merchant vessel—including the *Morgan*—was forward in a small portable house lashed on deck. Aboard whaleships, the galley eventually migrated aft as a stern shelter called the hurricane house became characteristic of whaleship design. In cargo ships, when the fo'c'sle crew quarters were moved out of the bow below decks and put in a house on deck, the galley was often incorporated into the structure.[6]

Whether the galley was forward or aft, somebody's dinner had to be carried from one end of the ship to the other, a risky trip in bad weather. Lloyd Briggs, a passenger living aft in the bark *Amy Turner* in 1880, said, "In the forecastle forward of the carpenter's shop was the galley. Our food had to be brought across the main deck, up the steps to the poop-deck, across the poop deck and down the Captain's cabin and it was therefore impossible in very bad weather for us to be served from the galley, as the deck was then often filled with water waist high."[7]

Briggs and the rest of the afterguard resorted to the steward's pantry, which was located aft, just off the saloon or common room. The *Morgan*'s pantry is located off the forward starboard corner of the saloon. Shelves, counters, bins, and cabinets line three sides of the space, which is comparable in size to many domestic pantries ashore. The open shelves are faced with wide boards to hold dinnerware. Bins and cupboards have room for the nicer cabin foodstuffs, and narrow counters make a place for the steward to perform his cooking duties.

Annie Ricketson's comments about the whaleship *A.R. Tucker*'s pantry suggest what it might contain: "At six a.m., heard my Husband making a raid on the Pantry to see how much dirt he could find! He soon discovered enough of it, three loaves of mouldy bread and the mixing pan about three inches thick with dough. I heard him tell the steward to carry everything on deck and give the pantry a good cleaning out and wash all the dishes and keep it clean after this. At 4 p.m. the pantry was finished and looked quite neat but how long it will look so is another thing."[8]

Cooking Utensils and Dinnerware

Details of the *Charles W. Morgan*'s original culinary outfit are buried in accounts of chandlery expenditures. The only specific reference is to the stove, which was called a "camboose." This was a misspelling or mispronunciation of the word "caboose," which by the early eighteenth century was used to denote the cookroom or kitchen of a merchant ship, and later meant a box or house for a chimney or fireplace, both on vessels and ashore.[9] In the middle of the nineteenth century the railroad borrowed the term, and a whole car was named for the stove within.

Cookware: Maritime supplies were sold by chandlers, nautical businessmen whose line of wares had expanded from candles to the full range of supplies needed aboard ship. Chandleries offered a wide range of cooking utensils for shipboard use. Not surprisingly, the lists parallel closely the outfits for the U.S. Life-Saving Service stations that we will discuss later. To promote their wares, some chandlers prepared order books listing all the items an owner or shipmaster might wish to purchase. Cooking equipment was listed under categories headed "Tin Ware," and "Crockery," and other sections included "Provisions and Cabin Stores," "Nautical Instruments," and "Cordage."

When cast-iron stoves were introduced aboard ship in the first half of the nineteenth century, makers customarily provided an outfit of pots, boilers, pans, and kettles—in fact, all the large cooking utensils needed. A well-found ship carried a spare grate, stove liner and piping, steamer, boiler, and tea kettle, so chandlery memorandum books listed extras in cooking equipment: tin cups, pots, pans, fry and sauce pans, tea kettles, dippers, bake pans, pie plates, graters, measures, coffee and tea pots, pudding bags (the utensil's name did not change even though the material it was made of changed from cloth to tin), colanders, and a wide variety of storage containers, including canisters for tea, tin flour boxes for dredging, and pepper boxes. Butcher knives, chopping knives and trays, ladles, "tormentors" (large two-tined meat forks), skimmers, ladles, cook's

"Dinner in the Forecastle" is the title of this drawing from *Scribner's Magazine* in 1893. Crew members brought their own knives, forks, spoons and sometimes plates to the rough table. The cook provided large quantities of coffee or tea in the slop-proof kettle shown on the cabin sole. [MSM 92-12-71]

spoons and basting spoons, scoops and sieves, a mortar and pestle, and a coffee mill made possible virtually any culinary effort. How much of this possible selection was actually carried aboard any ship is hard to determine, although a few chandlery order books survive to suggest the range. A book for the bark *Globe*'s "Third Voyage Outward," 1869, shows that the ship ordered tableware—a set of knives and forks, iron table and teaspoons, a carving set and table steel for sharpening—plus a ladle, skimmer, fork, and spoon for the cook, a chopping knife and tray, two sieves, two saucepans, and two fry pans.[10]

In 1901, the *Morgan* was outfitted in part by the Lewis E. Spear Company, Marine and Hotel Supplies, of San Francisco. The list included saucepan covers, an agate-ware coffee pot, two can openers, a biscuit cutter, five cake cutters, a doughnut cutter (by this time doughnuts had holes) three galley spoons, an egg beater, a coffee strainer, one large "melon mould" (a melon-shaped mold), a soup strainer, two deep agate-ware pudding pans, a flour sieve, a dozen pie plates, a large chop tray, a large mixing pan, a funnel, and a nutmeg grater. This equipment list reflects the increased number of specialized tools available to cooks at sea *or* ashore; for example, a tool specifically for cutting biscuits replaced an inverted tumbler, and can openers made it more convenient to use tinned food. The list also demonstrates the expectation of home-style cooking, at least for the cabin. Let's hope the steward was equal to it.[11]

Dinnerware: Shipowners made an effort to equip the cabin with all the pieces necessary for individual place settings and proper, home-style service. By the middle of the century, cabin dinnerware was available in tin *and* crockery. In 1839, aboard the whaleship *Mentor* out of New London, Connecticut, James Rogers recorded in his journal that "This day old Comfort finished a shelf to put crockery on; not exactly crockery, because it is all tin."[12] Tin's principal advantage was its durability; mishaps at sea because of bad weather or a sudden roll of the ship must have smashed thousands of crockery dishes.

Again, the chandlers' memorandum books offered a wide selection: soup plates, dinner plates, small plates, sauce dishes, cups and saucers, tumblers, and mugs for place settings. For table service there were platters, pitchers of many sizes, bowls, covered dishes, pudding dishes, oval serving dishes, castor bottles and castors, salts (tiny dishes to hold salt), butter and sugar dishes, molasses cups, tureens for soup, and bread trays. Eating and serving utensils included knives, forks, and teaspoons, tablespoons, ladles, carving knives and forks, and sharpening steels; even table bells were listed, so that the steward or cabin boy could be summoned.[13]

The ship *Hector* purchased a collection of dinnerware in 1852, and the list demonstrates how completely the cabin table could be set. In the account book, the name of the dish is given but the material it was made of is not consistently listed. The *Hector* went to sea with half a dozen plates at about nine cents apiece and a dozen at about a nickel each, possibly of different sizes or materials. In addition, there were another dozen flat plates, six dozen soup bowls, a dozen "bowls," a dozen and a half "saucers," which may have been sauce dishes, and a dozen mugs, plus half a dozen "blue" mugs. There were six pitchers; one of the largest-sized platters, plus three other platters; sugar and butter dishes; a "pr salts"; and one "castor complete." A "blanished" tin tureen, two tureen ladles, and two blanished tin teapots were among the unbreakables. The bread tray, listed just before these items, was also probably tin. Some of the *Hector*'s cookware in stone-, yellow-, or redware could be brought to the table: five "bakers" and two "nappies"—baking dishes with sloping sides used as we would use casseroles—were taken along.

For eating and serving the ship purchased four "setts" knives and forks, a dozen small tablespoons, a dozen each "Brita"—probably short for Britannia ware—tablespoons and teaspoons. A pair of carvers and a table steel anticipated large pieces of meat. A tumbler basket was purchased, but no tumblers; perhaps tumblers were already aboard. The ship also acquired a table bell.[14]

A tureen was used almost daily for a soup course; a platter carried the fresh meat served more often in the cabin; and other dishes like Captain Wendell's macaroni and cheese may have been served out of a nappie or baker. The castor bottles probably contained vinegar, a popular condiment, and pepper sauce, either similar to or the same as Tabasco sauce, and commonly listed among cabin stores. Salt came to the table in the salts, pepper in the pepper boxes, and molasses in molasses cups. It may have been hundreds of miles at sea, but the table was set just like home.

Cooks and Stewards

Despite the importance of food at sea, cooks and stewards were not the valued crew members one might expect them to be. In fact, early cooks were often the youngest or least experienced sailors; and even later, when men with some experience were employed, they were not usually trained in the culinary arts. Frequently they were black or Asian, particularly after 1840. Black sailors had once enjoyed the comparative equality of the fo'c'sle as able seamen, but by the 1840s they were often shunted into more menial jobs as cooks or stewards. At mid-century a whaleship cook was paid more than a greenhand and often more than an ordinary seaman, but less than a cooper or boatsteerer. Later in the century, the cook's pay dropped to the equivalent of seamen's pay, exceeding only that of greenhands.[15]

Sailors often had an ambivalent attitude toward their cook, due partly to his unique situation. Neither sailor nor officer, the cook was a crew member with his own distinct territory and duties on board. Unlike the sailors, he was regularly in and out of both the cabin and the fo'c'sle. The crew depended on him and needed his good graces for many of their creature comforts, but because of his ambiguous position between the fo'c'sle and the cabin, often because of his race, and because he did "women's work" at sea, they routinely discounted and demeaned him. His nickname "doctor" was meant both to flatter and to mock him.[16]

Dana testified to the cook's power in the little world of a ship at sea: "'The cook is the patron of the crew, and those who are in his favor can get their wet mittens and stockings dried, or light their pipes at the galley on the night watch." The crew had to appeal to the cook for permission to fix treats for themselves. Felix Riesenberg, aboard the *A.J. Fuller*, reported that "some of the crowd" in the fo'c'sle "constituted themselves his [the cook's] volunteer assistants, and almost every first dog watch, one of the them would be around the galley helping out. Chow rewarded them by allowing the use of the oven to make 'dandy funk.'" The cook (or steward) might provide succor to sick crewmen by slipping the patient cabin scraps or fixing special food. Charles Abbey was sick at sea and able to "eat nothing at all but rice which through the kindness of the cook I used to get once in a while." It was the cook, "a simple hearted African" who advised greenhand Dana about overcoming seasickness. He told the vomiting Dana to be glad to be rid of "your long-shore swash.....and turn-to upon good hearty salt beef and sea bread," which Dana did. "And getting a huge piece of strong, cold, salt beef from the cook, I kept gnawing upon it. When we went on deck I felt somewhat like a man, and could begin to learn my sea duty with considerable spirit."[17]

But the cook was also constantly the butt of racially motivated jokes and ridicule. "The poor old black cook!" wrote Herman Melville in *Omoo*. "Unlashing his hammock for the night, and finding a wet log fast asleep in it; and then waking in the morning with his wooly head tarred. Opening his soppers and finding an old boot boiling away as saucy as can be, and sometimes cakes of pitch candying in his oven." "'Hands about ship!' meant all hands, and the cook at the fore sheet, a time-honored station filled by the Celestial with all the importance in the world. It was all the work that Chow ever did on deck...we always hoped to have a sea come over and douse him, which often happened."[18]

On the other hand, the cook had the power of his skills and near-absolute control over what everyone aboard ate. "It don't do to scrap with the cook," was sailor Jimmy Marshall's sage advice. "If the dirty bum wants to be dirty

he can fix us all up. I knowed a cook once wot—[blank] in the soup an' bully on an English bark. The skipper, he caught him at it, an' puts him in irons. The cook had to be let out though because he was the only one wot could do the work, an' they was mighty careful aft not to rile him after they knowed wot he was. You got to leave them cooks alone."[19]

The most surprising thing about this account is that the cook was described as "the only one" who could do the work; shipboard cookery is hardly the complex craft that, say, navigating or carpentry is. Perhaps it was more a matter of the cook being the only who *would* do the work.

Still, references are common to the cooks or stewards being "sent forward" to join the fo'c'sle crew, while another man attempted to please everyone. Aboard the whaleship *Addison*, Mary Lawrence recorded a terrific turnover in galley personnel: "We have a very good steward but are not as fortunate with our cooks. We are trying the fourth now (five weeks out). The first was good for nothing; the second did not like being in the galley—it made his head ache; the third had sore hands, so he could not perform duty; and I cannot say what will befall the fourth." On a later cruise, Mrs. Lawrence reported "Think we have a cook worth having now, after taking up with all sorts."[20]

Stewards and sea cooks, like the man standing on deck at left, were often African-Americans or Asians. Because of their race, and because they did "women's work," they were subject to hazing and ridicule. At the same time their favor was curried since they had such power over the quality and quantity of the few creature comforts the men in the forecastle were allowed. [Hooper Collection, MSM 89-10-155]

Cook's responsibilities: It was usually the second mate who doled out the ship's provisions according to the daily schedule of rations. Using these provisions, and perhaps referring to the daily menu, the cook prepared three meals a day for the fo'c'sle and, with help from the steward, for the cabin. He also kept the galley clean and washed the boilers and pans, as well as the "kids" in which the crew's food was taken forward to the fo'c'sle. Although he did not stand watch, and he got to sleep all night, the cook did have responsibilities in sailing the ship. When the vessel was changing tacks the cook handled the foresheet, and at the call "all hands" he was expected to go aloft to handle sail or to pull and haul on deck.[21] The cook frequently lived in the fo'c'sle, though occasionally he had a bunk near the galley. Aboard whaleships his bunk might be in steerage, just forward of the after cabin.

Considering their few rights on board ship and their need for nourishment, sailors were jealous of their food rations. At the beginning of the Stonington, Connecticut, whaleship *Tiger*'s 1845 voyage, greenhand John Perkins complained, "The new cook took upon himself the duties of his office for the first time & proved himself wholly incompetent. He had not cooked near supper enough & one of the hands who has been three voyages whaling before declared he would not let the docter rest till he got something to eat." The cook was sometimes unjustly blamed for short rations, for he could work only with what he got from the officer doling out the food. Yet at times he might be at fault, either through incompetence or by intentional scrimping. For example, grease—which the sailors called slush—was saved up in the galley and sold at the end of the voyage to soap manufacturers. The cook was entitled to a certain percentage of the "slush" profits.[22] Fat was highly desirable at sea, and a cook withholding it to add to his slush fund deprived the crew of additional flavor and valuable calories.

Shipboard cooking was next to impossible in really severe weather, either because it was hopeless or dangerous to keep a fire going. But, oddly enough, little mention is made in narratives from American sailing ships about the plain day-to-day physical difficulties of the job. A sudden roll could send all the pots skidding to the other side of the stove, and hot liquids might slop around dangerously.[23] Because stoves were rarely gimballed they had the same cant as the deck, and the angle of the soup within matched the horizon. When the seas rose, a dutiful cook could not keep one hand for himself and a spare one for the ship if he hoped to keep the food together. He might prop up his pots to accommodate one tack, then be obliged to switch them around if the ship changed to the other tack.

Steward's responsibilities: Sixteen-year-old Ben Ely was recruited out of the fo'c'sle to become steward on the whaleship *Emigrant*, a berth he was glad to accept because he was "disgusted with the conversation of the forecastle." But he soon found "that I had jumped out of the frying pan into the fire....It humbled my pride not a little to wash dishes and make bread, and it was not long before I desired again to be a sailor bold and free, amid the tar and slush in preference to a lackey amidst flour and dishwater." Ely learned to make bread and pies, set the table, and clean knives and forks, all "useful accomplishments in the line of housewifery." Conflict with some of the boatsteerers, who stole pies and "disarranged" his pantry, finally drove him to ask the captain if he could resign the job.[24]

The steward was primarily the captain's servant, unless there was a cabin boy, but he—or occasionally she—served the whole cabin, which included the captain and sometimes his wife, the mates, and perhaps a few passengers. (Packets and steamers in the business of carrying passengers had several stewards with a variety of duties, but in this chapter we will concern ourselves with merchant and whaling vessels, which only occasionally carried passengers.) As the cabin servant, a steward was sometimes the object of sailors' resentment towards the cabin. In his journal, Amos Jenckes described the crossing-the-line ceremony as they passed the equator. The crew disliked the steward, and they used this ritual to get at him, treating him more roughly than any of the other hands who had not crossed the equator before.[25]

The steward's responsibilities included general housekeeping chores in the cabin, some of which would be done by a cabin boy, if there was one: cleaning the cabin and staterooms, setting the table, washing dishes, and washing heavy loads of laundry. At mealtimes he brought the food from the galley to the cabin and served it. Additionally, he handled the finer points of cooking for the captain's table, as Ely described, baking soft bread and making pies. Captains' wives mentioned teaching the steward how to make yeast, pie, and bread. Ann Brown wrote, "I showed the Steward how to make yeast today. I hope we shall have some sweet bread." The next day she reported happily that they did.[26]

Sometimes the steward rather than the second mate had charge of the ship's provisions and doled out the daily allotment to the cook, but this was more common on European vessels. Like the cook, the steward had *his* own territory; Dana reported that he "has charge of the pantry from which everyone, even the mate himself is excluded"—at least in theory, as Ely made clear.[27]

Both cook and steward were under considerable daily pressure, dealing with a valuable and finite resource, under awkward and sometimes downright difficult conditions. That pressure added to aggravations when cooks and stewards did not get along. They had to share galley space when the steward brought food prepared in his pantry to be cooked in the galley stove. And there are accounts of sometimes violent disputes between them over territory and responsibility, often provoked by interracial conflict. Aboard the *Clarissa B. Carver* in 1878 the black cook and the Chinese steward had a bloody battle, described by Sara Dow: "Cook and steward have had a pitched battle, they have been spatting for some time. The first steward, after putting him in the galley, wanted to boss over the Chinaman, the Chinaman has done very well as steward—but no one was satisfied with the cook—this morning they commenced in earnest, so the mate and carpenter had to separate them—the cook had the cleaver...but Chinaman, or pigtail as father calls him [he had a long queue] beat the old cook so he looked as if he was nearly murdered, blood all over his face—he threatened to shoot Chinaman and would not give up his pistol; Chinaman rushed down into the cabin for a carving knife, father had taken a pistol from him some time ago, he had it on deck firing it one day. They held the cook and got his pistol from him; they found his wounds were but scratches—took him out of the galley and put him in the forecastle—and Chinaman in galley again and took Jim, (that is, the boy we found in the coal locker [a stowaway]) in the cabin; he is 18 years old, very smart and active. Think we shall do finely with him with my help."[28]

The steward in the cabin: The steward had such an impact on life in the after cabin that few cabin seafarers failed to mention him in their journals. The steward's embellishments to the ship's fare, in the form of fresh bread, special side dishes, and proper desserts, were what distinguised cabin food from fo'c'sle grub. A steward's cooking ability made a big difference in cabin meals, and his attention to housekeeping details, something most nineteenth-century men were not trained to observe, maintained an aura of gentility in cabin life. Most journal and diary references to stewards (and cooks) are complaints—particularly from captains' wives, who best knew how a steward's housework should be done—so we must deduce the desirable qualities from descriptions of the undesirable ones.

Wives frequently mentioned cleanliness, as we saw earlier in Annie Ricketson's description of the pantry. As a passenger on the bark *Early Bird* in 1860, Richard Henry Dana, Jr. was moved to comment in his journal: "Great disappointment in the steward. He turns out to be far from neat. In dress, habits, ways is rather disgusting—though civil eno' to us." Dana admitted that a ship's captain was partly responsible for a steward's failings. The *Early Bird*'s captain had "no sensibilities, & is so incorrigibly careless & indifferent, that no hope of reformation of steward."[29]

On the *Clarissa B. Carver* in 1878, Captain Dow's wife commented: "I believe we have taken the worst steward in the lot. He doesn't know anything, and makes poor bread." He didn't keep his pantry clean either, and when the captain spoke to him he refused to continue as steward. Captain Dow assigned the cook to the steward's job, and Mrs. Dow recorded, "Our new steward does very well with my showing him a little."[30]

"A new steward came on board today," wrote Ann Brown on board the *Agate*, "Hope he will prove a good one. I like his appearance very much." He worked out, and she wrote later: "The passengers all look contented and happy. A good cook and steward go a long way on board ship to make passengers contented."[31]

The strict shipboard division of labor and the carefully maintained social hierarchy meant that the steward was indispensable: "The trials of life the changes on ship board Steward has been sick a day or two...the cook has taken his place and fills the office of both hope for more regular times," wrote Mary Brewster. It would not do for Mrs. Brewster to pitch in and set the table, even though having to do both jobs surely put much stress on the cook, who in turn may have given the crew short shrift. Yet, a captain's wife might take on some of the work if an acceptable substitute could not be found for a seriously ill steward. Ann Brown wrote: "Sarah and I have had to do all the baking since we left. Our horrid steward sick all the passage." Mary Brewster got up in the night to make herb teas and gruel for her sick husband, feeling free to go to the galley only when "all the stewards and cooks were abed."[32]

Stewards were sometimes recruited from among the crew, as was Ben Ely. Like the cooks, stewards were usually black, mulatto, or Asian, and sometimes they were women, especially in ships carrying passengers. The ship *Edward*, sailing from Philadelphia to Calcutta via Madeira in 1837, carried a number of passengers, including some missionaries

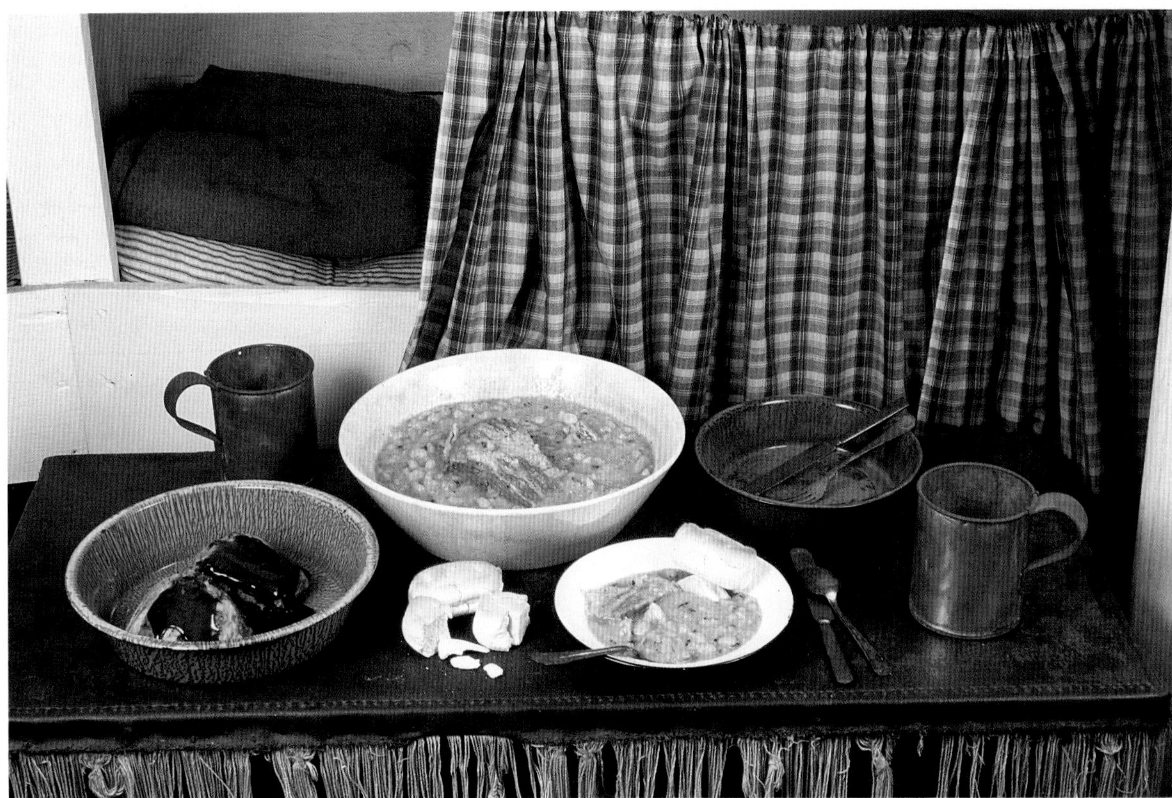

Dinner for the men before the mast, set on a sea chest in the *Charles W. Morgan*'s foc's'le— bean soup, center, recipe on page 115, with salt meat and hardtack. Dessert is plum duff, recipe on page 115, with a sauce of molasses. Enameled tin plates and tin cups were good enough for sailors.

to India. The steward was Norris Ballou of the East Indies; the steward's assistant was a Malaysian named Pancho; and the cook was Edward Hinton, a "colored American." On board the *Amy Turner* in 1880, Lloyd Briggs reported a husband-and-wife team: "Ben Dyer, our colored steward, was from Portland, Maine. His wife, Sarah, acted as stewardess. She was the only woman on board. Ben was a very good cook and had been with Captain Newell for six voyages." (Since Briggs did not describe any other crew member as cook, it may be that Dyer *was* the cook and his wife was stewardess.) Joanna Colcord reported that "Chinese were preferred as cooks and stewards, because they were more cleanly and efficient than whites who would take such jobs."[33]

Like cooks, stewards suffered racially motivated abuse, and because their work had a housewifely nature they were ridiculed for doing women's work. Thomas Larkin Turner referred to the *Palestine*'s steward as "kitchen maid" and "kitchen girl. Oh! but this said personage is a black man! No matter he answers our purpose."[34] In Ely's own account, it is apparent that learning housewifery was humbling; certainly it was a skill he anticipated never needing again in his life. Although stewards were insulated from the abuse of the crew by their position aft, they were often run ragged by the afterguard. Depending on their race, however, they also enjoyed some familiarity with their superiors, which occasionally led to a level of defiance few other crew members ever attempted.

On board the *Clarissa B. Carver*, according to a family member's journal, the afterguard "Had trouble with steward. Father spoke about keeping his pantry cleaner. He very independently refused to go steward any longer." When the fellow packed up and tried to go forward, Captain Dow put him in irons, but eventually Dow relented, let him join the fo'c'sle crew, and brought the cook aft to serve as steward.[35]

An 1863 confrontation between the *Charles W. Morgan*'s Captain Thomas C. Landers and the steward indicates that food could be a flash point for tensions about other issues. In this case, familiarity between cabin servants and officers, the captain's clear distrust of his first mate, and racial prejudice aggravated an already bad situation. Charles W. Chace recounted the incident in his journal:

"Tuesday the 17th January At 7 A.M. whilst getting Breakfast the Capt complained of his Coffee being poor asked the Steward what was the matter with it he [Steward] says nothing that he knew of the Capt then told him it was nothing but water and not to give him no words or he would muzzle him the Steward told him he had done everything he could to please him the Capt. then told him to shut up his head the Steward says I want to know what I have done the Capt then jumps up and goes to the Pantry clinches the Steward hauls him out & drove him upon deck Mrs.Landers [captain's wife] being at table gets up & leaves the Capt then sits down and says I expect I shall have the ship taken from me yet before we get home you officers will spoil a man if I get one I then said I thought that he [Captain Landers] talked to the men as much as I did & had the Steward talking with him in the aftercabin he said he had a right to I told him I had he then jumped up and came

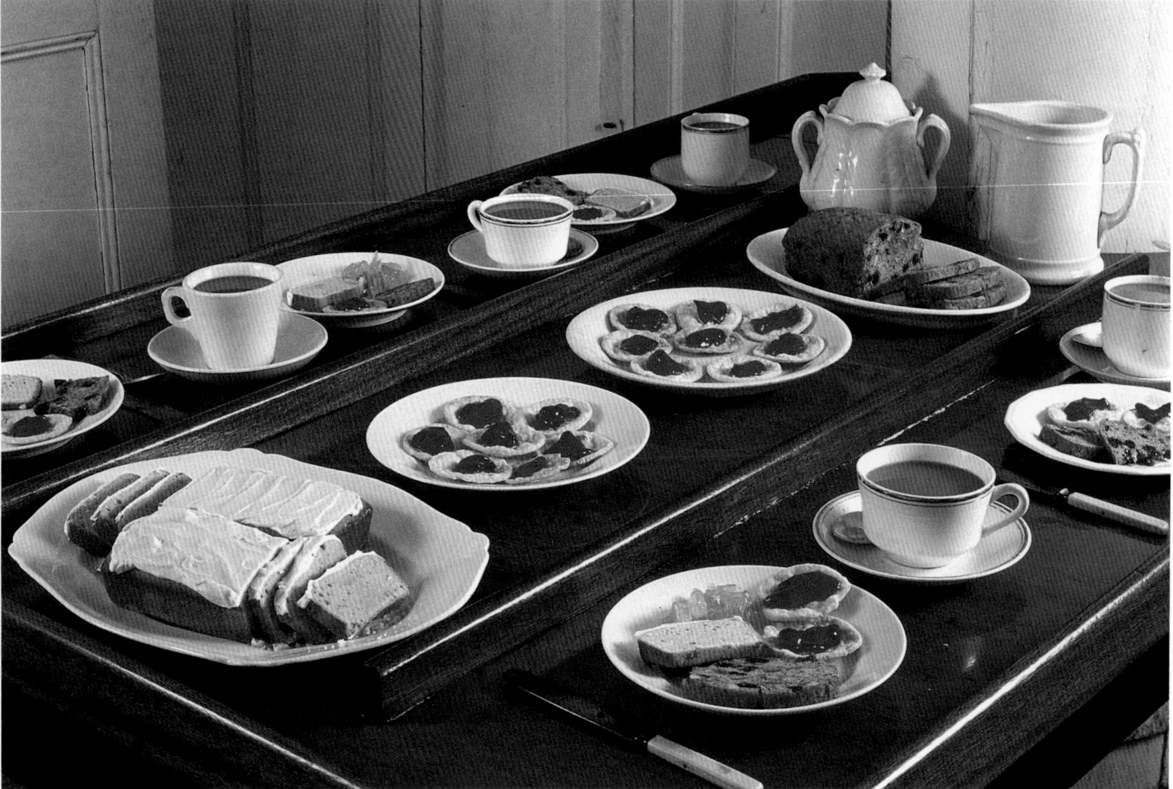

Minnie Lawrence entertained the men in the cabin on her birthday with a tea that consisted of, left to right, two loaves of frosted cupcake, two plates of currant tarts, and a loaf of fruit cake, recipe on page 186.

for me I got up he told me to go to my room I told him that I would finish my breakfast first he then called me the owners fancy mate that I had been corresponding with them all the voyage and that he ought to have put me on shore other masters would have done it and that the owners would build me a Silver ship and much more after this style I told him I would go off duty if he wanted me to he said I could go to the old harry if I liked, called me a liar &c

"Friday the 18th...The Steward told the Capt he was sick the Capt. told him he had the sulks & he would take them out of him sent for Hoss the previous Cook, put him in Steward & sent the Steward forward.

"Wed 23rd the Steward told the capt he was able to attend to his duty as steward the Capt told him he could not go into the cabin again that he could go to duty as seaman but he [the steward] said he did not ship for that and should do no duty & he might as well put him in irons the capt told him to go forward.

"Fri 25th steward in double irons...."

Other violence followed, with the result that the former steward remained in irons from December until May, even though the *Morgan* touched land and the case was taken to various American consuls, none of whom would allow the man to be released from his duty in order to leave the ship. Finally, homeward bound, the *Morgan* stopped at Barbados on 9 May 1864. Chace wrote: "On the 11th Friday took the darkey out of irons & sent him on shore to see the consul. May 13th went on shore with Landers, the Cook Steward & [illegible] to investigate the old stewards case the Consul ordered him on board but he did not come supposed a deserter."[36]

The only way out of this terrible situation was for Captain Landers to do as he did, essentially allowing the man to desert. Chace claimed that the captain charged the officers with "spoiling" the steward, a result, I suppose, of proximity; Chace countered that Landers himself talked with the steward in the after cabin, an extreme display of familiarity that may have led the steward to expect more civility from the captain. Frustrated by what he viewed as the uncooperativeness of his officers, Landers gave the steward a much harder time than the situation deserved. The casual racism of the time surely made it easier for the captain to vent his dissatisfaction and unreasonably punish the black steward.

Captains' wives and cooking: A captain's wife occasionally prepared food on board ship, but not whole meals. She often taught the steward his job and oversaw the finer points of yeast and pastry making. Wives' cooking projects made the cabin seem more homey, but when they prepared something like pie or cake their role was limited to mixing, having to entrust the dish to the cook for baking—a situation they sometimes disliked. On the whaler *Addison* in 1857, Mary Lawrence recorded: "I made our chickens into a pie today. The officers said it seemed like home. It was not baked well; the crust was not done. I should have more courage to make knicknacks if I could tend the baking of them, but of course it would not do for me to go into the galley."[37]

Mary Brewster made popped corn one day and hulled corn another: "whales being cried from mast head I knew they would be off and I should be alone accordingly got some corn and hulled it which has taken up my time all day but was paid for the trouble by the officers saying it was first rate." On the bark *Agate* in 1870, Ann Brown wrote: "I made some doughnuts this afternoon. Fixed them in the cabin."[38]

When ministering to an ill family member, a captain's wife might venture into the galley. Mary Brewster wrote "Was up during the night husband sick and vomiting" and, as we observed earlier, she went into the galley because "All the cooks and stewards were abed so I went and made a fire in the galley and made some herb tea Today I have been engaged in making gruel and waiting upon him This afternoon he felt better and went to work."[39]

Captain Dow's wife on the down-easter *Clytie* reported that during the time the ship was in the port of Naples she made cookies, doughnuts, a loaf of poor-man's cake, lemon pie, loaf cake. On the *Clarissa B. Carver* in 1878 she made Washington pie for her husband's birthday, and doughnuts, and a jar of some kind of mince meat, and her children made molasses candy. Her daughter reported that in Sicily "Mother took advantage of our stay in port to lay in a good supply of fresh fruits and vegetables, also to can cherries to supply our table on the voyage home," which she did at sea.[40]

"Our cook" is the title of this drawing from *Harper's Magazine* in 1860. [MSM 93-11-3]

In the late-nineteenth and early-twentieth centuries, ships might carry small kerosene stoves, or spirit lamps, functionally comparable to a modern hot plate, in the after cabin. Georgia Maria Blanchard reported: "When we could, at 4:00 pm. each day Banning and I had hot chocolate and bread and butter. I made the chocolate on a small oil stove."[41]

Provisioning

A ship began its voyage supplied with quantities of food and water required by a legalized scale of provisions: salt beef and pork, hardtack, water, as well as tea, coffee, molasses, some fresh foods like potatoes, cabbage, and livestock. Amounts of the basic supplies were regulated by laws revised periodically during the nineteenth century.

By an 1805 Act of Congress, all vessels were required to provide minimum amounts of water, meat, and bread: "Every American vessel, bound on a voyage across the Atlantic when she sails, must have on board, well secured under deck, at least sixty gallons of water, one hundred pounds of salted flesh meat, and one hundred pounds of wholesome ship bread, for every person on board; besides other such provisions, stores, and livestock, as may, by the masters or passengers, be put on board; and in like proportion for shorter or longer voyages." The penalty for failing to do this was specific: "Otherwise in case the crew be put on short allowance during the voyage, the master or owner must pay to each of the crew one day's wages beyond the wages agreed on for every day of short allowance."[42] It would have taken, however, extraordinary effort from a seaman to prosecute his rights; sailors were easily exploited because they were often unschooled, and once ashore they scattered to other vessels; a lone sailor had only his word against the captain and owners.

This scale was an absolute minimum, and most American vessels provided more. In fact, the U.S. Navy scale of daily rations shows a pound of meat, half a pound of rice or flour, fourteen ounces of bread, two ounces of sugar, an ounce of coffee or cocoa, or a quarter ounce of tea, and a quarter of a pint (half a cup) of spirits. In addition, a half-pint of beans was allowed three times a week, raisins or dried fruit were allowed twice a week, as were butter, cheese, pickles, or cranberries, and a half-pint each of molasses and vinegar were allowed once a week.[43]

Fresh meat could be substituted for salted; hardtack could be replaced with a pound of soft bread or additional flour or rice; peas, beans, and rice could all be substituted for one another. Vinegar was an American answer to the lime or lemon juice doled out on English vessels as an antiscorbutic. The English also understood sauerkraut to be as effective as lime juice, but if it was ever served to American crews it does not appear on bills of fare, provisioning lists, or in the narrative descriptions of shipboard life.[44]

In those pre-temperance-movement days, the U.S. Navy's daily ration of spirits reflected the national assumption that a person was entitled to and would want some alcoholic beverage every day. Anyone who did *not* want their allowance could be paid the value of it in money. People under twenty-one years of age were exempted from the daily ration, as were commissioned officers and midshipmen.[45] Gradually this daily allowance disappeared as temperance awareness entered every phase of life ashore and at sea.

The scale of provisions above was changed in 1872 and again in 1898. The 1872 scale varied little in *kind* from the earlier scale, but improved the quantity: the bread allowance went to a full pound, the beef allowance was increased by half a pound, the pork by a quarter pound, flour was allowed three times a week instead of two, but peas dropped from a half pound thrice weekly to a third of a pound. Peas, beans, rice, potatoes, barley, and yams could

A day's rations from the early 1800s: on the plate a pound of meat and a half-pound of rice. Clockwise from left: 14 ounces of bread, molasses, potatoes as a substitute for rice, an ounce of coffee or a quarter ounce of tea.

all be substituted for one another. Sugar was allowed, but molasses could take its place, and since it was cheaper it usually did.[46]

The real changes came at the end of the century, in 1898, when canned meats and canned tomatoes appeared twice weekly; onions, dried fruit, and molasses three times weekly; and *daily* rations were allowed of potatoes, butter, lard, sugar, and *fresh* bread in addition to hardtack.[47] As before, these were minimum requirements.

As the scale of provisions changed during the nineteenth century it reflected technological changes that made better food possible, changes in the nature of seafaring itself, and changes in society's nutritional expectations. Canning and refrigeration methods improved to meet increasing demands for fresh meat and produce. By then there was a growing awareness of the dietary importance of especially spoilable foods like vegetables and fruits; and more fresh meat diminished somewhat the disadvantages of heavily salted meat. It was *reasonable* to give deep-water sailors' better food and be more certain of its quality than ever before. As steam-powered vessels increasingly replaced sailing vessels on all but the longest ocean passages in the second half of the nineteenth century, the story of shipboard food changed. Steamships had to make frequent stops in port for fuel, and far more fresh stores ended up on the crew's table. In the middle of the nineteenth century, sailors were typically young men in their late teens and early twenties. Men in this age group often have mighty metabolisms and appetites to match. Sailing a ship was hard work, even when the weather was not cold and miserable. Sailors needed plenty of food, and they prized meat high in fat, as did their hardworking peers ashore. One scholar has calculated that the 1872 scale of provisions would yield from 3,252 to 5,548 calories a day, with a daily median of 3,762. At some point or another, we can assume that no matter how plain or even poor the food was, sailors ate it simply because they were hungry. As Lewis Eldredge confirmed, "our food, tho plain, was made quite endurable by the prodigious appetites we always had." The merchant sailor's diet was roughly comparable in kind and quantity to that of soldiers in the army and miners in California gold fields, and was greater, at least in quantity, than many of the urban poor enjoyed in the last half of the nineteenth century.

Smart owners and captains, at any point in the century, however, did not stick exclusively to the scale of provisions. They commonly provided more generous quantities, as well as fresh vegetables and fruit when possible, and fresh meat occasionally. Felix Riesenberg recalled a conversation with a shipmate who described bad grub as "Act of Parliament rations," i.e., the food on British ships. "Yes, we have about the same scale here," said Riesenberg, "but you don't see them follow it so close. The American shipowner knows better, he wants to get a lot of work out of his crew, to keep his ship up and to make fast passages; he knows he must feed the gang to make them do it without chucking overboard a lot of corpses."[48]

Nor did smart captains willfully withhold what Dana called "the little niceties of their meals, as for instance, duff on Sunday," as a mode of punishment—an allowable but injudicious practice.[49] But difficulties of storage and food quality could interfere with sailors getting their legal amount, as we will see.

Well-traveled grub?: Butchers in coastal towns, like Sarah Anna Emery's husband, made it their business to pack beef and pork for ships, and seaport bakers made plenty of hardtack, the sailors' bread. Owners purchased provisions directly from the makers or from chandlers who stocked all manner of ships' provisions. In case of a short trip, unused portions could be returned for credit, which perhaps accounts for the semi-apocryphal story of the well-traveled beef and biscuits, some of which were clearly sailors' exaggerations. In his account of a voyage on board the *Edward Everett*, 1869-71, George Bishop said, "The first piece of meat we had was very bad, by the taste of it I would dare say that it had been on 6 voyages, for it was so old and it made us all so sick so we could not keep anything on our stomachs." On board the *Tiger*, John Perkins claimed, "We have used up one cask of bread & part of another, both of which have been on a voyage to Chine [*sic*]," and Samuel Millet, in 1849, wrote of "our bread being so hard now we could hardly chew it for it had one or two voyages before."[50]

Meat was occasionally repacked; that is, the old brine was drained away, then the meat removed from the barrels and repacked in new brine. In fact, it was done ashore for domestic consumption, too; in some cases, the brine was drained off, reboiled, skimmed, and poured back into the barrels. Barrels were reused, and the packing dates were stamped on them. A succession of dates on a barrel may have led sailors to believe that their meat was old, but salt meat did not have to be old to be bad. Some owners may have tried to save money by having their captains return unused stores, but shipboard cargo space was generally valuable, so it behooved them to reckon their supplies closely rather than giving surplus casks of beef and bread free rides around the world.[51]

Water Supply

Water was taken on in tanks and casks. As the century progressed, ships were more often fitted with built-in water tanks, but casks—often reused casks—were the common storage vessels. Water tanks might be preferable in preventing contamination from earlier contents, but all too many stories tell of ships' water tanks being polluted by drowned rats, a condition that was sometimes not discovered until long after the rat had fallen in.

Of all the essential shipboard stores, water was the most difficult to keep well. Sitting for months in a hot hold, it could spawn all sorts of organic growth, it could interact with the wood or the previous contents of the cask, or it could simply go stale as the oxygen content declined. Staleness was the least of the problems. "Our water is about the color of new cider & tastes strongly of turpentine & tar, still I drink more of it than I ever did ashore," reported John Perkins of the *Tiger*'s water, which was clearly stored in reused casks. During a round-the-world trip he took in 1860, Dana wrote in his journal that "The water in the new casks is so bad that it made all the passengers sick yesterday. Could not drink it even in Chocolate. Mate ex[amined] & found all the casks the same. Gross negligence."[52]

Water from some sources gained the reputation of keeping well or perhaps "working" in storage and then becoming good. "Our water is rather salt, being taken from a well not far from the salt water, but they say it will keep longer", Perkins reported.[53] Whaling captains became familiar with many water sources during their Pacific cruises, and they frequently sent the boats ashore towing strings of casks to be filled at tropical island waterfalls.

Lewis Eldredge recalled that the water carried on the whaleship *Herald* in 1867 "had to purify itself. While it was 'working' and 'ropy,' it was hard to drink, but it became good again after a while." At Bangor, Maine, water was taken from the river, which "soon smelling to high heaven in the cask, later purified itself and became of rare keeping quality."[54]

There were remedies for bad water: *The New England Almanac* for 1820 said, "To purify Water: On long sea-voyages, or at a distance from wells and rivers, to render putrid water sweet, you have only to put into it, for every gallon of water, ten grains of calcined alum, and triple that proportion of powdered charcoal."[55]

While New Englanders might take good water for granted at home, on board ship it was a treat to be longed for. In her journal aboard the ship *Revely* in 1857, Sara Hix Todd wrote: "My preserves do not do me much good, I have no appetite for them. I would give *more for a glass of good ice water* than all the preserves ever made."[56]

Running low on water was annoying at best and dangerous at worst. Usually captains and owners planned well enough to avoid running out, but occasionally delay caused by unfavorable weather or contrary or light winds, combined with a lack of rain to replenish supplies, left a vessel short of water. A water shortage caused havoc with the bill of fare; it meant that rice, peas, beans, or even dried salt cod, which required too much water in cooking, were temporarily dropped from the menu.[57] Food items that could be boiled together, or prepared another way, were substituted, resulting in increased monotony. And short water rations meant the men would be thirsty all the time.

On the ship *Edward* in 1838, Spencer Bonsall described the difficulty: "We are now on an allowance of 2 qts water each per day. It is not near enough considering that we have to use it for Tea and Coffee and all the purposes of cooking....It is served out at 4 o'clock P.M. and is all gone by breakfast time next morning Scarcely having enough for coffee We then must go without the rest of the day—which goes rather hard with us especially as we must live on salt provisions. Those that keep their water in vessels by themselves generally save a little to drink throughout the day—but the rest of us not having vessels to put it in are obliged to put it together in a cask we then drink as much as we want through the night for fear of not getting our full share. And consequently are obliged

Ship's cooks and crews shared their grub with numerous vermin—weevils, roaches, rats. Here a fat little rat scurries before the cook in this drawing by Milton Burns in the collection of Mystic Seaport. [MSM 75.33]

to go with out through the day."

The two quarts that Bonsall and his shipmates did get were none of the best: "Sometimes we open a cask which is as black as Tar, and very dirty and stinking. So that we are obliged to hold our nose for fear of being suffocated and keep our teeth closed to prevent strangulation from the quantity of dirt &c. But we are now getting used to it and bad as it is, I hope we will not get on a shorter allowance."[58]

Under these circumstances the best the crew could hope for was a rainstorm. If it came, the sailors caught as much water as possible. Thomas Larkin Turner described it: "And how is this done? A close-rolled spare sail is laid across the deck a short way aft the scupper holes, the men's feet stripped of shoes and so-forth which might be dirty. Then all Buckets, half Barrels, tin pots etc are put in requisition for bailing...and containing; and carried below, to be put into the casks which are empty."[59]

Describing the operation aboard the *Edward*, Bonsall said, "It would have amused a landsman to see us all busy catching the rain as it fell, in Tubs, Buckets, Barrels, Tinpots and Pans—and bailing it up with our spoons." For the parched sailors nothing could have been more satisfying. "We had some of it for dinner," commented Turner, "by way of dessert, and all pronounced it fresh, safe, and good."[60]

Time to Eat

"The meal times and time for washing, mending, reading, writing &c., must all come out of the watch below," wrote Dana in his handbook for sailors, *The Seaman's Friend*.[61] As with everything at sea, meal times depended upon "weather permitting" and on a whaleship like the *Charles W. Morgan* it also meant whales permitting.

Mealtimes: Breakfast on most deepwater commercial ships was between seven and eight o'clock, with a half hour allotted to each watch. As John Perkins described it: "At half past seven (seven bells) the watch below takes the kids & gets their breakfast & coffee. When they get through the watch on deck gets their breakfast & coffee & goes below till noon."[62]

Just as it was ashore, the shipboard dinner was at noon. "The dinner hour is twelve o'clock if all hands get dinner together. If dinner is got by the watch, the watch below is called for dinner at seven bells (half past eleven), and the other watch dine when they go below, at twelve." Supper came at the end of the afternoon. "If both watches get supper together, the usual hour is three bells, or half past five; but if supper is got by the watch, three bells is the time for one watch and four [six o'clock] for the other."[63]

Sometimes a midnight snack was allowed at the end of the watch. Captain Samuel "Bully" Samuels reported that "In some ships the kid is allowed to remain in the forecastle, and in such cases Jack regales himself at midnight with a piece of pork or salt junk and biscuits."[64]

When whales were raised, whalers organized their meals around the work. Aboard the *Charles W. Morgan* during her 1871-74 voyage in the Indian Ocean, Hiram Look wrote, "The boats depart from the Ship about daylight haveing Breakfast before they depart taking food And water for the day, and they remain away til just before Sunset."[65]

During the *Morgan*'s first voyage, when whales were being processed alongside, the meals were arranged around the various tasks. For example, they might wait until the cutting-in was completed and all the blubber was on board, then eat, then light the tryworks to render the oil out of the blubber. This practice continued as long as this form of whaling continued. First mate William Griffiths, during the *Morgan*'s 1911-13 voyage, recorded that the starboard whaleboat struck a whale and towed it back to the ship, and "arrived 1 Pm had diner at 2 pm started cuting finished at 7 pm had super and set watch at 8 Pm so ends this day."[66]

Annie Ricketson, on the *A. R. Tucker* in 1871, described the confusion with meals that whales caused. After the lookout sighted whales early one morning, "They got things all ready to lower then had breakfast. All the men [Mrs. Ricketson meant the officers in the cabin] could stop for was a small peace [*sic*] of gingerbread." They were out all day, returning with a whale at four in the afternoon. "They got the boats up and we had dinner. It was late enough for supper but, as we had no dinner, suppose it must be called dinner." At least that day they got breakfast; another time, they "Did not stop for any breakfast and they left at half past six. They did not get aboard till five o'clock in the afternoon."[67]

Communal eating: With food playing such an important nutritional and attitudinal role for sailors, the common method of serving it in one container out of which all ate may have offended the sensibilities of a greenhand with any refinement. Ashore, in New England, hardly anyone ate communally, and had not for over a century. At mealtimes, wrote Dana, "There are neither tables, knives, forks, or plates, in a forecastle; but the kids (a wooden tub with iron hoops) is placed on the floor, and the crew sit around it." He claimed that "the kid and pans are usually kept perfectly clean," but this was certainly not true on all ships. John Perkins described the kid on the *Tiger* as "a black, greasy looking tub with wooden hoops," which was "attacked by tary hands & greasy sheath knives besides not a few rusty spoons." Perkins said that the crew "scared" the cook into washing the eating utensils, but Captain Brewster "forbid him saying it was not customary."[68]

The contrast between the serving and eating utensils in fo'c'sle and cabin highlights the great difference in status. The officers were supplied with a wide range of serving dishes and tableware. The crew forward were supplied only with coffee or tea pots, the food kid, and a wooden bread barge or bread bag, which held the crew's allotment of hardtack. The bread barge was "a kind of keg, made larger at the bottom than at the top....It contains about a half bushel which lasts a day, a hole in the side that will admit a biscuit and is the only opening."[69]

Unlike the officers, the sailors had to bring with them any other eating utensils. Men usually supplied themselves with a tin cup holding from a pint to a little less than a quart, a jack or sheath knife which they used for all purposes, and a spoon. Sometimes a sailor provided himself with a plate or bowl, though doing that may have been more common at the end of the nineteenth century than at the start.[70] Men in need could always buy utensils from the ship's slop chest, usually paying to the ship's owners an exorbitant price plus interest until they were paid off at the end of the voyage.

When it was time to eat, the sailors went to the galley to get their tea or coffee, and the youngest crew member brought the kid full of food back to the fo'c'sle, where it was set on the deck among the men. When the meal included salt meat, each person usually received one piece, although, on an unruly ship, there might be a scramble to grab the best portions. Aboard some ships, one man would turn his back to the food and name a member of the watch as each piece of meat was held up, thus ensuring a strictly equitable division of the meal. Divisible food, like a duff or hash, would be ritually divided. Sometimes the crew observed a hierarchy, with the oldest to youngest helping themselves, and sometimes the crew strictly divided the rations, share and share alike.[71]

Virtually all American sailors in the nineteenth century would have come from homes where food was served at tables with individual place settings. Spencer Bonsall, on the ship *Edward* in 1837, may have been commenting wryly when he described eating on deck in warm weather: "we were all sitting on the forecastle with our pots of tea on the deck (*not being used to the use of a table*)[emphasis added]". Perhaps a sailor well into a voyage, and having grown accustomed to the fo'c'sle manner of eating, would have found using a table aboard ship very strange; although, indeed, the late-century down-easters might have a rude table in their deckhouse fo'c'sles. Dana came from a privileged Boston background and was doubtless accustomed to elaborate table settings, yet even he found the fo'c'sle manner of eating simple and convenient.[72] The rub was, there were men who ate at table aboard ship. A sailor standing at the wheel and looking down through the skylight to the cabin below could see clearly that the table, though smaller than the one at home, was a symbol of shipboard authority and privilege.

A dining table in a "dining room": The shipboard name for the common eating room in the officers' quarters aft was saloon. The *Charles W. Morgan*'s saloon is situated just forward of the after cabin—the captain's sitting room—and on the starboard side it shares a wall with the captain's stateroom. The saloon can be entered from the deck by way of the after companionway, from the after cabin, from the mates' staterooms along its port side, and from the steerage forward of it. The steward's pantry is located at the forward starboard corner of the saloon. Overhead, a large skylight provides daylight for the saloon, another contrast to the dark fo'c'sle.

The 120-foot *Charles W. Morgan*'s cabin and saloon represent the scale of American seafaring in the first half of the nineteenth century. In the second half of the century, as ships grew to 200 or even 300 feet in length, the size of their cabins increased as well. For example, the 244-foot down-easter *Benjamin F. Packard* had a spacious cabin, which is now on exhibit at Mystic Seaport Museum. Yet, despite the size difference and the finer appointments, the layout is similar to the *Morgan*'s. Joanna Colcord described the saloons on the down-easters she and her family sailed in: "This room was long and narrow, with staterooms and pantry opening off both sides. It was lighted by a skylight, under which was sometimes a swinging rack for glass and condiments. The table, provided with 'fiddles' to prevent the dishes sliding off in rough weather, was flanked by two long fixed setees of mahogany or teak; the captain sat at the head in a revolving arm chair, also screwed down"[73]

As we have already seen, the cabin table was provided with tin or china dishes, a full set of flatware, cups or mugs, and tumblers, just as at home ashore. In anticipation of standard middle-class table service, platters, pitchers, castor sets, butter and sugar bowls, and tureens were acquired for the cabin. Occasionally, there was table linen.[74]

Two anecdotes help underscore the differences between fo'c'sle and cabin eating habits. A fo'c'sle hand was promoted to second mate aboard the *A.J. Fuller*, and the first mate came forward and told the crewman to lay aft. Alluding to the changes he was about to encounter at mealtime, the mate said "the steward has your dinner ready, and don't forget to bring your napkin."[75] Being served by someone and being expected to use a napkin were striking differences from the usual fo'c'sle routine.

Mary Lawrence, on the whaleship *Addison* in 1860, recorded the difficulty caused in the cabin by lost spoons. The steward accidentally tossed a meal's worth of teaspoons overboard with the breakfast dishwater, then compounded his error by doing it again the next day, leaving only one teaspoon. "So now we have one teaspoon left, that does execution for us all as a public stirrer, Samuel [Captain Lawrence] using it first, then I take it, then the mate, and so on down. It caused us a great deal of merriment at the table, but really I think it is no laughing matter. What we shall do when we have company is what troubles me."

Mrs. Lawrence and the others got along for a month with the one spoon, until, as Mrs. Lawrence feared, a captain visited aboard. After sharing the stirring experience, he sent Mrs. Lawrence some teaspoons from his ship.[76] This anecdote reveals two characteristics of the after cabin: first, the very clear hierarchy of the cabin—aboard ship there was no question of the order in which the single spoon was used, the captain always came first; and second, how important to Mary Lawrence it was to have a table setting that resembled what would be found at home, especially if there was to be company. As good a sport as Mrs. Lawrence was in other circumstances, one teaspoon was "no laughing matter."

Dinner is Served

Mealtimes in the cabin were the same as those in the fo'c'sle, although they could be adjusted to accommodate the desires of the captain and his wife, if she were aboard. As in the fo'c'sle, there were usually two sittings. The captain, his wife, the first officer, and any passengers on board ate at the first table. Diners at the second table changed over the course of the century and varied between vessels. On some vessels, the second officer, carpenter, and other "idlers"—sub-officers who did not stand regular watches—ate at the second table, but on a whaleship the cooper, carpenter, and boatsteerers messed in steerage, where they lived. These men were not especially welcome in the saloon. Felix Riesenberg described the *A.J. Fuller*'s carpenter, "Chips," "dining in dreary state at the second table....since the second mate had gone, the Jap (cabin) boy thought it beneath his dignity to wait on Chips, and the lanky carpenter found the table set with all that he was to have at one load, soup, meat, dessert, etc."[77]

On the whaleship *Tiger* in 1845, Mary Brewster decided that her husband's day began too early for her, so she "Arose at 8 this morning Took my breakfast alone and at 9 quite a genteel hour Husband has his at 5 which is altogether too early for me." Another time she recorded having breakfast at eight and "husband when he can comes below and takes a cup of coffee with me and says he will henceforth when business will admit of it will eat his morning meal with me."[78]

What's for Grub?

So much has been said—and so colorfully—about sailor's food that we might think it was entirely different from any food ashore. We might also imagine that the food and the various dishes made from it—hardtack, "salt horse," lobscouce, duff—were developed especially by and for sailors. We might even surmise that such food words all have some obscure maritime etymologies, or were names given to the food by a group of people determined to keep their identity distinct from everyone else. Some of each of those things were true, but we must remember that, until they went to sea, sailors and sea cooks were landsmen. Let's take a close look at the food; how *did* the cook come up with meals out of the provisions taken aboard? What did the sailors really think of it?

The "immutable bill of fare:" Sailors could usually identify the day of the week by the food they were served. There was some variation from ship to ship, but normally captains prescribed a regular rotation of beef, pork, and salt fish, accompanied with beans, flour, rice, and potatoes, as well as hardtack. As we have already seen, the scales of provisions allowed specific weekly quantities and frequencies of several foodstuffs. How this turned into a repeating bill of fare, and how that bill of fare was turned into specific seafarer's dishes, was at the discretion of the ship, and subject to the cook's skill and energy.

Some representative mess bills include:

On the India-bound brig *Reaper*, 1809:

Sunday	beef, potatoes, bread, flour and rum
Monday	beef, potatoes, bread
Tuesday	pork, beans, bread
Wednesday	fish, potatoes, bread, rum
Thursday	beef, rice, bread
Friday	pork, beans, bread
Saturday	fish, potatoes, bread, rum[79]

On the transatlantic ship *Edward*, 1837:

Sunday	
Breakfast	coffee, bread, and meat
Dinner	seapie or wheat duff, bread, and meat
Supper	tea, bread, and meat
Monday	
Breakfast	coffee, mush and molasses, bread, and meat
Dinner	bean soup, bread, and meat
Supper	tea, bread, and meat
Tuesday	
Breakfast	coffee, bread, and meat
Dinner	pea soup, bread, and meat
Supper	tea, bread, and meat
Wednesday	
Breakfast	coffee, meat, and bread
Dinner	rice and molasses, meat, and bread
Supper	tea, meat, and bread
Thursday	
Breakfast	coffee, meat, and bread,
Dinner	Indian duff and molasses, bread, and meat
Supper	tea, bread, and meat
Friday	
Breakfast	coffee, bread, and meat
Dinner	potatoes, meat, and bread
Supper	tea, meat, and bread
Saturday	
Breakfast	coffee, mush and molasses, bread, and meat
Dinner	codfish and potatoes, bread, and meat
Supper	tea, bread, and meat[80]

On the whaleship *Tiger*, 1845:

Sunday	duff, meat, bread, molasses
Monday	beans, meat, bread
Tuesday	meat, bread
Wednesday	beans, beef & pork, bread
Thursday	duff, meat, bread, molasses
Friday	rice, meat, bread, molasses
Saturday	hasty pudding, meat, bread, molasses

The *Tiger*'s crew was served coffee in the morning and tea at supper. "We have meat twice a day, about one-tenth of it pork," said John Perkins, which sounds as if the beef and pork were cooked up together. The molasses allowance was one quart to eight people, or one-half cup per person.[81] Earlier, Perkins had recorded in his journal that "We have rice twice a week, beans twice a week, duff twice a week, and potatoes the same." Given the perishability of potatoes, this part of the rations probably did not last for the whole passage. According to Perkins's scale of provisions, one day a week the crew must have received a generous portion of duff and potatoes together.

The 1872 scale of provisions, which Felix Riesenberg took with him from the fo'c'sle when he left the *A. J. Fuller*, showed the following specified daily bills of fare:

Sunday	beef, bread, and flour
Monday	pork, bread, peas
Tuesday	beef, bread, and flour

Wednesday	pork, bread, peas
Thursday	beef, bread, and flour
Friday	pork, bread, peas
Saturday	beef, bread

Allowable substitutions of barley, rice, beans, potatoes, onions, and yams would add variety to this basic weekly menu. The scale of provisions allowed the substitution of two pounds of fresh meat per man per day in lieu of salt meat. Coffee and tea were served daily; two ounces of sugar or three of molasses were also allowed daily.[82]

Some attempt was made at sea to parallel the patterns of meals ashore. The simplest meal would consist of a piece of salt meat, some hardtack, and a hot beverage. It was suitable for both breakfast and supper. Breakfast sometimes included hash, lobscouce, or hasty pudding. Dinner was the largest and most varied meal, as it was on shore. It included salt meat or fish, the vegetable, legume, or grain of the day, and whatever dessert might be offered, such as a "pudding" of duff or rice with molasses as sauce. Supper was a smaller meal, like a breakfast, tea, or supper at home. For a snack, thin slices of salt beef were shaved and eaten with hardtack. Whaleman Lewis Eldredge wrote, "One of our luxuries was to fill our tin cups about half full of water, then break into it some hardtack and fix to taste with vinegar and molasses. This was a special dish for our midnight watch on deck."[83]

When the daily allowable foodstuffs on the bills of fare were combined, they made dishes and meals often familiar to sailors. But even food items not made into specific, named dishes came together to form meals that were like very simplified boiled dinners, bean soups, or simple hashes—meals almost any New Englander would recognize.

Still, on the whaleship *Tiger* John Perkins claimed that "Our food is of a kind I am entirely unused to." Perhaps for this Yale student taking some time off for a sea adventure that was literally true, or perhaps the odd surroundings and lack of culinary care made the food seem more different from his shore food than it actually was. He recorded further descriptions of the grub, "At noon we have potatoes, cabbage, salt beef & pork. I generally take a double share of the beef & let it dry, then the next morning it is in taste like dried beef which I shave & it goes well on the hard biscuit. At night we have beef & pork again. For drink we have a quart of coffee in the morning, another of tea at night."[84]

The noon meal he described having just three days out was essentially a boiled dinner. When he said that the shaved shipboard salt beef was *like* dried beef he merely described reality: in the nineteenth century that is what dried beef was. Eating it on hardtack was the nearest possible replication at sea of a bread and meat breakfast or supper ashore. Farmer's son Stephen Walkley, who remembered that his family had boiled salt beef and salt pork dinners often, would not have been surprised at Perkins's dinner at sea, even to the molasses for sauce on the duff or the vinegar served as a condiment.

Familiar landsmen's dishes could be made from the daily shipboard combinations: pork and beans could become bean soup or stewed pork and beans, similar to baked beans; peas and pork yielded pea soup. A mixture of codfish and potatoes cooked together was comparable to a boiled codfish dinner ashore, especially when made as Isaac Hibberd reported it was when he was at sea in the 1880s and 1890s: "on all the ships I ever sailed on it was customary to serve fish on Saturday instead of Friday. This meal consisted of boiled fish, boiled potatoes, if we had any, and small pieces of pork boiled out and fried crisp like croutons." A shipboard mixture of codfish and rice was similar to a dish called kedgeree, but at sea it would have lacked the hardboiled eggs. Hasty pudding with molasses was alike ashore or at sea, unless, of course, the water was bad. Hibberd's supper on the *Jane Fish*, consisting of soft bread, stewed dried apples, gingerbread and tea, was very similar to the Story family's supper back in the shipbuilding community of Essex, Massachusetts.[85]

Fresh food: As we will see in chapter seven, fresh vegetables and fruit were brought aboard periodically, and fresh meat came from animals slaughtered aboard or from fish or mammals caught overboard. The fresh foods, especially the starchy ones—pumpkins, sweet potatoes, squash—were substituted for grains or beans. When a pig, lamb, sheep, goat, or bullock was butchered, the fo'c'sle customarily got one meal and the balance went to the cabin, though occasionally, as we will see, the foremast hands received more.

During the *Charles W. Morgan*'s first voyage, while cruising for whales in the Pacific, the ship returned to the Galapagos Islands off the South American coast every few months to resupply, bringing aboard potatoes, pumpkins, wood, and water. When they were at the island of St. Felix the crew caught terrapins and fish, and once "a Fishing about 4 o'clock got into the Rock. Caught about 200 Fish, Arrived on board at Sun set, made a Chowder."[86]

On board the ship *Edward*, Spencer Bonsall said that when a shark or porpoise was caught the crew did not get much of it, although after capturing a shark they had a "hearty breakfast of part of his flesh." At the beginning of another trip, Bonsall noted, "We have been living ever since leaving home on crackers, cheese, butter, and pickles, brought on board by the young hands." When these personal provisions were gone it was back to "old horse and ship's grub."[87]

While some of the sailors tolerated their regular fare, not everyone could endure shipboard food. Charles Abbey, an able-bodied seaman on the *Intrepid* during a voyage from New York to China in 1859, recorded in his journal that he was always hungry. Part of the problem was that he detested the food:

"O dear, I ain't very well & dont feel comfortable. Lets see beans for dinner = nothing for dinner my next wheel [turn at the helm], oh well not so bad after all I've got but 2 hours to work to'day & then I'll have a supper I can eat

Mess Bill for Brig Reaper

days	Beef	Pork	Bread	Water	Beans	Rice	Fish	Flour	Potatoes	Rum	Molasses	Vinegar	Sweet Oil
Sunday	12 lb	"	8 lb	25 gls	"	"	"	3 lb	8 lb	gills 12 "	1 Gallon pr Week	1 Gallon pr Week	1 Flask pr 14 days
Monday	12	"	8	25 "	"	"	"	"	8	none			
Tuesday	"	8	8	25 "	2 qts	"	"	"	"	none			
Wednesday	"	"	8	25	"	"	8	"	8	gills 12			
Thursday	12	"	8	25	"	3	"	"	"	none			
Friday	"	8	8	25	2 qts	"	"	"	"	none			
Saturday	"	"	8	25	"	"	8	"	8	gills 12 at night			
	36	16	56	175	4	3	16	3	32	36 gills	1	1	1

The above is a mess Bill pr week, for 10 Men. Half the above quantity is alotted the Cabin, for 5 Men - to be Regulated at the discretion of Isaac Hinckley

If this is beef, rice, and bread, it must be Thursday. This mess bill from the brig *Reaper*, in the Manuscripts Collection of Mystic Seaport Museum, shows the menu that repeated weekly. [MSM 92-7-5]

& relish too. No, by thunder, its too bad, today is pork day (I dont like pork) & I can get no beef, so I must hold on, lets see tomorrow is Wednesday, Rice, it would be good enough but that blasted steward is so afraid of his molasses that it is never sweet enough So to morrow 'brings no comfort' Well Thursday, Ah! ha! 'Duff & Applesauce' & plenty of it too, & well there need be, for from then until Sunday we get comparatively nothing & from Sunday to Thursday ditto again....After this voyage I will go where I have good food and sleeping apartments at the least. Oh, twould make an Epicures mouth water to see the cabin dinner sometimes. I've a notion to waylay the steward & steal it. Oh, no, though, never do, one week in irons, & a very unenviable time the rest of the voyage, never do; would it."[89]

Let's turn now to the cabin to see what "would make an Epicures mouth water."

Dinner in the Cabin

Meals for the cabin were prepared from the same basic provisions furnished the fo'c'sle, with differences both in quality and quantity, and were generally served on the same rotation as the fo'c'sle meals. Food aft *was* similar, but when Captain George Brewster of the Stonington, Connecticut, whaleship *George* told his rebellious crew that "their fare is precisely the same food as mine (a little butter and cheese excepted)", he was being a bit disingenuous.[90]

In addition to the salt beef and salt pork of general provision, the cabin had small stores of nice foods: in preparation for the *Morgan*'s first voyage in 1841, loaf sugar, olive oil, cinnamon, cloves, hams, chocolate, pepper sauce, various liquors, wine, and lemon syrup were all included in the cabin stores. Additional cheese, butter, and pickles may have been shared with the fo'c'sle on special occasions, but most was eaten aft.[91]

In the last part of the century, canned food was often carried as cabin stores: the *Mary Frazier* in 1876 was supplied with canned soup, tomatoes, ginger, pumpkin, clams, oysters, and roast beef. A wide variety of canned items was available to shipmasters: mutton, beef, green corn, lima beans, string beans, salmon, lobster, peaches, huckleberries, blackberries, and round clams. Captain John

A bowl of hulled corn, instructions on page 121, à la Mary Brewster and Mary Lawrence.

L. Williams, a New London, Connecticut, whaling master, made a neat list of all the stores needed to fit out a vessel, labelling provisions "pr man fore & aft," "pr man in cabin," or "For voyage." Among provisions he specified for the cabin were hams, salt mackerel, sugar, canned milk, and butter. Remembering her time aboard down-easters, Joanna Colcord recalled a "large variety" of canned foods, condensed milk, and canned Danish butter. "The meat," she reported, "was mostly the staple corned beef, and this was supplemented by frequent dishes of the good old salt beef used in the forecastle. The cook would select the best pieces of this for the cabin, and it was delicious; I still recollect the taste of it with pleasure." She observed that fresh potatoes and onions did not long survive the first crossing of the equator.[92]

One of the perquisites of the cabin was more frequent fresh meat and vegetables. Dana recorded that once the bullocks were gone aboard his *Alert*, "We, or, rather, *they* [emphasis added, meaning the officers] then began upon the sheep and poultry, for these never come into Jack's mess." Mutton, poultry, fresh pork, porpoise, and wild fowl all went to the cabin. When fresh vegetables were brought aboard, the cabin got preferred use of them too. On board the whaleship *Mentor*, cruising in the Indian Ocean in 1840, boatsteerer Rogers recorded in his journal: "There are a plenty of turnips and potatoes in the ship but they all go in the cabin. We have in steerage plenty of stinking meat and hard bread, while the passengers are eating up all our grub."[93] As a part of the steerage crew, Rogers was entitled to better fare than the fo'c'sle; it must have been particularly galling to be so near, but so far from, nice food.

Butter, and soft bread to put it on, pickles, preserves, side dishes, and desserts appear on the menus recorded by many cabin occupants; except for the exotic ingredients, the meals sound just like dinner at home. On board the whaleship *Ohio* in 1875, Sallie Smith mentioned roast chickens, fried dolphin, porpoise liver, quaohog chowder (quite possibly from canned clams), and apple "dumplins," green beans and new potatoes, whortleberry pot pie, asparagus, beans and corn, boiled turkey, and stewed apple. A few days out at sea on board the whaler *Coral*, Adelaide Wicks had steak, potatoes, and toast for breakfast.[94]

Mary Lawrence recorded the whole menu of a meal aboard the whaleship *Julian* as Captain Winegar's guest: "For dinner we had roast duck, potatoes, onions, some very nice biscuit, coffee, mince pie, and for dessert preserved peaches, pineapples, and quinces. For supper we had oysters, cold duck, biscuit, preserved pears, mince pie, doughnuts, and cookies, Capt. Winegar doing the honors very well." This dinner was served on the Kodiak whaling grounds for Sunday company. While it was hardly typical fare, the meal illustrates what was possible aboard ship. On other days Mrs. Lawrence mentioned corn and beans (possibly succotash), roast chickens, roast pork, and some sausage she made. "Killed a pig today. Tomorrow we shall dine on turtle soup and roast pork," wrote Ann Brown on the bark *Agate* in 1870. The Dow family's Sunday dinner on the brig *Clytie*, 9 June 1866, featured chicken; the next week they had roast goose, another day clam chowder.[95]

The excellent meals Joanna Colcord recalled eating aboard down-easters were similar to the ones she and her family and friends enjoyed ashore: "We always had a dinner of three courses, soup, meat or fish, and dessert. Split pea or bean soup was a meal in itself, and vegetable soup turned up long after the fresh vegetables were gone. Monday, not Friday, was fish day, the staple for dinner being salt cod and pork scraps with boiled potatoes. For supper we would have some form of hearty food, topped off with canned peaches or pears and cake. Always there were plenty of biscuits." These were hearty men's meals calculated to satisfy the appetites of the captain and mates.[96]

On down-easters, Colcord reported, "Breakfast was also a hearty meal, with cereal and possibly salt mackerel or tongues and sounds, or a cold meat." On the *Clarissa B. Carver* in 1878 breakfast one day was stewed chicken and sweet potatoes. Ann Brown had "broiled salmon, boiled eggs, hot biscuit, etc," for breakfast near Baker's Island in the Pacific, where the *Agate* stopped to load guano.[97]

Sometimes our glimpse of cabin fare comes from a fo'c'sle hand who had a chance taste. Charlie Abbey got some leftovers once when he was sick: "Got some 'curry' from the cabin table today. It was neither more or less than 'boiled' 'Chicken' highly seasoned & mixed with boiled rice & plenty of Gravy." When the *A.J. Fuller* made New York from Honolulu in 1898, the small number of crew left aboard were given "Cabin grub for supper," which Felix Riesenberg described as "corned beef hash made with real potatoes."[98]

Special Occasions

Special occasions brought better or extra food. We will talk about July Fourth, Thanksgiving, and Christmas celebrations and foods in later chapters. Birthdays and a whaleship's thousandth barrel of oil were occasions for celebrations. Jack Tar infrequently benefited from a birthday observance, usually held for someone in the cabin, though Bully Samuels was so pleased by the birth of his daughter at sea that he ordered "an extra allowance of grog, with a double-deck sea pie, and plum duff and wine sauce" for the crew's dinner that day.[99]

Captain George Wendell remembered *his* daughter's birthday by noting in his journal "Little May's birth day 1 year old," and recording that he observed the day "with a good dinner. Oyster soup. Fresh roast beef, green string beans, macaroni and cheese, and a nice plum pudding, ending with a glass of ale in which we drank your health, with many happy returns of the day."[100]

Shipboard cabin celebrations varied in expansiveness: Sallie Smith wrote "Fred's birthday today 36 years old had whortleberry pot pie for supper," a dessert they had frequently. In 1870 on the bark *Agate*, Ann Brown recorded on March 21: "This is my birthday. I treated the passengers to fruit cake. I brought it from home. It was as nice as when first baked. I had it sealed up in a tin case."[101]

When little Minnie Lawrence observed her eighth birthday at sea on the *Addison* in 1859, her mother Mary prepared a treat consisting of "a plate of sister Celia's fruitcake, two loaves of cupcake frosted, two plates of currant jelly tarts, and a dish of preserved pineapple, also hot coffee, good and strong, with plenty of milk and white sugar." Captain and Mrs. Lawrence had promised Minnie she could invite all the officers to share her birthday, and they "all united in saying that they had not sat down to such a table since they left home." The "ample supply" of leftovers were sent into the steerage. Recalling his own childhood days at sea, Scott Dow remembered: "The two five-pound boxes of candies in sealed tins given to us in New York were of great importance to the children. Mother only opened them on birthdays and holidays."[102]

The New London whaleship *Mentor* was the scene of a wedding in November of 1840, recorded by the boatsteerer Rogers: "the rest of the day was celebrated by splicing the main brace with all hands. Then we got the wedding supper, consisting of gingerbread and wine sweetened with a little gin."[103]

Yankees did a great deal of socializing wherever ships congregated—on various whaling grounds and in ports around the world. Mary Brewster recorded in 1846, at Margarita Bay, Lower California: "The days pass rapidly and we have plenty of company on board any quantity of fruit milk at times as much as we want fish Oysters and fresh beef Who could not enjoy themselves here and gossip enough from one ship to another."[104]

Joanna Colcord recalled the merchant vessels' long stops in port while discharging and loading cargo. The captains' wives shopped together ashore, or went sightseeing. "Several times a week, the masters and their families would all spend an evening aboard one of the vessels, sitting on the broad awning-covered quarterdeck if the weather permitted. The white jacketed steward would pass about with drinks—lemonade for the ladies and children, something a bit stronger for the men—the cigar tips would glimmer through the soft darkness and the talk went on."[105]

Doughnuts: It was an American whaling custom that for every thousand barrels filled with oil, the men would be treated to a big batch of doughnuts fried in the whale oil. Mary Brewster recorded the anticipation: "At 7 PM boats got fast to a whale and at 9 got him to the ship Men all singing and bawling Doughnuts Doughnuts to morrow as this will certainly make us 1,000 barrels." The next day she wrote, "This afternoon the men are frying doughnuts in the try pots and and seem to be enjoying themselves merrily." Similarly, on board the *Morgan* in 1863 Charles Chace recorded that the crew began the day cutting in and at 11:30 "made a Smoak, Middle Employed Boiling and frying Dough Nuts."[106]

This is the whaling bark *Charles W. Morgan* as she appeared early in the twentieth century near the end of her working career. Her owners' business records revealed how she was originally outfitted in 1841, including the cooking- and dinner-ware she carried. [Samuels Collection, MSM 71-3-262]

Doughnut-making required three scarce shipboard food resources: flour, sweetening, and lots of fat. But doughnuts were a common sweet treat at home, as we saw with the Walkleys and Sarah Anna Emery, and one that sailors would have missed very much, perhaps second only to pie. The tryworks were ideally equipped for doughnut-making, being full of fat and having skimmers right at hand to fish them out.

Doughnuts did not always have holes. Early doughnuts were like "nuts" made of "dough," dropped into hot fat. Shipboard doughnuts were probably made without eggs, relying instead on chemical leavenings. Early in the nineteenth century, pearlash was commonly used; later, saleratus or baking soda and cream of tartar replaced pearlash. Provisioning lists include saleratus and "yeast powders," which was one name for baking powder. There is an outside chance that doughnuts were occasionally raised with yeast, for yeast was made on ships for cabin bread. Landsmen's doughnuts were sweetened with sugar, if not loaf or white sugar then some variety of brown, which was more likely to be used on shipboard. Then too, molasses doughnuts are another possibility for a whaleship, which carried more cheap molasses than sugar for sweetening.[107] Deep-fat-fried food would have been a rarity at sea; fritters, crullers, and pancakes simply used too much fat.

For the whalers' doughnuts, the cook mixed the dough and the men did the frying, dropping small pieces into the boiling oil, then skimming them out by the tub or basket full. Aboard the whaleship *Merlin* out of Newport, Rhode Island, Henrietta Deblois apparently helped with the mixing: "The Steward, Boy, and myself have been at work all morning. We fried or boiled three tubs for the forecastle—one for the steerage. In the afternoon about one tubfull for the cabin and right good they were too, not the least taste of oil—they came out of the pots perfectly dry. The skimmer was so large that they would take out a 1/2 of a peck at a time."[108] In this case at least, the try pots were kept at a sufficiently high temperature that the doughnuts did not absorb fat, which they do when the fat is not hot enough. Besides a sturdy molasses or brown sugar doughnut's flavor probably held up well against the flavor of whale oil.

Here is the **Morgan** as she appears today at Mystic Seaport Museum. Her galley, steward's pantry, and the forecastle, all contain cooking and eating gear appropriate to the turn from nineteenth to twentieth centuries, a refurnishing based on recent research. [MSM 86-10-243]

Sailors' Dishes

A sea cook dealt with a limited range of ingredients: salt meat, hardtack, dried peas or beans, molasses, potatoes, and flour. He had to use a certain amount of each daily, which prescribed what he would cook; although each sailor's whack—allotted amount—determined the quantity of food the cook worked with, he was at least spared the necessity of cooking separate portions for each man. Rather, the food was cooked en masse and divided at serving. Variety in dishes was limited to the cook's competence and energy, and to his judgment about what little he could use at his discretion. Some sailors' dishes required a few more steps in preparation, and the crew of a ship with a lazy cook would never get them. The key ingredient available to the cook's discretionary use was fat. This precious stuff added flavor and valuable calories to food, but it was ferociously competed for by the fo'c'sle, the cabin, and the ship itself. As salt meat cooked, fat was rendered out and rose in the form of grease, which could be skimmed off and saved for many purposes on shipboard besides as an ingredient in cooking. For example, the masts were often "slushed" to lubricate them. And, as we saw, any "slush" not eaten or used earned money for the ship back in port.

As part of their occupational identity, sailors developed a distinctive jargon that included food terminology. Potatoes were called spuds, molasses was called long-tailed sugar and black cat; salt beef was known as salt horse and salt pork as salt junk; shortening or fat was named slush; food was called grub; bread of all sorts was tack, with dry sea biscuits named hardtack, and fresh bread, soft tack. Sailor's dishes had distinctive names, too, like duff, lobscouce, crackerhash, and dandyfunk.[109]

These words were certainly not used exclusively on board ship; nor did they originate there. For example, according to the *Oxford English Dictionary*, "spud" has a seventeenth-century meaning of "short stumpy person or thing," and by the nineteenth century in Scotland it was slang for potato. Scots-Irish immigrants to the United States may have used the term ashore. Similarly the word tack, for which the *Oxford English Dictionary* offers a large cluster of meanings, was used ashore; one form of the word designated "stuff," particularly "food stuff," and may have

Thursday August the 24th 1843 Gallapagos Islan
Comm'd with strong Trades at 4 oclock A.M. got the Ship under weigh in Company with the Ship Coral of New Bedford: about 9 oclock. Charles Island insight 4 Points of ou weather Bow Dist 25 miles. All Hands Employed Lashin the Anchors, and stowing away Turpin. Middle Part all sai set a Steering for the South Head of Albermarle, at Sunset shortened Sail. Brattle Island, bearing N.N.W. Dist 8 miles the South Head bearing West Dist 20 miles Last Part fine weather throughout. Lat by obs 00°=56 S. Long by Chro 90=33

Turpin

Friday August the 25th
Comm'd with thick weather the Watch Employed Blacking the Chains & Anchors, finished about 11 oclock AM. Middle Part about one P.M. saw Whales, at 3 oclock Lowered Struck to the W Boat. got the Whale along side at 5 oclock & Shortened Sail Last Part Laying by the Whale. The Island of Narbler bearing N. Dist 7 miles.

W Boat.

80bbls

Saturday August the 26th
Comm'd with light Trades, at 4 oclock A.M. hooked on to the Wha finished Cutting about ½ past 11 Cleared up the Deck. Mid. Par

The *Morgan*'s mate, James C. Osborn, sketched these terrapins in the log of her first voyage. Later they were cooked and eaten. [MSM 94-3-6]

been mixed up with one sense of the word that implied of good keeping or holding property.[110] Its nautical use to specify sea biscuits is the most enduring of the word's food meanings. That some words' nautical uses outlasted their use ashore will be evident when we look at individual sailor dishes.

Salt beef and salt pork: Captains could buy salt meats in three levels of quality Numbers One, Two, and Three. In her descriptions of dining aft, Joanna Colcord was probably describing Number One. Ashore, salt beef and salt pork were often soaked overnight in fresh water before they were cooked. At sea, fresh water was too precious to freshen salt meat in, so it was soaked in salt water, which was actually a good deal less salty than the meat. The process lowered the salt content of the meat, and rehydrated any meat that dried in the salting. This was done in a piece of deck furniture known as the "harness cask," which had two compartments, one for beef and one for pork. The "beef and pork came in 300-pound casks and were soaked in brine well saturated with saltpeter. When taken from its original cask the beef was as red as a flannel shirt. To freshen it, the cook put it into the oval wooden harness cask, which held about forty gallons and was larger at the bottom than the top to keep it from capsizing. The wood was usually scraped and oiled on the outside and bound with brass hoops, which were polished bright....The meat was allowed to soak for a day or so before it was fresh enough to cook."[111] Once soaked, it was cooked by plain boiling or was used as an ingredient in a dish.

When the barrels or casks of meat were opened, the steward picked through the contents seeking "choice pieces" for the cabin. Frederick Harlow said that once the choice pieces were removed, what was left was "lean pieces for the crew." Dana described the "best pieces" as "any with fat in them." Even the *lean* pork was "fought hard for." The lean, sometimes dry, pieces of meat were nicknamed "salt junk" and "salt horse." A sailor's story commonly repeated and widely believed early in the nineteenth century was that beef dealers actually sold horse meat for beef.[112] This may have been true occasionally.

Hardtack: North American bakers had been producing sea biscuits nearly since the colonies were settled. The biscuits might vary somewhat in shape, square and round being the most common, but otherwise they were the simplest form of dried bread, generally being made only of flour and water, mixed until very stiff, kneaded till smooth, formed, then baked. By the nineteenth century, they might be made from white as well as whole-wheat flour. John Perkins noted, for example, that "The bottom of a bread barrel is graham [whole wheat] instead of wheat flour [white] bread."[113]

Hardtack is a close kin to the beaten biscuits of the Middle Atlantic states, the principal difference being that beaten biscuits often had a little shortening or salt in them. Landsmen's crackers were also similar to hardtack, except they had shortening, too, and they were rolled thinner so they could be bitten through or broken into soup. Although it was hard and thick, hardtack could be chewed, especially if a sailor broke it into small pieces. Sailors apparently also soaked it before eating it in the manner of dry bread dipped into pot liquor, as brewis was eaten ashore.[114] On days when soup was served, hardtack could easily take the place of crackers. While hardtack was rarely eaten ashore—except by soldiers—it was analogous to certain breadstuffs ashore known to almost any Yankee sailor. Seafarers could, and probably did, adapt ways of eating dry bread to eating sea biscuit. And, as we will see, hardtack, like bread ashore, was used as a grain or in place of flour, being broken, sometimes finely, and combined with other ingredients.

Peas, and beans, and rice: In the nineteenth century these three were viewed—except perhaps subconsciously—more as a filling starch than as a source of protein.[115] The use of peas and beans as a primary foodstuff for the lower classes was centuries old by the nineteenth century, but they were a part of everyone's diet, as we have seen in preceding chapters. Pea soup and baked or stewed beans, especially in combination with pork or ham, were common fare ashore, and a shipboard weekly bill of fare that paired salt pork and beans created familiar dishes.

Nineteenth-century Yankees ate rice, but not in the quantities that Southerners did. As a staple grain, Yankees preferred corn, but they ate rice in puddings and used it in soups. So when rice and beef came together on the bill of fare they could have been cooked together in a rice-thickened salt-beef soup. Sailors' accounts suggest that rice was often sweetened with molasses. "Rice, it would be good but that blasted steward is so afraid of his molasses that it is never sweet enough," complained Charles Abbey; and Spencer Bonsall's list of meals shows that molasses was served whenever rice, hasty pudding, or duff were.[116] People ashore commonly used molasses to sweeten hasty pudding and as sauce for puddings; it may have been a convention for rice as well.

Potatoes and cabbage: As an essential part of Yankee diets ashore in the nineteenth century, potatoes were often served as much as three times a day. It was natural then that they were taken to sea and cooked for both fo'c'sle and cabin as long as they lasted. In fact, the phrase "as long as they lasted" is more applicable to potatoes than any other food at sea. Careful storage with adequate ventilation in a "potato-pen" lengthened their usefulness, but either heat, as vessels approached the equator, or the cold and damp weather of the higher latitudes, eventually soured them. Sailors were regularly put to work picking over potatoes to sort out spoiled ones, and every attempt was made to use them up before they went bad.

Potatoes, together with water and wood, were the most frequently obtained fresh provisions when a vessel came into port. When Irish potatoes (the white ones common in New England and actually native to Peru) were not available, sweet potatoes or yams were acquired. The "Irish" potato was carried to Europe by Columbus where it was only gradually adopted into a once grain-dominated European diet. In Ireland *Solanum tuberosum* was so widely grown and used that it became identified as "Irish" potato, and traveled back to the New World with settlers from the British Isles.

At sea, as elsewhere, potatoes were considered less a vegetable than a starch in a meal; in bills of fare they were sometimes substituted for the starch. Cabbage *was* considered a vegetable and was commonly taken to sea. It, too, kept reasonably well, and when cooked with salt meat would have seemed very like a boiled dinner ashore. Cabbage was often carried on foreign vessels in the form of sauerkraut, which preserved its high vitamin C content, but the American shipboard manner of cooking cabbage destroyed much of the benefit of its vitamins.

Coffee and tea: Nearly all bills of fare show coffee and tea each served once a day: coffee in the morning and tea at night. The *Charles W. Morgan* went to sea in 1841 with 1,000 pounds of coffee, 200 pounds of Sou[chong] tea, and 35 pounds of green tea, the latter probably for the cabin.[117] Since a dinner beverage was not specified in bills of fare and not mentioned in narratives, we must assume that water was served at noon.

Coffee was not always literally coffee, although the scales of provisions specified allowances of it. Coffee was costly, and if shipowners *or* housekeepers wanted to save money there were substitutes. In her *American Frugal Housewife*, Mrs. Child wrote, "Where there is a large family of apprentices and workmen, and coffee is very dear, it may be worth while to use the substitutes, or mix them half and half with coffee." Among the substitutes she recommended were roasted dry brown-bread crusts, roasted rum-soaked rye grain, and roasted peas, although Mrs.Child said peas "so used are considered unhealthy."[118]

Unhealthy or not, at sea peas and various grains—barley most notably—were roasted as coffee beans were, ground, and brewed into an imitation of coffee. Until the middle of the nineteenth century, consumers bought coffee beans green and roasted them at home, and we can assume this had to be done aboard ship as well. Some outfitting lists mention a coffee mill for grinding the finished beans.

The tea served to the crew was also subject to

substitution. "A battered tin can was handed me, containing about half a pint of 'Tea'—so called by courtesy, though whether the juice of such stalks as one finds floating therein deserves that title, is a matter all ship owners must settle with their consciences," wrote Herman Melville in *Omoo*. In his memoir, *Strange, But True*, Captain Thomas Crapo said that the bucket of supper tea that sailors got "will be about a quarter full of large leaves, and look as though they had been gathered in an apple orchard in the fall of the year; yet the tea is better than clear water."[119] Crapo may have been exaggerating, emphasizing more the strange than the true, but some shipowners surely cut corners.

After his service on the down-easter *Jane Fish* in 1881, Isaac Hibberd recalled that "The cook always started to make his tea about two o'clock in the afternoon and it was kept simmering on the stove until supper time....The blacker the tea was (and it was generally about the color of ink) the better the sailors liked it, for they judged its strength by its color."[120] With so much salty fare in their diets, sailors probably welcomed the astringent quality of extra strong tea, and they may have thought that very strong dark tea was more likely to be the genuine article.

Both tea and coffee were sweetened with molasses. Sugar was the prerogative of the cabin. When Charles Abbey was ill for a few days, the steward brought him biscuit with butter, and "A cup of green tea sweetened with sugar the greatest luxury I have tasted since we sailed." And Hibberd reported a skipper's thoughtfulness when the captain observed one day that Hibberd was not relieved at the wheel for coffee. Hibberd explained he did not like coffee sweetened with molasses, and so went without. The captain "made no comment, but after that the steward always saw that I had sufficient sugar to sweeten my coffee, which, of course, meant a great deal, for it is hard to make a landsman understand what a cup of coffee means to a sailor at five o'clock on a cold, stormy morning."[121]

Sea cooks and recipes: Sea cooks learned "recipes" for specific dishes from other cooks and crew members. They were not, of course, formulaic recipes, but rather general combinations and procedures.[122] In some cases, a cook may have learned the recipe by having merely seen or eaten the finished dish prepared by someone else. Occasionally the same name was applied to two different dishes, or to variations on them. To reconstruct such recipes, we must find as many descriptions as possible of each and look for common factors among them, then compare them to dishes similarly constructed ashore.

Lobscouce: The *Oxford English Dictionary* defines lobscouce "as a sailor's dish consisting of meat stewed with various vegetables and ship's biscuit or the like." The etymology offered for the word refers to "lob" and "scouce," and to an even older word "loblolly." "Lob" in brewing terms means a "thick mixture"; scouce is paired with "scuttle," which means "dish" or "bowl." Loblolly, a term in use by the early seventeenth century and through the nineteenth, usually specified an oatmeal gruel, and is defined by the *Oxford English Dictionary* as a "rustic or *nautical* [emphasis added] dish."

Dana described the scouce served on the brig *Pilgrim* in 1834: "biscuit pounded fine, salt beef, cut into small pieces, and a few potatoes boiled together and seasoned with pepper." John Perkins got a serving of cabin scouce leftovers, which he said was "a curious mixture, onions, potatoes, several kinds of meat, and everything eatable in the ship," but he reported that "Scouce for the forecastle is made of bread & meat soaked in water & then boiled." That was similar to the scouce described by Lewis Eldredge: "hard bread and salt meat well sprinkled with pepper, chopped into pieces and boiled in water." In 1882, George Boughton on the British ship *Archos* said lobscouce was "so simple that it may be made out of any old thing, although it was a kind of stew or hash with vegetables in it."[123]

George Brown Goode's *Fisheries and Fishery Industries of the U.S.* contains an elaboration on these descriptions: "Lobscouse is the most common of the fancy dishes....For a mess of this for all hands, about three buckets of hard bread, seven pounds of pork and beef, and about a quarter of a pound of pepper are required. The meat, usually the remnants of a former meal, is cut into small pieces and the bread is broken into fragments. Water is added and as the pot boils and simmers, the ingredients are mixed and stirred together with a large iron spoon; pepper is added, and the dish is served smoking hot." Captain Crapo's description of scouce says that the hardtack was broken up in a canvas bag with a hammer and soaked overnight, and that grease was added to the mixture. Goode also included information about potato scouce, which was the same thing made with more potatoes and less bread.[124]

Another description comes from the sea chantey "Paddy West's House," which tells about a boardinghouse master who promised to turn greenhands into seasoned tars by such activities as marching them around a table with a bullock's horn on it so they could claim to "have gone around the Horn." Paddy West served these aspiring sailors "American hash," which he called "Liverpool scouce." American hashes in the nineteenth century were made with leftover meats, warmed up in gravies, so it would have seemed similar to scouce—a near miss, like everything else at Paddy West's.

Narrators often used the terms "stew" and "hash," because that is what scouce seemed most like, but stews and hashes in nineteenth-century England and New England were usually made with fresh meats, and they contained vegetables that modern cooks call aromatics—carrots, onions, and celery—which were added for flavor, not for substance. What distinguished lobscouce from these dishes was the use of salt meat, which we know by looking at evidence from places ashore where lobscouce has survived: specifically Newfoundland and the north of England. According to one source, Swedish lapskojs and German labskaus, made with salt herring, were similar mixtures.[125]

Salt meat ashore was not valued as highly as fresh, so making a salt-meat stew was a coping strategy used wherever a living was hard to make. In the nineteenth-century British Isles that included the north of England where Liverpool is located—hence "Liverpool scouce"—and at sea. The connection between Liverpool, sailors, and the sea is famous, and this probably accounts for scouce on American ships, for New England seems never to have had a tradition of making stew from salted meat, or, if it did, the evidence has disappeared.[126] New Englanders preferred their salted meat—beef and pork—in boiled dinners with the ingredients served discretely on a platter, not chopped together and thickened as a classic scouce would be.

Scouce was described as a "fancy" dish, and sailors welcomed it because, seasoned with pepper and with bread softened to the consistency of dumplings, it was considerably more savory than plainly boiled meat and bread. It certainly required more work from the cook, who would have had to break up the hardtack, and chop the meat, and prepare what vegetables (if any) were in it.

Crackerhash: When there was less meat and fewer vegetables in a mixture, the names crackerhash or breadhash seem to have been given to the result. Hash ashore was usually leftovers chopped up fine, meat and starch together, and made moist, with gravy, water, or sometimes with fat. Crackerhash seems not to have had vegetables in it—keep in mind that nineteenth-century New Englanders viewed potatoes as a starch, comparable to grains or bread, not as a vegetable.

Dandyfunk: This was a sailors' dessert. The origin of this word is obscure, and it does not appear in the *Oxford English Dictionary*.[127] When soaked in water, hardtack has a consistency similar to dumplings or soft boiled puddings. Examples abound of sweets made from dried bread, specifically bread pudding, and hardtack lent itself to similar uses at sea. Dandyfunk was usually a dish of soaked, sweetened hardtack, sometimes baked, which sailors learned how to make from each other. Occasionally the cook made dandyfunk.

Charles Abbey noted one day "a slight variation in the 'duff' which was baked in a large pan & called in that state 'Dandy Funck' I liked it as well if not better than the boiled."[128] The cook, in this instance, may have done an extra good job of pounding the hardtack, or may have actually used flour, or the two together.

Hardtack was often off-ration—that is, the sailors could eat as much as they wished, and enough molasses could be saved up out of rations to use for dandyfunk, which at best tastes a little like graham-cracker crust. If shortening is added it begins to resemble short bread, so long as the hardtack is broken finely enough. Sailors on the *A.J. Fuller* made up a pan of "our favorite dessert," which Riesenberg described as "a baked mass of hard tack and molasses, a great delicacy with us and possible only at rare intervals when Chow would permit us to take up the space in his galley range." Captain Crapo claimed that dandyfunk was nearly the same thing as scouce, "with molasses put in to tone it up, as extra."[129]

While he didn't describe it as dandyfunk, John Perkins made a variation on it: "Last night I made me a mixture of biscuit soaked in water & put some of that sugar gingerbread (which I shall divide among our watch when we get on cruising ground) into it for sweetening, the cook baked it for me & it made a savory pudding."[130]

Bread, bread crumbs, and leftover dried cake were commonly used for other dishes ashore in New England. Bread with sweetened milk and eggs is, of course, bread pudding. Variations on Boston brown bread were made with bread crumbs sweetened with molasses and steamed into a pudding-like quick bread. So using pounded hardtack, the shipboard analog for bread crumbs, was based on established practice.

There are, in fact, *modern* hardtack pudding recipes in Newfoundland, one with pepper, onion, and salt pork is clearly a savory version, but another has molasses, finely chopped fatback (for shortening) and spice.[131] As with dandyfunk, the procedure in both recipes is to soak the hardtack. Whether these were landsmen's dishes to start with or sailors' dishes come ashore is hard to track, but dandyfunk and sweetened hardtack pudding seem to be closely related.

Duff: This famous sailor's dish is another whose name comes from northern England. The word comes from "dough," pronounced to rhyme with "enough," meaning a flour pudding, or dumpling.[132] At sea, this treat was served usually on Sunday, and sometimes another day as well. If flour appeared on the mess bill, duff resulted—at least until late in the nineteenth century, when flour was used to make fresh, soft bread, which sailors preferred even to duff.

As we have seen in preceding chapters, boiled or steamed puddings were popular accompaniments to meals in the 1800s. Depending on the ratio of flour to water, and length of time it was boiled, a duff could range from soft and pudding-like to almost cake-like inside. It, too, was served with molasses as sauce. "Plum duff" had raisins in it, which added to the sweetness, but at sea dried apples were used more often than raisins. Altogether, duff was a treat. Goode reported that, aboard whaleships, the Sunday duff was "served to all hands; one for the cabin; one for the boatsteerers, and one for each watch forward."[133]

The average duff recipe called for flour, shortening, saleratus, raisins or dried fruit (apples), and water. It was boiled in a cloth bag. Duff was comparable to the landlubber's batter pudding, but probably stiffer. The cook's generosity in shortening and fruit, plus his skill in mixing and boiling duff, made all the difference in its density and flavor. The condition of the fat he used was critical. Boiling puddings took skill and a watchful eye; if the pot got low on water, the pudding could stick and scorch on one side, a problem that was aggravated by a vessel's heeling.

John Perkins's description of duff would have applied to any batter pudding boiled in cloth. "At noon we had duff

This mad scramble for grub centered on the communal wooden kid. [From *Browne's Whaling Cruise*, 1846, MSM 94-2-14]

for the first time which I believe all sailors think to be the greatest feast possible. In appearance it was like bakers bread with the crust taken off & then wetted, four tablespoons of molasses were given to each man as sauce."[134] It is unlikely that Perkins had never eaten a boiled pudding before his voyage on the *Tiger* in 1845; by that time some puddings were being steamed in tin containers or molds, which made puddings with a drier surface than the shipboard duff Perkins ate. And perhaps the boiled puddings he knew were dark with spice and rich with shortening.

Mary Lawrence understood that duff was boiled pudding: on July Fourth 1857 she and her companions aft in the whaleship *Addison* had a very nice dinner followed by "a boiled pudding, or duff as we call it." And Spencer Bonsall recognized it too, only on his ship the mid-week duff was made of cornmeal: "We also have a dish made of coarse Indian meal, called Duff, it is boiled in a bag in the form of a Pudding and is eaten with molasses." Frederick Harlow described the differences between cabin and fo'c'sle duffs aboard the *Akbar* in 1875: "The cabin duff was seasoned with spice and plums or raisins and served with lemon or wine sauce. The crew's duff was steamed in a cloth sack and was seasoned with salt and dried apples and served with molasses. Too much spice and wine is not good for sailors. It is liable to ruin one's appetite."[135]

As we might expect, finicky Charles Abbey didn't like duff much either: "It is simply flour & water with dried apples mixed in & the whole boiled down hard & heavy as lead in a canvas bag. When first taken out of the bag it looks like a loaf of white sugar as much as can be. Two months ago I would have turned from it in disgust but now I am glad enough to get it." Abbey would not grow sentimental over duff: "Ever after shall I remember it in connexion with the hardest spots in my life."[136]

Sea pie: Sea pie was another dish for days when flour was issued. On Spencer Bonsall's *Edward* it was one of two once-a-week alternatives: sea pie or wheat duff, which was duff made with flour, as opposed to the Thursday "Indian duff" made with cornmeal. Bonsall describes sea pie as "a curious dish, made of lumps of dough, potatoes, and pieces of fresh and salt meat boiled together."[137] "Lumps of dough" may tell us that it was made carelessly on the ship *Edward*, for a truly well-made sea pie had pastry dough with meat filling in many layers, which required a good deal of labor to prepare. Bonsall's "lumps" seems to describe a short cut. In fact, sea pies were called "double-" or "triple-decker" by the number of layers.

Shoreside versions of sea pie were included in a number of eighteenth-century cookbooks, including Amelia Simmons's 1796 *American Cookery*. In describing western Virginia and Pennsylvania during the colonial era Joseph Dodderidge remarked: "The standard dinner dish for every log rolling, house raising, and harvest day was a pot pie, or what in other countries is called sea pie," suggesting that pot pie and sea pie were quite similar.[138] In parts of modern-day Quebec it is still possible to find dishes called six pates, or le cipaille, which are also multilayered casseroles.[139] The English "Cheshire Pork Pie for Sea" in Hannah Glasse's *Art of Cookery Made Plain and Easy* called for salt pork, potatoes, and crust, but land recipes usually included a greater variety of salt and fresh meats, poultry or fowl, and—particularly in Quebec—game. Clearly there was much room for variation in sea pie, but its essential character was a mix of ingredients separated by layers of dough or pastry.

Glasse's version, and the modern Quebècoise one, call for the dish to be baked. But the two American recipes call for gentle stewing, something entirely possible on board ship, maybe essential to make this in large quantities.[140]

Sea pie was usually not made of salt meat alone, so the cook might not make it until a porpoise or dolphin was caught or some of the livestock kept aboard was butchered. Spencer Bonsall described one time when the mid-watch was alarmed by cries from the pig pen, and the old sow was discovered to be in a "pig-arious situation, having delivered 9 grunters....Never did the soft breathing of a lady's Sute steal more sweetly oer the senses of a love stricken Swain than did the squeaking of those young choristers to the ears of us Jolly Tars." They all peered under the longboat, anticipating the destiny of the piglets while the sow looked on with maternal solicitude, little thinking the sailors were "longing for one of the little fellows to have him served up in that most exquisite style termed by sailors Sea pie. The Cook (bless his greasy trowsers which he has not changed these nine weeks) shakes his head as he looks at them, with a most malicious grin, saying, the way I'll spoil your profiles, some of these days will be a caution to grown folks."[141]

Not Getting Your Whack

The most enduring stories about food at sea are the horrific tales of stinking beef and weevily bread, of scurvy, and of being reduced to eating rats. We have to acknowledge that these things were part of life at sea but they need to be kept in perspective. Although such extreme conditions occurred occasionally, sailors were more often faced with tainted, partially spoiled, or pest-infested foodstuffs.

Food-storage problems: Getting food and water on board a ship was one thing, keeping it in good condition was another. A ship, unlike a house ashore, did not have ideal storage facilities; seawater, insects, and rodents could easily invade supplies. On the *A.R. Tucker* in 1871, Annie Ricketson noted: "Breaking out the after hole [hold] seeing to the casks of beaf they found some with the hoop bursted of[f] but the beaf was all right."[142] But this might happen in a cool cellar ashore, too, requiring the housewife to remove all the meat and repack it in a rehooped barrel.

Many sailors left accounts of knocking weevils and maggots out of the hardtack or soaking it in their tea to kill them, then skimming off what floated up. John Perkins reported after one month out that the *Tiger* had used one cask of bread and part of another: "one was wormy & the other contains litle black bugs."[143] Even into the twentieth century, hardtack infested with weevils had to be used up: Walter Bechtel, who sailed on the *Morgan* in 1900-01, recalled that "the cook split the hardtack and put 'em in a pail of water. The weevils were supposed to float on top and be skimmed off, but a whole lot of them didn't float. They went into the hash. When the hash got hot in the oven, they crawled up on top of the pan, and they couldn't get out of the pan so they baked right on top of the hash. They looked good, made a nice garnish on it, they were nice and brown. Well, they tasted all right too with vinegar."[144]

On board ship, cockroaches were everywhere. Riesenberg reported "Our tea was never without these disgusting vermin...lying drowned in the bottom of the can." One of his shipmates was very philosophical about them, saying "They's no worse nor shrimps." Food in the cabin was not necessarily better. One day Annie Ricketson recorded that "For dinner to day we had chicken soup flavored with cock-roach and my tea was flavored with spider."[145]

The meat, if not actually spoiled, was often described as being so hard and dry the men could carve "grotesque figures from a chunk of it before using it for food." Samuel Millet said that the beef on the whaling bark *Willis* was so coarse-grained "it was more like eating straw than meat." In letters home, even captains' wives complained about moldy bread and smelly meat.[146]

Sometimes meat even spoiled on the hoof. On board the *Hopewell* in 1838, Spencer Bonsall said: "three of our porkers died a day or two ago, and they cut the throat of an other to save his life. This they intended giving us for sea pie but they found we were not so green as to eat sick pigs, and after cleaning him right nicely they hove him overboard. So that I expect some Johnny Shark had quite a blow out."[147]

Food quality was sometimes a matter of taste, but evidence suggests that sailors had mixed feelings about shipboard food. When Captain Jonathan Dow died of a stomach ailment, his son Scott attributed it to the sailor's diet, saying "father's stomach trouble was of long standing, indeed dating back to his first years at sea as a boy." On the other hand, after being seasick a while, Richard Henry Dana said he got "the longshore swash" out of his system and "good sea fare" into it. John Perkins said "They tell me I have grown fat since we have been aboard, at any rate I have a steady good appetite," but Charles Abbey despised every bit of it.[148] Despite the variable quality of the food at sea, crews were often so mindful of their rights that they wanted their regular whack no matter what—even to the degree that they might resent certain fresh supplies, particularly fish and turtle, replacing their usual ration of salt meat. (We will look more closely at this in chapter seven—"Fresh and Exotic Provisions.")

Dining disasters: Heavy weather disrupted meals fore and aft. While the brig *Pilgrim* was rounding Cape Horn, "many a kid of beef have I seen rolling in the scuppers and the bearer lying at his length on the decks," remarked Dana. Under such conditions the crew would have eaten anything salvageable. Samuel Millet said that, during one bad storm, "I found the cook's pork washing fore and aft in the lee scuppers," and when the cook attempted to carry it forward he was knocked down. When the same bad weather prevented the cook from lighting a fire in the galley, "we all turned cannibals and ate the pork raw for breakfast."[149]

A lost kid meant lost dinner to the fo'c'sle crew, so sailors endured anything to prevent the loss. Millett scalded

himself when his foot slipped as he carried a kid of beans, but "I kept the kid right-side-up until I could set it down." He was burned badly enough that he had to stay confined below as result of the accident. "Sailors would never suffer a man to go without" when a shipmate accidentally lost his tea, said Dana, "but would always turn in a little from their own pots to fill up his, yet this was at best dividing the loss among all hands."[150]

Every time one thousand barrels of oil was stowed away, the crew of a whaler celebrated by frying donuts in the tryworks, shown here during its normal routine of boiling the oil out of whale blubber. Whale oil was used for cooking the doughnuts—then literally nut-sized balls of dough, with no holes—and at least one captain's wife reported that they had not the least off-taste. [Drawing from Robert Weir's journal in the collection of the G.W. Blunt White Library, MSM 75-12-23A]

Annie Ricketson, on the other hand, described one batch of lost food as "a very laughable affair." How funny it was depended on your point of view. "The Steward and the Boy had got everything on table all ready to sit down, when the ship gave a roll and over went the tureen of bean soup and stewed pumkin and boiled onion and various other things on the floor. The boy was trying to hold on to them to keep them from coming of[f] but could not keep from slipping himself....Lost all the bean soup but they had more in the cook's galley for the second table *so we had that and they had to go without.*"[151] The second table may not have seen the humor in the situation.

And Lloyd Briggs emphasized the inconvenience of handling food in a seaway: "It was amusing the see the steward, in weather—rough, but not so bad but he thought he could make the cabin—navigating his way across the decks with food for the Captain's table. He would often fall on his knees, squat or even sit, to save the dishes from being thrown from his hands when a specially bad lurch came, which would otherwise have sent him and his burden to the other side of the deck."[152] Lucky the ship with such a dedicated steward.

Food Conflict

Despite all the problems at sea with food and water quality, the major complaint was about food quantity, closely followed by complaints about the lack of variety. Within the closed shipboard society, the hierarchy of command was reflected in the allocation of food. Even though, ashore, members of the elite enjoyed better and more varied food, and plenty of it, aboard ship the distinctions were conspicuous, sometimes painfully so. Resentment resulted in conflict.

Not enough and "Too many persons in the cabin:" The cabin always had priority when better food became available. When the mate caught a barracuda on the *Edward*, Spencer Bonsall observed that "It did not fall to our lot to taste him as there are too many persons in the cabin." James Rogers noted that there were plenty of turnips and potatoes on board the *Mentor*, but they were all going into the cabin. "The passengers are eating up all our grub. We used to get a change once in a while but now we get dam'd little beef and pork."[153]

A few months later, when the *Mentor* ran low on flour, the crew "Went to the cabin and had our soft pap stopped—that is, pounded hard bread made into baby food. Have not got flour enough, as he [Captain Baker] says he lost, sold some, and gave some away." A few days later Rogers reported that the captain's pet disappeared, noting ominously, "We calculate he had gone to look for some duff that was thrown overboard a day before."[154]

Sometimes the crew took things into their own hands.

John Perkins recorded only three days out that "One of our watch managed to steal an excelent codfish & a good cabbage from the hold as well as to tap a barrel of vinegar for which a little quart demijohn was put in requisition & my pepper sauce bottle filled." Starting their voyage by stealing grub began a pattern of conflict over food on the *Tiger*. About a month into the trip there was a fracas over potatoes and onions. Perkins's watch ended up with potatoes and onions actually intended for the cabin, which the other watch saw them eat. Since it seemed unfair, a member of the potatoless watch complained to the captain who "was angry before because he was gouged out of his food thinking all the forecastle had a share & when he heard the man complaining he worked himself into a terrible passion & came forward scolding making threatening gestures &c. Damn it all says he & set the tryworks agoing & cook for yourselves, see then if you cannot get enough." When he got over his anger, Captain Brewster sent Perkins's watch a "pig that had broke his leg telling him to have roast pig as soon as he got a little fatter."[155]

Invidious comparisons: With better food aft being served right before their eyes, the fo'c'sle crew could not possibly avoid making comparisons. As Charles Abbey said, "It would make an epicures mouth water" to see what they ate in the cabin. Perkins explained the manner of living on the *Tiger* as "not owing to the owners, for our ship is well fitted out as it respects provision. But our captain is part owner & therefore wishes to spare all he can, he also has his wife [Mary Brewster] aboard & therefore wishes not to get out of potatoes, molasses, sugar, butter &c. He now denies us pork."[156]

Being denied the very desirable pork aggravated the *Tiger*'s crew more perhaps than it might have otherwise because of a gam they had with the crew of the whaler *Sheffield* from Cold Spring Harbor, New York. As Perkins reported, "Their descriptions of their living & manners made some of our crew discontented. Their cook brings their "scoff" into the forecastle, carries back the kids & washes the pans. A hogshead of molasses is open for them, pepper, vinegar & salt are free to them. Butter is also allowed them. They have chickens every Sunday, pancakes three times a week, scouce several times a week & potatoes & onions with limitations."[157] Well, the *Sheffield*'s potatoes and onions may have had limitations but her crew's sense of humor did not. Unfortunately, as outrageous as the *Sheffield* crew's claims were, the fellows on the *Tiger* swallowed the story.

After a couple of days of mulling over this inequity, the *Tiger*'s crew confronted the skipper about pork:

"One of the hands went aft & told the captain that we wanted pork. He denied that he ever said that we should not have it, though both steward & cook say that he told them to send the pork aft & not forward. He now told the cook to give us five barrels of pork to six of beef. Two of us determined to have potatoes & took a kid & filled it before the eyes of the officers who looked hard but never said any word, we cut them up with meat & carried them to the cook & threatened to take him over the windlass & give him a dozen if he did not cook it & put in seasoning."[158]

With a fo'c'sle crew highly aware of food, an unaware Mary Brewster did something impolitic. When some Mother Carey's chickens were flying about the ship, she recorded, " I have amused myself by throwing them bits of Cake."[159]

One Ship, Two Foodways

There were two societies aboard ship, one in the cabin and the other in the forecastle. The differences between these societies in their food and manner of eating were striking. But, as we will soon see when we look closely at the foodways of the fishermen, the differences were a matter of the shipowner's choice, not a matter of technological or even economic limitations.

Food in the fo'c'sle, by virtue of its being rationed and entirely subject to the owners' and captain's discretion within only legal limitations, was an extension of ship's discipline and a thrice-daily reminder of shipboard hierarchy. The quantity and quality of the fo'c'sle food was an extension of the owner's principle of maximum production for the least cost. As with most businesses, the owners did not increase their costs unless doing so increased productivity or unless change was negotiated at labor's insistence or by governmental intervention. Mutiny over food issues could be life-threatening for both fo'c'sle and cabin, and most captains and crews seemed to know how to tread the fine line between their sometimes conflicting desires or needs.

The fo'c'sle's communal eating helped create and maintain cohesiveness in the watch. Shipboard life thrived on a working class virtually undifferentiated internally; at the end of the voyage the greenhand would receive a lower rate of pay than the able-bodied seaman, but during the voyage he received the same food and shared the same quarters and working conditions. Yet, if this undifferentiated treatment enhanced cohesiveness it also reduced motivation to do anything more than an adaquate job, for there was little reward for individual achievement. That would come, if at all, when a sailor obtained a better berth, either during the voyage by promotion out of the fo'c'sle and into the cabin, or at the start of a new voyage.

Cabin food, on the other hand, did reward and recognize individual achievement, which was appropriate to the people who lived in the cabin. Individual place settings reinforced individuality. The quantity and quality of food, and its service at two distinct sittings, reinforced the hierarchy of the whole ship. The similarity of cabin food to landsmen's fare, and the manner of eating it, reminded the cabin crew where they were from, and perhaps it motivated them to consider what they would lose if they didn't succeed.

The Recipes

The following recipes are divided into fo'c'sle and cabin fare. For the fo'c'sle we have common sailors' dishes: bean soup, lobscouce, plum duff, and dandyfunk. For whalemen there are recipes for doughnuts to celebrate one thousand barrels of oil. Cabin fare is represented by recipes for roast chicken, sweet potatoes, Sallie Smith's whortleberry pot pie, and hulled corn like that made aboard ship by Mary Brewster and Mary Lawrence.

BEAN SOUP

Soak a quart of navy beans overnight. Then put them on the fire, with three quarts of water; three onions, fried or sauteed in a little butter; one little carrot; two potatoes, partly cooked in other water; a small cut of pork; a little red pepper, and salt. Let it all boil slowly five or six hours. Pass it through a colander or sieve. Return the pulp to the fire; season properly with salt and cayenne pepper.
A very good soup can be made from the remains of baked beans; the brown baked beans giving it a good color. Merely add enough water and a bit of onion; boil it to a pulp and pass it through the colander.
If a little stock, or some bones or pieces of fresh meat are at hand, they will also add to the flavor of bean soup.

From *Practical Cooking and Dinner Giving,* by Mrs. Mary F. Henderson, 1882, page 94

The ingredients for this soup would have been available on board ship. I am not sure if Mrs. Henderson meant salt or fresh pork when she said a "small cut of pork." I suspect she meant salt pork, but either would be acceptable.

This is just one of many recipes in which Mrs. Henderson instructed the cook to "pass it through a colander." She was fond of smooth-textured foods, and it would have been hard to prepare a meal from her book without dirtying up your colander. I doubt this was a procedure frequently done at sea, even though colanders appear in outfitting lists; instead, to thicken the soup, the cook would allow the soup to cook until the beans fell apart.

A modern interpretation follows.

4 cups navy beans, soaked overnight
3 onions
3 quarts of water or stock
2 Tablespoons butter
1 small carrot, diced
2 medium potatoes, diced
2 ounces salt pork, chopped
1/2 teaspoon red pepper (or more)
salt and pepper to taste

1. Put the onion in the butter in a large soup kettle and fry until soft.
2. Add three quarts of water or stock and the rest of the ingredients and cook for several hours (2-3 minimum) or put in a slow cooker for the day.
3. Mash through a colander or process at a low speed in a processor or blender. Some texture is desirable.

Yields a gallon of soup.

PLUM DUFF

1 pound of flour
1 teaspoon soda
2 teaspoons cream of tartar
2 oz. drippings
pinch of salt
6 oz. raisins
4 oz. sugar

Sift the flour, soda, cream of tartar, and salt together and add the drippings. Stone the raisins and add the sugar. Mix all together with water. Make into balls and boil for 4 hours or steam for 5 hours. If allowed, serve with sweet sauce.

From *The Yankee Whaler,* by Clifford Ashley, 1938, page 138

Clifford Ashley shipped from New Bedford on the whaling bark *Sunbeam* in August of 1904. The plum duff recipe he gives is typical of most simple boiled puddings of the period and probably is a top-of-the-line pudding for the fo'c'sle. Plain duff was for Sunday and possibly one other weekday, while plum duff was served in the fo'c'sle only on holidays and special occasions. During most of the nineteenth century cooks probably did not put sugar in fo'c'sle duff. Molasses was almost always served as sauce.

Frederick Harlow, a foremast hand on the *Akbar* in 1875, described a duff made with dried apples instead of raisins, which was one of the common shipboard variations on plum duff. Isaac Hibberd, you will recall, observed that too many raisins and too much spice ruins a sailor's appetite.

This duff is delicious. Like most batter puddings boiled in a cloth, its exterior is gummy, but inside the texture is moist and cake-like. You may prefer it steamed in a pudding bowl or mold. You can always add spices and more raisins if you aren't afraid of ruining your appetite. The recipe above makes two duffs, which is enough for two dozen people. At least once, try eating it with molasses drizzled on it as sailors did.

The interpretation below halves the original.

2 cups flour
1/2 teaspoon baking soda
1 teaspoon cream of tartar
pinch of salt
1/4 cup melted shortening
1/4 cup sugar
2/3 cup raisins
2/3 cup water

1. Set a large pot of water on and heat to boiling.
2. Sift together dry ingredients.
3. Stir in melted shortening, sugar, and raisins. Wet the pudding bag or cloth in the boiling water, and dust it liberally with flour.
4. Add the water to the dough and mix well; the dough should be fairly thick, but not stiff. Turn into the pudding bag, tie the bag leaving room for the duff to expand. Or put in a greased pudding mold.
5. Put the duff in the boiling water, suspending it by tying it to a spoon if necessary to keep it from touching the bottom of the pot.
6. If in a bag boil for four hours; steam for five hours if in a mold.
7. When done, turn it out of the cloth onto a serving dish. Let it stand a moment to set up. Slice it and serve with molasses, or one of the lemon sauces described on pages 59 and 145.

Yields 12 servings.

DANDYFUNK

...a pan of "dandyfunk," a baked mass of hard tack and molasses, a great delicacy with us and possible only at rare intervals when Chow would permit us to take up the space in his galley range....for once [we] enjoyed a complete meal of our favorite dessert.

From *Under Sail*, by Felix Riesenberg, 1919, page 71

A rough canvas bag was made into which hard ship's biscuits were placed; then we hammered the bag on the windlass until the contents were converted into what we termed flour. Next we courted the cook...offering to "wash up" for him all his greasy slushy pans,...in return for which voluntary service we secured a pinch of ground ginger, and the loan of a shallow square baking pan....We emptied the contents of the canvas bag,...mixed this with slush purloined from the tin containing the awful stuff we used for greasing down the masts....we added a little salt water until a lovely dough resulted, when it was flattened out in the baking-pan, and placed in the oven until nicely browned.

From *Seafaring*, by George Boughton, 1926, page 47

Dandyfunk was a sailor-made treat. Hardtack was often freely available to the sailors, and if they could negotiate with the cook for additional ingredients and oven space they could make this item for themselves. While there seems to have been some variation in the mixture, it was always made from pounded hardtack. Shortening or molasses could also be included. Shortening varied widely in quality on board ship; the chances of it being rancid were very good. Molasses was usually rationed, so sailors would have had to save a bit out of their daily whack to accumulate a supply of it for dandyfunk.

Felix Riesenberg sailed on the *A.J. Fuller* from New York to Honolulu as a foremast hand in 1897. George Boughton recounted his trip in the bark *Archos* from Sunderland, Scotland, which began in 1882 when he was twelve years old. Boughton romanticized his sailing past, so we may have to take his "recipe" for dandyfunk with a grain of salt, so to speak.

Dandyfunk has the texture of a sweet cracker-crumb crust. It seems to be related to shortbreads, and examples of fat, molasses, and flour confections can be found in traditional recipes from Newfoundland.[160] Recipes also exist in nineteenth-century cookbooks and manuscript sources for cake made with salt pork. These kinds of examples may have provided a prototype for sailors' dandyfunk.

I don't know why you would want to make this, but here is an adapted recipe in case you do. One cake of hardtack will pound out to about 2/3 cup of crumbs. The recipe below can be multiplied by the number of pieces of hardtack you use. Vegetable shortening is the best tasting, but miscellaneous drippings is most authentic. I don't like it at all made with water, à la Boughton, but if you want to try it that way add a quarter cup of lightly salted water to the recipe below.

1 piece of hardtack
1 tablespoon shortening
2 tablespoons molasses
Preheat oven to 350°.

1. Pound the hardtack until most crumbs are about the size of a grain of cooked rice. (There will be considerable variation as some of the hardtack becomes flour-like while other pieces remain larger.)
2. Mix in the shortening till it is evenly blended, then add the molasses and stir to mix well.
3. Bake in a small greased pan in a hot oven for fifteen to twenty minutes, until the molasses is all bubbly and the mixture is nicely browned. Eat warm.

DOUGHNUTS

DOUGH NUTS, No. 1.
Two eggs, one cup of sugar, half a pint of sour milk; a little saleratus; salt and spice to your taste; a small piece of butter or cream is better, if you have it; mix the articles together one hour before you fry the cakes; mould with flour.

From *New England Economical Housekeeper*, by Mrs. E.A. Howland, 1845, page 26

In 1845, when the *Tiger*'s crew had doughnuts to celebrate their one-thousandth barrel, recipes were available for both yeasted and quick-raised doughnuts. Because most doughnut recipes call for milk and eggs, I wondered how doughnuts at sea were produced. Milk was not always available. Eggs may have been, but were precious; of course, this was a special treat for which the captain might provide a few eggs.

A sweetened bread dough might have been fashioned into doughnuts and fried up for the crew in lieu of the kind of doughnuts you will get if you follow Mrs. Howland's recipe. In her *Complete Domestic Guide*, Mrs. Abell offered a doughnut recipe that called for butter, sugar, eggs, and spices to be worked into a bowlful of bread dough, with additional flour, which would be fashioned into doughnuts after the required rising time.[161]

Many stories purport to explain how doughnuts got their holes, and each story has loyal proponents. What is true is that doughnuts did not always have holes. They were sometimes fried up in small lumps, as a dough "nut," and at other times were cut into shapes. They were always fried in deep fat, and were considered an economical sweet suitable for filling up small boys or eating for tea. Cinnamon and nutmeg seem to have been the preferred spices for doughnuts.

To succeed, doughnuts need to be a soft, barely manageable dough fried in fat hot enough to cook them without their either burning or soaking up the fat as they cook. You may find it helpful to let the dough chill before cutting the doughnuts.

4-4 1/2 cups flour
1 teaspoon baking soda
1/2 teaspoon cinnamon
1/4 to 1/2 teaspoon nutmeg
1/2 teaspoon salt
2 eggs
1 cup sugar
1 cup sour milk
2 tablespoons butter, melted

1. Sift together dry ingredients.
2. Beat eggs well, slowly adding the sugar. When lemony, add the milk and melted butter.
3. Mix in the sifted dry ingredients, adding more flour till it is manageable, then set in the refrigerator for an hour to chill.
4. Turn out on a well-floured board and pat out to half an inch thick. Cut into desired shape and drop into the hot fat. Do not crowd.
5. Cook for about two minutes per side, turning over with a fork. When cooked, drain on paper towels. If you wish, put sugar (and cinnamon, if you like) into a paper bag and shake the doughnuts in the bag till they are coated.

Yields 20 doughnuts.

ROASTED CHICKEN

CAPONS AND CHICKENS.
Capons and chickens are prepared and roasted or boiled as turkeys. A capon weighing six pounds will roast in one hour and a quarter. A pair of chickens weighing six pounds, will roast in one hour. Make a gravy as directed for turkeys, and serve with boiled ham or tongue, on separate dishes.

From *The Practical Cookbook*, by Mrs. Bliss, 1864, page 79

Chickens were carried on board ship to provide a bit of fresh meat for the cabin. Captains' wives and cabin passengers noted from time to time that they had roasted chicken for dinner. Miss Hall commented that "A fowl may be roasted in a hot stove oven, so as to be nearly as fine as before the fire," referring to the nineteenth-century difference, which we no longer recognize, between roasting and baking meat.

I chose this recipe because I wanted to point out the real dissimilarity in old and modern roasting times: a six-pound capon today would be roasted for twenty minutes a pound for a total of two hours. The same goes for the chickens. Nineteenth-century chickens or capons were somewhat smaller than ours, but, even given birds of the same size, we are acustomed to roasting fowl longer than was done in the last century.

When Mrs. Bliss referred to making a gravy as you would for turkey, she meant to make a giblet gravy (recipe on page 249.) I offer these period roasting instructions for your interest, so no interpretation will follow.

SWEET POTATOES

Should be kept in earth or sand in cold weather, or they will be scarcely eatable after October. The best way to cook them, is to bake them. They may be boiled as other potatoes, peel them as others.

From *The Complete Domestic Guide Comprising the Mother's Book of Daily Duties and Skillful Housewife's Book*, by Mrs. L.G. Abell, 1853, page 102

Sweet potatoes should never be pared before cooking. If you wish to boil them, wash them clean, cut a bit from each end, and boil in clear water, without salt; the water in the boiling pot should always boil before the potatoes are put in; large potatoes require one hour to boil.

From *The Practical Cookbook,* by Mrs. Bliss, 1864, page 96

Wash them perfectly clean, wipe them dry, and bake in a quick oven, according to their size—half an hour for quite small size, three-quarters for larger, and a full hour for the largest. Let the oven have a good heat, and do not open it, unless it is necessary to turn them, until they are done.

From *Practical American Cookery and Domestic Economy,* by Elizabeth M. Hall, 1855, page 139

Sweet potatoes were not unknown to the New Englanders who bought them in foreign ports and ate them aboard whaling and merchant ships around the world. But they were not as common in the North as white, or Irish, potatoes. As you can see from the two recipes above, cooks did not always agree on the best way to cook them. Either boiling or baking would have been possible aboard ship, and I give the edge to boiling.

Personally, I like them baked and would follow Miss Hall's advice any day. The times she provides are perfectly suitable for an oven at 350°.

LOBSCOUCE

The cook had just made for us a mess of hot "scouce"—that is, biscuit pounded fine, salt beef cut into small pieces, and a few potatoes, boiled up together and seasoned with pepper.

From *Two Years Before the Mast, by Richard Henry Dana, 1834, World Classics Edition, pages 45-46*

The steward was bringing up the refuse food of the cabin...I got a panful of "scouce" as it is called, and a biscuit. The scouce is a curious mixture, onions, pepper, potatoes, several kinds of meat & everything eatable in the ship....Scouce for the forecastle is made of bread & meat soaked in water & then boiled.

From *"John Perkins's Journal at Sea, 1845,"* page 125

1 lb. salt meat cubed
1 med. onion
2 tbsp. rice
1 cup each of diced carrots, turnips, and potatoes
1 parsnip (diced)
1 cup chopped cabbage

Soak meat overnight to remove the salt. Drain. Add 6 or 7 cups of fresh cold water, and cook for one hour. Then add the vegetables and rice. Cook until vegetables are tender. (Spareribs may be used instead of salt meat.)

Lobscouce is a very thick soup or stew of vegetables and salt meat, A native of Liverpool, England, to this day is often called a "Lob-Saucer," so this is probably where this recipe originated. It has been used in Newfoundland for at least seventy years.

Recipe submitted by Netta Ivany of Sunnyside, Newfoundland, and Miss Alice Lacey of Wesleyville, Newfoundland, From *Fat Back and Molasses: a Collection of Favorite Old Recipes from Newfoundland and Labrador,* by the Rev. Ivan Jesperson, 1974, page 11

Here are two versions of scouce: a simple one suitable for the fo'c'sle crew, and a more elaborate one for the cabin. The Newfoundland recipe is a cabin as well as a landsman's version. Miss Lacey and Ms. Ivany are right about the origin of lobscouce: it is a common dish in northern England, associated with Liverpool in particular, and Liverpool's connection with the sea may explain why scouce appeared so often in the fo'c'sles of British and American ships.

Lobscouce tastes good. Sailors regarded it as a particular treat, and it certainly required more effort by the cook because he had to chop meat and potatoes, and break up hardtack—the sea biscuits referred to by Dana and Perkins. How carefully he did that determined how good the scouce would be. Potatoes were not always included in fo'c'sle scouce, but might have been if it were made on a day when beef and potatoes were on the mess bill. The hardtack served to absorb some of the liquid and thicken the whole thing.

Neither salt meat, particularly beef, nor hardtack are commonly available today. If you wish to produce an approximation of salt beef, purchase a cheap cut of beef, rub it thoroughly with pickling salt, and set it in a cool, dry place for a month or more. Check it frequently and add salt as needed. (Or follow salted beef instructions on pages 161 and 228.)

Hardtack is available in Newfoundland and Nova Scotia. Get a bag on your next vacation to Nova Scotia or convince a friend to pick one up for you. Don't worry about using it right up: it keeps as well now as it did a hundred years ago.

At sea the beef would have been freshened in the harness cask; be sure to soak your beef at least overnight. The interpretation below is for a fo'c'sle scouce. For a cabin-style scouce use the Newfoundland recipe above, which is clear enough that an interpretation is not needed.

1 pound salt meat, cubed
2 cups water
4 potatoes, cubed
1/2 cake of hardtack, broken up fairly small
pepper to taste

1. Put the meat and water in a heavy pot, and stew covered over a medium heat until the meat is cooked through.
2. Add the potatoes (and other vegetables) and cook, still covered, until tender.
3. Add the hardtack and pepper, reduce the heat, and simmer uncovered until the 'scouce has thickened.

Yields 4 servings.

WHORTLEBERRY POT PIE

Whortleberry-Pie.—Pick over the berries, and, if bought of berry-boys, or in the market, wash and dry them; but if you can trust the hands that gathered them, rubbing them gently in a coarse cloth is the best way, as you lose none of the flavor. Fill a deep plate, after having rolled the berries in sugar, and cover quite thick with sugar after they are put on the plate. No spice. Bake with upper and under crust. Some add a few currants to whortleberries, or a little juice of lemon, but we think nothing can improve their natural flavor.

From *All Around the House; or, How to Make Homes Happy*, by Mrs. H.W. Beecher, 1878, pages 425-26

Aboard the whaling bark *Ohio*, Fred and Sallie Smith, or their steward, combined a standard fruit pie recipe and the typical pot pie of the period, which had dumpling-like crust, to make a whortleberry *pot* pie. I have not yet found a printed or manuscript recipe for a fruit-filled pot pie; usually they were made with meat or poultry. Today we would call this dish a "cobbler" or a "grunt."

Whortleberries are not hard to find in the store these days, especially when you understand that the term was used in New England in the nineteenth century for what we call blueberries. If you buy them fresh, you are still well advised to wash them, though not for the same reason mentioned by Mrs. Beecher.

In her slightly earlier cookbook, Miss Hall disagreed with Mrs. Beecher about the matter of spice, instructing cooks to grate in nutmeg, and also dredge in flour to thicken the pie.[163] Certainly the filling in a slice of Mrs. Beecher's pie would have run out all over the plate.

Here is a slightly revised recipe for Fred and Sallie's favorite dessert.

2 cups blueberries
sugar to taste, about 2 tablespoons
nutmeg to taste
one-half the recipe for dumplings on page 25, or your choice of dumpling recipe.

1. Mix the blueberries, sugar, and nutmeg together and put in a deep baking dish.
2. Make a batch of dumpling dough, sweetening it with the addition of a couple of tablespoons of sugar, if you wish.
3. Drop bits of dough on top of the blueberries and set the dish into a pot with enough boiling water in it to come to within an inch of the top of the dish.
4. Steam for forty-five minutes to an hour, adding more water as needed from a hot kettle. Serve with whipped cream, which the Smiths probably could not have done.

Yields 4 servings.

HULLED CORN

Put two handfuls of clean hard-wood ashes in two quarts of cold water; boil fifteen or twenty minutes; let stand until the ashes settle and the water is perfectly clear. To this cleansed water (it should be strong enough of the lye to feel a little slippery), add as much cold water as is necessary to cover the corn. Put the corn in the water; let it boil until the hulls begin to start, then skim the corn out into a pan of clear, cold water, and rub thoroughly with the hands to remove the hulls and cleanse the corn from the lye,—rub it through two or three, or even four waters, that there may be no taste of lye; then put into clear water and boil until tender.

From *Mrs. Rorer's Philadelphia Cook Book,* by Mrs. S.T. Rorer, 1886, pages 355-56

Mrs. Rorer explained that hulled corn is "corn soaked in an alkali to remove the hull. In this way much of the oil is lost, and therefore it makes a good summer food." Indeed, "hulling" was a good way to make a breakfast food or vegetable side dish out of a long-keeping grain.

Corn and its various preparations have more regional names than nearly any other food item. Today hulled corn is generally called hominy and can be purchased canned. In the nineteenth century it was made and peddled by the "samp man," but it was also termed simply "hulled corn."

Mary Lawrence recorded that to make hulled corn on board the whaleship *Addison*, "we begged a few sticks of wood to make ashes, as ours is not suitable for that purpose."[164] You will not have to beg wood or ashes from a neighboring ship to make this. You can substitute baking soda for the ashes, using a couple of large spoonfuls in a half a gallon of water, which should be enough to take the hulls off a quart of dried corn.

For all the alarming mention of lye, when it was made from the wood ashes as Mrs. Brewster and Mrs. Lawrence did, a fairly weak solution would do the job. *Do not* use modern, commercial lye, which would be caustic unless very diluted. Instead, use the baking soda, which works just as well. Let the corn stand in the baking soda and water overnight. The next day, bring it to a boil in the water it soaked in. Then follow Mrs. Rorer's instructions for rubbing the hulls off in repeated changes of water.

To serve it, bring it to a boil, then eat it with butter and salt and pepper, or butter and sugar.

Fishermen's Fare

"The fare of the fishermen is far better than one would suppose who has heard stories of the poor living of other sailors. They live far better than any other class of seafaring men, and have provisions of a better grade and in greater variety," reported Henry Osborne after a trip to the banks in the summer of 1879, on the Gloucester cod-fishing schooner Victor. *Fishing romanticist James B. Connolly claimed that part of Gloucester's fame was "the beauty and staunchness of her vessels," and "the good grub served in them."*[1]

Above, the Gorton-Pew auxiliary schooner *Corinthian*, on the fishing banks in the 1930s, gives us a sense of the fishermen's appetite-building hard work. The shack locker, opposite, full of leftovers, was where the men grabbed a snack while "mugging-up"—having a coffee break. [Photo courtesy of Charlie Sayle, provided by Joseph E. Garland]

"The good grub served in them" was a marked contrast to deep-water fare. Equally striking was how it was served and who ate it; all hands sat down to a table and all ate the same food. "All the members of a schooner's crew, from the captain to the smallest boy...eat at the one table, and fare precisely alike."[2]

The fishing vessel's cook holds what appears to be a duff, while the men hold onto their mugs. The true horizon is apparent in the liquid in the large bowl at the center of the table. The fiddles which ran lengthwise on the mess table kept bowls and plates of food from sliding off the table and crashing to the sole under normal cruising conditions. Similarly, the stove behind the cook is equipped with iron fiddles to fence in the pots and kettles. Despite such unstable mealtimes, and the rough-and ready appearance of the table, there was good grub and plenty of it. [Drawing by Walton Taber for the *Century Magazine*, October 1886, MSM 94-3-12]

Fishing schooners were different from the deep-water whalers and merchant ships. The captain was the boss and commanded the respect of the crew, but he was not the privileged individual that a deep-water captain was. The crew of a Mt. Desert, Maine, fishing vessel responded to a reporter's question "where is the mate?" this way: "We're all mates, and scarcely any cap'n,' they said in a jovial way, 'and the cook is the best man.' "[3]

Fishing vessels had fewer layers of command and distinctions in pay among the crew. Early New England fishing voyages had been cooperative ventures, with all aboard contributing to the costs of the voyage and sharing in the profits. Fishermen aboard a vessel from a traditional fishing town were often neighbors and relatives at home, so there was already a community spirit, and this was reflected by and reinforced in the foodways as well.

"We lived jist so to home as we did on board of the vessels, pretty much," claimed one fisherman. But researcher George Brown Goode asserted that "There can be no question that fishermen, ordinarily, are provided with much better food than the people of the same class engaged in shore pursuits." This was true for some fishermen, particularly the Canadians or those from disadvantaged families, but fishermen's fare was similar to what working people preferred to eat whenever they could afford it. Fishermen took their home foodways with them to the banks, within the normal restrictions of equipment, shipboard storage, and the need to produce large quantities of food. In the context of men away from home cooking for themselves, this set of foodways strikes a mid-point between those of the Life-Saving Service and the foodways of deep-water vessels.

The earliest provisioning lists and meal descriptions sound like deep-water cabin fare of the same period, and the menu improved substantially through the nineteenth century and into the early twentieth century. Changes in food preservation and fishing technology meant canned grub and ice in the hold that kept both the vessel's catch and the fishermen's food fresh longer. The introduction of canned food "has been of great importance to the fishermen, and of course, there is dissatisfaction on the part of many of the older men, who think their successors are indulging in needless luxury, and also on the part of some of the fitters upon whom falls a portion of the increase in the expense." The Gloucester fishermen were credited with the improved fare on the schooners; the "shrewdest fishery capitalists" felt it was worthwhile to get good provisions and a good cook because it insured being able to recruit good fishermen who would stay with them.[4]

Some influences on the diet of the fishermen came from Newfoundlanders, other Canadian maritime provincials, and Portuguese fishermen. A look at traditional Newfoundland and Bluenose (Nova Scotia) recipes shows dishes mentioned aboard fishing schooners, variations of which were possibly common in early coastal New England but long gone from the tables of twentieth-century New Englanders. Portuguese people settled in New England coastal towns, worked on fishing schooners, and exposed Yankees to some of their traditional dishes as well.

The Galley

Fishing-schooner galleys and forecastles shared the same space. These galley-fo'c'sles got larger and more commodious through the nineteenth century as vessels used in the fisheries changed from the small pinky and chebacco types to the large, deep-hulled schooner type of which Mystic Seaport Museum's *L. A. Dunton* is an example.

In the first half of the nineteenth century, cooking arrangements were very simple. Between the 1820s and 1840s Provincetown, Massachusetts, vessels fishing on the Labrador coast could easily be identified at night: "From many a deck lurid fires flash and flicker in the gathering darkness, revealing dusky figures grouped around—the fishermen preparing their hasty supper. They use no stoves, but build their fires in halves of hogsheads filled with sand." Captain John Whidden described the fo'c'sle cooking arrangements in Gloucester and Marblehead fishing schooners during the 1830s and 1840s: "The old-fashioned forepeak, which was the fo'c'sle, was fitted with a fireplace built of brick directly under the fore scuttle, from whence the smoke escaped, or was supposed to, but as a matter of fact, the forepeak was so filled with smoke that one could not see across it. Above the fireplace hung a heavy iron crane, from which was suspended a huge iron pot in which all the cooking was done. Tea and coffee were made in it, the chowder and meat were boiled in it, and it was put to every other use in the culinary art."[5]

Fisherman Wesley George Pierce reported that the Maine pinkys fishing for mackerel and cod in the Gulf of St. Lawrence in the first half of the century had small fireplaces, *with* chimneys: "The men often cooked mackerel by hanging them on a wire in the chimney above the fireplace, where they cooked and smoked."[6]

After a mid-century mackerel fishing trip, with a crew of twelve plus cook, Charles Nordhoff reported: "The galley, or cooking stove and kitchen generally, was in the forecastle, a narrow and dark little hole, about six by eight feet, exclusive of the berths." A table occupied the center of the fo'c'sle, and "The whole smelled villainously of decayed fish."[7]

By the 1870s and 1880s, cooking facilities aboard fishing vessels had improved, just as the food itself had become more appealing. From that period through the demise of fishing schooners in the 1930s the fo'c'sle and galley arrangements were similar to the ample setup seen on the *L.A. Dunton*. A description of a fresh halibut schooner, ca. 1885, noted that the forehold was built to accommodate barrels for water and beef and flour plus firkins and half barrels of small stores such as butter, lard, and sugar. A pantry was on the port side, and the cook-stove was "always" on the starboard side, and the "berths abreast of the after row are used by the cook as lockers for putting his utensils &c. in." Pierce, who had gone to sea at age fifteen in 1884, recalled that one cupboard was designated the "shack cupboard," where food was kept for fishermen's coffee breaks and snacks. There was another for the cook, "where he keeps his whole loaves of bread, cakes, pies, etc., and the crew all understand they are not to use his cupboard."[8]

The *L. A. Dunton*'s galley in the fo'c'sle is arranged so that the coal-burning cook-stove is amidships behind the forward companionway. Cupboards with a work counter beneath line the bulkhead between the hold and the fo'c'sle; at the port end of the counter is a sink and pump. The coal bin is on the port side, and the ice chest is on the starboard, along with other storage lockers.

Thomas Norris recalled the galley of the 62-foot fishing schooner *Emerald*, (built at Essex, Massachusetts, in 1884) as it appeared when his father commanded the vessel early in the twentieth century. The shack locker, he said, was located on the port side, near the galley, and the cook hung all the cups on hooks over the sink area. For dishwashing, he recalled galvanized water containers hung on the side of the stove, as *Dunton*'s stove has today.[9]

Water Supply and Storage

In the early 1800s, water was carried in casks, but later in the century water tanks were installed beneath the cabin sole (floor). Cypress tanks were reputed to keep water the sweetest. The *Dunton* was built with cypress tanks, but they were later replaced with steel tanks. The cook used a hand pump in the sink to draw water for cooking and drinking.

In Gloucester and other New England ports, water was purchased from special water boats. "In Gloucester the water is purchased from...a boat called *Aqua Pura*," reported an observer around 1880. "The hold of this boat is one immense tank, filled from the city hydrants, and from it the water is pumped into the barrels of the schooner. Judging from the taste of the water and the untidy appearance of *Aqua Pura* one might think that the waterman was not quite as neat about his water tanks as could be desired." Some found Gloucester water more palateable. "The water taken at Greenland was excellent, as well as that taken from Gloucester," noted one fisherman. In the 1870s and 1880s vessels engaged in the banks trawl-line codfishery departed with just enough water to last till they arrived at Newfoundland, where they could fill the tanks with cheap, pure water.[11]

For washing, seawater sufficed, and this saved the fresh for drinking and cooking. Captain John Francis, who fished in the 1920s, recalled that aboard his vessel a barrel full of fresh water was kept on deck for washwater. "When it rained we tried to catch all the water we could," he said. Maine-coast fisherman Charlie York remembered that if the water supply ran short at sea, they chopped some ice and put it in the tank to melt.[12]

As we saw on deep-water vessels, it was hard to keep water good in any long-term storage, and it tended to get stale or off-flavored. Like sailors, fishermen preferred their tea and coffee exceedingly strong, perhaps because it disguised the taste of off-flavored water.

Cooking Equipment and Dinnerware

Through the nineteenth century, reflecting changes ashore, fishing-schooner cookery progressed from iron pots hung over open fires to the use of agateware on wood or coal stoves. By the turn of the century, a fishing vessel's galley was equipped as well as a modest home ashore, with all the usual cast-iron ware that came with stoves, and other items like tin stew pans, baking pans, bean pots, ladles, dippers, meat forks, molasses cans, tin pie plates, bread knives and boards, pepper boxes, butcher knives, sieves for flour, and even nutmeg graters. Potato mashers appeared, along with rolling pins, duff dishes, and table cloths that were made into dish towels when they wore out. Tableware included dinner and soup plates, and mugs made of tin, agateware, or stoneware, and knives, forks, teaspoons and tablespoons. An account book for the schooner *B.D. Nickerson* even included two large oval dishes, probably for serving food family style.[13]

As on deep-water vessels, the vessel's motion determined what the cook could prepare. To circumvent difficulties, stoves were fitted with iron railings to prevent kettles or pots from sliding off the surface. Of prominent interest on fishing vessels, and, as we will see later, at life-saving stations, were the big coffee and tea pots. "The cook's galley was just aft of the forecastle ladder. He had a big iron cookstove on which there were always two enormous pots, one for tea and one for coffee." Captain John Francis described "a kettle made out of tin and shaped big on the bottom and small on the top...with a handle." This pot sounds like a spoutless coffee pot which would enable the cook to prepare liquid or semi-liquid food like cereals and soup without much slopping.[14]

J. B. Connolly, who sailed on numerous fishing schooners, beginning in the 1890s, described a setup one cook used to prevent spilling: "Here a gang of oilskinned men were rummaging the grub locker...or helping themselves to another cup of coffee from the big coffee pot, which had been lashed to the stove while boiling, and was hanging from a hook in a beam just over the stove, swinging there like a hammock."[15]

Cooks

As food became a more important feature of life aboard New England fishing vessels, so the cook became a more important member of the crew. "The fishermen of former days [1830s] employed, as cook, a boy from twelve to sixteen years, whose pay was almost nothing," wrote Goode in 1880. "On European vessels the practice of having a boy for cook is still universal." During an 1806 fishing trip to Labrador on board the Newburyport schooner *Polly & Sally* John Synot earned $14 a month as cook, compared with others at $30 and the master at $50. Although we are not told John's age, his pay rate and title seem to point to a boy cook. Goode elsewhere explained that, previous to 1850, the fishermen themselves took turns. Either shared duties or a "boy cook" would have been practical on these vessels, which typically had fewer than ten crew members.[16]

By the 1860s, however, changes in fishing technology had caused a dramatic increase in crew size. The development of the purse seine—a vast net—for mackerel fishing required a crew of at least fifteen men, and the adoption of dory fishing, in which one or two men in each dory left the schooner to set their many-hooked lines on the bottom and haul them back, called for a crew of twelve to twenty-two men. To handle the complex job of feeding larger crews, an adult man began to be shipped as cook. From that time on, the cook was "expected to be a skillful cook and a generally capable and reliable man, and to him is usually entrusted the responsible duty of naming the quantity of the provisions which he selects." Under the description "generally capable and reliable" was the

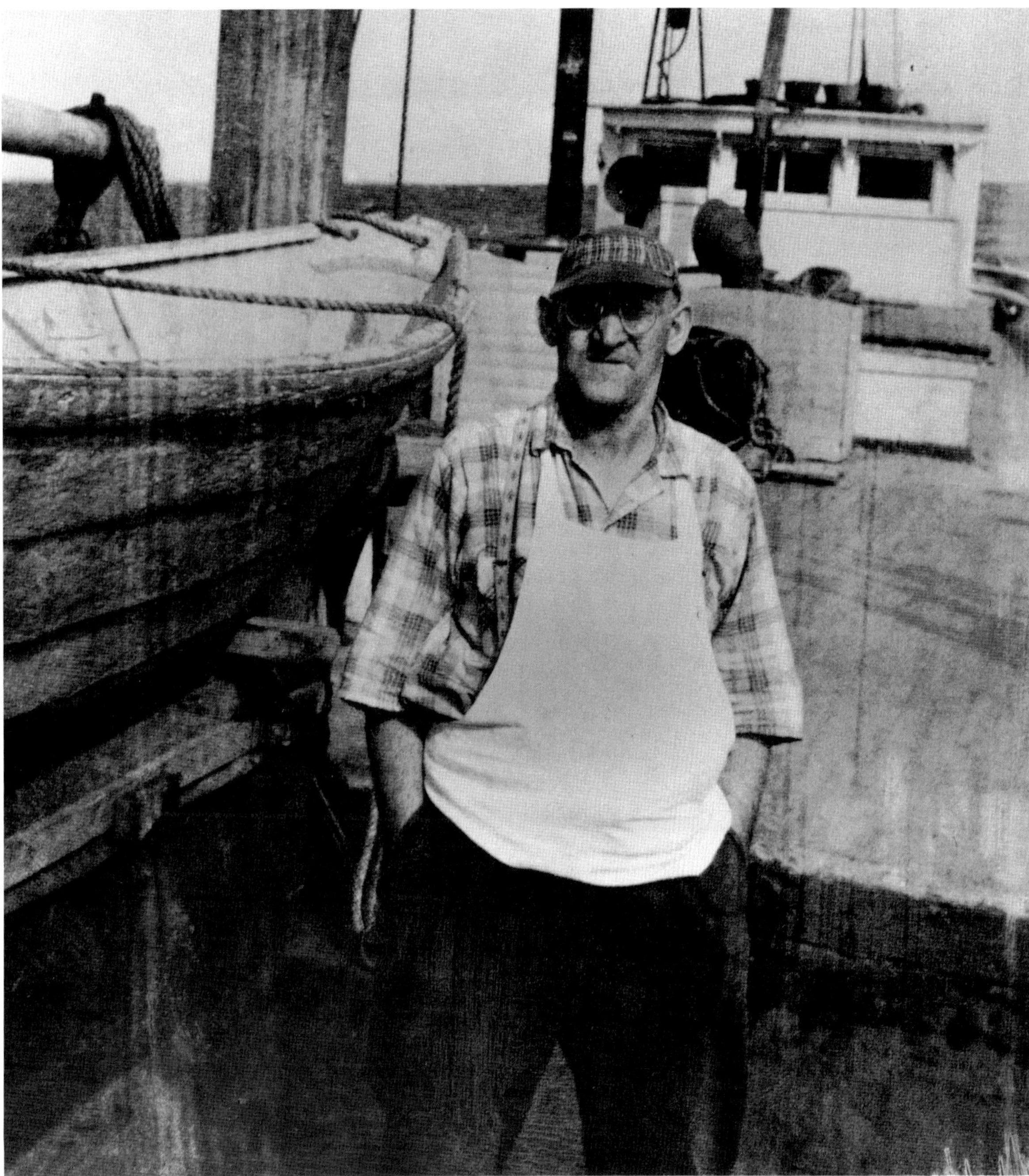

This is Randall Grandy, cook on the L.A. *Dunton* in 1963 when she arrived at Mystic Seaport Museum on her delivery trip from Newfoundland, where she was last owned. Unlike the cooks aboard deep-water vessels, Mr. Grandy and his predecessors in the fishing fleet were considered so important to a vessel that their pay was second only to that of the skipper. [MSM 87-7-11]

expectation that he fish, as well as cook, and if necessary come on deck to assist the skipper with handling the vessel when the men were off in the dories. He generally helped overboard the last dory to be launched and assisted aboard the first to return. On mackerel seiners, the cook frequently sailed the vessel by himself while the crew was off in the seine boat. In addition, he maintained the vessel's running lights and lamps and kept the fo'c'sle clean.[17]

"The cook, or 'Doctor,' as he is called, is a very important personage in more sense than one, for besides supplying the four, and sometimes five meals a day of the crew, he catches fish with the rest," reported Franklin North in 1886. The cook was entitled to half of any fish he caught on a handline or short trawl from the vessel, and, in fresh halibut fisheries at least, was permitted to save and sell for his own benefit the sounds (swim bladders) of hake caught on lines set for halibut and, in the cod fisheries, cod sounds. (The sounds were salted and sold as a source of isinglass used by breweries for clarifying beer.) The cook's perquisites varied but, unlike the other men on board, he was usually entitled to one.[18]

By the 1870s and 1880s, the cook was regarded as "one of the most important men on board; with the single exception of the captain." He was also "the best paid man on the vessel, and is often given a 'lay' [share] that makes his remuneration quite equal to that of the skipper." During nine "big trips" out of Gloucester between

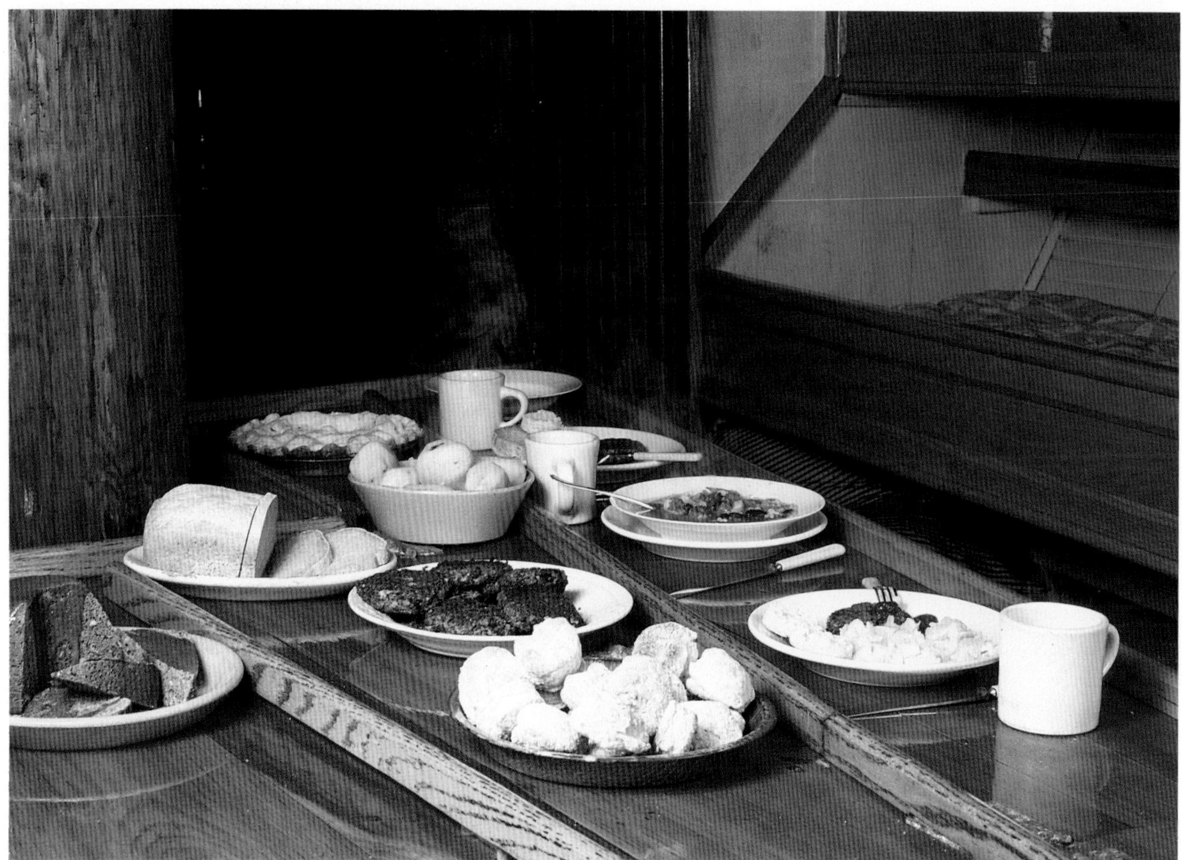

A fisherman's simple but plentiful supper is shown here—a hot Portuguese soup, recipe on page 142, in the bowl at center right, precedes meat cakes made from leftover pot roast. All this is accompanied by boiled potatoes; biscuits, recipe on page 144; and white bread, recipe on page 143. Dessert is a dried-apple pie, recipe on page 146, and gingerbread pudding, recipe on page 144, taken from the logbook of the schooner *William B. Herrick*. Beverages are coffee and tea in ample supply.

1864 and 1871, cooks averaged 20 percent more in pay than the rest of the crew.[19]

According to Wesley G. Pierce, at least some of the time the crew paid the cook's wages, either deducted from their half of the vessel's gross stock, when they went by the system of "share and share alike," or, when they fished "on halves," the cook earned half the money his fish brought, plus his wages.[20]

There seemed to be no particular identification of one race or ethnic group with the cook's job as there was on deep-water vessels. Goode reported that Portuguese fishermen "make good cooks or 'stewards,' and are often found serving in that capacity." While there were frequently black cooks aboard deep-water vessels, Goode reported that there were very few African-American fishermen among the New England fishing fleet, "though occasionally one is found serving as cook on a cod or mackerel schooner." Fishing vessel cooks in the early part of the twentieth century might be Yankee, Portuguese, or Canadian, and were often older men, sometimes experienced fishermen themselves. Captain John Francis shipped his father as cook in the 1920s, and Wesley Pierce went as cook at the age of fifty-seven after a long career of fishing. Barry Fisher, who went to sea very late in the dory-fishing era, remembered an eighty-one-year-old cook, "groaning, creaking, and cranking all...But he never missed a set on deck and he was cooking for thirty men and he baked for thirty men, and he put up his own corned beef and his own...what we used to call...'salt horse,' brisket. And he salted his own fish, he corned his own hake and baked bread and baked pies and baked cakes."[21]

The crew and the cook: The name "doctor" was often applied to a fishing-schooner cook; he was respected but not teased any more than the rest of the crew, unlike deep-water ships of the same period. But like a deep-water cook he could be irascible: "...one took his life in his hands if he disturbed any of Manuel's cooking or took any food other than that in the cuddy," which contained food specifically for crew snacks. The cook was clearly in charge of his domain. He and part of the crew shared the fo'c'sle; the skipper and the rest of the crew shared the cabin aft. When the men were at leisure, the fo'c'sle could get crowded. One account describes the cook chasing everyone back to the cabin which its inhabitants had just cleaned: "cabin is looking fit for gentlemen when down pitches the whole forehold, druv out by cookie." And Barry Fisher remembered: "The cooks ran the fo'c'sle. The skipper wouldn't say anything to a cook in the fo'c'sle. He wouldn't tell him to do anything or give any orders to him. The cook was boss of the fo'c'sle." Fisher also recalled the small ways in which the crew served the cook."You know, the gang would always look and if the slop bucket was full, just as a matter of courtesy you took it up and dumped it and brought it back for him. Or if...he wanted fish he'd just yell up and he says, 'I want some haddock for supper.' Or he'd say, 'I'm going to make a chowder. Get me a couple of haddock.' And you'd clean the haddock and chunk it up for him."[22]

Meeting the crew's expectations meant working very hard, which we will see further evidence of in the menus. "That poor cook he worked like a dog," said Captain Francis of the cooks he remembered. According to Barry Fisher, "A cook's day on one of these things would start at 2 o'clock in the morning, in the wintertime. It would start at *midnight* in the summer. And he baked every morning. One day he'd bake bread and the next day he'd bake his pastry." Maxon Langworthy of Noank, Connecticut, who fished with this father in the first quarter of this century, said "It was hard to get a good cook; it's a tough job."[23]

"If you had a slack cook, poor cook, or an unclean cook, he went ashore," recalled fisherman Elroy Johnson of Bailey Island, Maine. Wesley Pierce, who served as cook in the mid-1920s, observed that, "A cook who understands his business and knows how to cook well, can set a fine table. The fishermen expect it and if you are unable to give it to them, the 'Old Man' [skipper] will 'turn you ashore' and 'ship a new cook.' "[24]

Provisioning and Storage

The selection and storage of a fishing schooner's provisions depended on voyage duration, crew size, and the fishery it was engaged in. For example, salt fishing trips meant fresh meat for only the first few days out; when the fish were to be iced, fresh meat would keep longer. Another characteristic of fishing schooners was the practice of dividing the costs of provisioning between the "vessel" (its owners) and the fishermen, though the proportion borne by each shifted as the nineteenth century progressed into the twentieth, and varied among ports and fisheries.

"Great generals" and "small generals": The vessel owners bought the "great generals" and the crew paid for "small generals." Great generals consisted of the equipment needed for sailing a vessel and fishing from it: in the early days items like tubs, barrels, hardware, and later, ice, bait, wood, coal, wharfage, towage, and fishing lines.[25]

The small generals were the provisions. Provision lists for fishing vessels in the nineteenth century are comparable to the lists of goods carried for the cabin on deep-water vessels. In the early days, the crew paid for nearly all food consumed on board. During the first decades of the twentieth century the fishermen's lay systems had shifted so that the food cost was covered by the ownership; but in many instances the fishermen's share of the vessel's total stock (gross income) was calculated after the food bill was subtracted, so in a sense the men traded income for food.

Early nineteenth-century small generals: As an example of the kinds of provisions taken aboard early in the century, we can look at the small generals purchased in March of 1818 for the schooner *Betsy*: pork, beef, beans, rice, coffee, tea, flour, molasses, rum, chocolate, pepper, butter, pearlash (a leavening agent similar to baking soda) potatoes, vinegar, and meal (probably Indian corn meal). In June of the same year they stocked up again, quite possibly for a longer voyage, supplementing the basic provision list with navy bread (hardtack), and additional pork and beef.[26]

Pierce reported that, "In the old days (1830-1850) when Yankee fishermen went to Chaleur Bay and the Labrador coast after cod and mackerel (mostly in pinkys), the men lived very simply, and their diet was chiefly fish of some kind. Often they had fish three times a day...They carried hardtack for a bread supply...some salt pork, potatoes, Indian cornmeal, table salt, and molasses. They had no meat, sugar, or butter."[27] While such simple provisions were not universal, this description does emphasize the change in the fishing diet during the nineteenth century.

In the last half of the nineteenth century and into the twentieth the variety at mealtime aboard New England's fishing vessels increased quite a bit. The simpler fare of the early half of the century continued on vessels from the Canadian maritimes and some Maine vessels. But prosperity came to southern New England fishing ports like Gloucester, Marblehead, Boston, and Provincetown, and even smaller ones like Noank, Connecticut, and with prosperity came expectations of better grub. In Goode's description of the sailor-fishermen of New England, the report was that the changes were made slowly: "the Marblehead and Beverly fishermen began the innovations by carrying extra supplies of provisions, the property of individual members of the crew. Sometimes every man would have his own butter tub and can of sugar on board, and ketchup might be found on the table. Gloucester has always taken the lead in improving the food of its fishermen, and, as early as 1850, vessels were fitted out from that port in much the same manner as at the present time."[28] George Brown Goode's present time was the 1880s. Let us take a closer look at what that entailed.

Later nineteenth-century provisioning: "In the sixties, the owners put on board their vessels plenty of plate beef (salt beef), flour, beans, peas, butter, brown sugar, and some vegetables," claimed Pierce. But improvements followed quickly, and by the 1880s "a barrel of granulated sugar came aboard with evaporated apples, raisins, some canned goods, condensed milk and eggs." These last two—the condensed milk and eggs—"were extras, paid for by the crew," according to Pierce.[29]

If a vessel went salt fishing—as was most likely through the 1880s—it carried no ice that could also be used for preserving meat. But the Boston and Gloucester vessels going fresh fishing did, and, according to Pierce, "began to have more or less fresh meat...but the crew had to pay the difference in price between salt and fresh meat."[30]

By the 1880s, in addition to the beans, peas, rice, potatoes, meal, and meats, the provisions included items

Master Cooks of the Fishing Fleet

J. R. MURPHY
Cook, aboard
Schooner Edith Silveira

THERE'S NEVER ANY TROUBLE getting hands to ship aboard a vessel when J. R. Murphy is in charge of the galley.

FRANK JENNISON
Cook, aboard
Schooner Richard J. Noonan

THERE'S ALWAYS A HAPPY CREW with Frank in the galley, and his cooking certainly agrees with his own inner man; look at that "broad" smile.

ARTHUR NAUSS
Cook, aboard
Schooner Ethel B. Penny

GOOD GRUB REQUIRES good stoves says Arthur. He ought to know—he's used enough of 'em.

Household Marine Stoves are Popular among Master Cooks

For Years Household Marine Stoves have been the Standard by which others have been judged.

The step forward in good Ship Stoves made by the

HOUSEHOLD Marine Stoves

has had much to do with their rapid rise in popularity.

MADE IN MASSACHUSETTS

Repairs at 21 Union St. Boston

Truck service between foundry and Boston

Decide on the size you want by 4 o'clock in the afternoon and you are sure to have it by 8 the next morning.

Your dealer will be afforded prompt service from our Boston office.

No boat is too small or too big for the HOUSEHOLD MARINE LINE.

Made and Sold by

White-Warner Co.
TAUNTON, MASS.

Sales Rooms, 21 Union Street, Boston

JOE TAVES
Cook, aboard
Schooner Josephine De Costa

NO MATTER HOW TOUGH the fishing is, when Joe bestirs himself in the galley, the whole ship grins.

I have felt for a long time that insufficient attention has been paid to the many splendid cooks found in the fishing fleets. It gives me pleasure to publish their photographs, month by month, and so to give them a place in fisheries history.
R. E. Warner, Treas., White-Warner Co.

THOMAS FURLONG
Cook, aboard
Schooner Lark

TOM'S GOT A RECORD to be proud of. They say in all his years of cooking he's never yet botched a meal.

like lard, oatmeal, hardtack crackers, cornstarch, baking powder, hops (to be used in making yeast for the fresh bread baked aboard), brown sugar, condensed milk, onions, dried apples, dried peas, lemon essence, raisins, mustard, cloves, ginger, cassia, sage, and nutmegs.[31]

The quality of the food was generally very good. In testimony before a Senate committee in 1886, William H. Jordan, the owner of five Gloucester fishing vessels, declared: "The quality is good; the quality of the flour is best; as for the sugar we sometimes send white, but more frequently high grade yellow. The molasses is of good quality, not the best always; and the butter is of good quality...Pork is of the best quality; we send mostly clear pork, and pork shoulders; and the very best grade of plate beef we can buy; we also send pig's feet and tripe somewhat....Pure coffee and a nice quality of tea that sells for about 40 to 45 cents a pound. Strictly pure coffee and extracts and spices of all kinds."[32] If the men had any reason to complain about the fare it was that there was no fresh produce.

In the twentieth century: By 1910, fishing-schooner cooks had begun to order even more fresh meat for roasts, steaks, stews, and corned beef, cabbage, pickles, bacon, hams, cheese, eggs, sauerkraut, and turnips. They added more canned foods, including string beans, blueberries, green peas, peaches, and tomatoes in addition to whatever fruit and root vegetables would travel well. Evaporated milk replaced the sweetened condensed milk and prepared foods like condiments and packaged puddings and cereals made their appearance.[33]

When Pierce cooked in 1926, he questioned the skipper about how he should fit out: "'Skipper, I should like to order some fruit for the trip, a few bananas, oranges, and grapefruit, if you are willing.' He turned to me and said: 'Cook, get anything you want.' "[34]

Food storage: In the early nineteenth century, salt meat, flour, molasses, and other large stores were kept in the barrels they came in. Barrels continued in use, of course, but eventually only to hold bulky supplies like crackers. Canned goods were stashed in lockers; and on fishing trips that called for ice meat was kept on ice in the hold. Eventually fishing vessels were equipped with ice chests, though an informal arrangement was described by Captain John Francis: a tin garbage can with ice in the bottom and meat set in with more ice around. Put in the hold, this would maintain a low temperature for "a long while."[35] Generally, the quality of the meat would have been comparable to cabin fare on deep-water vessels, enviable by John Perkins or Charles Abbey's standards.

Mealtimes and Manner of Eating

Mealtimes: As fishing technology changed, meal hours shifted slightly during the nineteenth century and into the twentieth. Captain Gideon Bowley of Provincetown said the order of meals and times on a banks fishing trip in 1828—when the men fished from the rail—was breakfast at 7:30 A.M., dinner at 12, and supper at 6. By the end of the 1800s and into the 1900s—when fishermen had to bait their trawl lines and go off in their dories to set and haul them—the day became longer. Breakfast was served usually around 5 A.M.; dinner was eaten at 11 A.M.; and supper was around 4 P.M. "Lunches" or "mug-ups," eaten anytime between the regular meals, were interspersed between activities. "It was a fixed habit with the men to proceed below to 'mug-up' the instant they came in from a trawl or set."[36] Sometimes, on the other hand, meals were delayed until a particular chore was done.

The fishermen's daily schedule varied depending on the fishing they were engaged in, but here is one example of the day's rhythm when dory fishermen were trawl fishing in summer on the banks. The crew got up at daylight, ate breakfast, and lowered to haul the trawls. When they arrived back at the vessel, around 8 AM, they mugged-up, then began to clean the freshly caught fish and salt them down. When that chore was done, they ate dinner, then baited the trawls. Supper was served, then the fishermen set the trawls again, and mugged-up when they returned, usually by sunset. A watch was set overnight. On days when high winds prevented the men from lowering the dories, mealtimes were more similar to home.[37]

This was a leisurely pace compared to vessels engaged in market fishing where getting a full load of fish caught, dressed, and on ice as quickly as possible was imperative. Frederick Wallace described the relentless pace fishermen kept on March haddocking trips in the early 1900s. "I was to learn that hours mean nothing to a fisherman. The skipper sets the hour for breakfast and if he's a driver breakfast may be served at any time after midnight." On average they were called for breakfast at 4:00 to 4:30 AM and began a day of "flying sets." With the schooner under sail the fishermen were dropped off in their dories to set the trawls, wait a while, then "haul back" to take the fish off the lines. When they summoned the schooner with a raised oar, the captain and cook—the only men left on board—would bring the vessel alongside the dories while the fishermen pitched the fish aboard. Between his turns as a deckhand, "the cook toiled in his galley preparing food for the men as they came alongside. It was sort of a continuous feeding process. After pitching out their fish, the dorymates would go below, have a hasty snack, and then off in the dories again." But sometimes the men picked up a fresh tub of baited trawl and went directly out again without taking time for a bite.[38]

On one March trip in 1914, Captain Ansel Snow of the *Dorothy Snow* kept the men in the dories all day until 8:00 P.M. Back aboard, they dressed fish until midnight, then baited trawls for the next day. Only the men who quickly finished baiting won time for a catnap. As long as they were on fish, Captain Snow maintained this pace, one spell running for sixty hours. Meals during the day were limited to quick bites, but it was the food that sustained the men.[39]

Mealtimes on mackerel seining vessels were more subject to the vagaries of schooling fish. Few mackerel seiners fished at night, so breakfast came reliably after the men turned out in the morning. When a school was spotted, the seiners stuck with it until they had it surrounded or it clearly escaped. Mealtime must have been adjusted to the fishing. According to Wesley Pierce, it was the custom among them to dress and salt all the fish, a chore which had to be done before the easily perishable mackerel began to spoil. "When they got a large school, the crew must work on them day and night, without any sleep, until their fish were well under salt," a process that could

Fishermen's "three p's"—clockwise, pot pies, pancakes, and pudding—also known as smother, joe-floggers, and duff. Definitive recipes exist only for the duff, in this book on page 115. The servings of smother—salt pork and potatoes in gravy—and joe-floggers—pancakes with raisins, similar to drop scones—are the author's interpretations.

take from twenty-four to forty-eight hours.[40] Gallons of coffee consumed in mug-ups must have made it possible.

Manner of eating: Early in the century, the fishermen's manner of cooking and eating paralleled deep-water practice. An account from Captain Chester Marr described mealtime on a Gloucester schooner about 1830: "nor knife or fork unless we carried them ourselves. Each man had a pan and a mug. We had black tea boiled in an iron kettle. We had our food in one tin pan, and each man had a spoon and we'd all sit 'round and eat our victuals out of it."[41]

Later in the century though, and through the 1920s and 1930s, individual place settings were provided for the men: "Every man's place was set with his plate turned up-side-down and a knife, a fork, and a spoon," remembered Barry Fisher. "And a mug on the table for him when he sat down," all of which were of enameled tin or white ironstone ware similar to what was provided for the cabin on deep-water vessels. "There'd be a big pot of soup on the table...and usually the meal was broken in half with two platters of meat....And potatoes and whatever. And you'd just stand up and spoon the food out for yourself and...you always kept the plate in your hand when you were eating soup. Then you'd finish that and wipe it out with bread and then help yourself to your meal and then wipe that out with more bread and put your dessert in it. Then...you always had to carry your dishes to the sink. You'd dump out, in the slop bucket, anything that was left, and put it in the sink for the cook."[42]

The crew was usually divided into two gangs for eating because the mess table wouldn't accommodate the whole group. On some vessels the group was divided into starboard and port messes according to which side their bunk was on. The skipper ate in the first sitting, a modest sign of deference to his responsibilities, and if any preference was given to a crew member, it was according to age, the older men preceding the younger. Robert Merchant, recalling codfishing on the *Thomas S. Gorton*, reported that the skipper's seat was on the after starboard side near the companionway. He said that the gang who ate with the skipper were very likely to be quite civil, but that it was more interesting to eat with the second gang who felt free to express themselves at mealtime, occasionally commenting on how the skipper handled the vessel.[43]

The triangular mess table, with narrow end forward, filled the space between the bunks, and it was hinged to fold–making more room in the fo'c'sle when it was not mealtime. Benches lined the facing edge of the lower bunks. The table had fiddles—dividing bars that Barry Fisher called "keeper rails"—to prevent dishes sliding across or off the table as the vessel heeled. Sometimes, too, especially in later years, tablecloths were used to absorb spills. William Martell said that the cook brought tablecloths with him. In order for the cloths to be used with the fiddles, the cloths were fitted with holes through which spurs on the fiddles went into the table. At the mast end of the table was a little shelf, "and it had your butter dish, and your sugar, and some molasses, salt and pepper, ketchup, Worcestershire Sauce, mustard....oh, and canned milk. There was always two or three tins of milk on the table," Barry Fisher explained.[44]

Lunch "to go": Although dory fishermen spent much of the day away from the schooner in their dories, their sustenance then was their own responsibility. "As it is, the cook of a fresh fishermen puts in eighteen to twenty hours a day at full speed," noted James B. Connolly, suggesting why he couldn't make lunches, too. When John Francis fished, the men took firkins with "lunches" they put together *themselves* out of the shack cupboard or from things like apples brought from home. Even then, Francis said there was too little time to eat when dory fishing, so the food in firkins could have been emergency fare in case the dory was separated from the vessel. The rarity of dory lunches was underlined by the report from the *Fishing Gazette* about an exceptional cook on the *Tattler* who made up a lunch box for each dory.[45]

Meals disrupted: Just as on deep-water vessels, heavy weather disturbed meals, but spilled food did not mean that the crew went without as it did on deep-water vessels. Harry Eustis said that if the barometer was 29 and dropping, they didn't eat. As in the whale fishery, the act of fishing might interrupt meals. The most regular meal was dinner at noon; the other meals were "more or less interfered with by fishing," requiring the cook and crew to be flexible about meal times. "When the shoal [of mackerel] is in biting humor no time is lost; meals are hastily eaten or altogether neglected; even the cook sometimes renounces his ladle and sauce-pans, abdicates the galley and joins in the general onslaught" before the school "flashes" out of sight.[46]

Three Squares and Mug-ups

Frederick Wallace described meals through the day on fishing vessels as "a sort of continuous feeding process." The content of daily meals changed during the nineteenth century. Early in the century, each meal was nearly identical but by the later 1800s and early 1900s, at least on some vessels, traditional breakfast foods were served in the morning. Dinner was the main meal, and supper was hearty but might be leftovers or quickly prepared food. The cook concentrated his food preparation in the morning for dinner, and did *his* fishing, or sounds cleaning, after it. As on deep-water vessels, there was sometimes a weekly bill-of-fare rotation. During a 21-day swordfishing trip in 1902 Charlie York reported that "Steve [the cook] laid out a seven day rotation; whatever we had the first Monday, we had every Monday. On Friday it was fresh fish."[47]

Early menus: Marblehead fishermen in the first half of the century reported a bland menu: "The diet, while on the Bank, consisted largely of fish, chiefly halibut, prepared in various ways. Large numbers of birds, principally hags (*Puffinus major*), were eaten. The fishermen relished these birds very much, and since they would be obtained in large quantity they formed an important item in the bill-of-fare....Almost with no exceptions, hard bread was the only kind used, 'soft tack' being rarely cooked. Duff was boiled once a week and 'fat-cake' baked on Sunday, on which day no fishing was done. The fat-cake was a sort of short-cake, without sweetening, composed of flour, water, pork, &c. After being mixed, the dough was spread on one side of a barrel-head and patted down to about one third of an inch in thickness after which it was baked in front of the fire-place." Fat-cake was probably a type of unsweetened dandyfunk.[48]

Captain Chester Marr described life aboard Gloucester vessels at about the same time, the 1830s: "The manner of living on board of the vessels was very simple; the food was mostly fish, no meat at all, and no soft bread; no butter nor sugar." However, he remembered a trip to the Bay of St. Lawrence when a half-barrel of salt pork and a half barrel of salt beef were taken, which, along with molasses, hard bread, rice, potatoes, beans, pepper, and chocolate, were intended to last four months.[49] The small quantity of meat included just enough salt pork to use for chowder-making, and salt beef enough for a once-a-week meal.

These descriptions of Marblehead and Gloucester fishermen's food at sea parallel the following one of New Brunswick farmer/fishermen's fare at home in the first half of the nineteenth century: "He is kind and hospitable in his way; and the visitor who is treated to fresh *smother, duff, and jo-floggers*, may regard himself as a decided favorite." A footnote to this description describes smother, duff, and jo-floggers as "Potpie of seabirds, pudding, and pancakes—the fishermen's three ps."[50] The similarity of early nineteenth-century New England and Canadian Maritime fare and its persistence at sea reveals several things. This was a foodway shared by economically marginal people along the coast; more prosperous people, even those engaged in fishing, may have kept these dishes in their diet but added to them preferred meat along with richer puddings and cakes. When New England and Canadian fishermen sailed together aboard New England vessels in the last half of the nineteenth century, the improved fare of the New Englanders was a striking contrast to the Canadians' regular diet at home or at sea. We will see later that the tolerance of the Canadians for less-good grub could keep low the costs of outfitting their fishing vessels and made their stocks quite competitive with American vessels that provided better food. Canadian fishermen also flocked to New England to live better at their trade in American vessels.

However, Captain Gideon Bowley of Provincetown, Massachusetts, recalled a trip to the Grand Banks in 1828, in the schooner *Plant*, with more generous provisions similar to those of the Boston schooner *Betsy*'s ten years earlier. "The daily routine of meals was as follows: Breakfast at 7:30 A.M. consisting of brown bread, fish chowder, and tea and coffee sweetened with molasses. When there was no fish the chowder was replaced by a dish called 'smotheration' composed of potatoes and salt beef. Dinner at 12. We had sometimes soup, either made of salt beef with rice in it, pea soup or bean soup. Nothing under heaven but boiled beans. Brown bread, boiled potatoes, boiled beef twice a week, Wednesdays and Sundays (when there was

Mystic Seaport's fishing schooner *L.A. Dunton* is shown berthed at Gloucester about 1930. She was designed by Tom McManus, built by Arthur Story, and launched in 1921 as one of the last sailing fishermen to be constructed at a time when the Boston and Gloucester fishing fleets were dominated by motor-powered schooners. [Photograph courtesy of Charlie Sayle]

beef enough). When there was no fish on the table there was something else, such as corned fish [*sic*] and potatoes, or fried fish. Supper at 6: brown bread and the fish or whatever else was leftover from dinner."[51]

Breakfast: Breakfast descriptions from the mid-nineteenth century fisheries are scarcer than dinner accounts, but Charles Nordhoff on an 1850s mackerel trip recalled a "breakfast of coffee, hot cakes, bread and butter, fish, beef, sweet cakes and apple sauce."[52] Meat, hot breads, coffee, preserved fruit of some sort: this was fare similar to what we can imagine the Burrows and Greenman families putting on the table at breakfast, similar in *kind* if not *quantity*.

By the early 1900s, Maxon Langworthy reported that "Breakfast was just the same as any other meal, you know, steak, and pork chops and potatoes." Captain John Francis reported that breakfast was "practically the same every day." Eggs were served daily, sometimes with ham, or a piece of smoked shoulder, beans and bacon, or fish. There was usually a porridge of oatmeal or cream of wheat. Captain Francis's father, who cooked for him, used to make a porridge recognizable as a kind of brewis out of Royal Crown rye lunch crackers: "he used to get a bunch of them...we used to carry them by the barrel—and put warm water, cinnamon, a little sugar and evaporated milk" mixed and cooked together as oatmeal was. Breakfast "was always a hearty meal. You never went in that boat that you didn't have a hearty meal."[53]

Harry Eustis, who cooked aboard numerous Gloucester schooners, including the *L. A. Dunton*, cooked "scouce" for breakfast made like a beef stew but with spare ribs. "Eat two plates of that in the morning and you could stay in the dory all day," he said, claiming a fisherman would be good for handling six tubs of trawl before dinner, and once a man got used to that for breakfast he didn't want anything else. Barry Fisher remembered that "Breakfast was porridge....most fellas put butter and either brown sugar or molasses on it. And then you had eggs every day, and you had potatoes of some kind and you would always have a breakfast bread; French toast or pancakes or fried dough. And you had a breakfast meat; ham or bacon or sausages. Sometimes you had some salt or smoked fish that would be thrown on the table." Fisher also described the breakfast dish called "red flannel hash": "the salt fish, the potatoes, the beets, the fat, the onions, and the pork all thrown in together and fried up. People *liked* that."[54]

Dinner: As elsewhere ashore and at sea in the nineteenth century, dinner, in the middle of the day, was the main meal. Dinner centered on meat, the main distinction on fishing vessels being between fresh and salt meat. Vessels engaged in salt fishing—that is, long trips where the fish were salted for drying later—carried salt meat; vessels engaged in fresh fishing often carried ice for fish preservation, which permitted storage of fresh meat.

In his recollections of a salt halibut trip to Davis Straits on the *Bunker Hill* in 1879, Newton Scudder described the food as "excellent of its kind"—not fresh foods, of course—but "the salt meat could not have been better, and fresh halibut and cod, while the fishing continued, were ever available." There was neither milk or canned vegetables on this trip, and only enough potatoes to last a few days. "A little variety was noticed in the meals on Sunday, for on this day the cook added baked beans and brown bread to the bill of fare. Pea soup was common." "Rice pudding and the famous dish of 'duff' appeared occasionally. Neither were we without our mince pies, for the cook made some very fair ones out of dried apples and salt meat. Sugar, butter, and molasses were wanting only the last two weeks."[55]

"Though beefsteak or other fresh meat is rarely seen after the first few days out," explained Captain J.W. Collins of the salt-banker *Marion* in 1879, "the table is well provided with plenty of good raised bread, cakes, pies, duff &c., and last though not least the finest fish are served up in a manner rarely equaled elsewhere."[56] Fifty years later crews of the schooners still engaged in salt fishing ate well the first few days out, and when the fresh food was gone they turned to salted meat, potatoes, turnips, onions, and baked beans.

Early in the twentieth century, when icing fish was the preferred method of catch preservation, the fishermen enjoyed a lot of fresh meat: "We went heavy on meat, pot roast, roast pork, roast beef, beef stews come on the rough days," Leslie Stanton recalled of fishing in the 1920s. Captain John Francis remembered that "you had fresh meat and then it went into corned beef" as the trip wore on. The fishermen's meal that Francis described was a "hearty man's dinner" consisting of a good soup, a good roast or corned beef and cabbage with potatoes, and cakes, pies, and cupcakes—nicknamed "dory plugs" for their resemblance to the drain plugs in the dories. Leslie Stanton also remembered fresh beef at the beginning of a trip, and eventually corned beef, baked beans, and fish, and also raisins and dried canned apples made into apple pies or apple duff with a lemon sauce to go over it. "It was delicious," he said.[57]

Captain Francis reported that the cooks he knew did not use canned beans, even though they were available, but always prepared and baked their own. Bread, of course, was fresh-baked. Harry Eustis reported making eight to nine loaves of bread a day, and 480 biscuits in a day for a twenty-seven man crew. "Sometimes," he said, "you had to fall back on hardtack." Desserts included rice and tapioca puddings, plum duff, and even Boston cream pie. According to Barry Fisher, "they used to figure that a man...and these were big loaves...a man would eat half a loaf of bread per man per day....When they made bread they would make, generally, thirty loaves at a crack. And that would last two days." Fisher also recalled the desserts. "They made a good rice puddin'....Or they would have...'lad in the bag'....That was the favorite. It was steamed duff pudding. It was steamed in a cheesecloth and had quinces and dates and raisins in it, and then a hard rum sauce that was white....It was a steamed flour pudding with sugar and shortening and...allspice was in it and nutmeg and cinnamon and...rice puddin' was a big favorite. Bread puddin' was a big favorite, and they'd make chocolate/vanilla bread puddin'. And the cakes were generally like pound cakes, or a yellow cake, and they were heavy. They couldn't rise good at sea. They had plenty of dory plugs, muffins, and pies were generally fruit pies."[58]

Fishermen eating fish: As did most people ashore, fishermen preferred meat over fish for dinner. When fishermen ate fish at sea it was because they wanted to save money on provisioning, because they were Catholic or had Catholics aboard, or because they wanted variety in the menu. Fishermen early in the nineteenth century ate quite a lot of fish at sea; it kept food costs low and was an easy way to provision a vessel—fish directly from the water to the cook pot. When they made cod's head chowder they actually used refuse. Later in the century, however, fish-eating varied from vessel to vessel, as it did from household to household ashore.

Canadian vessels had the reputation of provisioning inexpensively, providing fish for part of the fare. Portuguese vessels had a reputation for fish, too, and nicely prepared by all accounts. Retired fisherman Barry Fisher reported that, "If you went on a Portagee boat, the food was different. Portagee boats fed well, too...A lot of fish, 'cuz they were all cheap-skates...I mean you'd have fish at least once a day." Fisher recalled that a cook might talk the crew into cutting out cod cheeks and tongues—actually the tongue muscles under the jaw—so he could corn them in brine for three or four days before frying them. "The batter was corn meal and evaporated milk. And, oh, they were good." Fisher also remembered "crungeons" as a popular accompaniment to salt fish. "You'd chunk up salt pork in pieces about as big as the end of your thumb and you'd throw them in the pan and let them try out," producing the crisp bits of salt pork called scrunchions or, as Fisher said, "crungeons." The fat was then used to fry onions, which the cook served up with the scrunchions to accompany a meal of salt fish, boiled potatoes, and beets.[59]

On vessels crewed by Catholic fishermen, fish was served on Friday, according to Maxon Langworthy. "They [the fishermen] wouldn't eat fish, the only time they would eat fish was Fridays, some of the guys were Catholic, but

they didn't like fish." Robert Merchant reported that they didn't eat much fish, although they might have a small halibut, or eat cheeks and tongues of large fish. But Elroy Johnson recalled that "strange as it may seem, the men might stay up all night handlining to get fresh fish to eat, because they got tired of meat." Even after the men put in a whole day of swordfishing, Johnson said, they would catch enough fresh fish for a nine-man crew to eat before they would stop.[60]

While salt-banking or catching cod or haddock for market, fishing vessels like the *Dunton* were equipped with dories nested on their decks, into which went tubs of baited trawl, and a pair of fishermen—"dory-mates." The dories were lowered over the side when the fishing grounds were reached, and the men rowed away from the vessel to set and haul the trawls. [Painting by Milton Burns for *Scribner's Magazine*, April, 1902, MSM 80-9-208]

Supper: Supper was the third hearty meal of the day. It was similar to dinner: meat, potatoes, bread and biscuits. In fact, it might be made of the leftovers of dinner meat, hashed or made into meatcakes, puddings, pies, cake. Captain Francis described a pudding his father used to make from leftover breakfast cream of wheat: "he would make a pudding out of it at night. He'd add a few eggs and a little flavoring,...Probably a little cornstarch or something. I don't know what he put...but anyway it was good."[61]

In the twentieth century, a good many Portuguese worked in the American fisheries, in their own and on Yankee vessels. Captain Francis himself was from a Portuguese family, and reported that "Even when I was skipper, once in a while I used to go and make soup. If I had an American cook, I'd go make this Portuguese soup. It's kale and red beans." Aboard the *Arthur D. Story*, Willard Boynton recalled "Our cook was a Portuguese named Manuel so there was usually a big pot of delicious soup with cabbage, peppers, onions, and so forth."[62] Compared to other more simply roasted or boiled meats and vegetables, and the fruit pies that Yankees wanted, the soup Portuguese cooks prepared was just about the only ethnically distinct dish a cook could make. The

Portuguese prepare fish differently than Yankees do, but fishing narratives don't reveal whether shipboard fish was in a Portuguese style.

Mug-ups: This fishermen's coffee break was part of the "continuous feeding process." All the leftovers that the cook didn't claim went into the shack locker, and the men could help themselves to that food plus all the coffee or tea they wanted to drink. As on deep-water ships, coffee and tea had to be strong. John F. Leavitt described the coffee on coasting schooners as "stronger than love and blacker than sin."[63]

Robert Merchant, recalling life on the *Thomas Gorton* out of Gloucester around 1905, reported that the tea was started when they left shore and every once in a while the cook would add another handful of tea leaves. Merchant said that Cap'n Billy—Captain William Thomas—used to say that the tea didn't start to get good until they'd been offshore for a week.[64] At the turn of the century, evaporated milk was carried on board to put in tea and coffee. The molasses used to sweeten it early on was replaced by sugar in the late 1800s: at first a cheap grade of sugar called "yellow"—essentially a light brown sugar—then later white sugar.

The word "shack," used here to describe the cupboard where leftovers were kept for snacks, interestingly has the very old meaning of grain fallen from ears available for feeding pigs or poultry.[65] Shack had two other meanings, specific to fishing: one was a catch of undifferentiated fish, another was the bait caught at sea. In other words, shack was a mixed lot, perfectly good bits of food for someone willing to root around for it, which fishermen were more than happy to do.

Henry Osborne, describing mug-ups on board the *Victor* out of Gloucester in the summer of 1879 said, "At evening, when he came on board from setting the trawl, the fisherman invariably went at once to the dish-locker and took from it one of the brown earthen mugs. This he filled from the tea pot, which the cook had left partially full of tea from supper. Then turning to the provision locker, he extracted thence bread, pie, cake or meat, according to his fancy and the state of the larder. From this he made a very enjoyable meal, talking meanwhile with those who were going though the same operations in their turn. This 'mugging-up' was also regularly practiced in the morning after the return from a haul."

Wesley George Pierce reported that on a hand-line dory fishing trip he made in 1884, the shack locker was "kept well filled with bread, butter, milk, sugar, meat, doughnuts, cake and pieces of pie left over from the table." The cook, according to Pierce, "makes his own bread, baking eight loaves a day, makes pies by the dozen, and fries doughnuts, half a bushel at a time."[66] Doughnuts were a perennial favorite and, although accounts of the cook and his domain do not mention it, must have been something a cook could make only in calm weather.

Mug-up descriptions underline how hard fishing-vessel cooks worked. Captain Francis commented, "They'd bake pies. Don't kid yourself, I'm telling you, them old cooks used to bake pies". Charlie York described Steve, the cook on a swordfishing trip in 1902, as a "true glutton for punishment" who made "fresh doughnuts, molasses and sugar cookies regularly," in addition to the raised bread and biscuits customary on fishing vessels.[67] Making cookies to keep up with a crew of hungry fishermen was no small task.

J.B. Connolly portrayed fishermen a little bigger than life, but his description of one captain's prodigious appetite was probably not greatly exaggerated: "from the grub locker he took a thin slice of bread and two thick slices of cold beef. He buried the bread among the beef and leaned against the foremast while he ate." He followed that with a wedge of dried apple pie. On another occasion, same trip, this fellow asked the cook to cut him two generous slabs of blueberry pie which he piled on top of one another to eat. "There, that's what they might call a blueberry pie sandwich ashore."[68]

The Fishermen's Seafaring Dishes

Many seagoing methods of preparing corned beef, smoked shoulders, salt beef, and vegetables were identical to methods used at home or for the cabin of deep-water vessels. For "at home" methods we can look to coastal New England and the Canadian Maritime Provinces, including Newfoundland. For example, one contemporary source for Newfoundland recipes names a boiled salt-meat dinner as "Jiggs dinner," "Newfoundland stew," and "Labrador stew," just as New Englanders named their version "New England boiled dinner." In Newfoundland particularly, there were (and are) traditional dishes that either never found their way to New England or had virtually disappeared from the region by the end of the nineteenth century. Newfoundlanders sailed with the American fishing fleets, and may have brought some of the traditional dishes with them.

Some dishes that we find reference to in fishermen's narratives and descriptions of the industry, however, don't appear elsewhere at sea.

Swanky: The cook might make the men, when they were hand-lining, a bucket of swanky–made of molasses, vinegar, and water.[69] Swanky was seafaring switchel, a beverage made for hayers and field workers ashore. Tart from vinegar, it was thirst-quenching, and the molasses in it supplied quick energy.

Fishermen's scouce: At sea, scouce was a salt-meat stew. Traditional Newfoundland recipes call sometimes for spareribs in scouce instead of salt meat. Winston Tibbo, who sailed on the *L. A. Dunton* in 1934 from Gloucester to Newfoundland, recalled that many Newfoundlanders ate inexpensive salted beef ribs from Chicago, never tasting fresh meat until they were grown, and that on fishing vessels they ate fish. Barry Fisher also remembered that fishermen, many of whom came from Newfoundland and

Nova Scotia, "generally liked things that were salty and smoked." As he reported, "a lot of the cooks corned their own meat. They'd get fresh brisket sent down and way up in the eyes of the fo'c'sle or under the fo'c'sle floorboards they had kegs that they would put the brisket in....And some of them used to brine their own...corn their own spare ribs."[70] Newfoundlanders eating a stew made from salt-meat, on either a fishing or deep-water vessel, would recognize it as a familiar dish from home.

Robert Merchant reported that the cook would make stew and on the first day call it scouce; the second day, he would add more meat and call it "mulligan."[71]

Smother: Smother or smotheration seems to be an early-to-mid-nineteenth-century dish mentioned less frequently in later years on the schooners. It was similar to sea pie, sometimes using potatoes instead of flour pastry to supply the starch. The descriptions of it vary quite a bit: a citation from 1826 says "a sailor's dish of beef and pork smothered with potatoes" while the 1852 reference from a Bay of Fundy fishermen describes it as "a pot pie of seabirds."[72]

Seabird pot pie suggests the Marblehead fishermen's hag-eating custom at sea. The "sailor dish of beef and pork" is reminiscent of Captain Bowley's accounts mentioned earlier of potatoes and salt beef. A Cape Cod cookbook dated 1916 provides what is termed "an old fashioned rule" for "smothered fowl and oysters." The recipe is for a refined dish made of steamed fowl stuffed with oysters and served with cream sauce with more oysters in it—an unlikely version of smother even on a well-found fishing schooner. The same cookbook gives a recipe for "smothered potatoes": potatoes sliced thinly with onion and salt pork, covered with water, and cooked covered—a dish more likely found at sea, though a fishermen's version would have more meat.[73]

Joe floggers: The earliest reference I have found to this familiar-sounding item dates from 1852 and speaks of Joe floggers with an "l." An 1889 citation describes "Joe-Floggers (peculiar pancakes stuffed with plums) for breakfast"—that is, pancakes with raisins in them.[74] Joe-froggers with an "r" simply didn't exist or were not widespread enough in the nineteenth century to be found in imprint or manuscript sources by that name. They seem to be a twentieth-century phenomenon, possibly derived from the fishermen's "floggers."

Chocolate rice: As a treat, particularly in the earlier part of the nineteenth century, chocolate and rice were cooked together in a pudding-like manner. As we saw on deep-water vessels at the same time, instead of using rice as starch with meat in place of potatoes or bread, sea cooks often boiled it and served it with molasses as they did duff and hasty pudding. As Captain Marr reported, "We used to boil our chocolate with rice, in a sort of pudding. I never saw a bit of sugar on vessels for years—nothing but molasses." Captain John Whidden wrote about the banks fisherman *Ceres*, in 1853: "Saturday nights at six o'clock the lines were taken in, and not put out until six o'clock Sunday night. The big kettle was filled two-thirds full of water in which rice was boiled, with chocolate added. It was sweetened with molasses, and imbibed during the evening, hot, as a great treat, the occasion being a gala one, interspersed with story and song."[75]

Special Occasions

Fishermen could arrange to spend significant holidays ashore. Accounts of holiday observances on the fishing grounds are not common; nor are accounts of birthday celebrations or visiting from vessel to vessel as whalers did. Fishermen socialized when they came ashore, however.

George Wasson described mackerel seiners driven ashore by "'spells' of weather and long-drawn 'fog-mulls' " at Isle au Haut, where a fiddler was recruited from one of the vessels, and a contra-dance was organized to which people from all over the island came. Snacks of peanuts, candy, dates, pilot biscuits, slabs of cheese, pickles, and tamarinds were provided and washed down by lemonade or "something more appropriate to the occasion."[76]

Ashore at Newfoundland baiting stations or while taking in ice, fishing crews went visiting or tried to get up a dance. "In accordance with the habit of Newfoundlanders, they enter any house that may seem attractive and talk with folks there about fishing, bait, their trip, etc., try to buy milk or other drinkables, and inquire if a dance can be 'got up' to which girls in town are invited, hire a fiddler, or if none can be found, someone who can make mouth music. Some one calls the steps to the dances and everyone has as good a time as possible."[77]

Home Cooking and Big Appetites

Fishermen expected and routinely got good grub. On fishing vessels there weren't the problems of poor quality, meager quantity, or food conflict common on deep-water vessels. Food's function as fuel was even more apparent among fishermen than deep-water sailors. Poor food as hardship was not part of the folklore of fishing; instead the dangers of fishing in fog and dreadful gales, stories of spectacular catches, and breathtaking races to market distinguished fishermen from other seafarers.

The parallel between the fisherman's and the working-class landsman's meals is very strong and was deliberately so. The fishermen themselves paid for their food out of the vessel's gross earnings and expected to eat as much as they pleased fixed in as familiar a way as possible. Their determination to have good food was demonstrated, for example, by their willingness, described by Pierce, to ante up for canned milk and eggs.[78]

And their appetites were remarkable. Maxon Langworthy took his wife to have dinner aboard a fishing vessel and "she said, 'boy, I never see men eat like that.' They could pack it away." Like other seafarers, fishermen

Here is the *L.A. Dunton* at Mystic Seaport today. Her forecastle has been restored, and can be viewed through a cut-away bulkhead from the fish-pen side of the hold. The galley is equipped with a Shipmate coal stove, the sink and pump are on the port side, and the triangular mess table butts up against the foremast. During the winter months, museum interpreters make big pots of strong coffee, and bake pies and cakes for mug-ups for fellow staff members, filling the foc's'le once again with warmth and good food smells. [MSM 80-9-208]

worked strenuously out of doors, often in cold weather, and quickly burned up calories from doughnuts and blueberry pie. As Captain Francis said, "See these young people, when they start fishing, they're not used to the cold and they'll stand and they'll shove their sleeves up and they're shaking like a cat." Captain Francis's sons went fishing with him for a while, and the captain advised them how to get warm. "I said, get busy and go cut them fish...'I'm cold'—I says, go cut them you won't be cold, and he'd limber up and he'd be all right..."

Captain Francis himself, once able to eat large quantities, struggled later in life with a slowed metabolism. His wife attributed his appetite to the salt water, which was true because when on it he and other men did appetite-building work at the same time they were eating just to keep warm.[79]

Eating large quantities, especially of meat and potatoes, may also have been a fisherman's way to identify himself with his occupation and gender. Entitled to good food and plenty of it, fishermen—especially those for whom it was true that the food on fishing vessels was better than home fare—may have felt obliged to "pack it away" while the packing was good. Meat and potatoes was then, as it is now, distinctly man-pleasing food. Hard-working men in an all-male setting were further distinguished by their lusty appetites and hearty, meaty diet.

Even though the fishermen used some nautical jargon for their food, compared to that of deep-water sailors most of their food was insufficiently different from the menu ashore to warrant its own lingo. From fishermen's foodways at sea we can learn about their foodways ashore, for the food and social setting of meals aboard New England fishing schooners were similar to home.

The contrast of this style of eating, common in the fisheries, to the style of eating on deep-water vessels, is revealing. The fishermen's egalitarian fare was partly a product of the nature of fishing communities and the business. Fishermen were not the exploited and powerless group that sailors very often were. Many owners, skippers, fishermen, and cooks were interrelated, if not by family ties, then by community, especially in the nineteenth century, and this was social reinforcement for the sound business practice and philosophy of feeding well to ensure a good fishing-vessel crew.

The practice of feeding fishermen well continued even when it put disadvantageous economic pressure on vessel

Entitled "Fall Fishing," this wood engraving from *Harper's New Monthly Magazine*, March 1861, shows a crew codfishing with hand lines from the vessel's rail—thirsty work. We may speculate that the black cook on the left is serving up swanky—a kind of seagoing switchel—from the bucket he's holding. A recipe for swanky—water flavored with molasses, ginger and vinegar—is on page 146. [MSM 93-11-38]

owners. In 1886, in testimony to the Senate Committee on Foreign Relations looking into the issue of Canadian frozen fish entering New England markets duty-free, one Gloucester fishing skipper reported, "They [the Canadians] live differently. We get the best there is in the market, in the shape of food of all kinds, to put aboard our vessels, but they go under a different system; they can eat a barrel of herring with a relish that at which our fishermen would turn up their noses. Our outfit costs nearly one half more. They get flour very much cheaper, and they live so differently in every way. We use a barrel of beef every twenty days, and they would take two months in consuming it; they use it only once a day, when we have it on the table all the time. They don't have any luxuries at all."[80]

The counterpoint to that argument was that the good food (along with opportunity to work on well-found vessels, promotion to skippers' slots, and the practice of paying cash) also made the Gloucester and Boston vessel owners competitive employers: they attracted Canadian provincial fishermen to work on New England vessels at a time when fewer Yankee men wanted the work.

Unlike deep-water vessels, there was virtually no command hierarchy on fishing vessels. "The captain or skipper is the sole officer, and, except when he has some order to give in relation to sailing the vessel or catching fish, he had no special authority over the crew, and the respect with which he is treated by the men is only that which his personal character obtains for him," reported a government investigator in 1880.[81] This fact was reflected in the fishermen's foodways as well; the captain had no different food than the crew.

The Recipes

The recipes that follow would make a fishing-schooner dinner and some extras for the shack locker. Many of these dishes would have been familiar to the Burrows family and to the men in the Life-Saving Service—a solid, simple diet characteristic of working peoples' foodways in the nineteenth century. A couple of the recipes here are also from the logbook of the coasting schooner *William B. Herrick*.

BEEF BAKED OR ROASTED IN THE OVEN

Place the joint in the bottom of a baking-pan, dredge it lightly with pepper; add one teaspoon of salt to one cupful of water, and pour it in the pan. Place it in a very hot oven; baste every ten minutes, lest it should burn. Turn it two or three times, and bake fifteen minutes to every pound. Serve with gravy made the same as for roast beef.

From Mrs. *Rorer's Philadelphia Cook Book,* by Mrs. S. T. Rorer, 1886, page 83

A POT ROAST

Trim off the rough parts of a nice brisket of beef, place it in a kettle over a good fire; brown on one side, then turn and brown on the other; then add one pint of boiling water, cover and cook slowly fifteen minutes to every pound. Add salt when the meat is half done. After the water evaporates add no more....

From Mrs. *Rorer's Philadelphia Cook Book,* 1886, page 84

Here are two possibilities for preparing fresh beef aboard a fishing schooner. Even though Mrs. Rorer was writing in 1886, her roasting instructions included directions for using a tin kitchen, a device you will remember reading about in the chapter on the Buckinghams. Many people continued using them at home in front of fireplaces, but more and more roasting came to mean baking meat in an oven, the only option in a galley stove.

These are perfectly usable instructions and clear enough that an interpretation is not needed.

SOUPA DA COUVAS PORTUGUESA

Take beef shank—1 lb. stew meat—Chourizo or linguica—med.size potato—1 cup red beans either dry or canned in water drained and rinsed—add water to cover—salt to taste and simmer—When meat is tender—take out potato and mash then put back in—add minced onion—a good bunch of kale, washed and chopped fine—1/2 cup rice. Lastly 1 tablespoon pure olive oil.

From Rose Camacho Hirsch, May 1988

Rose Hirsch learned this recipe from her mother, Maria Goulart Camacho, who was born at Fayal, the Azores, in 1901. Mrs. Camacho came to this country in 1918 and settled in Stonington, Connecticut, where she joined the Portuguese community, many of whom fished for a living. She brought with her the ways of cooking she had learned on her home island. Mrs. Hirsch pointed out to me that "every island had its own way of doing things," and that there are many "Portuguese" soups. On the island of St. Miguel, cabbage is used instead of kale. On others, split peas are used for soup. This red bean and kale soup is probably the same sort that Captain Francis and others in the Gloucester fishing fleet would have recognized.

Mrs. Hirsch said that her mother used old-fashioned-style beef soup bones, and picked the meat off herself, but modern cooks may prefer to follow Mrs. Hirsch's advice and get stewing beef. Red beans are also known as kidney beans. If you like "heat" in your soup, you may wish to choose chourizo which is the spicier of the two famous Portuguese sausages—linguica and chourizo. Plan on using a pound of sausage. Mrs. Hirsch routinely substitutes two packages of frozen collards for the kale.

Of course, the soup is better the second day—if any is left over. Here is the recipe in list form for easy reference.

beef shank bones and/or 1 pound stewing beef
1 pound chourizo or linguica sausage

1 medium-sized potato
1 cup cooked kidney beans
1 onion minced
bunch of kale, chopped
1/4 cup rice
salt and pepper
1 tablespoon olive oil

1. Put the beef bones and/or beef, cut into bite-size pieces, sausage (cut up), potato, and beans in a soup kettle, cover with water and simmer till the meat is tender.
2. If you use soup bones, remove the bones, and pick off all the meat and return meat to the pot. Remove the potato, mash it, and return it to the pot.
3. Add the onion, chopped kale, and rice. Cook until the rice is done. Taste and add salt and pepper to taste. Add the olive oil and serve.

WHITE BREAD

To Make the Bread
Ingredients:
Flour, one and a half cupfuls of yeast, lukewarm water, a table-spoonful of lard, a little salt.
Put two quarts of flour into the bread-bowl; sprinkle a little salt over it; add one and a half cupfuls of yeast, and enough lukewarm water to make it a rather soft dough. Set it one side [sic] to rise. In winter, it will take overnight; in summer, about three hours. After it has risen, mix well into it one table-spoonful of lard; then add flour (not too much), and knead it half an hour. The more it is kneaded, the whiter and finer it becomes. Leave this in the bread-bowl for a short time to rise; then make it into loaves. Let it rise again for the third time. Bake.

From *Practical Cooking and Dinner Giving*, by Mrs. Mary F. Henderson, 1882, page 64

This bread is made by setting a sponge (like thirded bread on page 26) using a liquid yeast (see recipe page 25) which is slower-acting than modern dried or cake yeast—as you will see when you try the recipe. A fishing-schooner cook in the nineteenth century would make his own yeast; hops were frequently listed among the provisions and were a common ingredient in yeast-making.

Mrs. Henderson said to "knead it for half an hour," which I do not think is literally necessary, though sometimes it seems like a half hour when you are doing it. Knead it until the dough is smooth and elastic and springs back when you poke it with your finger. The length of time spent will depend more on the flour and your kneading technique than anything else.

The bread is worth the wait during the risings. It has a smooth texture and crunchy crust. Here is an interpretation.

10-11 cups of flour
1 tablespoon salt
1 1/2 cups yeast (see page 25)
2 1/4 cups warm water
1 tablespoon lard or vegetable shortening

1. Set the sponge: mix the yeast and the water, then add salt and 4 cups of flour to make a soft dough or a very thick batter. Set in a warm place.
2. When it has doubled in bulk and has a light appearance, about 4 to 5 hours (if in a warm place), melt the lard, cool it slightly and mix it into the dough; mix in an additional 3-4 cups of flour until the dough is stiff enough to handle.
3. Turn out onto a floured surface and knead, using up to one more cup of flour, until the dough is smooth and elastic. Let rise till doubled (about 2 hours).
4. When doubled, punch it down, knead a bit more, and shape into loaves. Put the loaves into greased

bread pans and set to rise again until doubled (about 2 hours).
5. When the loaves have doubled, bake in a 375° oven for 1 hour, until the loaves are golden and sound hollow when tapped.

Yields 3 loaves.

GINGERBREAD PUDDING

Three and a half cups flour, half a cup butter, one and a half cup milk, one cup molasses, one teaspoon soda. Steam three hours. Sauce.
If condensed milk is used do not put in quite as much molasses.

From the Log of the schooner *William B. Herrick*, ca. 1875

This steamed pudding has the consistency of a dense, moist cake and could have easily been made in the *Herrick*'s galley. The recipe is another example of a manuscript source that omits the obvious seasoning—in this case, ginger—something rarely done by writers of published cookbooks who assumed nothing of the reader.

The note about condensed milk improves the probability that the *Herrick* recipes were actually used at sea. Canned condensed milk was a very common item in the provisioning lists of sailing vessels in the last part of the nineteenth century and would have been the obvious substitute for fresh milk.

The recipe above lists the ingredients clearly, but a recommended procedure for mixing and steaming follows. "Soda" of course means baking soda. A tablespoon of ginger is a good amount; you may also enjoy cinnamon or cloves.

1. Sift together the dry ingredients.
2. Mix together the molasses and milk. Melt the butter and stir into milk and molasses.
3. Add wet ingredients to the dry ingredients and stir all together.
4. Pour into greased pudding basin or mold, cover with a lid of foil loose enough to allow for swelling.
5. Steam three hours. Serve hot or cold with your choice of sauce.

Yields one large pudding.

SODA BISCUITS

1 pint Flour, 2 1/2 spoonsful
Cream Tartar, 1 Soda Salt
milk Peice [sic] of Butter

From an anonymous manuscript recipe fragment, ca. 1855, in the author's possession

...The success of the biscuits depends upon the even distribution of these ingredients...Pour in enough milk to make the dough consistent enough to roll out, mixing it lightly with the ends of the fingers. The quicker it is rolled out, cut, and baked the better will be the biscuits.
The biscuits are cheaper made with cream of tartar and soda than with baking powder...

From *Practical Cooking and Dinner Giving*, by Mrs. Mary F. Henderson, 1882, page 69

Soda or saleratus biscuits were a convenience food of the mid-nineteenth century. Biscuits could be mixed and baked so much more quickly than bread—only minutes from start to finish, especially since many people were using cookstoves, the oven of which could be heated very quickly. Mrs. Beecher, among others, abhorred the rise of biscuit-eating, citing the lack of care that housewives showed by avoiding the effort to make yeasted breads for their families.

Perhaps because biscuits were so simple to make—except for very inexperienced cooks—there were few printed recipes for them, even in the later nineteenth century. The printed recipes that do exist tend to be elaborately detailed, or include other less usual ingredients such as potatoes or graham flour. The following interpretation of the anonymous recipe above produces very light biscuits.

2 cups flour
2 1/2 teaspoons cream of tartar
1 teaspoon baking soda
1/2 teaspoon salt
2 tablespoons butter
3/4 cup milk
Preheat oven to 375°

1. Sift together dry ingredients.
2. Rub butter into the dry ingredients with your fingertips. Add milk about a quarter of a cup at a time, mixing with your hand or a spoon till the dough sticks together.
3. Working quickly, roll dough out on a floured board, cut into rounds, and put on greased baking pan.
4. Bake for about twenty to twenty-five minutes.

Yields twenty 2-inch biscuits.

COTTAGE PUDDING

One cup sugar, one cup milk, two eggs, one pint flour, two teaspoon cream of tartar, one teaspoon soda, butter the size of an egg, little salt. Make and serve with wine Sauce.
Sauce half a cup of sugar piece of butter size of an egg and little wine or nutmeg and extract lemon.

From the logbook of the schooner *William B.Herrick*, 1874-76, Log 713, G.W. Blunt White Library

Few fishermen's narratives specifically recounted eating cottage pudding on board, but it would be barely distinguishable from cake, which was frequently mentioned. Easy and quick to make, it could be frosted or served with a sauce as suggested. In fact, without a sauce it has little character.

Lemon extract—24 bottles of it on the legendary fishing schooner *Columbia*—and nutmeg both appear in provision lists. When I tested this recipe, I made lemon sauce, which I personally prefer over wine sauce, and found this to be a pleasant dessert. It rises nicely, but has a coarse texture. An interpretation follows.

Cottage Pudding
2 cups flour
2 teaspoons cream of tartar
1 teaspoon baking soda
1 cup sugar
1 cup milk
2 eggs
2 tablespoons melted butter
Preheat oven to 400°

1. Sift together dry ingredients, including sugar.
2. Mix together milk, eggs, and butter.
3. Stir wet ingredients into the dry ingredients and stir to blend.
4. Pour into a greased 8x8-inch pan, and bake for 30 minutes, or until a toothpick inserted comes out clean.

Lemon Sauce
1/2 cup sugar
2 tablespoons butter
nutmeg to taste

1/2 teaspoon lemon extract (or grated rind of one lemon)

1. While the pudding is baking, melt the butter and add the sugar to it, cooking over a low flame until the mixture is translucent.
2. Remove from heat and add the nutmeg and lemon extract or rind and mix. Serve over the warm pudding.

Yields 6-8 servings.

DRIED APPLE PIE

Stew the apples soft, turn them into a pan and mash them fine. Add half the peel of a lemon cut fine, or a little grated nutmeg, a sprinkle of salt, molasses or sugar to make them quite sweet. Bake them in a rich paste a little over half an hour. This will be quite as good as fresh fruit.

From *The Complete Domestic Guide*, by Mrs. L.G. Abell, 1853, pages 137-138

You might think that stewed and mashed dried apples cooked even more in a pie shell would be terrible. They aren't. And another nice thing about them is that they do not collapse as fresh apples do, leaving the top crust high and dry.

Because the apples are already cooked, the main object in baking is to get the crust done. If you wish, use the pastry recipe on page 252, rolling it out as the old recipe suggests with additional shortening to create a rich crust—though I doubt that extra step is one the ship's cook would be likely to take. This recipe makes a lemony flavored pie; if you prefer it less lemony, reduce the amount of peel, or just use a tablespoon of juice. A more specific interpretation follows.

3/4 to one pound of dried apples
water
grated peel of 1/2 lemon
1/2 teaspoon nutmeg
1/4 cup molasses or 1/2 cup brown sugar
salt
pastry enough for two 9-inch crusts
Preheat oven to 400°

1. Put the dried apples into a pan and add water until you just see it through the apples. Stew gently till the apples are quite soft. Then mash with the back of a spoon or potato masher.
2. Add the lemon peel, nutmeg, molasses or sugar, and a dash of salt, to the mashed apples and mix. Taste and adjust seasoning if you wish.
3. Fill the crust with apple mixture, top with another crust. Bake at 400° for ten minutes, then reduce oven to 375° and bake an additional twenty minutes, or until the crust is done.

Yields one 9-inch pie.

SWANKY

HARVEST DRINK

Mix with five gallons of good water, half a gallon of molasses, one quart of vinegar, and two ounces of powdered ginger. This will make not only a very pleasant beverage, but one highly invigorating and healthful.

From *Practical American Cookery and Domestic Economy*, by Miss Hall, 1855, page 117

As we observed, swanky was a seagoing switchel, which Miss Hall described as "a harvest drink." Similar in purpose to modern sports drinks, it slakes thirst and provides a bit of sugar energy. Molasses is high in minerals as well.

This recipe yields close to six gallons, which would be about right for a crew of people haying in summer months or a schooner full of handliners. The proportions for roughly a quart and a half are as follows: five cups water, half a cup of molasses, a quarter cup of vinegar, and three teaspoons of ginger.

One of our testers remarked that the swanky "tastes like something that's good for you." You may want to sample it after mixing and add additional water to taste. We liked it best when the water had been doubled.

SOFT MOLASSES COOKIES

1 cup sugar
1 cup melted bacon fat
1 cup molasses
2 tablespoons vinegar
2 tablespoons cold water
2 teaspoons baking soda
quarter teaspoon each of ginger, cloves, cinnamon
4 cups flour
Mix all well together, roll out to 1/4" thick. Bake at 275° for eight to ten minutes.

From Virginia Leavitt (Mrs. John F.), 1988

Virginia Leavitt got this recipe from her husband John's mother Grace, who was born in Norway, Maine, but who lived on the coast near Thomaston where John grew up. It is typical of most Maine soft molasses cookies, even down to the vinegar. Charlie York didn't say what kind of cookie it was that Steve made, but this one would be a good candidate—simple, easy, and the cook could use drippings for shortening.

The ingredient list in Mrs. Leavitt's recipe is clear enough that an interpretation is not needed, but I will elaborate on the process. You may wish to substitute melted vegetable shortening or margarine for the bacon fat, though on fishing schooners they would have used fat or lard. Ovens vary, and you may find that 300° for ten minutes gives you better results; take a taste from your first panful to decide.

Preheat oven to 275°

1. Sift together dry ingredients.
2. Mix together the sugar, melted bacon fat, and molasses. Then add the vinegar and cold water.
3. Stir in dry ingredients. Roll out on a floured board to a quarter of an inch thick, cut in rounds, and place on a greased cookie sheet.
4. Bake for 8-10 minutes. Put on rack to cool.

Yields 5 dozen 2-inch cookies.

COFFEE

We always measured our coffee in a glass that held exactly a quarter of a pound. We poured water into our pot up to a certain mark inside; it made eight mugs. I think the biggest factor was the old blue agate pot that would hold maybe two gallons. It had the essence of coffee in it, like a pipe carries tobacco. Soap never touched it; when it was time to make new coffee, we rinsed it overboard to dispose of the old grounds and some drops of sea water clung to it that helped to give it a flavor. We brought the water to a boil, poured in the coffee, and moved it off the flame. We had a long-handled wooden spoon that we beat it up with for a minute or two. Then we crushed up an egg in the hand and dropped it in, shell and all; that settled the grounds. After settin' for three, four minutes, it was ready to pour.

From *Charlie York: Maine Coast Fisherman*, by Harold B. Clifford, 1974, page 131

This is Charlie's "recipe" for the coffee that he made aboard his fishing boat, the *Fish Hawk*, in the early 1930s at Boothbay, Maine. The coffee was served with canned milk and sugar. The coffee made such an impression on a visiting doctor from New York City that he bet with a friend that it would be the best coffee his friend ever had—and the doctor won the bet.

A quarter of a pound of coffee to two quarts of water is a good proportion, assuming that Charlie's mugs held a standard eight ounces of water. Give this a try the next time you make coffee for a crowd.

The Life-Saving Service: Messroom Meals

Most men in the nineteenth century did not have to cook for themselves. Seafarers in fishing or deep-water merchant and whaling vessels had a cook, hired by the owners, who was considered an essential crew member. When seafarers were home, women in their households—mothers, wives, housekeepers—did the cooking, or they could find meals at a boardinghouse, often kept by women. If these men had left ship in California and headed into the hills to a mining camp, or joined a lumber camp in northern Maine or the western mountains, or if they had decided to try their hand at driving cattle from Texas to Kansas, they would have been provided with a camp cook. But if they went to work for the United States Life-Saving Service in the 1870s, they had to fix their own meals. This chapter investigates how the men of the Life-Saving Service arranged for their subsistence.

The Narragansett Life-Saving Station crew pictured here in 1873 with their breeches buoy cart and Captain Benjamin Macomber, keeper, at left, looked and perhaps felt better prepared to deal with ships breaking up in surf than with preparing the supper shown at left—clockwise: clam fritters, jonnycakes, salt pork and milk gravy, railroad cake, and frosted lemon pie. [MSM 75.449.2]

"The Mess-Room When the Wind is Off Shore," a sketch by Milton Burns from an 1879 *Scribner's Monthly* article about the Life-Saving Service, shows the stove with coffee pot and tea kettle and some laundry hung to dry—signs of domesticity in an all-male establishment. The scene conveys the literal calm before the storm. [Engraving by Milton Burns from *Scribner's Monthly*. [MSM 94-2-15]

When visitors to Mystic Seaport Museum step into the New Shoreham Life-Saving Station, which stood originally on Block Island, the surfboat on its cart, the metal life car, the breeches buoy and cart arrest their attention. The romance of shipwrecks and heroic rescues dominates the history of the Life-Saving Service, and rightfully so. Patrolling beaches during the coldest, stormiest time of year was miserable tedium, punctuated by periods of hazardous work in the worst possible circumstances. It is hard to remember that this building was also home to a crew of men who carried on daily household chores—cooking, cleaning, and making their beds.

The New Shoreham station building, constructed in 1874, is fairly representative of its type for the early period of the Life-Saving Service. This station was in town, on the east side of Block Island now known as Old Harbor. Other stations—for example, the Hull Life-Saving Station in Hull, Massachusetts—were fairly close to town, still others were remote, as were the West Side Station at Block Island and several Cape Cod stations we will mention here.

The Life-Saving Service, born of local volunteerism, became its own branch of government in 1878. The government had been appropriating money since 1871 to build a number of stations, including the New Shoreham facility. On Block Island, Nicholas Ball, a state senator and the station's first keeper, was largely responsible for getting two stations financed there, having campaigned for them since before the Civil War.[1] Eventually, in 1915, the Life-Saving Service was absorbed into the U.S. Revenue Service and both became the United States Coast Guard.

Six to seven surfmen recruited from among local farmer-fishermen [2] lived at the life-saving station. They were hired for their ability with small craft and their knowledge of local waters. At first, the active season for the service was the five to six months from November to early April; later the season was expanded to run from late August to the end of April. Eventually, patrolling the coast for shipwrecks became a year-round job. There were plenty of shipwrecks in the last half of the nineteenth century when schooners carried bulk cargoes that ranged from coal to pineapples up and down the U.S. east coast, and it has been estimated that loss of life from shipwreck on all U.S. coasts was reduced by 80 percent after the lifesavers came on duty.

Most of the men had families nearby. In some cases, the keeper's family lived at the station in their own cottage, an arrangement similar to lighthouse keepers and their families. Like fishermen, these men brought their food habits with them and tried to eat as they did at home. Some worked in the fishing fleet and brought that experience, and similar expectations of grub, to the Life-Saving Service.

At first, the government provided cooking utensils and fuel for each station and expected the men to work out the rest of the details themselves. But the food history of the Life-Saving Service was marked by the change from edibles being provided by crews themselves to being furnished by the government; and from a do-it-yourself approach to putting it in the hands of professionals.

The Kitchen-Messroom

Each station had a messroom and/or kitchen "sparingly furnished" and provided with appropriate equipment.[3] Early stations like New Shoreham's had a combination messroom/kitchen on the first floor in back of the main boat room. In later stations "the first floor [was] divided into four rooms: boat-room, mess-room (also serving as a sitting room for the men), a keeper's room and a storeroom...The more commodious stations have two additional rooms—a spare room and a kitchen," according to Sumner Kimball, a prime mover in establishing the service and a General Superintendent of the Life-Saving Service.[4] The building that succeeded the 1874 New Shoreham station was built in 1888 and, as Kimball described, had a separate kitchen, office for keeper, messroom, and pantry on the main floor.

Station food storage was like food storage at home, except that some stations lacked cellars. At one cellarless station, potatoes were stored in a hole in the dunes.[5] If a station was located close enough to a store that frequent shopping was possible, then the crew did not need much storage space. For more remote stations, supplies for a month or more would be stashed away in barrels and boxes wherever in the station they fit.

Water supplies varied at stations. At some there were wells, but in remote beach sites the water was not always good and the crew had to rely on cisterns filled by rainwater off the station roof. One official of the service reported that "the lack of fresh water on the beaches is one of the hardships of station-life."[6] In other cases, there were both well and cistern, the latter sometimes no more than a rain barrel. Plumbing was sometimes limited to an open drain to a cesspool for gray water.

Cooking and Eating Utensils

Mr. O'Connor, the Assistant Superintendent of the U.S. Life-Saving Service, reported in 1879 that the stations were equipped with stoves, cot-beds, mattresses, blankets, and "utensils for rude housekeeping. The crews find their own provisions."[7] The service provided very simple kitchen kits at first, and gradually made improvements. By the mid-1880s, if the officially allowable inventory was followed to the letter, the crew would be provided with a very complete kitchen and dining set-up.

The cooking utensils list on "Form 9, Inventory of Public Property" from 1873, which was to be completed and submitted by the keeper, reads like a simplified outfit for a fishing schooner. A cook could do basic cooking operations—baking, boiling, broiling, and, depending on the stove's capacity, oven roasting—with the items provided: a tea kettle, coffee pot, iron and/or tin mess cans, a one-gallon sauce pan, gridiron, large iron spoons, carving fork, knives, and tin pans. Tin cups, forks, small iron spoons, and the tin pans mentioned above were useful for eating. Dish washing made use of the dish pans and water buckets.[8]

Missing from this list are frying pans, although the stove surface itself would suffice if the fire were not too fierce—or so the author's father recollects. Amenities like dippers for scooping out soups and stews, which together with boiled dinners were the easiest meals to prepare with this kind of equipment, are also missing. Resourceful surfmen made do. To measure ingredients, drinking cups had to double, as mess cans would for mixing containers. "Form 9" aside, the New Shoreham station was fitted out with a more expansive collection. Bills and vouchers for the station show a copper-bottom boiler, two square cast-iron pots with covers, an iron tea kettle, two iron spiders, a tin dipper, both a one-and a one-and-a-half-gallon sauce pan, three different square sheet-metal pans—shallow, deep, and "middle"—and a dish pan. Coal hods, shovel, and an ash sifter were bought to use with the No. 2 Atlantic Plain Top stove.[9] In addition, the keeper selected two coffee pots, a pair of two-gallon mess pans, added a tin dust pan to housekeeping supplies, and equipped the station with a dozen each of knives, forks, spoons—large and small—and tin plates. The dozen tin cups he ordered had a one-quart capacity, and there were a dozen "tin pans." A butcher's knife and a meat fork—called on the form a "tormentor"—showed an intent to cook large cuts of meat.[10] An inventory of the contents of the building listed in the first logbook of the station fills in some descriptive details: The dozen tin pans were described there as "pie plates"; the tormentor was identified as a "beef tormentor." One of the tin pans was called a tin baker, another was specified as a "dripping" pan. The square cast-iron pots and covers were called "kettles," and the dipper was specified as a water dipper. Already one of the dozen teaspoons had disappeared, for only eleven were counted.[11]

In the next twenty years, the domestic furnishings of the life-saving stations improved substantially. The official annual inventory form provided places for Life-Saving Service keepers to enter the number of either stone-china or tin-ware place settings, glass tumblers, serving dishes of various sizes, tablecloths, and kitchen and dining chairs.[12] This form represented the allowable level of furnishing. Completed inventories from the Peaked Hill Bars and the Pamet River facilities reflected the reality of some stations between 1883 and 1887.

When the Peaked Hills station was outfitted in 1882, they had all the items listed on the new inventory form except a stone-china platter and pitcher, a chopping bowl and knife, and "dining" table and chairs, choosing instead, "kitchen" chairs. Nor did they obtain table cloths.[13]

Pamet River's five-year inventory from 1883 through 1887 shows that they did not have "dining" chairs and table either, but for some reason they never acquired a funnel, griddle, gridiron, butcher knife, meat fork, or baking dishes. The first year of the inventory, 1883, showed a spare collection of utensils: no mixing bowls, soup bowls, coffee mill, pitchers, and for a few years only single pieces of some items later present in multiples.

Over the five years, the station housed a changing population of spoons, stone-china cups, and plates. A pitcher was broken, a coffee pot sprung a leak, the "poor" chopping bowl was replaced. Extra bread pans, dish pans, and plain tin pans, plus a pepper box, were added.[14] It is easy to imagine utensils, dishes, and flatware getting dropped and broken or accidentally thrown out, so that a station might end up with a mongrel collection.

Not all stations were as well set up as these from southern New England. According to Aubrey Reynolds in Lubec, Maine, as late as the 1920s the station was equipped with a wood-burning cookstove, they had "probably only one" pot or pan, which was kept in the closet, and the surfmen "had to bring your own dishes in them days."[15]

Food Supplies at Life-Saving Stations

There were two separate food supplies at each life-saving station: one for the crew and another for shipwreck victims. Destitute and shipwrecked seafarers were sheltered at these stations at government expense as long as they were delayed by the wreck and weather.[16] According to Kimball, the stations would give them "every comfort it affords. They find hot coffee and dry clothing awaiting them, with cots for those who need rest and sleep."[17]

Food for succor: A supply of salt pork, beef, hardtack, corn, baking soda, coffee, and sugar was supposed to be stored for victims, though not all stations always had it on hand. The Pamet River inventory shows none of the above for five years.[18] Sometimes the crew provided food for care of victims out of their own provisions, and were reimbursed by the government.[19] Some stations were assisted by the The Women's National Relief Association.

This group, founded in 1879, assisted the government and life-saving stations in caring for shipwreck victims by providing money to help seamen get transportation home, and also found ways "to care for those sick from exposure or injured by accident."[20] It was they, Kimball reported, who maintained a constant supply of dry clothing. They also furnished home-canned foods and dry foods not supplied by the government. At Pamet River, for example, the Association placed tea, rice, oats, wheat, cocoa shells, "3 jars chicken soup, 2 jars beef soup, brunswick soup 4 jars" and some beef extract, all of which remained unused between 1883 and 1886.

Apparently the Pamet River crew kept some of the ladies' donations in their washboiler. In 1886, the inventory shows that the rice, wheat, cocoa shells, and tea were "expended from the supply chest on account of having been eaten by mice, cover to the wash boiler having been accidentally left off."[21] It was probably just as well that the mice ate the old supplies, which could hardly be expected to last forever, although they were apparently never replaced. The 1887 inventory shows that the same canned soups endured, awaiting a shipwrecked seafarer.

The surfmen's food supply: "The crews find their own provisions," reported Mr. O'Connor blandly in his article in Popular Science Monthly.[22] In some respects this was literally true, for some of the surfmen went fishing and fowling. Records of grocery shopping and meals were all off the official Life-Saving Service record in an otherwise exceptionally well-documented endeavor. For specifics we have to turn to oral histories, descriptions published in popular magazines, and details we can infer from regulations. Combined with what we know about the eating habits of the time and region, we can draw some conclusions about a typical bill of fare.

In the last quarter of the nineteenth century, men in the Life-Saving Service bought their food out of their pay, pooling money to form one fund for food. In 1882, one description reported that the crews bought food "out of their ten dollars a week, which, with the simplest coast fare, leaves them hardly ninety-three cents per day."[23] This is a weekly food expenditure of $3.49 each, equivalent to one-third of their weekly pay.

Later, the men were given a ten-dollar-a-month subsistence allowance,[24] and later still the stations were provisioned from district commissaries. Food for the twentieth-century successors to the New Shoreham station on Block Island came from the mainland, and the station no longer shopped at local stores.[25]

From the 1870s to the 1890s, the men's food supply came from local sources—stores or directly from farmers. The kinds of supplies and frequency of shopping depended on each station's location. The New Shoreham station was in town with both farms and stores nearby, and so the men could easily get fresh food weekly or as needed. The more remote stations, such as some on Cape Cod and Long Island, were provisioned with large quantities of food before the season began. The Fire Island station, for example, took on supplies "by ferry in September or early October before the docks were dismantled."[26] When the Cahoons Hollow station, near Wellfleet, Massachusetts, burned in February 1893 the provisions destroyed included such large quantities as seven barrels of flour, twenty pounds of lard, one hundred pounds of sugar, a bushel each of potatoes, beans, turnips, obviously in storage, and probably representing half or less of what had originally been obtained.[27]

The surfmen were permitted to supplement purchased supplies by fowling and fishing. At New Shoreham, Keeper Nicholas Ball's journal for the winter season 1874-75

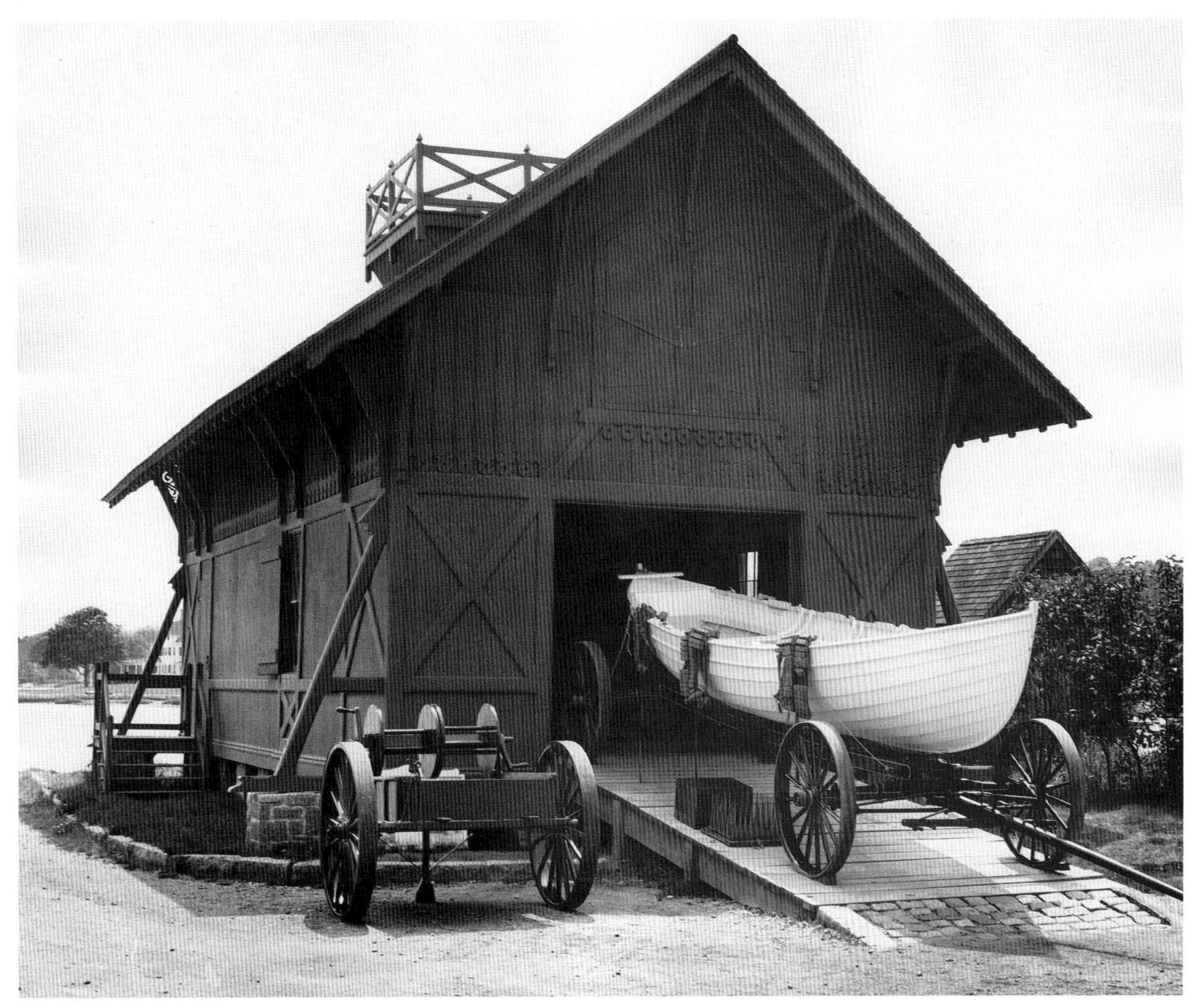

The New Shoreham Life-Saving Station from Old Harbor, Block Island, is restored and open to the public at Mystic Seaport Museum. Pictured here is the boatroom end of the building with the surf boat on the right, and the breeches buoy cart on the left. The crew's living quarters were at the opposite end. At a time when hundreds of coasting schooners trafficked up and down the coast from the West Indies to Canada'a Maritime Provinces, the life-saving stations were a necessity. [MSM 79-6-101]

reported that in one week in late November and early December, two or three surfmen a day went fishing, apparently stocking up, because no further fishing was mentioned.[28] Men in the Long Island stations fished, clammed, oystered, and eeled,[29] as did, in all likelihood, the Cape Codders. Aubrey Reynolds reported that the Lubec, Maine, surfmen would "go pollocking" and salt and dry enough fish to last all winter and have extra to sell.[30]

As the activities of the Life-Saving Service became increasingly regulated, hunting and fishing were officially permitted "in pleasant weather, between sunrise and sunset only."[31] But the surfmen apparently pushed their limits, and as seashore areas near the stations were bought up for leisure use, an amendment to this regulation in 1884 added the phrase "provided they do not trespass on private or club gunning grounds nor violate game laws."

The extra food the crews gathered certainly improved their bill of fare, and meant that they took home more of their ten dollars a week. But there was an enterprising side to their fishing and hunting. Surfmen with spare time could gather enough to sell—in effect a form of double-dipping, since they were paid to be at the station anyway. It created enough of a problem that in 1896 General Superintendent Sumner Kimball issued an order that "no member of a life saving crew shall, during the active season, engage in ferrying, boating, oystering, crabbing, fishing, shooting game, gathering [sea] moss, or in similar employment, for pay or market, in competition with other persons engaged in such business."[32] Nonetheless, Aubrey Reynolds and his fellow crew members picked blueberries for sale in the 1920s, and some crews continued to sell their surpluses surreptitiously.[33]

In the early years of the Life-Saving Service crews were not on duty during the growing season, so gardening was impossible. Later, when the season was expanded, a garden was feasible but depended on the station site. Stations in the middle of sand dunes could not have vegetable gardens. Others did, particularly if the station keeper's family was living nearby,[34] and, like some lighthouse keepers and

families, might keep a pig and a small flock of hens.[35]

The life-saver's "small generals:" Storeable supplies like flour, meals, sugar, lard, butter, smoked, salted, and corned beef and pork, beans, root vegetables—particularly potatoes—cabbage, molasses, vinegar, rice, tapioca, coffee, tea, raisins, rising agents, salt, and pepper yielded endless boiled dinners and biscuits, along with salt-pork-and-milk gravy, and pies or puddings for dessert.[36] Egg, milk, and cheese supplies depended on a station's location. Aubrey Reynolds admitted he "got used to canned milk," but a good many fishermen would already have been used to it.[37]

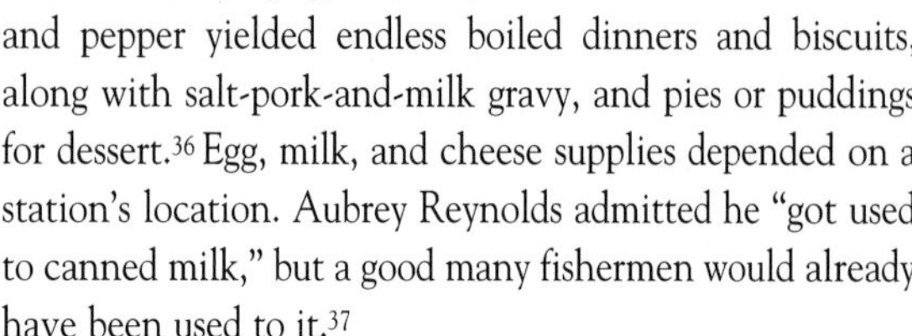

In at least one instance, the crew supplied extra food for themselves. When the government settled with the men at Cahoons Hollow after the fire, such items as fresh meat, hams, maple syrup, preserves, canned meat, spices, apples, various extracts, and canned preserves, plus extras of coffee, tea, rice, eggs, and rising agents were compensated. These were "articles which appear to have been kept at the station from choice and for personal convenience," apparently to vary and improve the regular diet. Given that many of these men had worked on fishing vessels, we can surmise that the shipboard share-and-share-alike ethic held for life on the beach too. A list like this made possible pancakes, ham and eggs, apple pie, and added spice to cakes or cookies.

The Meals of the Day

Most stations held to a watch system so that patrols came and went regularly. The crew performed certain drills on certain days, and routinely overhauled and checked out equipment. Saturday was cleaning day. The times of meals set at the discretion of the keeper revolved around the watch.[38] The station's daily meals were very similar in order and times to those elsewhere alongshore in the last quarter of the nineteenth century.

Breakfast, the first meal of the day, was served anytime from 6:30 A.M. to 7 A.M. Dinner, between 11 A.M.and 12 noon, was the main meal of the day.[39] Supper could be served as early as 4 P.M.[40]

If the keeper was married and his family lived at the station, he ate with his family; otherwise everyone ate together. In addition to the regular run of meals, a big pot of coffee was always kept on hand, just as on the fishing schooners. Specific menus from the Life-Saving Service are scarce. Period descriptions of the service and surfmen's recorded remembrances focused on wrecks, rescues, and the life-saving technology. The few available oral histories and observers' recollections mention mealtimes similar to home menus and schooner fare.

Who Cooked?

Stations handled cooking duties variously. In some, the cook's job was for one day a week, beginning with the dinner dishes and ending with preparation of dinner the next day. In other stations, the cook's tour lasted a whole week. The designated cook also cleaned the kitchen and washed dishes.[41] By the end of the nineteenth century the surfman serving as cook was officially excused from a day of watch during the winter months. The keeper was always excused from cooking.

Surfmen were picked for their strength, courage, and ability with boats, so cooking talent at the station must have been random. In the nineteenth century, except in special situations—like at sea, or on the trail, or in camps—cooking was women's work or in the hands of professional or practiced cooks. As at sea, food was an important part of a surfman's day, and there is no doubt that poor food could ruin the morale of a life-saving crew.

Who knows what led to the mealtime mutiny of January 1889 at the Truro, Massachusetts, Highland Life-Saving Station? Resentment at having to cook? The crew grumbling about the food? A long, boring winter? Two of the men at the station did not want to cook anymore and wanted to be excused from "culinary duties." The rest of the crew objected—as well they might. Each of the remaining fellows would have to cook more often if two of them were out of the rotation. The keeper wrote to the district superintendent, to see if a clear answer could be found in the regulations, and received this reply:

> relating to the proposition of two members of your crew to withdraw from the station mess and thereby seek to be excused from all culinary duties, and the objections of the balance of the crew to such proceeding, [I] would say in answer that while the Government makes no regulation whatever in regard to the subsistence of a Lifesaving Station crew, it provides all utensils and fuel for culinary purposes there the inference is plain that it (the Government) intends that all work relating thereto shall be performed at and within the Station but the method of so doing appears to be left wholly to the discretion of the Station Keeper [42]

His superintendent had tossed this hot potato right back to the keeper. Each station's crew and keeper had to work out kitchen duty themselves. A variety of solutions resulted.

At some stations, even in the twentieth century, cooking work continued to rotate from surfman to surfman.

At other stations, one man who either liked to cook or had a knack for it did the larger part of the job, sometimes paid by other men to pick up their days. In still other stations, the crew pooled money and hired an extra man to do the cooking.

At the turn of the century, at the Old Harbor Station, near Orleans on Cape Cod, the surfmen solved the problem by inviting their wives to the station for their "cook week." Rebecca Smith Ryder was married to Richard Ryder, a surfman at Old Harbor, and she recalled that "Each man had the cook week and they cooked whether they knew how or not!" But the married men could bring their wives down for the week to help out. As Mrs. Ryder remembered: "I made cookies and cake, whatever Richard thought I ought to make. And pies." Her lemon meringue pies were what the keeper's granddaughter remembered her making.

When asked if the wives did most of the cooking, Mrs. Ryder replied: "Oh, no...I wouldn't say that. My goodness no. Not for the number of men there were there you know." The women's role was to help out. That his wife made pastry meant that Richard Ryder at least felt more sure of plain cooking, and asked her to contribute fussier items to the station table. The surfman and his wife shared the station guest room for the week she was on hand to help, so this solution to the cooking problem was possible only in stations where there was an extra room.

There were other solutions. On Block Island, cooking was a job that George Jaixen could continue to do within the Life-Saving Service even when he grew too old to be a surfman, perhaps a solution to an individual and collective problem used at other stations as well.[43] And, over time, more and more crews hired a cook who was not a government employee. It meant less take-home pay for the men, but apparently they thought it was worthwhile. The billet of cook was not an official position at stations until 1949 under the Coast Guard, sixty years too late to help out the Truro keeper and crew.

Re-creating the Foodways of the Life-Savers

So far, we know what cooking utensils the New Shoreham station was equipped with. We know about sources for their fresh food. In order to recreate the New Shoreham life-savers' bills of fare, we need to know what staple foods the station bought, what Block Islanders' food habits and preferences generally were, and what men cooking for themselves felt capable of preparing. Fortunately, in the case of this station, we can come very close to knowing all of it.

The crew of the New Shoreham Life-Saving Station did at least part of their provisioning in 1878 at Lorenzo Littlefield's Store nearby in New Shoreham. We can reconstruct a season's worth of "grocery lists" out of the store's ledger entries.[44] The station's account begins in September 1878 and continues through April 1879. Littlefield's Store was probably not the only source of purchased food, but it appears to be where the crew bought all bulky staples and many other small items. Obviously missing from the account are fresh food: poultry and dairy items, vegetables, and fish.

The men who shopped at Littlefield's were contemporaries of the Burrowses, the Greenmans, and the fishermen described in the chapter about the *L.A. Dunton*, so we know what the regional food habits were, and what men who worked hard in cold weather expected when they gathered for meals. Narratives and descriptions of the Life-Saving Service have sketched in other details. And oral history recollections from Block Island and coastal Rhode Island give us more insights as information from the past and more recent time overlap to create recognizable patterns.

Life-saving service bills of fare: Among the few recollections of meals in the service come these menus: Breakfast was likely to consist of bacon, ham, eggs, bread, and/or pancakes. Dinner was boiled dinners of beef or ham with vegetables, baked or fried fish—haddock, hake, cod, whiting, eels—roasted wild fowl—both ducks and geese—beans, homemade bread, biscuits, chowders of fish or clams, puddings, and cakes. Supper was more of the same, or leftovers. One menu recorded from 1892 included corned beef, potatoes, tomatoes, and bread.[45]

Coastal Rhode Island and Block Island memories: Frances Jaixen Dodge and her sister are the daughters of a life-saving station cook, George Jaixen, who served at Old Harbor, Block Island. In addition, when the women were girls they visited the West Side station where their Uncle William Teal was the station keeper. Their grandparents lived in the house next to the station, and though their Uncle William lived and "messed" at home, the sisters recall what they saw, and heard about, being served at the station in the 1920s.

Mrs. Dodge said that the the men in the Life-Saving Service had pretty much the same fare as at home and on the fishing boats. She remembered seeing pies, cakes, and hot biscuits being made. Chowders were likely fare made on Block Island with and without milk, out of cod, haddock, or pollock and served loaded up with pilot crackers. Boiled dinners from corned beef, ham, and salted cod, nicknamed "Block Island turkey," would be followed with desserts of puddings, such as bread pudding, or cakes. Stewed haddock in cream, served with "cream lunch biscuits," and whole or filleted baked fish were common dinner items, as were baked beans. The cook frequently made jonnycakes and white bread.[46]

Virginia Saunders Allison also remembered jonnycakes. She is the granddaughter of Captain William Franklin Saunders, the first keeper of Quononchontaug Life-Saving Station, and recalls her grandparents' foodways from the 1920s. Her grandfather was a fisherman and farmer, and many of the men at his station were fishermen, too. Mrs. Allison reported that her grandmother had jonnycakes at every meal.[47]

Haddock stewed in cream and served over cream lunch crackers, recipe on page 401.

These recollections describe the "simplest coast fare" that Lamb mentioned in 1882, robust meals that would make use of the fish caught by the men, fowl hunted, and provisions of the kind stored at Cahoons Hollow. In New Shoreham, lists in the Littlefield account book support the probable menu suggested by oral history and written description.

The "grocery lists:" Here is what men from Block Island Life-Saving Station No. 2 stocked up on September 6 and 12, 1878: They provided the station with a barrel each of flour, beef, pork, and an additional 23 pounds of pork. They bought ten gallons of molasses and a keg to put it in; a gallon of vinegar, with a jug; twelve pounds of lard and a pail to store that in. Then they took a bushel of meal, probably Indian, a half bushel of beans, three bushels of corn, sixty-two pounds of milk biscuits, and four pounds of bread. For seasoning, they got a box of salt, a pound of pepper, one ounce of cinnamon, and a bottle of "pepper sos"—probably something like Tabasco. For convenient baking, they purchased "eight papers bred mixin"—probably the leavenings baking soda and cream of tartar, which at that time came in separate papers the cook combined when it was needed. To wash it all down, they bought twenty-five pounds of tea. They bought no coffee.

This basic provision list was maintained during the next seven months, with regular purchases to replenish the flour, molasses, pork, meal, and tea. They added ginger to their spice collection, and obtained a barrel plus several extra pounds of apples.

The menu: Several main dishes appear in this grocery list. The barrels of beef and pork to start the season probably contained salted or smoked meat and provided the makings for boiled dinners; if root vegetables were added to the dinner, they don't appear on the ledger; except for potatoes purchased in January other vegetables were bought directly from farmers. Additional pork and beef bought by the pound may have been fresh to form more main dishes. Salt pork was needed for chowders, and for baked beans and winter succotash, too, made possible by the dried beans and corn purchases.

Salted and smoked beef and salt pork were both made into a little-recorded, but very familiar dish: Fried up, with the rendered fat thickened with flour, and then mixed with milk to make what was called a milk gravy, salted pork and beef, as well as salt fish, were served this way in southern New England over jonnycakes. This was a quick-to-prepare meal, high in calories, just the thing to put under your belt before a long winter's walk along the beach.

In December, the New Shoreham life-savers purchased forty pounds of tripe; they may have eaten some fresh and pickled the rest. Sausage purchased in November and January probably varied the breakfast menu from hash made out of leftover boiled dinners. Sweet potatoes, twenty pounds worth, appear once on the station's store account.

For breads and desserts, cooks relied on the flour, he two spices of choice—cinnamon and ginger, and the leavenings. The only sweetening that appears here is the molasses; in that 1878-79 season, the station bought a total of twenty-eight gallons of it. If we recall that some stations had a molasses pitcher[48], we can surmise that it was used for sweetening hot beverages, as a syrup on pancakes, and as a general sweet sauce for desserts, just as it was used at sea. We do not know if the station ever bought sugar for this season.

A total of twenty-three pounds of lard was consumed that year by the life-savers, in all likelihood as an all-purpose shortening: in biscuits, pie crusts, cookies, to grease pans, to fry meat, doughnuts, fritters, or jonnycakes (unless as mainlanders did, they saved drippings for that purpose from sausage, ham, and pork.)[49] A barrel plus a few additional purchases of apples, together with the flour and lard, could have filled the dozen pie plates many times over.

The occasional large quantities of pilot bread by the pound—for example, a 62-pound purchase in January 1879—which they supplemented by milk biscuits also purchased in large quantities—were useful as a cracker in the chowder or stewed haddock dish Mrs. Dodge described. They could also serve as a breakfast or supper dish with milk, or as a snack.

Another possible interpretation of "bred mixins" bought by the paper frequently through the year, and the "Horsfords" bought by the paper, is that it was a self-rising flour identified by Mrs. Henderson[50] as suitable for fritter making, doughnuts, possibly biscuits. No yeast is mentioned, but if the cook ever made any breads besides biscuits and jonnycakes, the yeast could have been bought locally or made by the cook himself.

Pepper, salt, vinegar, and "pepper sos" for seasoning food at the table might have been augmented by private supplies of preserves that were not recorded.

Given the reputation of the life-savers as big coffee drinkers—and given that the station had two number-eight coffee pots, each capable of brewing two gallons—it is surprising to find no coffee on the list. Over the season, however, the station used thirty-four pounds of tea. If there was coffee here, it seems to have been off the record.

The only remaining item is the whopping nine bushels plus fifty-six pounds of "meal." In all likelihood this was made into jonnycakes, which, as Mrs. Saunders remembered, was served at "every" meal. It could also have become Indian pudding, which would have used up some of the molasses as well.

A few years earlier, in 1874, Nicholas Ball reported in the station journal that various crew members went fishing in November and December.[51] From what we know of life at the stations, going fishing was routine, and we can suppose it happened in the 1878-79 season as well, for at end of the season the New Shoreham crew paid part of their store account with 260 pounds of salt codfish. Perhaps they ate some cod fresh or salted as "Block Island turkey." In 1884, another Block Island station settled their old Littlefield Store account with 48 pounds of salt billet (bluefish).[52]

Since canned milk was not mentioned in the store account, we may surmise that the life-savers made arrangements, as other households did, for deliveries of fresh milk, cream, and possibly cheese.

The Life-Saving Service and its Foodways Evolve

The U.S. Life-Saving Service evolved gradually into an extensive network of stations—and a government bureaucracy to match. From its volunteer humanitarian start, the government built upon the earliest efforts without changing basic patterns. At first surfmen received fairly low pay, further eroded as they provided their own food and cooking. As the service's value became more obvious, proponents published articles, intended at least in part to encourage public support, describing the difficulty and danger of the work and the low pay.[53] The surfmen's early attempts to add to their income and diet brought on regulation, as we saw, with directives on hunting, fishing, trespassing, and competing with locals in various freelance occupations. Perhaps some of the neighbors of these stations felt the Life-Saving Service looked like a soft berth, and that government employees fishing on paid time was just too much to stand.

By hiring their own cook, some life-savers attempted to recreate the cooking arrangements some of them enjoyed on fishing schooners; it cost them but it guaranteed good food. And, as the Highland Life-Saving Station example suggests, it solved the problem, if there was one, of who *had* to cook. Eventually the government followed suit and installed cooks at stations, finally putting food preparation in the hands of professionals.

At other stations the men managed to save themselves some out-of-pocket costs by doing their own cooking, even if they ended up asking for help from their wives. Why more crews did not opt for this raises classic gender issues. It may have been one thing to hunt food, unquestionably a masculine task, but quite another to cook it. In *I Remember Cape Cod*, E. G. Janes described what he thought was a comical situation: a brawny six-foot surfman disclosing the culinary secrets of his apple pie;[54] and Elinor Dewire reported that another Massachusetts surfman took first prize at the Marshfield Fair for his coconut cream pie.[55] Obviously, not all surfmen felt uncomfortable in the kitchen.

The Recipes

The recipes that follow were all within the capability of the surfmen and their cooking. Some of them could have been made with ingredients from Littlefield's Store. Buckwheat cakes were a favorite in New England for breakfast, and you will remember them from the chapter about the Burrows family. Dried-beef gravy and salt-pork gravy were good for breakfast, too, or supper. This was high-calorie food for cold weather, best served over jonnycakes. Boiled corned beef (save the leftovers for breakfast hash) or baked billet were good dinner choices. Clam fritters made a good supper. Desserts included locally popular "railroad cake" and lemon pie.

BUCKWHEAT CAKES

One quart buckwheat flour, one handful Indian meal, four tablespoons yeast, one teaspoon salt, two tablespoons molasses—not syrup, warm water to make a thin batter. Let them rise overnight. If sour in the morning, add soda enough to sweeten the mixture.

From Mrs. *Winslow's Domestic Receipt Book,* 1876, page 4

There are no two ways about it: buckwheat makes a very heavy, even if good-tasting, pancake. Most modern recipes combine buckwheat with regular flour in order to lighten it. In the recipe above, the added Indian meal provides a bit more crunch to the pancakes. Be forewarned: they are thin but have to be baked on a very hot griddle in order to keep them from having gummy interiors.

If you wish, save some of the batter to start another batch. When the batter is new, there is relatively little chance that it will become sour overnight, so adding the soda is a step you probably will not have to take. The interpretation below halves the original recipe.

2 cups buckwheat flour
1 teaspoon salt
1/2 cup white cornmeal
2 tablespoons molasses
1/2 yeast cake
2 cups warm water

1. Dissolve yeast in the warm water.
2. Mix flour, cornmeal, salt together and add warm water and yeast.
3. Stir in molasses and mix well. The batter should be thin; if you need to, add a bit more warm water.
4. Set to rise overnight.
5. In morning, heat griddle and grease it well. Pour batter on and cook till pancakes are dry around edges and bubbles appear on top; turn and bake until done. If you wish, save half a cup as starter for another batch of pancakes.

Yields four servings.

SALT PORK GRAVY

TO FRY PORK.
If too salt, freshen by heating it in water after it is cut in slices. Then pour off the water and fry until done. Take out the pork, and stir a spoonful of flour into the lard, and turn in milk or cream enough to thicken. This makes a more delicate gravy and is very palatable.

From *The Complete Domestic Guide* by Mrs. L.G. Abell, 1853, page 90

Here is another high-carbohydrate dish just right for life-savers to eat before a cold winter beach patrol. This combination of salt pork and a gravy made with milk probably existed long before Mrs. Abell put it in her cookbook. It has endured under various names, the most common one in New England being "salt-pork-and-milk gravy."

This mixture could have been poured over potatoes or served on top of jonnycakes (on Block Island I would guess that there was about an even chance for either, although jonnycakes might have a slight edge over potatoes), in which form it would be good for supper or breakfast. It is delicious, and, for modern sedentary people, deadly. Try it once for the experience, but be sure to use the leanest salt pork you can find. An interpretation follows.

lean salt pork
flour
milk or cream

1. Cut the salt pork in thin slices or cut up in small cubes. Fry it until it is crisp; remove from the pan and drain.
2. Pour off some of the fat, but retain one to two tablespoons, adding about one tablespoonful of flour for every tablespoonful of fat. Add the milk gradually, stirring to mix, and cooking until it thickens.
3. Serve by putting the gravy over potatoes or jonnycakes (recipe below) and garnishing with the pork. Or mix the pork back into the gravy and then pour over the potatoes or jonnycakes.

DRIED-BEEF GRAVY

Dried Beef—Slice the beef as thin as possible; put into a saucepan, cover with cold water, and set over the fire until it slowly comes to a boil; then drain off all the water, add two gills of rich cream, if you have it, or rich milk, adding two tablespoonfuls of butter. If milk is used, wet to a smooth paste or cream a teaspoonful and a half of flour, and stir it in as it comes to a boil, and serve hot.

From *All Around the House* by Mrs. H.W. Beecher, 1878, page 397

This is a sibling recipe to the salt-pork-and-milk gravy recipe above, as nineteenth-century cooks worked with salted beef as they did salt pork. Even into the twentieth century, as they and their neighbors had done for generations, one farm family in North Stonington, Connecticut, kept a piece of dried salted beef hung in their cellar way from which they shaved the slices to be made into dried-beef gravy.[56] Like salt-pork gravy, this dish was also served on top of potatoes or jonnycakes, for breakfast or supper. In chapter sixteen, you will meet the salt fish equivalent of the preceding two recipes.

Nowadays dried beef comes all rolled up in a little glass jar. Get the kind that says it is not pre-formed or chopped. The recipe above is clear enough that an interpretation is not needed. Remember that a gill is equivalent to one-half cup. Four ounces of dried beef to a cup of milk is a good proportion, and will serve two amply. For rich milk you can use half and half.

JONNYCAKES

"With jonnycakes, a lot depends on the meal. Sometimes the meal takes up a lot of water, other times not so much. We'll use two large spoonfuls of meal for each jonnycake. Salt in the meal. The water has to be hotter than anything, and put in enough to make a batter that is loose but not liquid. Some people would stop adding water now and use milk, but I know that it will be harder than a rock in a minute, so I'll dump more water in it. It's a matter of judgment. If after a couple of minutes the batter just stands right up then it is too stiff. You add the milk till you get a loose batter again.

"Some people use sugar which causes it to brown, but I don't. It browns anyway. These jonnycakes get cooked at medium but they start up at hot. You have to cook them a long time. But you can feel safe if you have company coming and they are still on the fire, because they can cook longer and it doesn't hurt them any. Use plenty of grease, bacon dripping are good and put them on by the large spoonful. Flatten them with the spatula when you turn them over. You can turn them over a couple of times. Put the done ones in the oven until they are all cooked then serve them."[57] This description of jonnycake-making comes from Anna North Coit, whom I interviewed in 1988.

Anna Coit remembers watching her Aunt Jettie Boardman make jonnycakes at the Palmer family farm in North Stonington, and still makes her jonnycakes the same way. Jettie, a nickname for Juliet, was born in 1869, and made jonnycakes in the way the Palmer family had always made them, which in southeastern Connecticut was the way Rhode Islanders made them. While not all Rhode Islanders agree on jonnycake making, it is a distinctly regional food, and in the nineteenth century accounted for the use of barrels full of meal ground from flint corn.

Earlier in the century jonnycakes were known here also (and elsewhere in New England) as bannock and were baked on a board in front of a fire as related earlier by Grace Denison Wheeler.

You cannot make true jonnycakes with anything but flint corn meal, usually sold in southeastern New England as "jonnycake corn meal." And there can be no more specific a recipe than the one Anna provided above, because the meals do vary, some requiring more water, others less. About a half cup of cornmeal for two jonnycakes is a good guideline. Use boiling water. Cook them for about fifteen minutes, turning two or three times during the baking.

BOILED CORNED BEEF DINNER

Corned Beef
If dinner be at 12 or 1 o'clock, corned beef should be put on to boil as early as 7 o'clock. If boiled gently for this length of time, it will be very tender, have a fine flavor, and will cut easily and smoothly. Eat with mustard or vinegar. Hood's Sarsaparilla cures indigestion and dyspepsia.

From *Hood's Combined Cook Books* by C.I. Hood & Co., 1875-1885, page 8

The corned beef available today tends to be less salty and moister than it was in the nineteenth century. A good rule of thumb is one hour of simmering for every one pound of beef.

For a classic boiled dinner, follow the steps outlined below. Save the leftovers for hash for a breakfast or supper.

1. Put the corned beef in cold water and bring it up to a gentle simmer, and keep it at a simmer for one hour per pound of beef. Keep it covered with water by adding hot water from a tea kettle.
2. About an hour before serving, add turnips and carrots, peeled and quartered, to the pot.
3. About three quarters of an hour before serving, add peeled onions to the pot. If you like beets with your boiled dinner, put these on to cook whole and unpeeled, if you wish in a separate pan. Skin them just before serving.
4. About half an hour before serving, add peeled and quartered potatoes to the pot.
5. In the last fifteen minutes, add wedges of cabbage.

HASH

Chop the cooked meat and twice as much potatoes, cold, in separate bowls. Put a little water, boiling, and a bit of butter into an iron saucepan, stewpan, or spider; bring to a boil. Then put in the meat and potatoes, well salted and peppered. Add other vegetables, if desired. Let it cook through well, under cover, stirring occasionally, so that the ingredients may be evenly distributed and to keep the bottom from sticking to the pan. When done, it should be not at all watery, nor yet dry, but have sufficient adhesivenes to stand on a well-trimmed and buttered toast, on which it should be served. Hash from cold poultry can be made the same way. In the spring take Hood's Sarsaparilla, to purify and vitalize the blood.

From *Hood's Combined Cook Books* by C.I. Hood & Co., 1875-1885, page 6

Hash formerly was not the crispy fried dish it tends to be today. Leftover meat was often minced or "hashed" and warmed up in gravy, a dish that was sometimes termed "minced meat" (not to be confused with mincemeat, the preserve for pie-filling) or sometimes called "hash." By the last part of the nineteenth century it was customary to serve hash on toast—but I bet this was a refinement for the dining room, and not necessarily the way hash appeared on plates in the messroom of a life-saving station.

Many of the early nineteenth-century cookbooks do not give hash the great detail that the later recipe above does. The Hood cookbooks borrowed heavily from Mrs. Henderson's *Practical Cooking and Dinner Giving* for this hash recipe. In her book, Mrs. Henderson said this about hash: "Notwithstanding this distinguished dish is so much abused, I particularly like it." She went on to describe how one New York family she knew prepared it, using leftovers of large joints "purchased with special reference to this dish," and related that "Cold corned beef is generally considered best."[58]

The amount of potatoes or vegetables in hash is and was up to personal taste. The period cookbooks do not always agree, sometimes recommending half as much potatoes as meat, other times twice as much. Chopping the meat finely could be accomplished in a wooden bowl with a chopping knife, or it could be put through a grinder. Modern people can use a food processor, but must be careful to leave recognizable pieces of meat and vegetable.

The period recipe is clear enough that an interpretation is not needed. Allow about a half cup of chopped meat per serving, with as much of the cooked potatoes or vegetable as you like.

BAKED BLUEFISH

Score the fish down the back, and lay in a dripping pan. Pour over it a cup of hot water in which have been melted two tablespoonfuls of butter. Bake one hour, basting every ten minutes; twice with butter, twice with the gravy, and again twice with butter. Take up the fish and keep hot, while you strain the gravy into a saucepan; thicken with flour; add a teaspoonful of anchovy paste, the juice of half a lemon with a little of the grated peel, pepper and salt. Boil up, pour half over the fish, the rest into a boat. Garnish the fish with eggs, quartered lengthwise, lettuce hearts, and quartered lemons.

From *The Dinner Year Book* by Marion Harland, 1878, page 543

We saw how Block Island life-savers caught billet (bluefish), salted it, and sold it to their store, receiving credit against the station's account for provisions. Whether they ever decided to have some of the fish fresh for dinner is a matter of conjecture. The billet fishery was not a large one at this time, and billet does not appear very commonly at all in period cookbooks. Mrs. Harland's *Dinner Year Book* provided a new dinner menu for every day of the year, and she may have included this less popular fish out of desperation for something different.

Somehow I doubt that a life-saving station cook would have daintily garnished a baked billet with lettuce and wedges of lemon or added anchovy paste and lemon peel to the gravy. I do think they may have baked the fish, basted it with water and butter, and eaten it with a generous serving of potatoes on the side. But Mrs. Harland's ideas are good ones for us to follow. Another proviso is that this is a robust, delicious, oily fish that needs to be only hours out of the ocean to be at its best.

Mrs. Harland's recipe is clear enough that an interpretation is not needed. Because billet are now considered a fine sport fish, there is a good chance you can acquire a whole blue from a fisherman friend (who may even gut it for you). A whole three-to-four-pound billet will bake as above in thirty to forty minutes and serve four to six people. You can test for doneness by seeing whether the flesh flakes apart and the juice runs clear.

CLAM FRITTERS

CLAM FRITTERS (No. 2).
Strain one pint of clams, saving the juice; add to this juice sufficient water to make one pint; mix into it one egg, well beaten, and sufficient prepared flour to make a light batter, also the clams chopped, and some salt. Drop by the spoonful into boiling-hot lard.

From *Practical Cooking and Dinner Giving* by Mrs. Mary F. Henderson, 1882, page 230

One item that appears on the New Shoreham Life-Saving Station grocery list is "1 paper Horsfords." Mrs. Henderson, in her general fritter instructions, noted "The fritters are improved by using prepared flour, Horsford's or Hecker's being especially good."[59] While it would be difficult to know exactly what went into Horsford's brand prepared flour, it was probably similar to modern instant biscuit mixes, which contain leavening and shortening. The life-savers would not have had to dig many clams to make a fine mess of clam fritters.

Because the recipe calls for clam juice instead of milk, these fritters have a nice strong clam flavor. The interpretation below does not require prepared flour, but gives a proportion of flour and baking powder that yields light, crisp fritters. When you buy clams, keep in mind that if you order a pint you will get one generous cup of clams plus a cup of juice. This recipe has a high yield, and you may wish to halve it.

3 1/3 cup flour
2 teaspoons salt
5 teaspoons baking powder
pepper to taste
1 egg
clam juice with water added to make 2 cups
2 cups clams, strained and chopped

1. Put at least 3" shortening in a heavy pan and heat till it is at 365° or a 1" cube of bread will brown in 1 minute.
2. Sift together dry ingredients.
3. In a separate bowl, beat the egg well, and then mix in the clam juice and water.
4. Stir the wet ingredients into the dry ingredients and beat till you have a smooth batter, then mix in the clams and stir enough to distribute them evenly through the batter.
5. Drop the batter by large spoonfuls into the hot fat and cook for about three minutes each, or until they are golden brown all over. Do only a few at a time so that they are not crowded in the pot.
6. Remove and drain on paper towels. Keep finished fritters warm in the oven while you cook the rest.

Yields 30-40 fritters.

RAILROAD CAKE

1 cup of Sugar
3 Eggs
3 tablespoonful of melted butter
1 tea " " Cream tartar
1/2 " " " Soda
1 cup of flour
Flavor to taste

From the manuscript recipe notebook of Fannie Card, Westerly, Rhode Island, 1879

I would love to know why railroad cake is called that—but I don't. Like delicate cake, it was a locally popular dessert. Fannie Card had no fewer than three railroad cake recipes in her receipt book, and Julia Gates included it in hers as well.

One of the three Card recipes recommends "Bake in 3 or 4 thin layers while warm spread with jelly, frost the top layer." Another recipe, from the nineteen teens, recommends a chocolate frosting.[60]

In its ingredient proportions, it appears to be a gènoise-type cake. Because the nineteenth-century recipes are silent on the procedure for mixing it, I have adapted the gènoise mixing process.

1 cup flour
1 teaspoon cream of tartar
1 teaspoon baking soda
3 tablespoons melted butter
1 cup sugar
3 eggs
about 1/2 cup jelly or jam, any flavor
Preheat oven to 350°

1. Grease two round 8" pans and line with waxed paper.
2. Sift together dry ingredients.
3. Beat together sugar and eggs till the mixture is very thick and creamy, and creates soft peaks.
4. Fold in the dry ingredients, and last blend in the melted butter.
5. Divide the batter in the two pans, and bake 25 minutes until the center is firm when touched with finger.

6. Remove from pans and spread with jelly while cakes are still warm. Frost with your choice of icing.
Yields two 8" cakes.

FROSTED LEMON PIES

4 Eggs (Yolks)
2 Lemons
2 Spoons Flour
2 " Melted Butter
9 " White Sugar
1 Cup Milk
Whites of eggs and 3 spoons Sugar for frosting

From the manuscript recipe notebook of Fannie Card, Westerly Rhode Island, 1879

As you can see, this is really a recipe for what is now called lemon meringue pie: a lemon-custard filling with a "frosting" of meringue. Lemon pies seem to have come into fashion in the last half of the nineteenth century.

This recipe says that it is for pies, plural. Many of the lemon pie recipes of this period using these same proportions say that they yield a pie— but I found in testing them that the pie if baked in a standard nine-inch plate is, by our standards, very thin with barely enough frosting to cover. None of the recipes tell us what size pie plate to use. I have no idea whether nineteenth-century lemon pies were supposed to be thin, or whether they were baked in small pie plates.

In the interpretation below I recommend that you use a seven-inch pie plate, or double this recipe for a nine-inch pie plate in order to get a lemon pie that meets modern expectations.

Filling
2 egg yolks
2 tablespoons flour
1/2 cup sugar
1 lemon, grated and juiced
1 tablespoon butter, melted
1/2 cup milk

1. Prepare a baked pie shell.
2. Grate lemon peel, squeeze juice, mix together and set aside.
3. Mix a little of the cold milk with the flour, set aide, then put the rest of the milk on to heat up in a double boiler.
4. Bring milk just to the boiling point, then add flour and milk mixture, stirring constantly to avoid lumps; continue to cook, stirring till mixture has thickened. Remove from heat.
5. Mix well together the yolks and sugar and add to the milk; return to heat and cook, stirring, till mixture has the consistency of custard. Remove from heat.
6. Mix in lemon and juice and pour the custard into the pie shell. Let cool slightly before spreading the meringue frosting.

Frosting
Whites of the eggs
1 1/2 tablespoons sugar
Preheat oven to 375°

1. Make "frosting" by beating whites till stiff, gradually adding sugar.
2. Spread over the cooled custard, making sure that meringue connects with crust. Set in oven for about five minutes to brown slightly.

Yields one 7-inch pie.

Food in Foreign Lands

An important part of traveling is seeing new sights and encountering new things, including food and eating customs. Ships were obliged to stop periodically in ports to take on water and fresh food, familiar and strange. Sailors caught fish and sea mammals for a change from salt beef and pork. Seafarers went ashore and sought meals among local people.

The responses of seafarers to these new experiences is what the next two chapters will investigate. In "Fresh and Exotic Provisions" we will see that seafarers were likely to identify a new food in reference to a familiar one, with a "this tastes like" reaction, even though the analogy was often different from one person to another.

In "Meals Ashore for All Hands" seafarers tell us what was available for a good dinner, and what they liked or didn't. It will also be apparent that a New Englander's idea of what might be edible, and the circumstances under which he or she felt they could eat, were largely defined by their western culture.

Some of these travelers relished new experiences, sampled new foods every time they encountered them, even sought them out, and were completely unfazed by foreign customs. Others responded with distaste, even disgust. Their encounters with fresh and exotic, and with meals ashore from Frisco to Fiji, are other saltwater foodways.

Fresh and Exotic Provisions

"Although we had commenced to feel the lack of fresh provisions, scurvey did not bother us, possibly owing to the regular issue of lime juice, but the constant repetition of salt pork and salt beef, the weevily hard tack, and the abominable slumgullion, a stew made from canned mutton, made us crave something decent to eat," wrote Felix Riesenberg aboard the down-easter A.J. Fuller *on a passage from New York to Hawaii in 1897.*[1]

Seafarers supplemented a vessel's stored provisions with live animals and fowl carried on board and with fresh fare from the sea or from ashore. They purchased and gathered fresh perishables of all sorts at ports en route. They caught and ate fresh fish and sea mammals, sometimes even salting meat and fish on board or pickling and canning fresh fruits and vegetables. And people both fore and aft brought treats from home and exchanged gifts of food at sea with seafarers on other vessels. Sailors, particularly in the fo'c'sle, negotiated among themselves or stole to acquire fresh or otherwise desirable foodstuffs.

As they did with meals ashore, seafarers recorded varying responses to new and exotic foods. In their narratives and journals, some expressed ethnocentric suspicions and sometimes superstitions about strange foods, while others expressed curiosity and a sense of adventure. Naturally enough, when faced with a new food seafarers almost always attempted to think of an analogous food from their own experience. They wondered about edibility and how to prepare strange foods in palatable and familiar ways. In addition, their descriptions of new experiences often reveal how they felt about their everyday fare.

Acquiring Fresh Food

Acquiring fresh food met simultaneously at least three shipboard food needs: a sufficient supply for all hands, fresh fare for nutrition, and variety in the diet. As we have already seen, shipowners were required by law to provide a certain daily ration of basic food and water supplies. It was in the owners' interest to provide enough fresh fare to keep crews healthy and passengers, if any, happy. Everyone, fore and aft, came aboard with food memories and preferences well-established, and shipboard fare was constantly compared to these standards.

Nearly all sea travelers had in common a longing for fresh and familiar foods. Felix Riesenberg described the crew's reaction as fresh food came aboard the *A.J. Fuller* in 1898: "a boatload of fresh provisions, joints of clean, red meat, fresh vegetables, onions, green stuff, bananas and pineapples, and a big basket of real baker's bread, the loaves rich and mellow in the sunlight, like bricks of gold. Our eyes popped out at the sight and smell of this treasure cargo from the shore. Our salt ridden senses were starved for something fresh and clean."[2]

Plenty: There was a difference between having enough food and having enough of some particularly desirable food item. Ships usually began with enough, then resupplied at their destinations. Whalers' voyages were divided into several cruises, interrupted by reprovisioning stops. Much of Hawaii's early business history, for example, is dominated by the development of the provisioning trade because Hawaii was a convenient stopping place for vessels crossing the Pacific to Asia and for whalers cruising the Pacific and Arctic whaling grounds. Mate Charles Chase's journal documents the whaleship *Charles W. Morgan*'s efforts to resupply at Honolulu in November 1866: "got off 25 bblls Flour, & 2000 pounds of Bread and stowed them"; "took on 4 kegs of Sugar"; "Took in 40 Sacks of Potatoes then stowed and hauled off wharf."[3]

But accounts of food brought aboard ships reflect a much greater variety than would merely meet basic needs for salt meat, sea biscuits, and beans. As Riesenberg noted, "Our salt ridden senses were starved for something fresh and clean." Seafarers needed more than just sustenance.

Variety: Besides the nutritional advantages of food, the monotony of most voyages underlined the importance of *variety* in shipboard food. On the whaleship *Tiger* in 1846, bound from Stonington to Hawaii, Mary Brewster wrote: "A plenty of fish in sight caught a few and had them cooked for supper tasted very good though coarse meated anything for a change we are fond of a variety."[4]

Captain Alan Villiers claimed that a diet of salt pork and pea soup ruined a sailor's taste for life but sharpened his appreciation of many plain foods. In that vein, Mary Lawrence wrote in her journal of an 1856-60 whaling voyage that daughter Minnie missed apples more than anything. "She says sometimes she would eat the peelings and core that children at home throw away, even if they were covered in 'antimires.'" Mary herself reported delight in "a nice bushel of home corn" given the *Addison*'s crew by another whaling captain: "We have a mill for grinding corn, so now we can enjoy hasty puddings, johnnycakes, etc." Even the lowly potato was appreciated anew. Riesenberg wrote: "Have you ever been without potatoes for three months? If you have you will know how it feels to crave them." And Richard Henry Dana and his fellow sailors mightily enjoyed fresh onions sent forward from a batch acquired from a passing ship. They refused to have them cooked, "and ate them raw, with our beef and bread. And a glorious treat they were. The freshness and crispness of the raw onion, with the earthy taste, give it great relish to one who has been a long time on salt provisions. We were perfectly ravenous after them."[5]

Going ashore for provisions, and fishing and hunting, relieved monotony of activity as well as diet, as Mrs. Brewster reported: "Got a number of ducks they are good eating and the amusement serves to drive dull care away."[6]

Keeping a crew healthy: Stopping for fresh fare was particularly important before canned food was regularly carried aboard ship. Captain Samuel "Bully" Samuels recorded, for example, that "East Indiamen of all nations stopped at St. Helena for fresh vegetables as a curative for the scurvy, so common among crews on long voyages." Although American ships offered vinegar and sometimes citrus juice, and the English were famous for their lime-juice rations, scurvy still appeared at sea from time to time in the nineteenth century, as it did among landsmen similarly deprived of fresh food. Nineteenth-century New Englanders understood antiscorbutics because of work done by the British during the previous century, which showed citrus to be most

On page 167 is the harbor of Horta, Fayal, in the Azores, a frequent first stop by New England vessels for fresh provisions. [From panorama by Benjamin Russell and Caleb Purrington, New Bedford Whaling Museum] On page 166 is an array of fresh fruits frequently mentioned by seafarers. Above is a South Street, New York City, chandlery, circa 1870. Chandlers were found in major ports the world around. They provided ship captains with small memorandum books listing their wares under headings such as chains and anchors, provisions and cabin stores, cooper's tools, crockery, nautical instruments, tin ware, etc. Captains wishing to purchase items needed only to note the quantities desired next to this pre-printed shopping list. [MSM 40.246]

effective, but also endorsed apple cider, sauerkraut, and fresh vegetables and fruit for curing and preventing scurvy. We now know that vitamin C is the magic ingredient in all of these foods. Without understanding exactly why they worked, sailors themselves developed their own remedies for scurvy. As Riesenberg commented, "Someone, Old Smith, I believe, said that raw potatoes were good for the scurvey. We all tried eating them. Scouse and the Kanakas were the only ones who could stomach the raw tubers." Sixty years earlier, Dana had reported the benefits brought by a load of potatoes and onions that came aboard from another vessel at sea: "The chief use, however, of the fresh provisions was for the men with the scurvey. One of them was able to eat, and he soon brought himself to, by gnawing upon raw potatoes; but the other, by this time, was hardly able to open his mouth." For this man, the cook pounded the potatoes and drained off the liquid, which the sailor drank a teaspoon at a time, washing it over his gums. After a while the sailor showed improvement, and eventually he was able "to eat the raw potatoes and onions pounded to a soft pulp...and in ten

Orange Ambrosia with shreds of fresh coconut, from an 1878 recipe, page 185.

days...so rapid was his recovery, that, from lying helpless and almost hopeless in his berth, he was at the masthead furling a royal."[7]

Fresh fare from ashore: Because of their climates or their locations along the sea-lanes, certain ports became regular stopping places for all kinds of vessels to pick up water and fresh food. The Azores, 1,000 miles east of Portugal, were frequently visited by outward-bound whaleships in preparation for the trip around Cape Horn or the Cape of Good Hope. Aboard the whaler *Ohio* at the Azores, Sallie Smith recorded a typical journal entry: "Fred [Capt. Smith] went ashore in the afternoon and got Something to eat. Beef Chickens, Eggs and a few Potatoes & Oranges" In the Pacific, the list expanded to include bananas, plantains, breadfruit, papayas, pineapples, coconuts, sweet potatoes, and sweet and sour oranges.[8]

Goods were brought to a ship directly by local people or fetched by the crew in the ship's boats from shore, where the crew either gathered provisions in the wild or acquired food in local markets. Local people were often anxious to sell their goods, as Annie Ricketson described. At the Azores, Captain Ricketson ordered a boatload of stuff: "a nice lot of beats, potatoes, pumpkins, onions, and chickens and a lot of eggs and a few water mellons." When the local people delivered them to the ship, one little boy went to Mrs. Ricketson's cabin: "One of them had a little bag with two bunches of white grapes and three apples and he come to my room door and gave them to me and also a large mush mellon....Everyone of them had a basket of fruit, grapes, Apples and water mellons or a goard of milk to traide. My husband took a lot of fruit of all kinds and some milk so I had a real feast for a few days."[9]

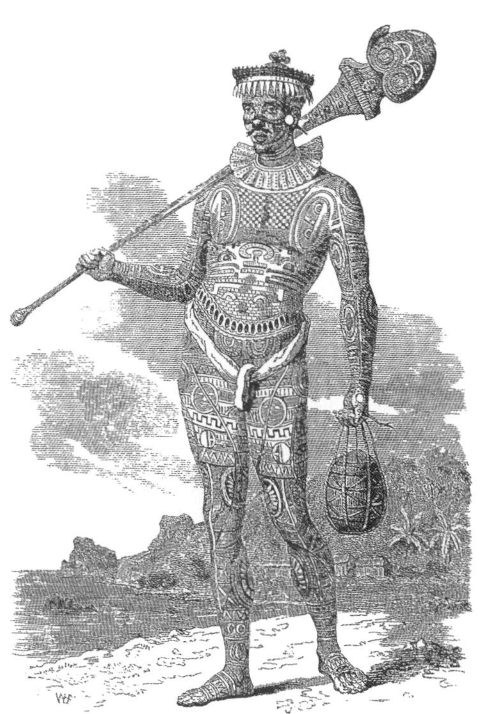

Mary Lawrence enjoyed the fresh and exotic provisions brought aboard her husband's ship in the South Pacific in 1878 by what she described as "frightfully naked tattooed men." [From *The Isles of the Pacific*, 1882]

Other stops, Mrs. Ricketson reported, were more chaotic. Near Madagascar, local people, mostly drunk, came on board the whaleship *A. R. Tucker*, and Mrs. Ricketson bought a straw hat, tamarinds, and lemons, noting, "I was so glad to get out of that place the natives were so noisy on deck and so many of them." Acquiring fresh food brought New England seafarers—and captains' wives—in contact with exotic peoples. When the whaleship *Addison* was at the Marquesas in the Pacific in 1857, Mary Lawrence, like many captain's wives, was alarmed at the approach of a canoe full of "frightfully tattooed naked men." The next day the ship was full of the native men and their goods. "We have had pigs, fowls, coconuts, breadfruit, bananas and pineapples brought off today....What would my friends at home say to see such frightful-looking creatures?"[10]

From the perspective of the South Sea islanders, the chance to trade their produce for exotic goods like cloth and metal tempted them or their leaders to exhaust their own food supplies. As Herman Melville described Tahiti in *Omoo*: "During the breadfruit season they fare better; but, at other times, the demands of shipping exhaust the uncultivated resources of the island; and the lands being mostly owned by the chiefs, the inferior orders have to suffer for their cupidity. Deprived of their nets, many of them would starve."[11]

Crews also went ashore to gather food growing wild. The whaleship *Tiger* stopped at Juan Fernandez off Chile, and, John Perkins reported, "we found wild peach trees loaded with peaches, there were also fig trees, grapevines, wild nasturtium, radishes & quince. The figs, grapes & radishes were not ripe....Took off our shirts & tied up the necks & arms & filled them with peaches & packed them down to the boats...about a hogshead & a half of peaches & a bushel of quinces." Mary Brewster "helped steward make peach pies" after this foray ashore on the island where Alexander Selkirk, the original Robinson Crusoe, was marooned in 1704.[12]

Food gifts and exchanges: In addition to books and newspapers, food was a frequent article of exchange between ships—a gift brought when gamming or in a trade, or sometimes an outright favor if one ship had anything to spare and the other had a need. Local people and friends ashore also sent food gifts to a ship, particularly when a captain's wife and family were aboard. The gifts were often reciprocated.

One of the nicest gifts was fresh meat. Annie Ricketson reported that when the *A.R. Tucker* met the *Benjamin Cummings* on the Indian Ocean whaling grounds Captain Brown and his wife came aboard and "she brought me a peace of fresh pork and a book to read." Along the coast of Lower California in 1859, Mary Lawrence on the *Addison* had a visit from Captain Willis, who brought a piece of fresh pork. A few days later "Captain Molde of the *Antilla* sent a fine pig as present to us this morning, also several tins of preserved meat put up in Germany, a nice present." Another time the Lawrences received a "a couple pounds of green tea, a couple tins of preserved pineapple, and a few shells...we carried him a little pig and gave him a piece of fresh pork." In exchange for a few pickled codfish and a salmon, the Lawrences gave another whaling captain two pigs.[13]

More often the exchanges consisted of fruits, nuts, preserves, and small treats from home. Annie Ricketson wrote that she had received "two kinds of cake and a dish of Bananas put up in a sweet pickle, and a string of eggs" from Captain and Mrs. Allen of the bark *Falcon* in the South Atlantic. Another time she visited an English merchant bark and came away with a can of blueberries, a jar of preserved ginger, and a half-dozen eggs. Mary Brewster received cake and candy from some women passengers on the passing ship *Charles*, and at other times oranges, apples, and a basket of bananas laid down in sugar.[14]

Mary Lawrence often recorded the gifts she and her daughter Minnie received and what she gave in return. Her journal brings us a detailed picture of the kinds of items exchanged between ships. For example, she received a jar of pickles, figs, currant wine, port wine, apples, peaches, a

Treats from home break the mealtime monotony aboard ship—cheese, frosted fruit cake, and sugar gingerbread.

"tin of very nice huckleberries," lozenges (candy), peach jam, flowers, milk, yams, dried bananas, honey, preserved quince, coconuts, almonds, walnuts, filberts, fowl, lemon syrup, cheese, and raisins. She gave figs, apples, eggs, peanuts, oranges, Indian meal, and salt fish, besides the pigs and pork mentioned above.

After a stay at Honolulu, the *Addison* was bound to the Bering Sea and Mary Lawrence noted that besides the sweet and Irish potatoes, onions, pumpkins, bananas, and oranges that they obtained in Hawaii, "Captain Barber sent me a California cheese and a half bushel of figs. Mr. Bigelow presented Minnie with a tin of gingersnaps and gave me two dozen tins of preserved fruits, which with crackers, preserved meats, codfish, fowls, and hogs, beside our common fare—I think will make quite a bill of fare for the season."[15] Food gifts amplified nicely the everyday diet.

Shore to ship: Gifts from ashore to the ship were usually destined for the cabin. At Corvo Island in the Azores, the island's governor's wife sent Annie Ricketson apples, grapes, and a sprig of lavender "which made me think of Home." At Akaroa Harbor, New Zealand, Mary Lawrence received a basket of peaches, and "A boy by the name of Willie Adams...came off today and brought me a basket of apples and peaches, a bouquet of flowers, and a bottle of milk. I gave him in return for his kindness some peanuts, oranges, and a book."[16]

Treats from home: Treats from home offered variety in the diet for both fo'c'sle and cabin. The shipboard ethic of sharing these things was strong, and even if it wasn't there was little or no privacy to eat alone. These foods had to be a preserve or at least something that kept a long time. Occasionally, family and friends at home attempted to send along special food items, but the vagaries of mail and package delivery at sea sometimes ended as Mary Lawrence described: "Found a box on board [the whaleship *William Gifford* during a gam] from Sarah, filled with bottled cherries, originally, and a loaf of cake. The bottles were all broken except two and the contents had penetrated all the reading and the loaf of cake was nothing but powder. Minnie said they had sent me a nice lot of ginger. It was some time before we found out what it was."[17]

In 1851 Ruth Post wrote her husband, Captain Francis Post, and inquired after a package of food: "Do let me know if your butter and cheese and dried fruit turned out well, and your Cake how did that taste like a chip I suppose."Some cakes fared well. As Annie Ricketson recorded, "We had a fruit cake for tea, one that Mother put in for my Husband's Birthday. It was Frosted and trimed very pretty. The men thought it to pretty to cut but not to pretty to eat after it was cut."[18]

As we saw in the chapter about the foodways of deep-water vessels, even the men in the fo'c'sle brought nice things—cheese, preserves—from home or from shore. John Perkins brought along sugar gingerbread. Felix Riesenberg noted that First Mate Zerk of his *A. J. Fuller* was a bit of a bully mate, but had a kindly side which he showed the men by sharing his supply of homemade jams and pickles.[19]

Generally these goods were divided among the group, although Melville described in *Omoo* a tin can of molasses so choice that the narrator "kept it hid away...in the farthest corner of my bunk. Faring as we did, this molasses dropped upon a biscuit was a positive luxury, which I shared with none but the doctor [cook], and then only in private." He claimed this made the molasses even sweeter. But there was a kind of retribution for his selfishness. One night when he tipped the can up to get the last drop, "something besides molasses slipped out. How long it had been there, kind Providence never revealed....The creature certainly died a luscious death."[20]

Ship to ship: Samuel Samuels described a food

exchange between his ship, *Manhattan*, and an English vessel. The *Manhattan* had just left St. Helena, where only a limited supply of fresh stuff was available, and the English vessel "loaded with wine, potatoes, cabbages, and onions...was a perfect godsend to us, as we had not tasted such luxuries in a six months." The English ship sent "potatoes, Spanish onions, a keg of wine, a box of Bass's ale and a cheddar cheese. As I would not be outdone in civilities, and the Englishman's debtor, I sent him in return a pig, a Westphalia ham, two Dutch cheeses, and a case of gin. It was a gala day; the monotony of the voyage was broken by a grand feast."[21]

John Perkins and his shipmates filled their shirts with fresh peaches from the island of Juan Fernandez.

Stealing and dealing for food: The men in the fo'c'sle, generally deprived of all the nice items being shared among ships or procured ashore, had other means for obtaining fresh or desirable foods. At great risk the crew might deliberately break into the ship's supply or lift from opened supplies. Three days out on the *Tiger*, John Perkins reported, "One of our watch managed to steal an exelent [*sic*] codfish & a good cabbage from the hold as well as to tap a barrel of vinegar for which a little quart demijohn was put in requisition & my pepper sauce bottle filled."[22]

When Riesenberg described some of the men eating raw potatoes for scurvy, it was from open supplies that the potatoes were lifted. "They always picked out the best sound potatoes and seemed to relish them; at any rate they robbed the cabin table of a good many messes of selected spuds." When the crew loaded sugar in Honolulu, Riesenberg reported that once in a while a bag broke. "The sugar as it comes from the island refineries is about twice as sweet as the white granulated article. To a crowd accustomed to black jack molasses as a sweetener for their coffee, the sugar was a powerful delicacy, for a time. Soon we became cloyed with the taste, and for weeks after my first gorging of sweets, I took my coffee and tea without it, though we always had a small keg of the stuff on hand forward during the remainder of the voyage."[23]

Tapping into barrels of molasses or spirits and sucking the contents out with a straw was a common enough shipboard practice to have its own name, according to Stan Hugill—"sucking the monkey." The term derived from drinking rum covertly "inserted into a coconut whose end resembles a monkey's face."[24]

Riesenberg introduced on the *A.J.Fuller* what he termed "a relic of my school ship days," a systematized trading among crew members to acquire favorite foods or get rid of unwanted items. "When I worked out a system of credits for different kinds of grub on the the *Fuller* it was found to be a source of diversion and made possible some adjustment along the lines of personal taste, in the matter of meals." Riesenberg would unload his ration of stockfish [dried cod] in exchange for "apple jack, a stew of musty dried apples." The trade was "a thriving business in the fo'c'sle, some of us even branching out into foreign trade with the starboard watch."[25]

Food exchanges and gifts reinforced social networks. Captains and wives exchanged food among their peers while the fo'c'sle crew exchanged among theirs. Vessels sharing abundance freely with vessels in need was common, as were food exchanges between vessels that met at sea, all expressions of the true brotherhood (and sisterhood) among seafarers. The sociable exchanges in mid-ocean reduced the isolation so many seafarers felt, particularly the women in the cabin. Mary Brewster, on board the *Tiger* in Magdalena Bay on the Pacific coast of Lower California, was able to comment with satisfaction, "The prospect is that I shall not get out of anything for what we dont have others do and send and give liberally."[26]

Food Storage

All this fresh stuff had to be stored on board ship. As small and crowded as vessels might be, ingenious officers could always find places to stash things away, even if some locations were far from ideal.

Live storage: Animals taken aboard provided fresh meat when needed. Pigs and fowl were most common among shipboard livestock, but just about every other creature can be found in documentary records. Live storage was usually proof against spoilage, though occasionally an animal sickened and died. Livestock also presented difficulties because they required food, water, and tending. Fowl might be kept in cages—a whaleship's carpenter's bench often had a cage built beneath it—and larger animals might be kept in pens or even loose on deck.

Spencer Bonsall on the ship *Hopewell* noted: "Today several of us went ashore after live stock, such as sheep, Pigs, Geese, Duck, and Chickens. These are intended for the cabin." During a transatlantic passage aboard the ship *Edward*, Bonsall recorded that the crew was disconsolate at the loss of a young passenger who came aboard at Madeira and had been in ill health. The young passenger, Bonsall wrote, kept to himself, paced the deck continually, perhaps with thoughts of a long voyage far from friends and relatives on his mind. When the "young passenger" died, Bonsall was reminded that in the midst of life is death. He observed that "It was a good thing for him, poor fellow, that he died a natural death, as he certainly would have been killed by the cook had he lived much longer, as sailors are real

Captains and wives preserved fruit aboard. Clockwise, canned whortleberries, figs, and preserved pineapple, page 189.

scroungers on seapie. Hah! Hah!! Hah!!! dont you think that a *Lamb* would make as good a seapie as anything else—"[27]

Mary Lawrence recorded in 1857 that her *Addison* "obtained a considerable fresh supply...twenty-six hogs, forty fowl, two thousand coconuts for the hogs to feed on." Goats kept aboard provided milk for coffee as well as meat for the table. On board the *Alert* in 1836, Dana counted the livestock the ship obtained at San Diego for the trip home: "four bullocks, a dozen sheep, a dozen or more pigs, and three or four dozen of poultry...the bullocks in the long-boat, the sheep in a pen on the fore hatch, and the pigs in a sty under the bows of the long-boat, and the poultry in their proper coop; and the jolly boat was full of hay for the sheep and bullocks." Spencer Bonsall said that at Mauritius it was possible to send a ship's geese ashore to be fattened, which the master of the *Hopewell* did.[28]

Pigs were the most compact of shipboard livestock, and fecund besides: on the New London whaleship *Mentor* in 1840 James A. Rogers wrote: "At 1 PM one of the sows that we brought from home was delivered of eleven pigs. The other is in a fair way to bring forth soon. Saturday 15th. This day had another family of fresh pork come into the world. Plenty of pork to fatten on now." During the whaleship *Charles W. Morgan*'s first voyage, Second Mate James C. Osborne recorded fresh pork dinners in his journal, celebrating one with a little portrait of two pigs killed for the occasion.[29]

Butchering was a mighty chore ashore and all the more trouble aboard ship. Still, as Annie Ricketson wrote, "This morning the morning watch killed the Ox that we got in Bima and we had some for dinner. It tasted very nice." The very next day she wrote that "The steward killed a goose for dinner and I have been stripping the feathers that come of him for a pillow."[30] The goose dinner seems superflous; it is highly unlikely the ox had been entirely eaten, but perhaps some of the beef was salted or corned.

Cabins festooned: Fresh food was stored anywhere in the ship there seemed to be room for it. Francis A. Olmsted on the New London whaleship *North America* reported the look of things after provisioning: "When the bananas, plantains, and other fruits were suspended upon deck and from aloft, the ship looked as if she had been dressed off with evergreens for some festive occasion, while the cabin and staterooms were full of the finest oranges, limes, pineapples, and coconuts." After the *Tiger* left Honolulu for home in 1847, the ship stopped at one of the Cook Islands for provisions, and Mary Brewster described her cabin: "Feel quite pleased with my room which is thus ornamented: two large bunches of ripe bananas were hung up, with Pineapples which helped fill up all the empty spaces." There was a basket of eggs in another place, and "a net of Oranges one of lemons and a string of Oranges hung up by the stems reaching nearly the length of the house."[31]

Second Mate James Osborne recorded in his journal of the *Morgan*'s first voyage: "watch employed making a Potato net" and "watch employed making onion baskets." At Point Malpelo two of the *Morgan*'s boats returned with "1500 hundred oranges, plantin, coconuts, etc." During this voyage on the west coast of South America the cruises were interrupted with visits ashore to get wood, potatoes, pumpkins, and terrapin—thirty-three in one haul.[32]

Just as at home, seafarers had to sort through vegetable supplies regularly to separate those that had gone bad or had to be used quickly before they spoiled. As Osborne on the *Morgan* noted in his journal, "watch employed picking over beans and potatoes." Felix Riesenberg referred to the crew who picked over potatoes as the "farmers" of the watch. Even little Minnie Lawrence helped the steward pick through the cabin supply of dried apples.[33] Minnie, as we recall, was partial to apples.

Shipboard preservation: Whatever food could not be stored for long or eaten soon enough was preserved, just as it would have been at home. Preserving made the bounty last. Mary Lawrence visited an orchard of "four hundred peach trees all bourne down with fruit. Such a sight I never saw before. It looked wicked to see them lying on the ground"—all the more so for one who went weeks without fresh fruit. Like many captains' wives, Mary Lawrence did a fair amount of shipboard preserving. "Have been engaged in washing, ironing, and putting up pineapples, besides my regular routine of work. We have been saving our white sugar nearly all the voyage for this occasion and have put up a famous lot in jars, bottles, etc.," she wrote.[34]

Mary Brewster recorded that when the *Tiger* was in Magdalena Bay, some Spaniards brought oranges and sweet lemons on board which her husband bought. "This forenoon I have been employed in putting some up in hopes they would keep." Another of her journal entries recorded, "I have been busy preserving Quinces which has taken most of the day—Had about a bushel."[35]

Annie Eliza Dow, the wife of Captain Jonathan Dow, on board the Searsport, Maine, brig *Clytie* at Naples in 1866, found cherries in the market, and the family bought many along with new potatoes, green beans, and peas. Her daughter reported that "Mother took advantage of our stay in port to lay in a good supply of fresh fruits and vegetables, also to can cherries to supply our table on the voyage."[36]

Sallie Smith "made piccalillie" and preserved some quinces—"had good luck quite rough but nothing happened," aboard the whaling bark *John P. West*. During her voyage on the whaleship *Ohio* in 1877 she reported, "I have preserved a few bananas today," although she didn't say how; and near the island of St. Catherine off the coast of Brazil she wrote: "Today I have been canning Whortleberries plenty of Fruite here. Fred has been squeezing limes." The Ricketsons also kept a supply of lemon juice: "Daniel and I squeeze them this afternoon and put the juice in bottles." Mary Lawrence explained how the juice was used: "Captain Diman sent me two bottles of lime juice, which was very acceptable, as I do not like to drink clear water now, it is so warm and poor."[37] The juice that fought scurvy also made water palatable.

Many of these preserves, besides improving the daily menu, gave the afterguard something to trade or to present as a gift.

Besides fruit, seafarers also salted or pickled meat and fish. The Lawrences and Brewsters caught, salted, and dried codfish, and the Lawrences preserved pork. As Mary Lawrence reported on a cruise into the Gulf of Alaska in 1859: "As soon as it is a little cooler, shall have some of the pigs killed, baked up, and put down in barrels with lard. Also have an abundance of sausage meat, hog's head cheese. etc." Part of the reason for doing this was an abundance of hungry porkers. "It takes too much for them all to eat. We had about forty when we left the last island."[38]

Consuming the Fresh Food

Sometimes captains acquired fresh provisions for the whole ship, providing a supply for everyone to dip into; other times the fresh food went primarily to the cabin. Much fresh meat, as we saw earlier, went aft, but on many vessels the fo'c'sle crew got a share, too. When passengers were aboard, there was extra pressure to provide fresh fare. A pig killed within sight of Cape Horn on the ship *John Q. Adams* provided fresh meat and

Juan Fernandez, the Robinson Crusoe island, was frequently mentioned in logs and journals as a stop for fresh food. About four hundred miles off the coast of Chile, this is where crewmen from the whaleship *Tiger* found peaches, fig trees, grapevines, radishes, quince, and wild nasturtiums in bloom. The *Tiger's* crew also caught thirty fish. It may be that Alexander Selkirk, the original Robinson Crusoe, who camped here from 1704 to 1709, found some of this bounty. [From panorama by Benjamin Russell and Caleb Purrington, New Bedford Whaling Museum]

inspired this from a passenger:

"Eat, drink your fill don't look forlorn,

There's roasted pork and there's 'Cape Horn'

So boys and girls we'll make no bother

But cut up one and pass the other."[39]

After John Perkins and his fellow crew members came back to the whaleship *Tiger* with peaches, "The chief mate gave to each of us a bucket of peaches apiece the greenest to put in our chests to ripen & left about half a hogsheadfull on deck to eat as we wanted."On the whaler *Mentor* near Ampanan in the Indian Ocean in 1840, James A. Rogers reported no such generosity from the officers: "Everyone that wants fruit must sell his clothes as the captain won't buy it for them." The *Mentor's* skipper seems to have been particularly mean-spirited about food for his crew. "We have been here," said Rogers at Ampanan, "about one week and have got one bullock. The captain bought some fowl and eggs, but forgot to return those that he borrowed from the steerage. Salt beef and pork—good enough for sailors!" Aboard the *Charmer* in 1856, Charles Abbey wrote: "At daylight this morning had Sumatra on the weather beam & Angier on the bow. Had two boats along side with yams, potatoes, pineapples, pumpkins, corn, monkeys, birds, &c but no fruit that we could get as the captain bought it all."[40]

But the crew did get some fresh food. On the *Surprise* in 1856 Abbey wrote: "we killed a pig yesterday which furnished us with fresh meat for the 'sea Pie.'" And on the *Tiger* Mary Brewster recorded: "For our dinner roast turkey fore and aft stewed fowls." Captain Jonathan Dow on the *Clytie* in 1866 made sure all hands had fresh cutlets when a porpoise was caught.[41]

Very often, as long as a ship was in port the fo'c'sle crew had fresh meat, fruit, and vegetables to eat, almost without limit. Knut Weibust quotes a Scandinavian sailor who worked loading guano in Chile in 1918—miserable, dry, dirty work—"But one enormous consolation was that we were able to quench our guano-snuff thirsts with extraordinarily cheap and good fruit such as oranges, apricots, peaches, and melons." John Perkins in Lahaina, Hawaii, made the journal entry, "We have had fresh beef since we have been in port."

Yankee response to exotic vittles: What is intriguing to modern people is the Yankee seafarers' reactions and attempts to describe fresh and sometimes exotic fare. Today many of us find these foods in grocery stores because such things as bananas, pineap-ples, coconuts, oranges, lemons, and limes are regularly stocked. Other items, if not always on hand, appear often enough that we have probably tried them, such as papayas, guavas, tamarinds, and mangoes. Let's take a closer look at some of the foods that appear most often in journals and narratives, starting with those from the sea and then the exotics from strange lands.

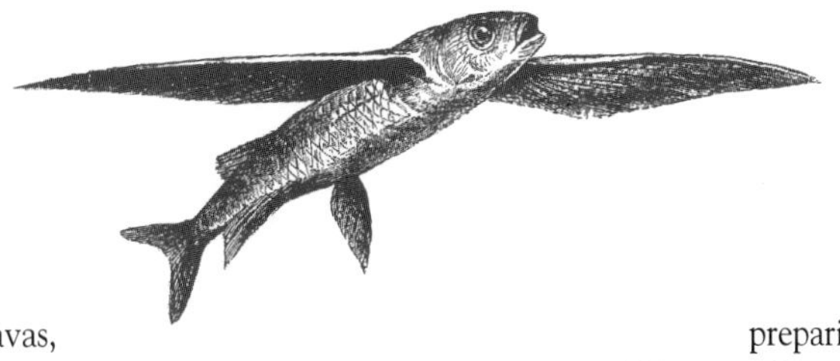

Fresh foods from the sea: At sea, presumably surrounded by an ocean full of fish, we might imagine seafarers spending every spare moment trying to catch some fresh food, and welcoming every opportunity to eat fish. But, as we have seen among fishermen, fish was less favored than meat, given a choice. Seafarers were also selective about what they would eat from the natural bounty around them, and certain favorites appear over and over in seafaring literature.

Porpoise: Hardly anyone went to sea in the nineteenth century and missed trying porpoise meat and liver. Usually special items like this were reserved for the cabin, but the crew ate porpoise occasionally, too. Porpoise, also known as dolphin by seafarers, had a very old place in English foodways, although this was not something most sailors would have known. Porpoise was one of the "royal fish," so called because they, along with whales and sturgeon, were reserved for royalty in late-medieval Britain. As sea dwellers, porpoise were considered acceptable meat for fish days. In the medieval kitchen, porpoise was used like venison in a number of dishes, including a kind of blood pudding made with porpoise intestines; in the 1700s, among those who still ate it ashore, porpoise meat was most often put into a venison-like pasty.[43]

Seafarers continued to catch porpoise for food, and at least one noted its similarity to venison. On his way to California from Haddam, Connecticut, forty-niner Cyrus Hurd, Jr., ate some "fried shack or porpoise, which," he observed, "is equal to any venison."[44]

Others likened porpoise to other meat. Thomas Larkin Turner reported in 1832 that "yesterday we ate his...liver for breakfast very much like a hog. Today with Beans, dined from it—no one could tell it from Beef, at least I could not." Spencer Bonsall thought "the meat is very dark colored and resembles in taste something between Beef Steak and Liver." Mary Lawrence thought "The meat looks very much like beef....Had some of the meat fried for dinner and some made into sausage cakes for supper. They are as nice as pork sausages." Mary Brewster said: "Had porpoise for breakfast. The liver tastes very much like beefs...and for a change it does very well." Jesse Campbell on the *Blenheim* in 1840 wrote: "Capt. Gray killed a large porpoise before dinner and the liver of it was nicely dressed and put down on the table. I tasted a small bit from curiosity and would not know it from sheeps liver. The sailors consider porpoise a great treat they say it eats like beef steak but dryer and coarser."[45]

The most popular method of preparing porpoise was to fry the meat and liver. Sallie Smith referred to porpoise and dolphin repeatedly in this way: "had him fried for supper." Annie Ricketson wrote, "Today Mr. Bourne struck a porpoise," which, instead of sinking as usual, floated. "It was quite exciting for a while all so anxious about them getting him. Of course we had porpoises balls and fried porpoises cakes for tea which tasted very nice as we had salt meat so long."[46]

Not everyone enjoyed the meat. Medical student Vernon Briggs harpooned a porpoise and dissected it on a voyage in 1880: "We had the meat and liver for dinner and the taste (and texture) of the meat reminded me of a description I have read somewhere in which it is compared to a fine sponge saturated with train oil." Georgia Maria Blanchard tried porpoise on her honeymoon trip in 1906 with husband Captain Banning Blanchard aboard the *Bangalore*. "We had some [porpoise] for breakfast next day. The meat is black, not good to look at and I don't like the taste."[47]

The numerous references to porpoise balls, cakes, sausage, and cutlets suggest that porpoise was a little bit tough and gamey, and was more palatable ground up. Even though porpoises can be large animals, the meat does not appear on table as a roast. Except for Cyrus Hurd, most seafarers failed to mention any similarity in taste to venison, perhaps because many nineteenth-century seafarers were not as familiar with venison as they were with beef.

Flying fish: Flying fish were identified as good eating as well as a great curiosity. They came aboard accidentally, or sometimes when lured, as Samuel Samuels reported: "the flying fish is caught in a flat net suspended under the martingale, with a light directly over it to attract the fish at night, but these dainty morsels are exclusively for the cabin table." Though there were exceptions to that rule, captains' wives' and passenger's journals provide most of the descriptions of the little fish. Flying fish were frequently fried for breakfast; as Georgia Maria Blanchard wrote of another breakfast aboard her husband's ship: "We had a real treat of flying fish for breakfast. It did taste so good."[48]

Most often flying fish were likened to small, oily pan fish of various sorts. Mary Lawrence wrote that "flying fish are very plenty. One flew over the side of the ship one day, and the steward cooked him for my breakfast. Was very nice; tasted some like a fresh herring." Vernon Briggs observed that flying fish "range in size from that of a large smelt to a common sized mackerel, and in color and grain of their flesh resemble the smelt. A few days ago one flew aboard and I had it for dinner and found it quite delicious, very much like smelt." Aboard the ship *Edward* in 1837, Spencer Bonsall observed flying fish caught in the forechains, which "were eaten this morning for breakfast. They are about the size of our Perch and taste very much like them."[49]

Isaac Hibberd, as first mate of the Thomaston-built ship *Cyrus Wakefield* about 1885 noticed that flying fish "rise up out of the sea to get away from bonita and the meat is very delicate, like trout." George Piper Boughton, foremast hand on the bark *Archos* enroute from England to Asia, recorded that "Apart from the fact that they are the sweetest fish to eat, their wonderful wings are a study."Mary Brewster studied these wonderful wings one day aboard the *Tiger*: "Whilst sitting by my stateroom window watching the flying fish one flew into the window which gave me a fine chance to examine it. This was a small but perfect fish in shape resembling our mackerels with the exception of its fins or wings which are quite curious. They are composed of a thin membrane which seems to be strengthened by ligaments which extend from the top to the bottom which serve to make them strong. They fly in flocks like birds and are a most excellent pan fish....Two...were saved and cooked for my breakfast."[50]

The ship *Cyrus Wakefield* built at Thomaston, Maine, in 1882, owned by Samuel Watts and Company, is the vessel Isaac Hibberd served aboard as first mate in 1885. Hibberd observed that flying fish "rise up out of the sea to get away from bonita." Sailors ate both bonita and flying fish, welcome as fresh, tasty additions to the often-monotonous menu aboard deepwater vessels. Isaac Hibberd reported that the flying fish "is very delicate, like trout." [MSM 80-3-193, painting by W. H. Yorke, 1885]

Herring, smelt, perch, and trout—flying fish reminded seafarers of all these. Their size and outward similarity to mackerel determined how they would be cooked. New Englanders almost always fried and ate small fish like this at breakfast.

Albacore and bonito: Albacore provided food for seafarers years before it won favor among landsmen as tuna. Sallie Smith watched her captain husband Fred catch albacore by line, bringing so many aboard that they salted them down in barrels for use later.[51]

Bonito, or skipjacks, were game fish. Felix Riesenberg described bonito as active, virile fish, which sailors caught by harpooning, although Cyrus Hurd said he caught them by line. Mary Lawrence wrote of "catching a few fish of the kind called skipjack, not the nicest that ever were caught, but very good in the absence of better."[52]

Charles Abbey, an apprentice on the clipper ship *Surprise* in 1856, reported, "Woke up this morning at 7 bells & found the men over the bows catching 'Bonita' of which altogether we had 8 & had fresh chowder & fried fish & duff & molasses in fact quite a treat."[53]

Bonita's similarity to the bluefish New Englanders knew at home may account for references to bonita cooked into chowder. Bluefish were used in chowder, especially at chowder parties where catching the fish was part of the event.

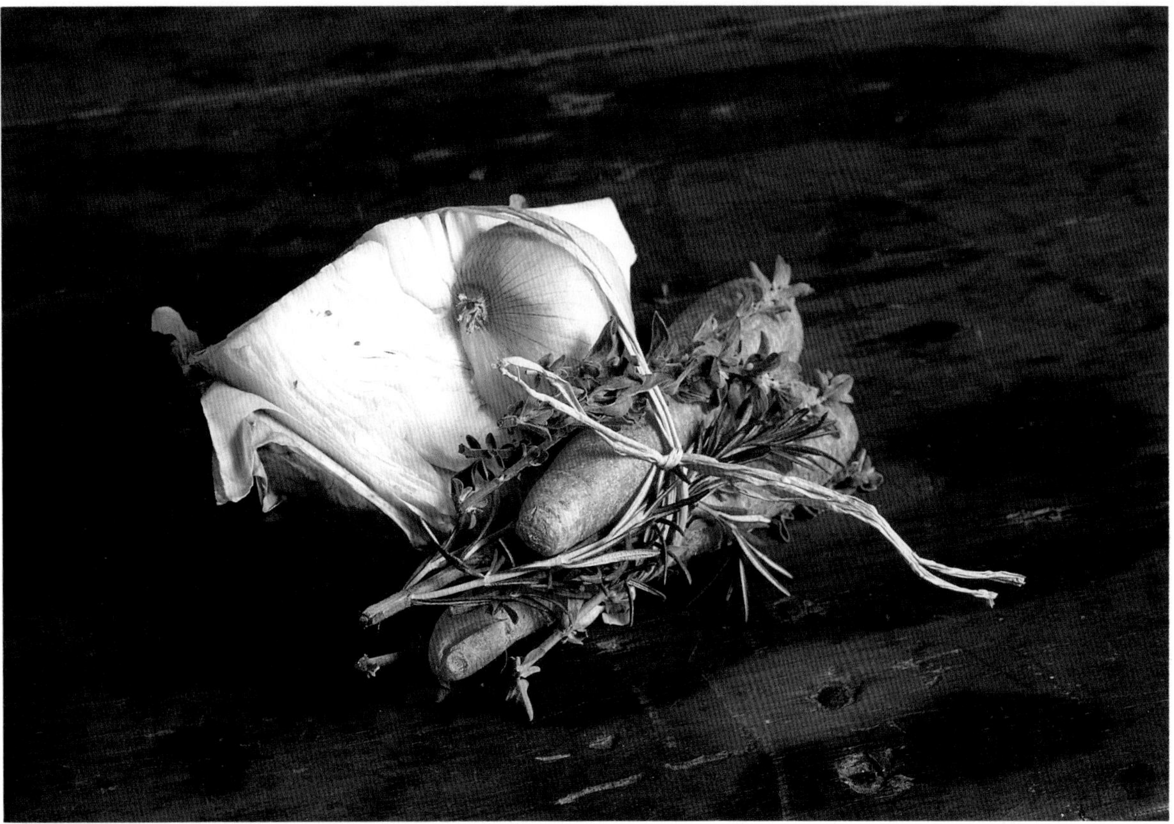

In 1862, Spencer Bonsall saw a quarter of cabbage sold with aromatics at Mauritius.

According to Captain Samuel Samuels, sailors sometimes resisted the fresh fish, and sometimes other meat as well. "The bonetta when a school is struck, is a godsend, and a clear gain to the ship-owner. We eat it cooked in various styles; but Jack tires of it after a few days, and asks for his salt beef."[54]

Turtle: Turtles caught at sea were another fresh food that apparently wore out its welcome in the fo'c'sle. As Samuel Samuels claimed: "When I was before the mast I saw turtles strangled to prevent the skipper from giving us steaks and soup after the fourth day."[55]

The *Charles W. Morgan*'s crew caught terrapin—"turpin"—so journal-keeper Norton spelled it, at the Galapagos and other locations. On the whaler *Tiger*, Mary Brewster in Margarita Bay reported, "We shall live high certainly," when the boats returned after a day of fishing, fowling, clam digging, and gathering turtles. A few days later she reported turtle soup for dinner. On the *Addison*, turtle was served as soup and as fried steaks, which Mary Lawrence decided "was very nice indeed."[56]

Annie Ricketson described her experience with turtle: "The mate Mr. Bourne caught a turtle this morning before breakfast and I had to come up on deck to see him. We had some of him made into soup for dinner. It was real nice and tasted very much like chicken soup. For tea we had some of the liver and meat fried. The liver was the nicest I ever eat, It was jest as tender as could be."[57]

Other fish and shellfish: Crews, especially on whalers where there was more idle time than aboard cargo ships, fished for quite a variety of other fish as well. Spencer Bonsall described a meal of shark: "we made a hearty breakfast of part of his flesh and found it pretty good eating, resembling catfish in taste, but rather coarser." There are many varieties of shark, of course, some more palatable than others. Mary Lawrence described pilot fish: "They are very pretty fish about the size of a trout, blue, striped around with black....Had some of those fish fried for supper last night and the rest for breakfast this morning. They tasted very nice." At Margarita Bay, Mary Brewster ate what she called sunfish: "For tea had some of it which in taste resembles lobster," she wrote. Mary Lawrence reported that one of the *Addison*'s mates went out in a boat "to see what he could find in the eating line. Came home about dark with several bushels of nice 'quahogs' and about a dozen mullett." As seafarers often did, Mrs. Lawrence and Mary Brewster both identified the round hard clams of the California coast as "quahog," which strictly speaking they were not. Mary Lawrence, Mary Brewster, and Sallie Smith all commented on oysters gathered in various places, particularly those that grew on mangrove roots along the shores of Lower California where whalers often gathered to hunt grey whales.[58]

Mary Brewster would have been familiar not only with oysters but also with lobsters, to which she compared some crawfish brought on board—which she seems not to have tasted: "They got quite a number of crawfish which resemble a lobster in looks and taste so I am told as respects the latter."[59]

Dana reported spectacular fishing in a bay of Juan Fernandez, where many vessels stopped after rounding

Cape Horn. "Two of our crew...caught in a few minutes enough to last us for several days, and one of the men, who was a Marblehead man, said he never saw or heard of such an abundance." They caught cod, perch, breams, and silverfish, "and other kinds whose names they did not know, or which I have forgotten."[60]

Whalemeat and other exotic seafoods: Whalemeat was regular fare for some of the world's people in the nineteenth century and, with porpoise, had been considered a royal fish in medieval Britain. But to most New Englanders whalemeat was exotic stuff. Their journals indicate that they occasionally ate it, but far less often than porpoise, flying fish, turtle, or bonito.

On the whaleship *Herald* in 1867, Lewis William Eldredge wrote about some blackfish they caught: "The carcasses were thrown overboard to the sharks after saving a large portion of the meat, as much as we would be able to eat before it began to spoil. It was hung up in the standing rigging forward and for two or three days we lived on meat that was as good as the porpoise had been. The meat was coarser but not as coarse as the meat of a small sperm whale we afterward once ate and were then glad to get back to our old stand by, 'salt junk.'"[61]

Mary Lawrence described some whalemeat they saved aboard the *Addison*: "We have been eating bowhead meat for several days, made with pork into sausage cakes, also fried, and it is good eating, far above salt pork in my estimation."[62] To us, who shy away from either whalemeat or salt pork, this may seem to be faint praise, especially considering the usual quality of the salt pork on board ship, which seafarers nevertheless often preferred over exotic foods. At least whalemeat was meat from a mammal.

Another whaleman, Robert Weir of the *Clara Bell* in 1855, reported about right whales, "On the end of their noses is a bunch of barnacles about 18 inches wide. This the whalemen call his bonnet...the barnacles are enormous as much as two inches deep—the boys often roast them and eat them the same as oysters. And many other tid bits do they have when a whale is 'trying out': cooking whale lean &c&c&c."[63]

Seabirds: We saw that among early nineteenth-century fishermen, shag—cormorants—were a source of fresh meat, and deep-water sailors caught seabirds occasionally, too. Charles Abbey reported the crew of the *Surprise* catching Cape hens and albatross—gooney birds: "A couple of the sailors & myself secured one of the 'Gooneys' & cleaned him & had him cooked for supper & I must say he was 'good.'" The *Charles W. Morgan*'s Nelson Haley, ashore on a South Pacific island, collected eggs laid by "a species of gull, called by the whalemen mutton birds, for what reason I know not; for the old birds have about as much flavor of mutton as carrion crow has." He reported that the immature birds were caught for food. "They are one mass of fat, not a streak of lean in their whole bodies, and they can be eaten by boiling; but one does not hanker after them. They are used as a substitute for meat by splitting them open on the back, taking the entrails out and the down off, and then packing them in salt for a time." Since fat was highly prized at sea, it may have been that salted mutton chicks were acceptable to fat-starved sailors. Eating sea fowl like these gulls had begun to go out of favor in eighteenth-century England, and along with much other wild food in New England as well. In remote Scottish islands, people still gathered sea birds and their eggs, and they may have continued the practice at sea where Yankee sailors observed it.[64]

Skewed menus: What could not be stored had to be eaten, and shipboard menus were sometimes freighted with a certain food item until it was gone. Mary Brewster reported "Mr. B dipping deeply in the egg basket," and shortly before mentioned "Egg nog twice a day." The whaler *Herald* stopped at Bird Island in the Seychelles, said Lewis Eldredge, and picked up "a number of bushels of eggs....After this visit we lived on hard boiled eggs for many weeks." Another time the *Herald*'s crew filled their water casks and bought peanuts and a bullock from local people at Fort Dauphin. "We lived lavishly on the peanuts, and the bullock meat last for a season."[65]

In 1836, Richard Henry Dana on the *Alert*, stowing hides at San Diego, reported that bullocks were purchased so regularly for the ship that "we lived upon almost nothing but fresh beef....A mess consisting of six men had a large wooden kid piled up with beef steaks, cut thick, and fried in fat, with the grease poured over them. Round this we sat, attacking it with our jack-knives and teeth, and with the appetite of young lions....This was done three times a day." The contrast of such plenty against the regular fare, and especially short rations, was great. "Once or twice, when our bullocks failed and we were obliged to make a meal again upon dry bread and water, it seemed like feeding upon shavings," wrote Dana.[66]

Fish-eating at sea: Bully Samuels may have been exaggerating about the bonito and turtles—he is particularly suspect because he included poultry and fresh meat in the list of fresh provisions that sailors resisted—but he may have been testifying to the general resistance to seafood in the fo'c'sle. Aboard the *A.J. Fuller*, Riesenberg reported that "I never cared much for fish and did not touch [the bonita]. Chow [the cook] certainly had made an ill-looking mess of it, garnished with broken tack, and basted with pork fat. 'You'll wisht you had a bit of this tucker afore we get to Honolulu,' was the comment of Joe who helped himself liberally." One conversation aboard the *Fuller* underlined a basic question about fish. "'If fish ain't meat, wot is it?' demanded Martin. 'Is it wegetables, or wot?'" While the crew determined that it was fish, in a class by itself, it was clear they did not consider it equal to meat.[67] As Samuels pointed out, the shipowners fared well if the crew would eat seafood, and that may have been sufficient reason for the crew to demand their legal entitlement of provisions, especially the more respected salt beef and pork.

Annie Holmes Ricketson, left, and Richard Henry Dana, Jr., right, both kept shipboard journals in which they often commented on food they ate aboard ship and ashore. Mrs. Ricketson married her whaler husband at age sixteen, and spent most of her married life at sea. The young Dana sailed before the mast in the 1830s, returned to sea as a mature traveler in the 1850s. [Right, carte de visite, New Bedford Whaling Museum; left, MSM 72-1-72 from *Richard Henry Dana*, a biography by Charles Francis Adams]

Another difficulty was knowing whether any given fish was actually edible, never mind palatable. Determining if an unknown food was good to eat was a matter of experience and some conjecture. A few bad experiences, or even just the report of one, could make a virtue of caution. Henry Blaney, a passenger on the ship *Mandarin* in 1853, reported that some perfectly familiar mackerel procured at St. Helena were broiled for the cabin breakfast. "Mr. Hanson (the mate) and myself ate heartily of them, and soon after we were attacked with vertigo and violent rush of blood to the head, which Capt. Stoddard said was caused by the mackerel poisoned by the influence of the moon." Mary Lawrence ate some pilot fish for supper one evening and breakfast the next day. "About ten minutes after I had finished my breakfast my face began to burn and my head ache badly. I looked in the glass and my face was a sight to behold, just as red as it could be all over, chin, forehead, ears and neck." Similarly, her husband and everyone else in the cabin who had eaten the fish became sick.[68] The Lawrences attributed the poisoning to keeping the fish overnight. Both accounts describe familiar symptoms of fish poisoning.

Fear of poisoning led to various tests, one of which, described by Riesenberg, was to lay a silver coin on the flesh; if the coin turned black the fish was considered poisonous. Frederick Harlow reported a similar test on the ship *Akbar*, bound to Asia from New York: "There were various arguments brought up by the crew [about] the edible qualities of the dolphin when compared to the bonito and albacore. Some claimed they were poisonous and not fit to eat." The *Akbar*'s cook refused to prepare the dolphin—in this case the dolphin fish—dorado—not the mammal dolphin or porpoise—because he didn't wish to be blamed for poisoning the crew. Harlow suspected the cook refused because he didn't want to clean and cook it, but the second mate said he'd eaten dolphin many times and he'd take responsibility for any results, and proposed that "he could put a coin in the water with the fish and if it turned green it would indicate that the fish was poisonous." The coin didn't change color and the dolphin was cooked for supper. On the *Bangalore*, Georgia Blanchard said: "We caught several dolphin which are good to eat but must be tested first. This is done by putting a dime in a piece of the fish and cooking it. If the dime turns black the fish is thrown back into the water but if it is bright and shiny the fish is cooked and enjoyed by all hands."[69] The dorado is still widely believed to be poisonous.

"Brought Off to the Ship"— Food From the Land

Their ship was the center of the New England seafarers' world, and food from the mainland or an island was usually described as having been "brought off" the shore to the vessel. This was done, we have seen, by the crew itself in the ship's boats, or by local people in theirs. Many of these foods were great rarities in New England, but, as modern travelers know, even familiar foods have a new taste in their native places.

Mary Lawrence was very fond of all the tropical fruits, and she listed them in her journal with obvious relish: "Pineapples grow in great abundance and in great perfection," she wrote from Aitutake, northeast of New Zealand. "Oranges, limes, bananas, plantain, breadfruit, yams, custard apples, etc. etc., all of which we procured a quantity." The pineapples were favorites: "I never had the pleasure of eating as much pineapple as I wished before. Oh, how luscious they are! It would be a mockery to put sugar on them as we do at home."Of coconuts she wrote, "The milk of a young coconut is delicious, and Minnie and myself have quite a feast with it."[70]

When the *Addison* was near Sunday Island, Mary obtained another familiar fruit: "Have been making pies and preserves of my strawberry tomatoes today, which we found very nice. They grow wild here....They are called cape gooseberries here, strawberry tomatoes at home, and powhas [pohas] at the Sandwich Islands." We know them today as husk cherries. When peeled they look very much like gooseberries, and Mary cooked them the same way she would have prepared gooseberries at home.

When Lloyd Briggs, a sixteen-year-old student traveling for his health aboard the bark *Amy Turner*, was in Honolulu in 1880, he noted that "Living here is fairly expensive unless you wish to live on vegetables and fruit...in the gardens and on the tables there are green peas, corn, summer squash, cabbage, beets, tomatoes, egg-plants, bread-fruit and strawberries in abundance, and bananas are only 25 cents for a bunch of 50 or more. The mangoes are delicious in flavor, but very juicy, and therefore awkward to eat. Mark Twain advises getting into a bathtub to eat them."[71]

Francis Olmsted, aboard the whaler *North America* in 1839, was especially fond of the exotic banana. "The banana in taste reminds me of the richest orange pears we have at home." The plantain, he reported, "when ripe, is a soft, sweetish, golden colored pulp...when sliced and fried it is one of the most delicious esculents I ever tasted."[72]

As we saw with his with meals ashore, John Perkins was fascinated by new foods. When the whaleship *Tiger* called at Hilo, Hawaii, in 1846, Perkins went ashore and "spent the forenoon wandering among the huts eating bananas, popas [pawpaws], watermelons, pineapples, coconuts, & other fruits of the island, but the pleasantest tasted of all was fresh sugarcane." Perkins also remarked on sweet potatoes and yams he ate as a guest in an islander's home—"these latter tasting like slippery elm bark. The potatoes tasted & looked like Irish potatoes but were the sweetest that I ever eat."[73]

Mary Brewster, also on board the *Tiger*, commented on the bananas, pineapples, and coconuts, too, but she also mentioned guavas, tamarinds, and "a delicious fruit called Custard Apple." Custard apple, also called Cherimoya, is a South American fruit with a sweet, smooth, juicy, cream-colored flesh, like a "custard of fine pears." Frederick Harlow tasted custard apples in Java: "Alligator pears or custard apples were very palatable. The outer shell resembled that of an alligator—a hard, bristly shell of brown green, growing as large as four or five inches in diameter, but when opened containing a yellowish, cream colored custard, with a few black seeds about the size of a hazel-nut meat. It was usually eaten with a spoon, but we sailors 'got outside of it' without wasting any time."[74]

Richard Henry Dana, visiting near Kilauea, Hawaii, in 1859, reported seeing guavas, oranges, mangoes, kukui, pandanus, breadfruit, banana, coconut, and papaya. He described guavas: "Guavas sweet & sour are plenty. Guava tree is like a quince tree, & guava like quince in form & color, seeds in middle ditto, tastes betw. insipid & sour."Twenty years later, Lloyd Briggs wrote of Hawaii's abundance: "The trees are laden with guavas, oranges, China oranges, limes, bananas, coconuts, mangoes, figs, loquats, papayas, tamarinds—all ripe!"[75]

Fruits seem to have gotten the most attention in seafaring journals, but occasionally other foods made an appearance, as they did in Spencer Bonsall's journal in Mauritius: "You see here a quarter of a cabbage and onion and carrot and a few sprigs of herbs tied together. This is to give a variety for a small cost." It was there he also saw and noted cinnamon, clove, and nutmeg trees.[76]

"We Have Everything Nice to Eat..."

The last of a fresh supply was often noted in journals: "Finished the last of the bananas today," Sallie Smith wrote, and when she polished off a treat from home she recorded the event: "Eat last roll of lozenges."[77] Having the last of the fresh stores or candy confections meant that anticipating the next stop in port had begun.

Fresh stores were allocated according to the same hierarchy used for dispensing the regular provisions. Seafarers fore and aft used fresh food to reinforce their social networks within their shipboard society, between their ship and others, and between their ship and shore. A captain and owners could expend fresh provisions wisely and guarantee both the crew's health and their loyalty as well.

Seafarers used exotic foods in ways that made them seem as familiar as possible: flying fish fried as panfish for breakfast, or porpoise made into sausage and the liver fried as domestic animal livers were cooked at home. When they ate strange fruits for the first time seafarers remembered fruit they knew at home and searched for ways to describe the new ones in reference to the familiar.

And when the vessel had been re-provisioned? We will let a captain's wife speak to that: "We have everything nice to eat," wrote Mary Lawrence when the *Addison* left Honolulu for the Alaska coast in 1857, "sweet and Irish potatoes, cabbage, onions, cucumbers, string beans, bananas, coconuts, melons, pumpkins, preserved meats, vegetables, oysters and lobsters, sausage meat, etc., butter and soda crackers, tamarinds, preserves, arrowroot, pigs, turkeys, ducks, and chickens, a goat, and a kid for a pet."[78]

The Recipes

The recipes which follow reflect some of the fresh fare found on ships in the nineteenth century. Directions for roasting fresh pork and for making turtle soup are followed by a recipe for fruitcake that Sallie Smith recorded at the back of her journal. It would have been a good cake to take to sea. A way to prepare both oranges and pineapples—fruits highly favored by traveling New Englanders—is followed by quince preserves from a cookbook printed the same year Mary Brewster went to sea and put quinces up on board the *Tiger*. You will also find ways to preserve whortleberries, as the Smiths did, and pineapples as Mary Lawrence did.

TURTLE SOUP

GREEN TURTLE SOUP (The Caterer)

The day before you intend to dress the turtle cut off its head; and to do this properly you should hang up the victim with its head downwards, use a very sharp knife and make the incision as close to the head as possible. You must not be surprised at seeing, many hours after the decollation, the creature exhibit extraordinary signs of muscular motion, by the flapping of his fins. Separate the upper from the lower shell, and in this operation be very careful not to touch the gall bladder, which is very large and if penetrated would destroy the flesh over which its contents ran. Cut the meat from the breast in half a dozen pieces; abstract the gall and entrails and throw them away at once. Separate the fins as near the shell as possible, abstract the green fat and put it on a separate dish from the white meat. Boil the upper and lower shells in water sufficient to enable you take away the bones. Then remove with a spoon the mucilage that you find adhering to the shells; put this also into a separate dish. Into the largest stewpan your kitchen affords put the head, fins, liver, lights, heart and all the flesh, a pound of ham, nine or ten cloves, a couple of bay leaves, a good sized bunch of sweet herbs (such as winter savory, marjoram, basil, thyme), a silver onion cut into slices and a bunch of parsley. Cover all these with the liquor in which you have boiled the shells and let it simmer till the meat be thoroughly done, which you can ascertain by pricking with a fork and observing if any blood exudes; when none appears, strain the liquor through a fine sieve and return it to the stewpan, which may remain at some distance from the fire. Cut the meat into square bits of about an inch. Put the herbs, onion, etc., into a separate saucepan with four ounces of butter, three or four lumps of sugar and a bottle of Madeira; let this boil slowly. Whilst this is doing, melt in another saucepan half a pound of fresh butter and, when quite dissolved, thicken it with flour, but do not make it too thick, and then add a pint of the liquor from the shells; let this boil very gently, removing the scum as it rises. When both these saucepans are ready, strain the contents of the first through a sieve, and this done, add both to the stewpan. Warm up the liquor from the shells, the green fat and mucilage and put them and the meat into the stewpan with the yolks of a dozen hard-boiled eggs, the juice of half a dozen green limes and two teaspoons of cayenne. Gently warm up the whole together, and you may regard your cookery as complete.

From Mrs. *Rorer's Philadelphia Cook Book,* 1886, page 31-33

Not a moment too soon. I offer this astonishing recipe for your interest. Personally, I think the cook deserved to add the bottle of Madeira to himself instead of the soup. Not only does turtle soup create a scene of violence and an unsavory mess, but you use practically every pan in the kitchen. Surely the ship's doctor cut some corners to produce this delicacy; but, unfortunately, no record exists to tell us how.

In many places, sea and green turtles are endangered and are now protected from being made into soup. And cooks are protected from having to make it.

ROAST PORK

To Roast Pork

When you roast that which has the skin on, take a sharp knife and cut through the rind, that it may crisp well. If a leg, cut a hole under the twist and stuff it with chopped bread, seasoned with pepper, salt, and sage, and skewer it up. Roast it crisp and handsomely brown. Make a drawn gravy of the dripping, and serve with apple sauce. This is called mock goose. The spare-rib should be sprinkled with flour, and pepper, and a little salt, and turned often, until nearly done; then let the round side lie up until nicely brown. Make the gravy of the dripping, prepared with flour, and seasoned well with salt; never send it to table without apple sauce, sallad, pickles, or slaw. Pork must be well done. To every pound allow quarter of a hour; for example, twelve pounds will require three hours. If it be a thin piece of that weight, two hours will roast it.

From *The Complete Domestic Guide,* by Mrs. L.G. Abell, 1853, page 88

Most of us would agree that Mrs. Abell was right when she said that pork must be well done, although modern pork is very safe. In order for fifteen minutes to the pound to work, she must have roasted at a higher temperature than is generally used today. Most cookbooks today recommend twenty-five to thirty minutes to the pound in a 325° oven. On shipboard, roasting was probably done in the galley stove's oven, a process, strictly speaking, known in the nineteenth century as baking; ashore some people might still have used a fireplace and tin kitchen.

Cabin diners might have been amused at Mrs. Abell's injunction against sending the pork to table without applesauce, salad, or slaw. But sea cooks—or stewards—made every effort to serve those with it if they could. Mrs. Lawrence commented once that a pitch of the ship dumped out some apples being stewed to accompany pork for dinner, resulting in a sauce-less roast of pork. I offer Mrs. Abell's recipe for your interest; no interpretation follows.

AMBROSIAS

Orange Ambrosia

Ambrosia

8 fine oranges, peeled and sliced.

1/2 grated coconut.

1/2 cup of powdered sugar.

Arrange slices of orange in a glass dish; scatter grated coconut thickly over them; sprinkle this lightly with sugar, and cover with another layer of orange. Fill the dish in this order, having a double quantity of coconut at top. Serve soon after it is prepared.

From *The Dinner Year Book*, by Marion Harland, 1878, page 212

Pine-apple Ambrosia

1 pine-apple, pared and cut into small squares.

1 coconut, pared and grated.

1 cup powdered sugar.

1 large glass good sherry or Marsala.

Put a layer of pineapple in a glass bowl; strew with sugar, and wet with wine. Next, put a stratum of coconut, and sprinkle more sparsely with sugar. More pineapple, sugar, and wine, and continue to add layers in the order given. The top coating must be of coconut. Eat soon, or the pineapple will wither in the wine and become tough. Pass light cake with it.

From *The Dinner Year Book*, by Marion Harland, 1878, page 273

Usually New Englanders, when given fresh fruits, put them into pies for dessert. Travelers like Mary Lawrence and Sallie Smith all remarked on the succulence of fresh tropical fruits. In the last half of the nineteenth century these exotics were increasingly available in good fresh condition in New England towns. Still, oranges were a special treat for many people, and so were pineapples. Period cookbooks comment on the tendency of pineapples to be fibrous and to need sugar. Eating them fresh was probably not a rewarding experience.

This is not a problem for us today. These two ambrosia recipes are wonderfully simple, probably not much used in the nineteenth century, and depend for success upon fresh coconut and fruit. As it stands, the pineapple ambrosia is very coconutty. One average-sized coconut will yield about six cups of fresh grated coconut while one cut-up pineapple yields about four cups. You may wish to reduce the coconut by half or more.

Use confectioners sugar or granulated sugar powdered in a blender and adjust the amount to your taste, keeping in mind that the Yankees of the nineteenth century had a sweet tooth. A large glass of sherry is about half a cup; a medium, golden sherry is a good choice.

The orange ambrosia yields 8-10 servings.

The pineapple ambrosia yields 4 servings.

Sallie Smith aboard the whaleship *Ohio* in 1876 wrote the recipe for this frosted fruitcake in the back of her journal.

FRUITCAKE AND FROSTING

Fruit cake
two lbs sifted flour
" " loaf sugar
" " butter
" " raisins
1 lb citron
1 " almonds
18 eggs
1 teacup brandy
a little soda
All kinds of spice

From manuscript recipes in the journal of Sallie Smith's voyage in the bark *Ohio*, 1876-77, manuscript collection, G.W. Blunt White Library, Mystic Seaport Museum

As we have seen, some voyagers took fruitcake with them to enjoy at sea; Mrs. Smith took her recipe, or perhaps collected it from another whaling wife and penciled it in the back of her journal along with a number of other recipes. Nineteenth-century fruitcake recipes do not all agree on ingredients. While Mrs. Smith's recipe does not include currants, a good many recipes from the same period did. Cinnamon, nutmeg, and mace are the most common spices.

This is a large recipe, and yields about sixteen pounds of fruitcake. You may wish to divide it. To help you calculate what pan sizes to use, you will find a 4 1/2-by-8 1/2-inch pan will yield a 2 1/2-pound cake. An interpretation follows.

9 cups sifted flour
2 teaspoons baking soda
1 tablespoon cinnamon
1 1/2 teaspoons nutmeg
1 teaspoon mace
allspice and ginger to taste
4 cups sugar
4 cups butter
1/2 cup brandy
18 eggs
5 1/2 cups raisins
2 2/3 cups citron
5 2/3 cups slivered almonds
Preheat oven to 275°

1. Sift together dry ingredients.
2. Cream together butter and sugar. Beat the eggs very well and mix into the butter and sugar, and add the brandy.
3. Beat in the dry ingredients. Stir in the fruit and nuts.
4. Divide batter among your pans which should be greased and/or lined with parchment or waxed paper.
5. Bake for 1 1/2 to 3 hours, depending on pan size, or until the cake pulls away from the side of the pan and a knife inserted comes out fairly clean.

Yields 16 pounds of fruitcake.

QUINCE PRESERVES

Preserved Quinces
Pare and core your quinces, take the cores and skins and boil them an hour, then strain the juice all out through a coarse cloth; boil your quinces in this juice till they are tender, then take them out; add the weight of the quinces in clean sugar to the sirup, boil it and skim it till it is clean; then put in your quinces again, and boil them three hours, when they are done. Preserves should not be covered up till entirely cold. They should be set away in stone jars.

From *New England Economical Housekeeper*, by Mrs. E.A. Howland, 1845, page 65

MARMALADES

They may be made of any fruits without seeds. The fruit should be boiled very soft with some of the kernals; and all of the pits of quinces, and parings, boiled and strained, added to the sugar. Mash to a fine pulp, and add sugar in the proportions of the sweetmeat, and simmer thick. It should be a smooth thick mass. Put up in tumblers.

From *The Complete Domestic Guide*, by Mrs. L.G. Abell, 1853, page 154

Preserved quinces could be served in a dish for tea. On shipboard, Mrs. Brewster may have used her quinces in that way once the supply of fresh fruit was gone. She may have also made marmalade from her supply of quinces.

"Pound for pound" was the rule of thumb for most nineteenth-century preserving; that is, one pound of sugar for every pound of fruit, or, as Mrs. Howland said, "the weight of the quinces in sugar." While Howland suggested putting the quinces away in stone jars, you may wish to can yours. Use a hot pack and process for twenty minutes in a boiling-water bath.

The second recipe is a good general instruction for that sort of preserve—as the recipe notes, for fruits that "do not have seeds" (as strawberries or raspberries have). Seeded fruits were usually made into jam. Again this is a pound-for-pound type of preserve. Quinces are high in pectin so you should have no trouble getting the marmalade to jell, which you can test by seeing if a spoonful sets up in cold water.

CANNED WHORTLEBERRIES

Preserved Whortleberries

#244. To preserve Whortleberries, for Winter Use.

Put the berries in a bottle, then cork and seal it, place the bottle in a kettle of cold water, and gradually let it boil. As soon as it boils, take it off and let it cool; then take the bottles out and put them away for winter use.

Gooseberries, plums, and currants, may be preserved in the same manner.

From *New England Economical Housekeeper,* by Mrs. E.A. Howland, 1845, page 64

TO PRESERVE FRUITS FOR TARTS OR OTHER FAMILY DESSERTS

Cherries, plums of all sorts, and apples, gather when ripe, and lay them in small jars that will hold a pound; strew over each jar six ounces of good loaf sugar, pounded; cover with two bladders, each separately tied down; then put the jars up to the neck in a large stewpan of water, and let it boil gently for three hours. All sorts of fruits should be kept free from damp.

From *Practical American Cookery and Domestic Economy,* by Miss Hall, 1855, page 241

CANNING

This is a most valuable manner of preserving vegetables and fruit....I also advise the canning of sweetmeats of every kind. In that case the same amount of sugar is not required, and the fruit does not have to be boiled until the natural flavor is entirely lost. If glass jars are used instead of cans, they must be put on the fire in cold water with a plate or piece of wood in the bottom of the kettle. They should not be filled until the water is boiling, and when they are cold the covers should be tightened, as the glass will contract a little after cooling.

From *Practical Cooking and Dinner Giving,* by Mrs. Mary F. Henderson, 1882, page 244-45

I include these three sets of instructions for your interest, and to demonstrate that Fred and Sallie Smith would have been familiar with canning procedures for fruits like whortleberries for pot pie. Imagine what a chore this would have been on board ship.

PINEAPPLE PRESERVES

Pine Apples.
Take those that are ripe and fresh; pare off the rind, and cut in slices about half an inch thick. Sprinkle between them powdered loaf sugar, and let them remain until the next day. Then with the usual syrup boil until tender, putting them in when it is cold. Keep in a cool place.

From *Practical American Cookery and Domestic Economy,* by Miss Hall, 1855, page 154

Preserved Pineapples
Pare the pineapple, and carefully remove the eyes with a sharp pointed knife. Either chop or grate the pineapple, or shred it with a fork, rejecting the core. Weigh, and allow three-quarters of a pound of sugar to each pound of fruit. Put all together in the preserving kettle, stir well, stand aside overnight. In the morning, bring to a boil, skim and cook slowly. Pour it into jars, and seal.

From *Ayer's Preserve Book,* ca. 1895, page 165

Miss Hall, and others, cautioned cooks that potential difficulties with making preserves were that they could ferment, get moldy, or become candied. On a ship at sea, fermentation and mold would be the two most likely storage problems. Candying was caused by processing the fruit too long at too high a temperature.

We have no way of knowing whether Mrs. Lawrence put up her "famous lot of pineapples," for long- or short-term storage. She may have made a pineapple jam or marmalade that she could have brought home to New Bedford, or perhaps she prepared the pineapples as canned fruit would be. Both of these methods could be regarded as "preserving."

The first recipe would be satisfactory as a method of short-term preserving. Its inclusion in Miss Hall's book gave cooks ashore a way of stretching a treat of pineapples a little longer.

The "usual syrup" could be whatever you prefer: a light syrup of half as much sugar as water, a medium of three quarters as much sugar as water, or a heavy syrup of equal proportions of sugar and water. Be sure to use the liquid that collects after the pineapples have stood with their light sprinkling of sugar. If you use this recipe literally, keep the pineapples in the fridge. Or you can can them by cooking them in the syrup for about five minutes, packing them hot in sterilized jars, allowing half-an-inch headroom, and processing in a boiling-water bath for twenty minutes.

The second recipe yields a jam-like pineapple preserve and comes from a later recipe book than Mrs. Lawrence's time. But the relative scarcity of pineapples for preserving until later in the century may account for the scarcity of pineapple-preserve recipes in the middle of the nineteenth century. The low-pectin pineapple does not set up as readily as other fruits so this jam is very tender. It is most suitable as a sauce or cake filling. Modern cooks may wish to take advantage of liquid pectin in the following adapted recipe.

1 pineapple (about 4 lbs.)
sugar
3 oz. liquid pectin

1. Pare and core the pineapple, and shred into a bowl to catch the juice. Measure the pineapple pulp and juice.
2. Measure out three quarters as much sugar (about 2 cups) as pulp and juice, and mix together well in a preserving kettle. Let stand overnight.
3. Next day, bring the pineapple and sugar mixture to a hard boil, and boil for a minute. Remove it from the fire and stir in the pectin, and bring to a boil again for a minute.
4. Remove from the fire once again and continue stirring for another five minutes to keep the bits of fruit suspended. Pour into jars and seal.

Yields about four half-pint jars.

Meals Ashore for All Hands

For some nineteenth-century seafarers, going ashore was sufficient reason for going to sea. The lure of the open sea was less of a motivation for travel than were all the world's sights, peoples, and customs. For better or worse, travelers inevitably encountered strange foods and foodways.

Port cities around the world were a complex of wharves, piers and an array of ship-oriented businesses including inns, boarding houses, and eateries of every sort and quality. Here is New York's South Street in 1856, shown in an engraving in *Gleason's Pictorial Drawing-Room Companion.* [South Street Seaport Museum] At the fictional Spouter Inn, Ishmael found a supper typical of small establishments, opposite, "fare of the most substantial kind—not only meat and potatoes but dumplings; good heavens! dumplings for supper!"

We of the twentieth century take foreign food for granted: we eat Chinese or Italian without leaving town or even home. Foreign food has come to us via immigrant neighbors, newspaper and magazine articles, restaurants, and cookbooks. Most large chain grocery stores have foreign-food sections stocked with items that nineteenth-century New Englanders could only hope to see in foreign ports. In urban centers, immigrant populations have created an import market for their native foodstuffs to which anyone has access. Some of these foods have become relatively common in people's diets, or at least in the cookery magazines—for example, Chinese vegetables like bok choy, or South American jicama—some only in the past twenty years or so.

As we have seen in preceding chapters, nineteenth-century New Englanders had a monotonous diet compared to today. Industry and transportation have changed ours. But when nineteenth-century Yankees traveled, some of them welcomed the chance to try new foods. Others sought the familiar, as some people do today. As with exotic provisions, seafarers' narratives and journals provide descriptions of their experiences. In some, we encounter suspicion and ethnocentricity; in others, curiosity and a lively sense of adventure. Some describe the new foods well and provide wonderful comparisons of exotic and familiar.

With the new foods came the eating habits of other cultures. Sometimes the unfamiliar habits caused more comment than the food itself. Nineteenth-century New Englanders were not a particularly tolerant group by our standards; it is important to keep what we now see as their racism and ethnocentricity in perspective. Travel and contact with new people and places—and food—broadened some people's minds, but had hardly any impact on others.

"Where's a Good Place to Eat?"

"Where's a good place to eat?" has been the tourist's question for years. Some sailors, of course, never had a chance to ask this question before they found themselves stowed away in some boardinghouse with a sizable tab already run up against their next advance. I will not discuss in great depth the landsharking that provided food, shelter, and entertainment for sailors in ports around the world. This topic has been covered well by others.[1] Besides, food is not usually the first thing that springs to mind when you think of sailors' accommodations ashore, nor is it the best-documented aspect of Jack's experience on the beach.

In all major ports and many smaller cities, inns, taverns, hotels, restaurants, and cafes of tremendously varying distinction offered food for travelers. The Spouter Inn of fiction and Mystic Seaport Museum depiction typifies small port eateries; but the range included, for example, in New York City, Delmonico's Restaurant, waterfront cafes, and street vendors. Boardinghouses accommodated a range of social classes and were often respectable establishments serving home-cooked food. A well-developed system of boardinghouses in Honolulu, Hawaii, for example, made a home away from home for New England seafarers and their families.

And there were kind hosts in every land—fellow American or English-speaking missionaries, merchants, colonial officials, ambassadors, as well as native people who proffered hospitality to seafarers. Sometimes these hosts reappear in several journals as one captain and lady after another visit the same place and record their experiences. In some ways, the nineteenth-century seafarer's world was very small.

Small Ports and The Spouter Inn

Small port-city taverns and inns provided food, drink, and lodging. A distinction should be made between hardcore waterfront places and the decent houses of which Melville's Spouter is an example. In *Moby Dick* Ishmael and Queequeg stayed at the Spouter for lodging, got their breakfasts there, but also ate at the Try Pots on Nantucket, where they had their choice of two chowders.

Mystic Seaport Museum's exhibit tavern is not a historic building, but houses the interior of two rooms from an inn in Stoddard, New Hampshire. Imagine a larger building, with several rooms—at least one for a bar room, plus at least one dining room, possibly more, a parlor, a kitchen, pantries, dwelling space for the innkeeper and family, guest rooms both private and shared, and, in the case of larger establishments, public rooms for meetings and possibly even a ballroom. Until mid-century, separate parlors were provided for women in the more respectable houses, but for the most part public accommodations were places for men.

Frederick Marryat devoted a chapter of his *Diary in America* to "Hostelry and Gastronomy," and said that the American innkeeper in the 1830s was seen in the same light as a personal host, someone who was likely to be met with in respectable company. In a very democratic fashion, he would greet travelers by shaking hands, and "he and his wife sit at the head of the *table-d'hote* at meal times...his authority, like that of captains of the steamboats, is undisputed; indeed the captains...may be partly classed under the same head," as innkeeper.[2]

Herman Melville's description of the accommodations and supper and breakfast at the Spouter Inn ring true. Ishmael had selected the Spouter because "I thought that here was the very spot for cheap lodgings and the best of pea-coffee."[3] It was just as well that he became accustomed at the Inn to pea-coffee—a coffee substitute made by roasting dried peas, grinding them, and brewing a beverage from them in the same manner as coffee—because a good many ships provided similar "coffee" for their crews. The Spouter, however, served beefsteaks for breakfast, which Queequeg preferred to all else, and "likes them rare," as we might expect of the strong and brave harpooneer.

Oysters were a nineteenth-century fast food. Oyster stands like this one at the Fulton Market in New York City served the public with raw freshly-opened and sometimes roasted oysters. Oyster saloons offered sit-down meals of oyster stew, or oysters roasted, fried, and broiled. Other food stands sold boiled corn, pastries, ice cream, sandwiches, candy, and hot and cold beverages to all comers. [Engraving from *Harper's Illustrated Weekly*, 29 October 1870, MSM 94.3.11]

The supper menu, Ishmael reported, was "fare...of the most substantial kind—not only meat and potatoes, but dumplings; good heavens! dumplings for supper!" He and the others ate this meal in a room adjoining the bar room. "It was as cold as Iceland—no fire at all—the landlord said he couldn't afford it. Nothing but two dismal tallow candles, each in a winding-sheet. We were fain to button up our monkey jackets, and to hold to our lips cups of scalding tea with our half-frozen fingers."[4]

Here is Melville's fictional description of how the men ate: "After we were all seated at the table,...I was preparing to hear some good stories about whaling; to my no small surprise, nearly every man maintained a profound silence....Here they sat at a social break-fast table—all of the same calling, all of kindred tastes—looking around...sheepishly at each other." Two English travelers in America, Frances Trollope visiting in the 1830s, and Capt. R.N. MacKinnon, writing twenty years later in the early 1850s, made similar observations about men eating hurriedly and silently in public places. Trollope described "long silent tables" and Captain MacKinnon wrote that people staying at hotels in New York City "will be struck by the absence of conversation. The solemnity is contagious."[5]

Small inns and eateries, then as now, offered foods that could be quickly prepared. A good example was "Gray's" in New London, Connecticut, which sold "Confectionery, Fruits, Nuts, and Toys" and advertised in 1859 that it served "at any time of day or evening, Oysters, roasted, broiled, fried, stewed, or raw on the half shell, Beef Steak, Ham and Eggs, Mutton Chops, Pies, Cakes, Tea and Coffee, and other refreshments usually found at a first class restaurant...This is a convenient and desirable place for people visiting New London to obtain meals and refreshments."[6] All the meats and the oyster dishes could be cooked quickly, and the cakes and pies done ahead to be served immediately.

Young Samuel Samuels ashore in Louisiana enjoyed a Creole Cook's corn cake, recipe page 207; gumbo, recipe page 206; and curried pork in 1835.

The silent dining and easily prepared food of early establishments like the Spouter and Gray's foreshadow the modern fast-food restaurant, where one can quickly buy a solitary meal and consume it without ever conversing with a fellow diner.

Large Ports and Many Choices

Big port cities offered a wide range of choices. New York and Boston featured, for example, fine fashionable restaurants like Delmonico's and Parker's, where businessmen, politicians, famous visitors, professionals, and well-to-do travelers ate—people, in fact, like Richard Henry Dana, Jr.

Dana, author of *Two Years Before the Mast,* became a Boston lawyer after his travels at sea. In 1859 he reported in his journal that "I have over-worked for the last ten years...One day a few weeks since, in the midst of arguing an exciting cause—the 'Smyrna Case'...I went into Parker's Restaurant & being hungry, I ate, hardly knowing what I did, a quantity of cold corned beef, & returned to court, & finished my argument, & went back to Parker's to dine. While at dinner, I was taken with a fit, from indigestion, & fell senseless." The fit resulted only from the hurried eating that kept him from adequately chewing his corned beef, but the incident convinced him he needed an around-the-world trip, during which he made detailed notes of many meals from which we will often quote in this chapter.[7]

Smaller eateries in the large ports included oyster saloons, which were tremendously popular in the last half of the nineteenth century and which will be described further in the chapter about shellfish. Other eateries offered plain fare at reasonable prices. They were decent houses suitable for anyone, even a woman traveling alone.

Mrs. Farnsworth, traveling in 1858 with her small daughter Annie, went "to the restaurant for breakfast and called for an oyster stew, giving Annie her first taste of the delicious bivalve, and by the time her appetite was appeased, there was no chance for my breakfast. In settling the bill my attention was diverted from her but on taking her in my arms found she was hugging half a loaf of bread she had taken from the table...It created a laugh among the onlookers, she was such a little tot."[8]

This 1825 menu from the Farmer's Inn in the Bowery in New York is similar to Gray's in New London a few years later: "Beef Steaks, Mutton Chops, Veal Cutlets, Broiled Chicken, &c." Later in the century—1872 to the turn of the century—Mike Lyon's famous restaurant in New York was never closed, and always had corned beef and cabbage on the menu.[9]

A sailor ashore in a port city like New York in the nineteenth century was more likely to seek a meal at the lower end of the price scale. Eateries abounded along the docks "to which," *Harper's Weekly* claimed, most of their readers "are really as complete strangers as they are to Kamtchatka or Patagonia." In a "low restaurant kept by an Irishwoman," Chinese, Irish, black, French, and German customers "mingled in perfect harmony," at least while the reporter was there. "The good-natured, broad-breasted, jolly-faced hostess was a stranger to national antipathies. She sold victuals to everyone who could pay for them and was not sufficiently hard-hearted to turn away the poor devils who sometimes came begging for a meal." [10]

The manner of food preparation and service was described as "rather promiscuous" but plentiful. The reporter asserted that these small places sold the leftovers from larger, expensive establishments. "The bit of steak, or roast, or vegetable you may leave on your plate at some first-class eating house, is not, as is sometimes horribly suggested, served to you the next day in some undistinguishable compound with a French name; it is sold as stated, and appears on the rude counter of some dock restaurants in the shape of soup or Irish stew, or beef pie...Prices at these eating houses are very low": ten to fifteen cents for a dinner.

Street vendors, both mobile and in small stands, abounded in cities. In 1870, the "three finest out-door stands in New York" were clustered at the junction of Wall and Nassau Streets. These were semipermanent structures, with roofs, counters, and doors; one sold French candy and tobacco, and the other two "tarts and cakes, sandwiches and pie." For beverages "ice-cold soda water" or "smoking hot coffee, were offered." Nassau Street had other vendors, including a banana, peach, and pear vendor and a peanut vendor with his roaster in a cart.[11]

The clientele of these stands and vendors were more prosperous than those of dockside coffee booths. Cheaper and more vulgar, but not vicious, these booths were "well warmed and cheerfully lighted," places where half-drunken beggars, poor little newsboys and girls, and "the tough and storm beaten sailor" could be found eating the "cakes and pies so tempting to the unfastidious appetite."[12]

Ready-to-eat food was provided by street vendors like the "female Falstaff, with blue bonnet strings and ragged royal purple dress, trimmed with black velvet, [who] vends suspicious cakes and pies, soggy yellow buns, and frightful red tarts, from a stand with a newspaper for a tablecloth." Hot corn and raw oysters, all sorts of fruits, candies, ice cream, and soda waters and lemonade were vended from carts by an economically marginal population.[13]

Hotel and Steamship Dining

The bill of fare at large hotels and restaurants in port cities received mixed reviews in the nineteenth century, but was mostly well-received. Marryat reported that there was good food to be had in America—in fact, better than some he recalled having in England, which, considering the reputation of English cooking, may have been faint praise. Captain MacKinnon was similarly impressed and said of New York hotels that "the cookery is admirable." The menus quoted by these writers show a wide variety of meat, game, poultry, wild fowl, and many dishes prepared in a French manner, or at least given a French name. [14]

An article in *Century Magazine* in 1885, however, promoted a change toward simplicity in menus that appeared to be underway: "When I have seen the lengthy bill of fare so commonly furnished at large American hotels...I have often believed that a reformer might succeed, by establishing [a hotel which offered] a variety well-cooked and served, through the cooks attention not being dissipated among a multitude of dishes." The author pointed out that improvements in hotel food reflected improvements in the diet of society as a whole: "Fruit and vegetables are consumed much more plentifully than before quick trains transported them cheaply and canning became a prodigious business. Baked joints and fowl, so often parboiled and sodden, are giving place to...genuine roasts. The gridiron, thank goodness, has well-nigh driven the frying pan out of the kitchen, and wholesome broiled steaks and chops have taken the place of hard greasy meats....Pie, too, is going....But hot bread and cakes still hold their own, and the baleful ice pitcher remains....Salt fish, salt meat, and pork are now little used. Fresh fish and oysters are consumed very largely."[15]

Passenger steamship menus paralleled those of large hotel dining rooms and restaurants here and abroad. Even if the variety of choices was comparatively limited on board ship, the same style prevailed: soup, fish, choices of boiled and roasted meats, with appropriate accompaniments, choices of entrees, sometimes even listed fashionably in French, vegetables, puddings and pastries, and desserts. A traveler of means could go from the steamship saloon to a hotel dining room and observe scant difference in menu offerings, except that the quality of the fresh food may have been more certain ashore.

Meals Ashore Around the World

Let's turn to the narratives and journals and see what people said about meals they ate in various places around the world.

San Francisco and California: Besides being the destination of many New Englanders in 1849 and years after, San Francisco was the major West Coast port for most vessels. Seafarers looked forward to the fresh foods they would get there, either to provision the ship or to enjoy ashore.

When her officer husband was stationed in San Francisco, Mrs. Farnsworth ate at the Officer's Mess House, "and as after any sea voyage, I had an enormous appetite....I had never tasted fresh salmon, and thought it so delicious that for some time I indulged in it twice daily, and the celery...was equally excellent."[16]

Captain John Whidden, ashore in California between voyages in 1863, took breakfast in a flower-filled room, with fresh air coming through open windows. "The table with its snowy linen and silver service, was spread with the most tempting repast of fruit, fresh eggs, and crisp bacon, tender steak done to a turn, and the crowning dish a large platter of fresh mountain trout."[17]

When the *Clarissa B. Carver* was in San Francisco in September and October 1878, the Dow family indulged in fresh fruit; Mrs. Dow, the captain's wife, wrote to her son Fred in Searsport, Maine, reporting, "When father came back to the ship last night with the letters, he brought a box of strawberries, pears, plums and grapes and a box of honey. You know he is partial to honey. We are glad, for the fruit was so poor in Yokohama."[18] The Dows looked forward to the fresh fruit and vegetables found in the city markets, something they enjoyed so much that they frequently mentioned it in their letters home, affirming that the reputation of California fruits and vegetables was already well-established.

Creole cookery: Samuel "Bully" Samuels, at about age twelve, sailed to Mobile Bay in the revenue brig *Jefferson*, around 1835. As the coxswain of the captain's gig, a trip ashore to the captain's home gave him a chance to hang around the kitchen. "The trip generally resulted in my having a good breakfast with Millie the black cook, with whom I had become a great favorite....She loved to talk as much as I love to listen while stowing away chicken gumbo, curried pig, corn-cakes and molasses, and all such delicacies."[19]

Samuels, a Northerner, did not record his reaction to what was probably spicy fare. The black Creole cooks of the Gulf ports were famous for their blending of Southern, West Indian, and—in New Orleans—French fare. Of all these dishes, the corn cakes, which were either the same as or similar to various Indian-meal quick breads made in New England at the same time, were probably the only food that seemed even a little familiar to Samuels.

These vendors of lemonade and candy set up a simple sales table on Boston Common, the prototype of the lemonade vending on the grounds of Mystic Seaport Museum. The gentleman on the left is a veteran of the War Between the States, whose injuries may have prompted customers to stop for refreshments. [Albumen stereograph, MSM 87.131]

Mexican and Spanish-American: Richard Henry Dana, Jr., visited California twice, once as a young sailor on board the brig *Pilgrim* and the ship *Alert* in 1835, and again as a mature traveler about 25 years later. When the *Pilgrim* was some distance down the coast from Santa Barbara, part of the crew went ashore and for supper they had "frijoles (the perpetual food of the Californians, but which, when well cooked are the best bean in the world) coffee made of burnt wheat, and hard bread." Later, on a liberty day in San Diego, the sailors went to a mission and, when asked what they wished to eat, Dana mentioned "frijoles which I knew they must have if they had nothing else, and beef and bread, and a hint for wine." When they were served they found their request answered with "dishes contain[ing] baked meats, frijoles stewed with pepper and onion, boiled eggs, and California flour baked into a kind of macaroni...the most sumptuous meal we had eaten since we left Boston."[20]

Later, Dana, aboard the *Alert*, stopped at Monterey, "the best place to go ashore on the whole coast." He and his companions "rode out to the Carmel mission...where we got something in the way of a dinner—beef, eggs, frijoles, tortillas, and some middling wine."[21]

The Bostonian Dana's apparent fondness and high praise for frijoles is an indication of the man's sophisticated palate; no stranger to the New England baked bean, he seems to have enjoyed these peppery Spanish bean dishes as a young sailor in foreign parts. But when he returned to the West Coast in 1859, Dana the gentleman went to French restaurants or inns.

French cooking: Dana stayed in San Francisco where he had "fresh meats & vegit., & excellent cooking, at French Restaurant. No one can conceive of the comfort of it, who has not been through a bad voyage at sea." Even when he went to San Jose, he stayed at a "French inn, where cooking was excellent," and then again, near Enriqueta, his hotel was "a little place, but kept by Frenchmen, & of course, well kept....The Frenchmen can make good bread anywhere, even in Boston. A Yankee can make good bread nowhere."[22]

Dana appreciated simple, basic things well done—in France in 1856 he noted that at Amiens he got off his train for a few moments and in the refreshment room purchased "the nicest cups of French coffee, and the neatest little pieces of bread and cake, a foretaste of that French tact and taste which no other people equal. Why should English coffee be unfit to drink, and French coffee excellent, with the intercourse there is between the people?"[23]

English fare: Dana did not think all English cooking was disappointing. He thought highly of English chop houses and admired the roast of mutton he saw at Simpsons, in London. "The joint kept hot, and under a cover, is rolled to your table on a small stand upon castors, the cover taken off and with the nicest skill and care, a hot slice is cut for you, with your due portion of fat, and the cutting so done that the juice of the meat runs into, and lies in the hollow of the meat, and not into the dish, and thence it is served out by a spoon. It was by far the best serving and eating of mutton I ever knew."[24]

Dana approved of the English tea "of muffins, tea, toast, and fried soles, so neatly set."[35] He also liked the English gentry's habit of leisurely breakfasts, like the one he attended at the Duke of Argyll's in Kensington, London, an informal event at which "the ladies are in easy morning dress, and the gentlemen in frock coats and boots. You take coffee or tea and toast, and fish or cold game, and fruit, and sit at table an hour or so and then lounge about the library, and converse....Everything is so easy and informal."[25]

Dana's impressions of the Portsmouth, England, waterfront in 1856, where the streets were full of soldiers and sailors, was colored by his knowledge of history: "the same lanes and streets, the same rooms in which the sailors of Nelson and Collingwood, Rodney and Howe, drank and sang, and rioted and were led to ruin."[26] But another English sailor, on an English whaler, far from home in the South Pacific, remembered breakfast in similar places:

"'Well, then,' said he, in a snugged tone, his eyes lighting up like lanterns, 'well, then, I'd go to Mother Moll's that makes the great muffins: I'd go there, you know and cock my foot on the 'ob, and call for a noggin' of somethink to begin with.'

"'and what then, Ropey?'

"'Why then, Flashy,...why then I'd draw my chair up and call for Betty, the gal wot tends to customers. Betty, my dear, says I, you look charmin' this mornin'; give me a nice rasher of bacon and h'eggs Betty my love; and I want a pint of h'ale, and three nice 'ot muffins and butter—and a slice of Cheshire...'"[27]

Ropey's account of such a succulent breakfast in the setting of a whaleship at sea so irritated a fellow sailor that Ropey was pounded for it.

Finally, here is Melville's description of supper in a Liverpool boardinghouse interestingly called "Sign of the Baltimore Clipper":

"Mounting a rickety staircase, we entered a room on the second floor. Three tall brass candlesticks shed a smoky light upon smoky walls, of what had once been sea-blue, covered with sailor-scrawls of foul anchors, lovers' sonnets, and ocean ditties. On one side, nailed against the wainscot in a row, were the four knaves of cards, each Jack putting his best foot foremost as usual. What these signified I never heard.

"But such ample cheer! Such a groaning table! Such a superabundance of solids and substantials! Was it possible that sailors fared thus?—the sailors, who at sea live upon salt beef and biscuit?

"First and foremost, was a mighty pewter dish, big as Achilles' shield, sustaining a pyramid of smoking sausages. This stood at one end; midway was a similar dish, heavily laden with farmers' slices of head-cheese; and at the opposite end, a congregation of beef-steaks, piled tier over tier. Scattered at intervals between, were side dishes of boiled potatoes, eggs by the score, bread, and pickles; and on a stand adjoining, was an ample reserve of every thing on the supper table.

"We fell to with all our hearts; wrapt ourselves in hot jackets of beefsteaks; curtailed the sausages with great celerity; and sitting down before the head-cheese, soon razed it to its foundations."[28]

Sicilian dining: Captain Whidden visited Sicily in 1858, and ate a dinner composed of "spaghetti, stews, macaroni, tomatoes, peppers, chicken fricasseed with tomatoes, sweets, light wines with fruit, black coffee and bread."[29] Yankees were familiar with macaroni by this time; it could be bought and taken home to be made into dishes—most usually a variation of what we would call macaroni and cheese. Some cookbooks even gave recipes for making macaroni from scratch. Spaghetti, the now-familiar string pasta usually served with tomato sauce, would not become common among New Englanders until the twentieth century.

Dana visited Venice, where he breakfasted "in Sq.[are] of St. Mark, wh.[ich] is lined with the best of restorants & cafes, where people eat & read, at tables in the open air,—where fruits are abundant and cheap—grapes, peaches, figs, & melons."[30]

Hawaiian cooking: The Hawaiian Islands, called the Sandwich Islands in the nineteenth century, contained a mixture of Pacific and Western influences. Island cooks included Pacific and Asian people—a great many Chinese people immigrated there—cooking western foods for their employers and customers, all foreigners to the Islands. Melville wrote that among the South Sea islands, in which he included Hawaii, "every evidence of civilization...directly pertains to foreigners."[31] Of course, he meant civilization in the Western sense. So the Yankee descriptions of food there range from the experience of the luau to familiar New England fare in island boardinghouses.

Because the Hawaiian Islands supplied provisions to vessels, food production there was skewed to meet the demands of Western ships. The following advertisement, quoted by Francis Olmsted in a letter written to his brother

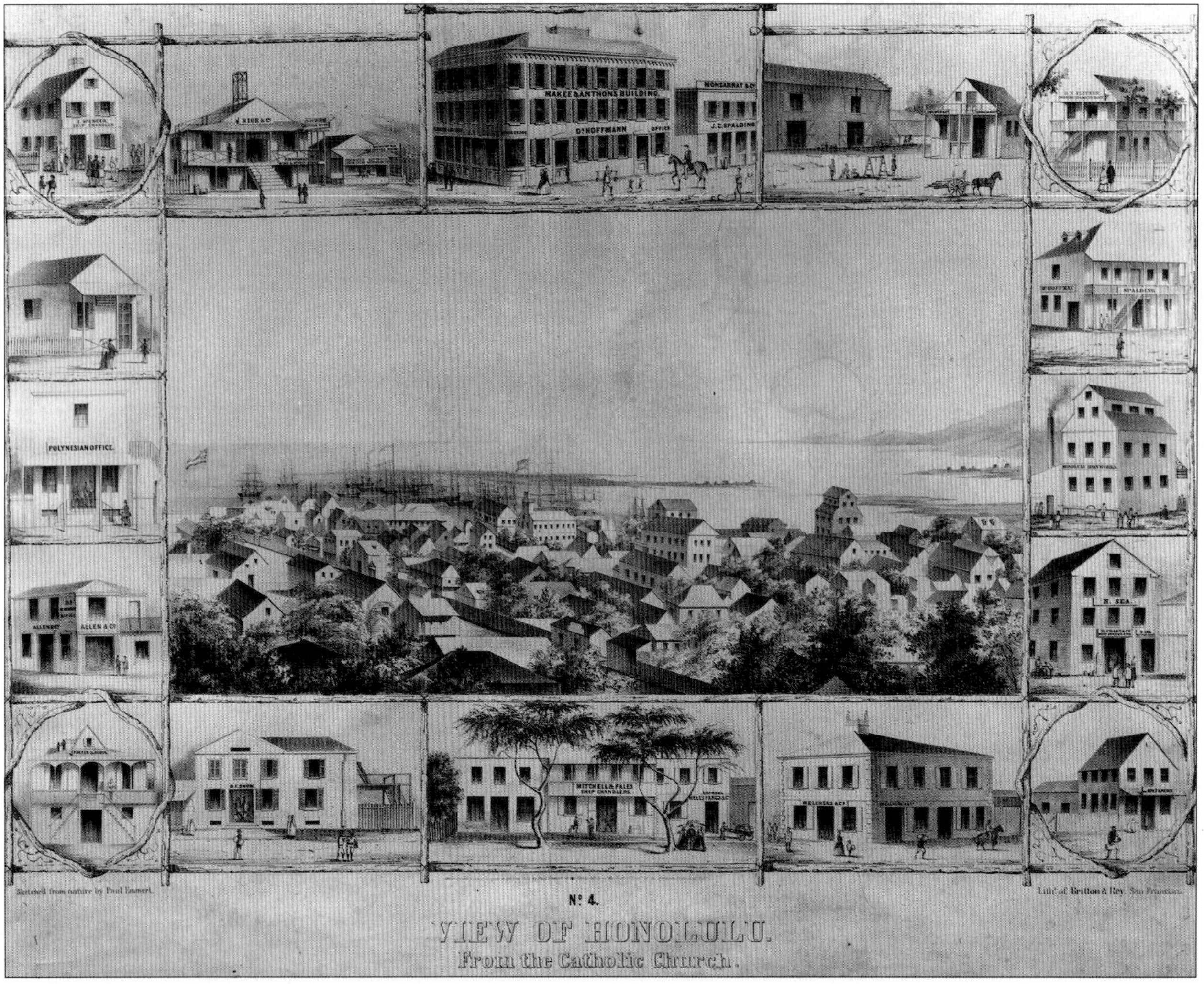

in 1840, illustrates a Chinese enterprise. Sam and Mow were from Canton and had established a bakery: "Good people all come near and buy Of Sam and Mow good cake and pie, Bread hard or soft, for land or sea, 'Celestial' made; come buy of wẹ."[32]

Cake and pie of the sort advertised to English customers were certainly not part of the Celestial Empire's regular foodways.

This view of Honolulu in 1854 shows a city familiar to Mrs. Lawrence and Mrs. Brewster, both of whom spent time living with other New Englanders in boarding houses kept by Yankees. Surrounded by Pacific foodways, the boarding-house owners and their guests recreated familiar New England fare instead. [Lithograph by Britton & Rey, San Francisco, 1854, MSM 32.265]

Hawaii was a destination for whaleships during nearly all their cruises in the Pacific Ocean, as well as other sailing vessels and, later, steamships. In Gold Rush days, before California developed farms, Hawaii supplied fresh provisions and vessels sailed between the islands and the West Coast carrying fruits, vegetables, and meats.

Between cruises on the various whaling grounds, a stop at Hawaii meant fresh provisions or a chance to transfer whale oil to a homeward-bound vessel. As more and more wives accompanied their whaling-captain husbands, the stop in Hawaii also meant a great deal of socializing with the many New Englanders doing business there, or serving as missionaries, as well as with the many families aboard other ships in port.[33]

When Mary Brewster arrived in Honolulu in 1849, she and Captain Brewster "Went ashore this morning have made calculations to take our meals at the Mansion house and have hired a room close by the lodge. It seems like being home to see so many familiar faces." Staying at one place and eating at another seems to have been common, as Mary Lawrence observed. The Lawrences stayed in "a room...at Mrs. Humphrey's; and we take our meals at Mrs. Carter's, a custom which prevails extensively at the Sandwich Islands." Mrs. Lawrence said that acquaintances from home in New England, together with new friends made during the voyage, would gather at a boardinghouse in Hawaii "five or six couples, and after spending an hour or two very pleasantly, would adjourn to an ice cream parlor."[34]

New Englanders in Hawaii could enjoy familiar home fare and island foods prepared in a Yankee fashion or, if they were so inclined, could eat among the native people, which some did. John Perkins did a little of both when the *Tiger*'s crew was at Byron's Bay in April 1846. "At noon we eat dinner at an Englishmans' who keeps an eating house for ships crews on liberty. Our dinner consisted of roast

A. WARNER & CO.,

DINING AND LUNCH ROOM,

No. 16 Dorrance Street, Cor. Fulton, Providence, R. I.

[OVER]

turkey & chickens, sweet potatoes & tarra a root like a potato fried like pancakes & boiled to be eaten with molasses. Their molasses is the best I ever tasted." The next day Perkins ate fried goat, sweet potatoes, and yams at a native's home.[35]

The taro was described by many Westerners, particularly the poi that was made from it. Taro is a root that grows in water to the size of a large sweet potato. Its texture is similar to potatoes, but more fibrous, and according to one observer "the taste, before dressed, is exceedingly pungent and acrid." Dana wrote that it is "the great vegit. of these islands, for foreigners as well as natives—is to them what the potato is to Ireland. Foreigners use it boiled or baked, as vegetable with meats," as in the meal Perkins reported. "Natives chiefly as poe."[36]

Poi varied in thickness, the density of which Felix Riesenberg claimed was measured by the number of fingers required to scoop some up to eat. The thickest was one finger poi. "Poi, one finger stuff, and none of your poverty stricken watery three and two finger poi of the stevedores and little island traders, was on the bill of fare," Riesenberg reported. Mary Brewster called poi "indispensable," and was generally dismayed to see the natives use their fingers for eating, especially when "it is quite usual for them to dip their fingers in the Poi Calabash and hold it for their dogs to lick and then the same for own palate."[37]

Contrast this with the islanders' own comments on poi—a food with many associations beyond mere sustenance. Dana was correct when he said that taro was to Hawaiians what the potato was to the Irish in importance as a staple; but the reverence islanders had for the taro root was closer to the Native American reverence for corn.[38] This was a cultural reverence to which the Yankee seafarers were insensible, a reverence that potatoes never stirred in the Irish, or in New Englanders either.

Poi-making was a fine skill, beginning with the judgment of when the taro was ready to be harvested—too soon and the taro was flakey; too late and it was gummy or watery. In the nineteenth century, taro for poi was cooked in an *imu*, an in-ground oven, about a foot deep, three or four feet in diameter, which was paved with stones and heated with a fire. When the imu was sufficiently hot, the taro was laid inside wrapped in leaves, with additional hot stones, and the whole sealed with leaves and earth to steam the roots inside. In later years, the taro was simply boiled.[39]

Once cooked, the taro was pounded till smooth, a process learned by islanders when they were still children. Using specialized tools and a particular method to insure cleanliness and a fine product, a whole Hawaiian family would cooperate to produce a batch of pounded taro to which some water was added, and the whole was then set away to ferment just a little. No part of the taro was wasted; the skin taken off was saved for fertilizer and the scrapings were fed to chickens or pigs. The taro crop was sustained by careful replanting.[40]

Most New England seafarers may have eaten poi without being aware of the effort and care that went into making the dish. If they were mindful of the lore and reverence around taro they seem not to have commented on it. Most of the time, they procured taro and cooked it as a root vegetable along with the sweet potatoes with which they were already familiar. It seems to have been a common table vegetable, as Mrs. Brewster reported.

Mary Brewster, either with friends or with her husband the captain, was likely to go sightseeing, taking along picnic food—once "a cold lunch of ham, bread, and cookys"—or eating at private homes. Ashore in 1847, she took a tour of East Maui, stopping at the home of Mr. Whittlesey, a missionary, at Kaupo, where they had two meals. "We had dinner about 3 consisted of roast Turkey, chicken, tarro and sweet potatoes and a good dish of coffee...had supper very late consisted of fried fish potatoes and tarro."[41]

A "dining saloon" stood on the main street of downtown Mystic in the last quarter of the nineteenth century. Their menu probably resembled "Gray's" in New London: oysters, chops, steak, pie, cake, tea and coffee. [Albumen print, MSM 77.92.599]

Her tour, in company with several missionary families, was partly a camping trip, with stops at missionary outposts, and occasionally at native homes. She frequently described the food they ate, which included roast duck, boiled ham, and bread, which they took along. At one native hut they were tired and hungry enough to be "all disposed to make way with roast pig with tarro and the best sweet potatoes I ever ate." On this trip they were also given currant cake and bread, sent along to them in a pail. As she reported, "the first move was made to the pail of food the bread and butter with the pan of currant cake though we eat sparingly the cake was soon devoured and one loaf of bread was left."[42]

Mary Brewster's experience of native cooking—particularly a luau—left her disinclined to eat. On a sightseeing trip to a volcano on Hilo, in 1846, she wrote "we had our own supper...which was a turkey liuou The company all relished it but to me it was very disagreeable It was cooked in true native style The fowl pig or what ever they have is dressed then rolled up in leaves with pork if they have it and the young tarro leaves put inside The whole taken and put in a hole dug into the ground and then filled with hot stones when the article is large the inside is also filled with hot stones before wrapping up it is then all covered up with leaves so none of the steam can escape and remains until wanted. When it comes out nicely cooked with them as well as foreign residents is considered a fine dish."[43]

This description will strike New Englanders as a process very similar to a clambake; whether Mary ever went to one of those, and what she would think of it, we have no way of knowing. Cooking in the ground this way is a universal technique, and was used, as we saw earlier, for cooking taro, too.

Lloyd Briggs, a 16-year-old student traveling for his health on the bark *Amy Turner* in 1880, had both Yankee and native fare at Hawaii a few decades later than Perkins and Mary Brewster. He was invited with the *Turner*'s captain to have dinner at Robert Lewers's house in Honolulu. "Mr. Lewers is head of the largest lumber concern in the island....The Lewers and Carters are more like New England people than anyone else I have met here." That was, of course, because they *were*, and appropriately their meal consisted of roast beef, green peas, fresh tomatoes, green corn, potatoes, and chutney, with taro and poi. Briggs was also invited to the home of H.A.P. Carter, the very wealthy brother of the *Turner*'s agent, for an elegant multicourse meal: "we had soup, followed by mullet, served with lettuce salad; chopped meat on toast; roast mutton with potatoes, tomatoes, green peas, fried sliced squash and fried bananas. For dessert there were floating islands with cake and afterwards fruits of many varieties."[44]

About 30 years after Mary Brewster's experience, young Briggs was treated to a luau: "a native dinner cooked especially for me by natives at Mr. Lewers." His description parallels Mrs. Brewster's: a young pig and chicken cooked on hot stones in holes in the ground, the pig with hot stones inside it, wrapped in ti leaves, but covered with matting; "...it was left for about an hour, after which the meats were taken out and served deliciously cooked...we enjoyed it all."[45] This was a gentrified version prepared at Mr. Lewers' home; I suspect they ate it with knives and forks. Too bad Mary Brewster could not have been along.

Mrs. Brewster was told that many of the natives had

been Europeanized, but she expressed doubts about this after observing a native feast at the church on Lahaina, where she saw tables set with dishes, knives, and spoons, but also natives seated on mats on the ground, still eating with their fingers with "no ceremony." In fact, of course, Mrs. Brewster was simply oblivious to the ceremony that did exist. Along with the great care and thoughtfulness characteristic of poi making, there was an etiquette of poi eating, which designated how many fingers to use, instructed eaters to keep fingers together, cautioned against scooping the poi towards the eater in a scratching fashion, advised on how far to insert them in the mouth, and specified the protocol of sharing a bowl. There were rules about not serving very soft poi to guests, which was considered bad manners, as was watching a person eat or commenting on how much they ate. Mary Kawena Pukui, a southern Hawaiian native, also reported "Heathen or Christian, my people were religious and believed in praying."[46]

Yankees eating poi with no knowledge of these rules were likely to offend their island hosts, as Richard Henry Dana did in the 1850s. Dana, ever open to new experiences, ate with natives at "a collection of huts, at a place called Kalaki-ki. People receive us well—gather around a calabash of poe & some fish. I begin to eat. No natives will eat. I ask them to. Look diffident, & one says must say Grace. Mortifies me. One of them says grace & all fall to."[47]

South Sea Islands: Similar to Hawaiians in most respects, other South Sea islanders showed hospitality to New England seafarers. In *Omoo* Herman Melville described a "dinner party" in Imeeo, one of the Society Islands, neighboring Tahiti. In the usual fashion, the diners were seated on the ground on mats and leaves, with "'pooroo' leaves, by way of plates,...by each was a rustic nut-bowl, half filled with sea-water, and a Tahitian roll, or small bread-fruit, roasted brown. An immense flat calabash, placed in the centre, was heaped up with numberless small packages of moist, steaming leaves: in each was a small fish, baked in the earth, and done to a turn. This pyramid of a dish was flanked on either side by an ornamental calabash. One was brimming with the golden-hued "poee," or pudding, made from the red plantain of the mountains; the other was stacked up with cakes of the Indian turnip, previously macerated in a mortar, kneaded with the milk of the cocoa-nut, and then baked. In the spaces between the three dishes, were piled young cocoa-nuts, stripped of their husks. Their eyes had been opened and enlarged; so that each was a ready-charged goblet."[48]

The description sounds like a Yankee dining room. Melville compared the mats to a green tablecloth; each diner had his or her own "plate," and individual service of sea-water, used as a condiment, and the "dinner roll"—breadfruit—was on the side of each. The main course is on its platter in the middle, with what sounds like a symmetrical arrangement of side dishes. Melville also pointed out that there was a side cloth, arranged as a New Englander might a sideboard, with the dessert course: bananas, guavas, oranges, and melons. There was enough familiar about the arrangement that even a non-adventurous traveler might have been comfortable. Though Melville and his companions were open to new experiences, they did as we all might, identifying what they saw in terms of a familiar metaphor comparing, for example, the sea-water to "pepper sauce" or catsup, the roasted breadfruit to toast, and the poee to pudding.

The food was good and the company comfortable. In a restaurant-review style, the narrator commented: "The fish were delicious; the manner of cooking them in the ground, preserving all the juices, and rendering them exceedingly sweet and tender. The plantain pudding was almost cloying; the cakes of Indian turnip quite palatable; and the roasted bread-fruit, crisp as toast." The narrator, relying on western etiquette, toasted his host, and observed, "No people, however refined, are more easy and graceful in their manners than the Imoeese."[49]

Eating Chinese: Not everyone desired familiarity. In Singapore in 1860, R.H. Dana stayed with a Scotsman named Anderson. "In the goodness of his heart," Dana wrote of his host, "he took pains to get me an American breakfast, with salt mackerel, balls of salt cod fish & such things, when I only wished to eat the products of the place. But he ended [breakfast] with some excellent mangoes from Bombay."[51]

Dana delighted in new food experiences, and at times his journal reads as though he were taking notes to remember how to prepare things at home the way he had seen them done in a foreign place. For example: "Tea must not be boiled. Pour upon the leaves boiling fresh water, as you need the tea. The water must not be allowed to stand in the kettle, simmering, but must be freshly boiled."[51]

In Hong Kong, Dana stayed at the hong of Russell and Company, where breakfast was served at 9 A.M., in the counting room, as was lunch, and dinner was served at 7 P.M. at the lodging house, with "a complete outfit of plate &c for each," and with all attending dressed formally, which Dana felt had a "civilizing" effect.

"Breakfast is of made dishes, rice & curry, eggs & omolettes, & fragrant tea." He was pleased with the food: "Cooking excellent, such rice as we never get at home. Rice is steamed here, dry & each kernal separate."

He observed shopkeepers' meals: "Two a day breakfast at 10 A.M. & dinner about 5 P.M....Breakfast of coolies was rice in abundance, tea, a dish made of vegitables, & some little cakes of flour or ground beans fried in oil. The tables and plates were clean & neat, & their food well cooked & neatly set out."

"Time for tiffin, which is lunch, in all Br.[itish] India, China, & Australia. Go to a China tea shop True Abundance. Little tables, 2 & 4 each, as in our eating houses. Place 2 cups on table, with tea leaves in each, turn hot water on them & cover cups with saucers. Little cups to dip out tea & sip it. Tray, with 15 little plates, each holding diff. kind of preserves & confection. Little cakes of black beans baked & ground to powder & mixed with a little oil & scented, & covered with a crust of baked wheat flour—very good. Little preserved oranges, not larger than olives—excellent. Other confections of nice, quaint contrivance. All Chinese drink tea pure, without either milk or sugar....Drank it pure, a la Chinoise, & found it refreshing & agreeable. Nice little tiffin."[52]

Annie Ricketson in Singapore in 1873 with her captain husband also had a tiffin. "We had dinner at one o'clock. They call it Tiffin here."[53] A New Englander used to the noon meal being "dinner," Annie nonetheless adopted the term tiffin for her whole stay ashore, promptly reverting to the word dinner when back aboard the *A. R. Tucker*. Because she did not recount the menu we have no idea whether her tiffin was dinner-sized or lunch-sized.

Charles Abbey and some shipmates, ashore in Canton in 1856, went into Acows Hotel, which had a sign in English and a menu intended to please English palates, which it almost succeeded at doing. The meal "was a nice one better than we had seen since leaving our own country. First came some vegetable soup, then some fish; next he brought on some roast beef, Macao potatoes beets turnips &c, and then a roast chicken, after which came a pudding, some walnuts, nankin dates & Lychees. We filled up with everything but the chicken; he was roasted claws head, comb and all and we didnt like the looks of him; he seemed to fresh, much as if the sun had caught him at some accidental focus and frizzled him up."[54]

That Abbey's was a western-style meal, despite the strangeness of the roasted chicken, is made clear by contrasting it to a Chinese banquet Dana described, which he enjoyed in 1860 at his host's home. "Now begins the series of courses. I did not count them, I am sorry I did not. We agreed that they must have been between 20 & 30. And such strange compositions, fins of sharks, sinews of dolphins, berries of the lotus, the most recherche & improbable things are the most prised [*sic*]. He [their host] told us fairly that many of them had no other merit, & were made eatable by condiments only. I ate too much of the first courses, not expecting so many, & the courses began to pall....I *tasted* of each."

Not only did Dana taste each, but he did it with chop sticks: "Chop sticks, of ivory! It is my first attempt, but I resolve to do or starve & after frequent failures get the nack of them pretty well."[55]

India and the Indian Ocean: Yankees traveled all around the Indian Ocean: whalers on the whaling grounds and merchant vessels visiting various ports for goods like spices, coffee, and tea. The variety of ethnic foodways encountered there varied from sophisticated to what seemed to some New Englanders primitive and very strange indeed.

Lewis Eldredge and the rest of the whaleship *Herald*'s crew in 1867 visited in Johanna in the Comoro Archipelago (north of the Mozambique Channel) where the "captain gave us a fine banquet in one of the old stone buildings of this ancient walled city. We feasted royally on curried chicken, fruits, cakes made of finely ground coconut meat. No wines of any kind were served for it is against the Arabian's religious vows. The feast was highly enjoyed by the crew, and we were indebted to the Arab host whose slaves fanned us while we ate."[56]

This was very elegant compared to the "Lewoua" Hiram Look saw in Madagascar in the early 1870s. Look's description demonstrates how seafarers' confusion hints at where else in the world they had been: "The Luowa was Where they had made the Fire just before I started,, Now I will describe it,, After the fire had burned long enough to thoroughly heat the stones all the ashes were removed and green stuff placed,, thick all over the Base. Then a grass Mat spread over the green Stuf. And Chickens,, Ducks,, Breadfruit,, Yams and Pumpkins placed there in. all were covered with another grass Mat,, The Grass Leafs and Bushes piled over,, it soon began to steam. They were cooking 3 hours. I witnessed Opening of the Luawa,, The Ducks and Chickens look fine. In fact, every Thing Was cooked thoroughly,,"[57]

Look had probably been to Hawaii or other Pacific islands, and had observed what is a universal method of in-ground cooking, and when he encountered it in Madagascar, called it by the same name he'd learned in the Sandwich Islands. He also reported on eating the "luawa."

He and others off the *Charles W. Morgan*, including Captain and Mrs. John Tinkham, were guests of Malagasys whom Look described as the "royal family." He was seated with two young women on either side of him. "One of them took a steaming Chicken And separated the Legs from body And passed me one,, takeing other and devouring it Rapedly,, there were large green Leafs placed on the Mat,, she took a wooden paddle after smashing a pumpken Yam and bread Fruit and placed some of each on a Leaf,, for me,, Likewise herself And commenced eating with her fingers. *I could not eat much as no salt, Knife, Fork or Spoon were used*,, [emphasis added] Neither could any of the crew,, We ate Pumpken Yams And bread Fruit."[58]

Were ideas so strong among these seafarers about what was required for eating—as Look says, salt, knives, forks, spoons—that they "could not eat," even though they were surrounded by good fresh food? Apparently. It would have been much better fare than they were able to get aboard ship, where they certainly did not eat under very refined circumstances. Or was the method of cooking so strange as to be repulsive? Some of Look's unflattering, even downright mocking, descriptions of their Malagasy hosts suggests that the seafarers may have treated the native hospitality cavalierly.

Interestingly, however, in 1872 Annie Ricketson (aboard the *A. R. Tucker* cruising in the Indian Ocean) reported that she and Daniel were visiting in a King's house in New Guinea, where "they got up a dinner for us

Barely visible at the stern of the bark *J.M. Thurston* is the end of the seawall that protects the Sicilian port of Messina. Captain John Whidden visited Sicily in 1858, two years before this painting was made by W. Bygrave, and dined on chicken and pasta. [MSM 62.476]

consisting of rice boiled and rice made in balls. We think they were made up with coconut oil, boiled sweet potatoes, fish fried some way with a gravy. The chicken got up the same ways as the fish but everything was seasoned up so high with red pepper that I could hardly eat it. They had a round table with legs to it, but they were only about an inch high. We had to sit on the floor and take the plates in our laps. *We had large spoons to eat with, some that they got aboard some ship* [emphasis added.]"[59] Had these native people earlier entertained seafarers, unable to eat without spoons, and concluded the best way to be hospitable to white people was to provide utensils?

That certainly seems to have been the case in an example from the Hawaiian Islands: "Occasionally, it happens that the Bishop or clergy in traveling about on their work are glad of a night's lodging in the house of some Hawaiian. In such a case, a fork or spoon, kept for the use of strangers, is brought out..."[60]

Even though New Englanders had "pepper sauce" and used vinegar for a condiment, overall Anglo cooking was mild. Seafarers encountering even garlic were sometimes startled. Annie Ricketson's response to red pepper is typical. Thomas Larkin Turner commented similarly. Ashore in 1832, at Batavia, Java (now Djakarta, Indonesia), Turner, the son of the captain of the brig *Palestine,* which was to pick up a cargo of coffee, wrote of the extraordinary hospitality of a Mr. Payne: "Who is this gentleman? This is a man we have never heard of before—eating his soups, his fish, his lamb, his capons, his fowls,...his ducks, his omelets, his geese, his fricasees, his mutton chops, his fruits of a dozen or more etc. to say nothing of the thousand little messes of one kind and another, we are constantly having served up for the education of the human stomach—that is mine—for it will be learnt to such a degree to relish such savory dishes that the garlics, the pepper etc, will put forth from my body their respective...shoots, in such numbers that I shall look like the devil within a few more hours."[61] It sounds as though Mr. Payne, a westerner, businessman, and avowed meat eater, had a native cook.

It would be interesting to know if Mr. Payne's cook was actually going easy on the red pepper, considering how hot the spicy cuisines of present-day Thailand, Indonesia, and Vietnam can be. Modern American palates are just now learning to enjoy them—but for Larkin, growing up in the same period represented by the Buckingham House, the food must have been quite a jolt.

Azores: The Portuguese islands of the Azores were often some of the first ports of call for American ships—especially whaleships—that crossed the Atlantic before dropping down to round Cape Horn to the west or to proceed east around the Cape of Good Hope. It was a place to get fresh food and water, and it often gave sailors their first liberty ashore.

Nelson Haley, a harpooneer on the *Charles W. Morgan* in 1849, encountered a garlicky Portuguese chicken stew in Fayal, Azores, which he described in his memoirs. "The table had quite a clean cloth on it, the tumblers and plates also looked pretty clean for a Porta'gee place, a bottle of wine was at each plate, and a brimming platter of chicken stew in the center. With fruit and flowers placed here and there, it made a display almost too grand for a common sailor to sit down to. We helped ourselves to chicken and commenced to eat.

"First one then another stopped at the first mouthful, laid down knives and forks and like myself almost spit out what we had in our mouths. Some of the boys said, What in hell is the matter with this stuff? I knew at once what the trouble was. The one who had cooked it had stuffed it full of garlic, and to all of us, if rotten eggs had been in it, the taste no doubt could not have been worse."

Haley then attempted to get the proprietor to bring some without garlic, but because the garlic flavor clung to the pots and pans, the food tasted of it anyway. Haley reported the second batch was not so bad, that he "could worry it down," and the proprietor wisely offered the others enough wine that they could scarcely notice what they were eating anyway.[62]

There were hotels in Fayal run by English people where American seafarers could find fairly familiar food. In 1871, Annie Ricketson stayed at one such place, and recorded, "We had a very nice dinner, a plate of soup first, always, for that is their Custom in all Foreign places, then we have fowl and meats of all kinds and also fruits of all kinds."[63] Actually, fashionable people in New England also prefaced meals with a soup course, but since Mrs. Ricketson seems to have been unfamiliar with that practice, she attributed it to foreign behavior.

Another frequent stop for American captains and wives during this period was with Mr. and Mrs. Dabney, the consul and his wife in Fayal. Mrs. Ricketson gave descriptions of two meals with the hospitable Dabneys: a lunch of "white bread and butter and preserves, prickly pears, apricots, figgs and cheese, also wine," and dinner that began with soup, followed by "something tasted like our fish and potatoes at home. Don't know what it was. Then they had a mutton stew which was very nice. Then the waiter came in with a brush and pan and brushed the crumbs off the table and brought on a pudding which I could not give a name. Then came the fruit, white grapes, figgs, apricots, almonds and raisins."[64]

Mrs. Ricketson seemed almost overwhelmed by the newness of the place. Did she expect everything to be so different that she would not be able to identify it? Certainly some of the food was made with unfamiliar ingredients, but Annie Ricketson was being entertained by a different class of people whose foodways were unlike her own. Had she been invited to a society dinner in Boston or New York, it would have seemed just as foreign to her there.

Differences and Similarities

Meals ashore for seafarers in the nineteenth century meant encounters with the familiar and the different. It certainly appears that by the middle of the nineteenth century a good many people around the world had encountered enough western seafarers, and recognized the economic opportunity they represented, to try to accommodate the foodways of the newcomers, providing western eating utensils or a familiar menu. This was not always a favor to the foreigners. Some seafarers, like Dana and Melville, seemed to relish the new and strange foods and settings—others like Mrs. Brewster and Hiram Look could not quite get past their ingrained ideas to give it much of a try. Most everyone else seems to have fallen somewhere in between, tasting and experimenting, dubiously sometimes, with pleasant surprises at times.

As the world grew smaller and smaller, seafarers could expect to find something familiar anywhere they went. And some fun could be had at the expense of innocent foreign hosts, as in this tale of a group of sailors in an Australian cafe in Melbourne: "Dan was a comical genius and at dinner, in a cafe, he had the waitress so puzzled that she couldn't wait on us. Pretending that he couldn't read he asked her if she wouldn't read the menu.

'We have soup—consomme, barley and oxtail,' said she.

'Oxtail!' said Dan, with a sober face, 'What kind of soup is that? I never heard of oxtail soup in America. What kind of soup—what does it look like?'

'Oh, it's very nice! All cut up in pieces and quite alright,' she replied.

'Small pieces!' said Dan in bewilderment. 'Has it got the hair on it? Ough! I don't want any,' said he, shrugging his shoulders as if disgusted."

The joke was up when the group burst into laughter, and Dan stopped pretending that he was a foreigner, or that Australia was such a foreign land.[65]

In twentieth-century New England, of course, oxtail soup is much less common a dish than it was even in Dan's lifetime, reminding us that the past is like a foreign country as well.

The Recipes

For a taste of a meal ashore in the past, I have assembled a few familiar items. Hardly anyone nowadays has had mutton, but much of the lamb offered today is closer to mutton than lamb by nineteenth-century standards. If you know someone who raises sheep you might be able to obtain the genuine article and fix up mutton chops like Gray's restaurant did in New London. Trout fishermen may recognize the standard way to fry up their catch, to prepare a plateful of the trout Captain Whidden enjoyed in California. Farm trout certainly can be used, but they will not taste the same. Bully Samuels enjoyed chicken gumbo with cornbread long before Creole and Cajun cooking became trendy, and a traditional recipe for both follows. There are instructions for making frijoles like the ones that Dana ate in southern California, which you can serve with chili sauce. A currant cake like the one Mary Brewster ate on her tour in Hawaii is included, and there are two slightly different recipes for floating islands, an elegant and popular nineteenth-century dessert, similar to ones that Vernon Briggs was served ashore in Honolulu.

CHICKEN GOMBO WITH OYSTERS

Take a young chicken or the half of a grown one; cut it up, roll it in salt, pepper, and flour, and fry it a nice brown, use lard or drippings, as if for fricassee. Cut up a quart of fresh green okras, and take out the chicken and fry the okra in the same lard. When well browned return the chicken to the pot and boil. Add to it a large slice of ham; a quarter of a pound will be about right for this gombo. Pour on to the chicken, ham and okra, half a gallon of boiling water, and let it boil down to three pints. Ten minutes before serving pour into the boiling soup two dozen fine oysters with half a pint of their liquor. Let it come to a good boil, and serve it with well-boiled rice.

From *La Cuisine Creole*, by Lafcadio Hearne, 1885, page 20

"Gombos" or gumbos were soups thickened with okra, as was the recipe above, or with dried and powdered sassafras leaves, called filé. Lafcadio Hearne noted that gombo is "an economical way of using up the remains of any cold roasted chicken, turkey, game, or other meats." He also suggested that "Oysters, crabs, and shrimp may be added when in season." Most gumbos have shellfish added.

Fresh okra may not always be available, but you can substitute two packages of frozen. The ham can be either leftover smoked shoulder or ham steak. Boil the rice separately, and at serving time put the rice in the soup plates and pour the soup over. An interpretation follows.

1 1/2 to 2 lbs. boneless chicken pieces
salt and pepper mixed in 1/2 cup flour
cooking oil or bacon drippings
4 cups sliced okra
quarter of a pound of ham, diced
2 quarts hot water
12 oysters in 1 cup liquor

1. Roll or shake the chicken pieces in the seasoned flour.
2. In the bottom of a heavy soup pot, fry the chicken in the oil or bacon drippings until it is golden brown all over, but not done through. Remove from the pot and, when cool enough to handle, cut into bite-sized pieces.
3. If the oil has all been taken up, add more to the same pot, and fry the okra till it is browned. Then return the chicken to the pot. At the same time, add the ham and water.
4. Simmer uncovered until the stock has been reduced by a quarter, about an hour. Ten minutes before serving add the oysters and their liquor. Let it come just to a boil, then take it off the heat.
5. Serve over rice.

Yields 8-10 servings.

FRIED TROUT

Scale, gut, clean, dry, and flour; fry them in butter until they are a rich clear brown; fry some green parsley; crisp and make some plain melted butter; the butter may be poured over the fish, but it is most advisable to send it in a butter tureen.

From *Practical American Cookery and Domestic Economy*, by Miss Hall, 1855, page 118

Anyone would welcome a "large platter of fresh mountain trout" as Captain Whidden did on his visit ashore near San Francisco in 1863. Brook trout, as fishermen and their families know, are good eating today, and are most easily prepared by frying. Whidden did not say anything about parsley accompanying the fish, or whether the butter was poured over it or came in a tureen. Miss Hall was being conscious of style and propriety.

It is an even bet that the trout was fried as often in salt pork fat as butter. Mrs. Abell said in her directions for frying fresh fish "A more common method is to fry them after salt pork, dipping them in Indian meal or flour."

Allow one eight-inch (or so) trout for each serving. Butter will do nicely for frying, or you can try it in salt pork or bacon drippings. The recipe above is clear enough that an interpretation is not needed.

MUTTON CHOPS

MUTTON CHOPS—BROILED.
Cut from the best end of the loin; trim them nicely, removing fat or skin, leaving only enough of the former to make them palatable; let the fire be very clear before placing the chops on the gridiron; turn them frequently, taking care that the fork is not put into the lean part of the chop; season them with pepper and salt; spread a little fresh butter over each chop, when nearly done, and send them to table upon very hot plates.

MUTTON CHOPS—FRIED.
The fat in which the chops are to be fried should be boiling when the chops are put into it. They should be pared of fat, and well trimmed, before cooking; they should be turned frequently,and when nicely browned, they will be done; of course, if they are very thick, judgment must be exercised respecting the length of time they will occupy in cooking.·

From *Practical American Cookery and Domestic Economy,* by Miss Hall, 1855, page 72

While Miss Hall suggested cutting mutton chops from the best end of the loin, Mrs. Abell said "Take pieces of mutton that are not good for steak, rib, or other pieces, have them cut small."[67] There is, of course, no way now to find out what part of the mutton Gray's in New London chose to serve as chops.

Chops, like the steaks, oysters, and ham and eggs that Gray's offered, were all small cuts that could be cooked up quickly as ordered. Broiling took more skill than frying; the "very clear" fire Miss Hall mentioned is a bright, smoke-free bed of coals. If, by 1859, Gray's was using a cookstove, chances are very good they chose to fry their mutton chops.

I offer this recipe for your interest, so no interpretation will follow.

MISSISSIPPI CORN BREAD

One quart of buttermilk, two eggs, three spoonfuls of butter, and a teaspoonful of saleratus; stir in meal, to the milk, until it is as thick as buckwheat batter. Bake in squares about one inch thick. It will require half an hour in a hot oven. If it is not nice, it will be because you put in too much meal, and made the batter too thick. But try again, and you will succeed.

From *La Cuisine Creole,* by Lafcadio Hearne, 1885, page 128

La Cuisine Creole, a Collection of Culinary Recipes "from leading chefs and noted Creole housewives who have made New Orleans famous for its cuisine," was published in 1885 and reflects established, traditional, Creole cooking practices.

This recipe yields a rich, moist, dense cornbread with a flavor similar to spoonbread—and quite unlike the cake-like cornbreads most of us are familiar with. One half this recipe will fill an 8-inch-square baking pan up to one inch thick. In testing it, I used a fine ground southern-style yellow cornmeal. The interpretation which follows is for a half-recipe.

1 pint buttermilk
1 egg
1 1/2 tablespoons butter, melted
1/2 teaspoon baking soda

2 1/4 cups cornmeal
salt
Preheat oven to 375°

1. Beat together buttermilk, egg, and melted butter.
2. Mix salt, cornmeal, and baking soda together.
3. Add the dry ingredients to the wet ingredients and mix only as much as is needed to combine.
4. Pour into a greased 8 x 8-inch pan. Bake for 40 minutes. Serve hot.

Yields one 8 x 8-inch cornbread.

CHILI SAUCE

Remove the seeds from fifty dry red peppers. Wash and put in saucepan with two quarts of cold water and boil one half hour. Mash through a cullendar until all of the meat is separated from the skins. Peel and chop very fine two heads of garlic. Boil in one half pint of water until soft. Add one rounding teaspoon of black pepper, one of salt, one small teaspoon of sage, two tablespoons of strong vinegar. Boil about three quarters of an hour or until smooth. Pour into fruit jars.

From the manuscript recipe notebook of Fred Bixby, ca. 1920

I cannot imagine what Richard Henry Dana thought of the spicy Spanish cuisine after a life of bland New England cooking. As we have seen, he was open to new food experiences, and he may have come to enjoy this very much, just as many modern New Englanders have.

The recipe above is clear enough that an interpretation is not necessary. You may wish to put this mixture through a food mill instead of a "cullendar."

FRIJOLES

Take four cups red beans. Wash and boil until tender. Do not soak. When half done add sufficient salt. When tender put one half cup of lard or bacon fat in a large frying pan. When hot pour in the beans. Add sufficient chili sauce to make hot and mash a few of the beans while frying to thicken gravy. Fry about fifteen minutes.

From the manuscript recipe notebook of Fred Bixby, ca. 1920

A bean similar in size and shape to present-day red Mexican beans and pink beans, and similar to kidney and pinto beans, has been found in the adobe clay of an early southwestern Spanish mission. Both kinds of beans were used to make the traditional frijoles of the Southwest that Dana and his crew mates were served at the mission near Santa Barbara.

Because frijoles, which means "beans," is a traditional food, period recipes for them are difficult to come by. This recipe is from Fred Bixby, the last rancher at Rancho Los Alamitos, now a museum in Long Beach, California. Fred was famous locally for his cooking, and the museum's curator feels sure that Fred cooked in the old style and that his recipe will give modern people an accurate replication of traditional frijoles.

This recipe produces a lot of frijoles; you may wish to halve the recipe. Use either kidney beans or pintos or, if you can obtain them, red beans. Notice that Fred specifies not to soak the beans. Drain the beans before adding them to the pan with the bacon drippings. Use Fred's chili sauce, made from the recipe that follows, or your choice of commercially prepared sauce. Notice, too, that only a few of the beans get mashed up, just enough to make a gravy. If it gets too thick, add a bit of water.

If you have any left over, you can make them into refried beans by adding fried onions, more fat, and chili sauce or powder.

Yields 10-12 servings.

CURRANT CAKE

1 cup of Butter
2 " " Sugar
1 " " Milk
3 Eggs
1/2 teaspoon of Soda
1 cup of Currants Flavor to taste

From the manuscript recipe notebook of Fannie Card, 1879

Similar in texture to pound cake, the recipe for currant cake did not change from one end of the nineteenth century to the other. Mrs. Howland (1845) and Fanny Farmer (1896) both provided recipes for it and suggested how much flour to use, which Fannie Card didn't bother to record. Mrs. Howland suggested nutmeg as the spice.

You can make this either as a loaf cake or in a square pan. I prefer it as a loaf for slicing to serve with tea or coffee. The recipe is adequate for two medium-sized loaves. An interpretation follows.

4 cups flour
1/2 teaspoon baking soda
1/2 teaspoon nutmeg
1 cup butter
2 cups sugar
3 eggs
1 cup milk
1 cup currants
Preheat oven to 350°

1. Sift together dry ingredients. In a separate bowl, cream together butter and sugar.
2. Beat the eggs slightly and beat into the butter and sugar mixture.
3. Add the dry ingredients alternately with the milk. Fold in the currants last.
4. Pour into two greased and floured loaf pans, and bake for about an hour, or until a toothpick inserted comes out clean.
5. Cool on a rack and when ready to turn out run a knife around the edges, then turn over and slide loaves out of pans.

Yields two medium-sized loaves, or two 8 x 8-inch cakes.

FLOATING ISLAND

Take the white of an egg or more as you want; beat to a froth, add a glass of currant jelly, beat them together until a spoon will stand up in it. Drop a spoonful at a time on a glass bowl of sweet cream.

From *The Complete Domestic Guide*, by Mrs. L.G. Abell, 1853, page 149

Scald one pint of milk, the yolks of two eggs, 3 tablespoons sugar, 1 tablespoon cornstarch which has first been stirred up in a little cold milk—[add] to the milk—as soon as it thickens pour it into a pudding dish & flavor lemon. Drop a spoonful of the beaten whites into boiling water & in a few seconds take out with a skimmer & place on the dish of float.

From the manuscript recipe notebook of Julia Gates, 1857-1930

There appear to have been two types of floating island in the nineteenth century. In the earlier part of the century, this dessert was made as Mrs. Abell described with egg whites beaten with currant jelly (seldom any other jelly) laid on top of bowls of cream. By the latter part of the century, the conventional floating island was poached meringue "islands" on a boiled custard "lake." Recipes vary mainly in the richness of the custards.

Both of these are delicious and pretty to look at. The Abell recipe produces a lovely pink and flavorful chiffon-like pudding, eaten with cream. The Gates recipe produces a very soft custard with snowy meringues. Since it was in 1880, Briggs probably enjoyed the latter type of floating island in Hawaii at H.A.P. Carter's.

You can make the custard richer by adding another egg yolk or two or using light cream instead of some of the milk. You may wish to use only a part of the additional whites, however, for a meringue, because just two whites produces quite a lot.

Both of these should be made the day they are to be served because they tend to deflate a bit after sitting around. Mrs. Abell's dessert is most easily served in individual dessert dishes, but Mrs. Gates's can be served either in one large shallow serving dish or in individual dishes. Interpretations of the two recipes follow. I personally prefer the first, but many people are squeamish now about eating uncooked egg.

MRS. ABELL'S FLOATING ISLAND

1 egg white
1/2 cup currant jelly
1 cup heavy cream

1. With a rotary beater, whip the egg white till it is frothy.
2. Continue beating, adding the currant jelly a tablespoonful at a time. Beat until it is glossy and makes medium stiff peaks.
3. Put a 1/2 cup of heavy cream in four individual dessert dishes, and divide the beaten whites among them. Chill.

Yields 4 servings.

MRS. GATES'S FLOATING ISLAND

2 cups milk
2 eggs, separated
3 tablespoon sugar
1 tablespoon cornstarch
1 teaspoon lemon extract

1. Put the milk in the top of a double boiler, reserving a couple of tablespoonfuls to mix with the cornstarch. Scald.
2. While the milk is heating, mix the cornstarch and cold milk, and beat the eggs.
3. Add both gradually to the heated milk, stirring constantly. Cook the mixture for about twenty minutes, stirring frequently.
4. Remove from the heat, let cool slightly, then add the extract. Pour into a serving bowl or individual dishes.
5. Beat the whites until stiff, and drop large spoonfuls on simmering water, and poach for a few moments, gently turning them over once.
6. Lift them and drain before putting them on top of the custard. Chill before serving.

Yields 4-6 servings.

Holidays and Special Occasions at Sea and Ashore

New England observed three major holidays in the 1800s—Fourth of July, Thanksgiving, and Christmas—at home ashore for most folks, but for some others at sea. The food in the Thanksgiving feast was the focus of the whole day, but New Englanders included food as part of their observances of the Fourth and Christmas holidays. In some cases certain foods were highly identified with a particular holiday.

We will see in the following chapters how holiday observances changed during the nineteenth century—how the Fourth of July increasingly became a family holiday; how Christmas, hardly observed at all in New England at the start of the 1800s, gradually engulfed Thanksgiving by the end of the century.

Food and drink mitigate social interactions, and so other special occasions often revolved around the preparation and serving of special food. "Clambakes" and "Chowder Parties," both outdoor events, had a particularly coastal flavor, while other special occasions such as weddings, church suppers, and socials were similar alongshore and inland. Menus for special occasions varied depending on who was to attend: certain foods were generally recognized to be feminine and others were suitable for male appetites, and this is one of the things we will investigate in "Refreshments Were Served."

Fourth of July: America's Day of Days

"Today is the anniversary of our independence and a glorious day it is. The sun seems to shine with greater briliancy [sic] than ever it has before. it came peeping over the top of The Rock of Gibralter in all its glorious Splender [sic]" wrote William Wainright on the Union Navy's steam screw sloop-of-war Kearsarge.[1] *It was his first Independence Day since joining the Navy, and he considered himself lucky to be where he was considering that it was 1862 and he might have been on a Civil War battlefield instead. On that day and in that place, the sun could not be brighter, the prospect of the day could not be more pleasant.*

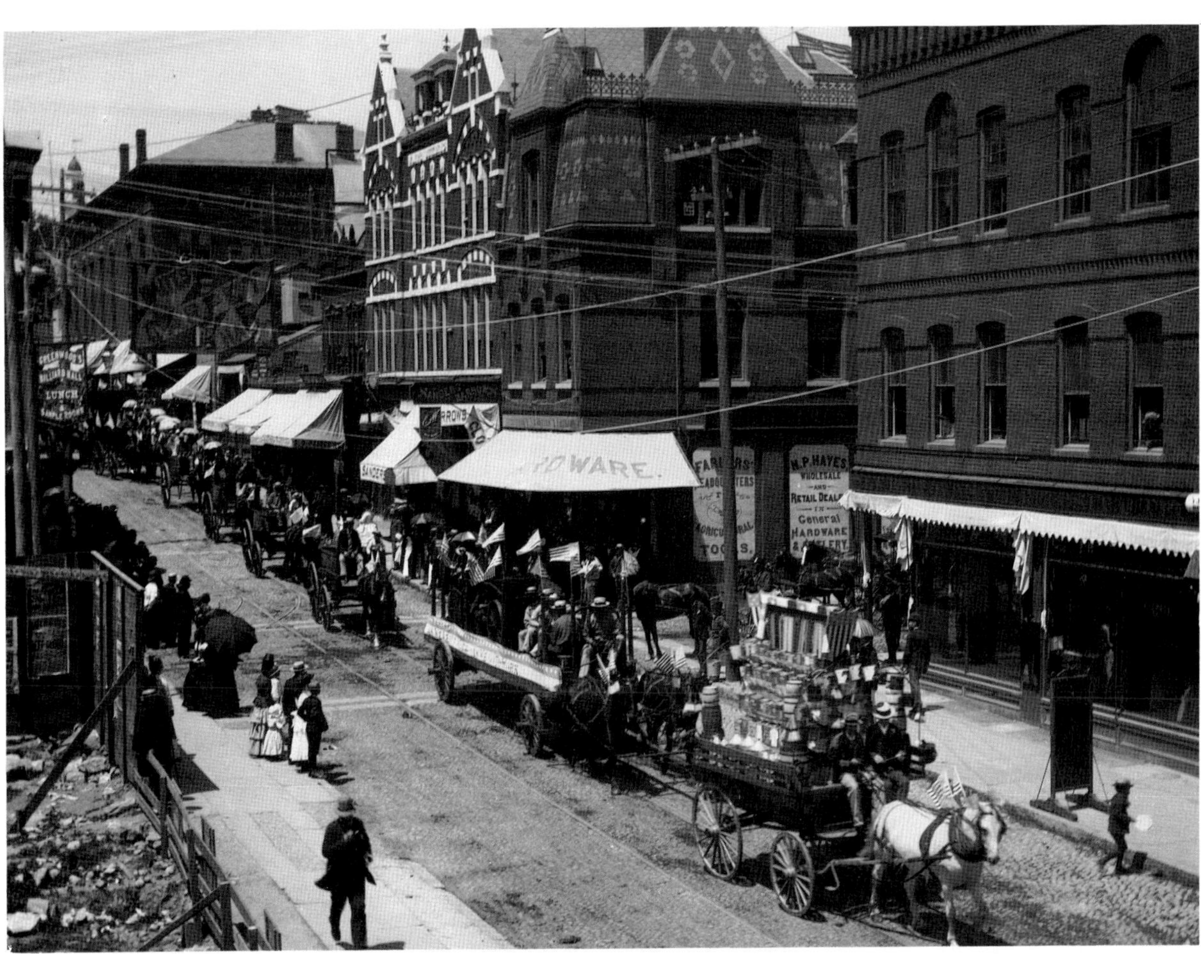

This parade marched down New Bedford's Union Street on the Fourth in 1888. [New Bedford Whaling Museum] Opposite, a pleasant at-home picnic with lettuce salad, chicken salad, boiled ham garnished with eggs, and French rolls.

A family gathering like this one, socializing around a picnic, was one of several ways to observe the Fourth in the nineteenth century. Sunday-school or church social groups held picnics at private homes or took excursions on the water to favorite picnic groves or beaches. Though it is hard to tell for sure, this photo has a post-postprandial look to it. [Photograph by E. A. Scholfield, MSM 75.294.506] At left, the Fourth among shipboard forty-niners featured elements of celebration ashore, including an oration. [*Century Magazine*, July 1891, MSM 86-2-73]

Ashore in New England that year was a population a little subdued by the anxiety of a war that was testing the country's unity. The usual pattern of early-morning noisemaking—from firecrackers, cannon shots, guns firing—followed by a parade led by a local military unit, accompanied by a band, if a town was large enough to have one, and all a prelude to patriotic speeches, had abated in some places, even though these things had been customary from the 1820s. There must have seemed little to celebrate; nevertheless, some observance of the Glorious Fourth would serve to encourage and reaffirm the endurance of the nation.

Fourth of July with its strong military and political overtones was a secular and patriotic holiday. There was only a little change in the manner of celebrating the Fourth from one end of the century to the other. The extent of a community's celebration depended mostly on how motivated and organized civic leaders were and to a lesser degree on the states of the economy and nation. For example, during the War Between the States, the tone of most public events was more patriotic than after the war; and the nation's centenary in 1876 stirred a more expansive celebration of the holiday, just as the bicentennial did in 1976.

In contrast to the private, family-centered celebrations of Thanksgiving and Christmas, the Fourth was a day of open public observance. After patriotic speeches and recitations, friends gathered for sociability, often outdoors, going on picnics or boating excursions. Annie Ricketson, away at sea in 1871, observed, "I suppose today they are having a general Holiday at Home. Friends come from far and near to see Friends and enjoy the forth of July [*sic*]." [2]

Public Celebration Ashore

Noise: Noise, noise, and more noise. Noise began as early on the Fourth as the celebrants dared—some years, young revelers began the holiday shortly after midnight. In New Bedford, Charles Morgan noted in his diary in 1854, "Roused at Sunrise by the bells and guns—and the crackers have been popping all night [much to people's annoyance]." One New Englander remembered that "The Fourth was ushered in with every variety of noise and natural discord the genius of man could devise and the prolific invention of boys could execute." Mary Channing, spending part of her girlhood in Boston in the 1830s, was delighted "to be waked up by the ringing of bells and the booming of cannon." Even small towns and villages, which

A parade of patriotic young people, with whistles and drums to make noise, was an essential element of the Victorian Fourth. Charles W. Morgan recalled seeing a parade of young people march in New Bedford in 1851, and in Mystic "troops of boys" were seen in 1870. [Unidentified image from The Spectre Collection]

had no other Fourth of July observance, enjoyed some noise. John Redfield, who grew up in the little village of Cromwell, Connecticut, said of the holiday, "In Middletown it was celebrated with some spirit, but I do not recall any special observance in our village except by squibs and gunfiring."[3]

The Mystic *Journal* reported in 1870: "At midnight, the troops of boys were under a full head of steam....We could easily believe that every boy in the village from seven to sixteen years of age was moving before our eyes. And every boy had a large fish horn, and every fish horn was tuned differently. And every boy had an immense horse pistol, and every horse pistol was fired off simultaneously and continuously. And every boy had a large tin pan, and several boxes of fire-crackers, and a horrid lot of torpedoes." Asa Fish reported that despite a light rain there was "puttering of firecrackers continuous." Charles Q. Eldridge, born in 1842, worked hard for his firecrackers driving horses that treaded oats, pounding bark for a local tanner, and husking corn. Although most of his money went for clothing he reported that, "Very few boys had much money 'to burn' and my largest outside expenditure was for material to celebrate Fourth of July, which was never neglected."[4]

Parades and public exercises: Public exercises—speeches, recitations, a reading of the Declaration of Independence, poems, and music—preceded or followed a parade or procession. At the early end of the century, the exercises might have centered at the meetinghouse. Later in the century they were more likely to be held in a public hall, truly separating church and state, although clergymen were still included in the program. Harriet Beecher Stowe reported that political parties "united to distribute as impartially as possible the honors of the day."[5]

In 1859, after some hesitation, the people of Mystic set what appears to be a fairly typical program for the day, despite the fact that celebrating the Fourth was not to "be a very showy affair, owing to a peculiar tightness in the money market which exhibits itself very uncomfortably just at this time." Asa Fish reported on it in his diary: "At 10 A.M. Washington Hall was filled to hear 4th July Address of Rev. Frederick Denison and the reading of a poem by a Lady of Mystic. After the Address or Oration the poem was read by M Slade. Evening—A great Display of Fireworks from the roof of P & H. new building—Guns fired—followed by a Ball at Washington Hall."[6]

In the first quarter of the nineteenth century, Fourth of July parades escorted speakers or honored citizens to the place designated for exercises. Elizabeth Dow recalled that the militia led "the Orator and other dignitaries up and down the streets, like the beasts that filed before Adam that they might be seen of men." Her town, Exeter, New Hampshire, in the 1810s and 1820s, was large enough to have a band of music, something Mary Channing did not see until she went to Boston, "to go out and see the military processions; to hear the bands—we who never in our lives had heard a band."[7]

Gradually other attractions were added to the

The Centenary Fourth of July

In Mystic, planning for the 1876 Centennial Independence Day was initiated as early as 2 June, but the first two meetings were so poorly attended that it prompted Mystic *Press* Editor Lucius Guernsey to write: "There have been two meetings called to take steps to secure a creditable celebration for our Centennial Fourth of July....This subject should receive the hearty support of all our citizens–Another meeting is called for Saturday evening at 8:00 in the YMCA rooms. The names already mentioned for committees are unobjectionable, but it seems to us that it would more fully secure the public confidence if more than one political party were represented in it."

In the 16 June paper, with only three weeks to go before the big day, Guernsey reported, "At last she moves," and "a good number were present who evidently meant business." Fund raising was commenced immediately and extended to the Upper Village (Old Mystic) and Noank as well.

The Antiques and Horribles issued an invitation to "all the Young Men who are thirty-five or younger and can walk alone and all who are older but call themselves young" to show up on the Fourth "in COSTUME, either on Foot, Horseback, or in Teams" and to "signify their intention and the CHARACTER they purpose to assume, by postal card or letter" to Flat Fish, Secretary of State of the colonies of the Mystics, Noanks, Quiambogs, Flanders, and Mason's Island.

In the week before the Fourth the paper's Home Brevities column anticipated festivities: "—Hot!—Large supplies of fireworks.—The Horribles will make fun.—Picnics and sailing parties are in order.—Let our boatmen practice for the Fourth." And even though a complete program of the day's events was unavailable the editor published the following, which he promised "will substantially cover the ground:

"At Central Hall Commencing at half past ten a.m.... Singing, Historical Address by Hon. Richard A. Wheeler, Reading Declaration of Independence by Capt. J.K. Bucklyn, Poem by Rev. Frederic Denison.

"The Committee on Festivities have arranged the following exercises:

Salute of fifty guns at sunrise.

Parade of 'Kurious Klans' procession to move at 7 o'clock: The prime minister will deliver an address in front of the Liberty Pole when the procession reaches that point.

At twelve o'clock, or at close of services in the Hall, Salute of 25 guns.

At 2 o'clock Target Shoot, Prize, Silver Cup.

At 4 o'clock Races:

1st. Single scull boat race, Prize: Silver Cake Basket.

2nd. Double scull boat race, Prize: Chromos.

3rd. Tub race, Prize: Pickle Caster.

4th. Wheelbarrow Race, Prize: Cup.

5th. Climbing Greased Pole, Prize: Ham

Entries must be made by July 3. Apply to J.B. Grinnell.

At sunset 25 guns.

Fireworks at 8:30.

Street Carnival during the evening by the 'Happy Klans.'

All are invited to join in the fun. No rowdyism will be tolerated, but all the fun must be had that kan be krammed in. Citizens are invited to decorate on the 4th, and illuminate in the evening. The happy Klans will sing some of their choice songs as a serenade to those who do honor the occasion."

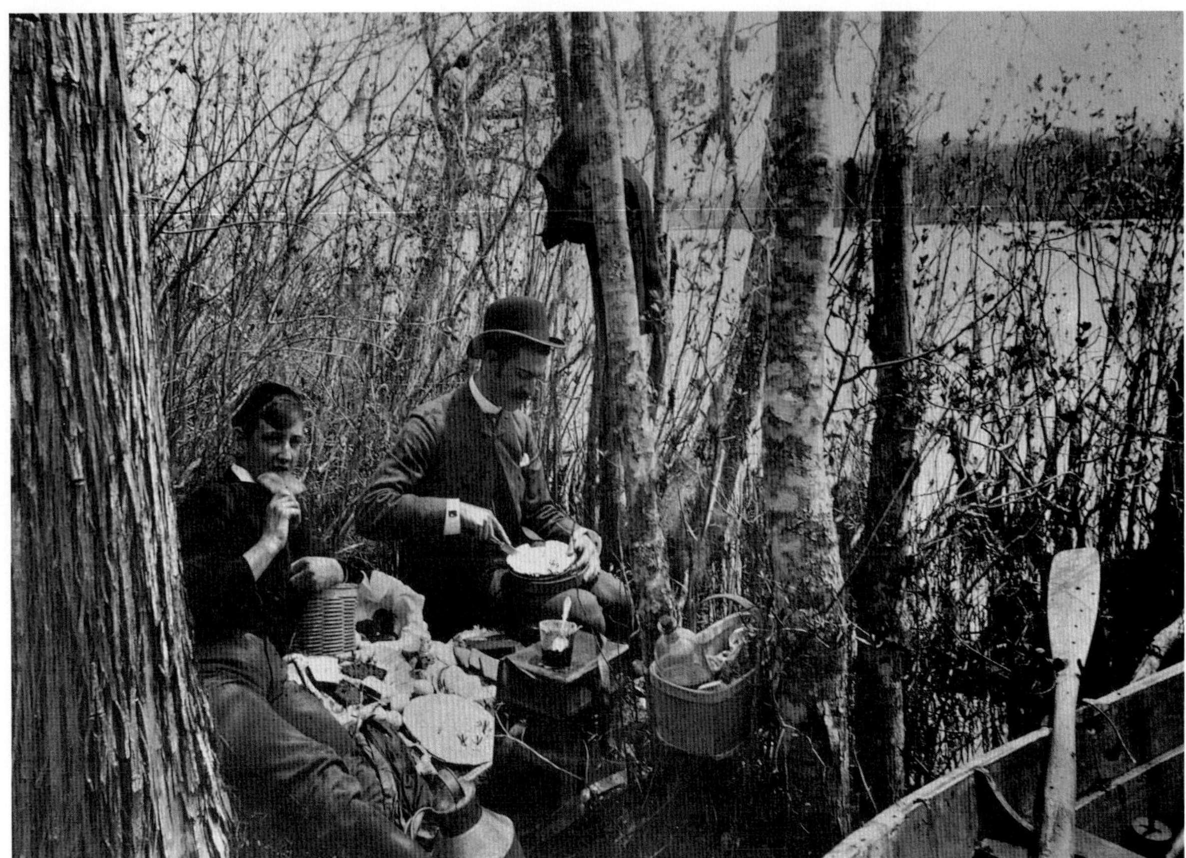

Charles E. Chase and C. B. Cottrell, Jr., eat a picnic lunch at Watchaug Pond, in Charlestown, Rhode Island, about 1885. Being on or near water for the Fourth was highly recommended. These gents packed a substantial spread in their rowboat, but other picknickers may have been along, including the photographer. [MSM 85.18.17]

procession. In New Bedford in 1851 the Fourth of July events included a "Floral Procession," described by Charles Morgan in his diary: "a beautiful spectacle it was—there were said to be about 2000 children a majority of them girls—with a profusion of flowers, many ornamented cars banners. bands of musick children mostly in white and all looking clean & happy—it was indeed a beautiful sight."[8]

In 1865, the order of march for the parade in Westerly, Rhode Island, was: Marshalls, Westerly Brass Band (16 pieces); Drum Band (6 pieces); Westerly Rifle Company; carriages with orators and other officials; returned soldiers, heroes of the war; a carriage drawn by six horses containing thirty-six misses representing the states of the Union; Pawcatuck Lodge of Masons; Palmer Chapter of Royal Arch Masons; Fenian Brotherhood; eighteen equestrians; and finally twelve vehicles of citizens.[9]

At about mid-century, a new feature of Fourth of July parades appeared in various towns. In 1865, in Mystic, a kind of mock parade was "extemporized by a company of Grangers....They sallied out, armed with new stable brooms, baskets for rations or ammunition, etc., and with the star bangled banner floating from a fish pole." This was a variation on what Charles Morgan described in New Bedford in 1860: "Soon the Bungtown Invincibles and the Squatery Hop Rangers came by—a most extraordinary and absurd looking body of disguised people whom no man could recognize—in all manner of grotesque costumes, and bands of discordant horns and drums which was exceedingly ludicrous & made everybody laugh—though how anybody could be foolish enough to engage in such absurdity I cannot tell."[10]

In some places, these comic bands became known as "Antiques" and/or "Horribles." Some marched in Mystic in 1872 with "Every age, sex, color, and condition...fully represented and many of the costumes, especially of the equestrians were very laughable."[11] These marchers, some in black-face, even sometimes called themselves the "Kurious Klans" or even the "Ku Klux" in interpretation and imitation of what was happening in the Reconstruction South.

Public dinner: At the early end of the century, many larger towns held public dinners after the exercises, to which the prosperous bought tickets. Joseph Anthony noted in his diary in 1823, "Nothing done in the village [of New Bedford] towards celebrating Independence but our Fairhaven neighbors had a public dinner."[12]

These dinners might be concluded with many toasts—to the nation, to the memory of George Washington, etc. Similarly, the 1865 Westerly observance included a procession to "tables spread in the vicinity, [where participants] partook with relish of the collation which had been provided....The collation being disposed of, the audience, still large and interested, returned to the stand, to hear the toasts and after dinner speeches."[13] The paper did

Coconut—a "prominent kind of cake" for picnics, made according to Julia Gates's recipe, page 229.

not specify whether the toasts were drunk with lemonade or something harder, but ten years later St. Michael's Temperance Society formed their *own* parade and marched off to Stillman's Grove for a picnic.

An association between drinking and the Fourth of July had been with the holiday since its inception. Alcohol use was prevalent in the early nineteenth century, so with the added impetus of holiday celebration normally sober citizens may have raised a patriotic glass. As the temperance movement gained strength, alternative beverages were encouraged. In New Haven in 1828 it was reported on 5 July that "The gardens and refectories wherever ice cream and lemonade were to be had, were filled in the evening; and the day passed with less of riot and intoxication than common."[14]

Still, forty-five years later, the Stonington *Mirror* reported wryly that the Fourth "was a good day for the grog shops and saloon keepers, and a select few improved the anniversary in an unmistakable drunk."[15]

Fireworks end the day: Mary Channing, who was delighted with all the novelties of her Boston Fourth of July, recalled that "above all other joys was the display of fireworks on the Common in the evening!" It took a substantial community in the early 1800s to afford fireworks, so John Redfield's village of Cromwell could not afford them, but his father woke him up to see rockets going off over Middletown.[16]

Charles Morgan reported that 8,000 people gathered on the New Bedford common in 1851 to see the fireworks. Most years—but not all—of the last quarter of the nineteenth century, in addition to larger cities, towns like Mystic and Westerly offered fireworks to conclude the day. Occasionally the show seems to have been provided by generous individuals. The Mystic *Press* reported in 1879

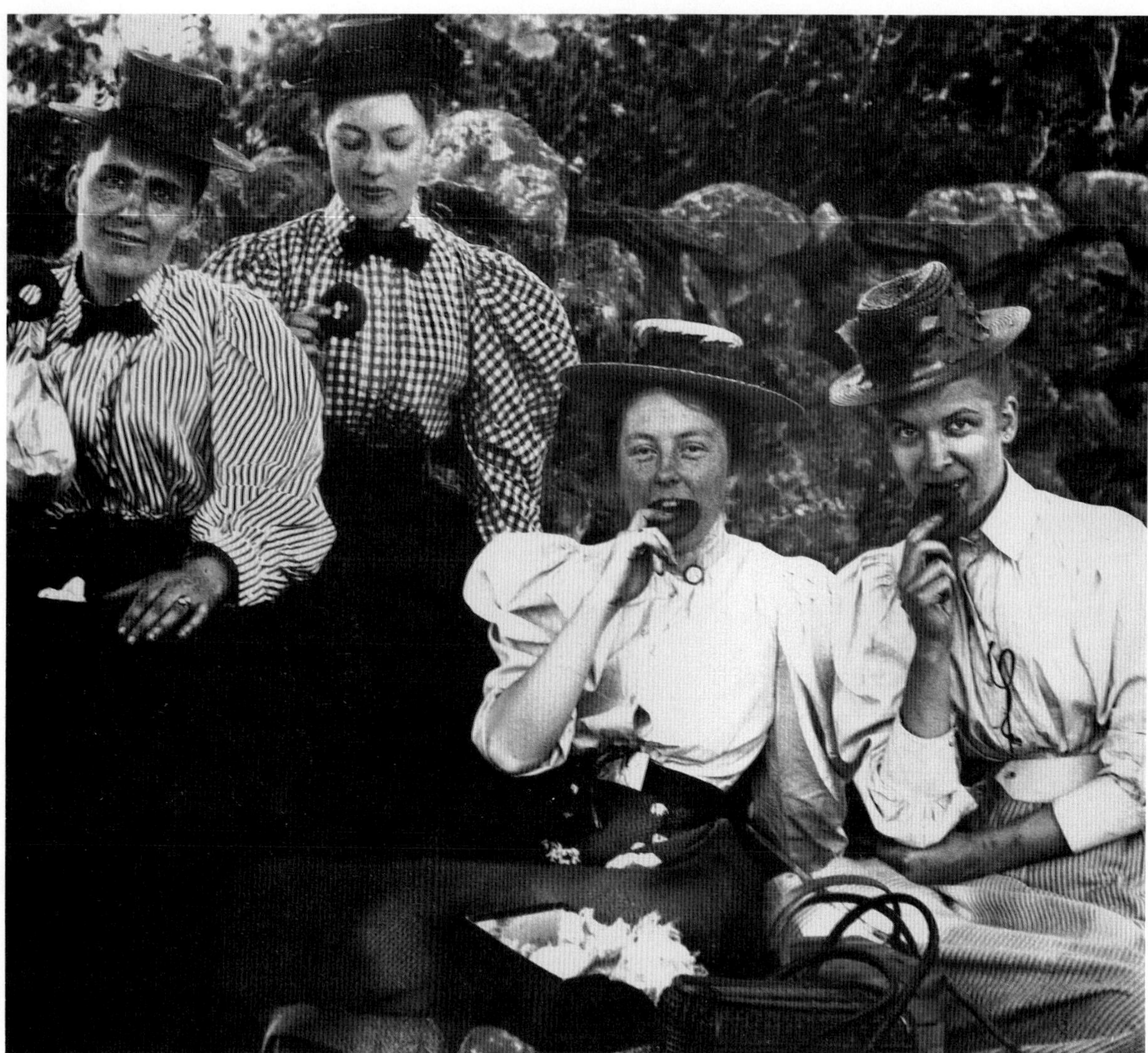

A quartet of doughnut-eaters on a picnic around the turn of the century are having a very good time. Transportation and balance of the meal, if any, unknown, although public transportation at the time could have been local trains, trolley connections, or excursion boats. [Glass-plate photograph by Edward H. Newbury, MSM 80.41.446]

that "Fireworks were displayed from the residence of Dr. Knowles."[17]

While communities repeated this general pattern of celebration when they chose to celebrate, they were not doggedly regular about it. Some years were quiet, even downright uneventful. In 1872, the *Weekly Mirror-Journal* of Stonington and Mystic Bridge reported: "In this immediate vicinity the birthday of our country passed without any elaborate celebration or display." But the Westerly celebration "was attended by hundreds of people from the surrounding country, and proved to be the best and largest affair of the kind in Rhode Island on that day. A delegation of Stoningtonians witnessed the parade and all were unanimous in declaring it to be a 'big thing' throughout."[18] Local train service between New London and Westerly meant that people from Mystic and Stonington could size up a local celebration, and if it was lacking could go where the action was. Improved transportation of this sort—combined steamer and rail—was built all through southern New England at this time, and many scenic locations were in easy reach of almost anyone.

In contrast, Captain Fred Smith had his wife, Sallie, with him aboard the bark *Ohio* of New Bedford, on a whaling voyage in the Centennial Year. In her journal Sallie Smith wrote on 4 July 1876, "Today is the Centennial Fourth it commenced with a Gale this morning but more moderate and cold tonight we have a fire in the Cabin very quite [*sic*] Fourth with us Lat 48:20 N Long 23:50 W."[19]

Decorating: Individuals as well as businesses decorated for the Fourth in the nineteenth century with draped red, white, and blue bunting and flags. Illuminating was a traditional way to mark a celebration, and it involved placing a candle in each window, much as people do now at Christmastime, or hanging strings of Chinese lanterns, as Mystic sparmaker William Beatty did in 1870 and "brilliantly illuminated" the grounds around his house.[20]

Social events: In the middle ground between the open, public observance of the day, and the family gatherings at home, were expansive private parties and excursions organized sometimes by groups like the St. Michael's Temperance Society, the St. Patrick's Church group that went to Mason's Island on a picnic, or students of Mrs. A.A. Murphy's school who picnicked on the academy grounds.[21]

Excursion steamers advertised well ahead the various trips planned for a holiday like the Fourth, and a day on the water had great appeal in coastal towns. The Good Templars took a group of 125 on the steamer *Loyalist* across the Sound to Greenport in 1866. Asa Fish noted in his diary that "The [steamboat] Liberty returns full of music and many passengers 5 P.M."[22]

Newspapers reported on large private celebrations like the Denison family's gathering at Mrs. Lavinia Denison's with an outdoor dinner and chowder in 1873. The same year, Captain Robert Wilbur entertained more than a hundred friends, neighbors, and invited guests at his home, where they, too, had chowder, and played croquet and various sports.[23] It was clearly a day for social gatherings and picnics, informal by Victorian standards but carefully planned.

In the last half of the nineteenth century, as more people took interest in boat racing, regattas became a feature of the Fourth of July. "For several years past it has been the custom of Stonington yachtsmen to celebrate the Nation's birthday by giving a grand regatta"—an event, the Stonington *Mirror* proudly asserted, "which is looked forward to with pleasurable anticipation, not only by the participators, but by the public generally." Fourteen prizes were to be awarded in 1870, ten in money, and four "splendid pennants...to be contested for only by boats belonging to Noank." However, the Mystic *Journal* reporter found, as many have before and since, that watching boats race was not fun: "A long and tedious boat race was arranged by the borough boat men....It was splendid enough for those who were fortunate to sail in the boats, but to the spectators...it was anything but agreeable."[24]

Observing Fourth of July with Family and Friends

Though the Fourth of July had a great deal of outward celebration, people gathered for small family parties as well as large public events. It is hard to quantify, but it is my impression that there was a trend through the nineteenth century toward more family gatherings and some fewer community-wide celebrations, possibly paralleling the trend for wage earners to work away from home. People may have valued what little holiday time they had and spent it with close friends and family members.

Early in the century, Ethan Denison noted in his diary, "Rainy weather though wind NW Independence Killed a lamb, had the company of Mr Page & his wife." When Joseph Anthony of New Bedford reported in 1823 that there had been a public dinner in Fairhaven, he didn't say whether he went or not. He did report that "This eve'n had a supper of Chowder &c"—an all-gentlemen's event, six of them—"had a pleasant time."[25] Can we speculate that he and his friends spent the day on the water and caught the fish that went into their chowder?

Charles Morgan went fishing on the Fourth in 1849, caught bluefish, and noted that many passing vessels "were decorated with flags in honor of the day." Another Fourth, he recorded that "Wm. & Emily and the children spent the day with us."[26]

The Stonington *Mirror* reported in 1873 that while some local people went to the regatta in Stonington, "Others looked landward for their bliss and devised select picnics in coy places by bubbling brooks." In 1885, the Mystic *Press* listed some favorite spots to spend the day: "Mystic people spent Independence Day mostly at Mystic Island, Lyle's Beach, New Haven, and 'home.' "[27]

Dinners and Picnics

New Englanders marked Independence Day with seasonal fare. Tradition has it that salmon, peas, and new potatoes made up one common menu. Nathan Fish confirms part of this in his diary entry for 4 July 1868: "Had salmon, Peas and beans."[28] A whole poached or baked salmon, often served with an egg sauce, made an impressive centerpiece. As we will see later, salmon, because of its size, firm texture, and flavor, conveyed more status and elegance to a meal than, for example, cod or haddock. Green peas and new potatoes at dinner meant the last of fresh peas before hot weather and the earliest of new potatoes. According to his diary, Nathan Fish didn't have new potatoes that year until two weeks after the Fourth. The beans he speaks of could have been early green beans; it was a little too early for shell beans.

For those who preferred meat, probably a majority, lamb and peas were served. Ethan Denison reported that he had lamb in 1809, and sixty-five years later the Mystic *Press* reported that, on 4 July 1875, "the larger portion [of our citizens] ate their lamb and peas at home."[29] July 4 was about as early in the season as anyone would wish to slaughter a spring lamb. The small size of the animal meant it could be consumed quickly, a concern with the onset of hot weather.

No particular dessert seems to have been traditional for the Fourth. The all-American apple pie was truly out of season, unless it was made with dried apples. The earliest new apples were still a month away, and any winter-kept apples would have been in tired condition. Fresh fruit pies from strawberries, cherries, or late rhubarb, were a possibility. An abundance of milk and eggs made almost any custard or pudding possible, as well as ice cream made at home or purchased.

Frederick Marryat, an English visitor to this country in 1837, described the food booths he saw in New York City on the Fourth of July. Besides oysters, clams, fruits, boiled hams, puddings, and pies, he remarked on the quantity of roast pig offered. He claimed every booth had one, for the

Captain Buddington's bunting-bedecked house on Monument Street, Groton, is a fine example of a citizen's celebration of the Fourth. Decorating structures with red, white, and blue was traditional on the Fourth in the nineteenth century, as it still is, and in the old days there were often "illuminations" featuring candles or Chinese lanterns. [MSM 65.407]

length of Broadway on both sides, for a total of six miles of roasted pig; he assumed that this was the case elsewhere in the country and asked "What association can there be between roast pig and independence?"[30]

Aboard ship, as we shall soon see, roasted pig and Fourth of July sometimes coincided, probably for the same reason they did on Broadway: one animal could feed many with no need to keep uneaten portions for long. But pig roasts as big outdoor events didn't catch on in New England as they had to the south. In coastal New England the thing to have was a "chowder" or clambake. (Both these events will be discussed in depth later in this book.) Picnics and chowders were sometimes synonymous, especially where clams could be dug or fish caught and eaten in the same place. So accounts of Fourth of July excursions for a picnic could mean that fish were caught on route, and the chowder cooked up and eaten on the beach before the party returned home in the boat.

A picnic was a fairly new idea in the nineteenth century. The word was from the French *pique-nique*. In France, it was an indoor *or* outdoor meal, to which each of the participants brought something to eat. By 1800 or so, the English were having picnics, too. By mid-century they were almost always outdoor meals. In New England picnics were sometimes enjoyed outdoors at home or conveyed, as we have seen, to a picturesque spot. At home picnics could be any menu at all, carted outdoors, eaten at a table brought outside, and set as it would have been indoors, if that was desired. Picnic pictures from the period show tables covered with tablecloths, set with dishes and flatware. Chairs plus benches, stools, or even boards and casks provided the seating.

Picnics away from home required transportable food to which chowder cooked on the spot could be added. Miss Parloa in her *Kitchen Companion*, in 1887, suggested: "ample supply of cold meat,...good bread and butter" as well as thinly sliced buttered bread, buttered rolls, pressed chicken, broiled chicken, tongue, ham, pressed corned beef, sardines, stuffed eggs, hard-boiled eggs, broiled smoked salmon, pickles, olives, crackers and cheese, orange marmalade, hard gingerbread, cake, cold coffee and tea, lemonade. To this generous advice she added that if ice was carried along the "bill of fare can be greatly improved" by ice cream. A picnic described in the Mystic *Pioneer* included "bread, pies, pickles, cheese, cold meats, &c, &c." Edward Knapp of Noank recalled "Family and Neighbor Pic-nics," which included a sail in a smack to "Gull island for gull's eggs and a good time," or over to Fisher's Island for a chowder on the beach. His Sunday school sponsored elaborate picnics on Mason's Island, to which, by his account, the whole village of Noank went. "What chowders, baked fish, great hams, potted meats–what biscuits, puddings, cakes, pies 'by the cord,' and lastly, Lemon Ice-Cream."[31]

Transporting and keeping food from spoiling required that meats be cooked and/or salted and smoked to begin with; hence ham, tongue, corned beef, sardines, and the like. The fish Knapp described were caught and eaten immediately. Bread, before or after being made into sandwiches, could be wrapped in damp towels. Even the stuffed eggs recommended by Miss Parloa, since they were not made with mayonnaise, traveled safely.

Sweets—pies and cakes—were not omitted. Cheap flour and sugar and wide use of chemical leavenings in the nineteenth century made cake-making very common. For the last quarter of the century, in coastal southern New England at least, coconut cake was a "prominent sort of cake for picnics and church suppers." An advertisement in the newspapers announced "COCOANUTS, Each one warranted sweet and sound, grated for Cake at a few moments notice at SPARKS MYSTIC BAKERY."[32]

Despite requiring as they did moving a great many people, a lot of food, and even cooking pots for the chowder, these picnics were served with what seems to us surprising elegance—cloths, dishes, knives, forks, spoons—all went along and were laid out in style.[33]

The Fourth of July At Sea

William Wainwright had his Fourth of July off to a good, even glorious, start, as we already observed, with his ship at anchor off Gibraltar. He went on to report that "it got so warm that we were compelled to spread awnings at 8 o'clock." After that they dressed ship completely fore and aft. "After the ship was dressed breakfast was piped I had a jolly old breakfast consisting of fried fish and potatoes. There was nothing of account occurred during the day"—at least until 4 o'clock in the afternoon. Then to his delight the captain ordered a ration of whiskey all around for the crew: "What is that I hear do I hear aright? yes my ears do not deceive me. It is the boatswain piping all hands to 'splice the main brace' There was no need of passing the word more than once this is my first 4th of July on board a man of war God only knows where I shall be when another comes around."

The next year, 1863, the USS *Kearsarge* was at sea, and his Fourth of July was a disappointment. Wainwright had already figured out that the Navy was not to his liking. "This is the second fourth of July I have passed in this ship. I don't want to pass the third. This would suit some of you at home who dont like the smell of powder or hear firecrackers for we being at sea we never took any notice of it all. as whiskey is abalised in the Navy we [can't] even splice the mainbrace which I would have done if I could."[34]

Wainwright's experience shows that, as we shall see with Thanksgiving and Christmas, the Fourth was not consistently or uniformly celebrated at sea. Working ships under sail such as whalers, merchantmen, and packet ships with few idle hands, were hard put to observe the holiday, except with noise or a little special food. The exception to this was vessels with passengers aboard who were not subject to the discipline of running the ship.

This was the case with many bound to San Francisco in 1849. Fourth of July celebrations aboard California-bound ships in 1849 were planned and implemented by passengers. Both the manner of organizing the celebration and the individual elements of the observance parallel the event ashore. Because so many forty-niners traveled to California in company with friends and business partners, there was an internal structure to groups that eased celebration planning. Committees were formed, orators selected, readers of the Declaration designated, prayer leaders chosen, and other details arranged for a celebration as similar as possible to what they had known at home.[35]

Not surprisingly then, the forty-niners' day at sea began with noise, followed by breakfast. Then came a program very similar to those we have seen already, with speakers, music, and toasts—on some ships with alcohol, on others, in a time of temperance-consciousness, with water. As decent a dinner as provisions and conditions allowed was served at noon.

Parades, even a variation on Antiques and Horribles, might be part of the celebration. On the ships *Belvedere* and *York*, groups of men formed up mock militias close in spirit to the Squatery Hop Rangers that Charles Morgan described. The forty-niners' day ended, as many Fourths did ashore, with a ball, or alternatively some musical or theatrical entertainments. The only missing element seemed to be fireworks.

A post-forty-niner, an anonymous passenger who left Boston in May 1852 to travel to San Francisco on the ship *John Q. Adams*, reported in his narrative journal: "On the 4th of July had a visit from the 'honorable' John Q. Adams who made a long speech very appropriate to the occasion, but in the midst of our merriment the wind suddenly changed to the SW and blew with great violence." With no need of fireworks to provide excitement, everyone scurried below and didn't come back on deck until the crew had squared the vessel away. We have no way of knowing what else the *John Q. Adams* passengers might have done that day if it hadn't been for the storm.[36]

New Englanders in port on the Fourth predictably recreated their at-home celebration, just as the forty-niners did at sea. In 1878, the ship *Clarissa B. Carver* of Searsport, Maine, was in San Francisco with a dozen other American ships. All the American captains met to plan the event and choose a location. They concluded that the *Carver* "had the best accommodations for the Fourth of July celebrations and was the best by far and the finest looking ship in port. We are to have a picnic dinner, all contributing."

The wife of the *Carver*'s Captain Jonathan Dow reported to her son Fred that "It was a rainy day but nevertheless the ship and the men of war were gaily decked with bunting. I never saw so many flags flying in one day before. We had but 25, some had 50....It was a a gala day....We had the cabin all trimmed up with green. They commenced bringing a roast pig and roast turkey etc....Several stewards came on board from other ships to help." The only disappointment was that "Father forgot to get Scott any firecrackers with so much excitement."

The vessel's guest list was extensive: there were the

families from the other American ships, shipping men from on shore, and officers from American, British, and Russian men-of-war. "Dinner was served between decks, where the side of our ship was all covered with flags." Bands from the men-of-war provided music for dancing. Fred Dow later wrote that his sister Sarah "said she remembered having danced with two of the Russian officers."[37]

Even though not all Fourths of July at home were remarkable, people at sea were thinking of home, and often assumed that something special was going on. Annie Ricketson wrote in 1873, "I suppose they are having a Celebration at home as It is the glorious Forth." Charles Abbey, apprentice on the ship *Surprise* in 1856, anticipated the Fourth a month ahead and wrote in his journal: "In month from today it will be the 'Glorious 4th' & then what rejoicing there will be in the States How queer it seems to talk about the States as a foreign country." And finally the day came: "This is the 'Glorious 4th' in the States but oh how far from that was it with us." Not only did it rain, but the crew expected something different for dinner and merely had "that ('I cant give it a name bad enough') apology for bean soup." There were a few firecrackers on board, which the captain and mate lit off, and the gloomy weather cleared in the afternoon, but it was not much of a Fourth for Abbey and his mates.[38]

On most ships there was little more observance. On the whaleship *Mentor* of New London in 1840 a boatsteerer wrote in his journal: "Celebrated the 4th by firing a gun at sunrise." They spent the rest of the day catching whales. Mrs. Ricketson reported a small bit of fireworks: "In the Evening we had some Sky Rockets which my Husband and Mr. Bourne sent up. They looked very pretty when they come down in the water." Robert Weir on the *Clara Bell* in 1856 wrote that they "wound up the day by firing salutes with a couple of packs of fire crackers—and a grand consertino given by the Steward and Myself on an old tin pan and a cracked flute." Captain Fred and Sallie Smith managed fireworks from the bark *John P. West* on the Fourth in 1882.[39]

Besides these opportunities to make noise, seafarers luckier than poor Charles Abbey might mark the day with a special meal. As with Thanksgiving and Christmas, any kind of holiday meal was most likely to be enjoyed in the cabin, with occasional largess extended to the fo'c'sle. Lamb or salmon with fresh peas was unlikely at sea, although in 1871 Mrs. Ricketson, captain's wife on the *A.R. Tucker*, reported that, even though "I should enjoy one of Mothers good dinners", a satisfying 4th of July feast was enjoyed at sea that day: "Had Oysters, soup and fresh meat pie and *green Peas* [emphasis added] and they tasted good to us although not so fresh as those picked right out of a garden." In 1873 she wrote, "We had baked goose and all the fixings for dinner to day. That was the only Celebration we could have."[40] The oysters one year, the extra effort that went into a meat pie, and the roasted goose another year would have made the day special.

In fact, a roast of meat or poultry alone could signal a special occasion or the importance of the people eating it. For example, the Lawrences, who spent a couple of Fourths of July at sea, one year ate a pair of stuffed and roasted ducks, with cranberry sauce, potatoes, pumpkin, boiled pudding, or duff. The next year they had stuffed and roasted turkey with wild ducks. A turkey certainly meant festivity, even if it was strongly associated with Thanksgiving.[41]

Sallie Smith wrote in her journal that they "had beans & corn for dinner and roast Beef for supper Mr. Hammond had a nice cake from home...and we had that for Supper."[42] Mrs. Smith's punctuation raises some question about exactly when the roast beef appeared, but since the dinner was the main meal of the day, I think probably the beef was served then, with the supper menu similar to a tea in early evening.

The "picnic dinner, all contributing" that Mrs. Dow and her family enjoyed in San Francisco was in the tradition of the early meaning of "picnic" as a kind of potluck. The menu was roast pig and turkey, just right for serving a great many people and making a large enough presentation to convey festivity.

Among the forty-niners, who, as passengers, regularly fared a cut or two above the crew, sometimes almost as well as the officers in the cabin, Fourth of July menus were quite varied. On the *Belvedere* the meal was like a picnic—boiled ham, biscuits, gingerbread, cheese, and other stuff unnamed. Celebrants on the *Magnolia* had beef and veal pies, green corn, green peas, green beans, preserved peach sauce, mince pies, apple pies, English walnuts, apples and pears, and various liquors.[43] The sheer abundance and variety on the *Magnolia* made it a special meal for one eaten at sea; quite a bit of effort had to go into the meat, mince, and apple pies.

In the fo'c'sle, the usual round of rations was served unless the skipper was feeling expansive as he was on *Clara Bell*. As Robert Weir reported: "This day has been one of a little enjoyment with us—coconuts, roast pig, minced pie, soft tack, ginger cake, pepper sauce, Molasses, pepper, rice, and pickles, was our bill of fare—quite extensive for sailor's." On board the *A.J. Fuller*, Felix Riesenberg and his mates ate a fine dessert: "On the glorious Fourth, Chow [the cook] had spread himself to the extent of favoring the fo'c'sle mess with two large pans of gingerbread, nicely cut into squares, so that everyone would get his lawful whack."[44]

Considering the meaning of the day, Horatio Gray, master of the ship *Medford*, on the Fourth of July in 1885 paused for a moment and wrote in his journal: "This the glorious Fourth of July has been a lovely day and through it I have been in any other than a *patriotic* mood, yet I have not forgotten the day, and trust that as an American I may ever possess that national spirit that should flow in the veins of every true lover of liberty, and cause him to reflect with sincere devotion, this the anniversary of the day that declared us 'a free people.' "[45]

The Recipes

Some of the recipes that follow are for nineteenth-century picnic food. The recipe for corned beef to serve cold makes the beef easy to slice for sandwiches, and a simple dressing for sandwich bread is also here. A sugar gingerbread, which makes crunchy gingerbread bars, and a coconut cake are good for dessert. Poached salmon and egg sauce is for the traditional Fourth dinner. Some of the forty-niners recorded that they enjoyed veal pie on the Fourth, and a recipe for that is included. Lemonade, a good all-purpose summer beverage, especially for the temperance-minded, is also here. The cold stuffed eggs are good for a picnic at home or away. Early July was, and is, a good time to enjoy berry pies and peach ice cream.

POACHED SALMON

FRESH SALMON, BOILED
From the middle of a salmon weighing sixteen or eighteen pounds, take four pounds, wash it carefully, rub the inside with salt, tie it up in a cloth, and boil it slowly forty minutes; when half cooked turn it over in the pot, serve with egg sauce, or drawn butter and parsley.

From *The Practical Cookbook,* by Mrs. Bliss, 1864, page 30

Hardly anyone I know would whack a choice four pounds out of the middle of a sixteen-pound salmon, even if they could get such a large fish in the first place. Most of us will be very glad to buy a medium-sized salmon, preferably in the round, at a fish market, allowing at least half a pound per serving. Salmon is also frequently sold in steaks; allow one steak per serving. At the very best, a fresh-caught salmon is easier poached whole than filleted.

The modern rule of thumb for determining the amount of time for preparing poached fish is ten minutes per inch of thickness. By this rule, Mrs. Bliss's would have been at least four inches thick at its thickest. Wrapping the fish in cheese cloth enables you to handle the fish with less risk of its falling apart. If you have a fish poacher, all the better. More sophisticated cooks may wish to use court bouillon (stock made from fish bones, heads, etc.) or white wine in a poaching liquid.

Serve with the egg sauce recipe that follows, either poured over the fish or served in a gravy boat on the side, and garnish the fish with additional boiled egg. If it is the Fourth of July, have fresh peas and new potatoes with it.

EGG SAUCE

NO. 1 MELTED BUTTER
Melted Butter, sometimes called Drawn Butter, is made as follows: Braid two tea-spoonfuls of flour into a quarter of a pound of nice butter, stir this into four table-spoonfuls of boiling water, keep stirring until the butter is all melted; then let it boil up once, and it is fit for the tureen. If the butter and flour are not well braided, the sauce will be lumpy.

NO. 2 EGG SAUCE
Egg sauce is made by putting four hard-boiled eggs chopped fine, into the melted butter as above. A little more water is needed in the melted butter when egg sauce is to be made.

From *The Practical Cookbook,* by Mrs. Bliss, 1864, page 7

Mrs. Bliss's term "braiding" means rubbing the flour and butter together well. You might consider using some of the poaching water for making the sauce.

For your convenience, here is an egg sauce recipe adapted from the two above:

1/4 lb. or one stick of butter
2 teaspoons flour
1/2 cup hot water or fish stock
4 hard boiled eggs
salt and pepper to taste

1. Rub the butter and flour together. In a heavy saucepan over a low heat, cook the mixture a few moments, then add a 1/2 cup of hot water or stock, and bring it up to a boil.
2. Chop the eggs finely and add to the butter and flour mixture; add another 1/2 cup of hot water or stock to make the sauce a pouring consistency.
3. Taste and add salt and pepper to taste.

Yields nearly 2 cups of sauce.

VEAL PIE

Take a shoulder of veal, cut it up and boil one hour, then add a quarter of a pound of butter, pepper and salt, cover the meat with biscuit dough, cover close and stew half an hour, and it will be ready.

From *Mrs.Winslow's Domestic Receipt Book for* 1871, page 19

This recipe is merely a veal stew with biscuit crust similar to dumplings—a pie that did not require an oven. Using this absolutely unprepossessing recipe would be entirely possible on a ship like the *Magnolia.*

Modern veal has less fat than other meats because of the age of the animal; in the nineteenth century veal was leaner, and this helps explain the quarter of a pound of butter. A veal pot pie recipe in Miss Hall's 1855 cookbook suggests cooking the veal with salt pork, which was even more likely to be done on a ship.[46]

Miss Hall also included elaborate plans for lining a pot with a side crust of biscuit dough, placing the stewed veal and its gravy inside, with a top crust carefully supported by skewers, all closed up and set over a fire to cook. But at the end of the recipe she tells us that if we wish we may omit lining the pot with dough—which I think most people did. A pot pie today almost always has only a top crust.

This recipe is clear enough that it does not require an interpretation. The shoulder of veal Mrs. Winslow described is difficult to find today, and very expensive; it is usually boned and rolled. Generally, stewing veal is available already boned and cut in stewing pieces. Cook the meat, barely covered with water, about an hour, not literally boiling the veal, as the old recipe says, but stewing it. Use less butter if you wish, or use both a little salt pork and butter. Salt and pepper to taste.

Use the biscuit recipe on page 144 for the crust or any biscuit recipe you prefer. Spread the mixture over the top of the stewed meat, cook covered for about ten minutes, then uncovered another ten minutes. You can do this on top of the stove or in the oven.

Yields 4 servings.

DRESSING FOR SANDWICHES

One-half lb. of nice butter, two tablespoonfuls of mixed mustard, three tablespoonfuls of salad oil, a little red or white pepper, a little salt, yolk of one egg; rub the butter to a cream, add the other ingredients and mix thoroughly, set away to cool; spread the bread with this mixture and put in the ham, chopped fine. Cheap-One hundred doses Hood's Sarsaparilla one dollar.

From *Hood's Combined Cook Books,* by C.I. Hood & Co., 1875-85, Hood's #2, page 6

This is very simple and quite good—but remember that the nineteenth century was not a time of highly spiced foods in New England, so this may seem a bit plain. Add more mustard if you like or be generous with the red pepper.

"Mixed mustard" is prepared mustard. Use whatever sort you prefer, though a plain, unsweetened mustard made from ground mustard, water or vinegar, and salt only, not thickened with flour, nor with turmeric added, will give you a more authentic taste.

Even though the recipe suggests ham for a sandwich, you certainly could use this spread with cheese, corned beef, or anything you like mustard on. Whether you chop your ham for the sandwich or use thin-sliced ham is up to you. Chopped ham was by nineteenth-century standards more refined and could have been easily accomplished then by running it through a meat grinder, making these sandwiches suitable for a ladies luncheon.

The recipe is clear enough that it does not need interpretation. Let the butter sit at room temperature before you work with it. The recipe provides enough dressing for quite a few sandwiches; halve the recipe or refrigerate the unused part.

Yields 1 1/2 cups of dressing.

PRESSED CORNED BEEF

CORNED BEEF TO SERVE COLD (Mrs. Gratz Brown)
If it is too salt, soak it for an hour in cold water, then put it over the fire, covered with fresh cold water, four or five cloves (for about six pounds of beef), and three table-spoonfuls of molasses. Boil it slowly. In an hour change the water, adding five more cloves and three more table-spoonfuls of molasses. In two hours more, press the beef, after removing the bones, into a basin rather small for it; then, turning it over, place a flat-iron on top. When entirely cold, the beef is to be sliced for lunch or tea.

From *Practical Cooking and Dinner Giving*, by Mrs. Mary F. Henderson, 1882, page 139

The recipe above suggests a couple of things that might surprise modern cooks, but were included in 1882 because a great many people, especially those in rural areas, were corning their own beef even in the later nineteenth century.

For example, the recipe says to remove bones: today our corned beef is made from the rump or brisket and is boneless, but in the past other parts of the animal were also corned. Mrs. Henderson suggested that if it was too salty, the beef might need to be soaked because not only could there be variability in saltiness of home-corned beef but generally it was a saltier and drier product than it is today. Soaking and cooking it for a long time would have rehydrated it to a certain extent.

I have included this recipe for your interest. You may want to follow this process, which is clear enough that an interpretation is not necessary.

SUGAR GINGERBREAD

One quart flour, one cup shortening (pork fat and butter) rubbed into the flour, one and a half cup sugar, one tablespoon ginger, one cup sweet milk, 1 teaspoon soda.

From Mrs. *Winslow's Domestic Receipt Book for 1868*, page 13

A gingerbread or ginger cookie without molasses seems a little odd today, but a standard hard or "sugar" gingerbread in the nineteenth century was usually made with sugar instead of molasses; hence its name. It was mixed stiff and rolled out on a baking pan or sheet and cut into pieces after baking.

This recipe is fairly typical of the type. I personally think it could use more ginger, but that is up to you. Add it to taste. The suggested mixture of lard or pork fat and butter can be replaced by vegetable shortening and butter, if you wish, but it would change the flavor some. Miss Farmer's cookbook in 1896 suggests sprinkling sugar on the top.

This recipe yields two cookie sheets of gingerbread; if your oven cannot accommodate a full batch, consider dividing the dry ingredient mixture, adding half the milk to one half and baking it before adding the rest of the milk to the balance. Here is an interpretation:

4 1/2 cups flour
1 tablespoon (or preferably more) ginger
1 teaspoon baking soda
1 cup shortening
1 1/2 cups sugar
1 cup milk
Preheat oven to 350°

1. Sift together the dry ingredients.
2. Using your fingers or the back of a spoon rub together the dry ingredients and the shortening. Then mix in the sugar.
3. Add the milk and mix thoroughly; turn the dough out on a floured board and knead lightly till it forms a smooth mass.

4. Divide and roll out on two greased cookie sheets to about a half-inch thick. Sprinkle with sugar if you wish.
5. Bake for twenty-five minutes till golden brown. Cut into squares, diamonds, or rectangles while still warm.

Yields two 15- x 10-inch sheets.

COCONUT CAKE

1.2.3.4.*Cocoanut Cake*
1 cup butter
2 cups sugar
3 cups flour
4 eggs whites only
1 cup milk
1 teaspoon cream of tartar
1/2 teaspoon soda
1 small cocoanut

From the manuscript recipe notebook of Julia Gates, 1857-1930 in the collection of the Mystic River Historical Society

Coconut cake was "a prominent kind of cake" in the last quarter of the nineteenth century and early twentieth century, especially for picnics, according to the recollections of a woman from an old North Stonington family. But Mrs. Harland in *Practical Cooking and Dinner Giving*, 1882, says, "This cake looks most beautiful mixed with fruit-cake in a cake basket."[47] This would be especially true if some of the coconut is reserved to sprinkle on the icing.

"One, two, three, four cake" gets it name from the recipe content: *1* cup butter, *2* cups sugar, etc., and early in the century it was also called cup cake because the measuring was all in cups. It is moist and buttery.

There is no doubt that using freshly grated coconut is the best way to make this cake. With a food processor, it should be no trouble. You can imagine Mrs. Gates's relief when Sparks Mystic Bakery offered to grate coconut upon a moment's notice; consider the effort required to produce this cake when grating the coconut by hand was the only alternative. Do *not* use sweetened coconut. I found that one average-sized coconut gave me about five cups grated coconut, which was enough for the cake and frosting. Mrs. Gates may have been using very small coconuts when she called for one each.

This cake is simply rich and delicious.

1 cup butter
2 cups sugar
3 cups flour
4 egg *whites*
1 cup milk
1 teaspoon cream of tartar
1/2 teaspoon baking soda
1 small coconut, grated, or 2 1/2 cups coconut
Preheat oven to 350°

1. Grease two 8-inch pans and line with waxed paper.
2. Sift together the dry ingredients.
3. Beat the egg whites till stiff.
4. Cream together the butter and sugar. Beat in the milk.
5. Add the dry ingredients to the wet ingredients. Mix in the grated coconut.
6. Fold in the egg whites and gently pour into the cake pans.
7. Bake for 45 minutes, or until a toothpick inserted comes out clean.

FROSTING

Cocoanut icing between is nice—
1 grated coconut, to 1/2 of this add whites of 3 eggs beaten to a froth & 1 cup powdered sugar. Lay this between the layers. Mix with the other half of the cocoanut, 4 tablespoons sugar and strew thickly on top.

From the manuscript recipe notebook of Julia Gates, 1857-1930

Mrs. Gates's comment on this icing pertains to the White Mountain cake recipe she included in her notebook, copied from Marion Harland's *Dinner Year Book* published in 1878. But I think this icing is good between layers of coconut cake as well.

Incidentally, the yolks from the eggs used in the cake and frosting can be used in a custard (page 210) or for gold cake (page 323), or in the vanilla ice cream (page 233). The instructions Mrs. Gates provided are clear enough that no interpretation is needed. Use confectioners sugar or pulverize granulated sugar in a blender.

Yields enough icing for one cake.

LEMONADE

Take good lemons, roll them; then cut and squeeze them into a pitcher. Add loaf sugar and cold water, till it makes a pleasant drink. It should be sweet; it is sometimes too acid to be agreeable. Send round in small glasses with handles, or tumblers a little more than half full. The best drink for parties.

From *Practical American Cookery and Domestic Economy*, by Miss Hall, 1855, page 117

There you have the drink of choice, next to water, for temperance advocates everywhere in the nineteenth century. Loaf sugar, of course, was sugar in a hard, cone-shaped form, which had to be pulverized for baking but could be dissolved by stirring into drinks. If you make your lemonade from scratch, you may find that bar sugar dissolves in beverages more readily than regular granulated sugar does; you can make your own by whirling granulated in the blender for a few moments.

FRUIT AND BERRY PIES

In England, only an upper crust is made. In this country there is generally only an under crust, with bars of paste crossed over the top. I prefer this mode; but these tarts should always be served fresh, or the under crust will become soaked and unwholesome. The berries or fruits are first stewed with sugar to taste, then baked, or not baked in the crust, as preferred.

From *Practical Cooking and Dinner Giving*, by Mrs. Mary F. Henderson, 1882, page 447

Mrs. Henderson in *Practical Cooking* provided a pastry recipe as well. "For Pies," she said "I mean Yankee pies," distinguishing the favorite American dessert from English tarts. I once heard a story that illustrates the New England attitude toward pie.

An elderly New Englander known for her pies was interviewed by a cookbook writer who asked her what kinds of pies she made.

"Why," she said, "all three kinds."

Amused and a bit condescending, the writer asked her "What three kinds is that?"

"Open, shut, and barred," she answered.

The moral of the story was that New Englanders thought, and still do, that just about anything can be put in a pie. The conventions were and are "open" pies for custard-types, like pumpkin or lemon meringue, "shut" for solid fruited pie such as apple and peach, and "barred" for berry or mince pies, although, of course, there were always variations from these according to personal preferences.

Cherry pie
fill with a mix of sour and sweet cherries; sweeten plentifully....Eat fresh....but not warm, with white sugar sifted over the top.

Blackberry pie
fill with ripe berries, sweetening plentifully....Eat cold with white sugar sifted over.

From *The Dinner Year Book,* by Marion Harland, 1878, pages 359 and 447

Once nineteenth-century cooks decided anything could be made into a pie, then pie-filling choices depended on the season or the contents of the preserve cupboards. The cherry and blackberry pie recipes above are offered as possibilities for early July picnics. Interestingly enough, cookbooks included a wide range of berry and fruit pies, but usually left out strawberries, which were favored for eating fresh or making preserves.

The "recipes" for fruit and berry pies are usually little more than suggestions for the kind of spice and comments on the amount of sweetening—"plentifully," "enough," "less," or "more" than some other sort of fruit. Today we like pie filling thickened, but the period recipes seldom specified a thickening: once in a while a recipe will say "strew some flour over" the fruit in question.

Frequently the filling was cooked before being put into the pie. Apparently a cook could choose to bake the crusts first and put the filling in later, because cookbooks often cautioned the cook to "lift the lid (top crust) carefully" to pour the filling in.

In the spirit, then, of nineteenth-century fruit pie recipes, you are on your own, and no interpretation of the recipes above will be provided. Figure on using about a quart (4 cups) of filling for the average 9-inch pie. Use the spice you like best, and sweeten to taste.

COLD EGGS FOR A PICNIC

Boil hard; halve them lengthwise; remove the yolks and chop them fine, with cold chicken, lamb, veal, or any tender roasted meat; or with bread soaked in milk, and any salad, as parsley, onion, celery, the bread being half the whole; or with grated cheese, a little olive oil, drawn butter, flavored. Fill the cavity in the eggs with either of these mixtures, or any similar preparation. Press the halves together, roll twice in beaten eggs and bread crumbs, and dip into boiling lard. When the color rises delicate, drain. The testimonials to Hood's Sarsaparilla deserve a careful reading.

From *Hood's Combined Cook Books* by C.I. Hood & Co., 1875-1885, Hood's #2, page 10

Mrs. Rorer in *Mrs. Rorer's Philadelphia Cook Book*, 1886, offered a similar recipe for stuffed eggs, but commented "These are delicious but difficult to make."[48] Modern people would agree to this method of stuffing eggs, similar to deviling eggs, up to the point where the eggs are fried in lard. But this was the conventional way of preparing stuffed eggs to be taken cold on picnics and to serve hot at home with a sauce over them.

This recipe is several in one: there is a meat filling, a bread and greens filling, and a cheese filling. In the interpretation that follows there are three separate recipes for each filling, followed by instructions for deep-frying the eggs when stuffed. They *are* delicious and difficult to make. You might want to skip the frying.

Meat Filling
1 hard boiled egg per person, halved
1 tablespoon finely chopped chicken, ham, lamb, or veal per egg
some melted butter
salt and pepper to taste

1. Mash yolks finely and blend well with chopped meat, using butter to moisten and bind. Add salt and pepper to taste.
2. Put filling in hollows of the whites and press the two halves together. Proceed to frying step below.

Bread and greens filling
1 hard boiled egg per person, halved
bread crumbs
1 tablespoon finely minced onion, parsley, or celery (or all three combined)
milk
salt and pepper

1. Mash yolks finely and blend well with finely minced vegetables. Add an equal quantity of bread crumbs, and moisten to taste with milk. Add salt and pepper to taste.
2. Put filling in hollows of the whites and press the two halves together. Proceed to frying step below.

Cheese filling
1 hard boiled egg per person, halved
1 tablespoon finely grated cheddar cheese
melted butter or olive oil, about 2 teaspoons per egg
salt and pepper

1. Mash yolks finely and blend well with finely grated cheese, moistening with the butter or oil. Add salt and pepper to taste.
2. Put filling in hollows of the whites and press the two halves together. Proceed to frying step below.

To fry the stuffed eggs:
1 egg beaten
1 cup dry bread crumbs finely crumbled
lard, vegetable shortening, or oil
(above is sufficient for 4 eggs)

1. Put at least 3 inches of shortening in a heavy pan and heat till it is at 365° or a 1-inch cube of bread will brown in 1 minute.
2. Roll stuffed eggs in beaten egg, then in crumbs. Then repeat. You may wish to repeat this once more.
3. Put eggs in hot fat, making sure they do not touch one another. Cook until golden brown, then remove them with a slotted spoon. Set on paper towels to drain.

PEACH ICE CREAM

1 quart of rich milk and as much sweet cream; 4 cups of sugar; 6 eggs; 1 quart of very ripe peaches pared and cut small.

Make as directed in full on Sunday of Second Week in July; but stir in the peaches just before closing the freezer for the second time, beating them well into the congealing cream. Unless they are very sweet, you would do well to dredge them in sugar before they go in.

From *The Dinner Yearbook*, by Marion Harland, 1878, pages 485-486

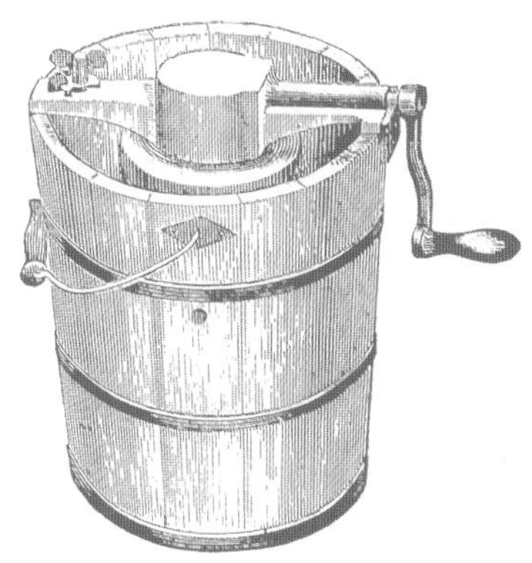

SELF-FREEZING ICE-CREAM

(Instructions from Sunday, Second Week in July)
Heat the milk; pour it upon the eggs and sugar. Cook, stirring steadily fifteen minutes, or until it has thickened well. When perfectly cold, add the cream. Make the custard on Saturday, and set on ice. Early Sunday morning, beat in the cream, and put all in an old fashioned upright freezer, set in its pail.

From *The Dinner Year Book,* by Marion Harland, 1878, page 414

"With a patent five-minute freezer (it really takes, however, from fifteen minutes to half an hour to freeze anything), it is as cheap and easy to make ices in summer as almost any other kind of dessert," said Mrs. Henderson in the introduction to her "Ices" recipes.[49] A half hour of slow, steady ice-cream cranking, even speeded up by improved ice-cream freezers, was something nineteenth-century New Englanders hoped to cut short. Mrs. Harland's instructions for "self-freezing" ice cream essentially meant leaving the chilled custard in the freezer, scraping down the sides occasionally until it was all frozen, which probably produced an ice cream too icy to be the smooth, frozen dessert most of us enjoy.

Vanilla- and fruit-flavored ice creams seem to have been the nineteenth-century favorites, though recipes for chocolate are not uncommon. The Victorian love of a highly molded and decorated dessert included ice cream as well. Putting the frozen ice cream into a mold, or putting two or three different flavors together in a block that could be trimmed with nuts or circled with whipped cream, took effort and had to be eaten quickly in the summer. Ice cream served at a picnic was probably served less formally, scooped directly from the freezer container onto cake-laden plates in the hands of happy eaters.

You can use half-and-half in the place of rich milk in the interpretation below. Whipping or light cream are good choices for "sweet cream." You can make this as rich as you like.

1 quart milk or half and half, or a blend of the two
1 quart cream
4 cups sugar
6 eggs
1 quart crushed, fully ripe peaches

1. Scald the milk in a double boiler.
2. Beat together eggs and sugar; when the milk is hot, pour it into the egg mixture gradually and blend, return to the double boiler and cook till it has thickened slightly.
3. Chill. (You can keep it in the refrigerator overnight and freeze it the next day; it will make a better ice cream if you do.)
4. When you are ready to freeze the ice cream, fold in the cream. Pour into the freezer.
5. Following the instructions for using your freezer, churn the ice cream until it is thick enough for you to feel resistance as you turn the crank. At this point, remove the top and add the peaches.
6. Continue churning till the ice cream is frozen. Eat immediately or repack to freeze harder to eat later.

Yields 3 quarts.

Thanksgiving: New England's Premier Holiday

Thanksgiving in nineteenth-century New England, coastwise and inland, was widely observed and hopelessly romanticized. For most of the century its observance outranked Christmas as the premier annual holiday. Narrative and memoir descriptions echo one another and, if we can believe them, show great similarity from household to household in the day's events, social interactions, and bills of fare.

"Sarah and Friends Going into Turkey" shows a festive board, including a molded dish on the sideboard. [Benjamin Russell watercolor, New Bedford Whaling Museum] Opposite, *at least three* kinds of pie for Thanksgiving dessert: left to right, mincemeat, pumpkin, and apple. Mince and pumpkin pie recipes at the end of this chapter; apple pie recipes on pages 73 and 146.

"Birthdays were almost unnoticed, and Christmas was for the 'church' people—not for those who worshiped in New England meeting houses. We wished each other happy New Year on the first of January, but no gifts were exchanged. Our one great holiday was Thanksgiving Day; to it we children looked forward as soon as autumn began." So wrote the daughter of a middle-class family who grew up in Great Falls, New Hampshire, during the 1830s.[1]

Harriet Beecher Stowe, one of the holiday's chief romanticists, provided a fictionalized account of the day, which may have influenced some of the more glowing narratives that have come down to us; but there is enough similarity of detail in all of these accounts, both straightforward and overblown, to give us an accurate picture of a New England Thanksgiving. John Howard Redfield, in his recollections of life in early Cromwell, Connecticut, said that, since Thanksgiving had been so graphically described by everyone who had ever written about New England, "I shall only attempt to give a few of my recollections," and as we shall see the accounts of the holiday he provided are similar to those from all around the region.[2]

Even as Thanksgiving became a regularly observed national holiday, there were subtle changes in its celebration. It became a great deal more secular; it became burdened with Pilgrim mythology; and, to a certain extant, it became an emblem, even in the nineteenth century, of the "good old days."

A Brief History of the Holiday

At the end of the eighteenth century and the beginning of the nineteenth, Thanksgiving was what was left in New England of a traditional autumn English harvest feast. "Feasts" are practically meaningless today without the observance of a fast day, which was in early New England usually declared in the spring. Thanksgiving, with a small "t", could be declared at any time by the colony—or later the state—or by the church (sometimes there was little distinction between them) for the purpose of giving religious thanks for any manner of blessing, just as fasts could be called to devote time to hopeful prayer in times of stress or trouble.

A boiled turkey with gravy sauce, recipe on page 247, inspired by the one Charles Morgan enjoyed.

Examples of this pattern are the fasts called by the Continental Congress during the Revolution, with thanksgivings declared when General Burgoyne surrendered and when France joined the American cause; and again the fasts called for by President Madison when we were back at war with Britain in 1812, followed by a national thanksgiving declared for 13 April 1815, when the war ended.[3]

At the beginning of the nineteenth century, the New England states were the likeliest in the country to observe Thanksgiving, and of these Connecticut was most likely. The state had a steady custom of annual proclamations, from the middle of the seventeenth century right up to Independence, long before Thanksgiving became a

BY HIS EXCELLENCY

OLIVER WOLCOTT,

GOVERNOR AND COMMANDER IN CHIEF, IN AND OVER THE STATE OF CONNECTICUT,

A PROCLAMATION.

WHEREAS demonstrations are constantly exhibited, that all events are controlled, by a merciful wise and benevolent Being, to whose Providence we are indebted, for those distinguished manifestations of divine favor and protection, which we enjoy :

I have, therefore, thought proper to appoint, and I do hereby appoint, *Thursday, the sixth day of December next*, to be observed throughout this State, as a day of publick *THANKSGIVING* and *PRAYER*. And I do accordingly invite the ministers and teachers, of all denominations, with all the good people of this State, to assemble on said day, and, with grateful, sincere and devout affections, to present a solemn and united homage to ALMIGHTY GOD, to offer our humble thanks, for His inestimable bounties, to our State and Nation; especially, for the continued blessings of peace and internal tranquility; for general health, and the ample supplies, which have rewarded industry, during the current year: above all for the divine revelation, and perfect example, of HIS SON, our Saviour and Judge, and the assurance which his resurrection has established, of a glorious and happy immortality, to be attained, through faith, penitence and conformity to His will. At the same time, to supplicate the Divine guidance and protection, in behalf of the President of the United States, and all others entrusted with rule, counsel and authority; that they may be enlightened by the true spirit of their stations, and may cause right and justice, on all occasions, to prevail; that all institutions, for promoting piety, science, morality, benevolence and charity may flourish: that liberty, happiness, peace and security, may be continued to our country, to the latest generations, and be speedily extended to all mankind.

All servile labour and vain recreation, on said day, are by law forbidden.

Given under my hand, at Litchfield, this twenty-second day of October, in the year of our Lord one thousand eight hundred and twenty-one ; and in the forty-sixth year of the Independence of the United States of America.

OLIVER WOLCOTT.

By His Excellency's Command,

THOMAS DAY, *Secretary.*

national holiday. The proclamation from the governor set the date for Thanksgiving, and in the seventeenth and eighteenth centuries this could be any time from mid-October to the end of December. By the nineteenth century, the day set aside was almost always in November, and most often the last Thursday.[4]

Harriet Beecher Stowe, who spent part of her childhood in Litchfield, Connecticut, and John Howard Redfield, who grew up in Cromwell, described the mood of anticipation created by the arrival of the Thanksgiving proclamation: "On the Sundays of two or three weeks before the appointed day, the minister would unfold a large printed document...which was read to the Congregation. It concluded, as did also the Fast Day proclamation with these words: 'All servile labor and vain recreation are by law forbidden on said day.' "[5]

Stowe wrote that even before the proclamation arrived there were early holiday preparations in which children participated—stoning raisins, chopping suet and meat for mincemeat, powdering spices, and cutting citron, all of which "were only dawnings and intimations" of what was to come. "The glories of that proclamation! We knew beforehand the Sunday it was to be read, and walked to church with alacrity, filled with gorgeous and vague expectations....We children poked one another, and fairly giggled with unreproved delight as we listened to the crackle of the slowly unfolding document." [6]

Few at sea, of course, knew the proclaimed date for Thanksgiving early in the nineteenth century. Richard Henry Dana, Jr., in a foreign port in 1831, saw an Italian ship's crew going ashore for a holiday, and reflected: "American ship-masters get nearly three weeks more labor out of their crews, in the course of a year, than the masters of vessels from Catholic countries. Yankees don't keep Christmas, and ship-masters at sea never know when Thanksgiving comes so Jack has no festival at all."[7]

In later years, if the captain knew or could surmise the date, there might be an attempt at observance, if only a special meal, weather and state of provisions permitting. Mary Lawrence, on the whaleship *Addison* in the Pacific whaling grounds, wrote in her journal for 26 November 1857, "Probably this is Thanksgiving at home," hoping that her family was thinking of them at sea. "As it was blowing quite fresh and a heavy sea, we made no preparation for a special dinner," she noted.[8]

On the *Mary & Helen* in 1879, Irving Reynolds wrote in his journal "Thanksgiving Day at home." Two years later, the ship's crew spent the day fighting a gale, and the journal reported only "Thus ends Thanksgiving 1881."[9]

Between the national day of Thanksgiving declared at the end of war in 1815 and 1862, there were no *national* Thanksgiving holidays proclaimed, although individual states did so, keeping alive a tradition of an annual holiday. Sarah Josepha Buell Hale, editor of *Godey's Lady's Book*, is generally credited with having persuaded President Lincoln to create a national Thanksgiving holiday, which he did in 1863, to be celebrated on the last Thursday in November. After Lincoln's assassination, President Johnson maintained the custom at the urging of Reverend Benjamin Morris of the First Congregational Church in Washington. We have had a national holiday ever since.[10]

Observing Thanksgiving in the Nineteenth Century

Church attendance and charity characterized the public celebration of the holiday, while reunion, dinner, especially pies, and recreation were main themes of the private observance.

Going to church: In the early eighteenth century, the day was similar to a Sabbath, with two services to attend, one morning and one afternoon. By the early nineteenth century the service was squeezed down to one, followed by the family gathering for the meal. Redfield tells us that on Thanksgiving "the religious service began at 11 a.m. instead of 10:30 as on Sundays, and it rarely finished before 1 p.m. The sermon was long, the meeting-house cold, but boyish hope on exultant wing looked beyond the tedious service to...the Thanksgiving Supper, as we called it. Generally, my grandfather invited his children and grandchildren to this feast," which was served at 3 P.M. The advantage, he reported, to this late hour was that "it sharpened the appetite prodigiously, and the feast served for both dinner and supper."[11]

Even with a big dinner in the works, church attendance was usual for as many of the family as possible. Charles Morgan in New Bedford wrote in his diary, "Thanksgiving Day and a beautiful mild day....Attended church with wife & daughters and well were we repaid by a glorious sermon," of which he recorded the text.[12]

In a more strenuously Calvinist tradition, such as the one Harriet Beecher Stowe grew up in, "Great as the preparations were for the dinner, everything was so contrived that not a soul in the house should be kept from the morning service of Thanksgiving in the church and from listening to the Thanksgiving sermon in which the minister was expected to express his views freely concerning the politics...in a somewhat more secular vein of thought than was deemed exactly appropriate to the Lord's day." Pressure on the length of the service came at least in part from culinary considerations, said Mrs. Stowe, because, although the minister was expected to hold forth, "it is to be confessed, that, when the good man got carried away...anxious glances, exchanged between good wives, sometimes indicated a weakness of the flesh, having a tender reference to the turkeys and chickens and chicken pies, which might possibly be overdoing in the ovens at home."[13]

By mid-century, at least one Mystic-area family solved this problem. As Grace Denison Wheeler, describing Thanksgiving around the late 1860s in Stonington, reported: "Always some of the family went to church for the morning service while the rest stayed at home to get dinner, and at 12 o'clock it was on the table."[14]

Charity: In the early nineteenth century, Thanksgiving was the season of charity later assumed by Christmas. "It was the custom in that homogeneous age," wrote Elinor Stearn, describing life in a seacoast town in 1825, "to weigh out and measure flour, sugar, tea, potatoes, butter, etc., and with small turkeys, chickens, legs of mutton to pack tempting baskets for families less fortunate than our own in worldly goods, for their Thanksgiving celebration."[15]

Caroline Howard King in Salem, Massachusetts, about the same time, reported: "For two days before Thanksgiving, our back door was besieged by pensioners, who all came with the same whining request, 'Please give me something for Thanksgiving.' My mother always had ready a store of rice, flour, Indian meal, and apples, which were dispensed to the crowd, while the more favored family retainers were given in addition tea, sugar, raisins, and oftentimes a pair of chickens or a turkey."[16]

"Thanksgiving time was the time for errands of mercy and beneficence through the country," wrote Mrs. Stowe, and reported that the fictional grandmother of Oldtown shamed the arguments of any in her family who resisted the beggars at the kitchen door. "How many times must I tell you, Lois, to read your Bible...'If there be among you a poor man in any of the gates of the land which the Lord thy God giveth thee, thou shalt not harden thy heart, nor shut thy hand from thy poor brother.' "[17]

Charles Morgan took time to comment in his journal, "Still I like the season of thanksgiving to renew & strengthen social ties and to open & invigorate the benevolent feelings. It has this effect generally I think and our poor community generally I think have had a good dinner today and mostly of turkey—of which wife & I distributed several to poor friends and dependents."[18]

Reunion: Lydia Maria Child's Thanksgiving poem, which begins "Over the river and through the woods to grandmother's house we go," has basis in fact. Thanksgiving was then, and has been since, a family reunion, even though *Scribner's Magazine* said of Thanksgiving in 1871, "a family sacrament, to which long scattered members of the same household sat down together beneath the old roof tree which sent them forth, is rapidly dying away. Year by year sees fewer of these beautiful festivals....Old customs are decaying. Families

Caroline King described "squash with queer designs in pepper" for a dinner party, a novel garnishing idea for plain boiled squash, and an attractive ornament to the Thanksgiving table.

A National Thanksgiving was proclaimed for 7 December 1865 to give thanks for the end of the Civil War. This image of three generations of a family gathered around the Thanksgiving table on that significant day matches many of the descriptions of mid-century holidays, like those from the Fish and Morgan families. Here we see the Victorian ideal of a family gathered around a feast. [*Harper's Weekly*, 9 December 1865; drawn by Thomas Nast]

separate more widely and radically than they used, and the spell which once hallowed the day has grown to be, in great measure, a thing of tradition and the past."[19] This was eight years after Thanksgiving had become, in proclamation if not in fact, a national holiday. And it seems to have been a premature obituary for both the feast and its family folklore.

Of course, not everyone before that time always gathered with family, even if they lived in or near the same town as revered parents and grandparents. John Redfield, for example, remembered that at age seven he spent a Thanksgiving with the family of his father's store clerk fifteen miles away from Cromwell.[20] Families certainly were more scattered at mid-century than before, but if their accounts are to believed they made an effort to get home for Thanksgiving.

In 1861, Benjamin F. Fish highlighted Thanksgiving in red in his diary, and recorded that he and other relatives traveled back to Mystic from New York City, where they worked, leaving the night before the holiday by the steamer *Plymouth Rock* and arriving Thursday in time for dinner. The year before he had reported a "Fine night for sailing through Long Island Sound." That year Thanksgiving dinner was "ample and recherche." Among the 25 people "who sat down to discuss it" were his parents, sisters, brothers, in-laws, nieces, nephews, and some of his mother's relatives.[21]

During her Salem childhood, Caroline "Kiddy" King described the entourage that went to church on Thanksgiving. "After church was over, there were greetings from friends and neighbors, and if necessary, introductions of 'my son from the West,' or 'my daughter-in-law from the South,' or 'my friend from the North.'" A little to the north, in Newbury at about the same time, Sarah Anna Emery's family went to the maternal grandparents on Thanksgiving, and to the paternal grandparents the day after. And in Stonington, Connecticut, Grace Wheeler reported that on the Thanksgiving when she was eleven, she was taken "to my grandparents Mr. & Mrs. Noyes at Anguilla Hill." Charles Morgan recorded a family Thanksgiving arrival the day before the feast: "Wednesday November 29, 1848...Nothing occurs to record except that daughter Bessie came from school to spend Thanksgiving."[22]

Reunion's other side was absence and departure. It underlined the lonesomeness of those at sea and of those left at home, and it stirred the emotions of those bereft. Nathan Fish noted in his 26 November 1868 diary entry all who attended that year's Thanksgiving dinner; and, fortunate man, was able to note, "What good reasons we have for Thankfulness. Death has not been permitted to enter our ranks." Charles Morgan's family was not so lucky in 1860: "Bessie was not with us, She could not take part in the lively scene the loss of her little Edith being so vividly recalled this last Thanksgiving when the dear little child was here."[23]

Kiddy King reminds us that in a time before jets and freeways the end of Thanksgiving holidays was "a sad time of good-byes, for in some cases it might be years, it might be forever, but finally the last words were said, the stage door was shut with a clang."[24]

Benjamin Fish and the others were lucky to get home. There were families in New England who had members among settlers in the West, or who perhaps could not afford steamer fare even from New York, and in coastal towns there were family members at sea. Julia Gates, at home in Mystic River, writing to her husband Captain George Gates in 1876, said, "We talked of you Thanksgiving and wished you were one of our party at mothers. It would have been pleasant to have your company, Harriett wished for you to carve the Turkey...I hope your Cook and Steward take good care of you."[25]

"Thanksgiving Dinner Among the Puritans" is the title of this drawing from *Harper's Weekly* in 1867. Most Puritans of the seventeenth century would have been surprised to see themselves pictured as the Victorians romanticized them here. In fact, Puritan settlers used tablecloths and napkins, were likely to share plates, did not include children at table, and often reserved the armed chair for the elder male. [*Harper's Weekly*, 30 November 1867; drawn by J. W. Ehninger]

Recreation: Genuine recreation, even playfulness, marked this day in a New England devoted to simplicity and industry. Mary Channing's memories of the late 1830s were that "for once in the whole year, our elders unbent, and in place of the strictness and severity of other days, actually played games!—blind man's bluff, fox and geese, hunt the slipper and twirling the plate."[26]

Grace Wheeler remembered that, "After dinner was eaten the men would go out into the big field nearby and play ball or pitch horseshoes or try throwing barrel hoops over a stake to see who could ring the most, the fastest." Even if it was cold, she says, they would be shirtless, heated by the exercise, and working up an appetite for cake and pie later. Benjamin Fish recalled some of the younger people "playing ball and tramping around the village."[27]

Kiddy King said that the holiday was "happily kept. If there were family skeletons they were always safely locked up in their cupboards on Thanksgiving Day. Old family jokes were laughed over, healths were drunk and toasts given, old songs sung, and friends passed away lovingly remembered." In her family, the evening might be spent with music, charades, and dances.[28]

All this in spite of the Thanksgiving proclamation's prohibition of "all vain recreation." John Redfield said that "The Friday and Saturday which followed Thanksgiving were always holidays. If the ground was uncovered the days were given to ball; but if winter had set in...sleighing, sledding or skating filled up the time merrily."[29]

Sledding and skating, among other things, were what Charles Abbey, at sea on the ship *Intrepid* in 1859, remembered about Thanksgiving: "'Thanksgiving day' & a holiday at home....Wonder if theres any snow. Visions of sleigh rides rise before me. Is the creek frozen—No; not the creek but the mill ponds." The always-hungry Abbey naturally remembered dinner, but he also imagined the happy holiday social scene at home. "Now friends & families collect & have general jubilee, beginning with church service & Sunday clothes; flanked by a 'huge' dinner, & the reserve brought up in the shape of music & dancing, when pretty girls, display their vocal powers & their pretty ancles, to the immense delight of—ahem. Oh.—h—h, dont I wish I was home, how I would carry on."[30]

What Abbey did instead was prepare to take his turn at the wheel. Thanksgiving day at sea tended to be the same as every other day. Lloyd Briggs, a passenger on the bark *Amy Turner* in 1880, reported, "Thanksgiving day at home, but here no change in routine, The crew are employed scraping decks, spars and masts, scrubbing and painting the ship inside and out."[31]

The *W.W. Brainard*, a coasting vessel out of Mystic, spent Thanksgiving in 1868 loading barrel heads in Portland, Maine. On the *Charles W. Morgan* in 1883, a seaman named Russell was buried at sea on Thanksgiving, and there must have been a whale alongside, for the tryworks were started up. Most journals and logs from this time contain no comment on the holiday, and we are left to gather that there was, as Richard Henry Dana, Jr., said, "no festival for Jack."[32]

Mostly those at sea thought of those at home, remembered past Thanksgivings, and hoped for a safe return. Annie Ricketson, on the whaler *A. R. Tucker* out of New Bedford, wrote in her journal in 1871, "I suppose they are enjoying a nice Thanksgiving dinner at home." Recollecting his previous two Thanksgivings, one at home, one at sea, Charles Abbey wrote, "But today bids fair to be as sad & lonely a one as e'er I experienced," even though he noted that he had a good ship and good fellows to talk to on a holiday with no celebration.[33]

Thanksgiving Dinner

The central feature of Thanksgiving ashore or at sea was food. There are few descriptions of the day that lack mention of dinner. As a result, this meal is the most thoroughly documented one for the whole of the nineteenth century: many menus still exist and details of food preparation dominate descriptions of the holiday.

While the 1871 *Scribner's* essay on Thanksgiving was romanticized, it still rung true: "the men, though they say to each other on the way out, 'First rate discourse, minister, wasn't it now?' are on the whole glad to have it over, and be free to turn with undivided interest to what has grown to be considered the real event, the raison d'etre of the day—namely, the dinner."[34]

Actually, the feast was the focus of the day even earlier. A century before, in 1784, Shubael Breed of Norwich, Connecticut, wrote to Mason Fitch Cogswell in New York City: "Thanksgiving with its multitude of good eating and good drinking is gone. Yesterday was the festival and today the puddings with all their dimensions have disappeared. What a glorious thing it is, my boy, once a year to eat and to drink and to be crammed to bursting—to be six months at least in preparing our stomachs to swell, that profusion may be loaded into them and then be six months in getting rid of the heart-burn and indigestion occasioned by it—charming—charming....What a sight of pigs and geese and turkeys and fowls and sheep must be slaughtered to gratify the voraciousness of a single day."[35]

John Howard Redfield in Cromwell in the early 1800s described "this feast, where roast turkey, chicken pie, and sometimes roast pig, with all due accompaniments were followed by mince and pumpkin pie ad libitum." Mary Channing declared: "A turkey was the principle dish; then there were chicken pies, and vegetables, sauces, pickles, preserves; pie of mince, apple, squash, pumpkin, and custard; nuts, apples, and raisins."[36]

Grace Wheeler provided a few more details: "The big turkey, brown and shining, accompanied by two big pans of chicken pie and roast pork, crisp and brown, clove studded so it had a spicy odor. There were vegetables of many kinds, cranberry sauce and brown bread, butter from the old churn....Dishes of cucumber pickles and pickled pears and peaches crowded the table, jugs of sweet cider, milk, tea, and coffee. Then came the pies—mince, apple and pumpkin—and cheese grandmother had made, both sage and plain."[37]

The centerpiece turkey: Even where there is small reference to the meal eaten on Thanksgiving, turkey is clearly identified with the holiday in the nineteenth century. Silas Fish, in New York, wrote to his mother in Mystic the day before Thanksgiving in 1847, saying: "I expect to take dinner (tomorrow) on board the [bark] *Montauk* (Capt Gates Vessel) we intend to have Roast Turkey & cc I think I shall enjoy part of the day at least....Hoping you will all have a pleasant time picking Turkey Bones & eating Pumpkin Pies & ccc." In New Bedford, Massachusetts, Charles Morgan's 1860 dinner featured roasted and boiled turkeys. The young Mystic soldier Simeon Fish, writing in his diary at Camp

Somebody's turkey dinner still foraging for itself; but since the leaves have fallen it won't be long before these birds find themselves at Thanksgiving or Christmas dinner. [Glass-plate photo by Edward H. Newbury, MSM 80.41.783]

Buckingham in Norwich while waiting to be sent south to war, celebrated Thanksgiving 1862: "Had a gay time had a number of female friends to visit and also had our regular Turkey, Pies, etc." Even in its absence, turkey was noted in association with Thanksgiving on the barkentine *Good News* in 1894: "Thanksgiving Day & no turkey."[38]

But turkey was not necessarily universal, as Joseph Anthony reported in 1823 from New Bedford: "Nov. 20th. Thanksgiving Day. Dined at Nat. Hathaways on a roast leg of venisoned mutton." Francis Gifford's family in the Little Compton area of Rhode Island killed their hogs just before Thanksgiving in the early 1860s and "Had a sparerib for our Thanksgiving dinner." Phebe Sherman wrote to her husband Captain James on the whaler *Milton* in 1873, "We had our Thanksgiving dinner, a stewed chicken, the next day after Thanksgiving Day."[39]

Why turkey?: Turkey was an all-purpose celebration roast in nineteenth-century New England. In Great Britain, at the same time, it was a special-occasion meat, too, but rivaled by beef. A New World fowl, the turkey was introduced to Europe and adopted by sixteenth-century French gentry as a luxury food. Similarly, in sixteenth-century England, turkeys were domesticated and sold expensively in markets.[40] So the wild native turkeys the first settlers encountered were familiar, and the quantity of them, together with the venison which had been for so long in England the prerogative of the gentry, must have seemed nearly luxurious.

On Thanksgiving, turkey had special significance to New Englanders because of its associations with the "Pilgrims" whom Victorian Yankees increasingly identified with the folklore of "the first Thanksgiving."

As the nation neared its Centenary, a great many people became interested in the country's colonial past and the earliest settlers. By the middle of the nineteenth century New Englanders—particularly Plymouth and Boston people—had observed the old eighteenth-century Forefather's Day marking the Pilgrims' landing date for nearly a hundred years. This custom was overshadowed as Thanksgiving became more popularly celebrated; but the renewed interest in the Pilgrims underlined an interest in *their* Thanksgiving dinner.[41]

Two brief descriptions of the day and the meal were left by Puritan settlers at Plymouth. One, William Bradford's, identified some of the meat served: "And besides waterfowl there was a great store of *wild turkeys*, of which they took many, besides venison, etc."[42]

In addition to its venerable associations with the first Thanksgiving, a turkey met the requirements of a substantial presentation roast, which in our Anglo-American culture signals a significant meal today as much as it did in the nineteenth century. In order to provide enough food for all, the turkey was bolstered by other joints of meat like roast pork, even a suckling pig, beef, wild fowl, and substantial chicken pies, all of which reassured the gathering that this was a major feast. Kiddy King's family included ducks and partridges in Thanksgiving dinner. Numerous menus list roast pork.[43]

Seafarers lacking a turkey attempted to provide a centerpiece joint or roast to convey festivity. On the *Mary & Helen* in 1879, Irving Reynolds's dinner that day was roast beef with green peas, potatoes, and apple pie and raisins. On one Thanksgiving at sea Annie Ricketson reported: "For our dinner here aboard ship we had Boiled Chicken and the fixings and also a boiled pudding which was very nice, a peach pudding."[44]

How to cook a turkey: By mid-century, most homes in New England, particularly in coastal areas, were equipped with a cookstove. Nostalgia for open fireplaces and ambiguity about modern improvements combined at Thanksgiving—powerfully enough in a few homes that the centerpiece turkey was roasted before the fire.

The *Scribner's* essay hints at this, saying that "No wonder that we cannot in these days of water-backs, improved ranges, and anthracite, emulate [the old fireplace's and oven's] perfection. No wonder the turkeys of the period all taste alike, and not one of them in the least like that lordly bird which in the good old days presided over grandfather's Thanksgiving feast."[45.]

Some people agreed. Kiddy King wrote that her father had great contempt for any meat baked in a range, and his opinion was shared by another old Salem resident who "used to roast the Thanksgiving turkey herself, in a tin kitchen, before the fire, in her back parlor. She is remembered...shrouded in a large white apron with her elegant silk dress carefully pinned up" This well-dressed cook visited with her family in the front parlor between trips to check on the roasting turkey.[46]

Pie and Thanksgiving: Besides turkey, pies seem inextricably connected with the great feast. "The Yankee Thanksgiving, with its turkey, cranberry sauce, mince, pumpkin, apple pie and cider," is how one writer styled it in 1871.[47] Thanksgiving was pie season, and great quantities of pies were made for long storage.

"I have known of my mother to make seventy pies to eat and give away!" wrote Elizabeth Dow Leonard, who grew up in Exeter, New Hampshire, in the 1820s, "such exhibitions of every kind of pastry that the soul of woman ever conceived." The Dows were prosperous and could afford generosity with pie. Other families baked enough for the holiday plus some extra for storage. Captain John Whidden in his memoirs wrote that regularly, but especially at Thanksgiving and Christmas, "my grandmother made up what she called a 'batch' of pies—mince, apple, and squash predominating." Whidden reported that a batch consisted of thirty or forty pies and that he "was very fond of pie, and at these times I was in great demand to peel and core apples, seed raisins, chop meat and suet for the mince."[48]

The *Scribner's* essay rhapsodized over "those magic spheres, one for each person, whereon, in many colored segments, cranberry pie and apple, mince, Marlborough, peach, pumpkin and custard, displayed themselves like a gastronomic rainbow."[49] But Channing, Wheeler, Emery, and others attested that apple, mince, pumpkin, and custard pies regularly put in a Thanksgiving appearance.

Narrative writers claimed that children participated in preparing for the holiday dinner, and much of their work was for the pies. "For as much as a week before hand 'we children' were employed in chopping mince for pies to a most wearisome fineness, and in pounding cinnamon, allspice, and cloves in a great lignum vitae mortar,"[72] recalled Harriet Beecher Stowe. As Mary Channing testified, "We were willing helpers in all the preparations—the chopping of meat and apples, the picking over of currants and raisins for mincemeat pies...." "At other times of the year we sometimes murmured at these labors, but those that were supposed to usher in the great Thanksgiving festival were always entered into with great enthusiasm."[50]

Making mincemeat was not done just for Thanksgiving but for consumption all winter. It was frequently made in large quantities as a form of meat preservation; not just for holiday pies, but also put in a crock down cellar to be made up into pies anytime it was wanted. Belinda Smith wrote from her home in Middle Haddam, Connecticut, in 1837 to her brother Hemen on a trading voyage to China, "I will just mention that when mama heard *Niantic* had arrived [in New York City] she went to making mince pies for you."[51] Quite possibly she made them from a crock of stored mincemeat.

According to Kiddy King, the great quantity of pie-making puzzled one four-year-old boy in Salem who asked his mother what all the pies were for. "'For Thanksgiving Day, my dear'....'Do men eat pies?'" he asked, and his mother assured, "'Certainly my dear, I am making these for you and Edward and Papa.'" Thanksgiving morning the little boy got up early, and wakened his father saying, "'Get up Papa, get up. This is Thanksgiving morning, and you know that you and Edward and I have got to eat all those pies today.'"[52]

Any pies that were left uneaten could be stored in a pie safe or a cold room or cupboard. In the years before central heating, various corners of houses were suitable for food storage, as cold—or nearly—as a refrigerator, occasionally even freezing cold. Captain Whidden's Grandmother Appleton had such a cupboard. Unexpected company could be treated to a pie freshened in front of a fire or in a bake kettle.

Chopped meat, suet, raisins, apples, currants, fragrant with spices and brandy, ready for pie; recipe on page 252.

Pie Was Why Whidden Went to Sea

John Whidden lived with his grandparents near Newburyport in the 1830s, and at age 12 longed to go to sea. A misadventure with his grandmother's pie supply, he believed, was "the predisposing cause of her consent being obtained for my going to sea." It happened this way:

His grandmother, as we noted before, baked pies in large batches of up to 40, which were then stored away in a cool cupboard. When a pie was needed, she took one out, warmed it up in the fireplace, and served it.

Whidden's grandmother kept her pie cupboard locked, as any smart woman would with a teenager in the house. But John tested the cupboard door nearly daily, and one day, to his joy, found it unlocked. He snagged a case knife from the kitchen and "Standing on a chair, and taking a pie from the top shelf, knowing these would be the last used, I inserted the thin knife between the upper and lower crusts, and working carefully round was able to lift the top crust...and eat all the mince from the inside." Then he replaced the crust and put the empty pie back on the shelf.

Whidden worked his way through the pies for quite a while. One day, returning home from school, he found that his grandmother had company in to tea, with the table nicely set and pies warming on the hearth.

"At the right moment one of the pies was placed in front of the old lady. As she took the knife and fork in her hands to cut it, she made a few remarks on how she made her pies, how careful she was to select the ingredients, etc., ending with the query whether Mrs. Jones would prefer apple or mince? 'Well, really, Mrs. Appleton,' replied the lady, 'they look so nice, I believe I'll take a small piece of each.'

" 'Why, certainly,' replied my grandmother, laying her knife upon the pie, which crashed through it like eggshell!"

This performance was repeated with a second pie, with the same results. Whidden's grandmother looked at her husband and then at young John, who, though not a word had been spoken, blurted out, "I didn't do it." As he observed, that was a dead giveaway.

Within weeks of this episode, Whidden found himself aboard a half clipper named *Ariel* bound for Liverpool and China, and on his way to a captain's berth.[53]

As the nineteenth century progressed, the Yankee taste for pie was subject to some ambiguity. "Indigestible" and "dyspepsia" became words that described a nineteenth-century concern with health that we continue today with words like "cholesterol" and "fiber." Occasionally pie came under fire.

When the *Scribner's* essay said that even on Thanksgiving "pie and penalty are too inseparably connected," and "We have wandered far from those times of cheerful excess and reckless indigestion" of the good old days, the author was acknowledging some of the dietary—or at least digestive—concerns of the time. "The most indigestible of all foods are fatty and oily substances, if heated. It is on this account that pie-crusts and articles boiled and fried in fat or butter are deemed not so healthful as other food," announced the Beecher sisters in *The American Woman's Home* in 1869.[54]

The changing metabolism of the average New Englander at mid-century, as many more people switched from vigorous outdoor work to more sedentary occupations in business or professions, or relatively passive industrial jobs, meant that high-calorie diets, replete with pies made by "little grown women who have learned from the cradle that man is born to eat pastry and woman to make it,"[55] were less suitable than they had been half a century earlier.

After-dinner dishwashing: No one in the nineteenth century or today can get out of a grand Thanksgiving meal without a pile of dirty dishes. Who tackled the job while the men pitched horseshoes and the younger children went outdoors to play? One early narrative actually referred to the dishwashing process. Sarah Anna Emery recalled seeing her young aunts, girls in their teens, who had had major responsibility for preparing the meal while their elders went to church, as they "fell to clearing the table, having first stirred the kettle of boiling dish-water with the knives and forks....The girls washed the dinner things; the others repaired to the 'fore room.' "[56]

Did anyone ever have a bad Thanksgiving? You would hardly think so—the record is so replete with glowing accounts. Perhaps the diarists and letter writers who were miserable that day withheld comment. But here is one sardonic view from Asa Fish in his diary of 1811: "Wednesday, 27 [November] The preparation Day, that is, the day before Thanksgiving. Many are now flattering themselves with an approaching feast & a joyful season. Children preparing to visit their parents & make merry with their friends....Thursday, 28 the day appointed by his Excellency Gov. Roger Griswold to be observed as a day of Public Thanksgiving & Praise by us the inhabitants of [Connecticut]. At home & unwell." Things did not seem much better three years later: "Thursday Dec. 1, 1814. Appointed by Governor John Cotton Smith's proclamation as a day of Thanksgiving.... Dull Thanksgiving."[57]

Asa seems to have been a cold Fish.

The Recipes

The recipes that follow provide instructions for making all the essential Thanksgiving dishes we have read about in the narratives and letters. You will find both roasted and boiled turkeys, as Charles Morgan had for his dinner, together with a basic stuffing recipe. There is also an oyster sauce and "gravy sauce for boiled fowls," the usual accompaniments to boiled turkey. The chicken pies mentioned by many follow. An idea for preparing turnips with potatoes, plus an early boiled-onion recipe, are also here. Pickled peaches like those mentioned by Grace Wheeler are included. And finally there are instructions for making mincemeat along with both mincemeat and pumpkin pies.

ROAST TURKEY

212. Roast Turkey.
Let the turkey be picked clean, and washed and wiped dry inside and out. Have your stuffing, No. 2, prepared, fill the crop and then the body full, sew it up, put it on a spit, and roast it, before a moderate fire, three hours. If more convenient, it is equally good when baked.

From *New England Economical Housekeeper*, by Mrs. E.A. Howland, 1845, pages 55-56

...fasten it to a spit; dredge it with flour; if the turkey is not very fat, put small bits of butter on the breast; if it is fat, no butter will be requisite; place it before a slow fire and turn it frequently until all the flour begins to brown; baste it continually with salt and water from the dripping-pan, and when half done dredge it again with flour. If the breast is browning too fast, put a piece of paper over it. Fifteen minutes before you wish to serve it, drip a little melted butter over it, from the basting spoon; dredge it with flour, let it brown,—and the turkey is roasted.

From *The Practical Cookbook*, by Mrs. Bliss, 1864, page 77

Time to Roast.
Turkey, 10 pounds, stuffed, 3 hours; over 10, 4 hours; under 10, not less than 2 hours.

From *Hood's Combined Cook Books*, by C.I. Hood & Co., 1875-1885, *Hood's #3*, page 11

I have included these instructions for your interest. If you think you would enjoy trying to roast a turkey in your fireplace, and if you have a tin kitchen at your disposal, as surely Mrs. Howland and Mrs. Bliss would have, these instructions can serve you well.

Roasting times for a turkey, which averaged three hours for a ten-pound turkey stuffed, seem underdone according to modern preferences, and you will probably want to cook your turkey longer than these instructions specify—four to five hours for an eight- to twelve-pound stuffed turkey.

Depending on your skill in the fireplace, it need not take longer than it would in a standard oven at 325°, and you can tell if the bird is done by pricking it with a fork at a joint to see if the juice runs clear, or by wiggling the drumstick up and down. It will move freely when the turkey is done.

BOILED TURKEY

The turkey should be prepared as for roasting, with the wings twisted over the back. Stuff the turkey as follows: Pour boiling water on wheat bread or mashed potatoes; season high with pepper and salt, and if liked, a teaspoonful of sage or thyme, or a bunch of fine chopped parsley; fill the crop, and turn the skin of the neck over against the back and fasten with a small skewer.

Dredge with flour over the outside; tie it in a cloth, and put it in a pot of hot (not boiling) water; cover the pot, and let it boil gently about fifteen minutes to the pound; take off the skum; serve with drawn butter, celery or parsley sauce.

From *Practical American Cookery and Domestic Economy*, by Miss Hall, 1855, page 90

Few people today think they would enjoy a boiled turkey even though this method of preparation was very common in the nineteenth century. Let me mention a few advantages to this method. One is that there is no danger of the bird getting dried out as it sometimes does in roasting. The other is that there are fewer calories in boiled turkey unless you serve it with drawn butter as the recipe above suggests or unless you are one of those people who can actually decline eating the crispy roasted skin of the standard roasted turkey.

"Some people," wrote Mrs. Bliss, "object to boiling a turkey in a cloth, and I think it equally nice boiled without a cloth, provided the cook will watch it closely, and take off all the scum that rises."[58] The scum these writers speak about is the grayish stuff that gathers on the top of the boiling water of most fresh meats and which can discolor the meat. You would not want to send anything to table with dried flecks of this clinging to the meat, but doing a bird up in a cloth is a bit of a bother.

If you are game to try this method, allow 20 minutes to the pound. Mrs. Bliss also recommended mixing the stuffing for boiled poultry with egg rather than water so the stuffing will not get soggy. In the stuffing recipe that follows, substitute beaten egg for the liquid.

Oyster sauce was a usual accompaniment to boiled turkey, and there is an oyster-sauce recipe below.

BASIC STUFFING

211. Stuffing, No. 2

Take dry pieces of bread or crackers, chop them fine, put in small pieces of butter or a little cream, with sage, pepper and salt, one egg, and a small quantity of flour, moistened with milk.

From *New England Economical Housekeeper*, by Mrs. E.A. Howland, 1845, page 55

Pounded crackers and bread crumbs were used interchangeably in the nineteenth century for stuffings. Sometimes salt pork or sausage were included. Seasonings also included from time to time lemon and such spices as cinnamon and nutmeg. The recipe above describes a very basic stuffing that you can add to as you wish.

The rule of thumb for stuffing is to provide one cup of stuffing for each pound of bird. You will find that three to four slices of bread will make one cup of crumbs; use one ounce or two tablespoons of butter per cup of crumbs, less if you add sausage or salt pork. If your crumbs are very dry, you will need to add some water or milk, but only enough to moisten them. If you use an egg, plan on one for every three to four cups of crumbs. The seasoning must be done to your taste, but start with at least a quarter teaspoonful of sage per cup of crumbs.

OYSTER SAUCE

12 oysters, cut into thirds.
1 cupful of milk.
2 tablespoonfuls of butter.
2 teaspoonfuls rice or wheat flour.
Flavoring to taste.
Chopped parsley.

Drain the liquor from the oysters before you cut them up. Boil the liquor two minutes, and add the milk. When this is scalding hot, strain and return to the saucepan. Wet the flour with cold water and stir into the sauce. As it thickens, put in the butter, then pepper and salt, with a very little parsley. The juice of half a lemon is pleasant flavoring. Stir it in after taking the sauce from the fire. Before this, and as soon as the flour is well incorporated with the other ingredients, add the oysters, each cut into three pieces. Simmer five minutes and pour into the gravy tureen. Some also pour a little over the turkey on the dish. Garnish with slices of boiled egg and celery tops.

From *The Dinner Year Book*, by Marion Harland, 1878, page 78

Serve this by itself, in connection with other gravy, for every person does not like oyster sauce.

From *Practical American Cookery and Domestic Economy*, by Miss Hall, 1855, page 90

This recipe is clear enough that no explanation is needed. Serve in a gravy or sauce boat to be poured on the turkey and stuffing.

Thanksgiving dinner at Pachunganuc Farm, with two turkeys.

GRAVY SAUCE FOR BOILED FOWLS

Gravy Sauce

Boil the neck, wing, gizzard, liver, and heart of the fowls, till they are tender; put in a boiled onion, chop it all up fine, then add two or three pounded crackers, a piece of butter, and a little flour thickening; season it with pepper and salt.

From *New England Economical Housekeeper,* by Mrs. E.A. Howland, 1845, page 72

In most ways this is similar to the giblet gravy we know today, although not many people thicken anything with pounded crackers anymore. How closely you wish to follow the original is up to you; most of us leave the wings on the bird, and would be unhappy at finding bits of neck bones in our gravy, if that is really what Mrs. Howland meant. Other cookbooks of the period mention only the gizzards and liver for gravy. Remember, too, that this was for boiled fowls so there are no pan juices to use. The following adaptation leaves bones out of the final product.

neck, gizzard, liver, and heart of turkey
1 quart water
1 onion
1 tablespoon butter
2 common crackers
2 tablespoons flour shaken in 1/3 cup water
salt and pepper

1. Put the neck, gizzard, liver, and heart, and the onion, in a saucepan with about a quart of water to boil together till all are well cooked. Add water as necessary so it does not cook dry and so that you'll have 2 1/2 to 3 cups of broth.
2. With a slotted spoon, remove the meat and onion from the broth, discard the neck (if you wish, after removing shreds of meat), and chop all finely and set aside.
3. Add the butter to the hot broth. Shake the flour and water together in a jar, and pour that mixture and the crackers into the broth.
4. Cook and stir till thickened; add salt and pepper to taste, and then mix in the chopped meat and onion.

Yields about 3-4 cups gravy sauce.

Note: You may adapt this recipe to make gravy for a roasted turkey or chicken by allowing the broth the giblets cook in to reduce, omitting the butter, and adding the pan juices to the broth.

TURNIPS

For Turnip Sauce. — Boil your turnips and mash them fine; add the same amount of mealy mashed potatoes; season with salt and pepper, moisten it with cream or butter.

From *New England Economical Housekeeper*, by Mrs. E.A. Howland, 1845, page 275

The combination of potatoes and turnips cuts the strong flavor of turnip that some people object to. In Scotland this combination is called clapshot, and yellow (swede) turnip is used. Either purple-topped white or yellow turnips are good fixed this way. The original recipe is clear enough that no adaptation is necessary. The term "sauce" was used in earlier days to refer to cooked vegetables and does not mean that this should be sauce-like in texture.

CHICKEN PIE

Take two full-grown chickens (or more if they are small), disjoint them, and cut the backbone, &c., as small as convenient. Boil them with a few slices of salt pork, in water enough to cover them; let them boil quite tender; then take out the breast bone. After they boil and the scum is taken off, put in a little onion, cut very fine, not enough to taste distinctly, but just enough to flavor a little; rub some parsley very fine when dry, or cut fine when green; this gives pleasant flavor. Season well with salt and pepper, and add a few ounces of good fresh butter. When all is cooked well, have liquid enough to cover the chicken; then beat up two eggs and stir, also some sweet cream.

From *Mrs. Winslow's Domestic Receipt Book for 1868*, page 19

...Have ready a baking dish, lined, on the sides, with a light paste...put the pieces of chicken into this dish...pour over it the liquor from the stew-pan, cover with the light paste, ornamenting the cover with leaves cut from the paste, and bake forty-five minutes.

From *The Practical Cookbook*, by Mrs. Bliss, 1850, page 82

A chicken pie served at sea might have been quite different from the one served ashore. The recipe for chicken pie provided by Mrs. Winslow is really more suited for ashore unless a ship was lucky enough to have a cook or steward versed in the finer points of egg-thickened sauces and fine pastry techniques. A chicken pie at sea could also, but not necessarily, have been a simpler affair made with a flour-thickened filling, and a biscuit-like bottom and/or top crust.

Chicken pies vary quite a bit in complexity. For the filling, some sources say to prepare the chicken as for a fricassee; others merely have you fix boiled chicken with a flour-thickened gravy. The simplest fillings are pieces of cooked chicken with some flour sprinkled on and broth poured over. Crusts vary from biscuit-like crusts top and bottom, or just top, to pastry made with lard or drippings, either top and/or bottom or just top.

Mrs. Winslow's filling is a simplified white fricassee. Fortunately, you will be able to buy your chicken already cut up, and even boned, if you wish. Chickens are bred to be fat, so the "few ounces of butter" Mrs. Winslow suggests may be superfluous for your taste. Keep in mind that people in the nineteenth century liked foods richer than we do now.

Mrs. Bliss's suggestion to ornament the top with leaves would create a very festive-looking chicken pie for Thanksgiving. Any plain pastry recipe you like would be suitable for this. The following interpretation halves the original.

1 stewing chicken, cut up and boned
2 slices of salt pork
small onion
parsley to taste
salt and pepper

3-4 tablespoons butter (optional)
1 egg
1/2 cup cream
Preheat oven to 425°

1. Stew the chicken pieces and salt pork in water enough to cover, with the onion chopped up and added.
2. Prepare pastry enough for two crusts. Line a deep pie plate with one. Roll out the second and set aside. Reserve enough pastry from the scraps to make leaves for the top.
3. When the chicken is cooked, remove it from the pan and keep it warm while you prepare the sauce. To broth enough to cover the chicken in the pie plate, add parsley, salt and pepper, the egg well beaten, and the cream; cook till thickened slightly.
4. Put the chicken into the pie plate, pour the sauce over it, and cover with the top crust. Attach the leaves by moistening the undersides with a bit of water and laying them on the surface.
5. Bake the pie at 425° for ten minutes, then reduce the oven to 350° and bake for an additional 20 to 25 minutes, or until the crust is golden.

Yields six servings.

ONIONS

It is well to boil onions in milk and water, to diminish their strong taste. They require an hour or more, and when done, press out the water a little, and season them with a little salt, pepper, and a little melted butter. They should be served hot with baked or roasted meats. They should be kept in a dry place.

From *The Complete Domestic Guide*, by Mrs. L.G. Abell, 1853, page 104

No adaptation is necessary for this a straightforward set of instructions for preparing onions. You will not want literally to boil the onions, but rather simmer them. Otherwise, the milk will curdle. Nineteenth-century cookbook writers used the word boil rather loosely at times.

And, of course, Mrs. Abell meant that you should keep the onions in a dry place *before* they are cooked, not after.

PICKLED PEACHES

Take those of full growth, ripe, but not soft; wipe them with a flannel cloth, or pare them; stick three or four cloves into each peach; lay them in a stone jar. Put half a pound of sugar to a quart of good vinegar, add cinnamon and other spices to the taste; let the vinegar come to a boil, skim, and pour it on the peaches. Let them stand two weeks, then pour off the vinegar and boil it, and pour it on again, and they are then fit for use.

From *Practical American Cookery and Domestic Economy*, by Miss Hall, 1855, page 257

When Grace Wheeler was a child, pickled peaches were more pickles than peaches. As the century wore on, this dish became sweeter. By the turn of the century it was even named "sweet pickled peaches," and had the generous modern ratio of two parts of sugar to every part of vinegar, instead of the one to four parts suggested by Hall. Pears were routinely treated like peaches in pickling.

I offer this recipe for your interest, and no interpretation will follow. You could try it as it stands, canning the peaches instead of keeping them in a stoneware jar. Brown sugar is often mentioned by later cookbooks for pickled peaches, so you may wish to use that instead of white sugar.

MINCEMEAT

Boil a tender, nice piece of beef—any piece that is clear of sinews and gristle; boil it till it is perfectly tender. When it is cold, chop it very fine, and be very careful to get out every particle of bone and gristle. The suet is sweeter and better to boil half an hour or more in the liquor the beef has been boiled in; but few people do this. Pare, core, and chop the apples fine. If you use raisins, stone them. If you use currants, wash and dry them at the fire. Two pounds of beef after it is chopped; three quarters of a pound of suet; one pound and a quarter of sugar; three pounds of apples; two pounds of currants, or raisins. Put in a gill of brandy; lemon brandy is better, if you have any prepared. Make it quite moist with new cider. I should not think a quart would be too much;... A very little pepper...One ounce of cinnamon, one ounce of cloves. Two nutmegs add to the pleasantness of the flavor;...If your apples are rather sweet, grate in a whole lemon.

From *The American Frugal Housewife,* by Mrs. Child, 1833, page 66

Old mincemeat recipes vary to include lemons and oranges, both juice and rind, citron, and wine, in addition to the standard meat, apples, suet, raisins, currants, and spices. Allow the mincemeat to season for a week or two before you use it in a pie; the flavor will develop and mellow. You can refrigerate it, process it in canning jars, or keep it in a crock in a cold place.

2 lbs. lean beef
3/4 lb. beef suet
3 lbs. apples
2 lbs. currants or raisins or 1 lb. of each
3 cups brown sugar, firmly packed
1/2 cup brandy
1 quart sweet cider
1 teaspoon pepper
2 teaspoons salt
2 1/2 tablespoons cinnamon
2 1/2 tablespoons cloves
2 tablespoons nutmeg

1. Boil the beef till fork-tender. Cook the beef suet for a half hour in the beef liquor. Allow both to drain and cool enough to be firm. Chop finely by hand in a wooden bowl, by running through a grinder or processing coarsely in a processor.
2. Peel, core, and chop apples finely. Chop the currants and raisins. Mix all the meat, suet, and fruit together.
3. Add the spices, brandy, and cider. Mix altogether. Pack into a crock and store in a cool place, or pack into canning jars and process to seal.

Yields 4 quarts.

PASTRY

Take a quantity of flour proportioned to the number of pies you wish to make, then rub in some lard and salt, and stir it up with cold water; then roll it out, and spread on some lard, and scatter over some dry flour; then double it together, and cut it in pieces, and roll it to the thickness you wish to use it.

From *New England Economical Housekeeper,* by Mrs. E.A. Howland, 1845, page 41

Mrs. Howland's recipe for pastry seems vague to us but would not have been for the experienced nineteenth-century cook. Lard was a common shortening, as was butter, and puff pastry was popular.

A good rule of thumb when making crust, if you don't measure for flour and shortening, is enough shortening rubbed or cut into the flour so that if you squeeze a handful of the mixture it will cling together; then add enough cold water till it all sticks when mixed. My own favorite pie-crust recipe follows.

2 cups of flour (half whole wheat and half white, if you wish)
1 teaspoon salt
2/3 cup shortening
6-8 tablespoons ice water

1. Mix together the flour(s) and salt.
2. Cut the shortening into the flour with a pastry blender.
3. Add the ice water one tablespoon at a time, tossing the mixture with a rubber spatula until it all will stick together. Put in the refrigerator to chill.
4. When you are ready to make a pie, divide the crust into two parts, and, handling it as little as possible roll out quickly to size; fold in half, and in half again, place point in center of the pie dish and unfold.
5. Put in filling, and if the pie requires a top crust repeat the process above, crimping the edges to close them.

Yields two 9-inch pie crusts.

MINCEMEAT PIES

...Small pieces of butter sliced over the mince before laying on the top crust, will make them keep longer...

From *New England Economical Housekeeper*, by Mrs. E.A. Howland, 1845, page 41-42

...Baked three quarters of an hour.

From *The American Frugal Housewife*, by Mrs. Child, 1833, page 66

Weight- and cholesterol-conscious modern people will probably be reluctant to add butter to the suet-laden mincemeat. Mrs. Child says bits of sweet butter "makes them [the pies] rich; but these are not necessary."[59] Most of us will agree. Two to two-and-a-half cups of mincemeat per nine-inch pie is the usual amount of filling these days, but I think that makes a skimpy pie so I use up to a quart per pie, topped with a lattice crust. Bake at 350° for 45 minutes.

PUMPKIN PIE

Pare the pumkins, cut them into small pieces, and stew them in just enough water to prevent their burning; let them stand over a slow fire until they are quite soft, then strain them through a collander, and to one quart of pumkin, add one quart of rich milk, one table-spoonful of ginger, one tea-spoonful of salt, one nutmeg, two tea-cups of sugar—more will be necessary if you use brown sugar—and four eggs, well beaten; when cold, put into deep plates, lined with Paste, No. 1, trim and bake forty-five minutes.

From *The Practical Cookbook*, by Mrs. Bliss, 1864, page 171

This recipe is obviously for more than one pie. Most modern recipes for a nine-inch pie call for two cups of cooked pumpkin, or half a quart, so the recipe above should yield two pies.

The secret, if there is one, to good pumpkin pies is how well the pumpkin is prepared. Mrs. Abell said to let the cooked pumpkin "remain over the fire, stirring it often until quite dry."[60] If you make this pie from scratch, cooking the pumpkin yourself, this is good advice. No liquid should gather in the pumpkin pulp if you have either cooked the pumpkin or drained it long enough in a sieve.

Usually, the sweet little pie pumpkins available in the fall in fruit and vegetable stores are good for one pie apiece. For "rich milk" you can substitute half and half. One nutmeg grated is equal to three teaspoons, and a tea-cup is equivalent to about half a cup.

The recipe above is clear enough that an interpretation is not needed. If you do not customarily make more than one pie at a time, halve the recipe.

Christmas at Sea and Ashore

"Plum Duff in Danger: Christmas Dinner at Sea," above, shows us a treat too precious to lose. Opposite, roasted fresh pork and potatoes are served in the fo'c'sle on a sailcloth-covered sea chest in honor of the holiday. Sallie Smith made popcorn balls like these for the whalers on her husband's ship. [Engraving by Milton Burns from *Harper's Weekly,* 22 December 1883, MSM 83.110.1]

If you were born at the very end of the eighteenth century, or sometime during the first quarter of the nineteenth, as was Charles Waln Morgan of New Bedford, you might have found yourself confused about your holidays, as Morgan himself was in 1850. His diary entry of December 24 reported, "Family preparing presents for New Years," which he was obliged to scratch out. "Christmas" he wrote in its place, " - a troublesome affair."[1]

We can imagine Richard Henry Dana as a mature Boston lawyer enjoying this kind of formal dinner at Christmas with his family. New Englanders often repeated Thanksgiving's menu for Christmas. The older gentleman is carving a turkey, which, in preference to the goose romanticized in our time, often appeared for both major holidays. [Engraving from *Harper's Illustrated Weekly,* November 30, 1867, MSM 84-7-117]

Christmas in nineteenth-century New England reflected changes in American society as it assimilated new people and customs. There are also undercurrents of Anglophilia, class stratification, crass commercialism, and the increasing secularism of society in this Christmas story. At the early end of the 1800s Thanksgiving in its autumnal glory was the highlight of the New England year. At the later end, Christmas had assumed many of the Thanksgiving features of charity, family reunion, and feasting, and, at least in urban areas, outshone Thanksgiving. Christmas was on its way to engulfing the November holiday, something that finally happened in our time.

A period of non-observance: There is virtually no such thing as a "colonial" Christmas in New England. By now, most people know that the Puritan settlers did not observe the day. School, work, government, and home life were business as usual on December 25. Christmas, as Christ's birthday, if mentioned in Protestant meetings at all, was discussed on a Sunday close to December 25. Various doctrinal reasons were offered to support the Puritan rejection of the holiday, including such arguments as a lack of Biblical warrant to observe the day, compared, for example, to the clear charge to take the Lord's supper. Nor was there any way to know with certainty the date of Christ's birth. Mystic schoolmaster Asa Fish in his diary in 1811 noted, "Wednesday 25 Dec Which day we all know to be called Christmas, but whether it be the anniversary of the birth of Christ demands a doubt. Yet, whether it be or not is not, I think material. Tis enough for us to know that Christ is our Savior."[2]

In addition, early Puritans were offended by the Popish pomp and ceremony that the old Church had added to the observance, and by the holiday's "reckless feasting and mirth." It wasn't that Puritans and the conservative Protestant denominations that followed were offended by feasting and mirth per se—we saw how they celebrated Thanksgiving wholeheartedly. They just felt that Christmas should be a religious occasion, not a secular festival. Further, and more powerfully, as Harriet Beecher Stowe wrote in her fictional autobiography, *Poganuc People*, the "forms and ceremonies were all associated with the persecution that drove the Puritans out of England and left them no refuge but the rock bound shores of America."[3]

Besides, those who did observe Christmas in New England at the beginning of the nineteenth century were likely to be Episcopalians, a church that represented not only a doctrinal, but also a political, threat to the old Calvinist theocracy that had managed to prevail until the years after the American Revolution, when finally people could join another church or "sign-off" membership in the town's Congregational or Presbyterian Church.

The state and church were so closely aligned in the early days of New England that taxes supported the church and minister, church attendance was virtually required, only members of the church were elected to public office, and Sabbath-keeping—not working on Sunday—was strictly observed and enforced. Beecher, whose own father was a Calvinist minister, writes that all this "justified the sarcasm which said that they had left the Lords-Bishops to be under the Lords-Brethren."[4]

There were many New Englanders, however, especially those who settled in the region during the eighteenth century, who would have remembered the traditional Anglican Christmas they observed in England. They provided a chink in the social armor that allowed for the eventual renewal of the holiday as part of the dissolution of the state theocracy.

Caroline "Kiddy" King's family were part of this process during the 1820s and early 1830s. Caroline wrote: "There was no observance of Christmas in those days in Salem. It was not a holiday, and no schools or shops were closed. There was still too strong a Puritan element in New England to admit of the chief festival of Episcopal Church....But in our family we had a small celebration on Christmas Eve, when my father always read to us the Christmas Canto in Marmion, and Milton's Hymn of the Nativity."[5]

King's family kept alive some Christmas tales and traditional beliefs. As she reported, "I remember, too, when I was a child, stealing to the window at midnight on Christmas Eve because I had been told that at 12 o'clock, all over the world, all cattle knelt to do homage to the Savior, and I was woefully disappointed because I could not see our neighbor's cow saluting the Star in the East in the traditional manner."[6]

Harriet Stowe's fictional description of Parson Cushing's little daughter Dolly sneaking off to the Episcopal Church to take in the sight of the evergreen decorations and to attend Christmas Eve illumination, seems to describe at least Stowe's own childhood ambivalence about the celebration. In her story, on Christmas morning Parson Cushing gives Dolly a special treat of candy with a kiss, saying, "Papa gives you this, not because it is Christmas, but because he loves his little Dolly."[7] So not just children may have been confused about how to handle the attractive nuisance of Christmas.

New Year's observance: Early New Englanders, like many other settlers from the British Isles up and down the eastern seaboard, *did* observe the New Year with visiting, eating nice foods, and exchanging gifts. As Kiddy King noted, "We rather inconsistently substituted the pagan New Year" for the Christmas holiday. The notion of a New Year's gift may have persisted even into the later nineteenth century as well, if Annie Ricketson's account of her gift for husband Captain Daniel is an example. She was making a shaving tidy that she had not quite finished, but planned to give him at tea, anticipating his turn at the masthead of the whaleship would leave her time enough. She had tucked it away in a drawer in the cabin, but "he must go down and look for his Account book in the drawers and found It."[8]

Quakers were another group that had rejected traditional Christmas observance. Raised a Quaker, Charles Morgan may have celebrated New Year's Day in his early years. He joined the Congregational Society in New Bedford not long after his marriage, and he and his peers in the merchant gentry may have begun to observe Christmas both in the church and socially. But the holiday was something new for him, overlaying and replacing the familiar, hence his confusion about the day. It's unclear whether "troublesome affair" meant to Morgan the fuss of getting presents together, or trying to keep his holidays sorted out.

Southern coastal New England's proximity to New York not only promoted the New Year celebration in the combined English and Dutch fashion, but ultimately exposed the region to the vigorous, urban Christmas influence as well. Fashionable and wealthy urban Americans were among the first to adopt and adapt old-country and ethnic traditions like St. Nicholas and decorating with evergreens.[9] These exotic plantings did not readily take root in the old Calvinist sod, however.

Christmas confusion: "They were noble and high souled men—the Puritan fathers of New England," wrote Rev. S. K. Lothrop in the *Monthly Religious Magazine* in 1846. "But it is certainly a matter of rejoicing that their descendants have so far outgrown their feelings or prejudices in regard to Christmas that the custom of marking the day by religious observance and social rejoicing is fast spreading among the Congregational Churches planted by their labors and watered by their tears."[10]

Lothrop's assertion that prejudices had been outgrown was not at that time entirely true, but was becoming more so. Connecticut was the first of the New England states to declare the day a holiday, which it did in 1845, the neighboring states of Rhode Island and Massachusetts recognizing it in 1852 and 1855 respectively. But family and personal observance was another matter.

Grace Wheeler, who was born in Stonington in 1858, wrote, "Christmas was not observed at all in many homes when I was a little girl. Father did not believe in hanging up stockings for Santa Claus to fill, but mother thought it was well enough for the children to have some presents."[11]

A look at Charles Morgan's diaries over a dozen years between 1848 and 1860 shows a shift in his observance, which probably reflects that of New Bedford's gentry and perhaps others as well. In 1848 he reported mild and rainy weather for Christmas, a Monday that year, and observed that "It has been a very quiet day also being Christmas." He attended a lecture by Ralph Waldo Emerson but said nothing further about the holiday. We already noted the confusion he felt in 1850; but on that Christmas he noted how his grandchildren were "happy with the gifts Christkinkle *(sic)* left in their stockings." He also wrote that he "worked all afternoon on the books." In the next few years, 1853-56, Morgan usually identified the day as Christmas but described it as quiet, made the usual mention of vessel arrivals, commented on his own and family's health. In 1856 he wrote that "it has been a very quiet Christmas except among the Catholics who observe it very strictly."

By 1859, it appears that having a Christmas tree caught on, and the church was likely to be decorated. As Morgan reported that year, "Clara [his daughter] & I went to Rotches where the children had a Christmas Tree — and enjoyed the distribution of its fruits....The church has been decorated with evergreens in honor of the approaching Christmas," which was the next day. Christmas fell on a Sunday that year, and he attended church in the morning and evening, the text both times being from the Christmas story.

In 1860, on December 24th, he reported a Christmas that we would recognize: "Children are all preparing for Christmas & hanging up of Stockings," and "Clara goes to Stay at her sisters to see the fun in the morning when Santa Claus gifts are to be examined." On the 25th he wrote that "This holiday of the Christian world opens beautiful & bright." He worked in the morning, but spent the afternoon at W.J. Rotch's "to see the pretty Christmas tree they had there."[12]

J.D. Fish, living and working in New York City in 1864, wrote his mother the day after Christmas: "We had a lovely day yesterday for Christmas being but Sunday it was not celebrated. You are aware that this day is made very much of in this city—as much as Thanksgiving Day. So it is in old England—and all Catholic countries." After these observations, he added dubiously, "I suppose it is the greatest day in the year."[13]

J.D. Fish mentioned three noteworthy things about the holiday. One is that at that date Christmas was widely enough celebrated to be noticeable to a conservative New Englander. Another is that the holiday's connection to England was obvious, and lastly there was a sufficient presence of Catholics that their participation was apparent. These underline the urbanity of Christmas celebration, the awareness of England's example—which was promoted in popular literature and periodicals–and the presence of Catholic immigrants, a good many of which at this time were probably Irish. These forces—urban life and immigration especially, but Anglophilia, too—would grow in influence as the century progressed and help shape the holiday celebration we now consider the way it always was.

St. Nicholas comes: In 1840, Samuel Rodman of New Bedford showed his unfamiliarity with Good St. Nick: in his December 24th diary entry he wrote, "I went to see mother after tea and then called at a shop or two for some little tokens for our children to enjoy on the morrow as the bounty of their friends under the fiction of 'St Aclaus.' "[14]

Clement Clarke Moore's poem was written in 1823, and helped popularize the idea of St. Nick. Shifted from December 6–when the Dutch observed the saint's day–to Christmas Eve, this blending of traditions caught on gradually through the early nineteenth century. Helped along by popular literature and commercial interests, it had penetrated New England by the mid-1800s.

One little book printed in 1842 contained a fictional letter from a country girl visiting city cousins. Writing to her mother at home, she described what she called "one of the oddest things...the frolic they have the night before Christmas. You must know it is the fashion here." The fashion was to hang up stockings so that St. Nicholas would bring presents for the good and rods for the naughty. She is quite frank about how this is done: each member of the household buys or makes gifts which are turned over to "my aunt who was to to act the part of St. Nicholas; and I am so faithless, I do not believe that without such arrangement the stocking would ever be filled."[15]

The country girl's description provided a complete set of instructions for anyone unfamiliar with hanging up stockings and making sure they will be filled. Individual families soon devised their own plans for Santa's visit.

In Mystic Bridge, on 16 December 1864, Julia Gates wrote to her husband, Captain George, shortly after the birth of a daughter, an experience from which she was gradually convalescing. "Cliffy teases for something to play with, and I wish he had something like a box of blocks...or something of the kind. So that if you have an opportunity you must remember that Christmas is coming, and the little folks expect their Stockings filled. It is not likely I shall get out to look up Santa Claus."[16]

Grace Wheeler reported that, despite their father's objection, she and her sister hung under the mantle a pair of his long, hand-knitted stockings. The Wheelers had live-in help, a young woman from a nearby town, who removed the fireboard that covered the fireplace in back of the stove

A collection of Christmas sweets: Clockwise from upper right, sugar gingerbread, the once-a-year orange, candied orange peel, peanut brittle, orange peel rolled in sugar, and popcorn balls. Recipes at the end of the chapter.

and set a basin of dirty water on the hearth to prove that Santa had washed his hands after coming down the chimney. The girls' stockings contained "an apple, or orange, or maybe as great a treat as a pencil-like stick of red and white candy, and a little cake or cookie." Shagbark walnuts filled up the rest of the space.

"We had as much for Christmas as other children about here and felt very grateful to Santa Claus for his presents, which we rushed to get Christmas morning very early," Grace Wheeler wrote. "We always shouted, 'Merry Christmas, Merry Christmas' to all in the house and it was indeed a merry day for us." Santa was such an accepted feature of Christmas by the 1870s that the Stonington *Mirror* was able to report "Santa Claus was round as usual and notwithstanding the hard times, shelled out liberally. Manifestly there has been no panic in the goodly land from which he comes."[17]

By this time Santa Claus was putting in an appearance at Sunday-school Christmas parties as well. In Mystic in 1877, "the Episcopal Church had, at Morgan's Hall, on Tuesday evening, a beautifully arranged winter home, from which Santa Claus made his appearance (through the chimney,) and the distribution of presents was made..." The Mystic Congregationalists were visited in 1880: "old 'Santa' personated by Mr. Frank Foote, made his appearance during the evening."[18]

Sunday-school Christmas parties: Sunday schools may have helped cultivate Christmas observance. The custom by the last quarter of the nineteenth century was to have one evening, sometimes Christmas Eve itself, given over to holiday celebration, usually with seasonal music or recitations, often from the youngsters. Newspaper accounts draw the picture for us.

A Christmas tree was a standard feature. In 1874, Stonington Congregational Church Sunday School had a "large Norway spruce [which] was illumined with candles and festooned with presents of various kinds." The trees were loaded with "fruit," sometimes literally—apples, oranges, nuts, sometimes metaphorically with various small gifts, such as cornucopias filled with candies, "books, dolls, games, all sorts of toys, and candy and oranges." Another description related that pen wipers and pocket testaments were the usual Sunday-school present. Parents, friends, and neighbors brought small items for one another and children, sometimes providing gifts (or at least trying to) for those who might be otherwise forgotten.[19]

A particularly maritime wrinkle in Sunday-school Christmas parties appeared at the Mystic Baptist Church: "a boat transformed into a full-rigged ship and called the *Merry Christmas*, brought the gifts...rigged by Messrs. Chas. and J. Dudley, and Charles Haynes, and when trimmed with fine taste by the ladies presented a beautiful appearance." The cargo was bags of confectionery and peanuts for the children.[20]

Refreshments for the party-goers apparently varied considerably from church to church and year to year. The Mystic Methodist Church had a supper along with their Christmas tree in 1875; the Stonington Congregationalists offered a "fine collation of fruit and cake" for 150 children accompanied by their parents and friends.[21] "Extensive supper" and "bountiful collation" described the party food other years. Lacking refreshments,

Special food for the Christmas table in the nineteenth century might include, clockwise, a roasted turkey with gravy, a plum pudding, oyster stew, and a molded gelatin salad. The pudding is made from a rhyming recipe published in *Godey's Lady's Book*, and reprinted at the end of this chapter.

the youngsters could always fill up on the treats from the tree before participating in the games that sometimes followed.

At the Life-Saving Station: The men tending the Life-Saving Stations along the coast were not forgotten. This description comes from the end of the nineteenth century: "About Christmas time the neighbors around some of the stations give the men a party—not wholly a surprise, for the boats and buoys must be moved out before the musicians can take possession of the boat-house. After a rousing dance they all repair to the adjoining mess-room to partake of the supper which the guests have provided."[22]

Whether this ever happened at the New Shoreham Life-Saving Station, now preserved at Mystic Seaport Museum, we don't know for sure. Neither Nicholas Ball nor William Card, who were keepers for New Shoreham Station No. 2 on Block Island in the years 1874 and 1875, respectively, reported any kind of Christmas observance. Perhaps they viewed their journals as seafarers regarded their logs: just for facts about work and weather. By the early twentieth century, Block Island men in the Life-Saving Service staggered their shifts off so each could spend part of the day at home with families, and they may have done this in earlier years, weather permitting.[23]

Observance at home: "Christmas was more generally observed than usual as a holiday," wrote the Stonington *Mirror* editor, discussing the Christmas of 1873 which fell on Thursday. "Many of the places of business were closed. The School Bells did not ring and the bell of St. Mark's did. There were church services, family gatherings, little dinner parties and the usual number of Christmas greetings at home and on the streets."[24]

Stonington and neighboring Mystic and Westerly were small, nearly rural towns at that time. Christmas celebration was a little slower to catch on in places like these, and one editorial comment refers perhaps to a lingering doctrinal resistance: "The observance of Christmas was very thorough and hearty by almost all classes and churches, socially if not otherwise. All felt the genial warmth of the season even if they did not recognize the sun from which it came."[25]

In Boston, a full two-dozen years earlier, Richard Henry Dana, Jr., recorded his celebration: "To Ch.[urch] in the morning. H. N. Hudson preached. Dined at fathers & came out early. Our rooms are prettily dressed in greens, as well as my office, as usual, & last night the presents were shown to the children." A year later, in 1852, he reported in his diary that "In the afternoon, had the Longfellow & Mackintosh children & a few others, at a tree & children's entertainment."[26]

In New York City, James D. Fish wrote to his father back in Mystic, on 27 December 1851, with news of Christmas with James's seven-year-old son: "Asa got his Orange Tree it was the principle subject of conversation for some days previous–The Sparib *[sic]* & things were received just in time for Christmas, were very acceptable, & in good order"[27] Because he does not describe the tree in detail, we may surmise it was a kind of Christmas tree with oranges on it. Apparently the grandparents themselves supported the holiday to the extent that they would provide family members something to celebrate with.

New Year's gift exchanges gradually shifted to Christmas. As we saw with Charles Morgan, this progressed unevenly. In 1855, the Morgans did little on Christmas, but on New Year's Day Charles wrote, "we have had a great many beautiful presents– A box arrived from Rod...with many pretty mementoes–our little grandchildren all remembered [with] toys, books, & goodies."[28]

Dana recorded the gifts he received and gave in 1852: "My presents are Burns' complete works fr.[om] Aunt E., Bryant's Poems fr. Aunt S., a silver napkin ring from Aunt M., & a pocket book from Sally (in part). I gave Sarah a needle case made on the inside of Cedar of Lebanon, & on the outside of Olive Wood from the Mt. of Olives. This is bot, with a few other things of M. Murad, therefore know them to be genuine...two napkin rings of olive-wood to Mrs. Watson & Miss N. Marsh, a necklace of olive stones to Charlotte, & a folder to Lilly." All were the kind of thoughtful and useful gifts that were highly recommended by the author of "The Month Before Christmas," a guide to gift-buying, who cautioned against giving books that "will not bear reading more than once," and listed napkin rings among "the presents which will do equally well for father or mother, brother or sister."[29]

Clearly, by 1889 at least, when the gift-buying guide appeared in *St. Nicholas Magazine*, Christmas had been so commercialized in some quarters that a whole magazine article could be devoted to helping consumers find their way through a treacherous season of buying and giving.

How much did commercialism affect the general population? There are a few hints here and there. For example, when the Stonington Congregational Church Sunday School passed out presents in 1873, the newspaper commented that "They were entirely different from the usual pocket-testament-and-penwiper style which Sunday School presents usually follow and were both numerous and valuable..."[30] While the gifts are not described, it is interesting that they were described as "different" and more interesting still as "numerous and valuable." This is beginning to look a lot like Christmas.

Maria Stover of Bucksport, Maine, writing to her husband Captain Joseph at sea in 1866, described the Christmas exercises at her church and reported that "The trees...were covered with gifts and our minister's family were well remembered. The ladies contributed money enough to buy Mrs. H. a nice winter dress and a beautiful worsted breakfast shawl and a gold pen for Mr. H. The free masons have made him a present of two handsomely bound volumes the life of 'Michael Angelo' and the Good Templars gave him a large picture framed." Mrs. Stover also reported a flutter in the church caused by the present from the minister's wife to her husband—a costly gold watch. The one hundred dollars spent seemed like "a large sum for a Methodist Minister's wife to spend for a watch," especially considering he already had a perfectly good silver one. Some in the community obviously felt that Mrs. H. should have avoided the commercial temptations of Christmas. They might have approved of napkin rings.

The gifts must have been distributed for all to see, as were gifts for others in the church community. "Mr. Beal I fear felt hurt, for I do not think his name was called at all. I put on a present for his wife but did not think of him. I hear he said that he wished the trees had been in the woods for he thought unpleasant feelings were excited by some having many more gifts than others." Mrs. Stover pointed out what anyone engaged in giving or receiving gifts has known: "it is quite impossible to please all or to satisfy each one with the gift they would like."[31]

Christmas dinner: For Christmas, New Englanders largely repeated the festive meal they enjoyed on Thanksgiving. The Cratchit family's roast goose of Charles Dickens's *Christmas Carol* had some, but not much, appeal to nineteenth-century New Englanders. It actually had little appeal to any Englishman who could afford a turkey. While geese today are costly, and have romantic holiday associations, they were the poorer, working-class holiday roast in the middle of the nineteenth century. That is why, when Scrooge wakes up after his three ghostly visits, he sends the young fellow to the poulterers for a *turkey* to be sent for Tiny Tim and family to enjoy. During the seventeenth and eighteenth centuries, according to C. Anne Wilson, geese and turkeys were driven into London markets from the English countryside. Before being used for food, the geese "were plucked regularly five times a year to supply quills and down" which resulted in "uncommonly tough and dry" fowl, and this accounts for why they were held in low esteem.[32] Still, there is evidence that geese and other waterfowl were part of New Englanders' dinners.

A good many families added plum puddings to Thanksgiving, and had them again at Christmas. A love of boiled pudding was something shared across the Atlantic, but Yankees were just as likely to have an array of pies with their dinner.

Richard Henry Dana recorded a whole dinner menu from 1842: "to celebrate Christmas, we had our friends to dine with us–Aunt Martha & Mr. Allston, Aunts

This orange jelly from an 1882 cookbook is delicate and flavorful, an elegant finish to a Victorian Christmas dinner. The recipe is on page 274.

C[harlotte] and S[arah], Father, Ned, & cousin Mary. Dined at 4. First course, raw oysters, in the shell with lemon to squeeze on; 2nd. soup; 3rd., roast turkey, with apple sauce, potatoes & squash; 4th., roast duck with cranberry sauce, potatoes & celery; 5th., mince & squash pies, & custard. After this, olives, old cheese & crackers out on the table for about 10m[inutes]. Then the dessert, of nuts, raisins, & apples. Took plenty of time & were 3 1/2 hours at table."[33] This menu is stylish and a far cry from the meals Dana ate around the kid in the fo'c'sle. Dana was part of the Boston gentry in the 1840s and such a complex meal is perfectly appropriate for his family. But even middle-class families would have enjoyed a similar main course.

Turkey and oysters are the primary features of an ideal Christmas dinner described in a story from *Godey's Lady's Book*. The fictional small-town family, suffering financial reverses, essentially pooled resources to make what was called a "donation-party" (what we would call a potluck today) and planned to enjoy "the splendid turkey that Dr. C— sent for a Christmas dinner." "I will send a well-filled cake basket," said one; "and I grapes and apples–and I candies–and I oranges, nuts, almonds and raisins." "And I," said Uncle Ellis, "will get as many first rate Baltimore oysters as you can eat." "And Auntie must cook them," said Kate, "for there is no oyster soup like hers."[34]

Sailors at sea remembering Christmas dinner ashore shed light on the usual menu. In 1837, the Pennsylvanian Spencer Bonsall on the ship *Edward*, spent Christmas in the fo'c'sle where he and the crew thought of home. "Our thoughts then reverted to the poor Turkeys, Geese, and others of the feathered tribe, that had suffered the three previous days to grace the tables of our friends. Whilst we poor outcasts from society are denied any one of the dainties that made the tables on shore groan under their ponderous weights."[35]

Christmas cookies and candies: Christmas was, in the nineteenth century as it remains today, a prime season for the sweet tooth. Many of the accounts we have seen so far mention confectionery and nuts. Fresh and dried fruits like oranges and raisins were part of the seasonal treats. Where fancy molded cookies and cakes had been a significant part of holiday celebrations in many cultures, including some baked goods seen only at Christmas, their seasonal impact was about to be eroded because cheap flour and sugar, and easier baking technology, meant that more people could enjoy cookies more often.

Christmas candy could come from the store or be made at home. Edward Knapp, who grew up in Noank in the late nineteenth century, described the array of candy in William "Boss" Latham's store: "on the North side, was a counter with show case, and a great display of Candies: Peppermint, Clove, Wintergreen, and Cinnamon. The Clove was transparent with fine red stripes twisting around it spirally. There were Chocolate Beans, Conversation Lozenges and long Licorice bars, and sticks of Licorice-root-woody and sweet....Coconut cakes, thin and delicious, were 1¢ ea. Lemon Balls bigger than the largest Glass Alleys, make the lucky boy's cheeks look like a well developed case of mumps. Horehound sticks, and pride of the boys, Maple Sugar Cigars, alight with a strip of brilliant red paper at the ends....There were red hot cinnamon drops, the like of which cannot be found in these degenerate days-whew! They *were* hot."[36] From such a selection the Sunday-school party organizers could assemble the contents of the little bags or cornucopias.

Some holiday candies were homemade. Most cookbooks of the time contained candy recipes, and household cooks could make sweets like caramels, molasses candy, taffy, peppermint drops, and creams of various kinds.[37] Most candy-making was the province of the confectioners-bakers. By the middle of the century most towns had a business or two that provided sweets, baked goods, and ice cream, too.

Candied peels and preserved fruits were by the end of the nineteenth century done both in the home and by confectioners. Nineteenth-century domestic preserve-making encompassed all processes for keeping large quantities of fruit for use at any time, and the distinctions we make today between jams, jellies, and preserved fruit were not so finely drawn. Fancy sweetmeats made of fruits were something to buy from the confectioner, while recipes for simpler sweets, like the candied orange peel which appears at the end of this chapter, continued to be printed in home cookbooks, though increasingly women chose to buy them.

Modern children who drink orange juice every day at breakfast would be astonished by the significance of an orange as a special treat off the Sunday-school Christmas tree. In the middle of the nineteenth century, eating oranges was sufficiently prestigious and uncommon to warrant special table utensils and instructions in etiquette books for gracefully handling the fruit. Even into the twentieth century, for many New England children, an orange was a annual event. Florence Button, born in 1894, recalling her childhood near Center Groton, Connecticut, as the nineteenth century became the twentieth, said that she and her little sister attended the Christmas tree at the church, where they "got a small box of ribbon X-mas *[sic]* candy and an orange the one and only one we got through out the year."[38]

Today cookies and Christmas are synonymous, but in the nineteenth century there is little mention of them in recollections and descriptions of the New England Christmas. Fancy baked cakes and molded cookies especially made for the Christmas holidays seem prominent in the later eighteenth century and early nineteenth century among the Dutch and Pennsylvania Germans, and later in the century in the Christmas celebrations of Scandinavians and eastern Europeans. There seem not to have been as many traditional Christmas *baked* goods among the British-descended except for Twelfth Night Cakes for Epiphany (Christmas plum pudding was boiled).

But for any special occasion the English and their North American descendants did make what we would recognize as cookies: in cookbooks and manuscript sources these are often called "cakes," plural, not to be confused with cake, singular, which was one large baked item. Shrewsbury cakes, naples, craknells, jumbals, seed cakes, gingernuts,

and hard gingerbreads were among the popular cookie/cakes of the early nineteenth century. As the century progressed the number of cookie recipes burgeoned, one result of cheaper flour and sugar and easier baking technology. A stove oven was much easier to heat and keep hot than the brick ovens of earlier times.

The word cookie and perhaps even the association of Christmas and cookies seems to be Dutch. The first use of "cookie" in a cookbook printed in America was in *American Cookery* by Amelia Simmons in 1796. The word derives from the Dutch word *keokjes*. Part of the New Year's observance, koekjes were offered to the guests who attended the customary open houses, especially in New York, where the Dutch started it and the English picked it up.[39] Along with other New Year's Day customs, cookies may have slid over and gotten attached to Christmas.

Miss Simmons provided a recipe for "Christmas cookies," a kind of sugar cookie flavored with ground coriander. Another early New England recipe for "Christmas cookies" specifically appeared in Mrs. E.A. Howland's *New England Economical Housekeeper*, published in Worcester in 1845. It is similar to the Amelia Simmons recipe, except that, in the tradition of English seed cakes, it is flavored with whole caraway seeds. (Mrs. Howland is not famous for original recipes, so this one may have been borrowed as well.) She does say to "Roll out and cut in hearts or diamonds and bake on buttered tins."[40] Tinsmiths made cookie cutters at the time Mrs. Howland published her book, but it was not long before they were manufactured items. The dozens of rolled and cut cookie recipes did not all require cutters: cooks could use inverted glasses for circles, or just score out bars, diamonds, or squares with a knife.

By the late nineteenth century, decorative cookies were generally associated with Christmas, as illustrated in 1877 by a sentimental story in *St. Nicholas Magazine* for children. The mother of a poor, cookie-cutter-less family made some cookies for her children's Christmas: "That night she sat up—I wouldn't dare tell you how late—making cookies—something that hadn't been seen in the house before that winter. She cut them out in all manner of shapes that feminine ingenuity and a case knife could compass, not forgetting a bird for Janey, with a remarkably plump bill, and a little girl for May with the toes turned out."[41]

Plum pudding and mincemeat pie: A rich, raisin, suet, and dried-fruit pudding well-laced with brandy had been associated with Christmas among the English for several centuries by the time the Cratchit family enjoyed theirs. Mincemeat pies were a Christmas tradition by Elizabethan times.[42] Mincemeat was so closely associated with the holiday celebration that the early Puritans forbade eating it on December 25. Since both pudding and pie bespoke festivity, early New Englanders included them on Thanksgiving's menu. When the Thanksgiving menu was extended to Christmas, plum pudding and mincemeat pie were reunited with their older holiday.

But with these two exceptions there was much that New Englanders had forgotten during the Puritan era about celebrating the holiday. As Christmas became more popular, they turned to England to be reminded how it should be done. One example of this is in *Godey's Lady's Book*, where many Christmas articles made reference to English celebration: the December 1856 issue contained nineteen plum pudding recipes, many of them with recognizably British names such as Haddon Hall plum pudding, Nottingham, Derbyshire, etc.[43]

Christmas trees were popularized by Queen Victoria after her marriage to Albert, who brought the custom from Germany. Charles Dickens read his *Christmas Carol* on tours around the United States. Washington Irving wrote his romanticized but very popular set of essays describing an old English Christmas celebration in his *Sketch Book*, virtually an instruction manual for a traditional holiday.

Scribner's Magazine tried at least once to reestablish the English tradition of a Twelfth Night party with the great frosted, fruited Twelfth Night cake. It never really caught on in New England, where celebrating beyond the New Year would have seemed excessive; Virginians and Pennsylvanians were more likely to continue the custom. After explaining all the details, the editors of the Home and Society column wrote, "what with the quaint character of the entertainment, and its novelty, we are not sure but it might be advantageously introduced as a holiday pleasure on this side of the sea." It was especially recommended for children's parties.[44]

As we observed before, pudding-eating had declined from the early to the late nineteenth century. Plum pudding (like plum duff) was not literally made with plums, but with raisins, and the Christmas version often had liquor in it. Temperance recipes for it were developed for those who wished to be strict, and the Christmas pudding recipe at the end of this chapter is one.

Christmas mince pies merely used up more of the mincemeat New Englanders put away before Thanksgiving. In some parts of England at Christmas mincemeat pies were baked in an oblong shape to suggest a creche, but that custom did not survive the Puritan era in New England.[45]

Food in Christmas charity: Charity from the prosperous to the less-fortunate was already an important part of the Thanksgiving holiday in New England, and often took the form of food gifts. It had continued to be important at Christmas in Old England, and gradually caught on here as well.

Popular literature—for example, *Little Women* by Louisa May Alcott and Dickens's *Christmas Carol*—did its part to promote generosity at Christmas. "How Effie Hamilton Spent Christmas" in *Godey's* depicts a rich man's sister assembling her charity baskets: "'this one is for Mrs. Thomas, a poor washerwoman with three children,' she said. 'The basket contains a turkey, you see, two pies, a peck of potatoes, some currant jelly in that jar, and, in this tightly covered kettle, some oysters. That is for Christmas

Captain Fred Smith, and his journal-writing wife, Sallie, spent several Christmases at sea aboard New Bedford whaleships. Mrs. Smith recorded dinner menus, and for Christmas at sea in 1876 they had roast chicken, stewed apple, pickled pears and apples, and sweet and Irish potatoes. It was Sallie who reported on Christmas in 1882 that she made "fifty-five corn balls for all hands"—a treat for the crew. [MSM 91.294]

dinner. At the bottom of the basket there is a box containing a five dollar gold piece...and candies, cakes, and bon-bons for all. All the baskets are alike, excepting that some contain wine and invalids foods, extra for the places where there are sick.'" Effie also packed in some toys and baby dolls for children, as well as all the eatables.[46]

Scribner's supported Christmas charity in an article entitled "Holiday Shopping." "Of another kind of shopping we have not trusted ourselves to speak, though it is most delightful of all, and its reflected glow does more than any other to brighten our homes at this Christmas time. There they lie, the piles of coal, the warm blankets, the barrels of flour. A touch from us, and lo! they become Christmas cheer to bare homes and cold hearths—the best and truest work of the Christ season. Try it, dear everybody, and see if we are not right."[47]

Christmas at Sea

While Thanksgiving's date was moveable and seafarers might not have known exactly when it was, Christmas always came on December 25. To celebrate or not became the skipper's choice, and among New Englanders this would likely reflect his opinion of the holiday and when in the century he made his choice.

Families together at sea attempted to replicate as many of the day's features as they could: a good meal, gifts, decorating the cabin, and hanging stockings. Nice food might be provided the fo'c'sle, in what seemed to be an at-sea variation on charity to the poor, or a turkey for the employees from the boss. Sailors lacked virtually all other ways to observe the holiday; if they celebrated the day at all it was with food, with or without help from the cabin.

This hearkened to an earlier time when a festival day was distinct from other days in the year for the quantity and quality of viands. Our modern daily diet is plentiful and varied in all seasons, regions, and even households, so there is less contrast between festival meals, such as might be enjoyed at Christmas, and ordinary meals. But shipboard food in the nineteenth century, with its repetition and daily plainness, provided a flatness of fare against which any special food stood in high relief.

Missing and being missed: One theme reoccurs in at-sea accounts of Christmas: that the seafarer misses his or her family, and believes they miss him, too, and will think of those far from home.

Charles Abbey, a sailor on the ship *Charmer* at Christmas in 1856, wrote, "What are my friends doing today I wonder if any of them are thinking of Careless Charlie & where he is....They are all wishing each other Merry Christmas, & I hope they are having one, but there is none for me."[48]

Horatio Gray, master of the *John and Albert*, wrote on Christmas Eve in his journal: "Happy Christmas to you all at home, and friends everywhere. I cannot but feel I shall be with you in spirit if not in person...I know that the 'absent one' will not be forgotten, but his name and his memory will be subject of the thoughts of many kind and dear Friends."[49]

Mary Brewster spent several Christmases at sea between

Nehemiah Hayden recorded the menu for this Christmas 1858 spread in the cabin of a packet ship. It included, center, roast fowl, green corn and beans, beef, potatoes, pickled beets, bread to right of the mast. Whortleberry—blueberry—pie is left of mast, and front left is salt cod with salt pork. There's whiskey in the glasses.

1845 and 1849. Writing of one, she noted, "I have passed as merry a christmas here as I should at home." Of another, she observed that it was very pleasant, but she seemed homesick: "Surely I would not remain long could I help it but would be on land by my own fireside and a prayer is often breathed Oh God preserve prosper and return us to the land of our birth where we may live & die."

On still another voyaging Christmas, in 1846, Mary seemed almost gleeful: "A merry Christmas to all the dear friends in Stonington think possibly they may have spoken of me today with the like phrase I wonder where Mary is today imagination pictures me to them eating salt beef and sailing on the deep–But dear friends you are mistaken Here I am in a most beautiful Bay [Margarita Bay, Lower California] with everything to make me happy and comfortable." The California comforts included fish, fresh beef, plenty of milk, oranges, figs, and pomegranates.[50]

Celebrating in the cabin: As might be expected, the presence of the captain's wife and children vastly improved the chances that Christmas would be observed aboard ship, fore and aft. A special meal was the focal point of the day. If provision had been made for live fowl or a pig, then roast chicken, possibly turkey, or pork was on the menu. A slightly expanded array of vegetables, fresh or pickled, would be served, and plum puddings and pies of various sorts would be the dessert. Treats from home might be dug out and shared in honor of the day.

As Captain Horatio Gray aboard the *John and Albert* recorded in his journal on Christmas Day, 1858, "Not withstanding the gale that is blowing, the violent motion given the ship by the high sea now running, we had our 'Christmas Dinner' and as I do not want people to think we had any mean one, because we were at sea, I'll just mention that fact that I saw Chicken Pie, Roast Chicken, Meats, etc, with Fresh Beets, Irish Potatoes, tomatoes, etc. and to cap all I saw Rhubarb pies, Plum Pudding—"[51] Unfortunately, Gray was "unwell" and did not get to enjoy this meal which compared very favorably with a Christmas dinner ashore. The cook and steward did admirably for the afterguard, considering the weather conditions.

In 1873, Captain and Mrs. Ricketson on the whaler *A.R. Tucker* dined more modestly on spare-rib from a freshly killed hog, Irish potatoes, stuffing, and stewed pumpkin. Captain Fred and Sallie Smith on the bark *Ohio* had roast chicken in 1876, accompanied by stewed apple, pickled pears and apples, and sweet and Irish potatoes. Three of their other Christmastimes at sea saw them dining on pork—once, the captain's wife reported, "with the fixings."[52]

Nehemiah S. Hayden, first mate on the packet ship *Frederick Gebhard* in 1858, reported "For dinner we had chicken, beef, pork, codfish, onions, green corn and beans, boiled tongues, pickles, pickled beets, bread and butter and Whortleberry pie and Whiskey. Many a poor fellow has had a worse dinner than that and some have had nothing at all."[53]

The Lawrence family on the whaleship *Addison* at Christmas in 1856 had a roast-chicken dinner with potatoes and four vegetables, and even enjoyed stewed cranberries. By tea they had room for a tin of preserved grapes and a loaf of fruitcake that Mary had brought along.[54]

At sea, the most festive meal that provisions and conditions would allow might be accompanied during the day with some gift-exchanging—but mostly when there were children aboard. Minnie Lawrence always hung her stocking up, although one year her mother reported that "She was fearful that she should get nothing in it, as we could not go to the store." But the Lawrences always seem to have been prepared with nuts, candies, oranges, and small gifts like books, a gold piece, and one year a portmanteau and a cake of soap from the captain of another New Bedford ship with whom Captain Lawrence had visited.[55]

Fred Duncan, sailing with his family on the down-easter *Florence*, reported that "Christmas was the day of days in our lives." The Duncan children did not believe that Santa would ever find them at sea, so they did not hang up stockings. But they emptied their clothes hamper and trimmed it with red and green ribbons, then filled it with presents which they distributed from the hamper as if it were a Christmas tree.[56]

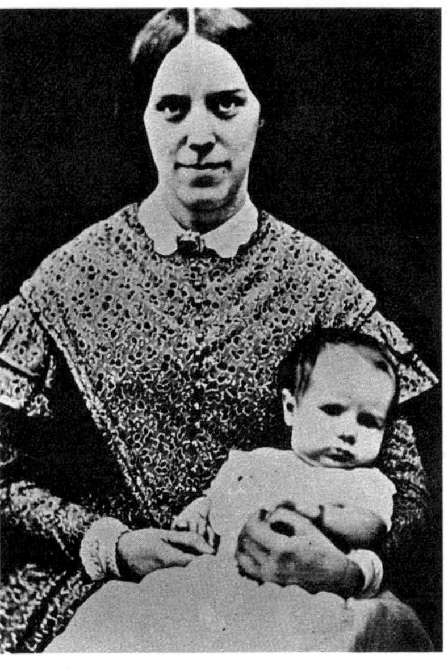

Mary Chipman Lawrence, wife of Captain Samuel, with Minnie on her lap, is another whaling wife who spent Christmas at sea, arranging for Santa Claus to leave gifts, and for relatively sumptuous Christmas dinners to be served, even though they were far from home. [Lawrence, *The Captain's Best Mate*, 1966]

Annie Ricketson gave her husband Daniel "a present of a Cigar holder, that I got for him in St Helena, he was very much pleased with it for he had been wanting one for a long time." This seems to have been unusual; for the most part there is little record of gifts between captains and wives at sea, and exchanges among crew members were rare or unreported. Exchanging Christmas greetings was another matter. Mrs. Ricketson said that the crew "were all looking out to wish me [Merry Christmas] first." The cabin boy beat everyone by tip-toeing down before she got up. She wished Mr. Harris and Mr. Vanderhoop an early Merry Christmas but found that the cook had gotten to them first.[57]

Aside from the Duncans' beribboned clothes hamper, there is little evidence that the cabin was decorated for the day if the ship was at sea. In port, with the possibility of visiting among gathered ships, more effort was made for festivity.

Sarah Dow, spending Christmas with her mother and captain father in port at San Francisco in 1878 on the ship *Clarissa B. Carver*, described in a letter to her brother home in Searsport, Maine, how the Dows celebrated with friends in the fleet. "they had the tree in the aftercabin they moved the table away and took the lamp down and had japanese lanterns around the tree It looked splendid there were over 100 presents on it."[58] Miss Dow went on to list the gifts. These were exchanged among the captains and wives, who also provided presents for the Dow children. The group replicated just the kind of event they would have had at home.

Frozen in the harbor at Marble Island in Hudson's Bay in 1878, the whaling fleet pooled resources. All the captains gathered on one ship, the first mates together on another, and so on. Captain Elnathan Fisher reported that the skippers ate roasted venison, baked salmon, baked beans, raisin-filled duff, gingerbread, and ice cream made from condensed milk, "and plenty of good coffee. There was no liquor. Some of the men put some cake on the table. They had brought it from home in sealed cans."[59]

In foreign ports, seafarers sometimes had the opportunity to observe or even participate in a different kind of Christmas celebration. Vernon Briggs traveled from Boston to Honolulu in 1880 at age 16 on a voyage for his health aboard the bark *Amy Turner*. Once in Honolulu, he made friends among the American community and spent Christmas helping to trim Christmas trees at the sailor's Bethel and at a Mr. Carter's. This was all familiar; but once he went to bed at his rooming house he was serenaded by groups of Hawaiian boys and girls who "form in bands to sing on Christmas Eve and other festive occasions beneath the windows of their acquaintances or of people of prominance....At 2 a.m. I was awakened by the band again—and thus ended Christmas Eve in the Sandwich Islands. A very strange but exceedingly pleasant one it was."[60]

Christmas in the forecastle: Whether the crew got to observe the holiday depended entirely on the captain. William B. Whitecar, Jr., spent Christmas on a New Bedford whaler in 1855. Whitecar was a Philadelphian, expected a treat or two on this day, and was disappointed when the Yankee captain observed the day only by sending a cheese forward. Another year, he recorded, there was not even a cheese and no change in the day's work routine. But on another Christmas they were "agreeably surprised by the steward's making mince pies for the whole ship's company." Mary Brewster recorded that Christmas 1845 found her "busy most of the forenoon in shewing Steward how to make Ginger bread and pies." She didn't say whether *Tiger*'s crew got to enjoy any.[61]

Although Sallie Smith didn't mention it, Captain Fred Smith may have sent forward to the *Ohio*'s crew some fresh pork from the hog they slaughtered at Christmas, 1877. It was a small pig—she reported that it weighed 51 1/2 pounds –but some fresh meat may have found its way into the crew's mess. Sometimes the skipper would have an animal designated for the crew's use. Mrs. Lawrence recorded that her husband, Captain of the whaler *Addison*, "Had a goat killed for the benefit of those living in the forecastle, to which, I should think, they did ample justice, as there are but two legs remaining." (Most modern people are not familiar with chevon, but as Mrs. Lawrence observed earlier the goats they picked up "were very good eating. The taste resembles very much that of mutton."[62]

Spencer Bonsall on the ship *Edward* in 1837 reported that the crew's Christmas dinner was "Roast Pig, or at least, a part of one. It had that fault, common to all such dishes at sea, that is, there was a leetle too leetle *[sic]* or not enough of it."[63]

If there was no fresh meat for the fo'c'sle Christmas, the crew might hope for a plum duff, pie, or some similar treat. R.H. Dana, Jr. in 1834 on the *Pilgrim* recorded that the crew did not get the day off but "we had a 'plum duff' for dinner, and the crew quarreled with the steward because he did not give us our usual allowance of molasses to eat with it. He thought the plums would be a substitute for the molasses, but we were not to be cheated out of our rights in this way." Dana's next Christmas was in San Francisco aboard *Alert* which the crew was loading with hides. They got a plum duff *and* the day off, but only because it was raining and there were no hides to load.[64]

Felix Riesenberg and his messmates sitting down to their usual cold salt beef, hard bread, and tea, on Christmas in 1897, heard about the plum pudding that the cabin was enjoying. "Plum pudding! Christmas! The thoughts of loved ones far away, and those distant homes...came as a pang." But they ended up treated to pie, after all, which they very carefully divided and shared.[65]

On the bark *John P. West* at Christmas in 1882, Sallie Smith "made corn balls for all hands I made 55." These were probably *pop*corn balls, just about the easiest confection that could be made at sea.[66]

Sailors were resourceful in providing some festivity for themselves. Spencer Bonsall, from whom we have already heard, described in great detail the holiday he and the rest of the crew enjoyed in 1837: "...we made the best show that we possibly could, of what little we had. At 7 bells we hauled out two of the chests and getting boards we laid them across the chests forming a table, we then spread some pieces of old sail over it, which answered the purpose of the finest tablecloths. At 8 bells, the Captain hauled out the brandy bottle, giving a glass to all that chose it. We then prepared to serve up our dinner in the most fashionable style. First course, Roast Pig...Second Course, Wheat Duff with raisins in it, but the Black rascal of a Cook, not being accustomed to cooking such rich dishes, put all the raisins in one end consequently those who were served first had the best part of the pud*[sic]*. Third Course, A large quantity of figs which we brought from Madeira and about 1/2 bushel of Chestnuts and English Walnuts which the captain gave us. We then had a bucket of switchel (molasses and water) with which we drank the health of our friends, and of each other, not forgetting the girls, who were toasted and cheered. After numerous songs, we adjourned to the deck to get a little fresh air as it was almost suffocating below. Take it all together it is the happiest day we have spent since leaving Philada *[sic]* and long will it be remembered by the crew of the ship Edward. In the evening we fired two guns in honor of the day.[67]

These accounts of Christmas at sea provide descriptions only of what someone chose to record. A great many logs say nothing about the holiday—after all, their function was to record the movements and condition of the ship. Many journal-keepers skipped the day or described only work accomplished, with hint of either homesickness or good cheer aboard. Some journal-keepers marked the day as Harry Mitchell did in 1816: "This is Christmas but I forgot till noon. It doesn't seem like Christmas here. We didn't even have plum duff."[68]

What Happened to Thanksgiving?

Dana's comment that even his offices were decorated "as usual" underlines the differences between urban and rural acceptance of the holiday, considering that little Grace Wheeler barely got a stocking at Christmas in Stonington in the 1860s.

While it is apparent that some people celebrated the holiday as we imagine they would with greenery, in church if not home; with Christmas trees at home and Sunday school; with the exchange of gifts; with special meals and social gatherings, the details do not often appear in diaries or letters. Popular magazines and literature which gave complete instructions for everything to do with Christmas, from decorating the house to buying gifts, still sound, by the last half of the century, as though they are suggesting something new.

"Talking of Christmas and fashions, we must not forget the home-trimmings soon to be worn. Fortunately the old, old fashion of the evergreens becomes newer and newer every year," wrote the author of *Scribner's* Home and Society column in 1871, following up with how-tos for wreaths, festoons over and around pictures, Christmas mottoes, and how to select a Christmas tree. The author of *Our Homes; How to Beautify Them* included a section on "Dressing the House for Christmas" in 1888, and reported that "The observance of Christmas as a merry holiday has now become almost as general in this country as in Europe." But only almost.[69]

By the end of the century, the holiday season was bracketed by two major holidays. As the author of *Our Homes; How to Beautify Them* wrote, "The Puritan forefathers sternly frowned on what they regarded as unseemly levity at Christmas-tide, and Thanksgiving very largely supplanted the older holiday in the Eastern States. But we have changed all that, and now have the two holidays."[70]

In the following group of recipes are dishes for every course of a nineteenth-century Christmas dinner, plus some cookies and candies for Christmas treats. Oyster soup like "Auntie's" mentioned in the *Godey's* story is here. There are directions for roasting ducks and geese, together with a variety of stuffings for them. For vegetables there are nineteenth-century instructions for preparing celery just like Dana had; pickled beets like Mrs. Lawrence may have eaten aboard the *Addison*; and a very elegant orange jelly. For dessert you can use a rhyming recipe for a Christmas pudding and instructions for making your own preserved orange peel. For Christmas cookies there is a recipe for gingersnaps from Mrs. Gates. If you would like to try making popcorn balls, as Sallie Smith did for the crew of the bark *John P. West* in 1882, you can use the molasses candy recipe included.

OYSTER SOUP

NO. 16. WHITE OYSTER SOUP

Separate the oysters from the liquor, and to each quart of liquor add one pint of rich milk; set it upon the fire, let it come to a boil; add the oysters; mix a heaping table-spoonful of flour with a table-spoonful of butter, and stir it into the liquor as soon as it boils; season with a little salt and pepper; serve on sippets of buttered toast.

From *The Practical Cookbook*, by Mrs. Bliss, 1864, page 21

The line between oyster soup and oyster stew was sometimes a fine one in the nineteenth century, with variations occurring in the amount of liquid and manner of thickening. Mrs. Henderson said "An oyster soup is made with thickening; an oyster stew is made without it," but not all period recipes bear this out.[71]

This is basically a roux-thickened soup with milk. Some oyster-soup recipes were milkless, using the oyster liquor for a broth and yielding a fairly homely dish. This milk recipe is more attractive. Mrs. Henderson also suggested that oyster crackers and pickles were often served with an oyster soup, especially if it was the first course of dinner.

For "rich milk" you may wish to use half-and-half. A more specific interpretation follows.

1 pint oysters
1 cup half milk and half cream
1 tablespoon butter
2 rounded teaspoons flour
salt and pepper

1. Separate the oysters from their liquor and reserve the liquor, adding milk and cream to make one cup. Heat this over a medium flame.
2. Rub together the butter and flour, and add to the heated milk and liquor mixture, stirring and cooking together for about three minutes.
3. Add the rest of the milk and cream, and when it is hot add the oysters and cook only until their edges curl. Serve.

Yields two servings.

ROASTED GOOSE AND DUCK

TO ROAST A GOOSE.—*Goose in itself is of a strong rich flavor, and requires both nicety in the cooking as well as in the stuffing to obviate that strength of flavor. There are many modes of stuffing: for one mode take two moderate sized onions, and boil them rapidly ten minutes; then chop them finely; mince sage to the quantity of half the onion; add of powdered bread twice as much as onion; pepper and salt in it; introduce a little cayenne, and then bind it with the beaten yolk of an egg. Potatoes mashed are sometimes introduced, but not frequently, into the body. They should be mashed with floury potatoes mixed with a little cream and a little fresh butter rather highly seasoned with cayenne and salt. Both ends of the goose should be secured, when trussed, that the seasoning may not escape. It should be roasted before a quick fire, and kept constantly basted. A piece of white paper may be placed over the breast, while roasting, until it rises, and then it may be removed. It will take from an hour an a half to an hour and three quarters…*
Boil some sage and some onions, and some apples; chop all fine together; a little pepper and salt, a little mustard, juice of lemon, a few bread crumbs; bind all together with a little good stock, or milk, or butter; …

From "Receipts &c.," *Godey's Lady's Book*, 1857, page 554

> *...Make a stuffing of boiled potatoes, seasoned highly with pepper and salt, add a table-spoonful of vinegar, if you like it, or a little sage and onion chopped fine; but the stuffing will need no butter, as the goose will supply it with plenty of oil while cooking; fill the body of the goose with stuffing and roast before a moderate fire...*
>
> **From *The Practical Cookbook*, by Mrs. Bliss, 1864, page 21**

Again we can see the nineteenth-century preference for what we would consider underdone poultry. Mrs. Bliss's recipe notes that "A goose weighing eight pounds will roast in two hours." Today we allow half an hour per pound for roasted goose and duck.

Almost all early recipes comment on the fattiness of goose and duck, and nearly all recommend onions or apples in the stuffing and that the cook serve apple or onion or a "sharp" sauce to help cut the oiliness. A "sharp sauce" recipe included in this 1864 issue of *Godey's* follows on the next page.

Modern cookbooks will caution you against basting a goose or duck as it roasts. It is a good idea to place the bird on a rack so the fat can run freely and, in fact, you may want to prick it in several places as it cooks to allow the fat under the skin to run off.

I think it is interesting that even though the editors of *Godey's Lady's Book* declare that mashed potatoes are seldom used as stuffing, they provide a recipe for a potato stuffing anyway. I think it was more common than they claim. A potato stuffing makes a very good side dish in a roast goose or duck dinner, and contrary to what you might think it does not take up fat from the poultry.

When bread crumbs are called for, consider using whole wheat bread and increasing the liquid a bit. Following are more specific versions of the three stuffing recipes above.

ONION AND SAGE STUFFING

2 onions
handful of fresh sage or 1 1/2 tablespoons dried
4 cups bread crumbs (about 12 slices of bread)
pepper and salt
1/4 teaspoon cayenne
1 egg yolk, beaten

1. Boil the onions for ten minutes. Remove from the fire and chop finely.
2. Toss together the onion, sage, and crumbs to mix well. Add the seasonings to taste.
3. Mix with the beaten egg yolk and put in the goose, and proceed with the roasting instructions that follow.

Yields 2 3/4 cups stuffing.

APPLE AND ONION STUFFING

2 cups quartered apples
2 onions, halved
handful of fresh sage or 1 1/2 tablespoons dried
1/2 cup dried bread crumbs
salt and pepper
1 teaspoon ground mustard
juice of 1 lemon
broth or milk

1. Briefly stew the quartered apples and onions with the sage. Then remove from fire and chop them all up finely.
2. Toss all together with the crumbs, salt and pepper, mustard, and lemon juice to mix well. Add enough stock or milk to bind loosely.

3. Stuff into the goose and proceed with the instructions for roasting that follow.
Yields 1 1/2 cups stuffing.

POTATO STUFFING

2 cups hot mashed potatoes
1 medium onion
1 tablespoon dried sage
salt and pepper to taste
1 tablespoon vinegar (optional)
cayenne pepper (optional and to taste)

1. Chop the onion and sage together (if you are using fresh sage).
2. Mix the potato, onion, sage (if dried), salt and pepper, vinegar, and cayenne together well.
3. Stuff into the goose and proceed with the instructions for roasting that follow.

Yields about two cups of stuffing—six moderate servings.

TO ROAST A GOOSE

Note: Most of the stuffing recipes will yield enough for a duck, but you may need to increase the recipe for a goose weighing between 10 and 12 pounds to about 3 cups of stuffing.

Preheat oven to 325°.

1. Remove as much of the visible fat from the bird as you can and prepare for roasting as you would a turkey.
2. Prepare stuffing and pack it in loosely, truss, and place on a rack in a pan.
3. Roast allowing half an hour to a pound, pricking occasionally, basting only if it appears to be drying out.
4. Remove from oven and allow to continue draining fat while you make a gravy which you can do by draining some of the fat from the drippings and proceeding as you would for turkey gravy.

SHARP SAUCE FOR GOOSE

Previous to sending [a roasted goose] to table, a flavoring may be made as follows: To a dessert-spoonful of made mustard, add a quarter of a teaspoonful of cayenne pepper, about the same quantity of salt; mix it evenly with a glass of port wine and two glasses of rich gravy; make it hot; cut a slit in the apron of the goose, and pour it through just previously to serving.

From *Godey's Lady's Book*, 1855, page 90

This snappy sauce would help cut the fattiness of a roasted goose or duck. It has to be prepared after the gravy has been made. "Made mustard" means prepared mustard. Use whatever sort you prefer, although a plain, unsweetened mustard made from ground mustard, water or vinegar, and salt only, without flour or turmeric, will give you a more authentic taste.

2 tablespoons prepared mustard
1/4 teaspoon cayenne pepper
1/4 teaspoon salt
1/4 cup port
1/2 cup of gravy made from goose drippings

1. Mix all the ingredients together well, whisking out any lumps. Heat it till it bubbles.

2. Remove from the fire. If you wish to pour it into the goose, cut a slit in the hollow below the breast, and pour it in. Or serve it separately in a gravy boat.

Yields about 3/4 cup sauce.

ROASTED DUCK

214. To roast Geese and Ducks.

Boiling water should be poured all over, and inside, of a goose or duck before you prepare them for cooking, to take out the strong oily taste. Let the fowl be picked clean, and wiped dry with a cloth, inside and out: fill the body and crop with stuffing, No. 1 or 2. If you prefer not to stuff it, put an onion inside; put it down to the fire, and roast it brown. It will take about two hours and a half.

From *New England Economical Housekeeper*, by Mrs. E.A. Howland, 1845, page 56

TIME TO ROAST

Duck (young) 50-60 mins. duckling 25-35 mins.

From Hood's Combined Cook Books, by C.I. Hood & Co., 1875-1885; Hood's #3, page 11

Most early cookbooks treat ducks and geese the same way. Modern people will find these cooking times inadequate for their tastes. The general rule today for ducks and geese is thirty minutes per pound. You may use any of the stuffings suggested for roasted goose on pages 271 and 272, or Mrs. Howland's Stuffing #2, the adaptation for which is on page 248 in the Thanksgiving chapter. Or you may wish merely to put an onion in the duck instead of stuffing.

Preheat oven to 325°.

1. Remove as much of the visible fat from the duck as you can and prepare for roasting as you would a turkey. If you wish, pour boiling water inside and outside the duck, then drain well. Take up excess water with paper towels.
2. Prepare 2 to 4 cups stuffing. Put stuffing in loosely, truss, and place on a rack in a pan.
3. Roast allowing half an hour to a pound, pricking occasionally, basting only if it appears to be drying out.
4. Remove from oven and allow to continue draining fat while you make a gravy which you can do by draining some of the fat from the drippings and proceeding as you would for turkey gravy.

CELERY

Scrape and wash it well; let it lie in cold water until just before being used; dry it with a cloth; trim it, and split down the stalks almost to the bottom. Send to table in a celery glass, and eat it with salt only; or chop it fine, and make a salad dressing for it.

From *Practical American Cookery and Domestic Economy*, by Miss Hall, 1855, page 133

As we saw with Kiddy King's description of her father's elegant dinner, celery was a special-occasion food. It had enough status to have its own specific serving glass in which it probably graced Dana's Christmas table. Celery, according to Mrs. Child in 1833, was harvested whole, and stored with the roots kept damp, but it probably lost some moisture, requiring the soaking specified by Miss Hall, still a good idea today.

PICKLED BEETS

BEETS. Break off the leaves, but do not cut beets, as that spoils both flavor and appearance; wash them and boil them till tender; then take them out into basin of cold water, and rub all the outside skin off, with the hands; then slice them thin in a dish, and just cover them with cold vinegar, and sprinkle them with pepper and salt, or quarter them, and lay them for a day or two in cold vinegar, as they are then fit for use. The tips of young beets are dressed as asparagus.

From *Practical American Cookery and Domestic Economy*, by Miss Hall, 1855, page 132

Beets would travel well on a ship. Pickling them would have been a good way to use leftover boiled beets. Mrs. Lawrence didn't say how the pickled beets she had for Christmas dinner were prepared, although one period cookbook recommended spiced vinegar.

This recipe is clear enough that an adaptation is not needed. You may find today's vinegar a bit too sharp, and you may wish to dilute it to taste with water. If you decide to use spices, a bit of whole allspice, ginger, mace, and mustard seed would be appropriate.

ORANGE JELLY

Ingredients: Eight oranges, two lemons, three-quarters of a box of gelatin soaked in half a pint of cold water, three-quarters of a pound of loaf-sugar, one pint of boiling water, beaten whites and shells of two eggs. Rub the loaf-sugar on the peels of two oranges and one lemon; squeeze the juice from six or seven oranges and two lemons, and strain it. Take off the peel carefully from two oranges, leaving only the transparent skin surrounding the quarters, and separate all the sections without breaking them. Soak the gelatin half an hour in half a pint of water; boil the other pint of water and sugar together, skimming all the time till no more scum rises; then put in the sections of oranges, and when they have boiled about a minute take them out, and put them one side. Pour this sirup over the soaked gelatin, adding the orange and lemon juice, the beaten whites and the shells of two eggs. Put it on the fire, and let it boil about a quarter of a minute without stirring; then place it at the side of the fire, skim off carefully all the scum at the top, and pass it through the jelly-bag. When half the jelly is in the mold, put it on the ice, and let it set hard enough to hold the orange sections, which place in a circular row around the edge of the mold; then add enough more jelly to cover the sections; when this has hardened, pour over the remainder of the jelly, which should have been kept in a warm place to prevent it from hardening. All the sections of orange may be put in with the first half of the jelly, as they will rise to the top, although they will not hold their places evenly. Or, if time is valuable, mold the jelly without the sections, and save them to garnish the jelly on the dish.

From *Practical Cooking and Dinner Giving*, by Mrs. Mary F. Henderson, 1882, page 291

Mrs. Henderson's recipe is enough to discourage anyone from ever making a jelly. That would be too bad, because this delicate, light dessert has a *very much better* flavor than its twentieth-century instant counterpart. Besides its wonderful taste, it has a simply beautiful color.

The women authors of the *High Street Cookbook*, a community cookbook in *Hood's Combined Cookbooks*, used Mrs. Henderson's orange jelly recipe, but streamlined it considerably: "The juice of six oranges, juice of two lemons, one pound of white sugar, three-fourths of a box of gelatin, soaked in one pint of water for half an hour, then add three-fourths of a pint of boiling water, stir thoroughly, and strain through a flannel bag into moulds."[72]

Earlier in the nineteenth century and before, jellies were very fashionable and were served on special occasions. Gelatine was extracted from calves feet, with an involved process. A statuesque jelly presented at dinner was a sign of ample kitchen help. Isinglass extracted from fish was also available for jelly-making;

but commercially prepared gelatine, similar to the sort we have today, finally simplified jelly-making for ordinary households in the last quarter of the nineteenth century. Jellied deserts and salads finally became daily items in the twentieth century, with instant mixes that would have made Mrs. Gates and Mrs. Greenman envious.

Nineteenth-century gelatine seems to have been less instant than our modern gelatines since most period recipes require you to soak the gelatine before using it. In her 1896 cookbook, Fannie Farmer equates a half box of gelatine to two and half tablespoonsful. Apparently a box typically contained five tablespoons.

In the interpretation below, I have taken the liberty of simplifying the recipe considerably. The egg whites and eggs have been banished (I think their function was to help settle impurities from the gelatine and sugar, which is no longer a problem). And I have substituted the straining through a jelly bag with running the mixture through cheesecloth. You could substitute juice made from a concentrate if you wanted to; you will need about 3 1/2 cups. But it won't taste as good as freshly squeezed juice.

8 juice oranges
2 lemons
3 3/4 tablespoons unflavored gelatin
1 cup cold water
1 1/2 cup sugar
2 cups boiling water

1. Squeeze juice from seven oranges and two lemons; strain through a sieve to remove pulp. Set aside.
2. Peel the remaining orange to use for garnishing.
3. Dissolve the gelatine in a large pan with the cup of cold water. Meanwhile, boil the sugar and two cups of water together in another pan.
4. When the syrup comes to boil, dip the orange sections in it briefly, using a slotted spoon, then set aside.
5. Pour the syrup into the gelatine, add the juice, and bring to a boil together, then take it off the heat immediately.
6. Wet your mold(s) with cold water, or oil it. Lay a piece of cheese cloth in a strainer, and strain the jelly mixture through it into the mold(s). If you use the orange sections in the jelly, fill the mold(s) only half full and place in the refrigerator to partly set up. Keep the remaining jelly just at a liquid point by warming it slightly.
7. When the refrigerated jelly has set up enough to hold the orange sections, lay the sections in the jelly as suggested by Mrs. Henderson, then pour the remaining jelly through the cheesecloth and sieve into the mold(s). Put back in the refrigerator to chill thoroughly.
8. To serve, remove from the mold(s) by warming a towel repeatedly with hot water, and holding it on the mold inverted on a serving plate until the jelly comes free. Garnish with more orange sections, or orange and lemon zest.

Yields a 1-1/2-quart jelly.

GINGERSNAPS

1 cup sugar, 1/2 cup molasses,
1/2 cup melted butter–
1/2 cup water, 1/2 tablespoon soda–flour spice.

From the manuscript recipe notebook of Julia Gates, 1857-1930, in the collection of the Mystic River Historical Society, Mystic, Connecticut

This is the perfect cookie for making in large quantities, ideal for a Christmas open house and at other times of the year to grab by the handful to eat with milk; I love these to dunk in tea. This and other period recipes for gingersnaps don't bother to include ginger in the ingredient list, while others include other spices in addition to ginger.

Some period recipes require you to boil the butter and molasses together, which yields a crisp, brittle cookie, while others have you mix the ingredients cold which produces a shorter cookie. All agree that gingersnaps should have a very stiff dough and be rolled thin.

An interpretation of this gingersnap recipe, one of three in Mrs. Gates's notebook, follows. It has a high yield; you may wish to halve the recipe or freeze some.

3 cups flour
1 tablespoon ginger
1/2 cup butter
1 cup sugar
1/2 cup molasses
scant 1/2 cup water
1 tablespoon hot water
2 teaspoons baking soda
Preheat oven to 375°

1. Sift together flour and ginger.
2. Melt the butter; mix it with the sugar, molasses, and water and bring to a rolling boil for a couple of minutes.
3. Mix the hot water and baking soda, and add to the ingredients above. Gradually add this mixture to the flour and ginger, mixing well. Dough will be very stiff.
4. If you have time, you may wish to chill the dough before rolling it out. On a floured surface, roll dough very thin, 1/16 of an inch at least. Work quickly so it will not have time to take up flour. Cut into desired shapes and bake on a greased cookie sheet for 7 minutes.

Yields 24 dozen 2-inch cookies.

PRESERVED ORANGE PEEL

Weigh the oranges whole, and allow pound to pound; peel the oranges neatly, and cut the rinds into narrow shreds; boil until tender, changing the water twice, replenishing with hot from the tea-kettle; squeeze the strained juice of the oranges over sugar; heat this to a boil. Put in the shreds, and boil twenty minutes. Lemon-peel can be preserved in the same way, only allowing more sugar.

From *The Hearthstone; or Life at Home, A Household Manual,* by Laura C. Halloway, 1887, page 501

Preserved peel of either lemon or orange is a frequent ingredient for steamed puddings and mincemeat in the nineteenth century. The recipe above calls for sugar in an equal proportion to the weight of the oranges ("pound to pound"). An average orange weighs approximately six ounces, so 3/4 of a cup is a good proportion to each orange.

I prefer a thinner-skinned juice orange to the thick-skinned navel oranges for this project. Cutting the peel into the julienne strips needed is easier to do if you use a sharp pair of kitchen scissors.

This recipe makes the most delicious candied orange peel I have ever tasted. If you want sugared peel, roll the shreds of orange in granulated sugar and lay them on waxed paper to dry before putting them away in a jar.

thin-skinned oranges
3/4 cup sugar per orange
1 1/2 cups hot water per orange (or plenty of water to cover)

1. Cut the oranges in half; squeeze out juice and set aside.
2. Scrape away the white part of the peel and cut the skin into julienne strips; using scissors makes it easy.
3. Put the shreds into the hot water and boil for about five minutes; drain; pour on more hot water; boil another five minutes; drain; boil a third time for five minutes, and drain.

4. Strain the juice and add to the sugar in a heavy saucepan, bring to a boil, then add the cooked orange peel. Boil gently for twenty minutes.
5. Remove with slotted spoon and cool on waxed paper, separating the pieces of peel and rolling them, if you wish, in sugar.

Yields about an ounce of candied peel per orange, but this will vary depending on your oranges.

CHRISTMAS PUDDING

To bread crumbs and flour, three ounces of each,
Add three eggs and six ounces of suet
Chopped fine, and one-sixth of a nutmeg or more,
So long as you don't overdo it.
A good pinch of mace, and of cinnamon ground,
Or in other words carefully grated;
Half a pint of new milk, a spoonful of salt —
A teaspoon I ought to have stated.
To this add some raisins (Malaga) well stoned,
And some currants washed clean and washed nicely,
Of each half a pound, or as some people say,
Of either eight ounces precisely.
Then of citron and lemon an ounce and a half,
Half the former, and one of the latter;
Four ounces of sugar — the moist kind will do —
Which will form an exceeding rich batter
Or mixture. The eggs to a cream should be beat
With the spices, and then by degrees
The milk may be added according to taste,
And the other ingredient to please.
Now taking for granted the pudding is made,
And the water is boiling like fun;
Tie it up in a cloth, pop it into the pot,
And boil — seven hours — till done.

From "Receipts, &c.," *Godey's Lady's Book,* December 1857, page 552

This recipe from *Godey's* is one of several rhyming recipes for various holiday treats. Holiday puddings can be boiled in pudding basins or molds, ceramic or metal, or in cloth bags. Molds are nice because they are more decorative and it is easier to manage the steaming process. Boiling in bags à *la* Mrs. Cratchit with the smell of laundry day makes a homely pudding and is trickier to manage if you are not familiar with it.

This recipe really does make "an exceeding rich batter"—a very dark, very rich pudding which is not beautiful sitting all alone on a plate. Dredge it with some confectioners sugar and stick some holly in it to spruce it up. The flavor is very good.

If you decide to boil it in a bag, saturate the cloth with hot water, and dredge it thoroughly with flour. Maintain a constant level of water in the pot, adding to it from a hot teakettle, and don't allow the bag to hit the bottom of the pot. You can keep the bag suspended by tying it with a string from a long handled-wooden spoon or a stick resting across the top of the pot.

Following is a more standard version of the poetic recipe above.

1/2 cup flour
1 1/3 cup bread crumbs
3 eggs
1 1/2 cups suet, chopped finely

1 teaspoon nutmeg
1/8 teaspoon mace
1/2 teaspoon cinnamon
1 cup milk
1 teaspoon salt
1 1/2 cups raisins
1 1/2 cups currants
2 tablespoons citron
peel of 4 lemons, grated
1/2 cup brown sugar
Set a large kettle of water to boil

1. Beat eggs with the spices.
2. Mix everything together till well blended.
3. Grease your pudding bowl, or prepare your cloth. Empty the pudding into it, allowing room for the pudding to swell.
4. Boil or steam for seven hours. If you boil the pudding in a bag, don't worry about a scum which may form as the suet melts a bit and soaks out through the bag.

Yields pudding enough for 24 servings.

MOLASSES CANDY

1 cup New Orleans molasses
1 cup of brown sugar
1 tablespoonful of vinegar
1 ounce of melted butter

Mix all together, and boil without stirring until it hardens when dropped in cold water; then add a teaspoonful of baking soda, and pour into buttered tins.

Or, when cool, pull and cut into sticks. While pulling, brush the hands with butter or moisten them with ice water.

PEANUT MOLASSES CANDY

Peanut molasses candy is made precisely the same as Walnut Molasses Candy.

From Mrs. Rorer's *Philadelphia Cook Book*, 1886, page 510

This three-in-one recipe will give you two sorts of nut brittles plus a hard molasses candy. All have a sturdy molasses flavor. The peanut candy should be made with roasted peanuts. When pulled and snipped into pieces, the molasses candy has a lovely golden-brown satiny appearance and sticks wonderfully to the teeth.

You can use the recipe list above with the following instructions. Remember that one ounce of butter is two tablespoons.

1. Mix together the molasses, brown sugar, vinegar, and butter. Set it to boil till it reaches the hard ball stage or 270° on a candy thermometer.

2. Remove from the heat and stir in 1 teaspoon baking soda. The candy will foam up slightly and change color.
3. Pour onto a greased cookie sheet, and when cool enough to handle, and *working quickly* pull it as you would for taffy, folding it back on itself a few times until it it almost too stiff to pull.
4. Stretch it into sticks and snip the pieces off with kitchen scissors, allowing them to cool on waxed paper. Store in an airtight container.

WALNUT MOLASSES CANDY

Make a plain molasses candy, and, when done, grease deep pans with butter, fill nearly full with walnut kernel, pour the molasses candy over them, and stand away to cool.

PEANUT OR WALNUT MOLASSES CANDY

3 cups roasted peanuts or walnut pieces
1 batch of molasses candy (recipe above)

1. Mix together the molasses, brown sugar, vinegar, and butter. Set it to boil till it reaches the hard ball stage or 270° on a candy thermometer.
2. While the syrup is boiling, butter well a large baking pan or a cookie sheet. (I recommend the cookie sheet because it is easier to break the candy up into chunks when it is in thinner sheets.)
3. As soon as the syrup reaches 270° on a candy thermometer, remove from the heat and stir in 1 teaspoon baking soda. The candy will foam up and change color.
4. Pour over the nuts in the pan, spreading with a greased spatula to cover the nuts as evenly as possible. Set aside to cool.
5. When the candy has cooled, break up into smaller pieces and store in an airtight container.

POPCORN BALLS

The versatile molasses candy recipe above can be added to popped corn, and formed into balls. Nineteenth-century narratives and diaries mention popcorn as a treat and Mrs. Smith tells us she made popcorn balls for the crew of the the *John P. West*, but there are very few historic recipes for preparing them. One calls for gum arabic and suggests various combinations of white and brown sugar and molasses.

The ingredients for Mrs. Rorer's molasses candy would all have been available on shipboard. Mrs. Smith could have used an even simpler molasses and vinegar mixture boiled to just under a hard crack stage. Following are instructions for making popcorn balls with molasses candy. Half a cup of corn will yield about three quarts of popped corn. This recipe is now a personal favorite and I make popcorn balls for Halloween and Christmas both. I prefer the molasses flavor, and modern corn-syrup-based popcorn balls taste bland to me.

8 quarts popped corn
1 batch of molasses candy from recipe above

1. Pop enough corn to yield 8 quarts. Keep warm in a large pan in the oven while you prepare the molasses candy.
2. As soon as the candy reaches 270° on a candy thermometer, stir in the baking soda to mix.
3. *Working quickly*, pour the candy over the popcorn, stirring to coat the popcorn evenly. Butter your hands, and shape handfuls of the coated corn into the size ball you like best. If the mixture gets too hard to work, set it in the oven a moment to soften slightly, then continue. (Better yet, get a friend or a couple of children to help you.)
4. Set the balls on a greased cookie sheet to cool.

Yields 18-24 balls about 3-4 inches in diameter.

Clambakes and Shore Dinners

"Ladies, life will be a continuous watermelon pic-nic and clambake holiday if you will use Brussels, the no rosin soap, for all household purposes."[1] *Now there was an attractive notion, especially to the women of coastal southern New England, who were familiar with clambakes in the late nineteenth century.*

Clambakes and chowder parties were similar but not at all the same thing. Both were distinctly outdoor events that took place at the seashore, at least at first, and seemed to be typical of southern New England. Both involved seafood, and both included a typically nineteenth-century array of other eatables such as pies, bread, and cakes.

Too bad the photographer didn't step back a foot or two to give us a better look at the comestibles. But his job was to capture the image of this Mystic, Connecticut, group having a pleasant clambake around the turn of the century. Opposite, the opened bake yields clams, corn, and lobsters. [MSM 82.8.55]

Anyone who didn't wish to dig clams and lug rocks and seaweed for their own bake could go to one of many shore dinner establishments like this one, possibly Rocky Point, Rhode Island, around 1870. These places accommodated all social classes on their day off. [MSM 81.87.10]

Or did when the occasion called for an elaborate spread. Both had recognized practitioners in their respective arts: the chowder master and the bake master.

Chowder parties seem to have arisen from a matter-of-fact desire or need to cook food outdoors, were enjoyed in their time, and have since disappeared. Clambakes, on the other hand, seem to have been self-consciously invented, were given all kinds of cultural symbolism and social significance, and are still with us today.

A History of an Invented Tradition

Cooking outdoors as *recreation*, something we take so much for granted in the late twentieth century, is a fairly recent phenomenon and has much to do with increased leisure in the nineteenth century. Coastal New Englanders situated their outdoor cooking at the beach. Southerners have long had a barbecue tradition, one variety of which is fish planking—often with shad—to which I have not yet found early New England reference. While easterners, north and south, were cooking outdoors for recreation in the nineteenth century, westerners were still doing it out of necessity along trails and in mining and cow camps. When they finally enjoyed leisure themselves, some of their outdoor cooking traditions were continued. Pit barbecuing is one example. Chowder-making in New England may have been a similar leftover from fish-camp days, as New England bean-hole bean baking seems to be a relic of lumbermen's log drives.

Clambake explanations, on the other hand, usually begin with Native Americans: "When the earliest explorers landed upon the shores of North America, they found that the Indians ate all the various shell-fish we now make use of. They understood the superior value of the clam and oyster, and everywhere along the New England coast were accustomed to assemble at favorable points and have feasts on mollusks and maize, with much merry-making. That fine old institution of Rhode Island and Connecticut, the clam-bake, almost the only thing allowed to warm the cockles of a Puritan's heart, and still the jolliest festival in summer experience along shore, perpetuates this practice of the aborigines."[2]

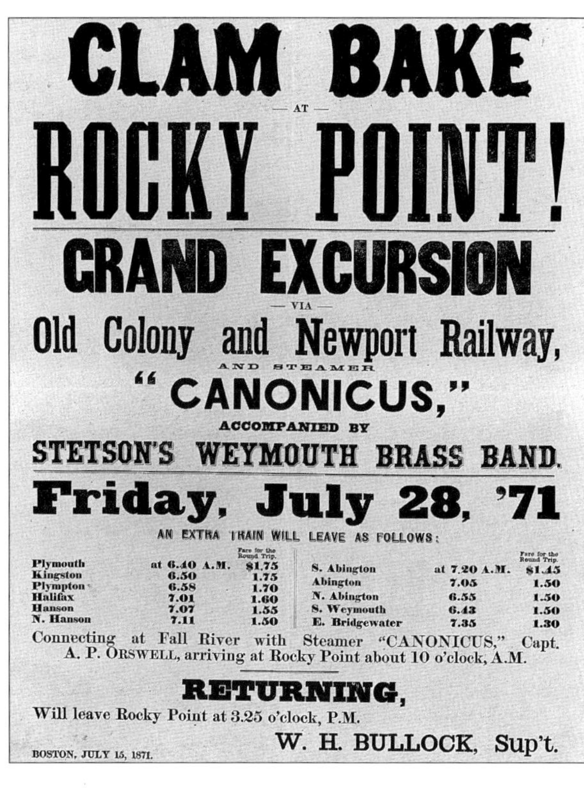
CLAM BAKE
— AT —
ROCKY POINT!
GRAND EXCURSION
— VIA —
Old Colony and Newport Railway,
AND STEAMER
"CANONICUS,"
ACCOMPANIED BY
STETSON'S WEYMOUTH BRASS BAND.
Friday, July 28, '71
AN EXTRA TRAIN WILL LEAVE AS FOLLOWS:

		Fare for the Round Trip.			Fare for the Round Trip.
Plymouth	at 6.40 A.M.	$1.75	S. Abington	at 7.20 A.M.	$1.45
Kingston	6.50	1.75	Abington	7.05	1.50
Plympton	6.58	1.70	N. Abington	6.55	1.50
Halifax	7.01	1.60	S. Weymouth	6.43	1.50
Hanson	7.07	1.55	E. Bridgewater	7.35	1.30
N. Hanson	7.11	1.50			

Connecting at Fall River with Steamer "CANONICUS," Capt. A. P. ORSWELL, arriving at Rocky Point about 10 o'clock, A.M.
RETURNING,
Will leave Rocky Point at 3.25 o'clock, P.M.
W. H. BULLOCK, Sup't.
BOSTON, JULY 15, 1871.

Steamers and railroads delivered hungry excursionists to clambake pavilions. [Paper broadside, MSM 81.98.3]

This excerpt from George Brown Goode's history of the American fisheries (1887) brings us the romance of the clambake as created by Victorian Yankees. It was *their* notion that settlers learned clambakes from Indians, as it was *their* notion that Puritans lived grim lives. The author seems to be speaking from personal experience of clambakes as the "jolliest festival" of summer; clambake fun was certainly well-established at the time Goode's work was published. However, despite even modern assertions to the contrary, folklorist Kathy Neustadt's recent research and thinking shows that there is no proof that settlers learned clam-baking from Indians.[3] Native Americans did enjoy shellfish feasts—middens (shell heaps) are evidence of that—but there is no absolute archaeological verification of shellfish cooked in seaweed on hot rocks in classic clambake fashion.[4]

Kathy Neustadt's work on the origins of clam-baking further points out that there is almost no evidence for an uninterrupted tradition of "Indian-to-Pilgrim transference of knowledge." Instead, English settlers greatly preferred their own foodways. As previous chapters have discussed, they certainly adapted Indian-introduced ingredients to basic English dishes. But there is simply little evidence that New England's early settlers were willing to learn much, if anything, from the native population. What little inclination there was, as Neustadt points out, evaporated after King Phillip's War.[5]

So, George Brown Goode notwithstanding, clambakes didn't warm the cockles even of *Puritan* hearts. In fact, clambakes did not appear until most of the Indians in southern New England were entirely eliminated, and the country's origins had become sufficiently remote for Yankees to romanticize and commemorate both the original population and the earliest settlers.

Clams and corn, to some early New Englanders, were symbolic of the earliest years. Neustadt identifies the centennial celebration in 1720 of the "Pilgrim's" landing, held in Plymouth, as one, if not the earliest, appearance of clams as a symbolic New England dish. The meal included two parts, the first part consisting of a wooden dish full of corn and clams to signify the food of the settlers. The second part of the meal was an elegant dinner of 1720. The message clearly was one of progress, improvement and self-congratulation. In this instance, and in subsequent meals which featured clams, New Englanders found in the shellfish a way to identify with the earliest settlers and to express New England's unique identity.

When the Old Colony Club was founded in 1769 in Plymouth, its members began an annual observance of "Forefather's Day," and by the end of the eighteenth century this featured a meal called "The Feast of Shells."[6] Added to these ceremonies was the creation of an event called a "Squantum," also an outdoor occasion at which clams were cooked and eaten in what the participants believed was an Indian manner. The name reputedly recognizes "Squantum," the last surviving Indian woman to live on the shores of Boston Harbor. Once Indians were no longer a threat to white society, they were romanticized and mythologized, and in the case of the squantum/clambake, imitated even though the imitation was largely fiction. Squantums were held during the years of the American Revolution, with strong overtones of political rallying, and in the early nineteenth century were annual events in Nantucket and around Boston.[7] Kathy Neustadt has found squantums to be "an essential link in the development of the New England clambake as invented tradition."[8]

Although clams, so associated with Pilgrims and Indians, may have been a symbol of New England's past, they were also ideal for the creation of outdoor events like clambakes. Clams were not serious food, much as hot dogs are not serious food today,[9] and this made them particularly suitable for recreational eating. People certainly enjoyed their flavor, and found a use for them in other dishes, usually as an embellishment, but most shellfish was considered insubstantial fare in the eighteenth and nineteenth centuries, especially in proportion to the effort required to obtain them.

Digging clams to be eaten immediately was part of the recreation, and like most food-hunting and gathering at this time, it was done by the economically marginal for subsistence or the leisured for pleasure. Even though the digging was work, New Englanders often combined work and social fun: husking bees, barn raisings, berrying expeditions, quilting parties, even chowder parties.

Clambakes in the Nineteenth Century

Within not many years of its origin, "squantum" was a generic term for picnic/clambake, and clambakes were a common activity for children and adults. A Nantucket whaling captain's daughter, Elizabeth C.P. Bennet, recalling her childhood during the 1840s and 1850s, wrote that her family, "especially on the 'liberal' side of the house, liked squantums and berry-pickings and graping expeditions. Of course, one dressed suitably for going into a swamp or roaming the commons. Nobody dreamed of wearing best clothes to a clam-bake."[10]

Mary Emma Weaver Farnsworth recalled children's amusements in the 1830s and 1840s in New London. Sometimes, she wrote, the children would go to the lighthouse and play on the beach and wade in the water there, and "Sometimes the boys would bring baskets and dig clams, and gather crabs to take home, when we would make a fire in a clay furnace under the grape arbor and filling a big iron pot with the clams, cooked them and ate from the pot using the shells for drinking the broth. We had also a tin baker mother gave us in which we roasted potatoes and corn which we gathered from the garden..."[11]

Mary Emma and the other children seem to have been imitating, with the exception of building a stone-and-seaweed cooker, what they had seen the grown-ups do at squantums, even to using clam shells for spoons.[12] Mary Emma's "clambake" is paralleled by Charlie York in Harspwell, Maine, at the other end of the century. Born in 1887, Charlie remembered clambakes on Cedar Island. He and his friends knew of tide pools where they could catch soft-shelled lobsters which had crawled under rocks to wait out the change of tide. "What yellin' and splashin' as the lobsters backed away trying to escape, and us kids after 'em. With a driftwood stick we could easy dig enough clams to go with 'em. They was an old iron kettle on the bank and somebody has rocked up a small fireplace. Storms had piled plenty of wood above high-tide mark for our fire. We'd put a quart or two of sea water in the kettle and heat it, then in would go the lobsters, followed by the clams and seaweed on top. We didn't need no melted butter nor other fixin's to make 'em perfect..."[13]

Youngsters cobbled together informal clam and lobster bakes on the beach. [Winslow Homer engraving "Seaside Sketches—A Clam-bake," *Harper's Weekly,* 23 August 1873]

These simple productions cobbled together by youngsters were not strictly clambakes, but fell somewhere on a continuum between chowder and bake. When a full-scale clambake was organized as an outing, things got a little more complicated. The basic technology of a clambake has ancient precedents, long predating white men encountering Native Americans. Using heated rocks for cooking, creating an in-ground oven or cooking pit, was known to early Britons, and even if it wasn't this outdoors baking was such a universal cooking method that it did not have to be consciously invented. Once observed, it could be imitated. Children growing up with clambakes as part of their family tradition could continue it as adults, teaching their children in turn.

Clambakes were conducted purely for pleasure as family, social group, or even community-wide events. Clambaking was also done commercially, even in the nineteenth century, and as a fund-raising activity for various organizations.

Portrait of a Family Clambake

One family-sized clambake is described in *Summer Yesterdays in Maine* by Willard Sperry, who was born in 1882 in Peabody, Massachusetts. The Sperrys summered in the York, Maine, area, and occasionally went on clambakes during their summer-long stay. For them in the late 1880s and early 1890s clambake and picnic were synonymous.

Besides clams, the picnic included "making sandwiches, getting butter and vinegar and salt and pepper for the eventual 'melted butter,' putting up coffee and sugar and cream, perhaps frying some doughnuts....If time allowed, Aunt Annie made the *specialite de la maison*...her Banbury tarts....They were filled with chopped lemon peel, currants and raisins. I have never met them in the open market. The rule cannot have been in general circulation."[14] (It was, though Sperry did not realize it.) In addition, the Sperrys brought fruit in season, preferably watermelon, and sometimes ginger ale and crystalized popcorn, too.

Willard and his father had the responsibility of obtaining the clams. "Of course we could buy clams if we were lucky enough to catch the fish cart on its rounds, but bought clams cost fifty cents a peck, and it was with us a matter of economy as well as of pride to dig our own. Furthermore, if we bought our clams we knew nothing of their life history—where they came from in the first instance, and more particularly how long they had been thence."[15] Usually the Sperrys dug them –"no work for weaklings." They washed their clams to rinse off grit and, he says, "...to encourage the creatures to wash themselves out inside. At this point, if the truth be told, a freshly dug clam is uncooperative... When we could give ourselves a couple of days and could physic our clams in their baskets by occasional washings in fresh water, they would help us out."[16]

A boat—at first sail, later power launch—was the preferred method of transporting a group of clambakers or chowder partyers to a favorite spot along shore as seen here in the Mystic area around 1900. [Glass-plate photo by Edward H. Newbury, MSM 80.41.405]

Occasionally, they procured short lobsters straight off a lobster boat and some green corn, but nothing else was added to the bake: "I have been to clambakes that produced sausages...Why anyone should want sausages at a clambake passes me. The whole point of a clambake is to eat all the clams you can and stop there," wrote Willard.[17]

The Sperrys had a favorite spot to go to for their bake, and had a ring of stones that they used year after year. "Family size, to accommodate a couple of pecks of clams and feed five persons will be, let us say, two or three feet across its pit. Ideally the pit should be built on an outcropping ledge which provides a stone floor, Otherwise it must have a cobblestone pavement built of small flat rocks. Its circular wall will rise a foot or eighteen inches from the base."[18]

Willard's sisters helped with gathering wood and seaweed. He remembers finding

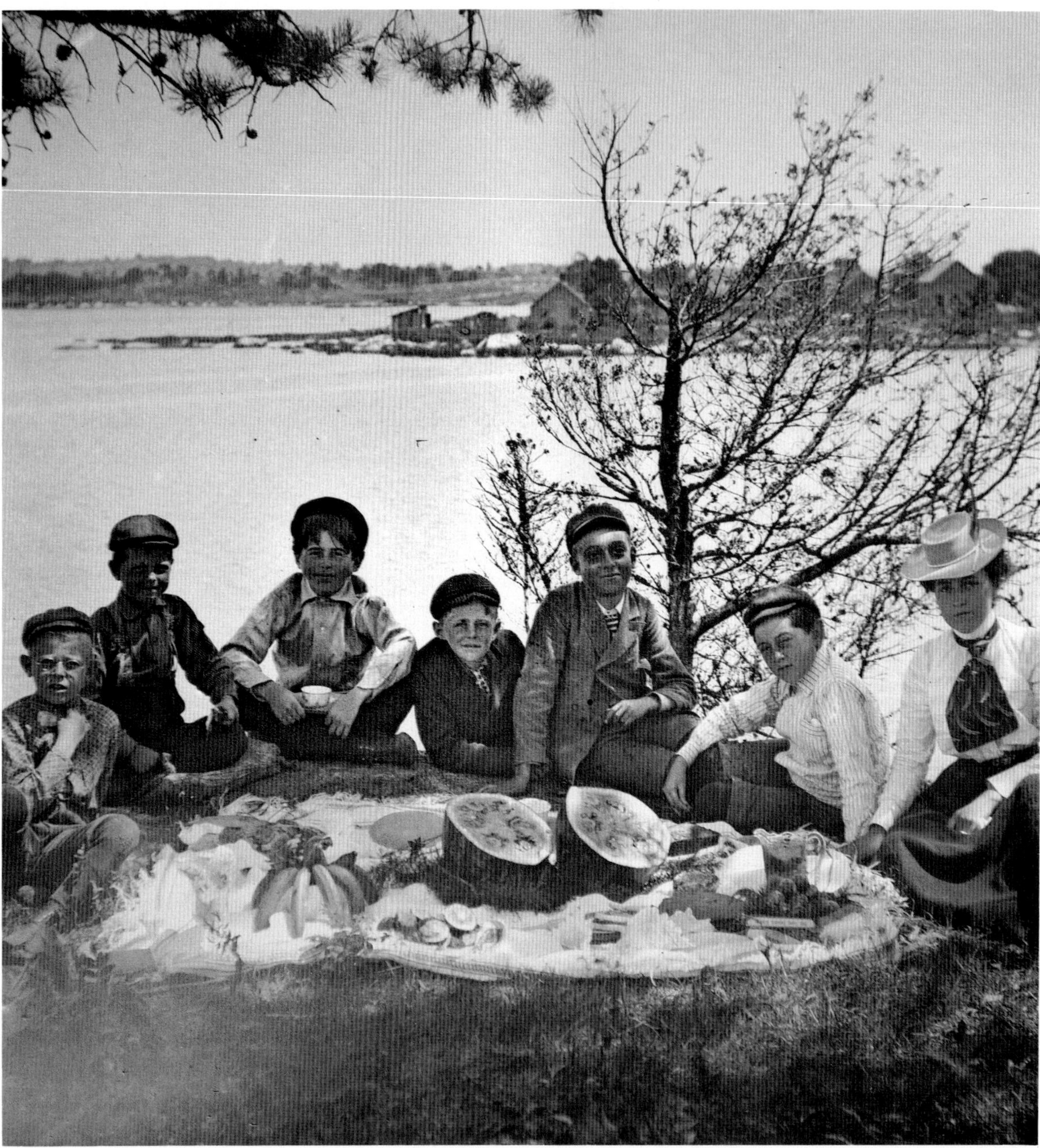

many shingles that washed off coasting-schooner deckloads, bits of broken lobster pot, and driftwood of all sorts. A fire, built on the stones in the pit, burned fiercely for an hour. "Finally the embers were cleaned out and the fire pit, which consisted of the stone floor and the circular wall of rocks, was lined with seaweed, the familiar olive brown rockweed that grows right up to the high tide mark. The clams were then turned out of the basket onto the weed and leveled off."[19] The clams, and lobsters and corn if included, were covered with another thick layer of seaweed, piled high and wide so that its fringes hung well over the stone circle.[20] They left it to sizzle for a half-hour before opening it.

This "watermelon picnic" may be a turn-of-the-century Sunday-school outing according to the family friend who identified the woman at the right as Eva Collins Grinnel (1879-1969). Watermelon was nearly indispensable at clambakes which, in the most expansive versions, included other picnic foods of the sort pictured. The bake itself, to be genuine, would have only clams, potatoes, and corn. [Glass-plate photo, MSM 93.136.32]

When the bake was opened, "Father scooped the clams out and piled on each tin plate as much as it would hold." Each person had a large clam shell with melted butter and vinegar in it; the trick was to keep it from tipping over. Willard reports that each of them sat away from the heat of the bake to eat.

"For the sake of variety," during the meal, "we often intruded a sandwich or two along the way; but the main thing was clams and more clams...doughnuts that Aunt Annie fried often had to be passed up and packed away to be carried home. Don't worry, their turn will come. Though we were always good for a Banbury tart. Ideally, we polished off with a slice of watermelon...Even the lobsters and the corn were there any en route, had faced a bear market. It was no good pretending otherwise; we set out to eat all the clams we could and eventually we had done so."[21]

This family bake was probably typical of its kind for most of the nineteenth and early twentieth century, part of the usual round of summer activity in coastal New England, for summer people as well as locals. A clambake could be the featured event for the Fourth of July, as it was for the Warren Brewer family who arrived from Newton Center, Massachusetts, to summer in North Islesboro, Maine, in a farmhouse overlooking Coomb's Cove and Hutchins Island, a locally famous clam flat until the 1930s. The Brewer family caretaker, Frank Ladd, was the bake master, and the Brewers invited their year-round neighbors along the Bluff Road to participate. One family that attended were the Bunkers, Adrianna and sons Henry and Newton.

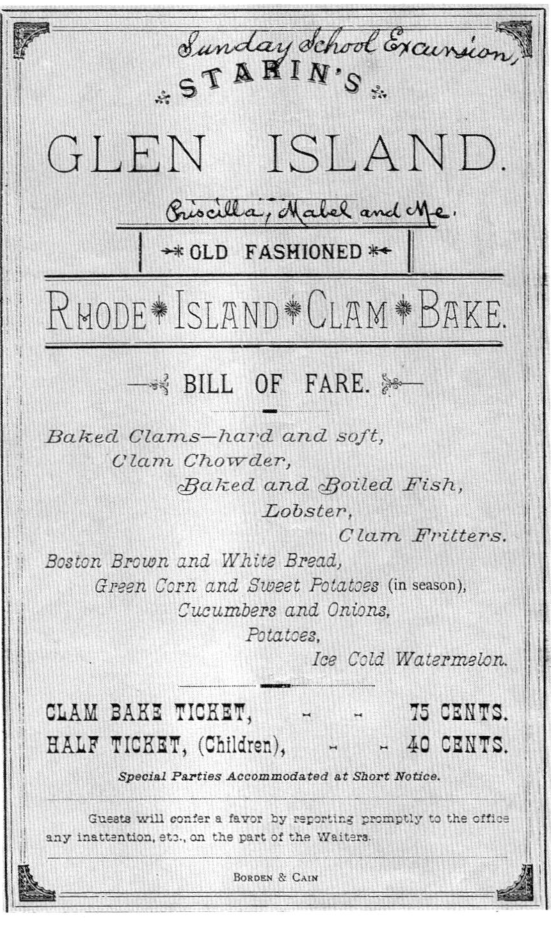
Sunday School Excursion,
STARIN'S
GLEN ISLAND.
Priscilla, Mabel and Me.
OLD FASHIONED
RHODE ISLAND CLAM BAKE.
BILL OF FARE.
Baked Clams—hard and soft,
Clam Chowder,
Baked and Boiled Fish,
Lobster,
Clam Fritters.
Boston Brown and White Bread,
Green Corn and Sweet Potatoes (in season),
Cucumbers and Onions,
Potatoes,
Ice Cold Watermelon.
CLAM BAKE TICKET, - - 75 CENTS.
HALF TICKET, (Children), - - 40 CENTS.
Special Parties Accommodated at Short Notice.
Guests will confer a favor by reporting promptly to the office any inattention, etc., on the part of the Waiters.
BORDEN & CAIN

But the Bunkers went to clambakes before the Brewers began to have theirs. In a letter to a friend written by Emery Bunker on 5 September 1893, describing his home activities between voyages, he reported "Yesterday we had a clambake at the narrows and a game of ball and of course that was resting."[22]

These northern New England bakes notwithstanding, the classic clambake seems to have been the one that originated in southern New England, particularly Rhode Island and neighboring southeastern Massachusetts. When George Brown Goode's *The Fisheries and Fishing Industries of the United States* was written in the 1880s, it was to Rhode Island that one of the authors—Ernest Ingersoll—turned.

The Genuine Rhode Island Clambake

Ingersoll wrote the section on the clam fisheries for Goode's history. His description of "modern clam-bakes" correctly reported the social significance of the event, but some of the technical procedures and the food content of the bake he described are questionable:

"A 'clam-bake' expresses the sum of all human happiness to the Rhode Islander, and to gather all his relatives and friends on the sea-shore, bake the roystering clam in dried seaweed[23] and eat it with other good things, fills his cup of joy. As enthusiasm and emotion always seem odd, and perhaps ludicrous to those who are not under its influence, the New Englanders get much fun poked at them by outsiders. It is related, for example, that a Sunday-school teacher in Rhode Island told the pupils that there were poor children in Illinois who had never experienced the supreme delight of a clam-bake, and the last penny in the juvenile pocket was dropped in the plate in the aid of the benighted sufferers."[24]

The menu of the "modern clam bake"—modern for 1887—that Ingersoll described was "a layer of clams about 3 inches thick covered by more seaweed; then follows a layer of green corn in the husk, intermixed with potatoes and other vegetables; then a layer of oysters, crabs (in sacks to prevent their escape), and poultry, dressed and seasoned; then more seaweed." Mr. Ingersoll doesn't say if he actually attended this bake, but the oysters, crabs, chicken, and "other vegetables" are a little at variance with a classic clambake menu. During the last half of the nineteenth century, clambakes were undergoing changes, particularly because of commercialization.[25] These ingredients may have been added to the bake he observed to make it more palatable to paying customers.

This raises the question of what a "genuine Rhode Island" clambake was exactly. In an account of a clambake in the 1865 Mystic *Pioneer*, the writer assures readers that the event *was* a genuine Rhode Island clambake, because "The committee on clams Capt. P.E. Rowland, had procured about thirty bushels of round and soft clams, and secured the services of a Rhode Island man to take charge of the bake."[26] In addition, "About fifteen bushels of green corn and a full supply of Irish and sweet potatoes were provided..."[27] The manner of preparing the bake was described: "A bed of stones was thoroughly heated, when about fifty bushels of clams, corn and potatoes were poured upon it, and covered with an old sail and a quantity of rockweed and allowed to remain about fifteen minutes when they were found to be well done. You never saw clams, green corn and sweet potatoes better cooked."[28] So much for the edible content of a Rhode Island clambake.

The reporter went on to note that, "At a genuine Rhode Island clam bake all distinctions of wealth and position, differences of opinion and all the perplexities of domestic, and active business life are for the time forgotten; self seems merged and lost; care, trouble, envy and hate are lulled to slumber by the music of our better feelings. Such gatherings are schools for the unfolding and strengthening of the best faculties of the mind. They are resting places in the journey of life. Spots around which in after years memory will linger and be refreshed."[29] Allowing for some hyperbole, it is plain that a clambake was not just food, but had a large package of pleasant associations to accompany it.

The idea of an "old-fashioned" or "genuine Rhode Island" clambake is one that grows as the century passes, increasingly as there are *fewer* genuine and old-fashioned bakes available to the larger population, who mostly experience clambakes as customers of clambake professionals.[30] You can see a good example of this in the menu (see illustration, page 287) saved as a souvenir of a Sunday-school excursion in June 1883. Starin's Glen Island pavilion wished to assure its customers they were getting the real thing. The menu comes close: clams, lobsters, corn, potatoes and sweet potatoes, along with watermelon. Overall, the embellishments reinforced the seafood theme with fish, clams again in chowder and in fritters, and the Boston brown bread, a nostalgic fillip to support the "old-fashioned" quality of the meal.

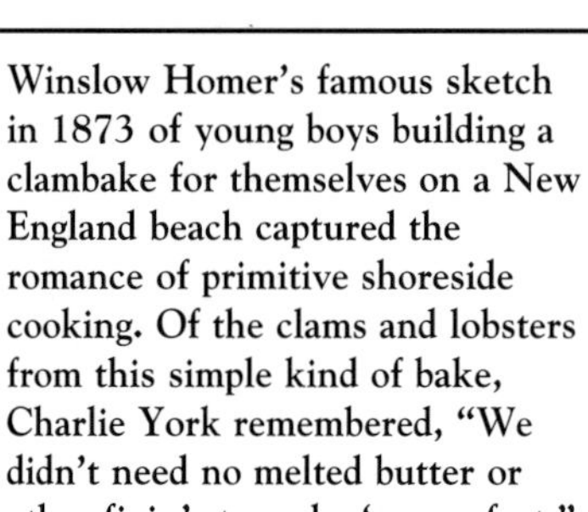

Winslow Homer's famous sketch in 1873 of young boys building a clambake for themselves on a New England beach captured the romance of primitive shoreside cooking. Of the clams and lobsters from this simple kind of bake, Charlie York remembered, "We didn't need no melted butter or other fixin's to make 'em perfect."

Not everyone was fooled. An unidentified newspaper article, cut out and glued into a scrapbook at the turn of the twentieth century, asserted "Simon Pure Clam Bake is a Triumph, Rhode Island Stands By the Real Thing—Differences in Bakes and Shore Dinners."[31] The article went on to describe a debate between the Boston *Transcript* and the Providence *Journal*. The Boston paper apparently stated that "no clambake is right up to the hour that doesn't include fried chicken." This was roundly denounced by the *Journal*: "Whatever may be the proper name by which to call an amorphous aggregation of incongruous foods that includes baked clams and fried chicken it is most certainly not a clambake."

The writer contended that the "simon-pure" clambake occurs when "...the farmers of Rhode Island, not in lone families usually, but in groups sufficiently varied in paternity and sex to add to the zest of the recreation, would go down on the shores of the bay, collect wood for the fire, stones to be heated, fresh and dripping seaweed and rockweed...and with these simple agencies cook the clams which they themselves have freshly dug on the spot, throwing in with them, perhaps, a few potatoes and ears of corn from a neighboring field."[32]

He accounts for the changes in clam-baking when he says that every true Rhode Islander, even the middle-aged veteran, thinks he ought once a year "test the old delight," for himself and friends. "Unhappily, however, they find that each year the stones and wood grow heavier to bring together, the clams more taxing on the back to dig and the squatting around the bake less practicable. For these and other reasons that will readily occur, the modern form of the clam bake has now come to be the more common offering."[33]

The modern form was, of course, the commercial bake or shore dinner. Even so, the writer insists that these should conform in "three absolutely essential respects"—specifically: "it must not be cooked with any other steam than that made by seaweed on hot stones, that it must be served in the open air, and that, except for the watermelon...it must not include any kinds of foods which cannot be cooked altogether in the bake."[34] Exit fried chicken.

Many large clambake pavilions were built after the middle of the century along the southern New England coast, especially near steamer or train terminals or trolley lines. Sometimes they provided piers of their own for excursion-steamer convenience. One of the most famous was Rocky Point in Rhode Island. These establishments provided a meal, no longer strictly a clambake, which became more widely known as a "shore dinner." Often they had facilities for entertainment as well, from swimming to dancing. Clambake and shore-dinner resorts continued until the great 1938 hurricane destroyed many of those that had survived the Depression. World War II and the 1954 hurricane put an end to the last of them, with a few exceptions.[35]

Some Local Clambakes

Some clambake accounts, like this Connecticut one from Mystic in 1865, sound like chowder parties and picnics with their addition of pies and cakes. "At about one o'clock the table cloths, loaded with pies, cakes,

This scene from a stereograph is entitled "New England Clam Bake." These eight gents apparently arrived by rowboat and spritsail-rigged sailboat in the spirit of Mystic's Captain Lanphere and the *Bivalve*. We don't know if they dug clams or bought and carried them in the baskets pictured. Small outings like these for family and social groups were in counterpoint to large public clambakes and commercial shore dinners. [Stereograph by Kilburn Brothers, circa 1880, MSM 87.1.2]

sandwiches, peaches, Ice cream, Watermelons, &c, &c., were surrounded by a hungry crowd." Presumably the clams, potatoes, and corn were there as well.[36]

A "monster clambake" held the year before at a grove near the mouth of Quiambaug Cove, a little east of Mystic, was attended by about one thousand people, and the menu was the orthodox clams and corn (no mention was made of potatoes, sweet or Irish). However, "The Ladies had...spread out their donations of excellent cakes, pies, jellies, etc.,..."[37] This bake was sponsored by I.W. Denison, and featured, in addition to food, some speeches. It went over so well that a committee was appointed to plan the 1865 monster clambake. The committee included Mr. Denison, again, J.D. Spicer, A.B. Taylor, D.W. Stewart, Joseph Watrous, Mrs. Thomas S. Greenman, Maria Stanton, Mrs. Charles H. Denison, and Mrs. D.W. Denison,[38] all substantial citizens.

This tradition of large clambakes, often held to raise funds or to bring together a community in the celebration of an "Old Home Week,"[39] continued from the nineteenth century into the twentieth. In some places the technology shifted a bit from rock-filled circles to barrels filled with ingredients and seaweed. This was the method chowder master Fred Hermes favored for large parties.

The clambake continues to evolve—not necessarily in ways that old-timers would approve. Today it is possible to buy a clambake in a tin can to take home or aboard a boat, a self-contained meal with lobsters and clams to be steamed together atop a stove. This is about as far as can be from the "pristine simplicity of aboriginal culinary skill"[40] that characterized the old-fashioned clambake.

Clams are getting harder to find and more expensive. The clam flat that the Brewers and Bunkers could raid at will in North Islesboro, Maine, is played out now. New Englanders might, in our lifetime, lose the clams. If they do, how will they keep their symbol of the simpler past—the clambake—in the complex present and the perhaps-frenzied future?

The Recipe

Even if you don't want to go on a clambake, you might want to try some of the Banbury tarts for which Willard Sperry saved room. Sperry wrote that "the rule" for the Banbury tarts he remembered from his childhood "cannot have been in general circulation." Perhaps not in the Maine town he summered in, but it appeared in Fanny Farmer's first cookbook in 1896, and here it is from a Stonington, Connecticut, source.

BANBURY TARTS

Bann Berries

One cup of sugar, 1 cup seeded raisins chopped, 1 egg, juice of 1 lemon. Put all in a double boiler and cook two minutes.

Make pastry of 2 cups of flour, 1/2 cup lard, 1/2 teaspoon baking powder, a little salt. Roll out and cut thin. Put a teaspoon of raisin mixture in each puff, and bake.

Miss E. Agnes Stewart. From *The Stonington Cookbook,* Reprint of the Cookbook of the Young People's Society of Christian Endeavor of the Second Congregational Church (Stonington, Connecticut), ca. 1900.

Banbury Tarts by name originated in Banbury, Oxfordshire, England, a town known for the number and zeal of its Puritan inhabitants, according to the *Oxford English Dictionary*. The early Banbury cakes were "a small oval cake, of rich pastry with a filling of mincemeat."[41] The filling recipe above has a taste reminiscent of mincemeat.

These are really delicious and easily made from ingredients on hand in nearly anyone's kitchen. The recipe above is clear enough to follow, so an interpretation is not necessary, but I suggest the following procedure: Double the pastry recipe because the filling recipe makes enough for up to 40 tarts, or use your favorite pastry recipe.

Preheat oven to 425°.

1. Chop the raisins coarsely by rocking a knife through them.
2. You may substitute vegetable shortening for lard in the pastry, if you wish. You will need 6-8 tablespoons of cold water for the pastry, even though it is not mentioned in the original recipe.
3. Mix the filling ingredients well before cooking. You may also add the grated rind of the lemon for a more lemon-flavored filling (which is done in the Farmer recipe). Cook the filling, stirring constantly, until it is slightly thickened. Let it cool completely.
4. Cut the pastry in rounds providing two for each tart. Put the filling on the bottom round, and moisten the edges; then place the top round over, pressing the edges together with a fork.
5. Bake for 15-20 minutes.

Yields up to 40 tarts made with a three-inch cutter.

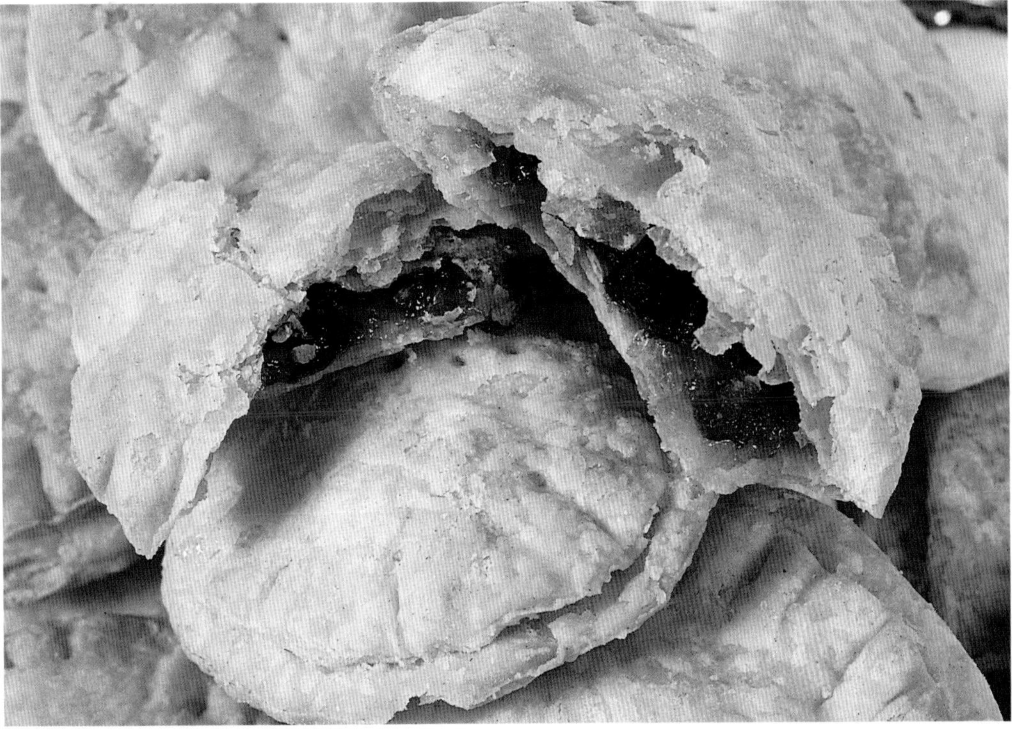

Chowder and Chowder Parties

This party is waiting for their chowder to cook on the granite coast of New Hampshire about 1890. A tripod, a kettle and a fire were all that the feast required. Opposite, picture as recipe: bluefish, salt pork, crackers, onions and potatoes. [New Hampshire photo from The Sandler Collection]

In nineteenth-century southern New England, "chowder" was both a dish and an event. Most culinary historians agree that chowder-making is several centuries old and that the dish was named for the pot it was made in. The word comes from the French chaudiére, a type of cauldron.[1] According to Karen Hess, a French word for a fisherman's stew is la chaudrée, a dish that appears along the coast of France from Bordeaux to Brittany. The Celtic connections between Brittany and Cornwall in England, and Wales and Ireland, suggest that at least among fishermen, chowder, even if not called by that name, could have appeared in Great Britain sooner than the first recorded dates. (In Cornwall, a variation on the word appears as early as the middle of the sixteenth century).[2] But among the first settlers to New England, many of whom hailed from East Anglia, making a chowder was not the first thing that would come to mind if they were presented with fresh fish, salt pork, and dry bread or hard biscuit.

Chowder was ideal stuff to feed a crowd. There are a great many photographs like this one of outdoor gatherings around a table, and while we can't be sure they're putting chowder into the cups and bowls in evidence, it seems a good possibility. [E. A. Scholfield photo, MSM 77.92.209]

More probably, chowder-making was dispersed by the mixing of French and English fishermen in the early banks fishing fleets, and possibly in the fishing camps of Newfoundland, Nova Scotia, and Maine. The *Oxford English Dictionary* tells us that Breton fishermen carried it to Newfoundland, "long famous for its chowders whence it has spread to Nova Scotia, New Brunswick, and New England."[3] As a vernacular dish, though, chowder need not have spread to New England from anywhere, but could have come directly here with fishermen settlers.

One of the earliest written recipes for it was in Hannah Glasse's 1789 edition of *The Art of Cookery* in which she wrote "To Make Chouder, A Sea Dish." This connection between the sea and chowder is intriguing: a look at the ingredients—cod, salt pork, onions, water and, to thicken it, sea biscuits—all point to the provisions carried aboard ship or fished right out of the ocean.[4] These ingredients were also in the larders of coastal people. The sea biscuit had its parallel ashore in dry bread. As we have already seen, within the limits of what foods were seaworthy, people chose to take to sea with them foodstuff to which they were accustomed and which they could make into familiar fare. Chowder certainly fit the bill. Chowder ashore could easily become chowder at sea or vice versa.

The orthodox nineteenth-century chowder contained potatoes in addition to Mrs. Glasse's ingredients above. They were added after potatoes were more widely accepted in Great Britain and New England in the eighteenth century, but the adoption process was uneven enough that New Englanders may have been including potatoes in their chowders at the same time Glasse was recording the recipe without them. Also, potatoes, a common part of the rotating bill of fare at sea, eventually ran out or spoiled, so seafarers could, and probably did, make chowders without them.

In the course of this chapter we will also examine how milk got into chowder. It was not always an essential ingredient and, as we will see, there are milkless regional varieties of chowder.

Chowder: The Event

In August 1859, the editor of the Mystic *Pioneer* rhapsodized on summer's recreation: "hardly a day passes that crafts of various descriptions do not glide gaily down the river, freighted with merry men and fair maidens and amply provided with the good things of this life for an eight hours campaign among the green carpeted groves of Mason's Island. God bless the man—or was it woman—who invented picnics." A few weeks later he went on to praise "the bountiful fishing, the huckleberrying parties, the pic-nics, and *most glorious of all, the chowder parties.* [emphasis added].[5]

By mid-century, when picnics, by name, were more common, chowder parties and picnics were sometimes synonymous. People who went on chowder parties then did not eat only chowder. Or if the event was named "picnic," chowder might have been made during it. The custom of making chowder at the beach seems to have coincided with, but also to have been a little more common than, clambaking and "squantums," which were also beach recreations.

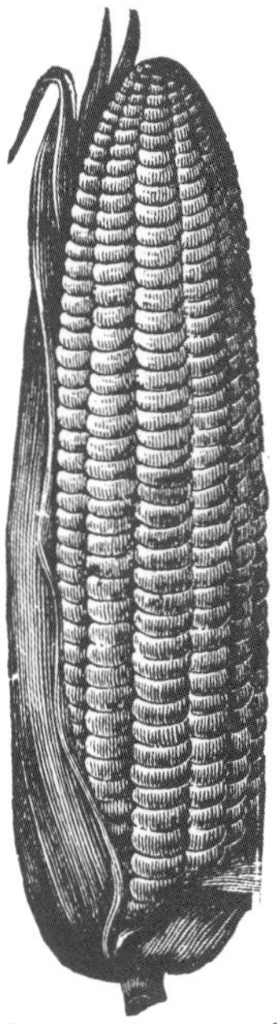

Chowder parties were sometimes all-male events, sometimes coeducational. In 1823, Joseph Anthony of New Bedford went out with eight other fellows in the sloop *Experiment*, and they "anchored under the large Weepecket island [and] commenced fishing....We did not get many fish, though more than we needed. I was so fortunate as to catch more than anyone else, which was but twelve. We had a very good chowder, got under weigh for home about two o'clock."

About a month later Anthony and a group of men and women "took a ride to Horse Neck beach to spend the day. We had a fine ride on the beach where we found some men a seining. We bought some Bass and made a chowder, and dined on the Rocks from Provisions carried with us, and the chowder."[6]

The first chowder Anthony mentioned may have been made aboard the sloop, and it provided a decent and fairly easy meal for a large group, with the freshest fish possible. The second took a little more planning, because a pot to cook the chowder in, plus their choice of other ingredients—salt pork, onions, and biscuits or potatoes—had to be hauled to the beach, along with the "provisions" they took. We don't know who did the cooking, but it could have been either the men or the women, or maybe both together. In this setting, customary gender roles softened some.

The "boss chowder of the season" in 1878 was a bluefish chowder cooked up on Mason's Island by a professional—a woman, this time—for "a large party of picnickers...under the immediate supervision of the illustrious caterer, Mrs. A.J.F." At the end of the century, the "Mystic Clam Club" went up-river to their "camping ground in their new and commodious boat the *Bivalve*, Capt. Lamphere. They expect to have a chowder and all the delicacies of the season."[7]

Besides these private parties, chowder feasts sometimes served as fund-raisers: "That Clam Chowder advertised to come off this Thursday evening under the auspices of St. Mark's Church is postponed one week to await a 'clam tide and pleasant weather,'" announced the Mystic *Press* in January of 1876. Clambakes were sometimes political events, and chowder parties could be, too, or else the focus of a gathering by a fraternal or professional group, such as one that took place in New London in 1848: "A grand clam and fish chowder was served up at the Astor House yesterday by the 'Willimantic Association' of ship carpenters, of which some dozen of the craft, together with several invited guests of distinction, partook."[8]

Chowder at Home

As one of New England's plain, everyday kind of dishes, chowder was eaten at home as part of a meal or even the whole meal. How frequently is hard to determine.

Caroline "Kiddy" King's prosperous Salem family in the 1820s and 1830s ate "always a chowder once a week...not the prefix to a dinner, but the piece de resistance of the dinner itself."[9] But few recollections and narratives from the early nineteenth century mention chowder at meals, even though recipes for it are plentiful. We will see later, when we discuss fish-eating, that fish was not a preferred food if one could afford meat. Chowder-eating may have increased as income decreased, and not many descriptions of life in earlier times come from the poor. Chowder was probably eaten more often by people who could afford little meat and occasionally by other people because they liked it or desired variety in their menus.

Chowder was also most commonly eaten in coastal areas where fresh fish could be obtained. When the ability to transport fresh fish away from the coast improved later in the nineteenth century, cookbooks with inland distribution might include it. Mary Whitcher's 1882 cookbook contained seven dinner menus; Friday's is "Fish Chowder, Beef, with Puree of Potatoes, and Cottage Pudding." At about the same time, *Hood's High Street Cookbook* also recommended chowder on Friday (followed with salmon), but listed it under "Plain Family Dinners." Hood's put chowder among its July menus, but did not include it in winter menus.[10] Marion Harland's *Dinner Year Book* included chowders, but with a need for 365 soups to provide her readers with a different dinner menu a day for a year, she included everything she could think of.

Making Chowder

There is—and was—room for discussion about how to make chowder. As we already observed, the essential ingredients were fish–preferably fresh–salt pork, hard biscuits or bread, and water. Onions, potatoes, and milk were optional. Whether someone chose to make a chowder out of those ingredients instead of some other dish depended on their idea of what chowder required. One literary reference to chowder shows that onion made the difference. Sarah Orne Jewett's story, "The Country of the Pointed Firs," tells of the narrator and Mrs. Todd's visit to the latter's mother on an island. Mrs. Todd picks a haddock off her brother's trawl line and brings it to the house. "I just made one stop to underrun William's trawl line till I come to jes' such a fish's I thought you'd want to make one o' your nice chowders of. I've brought an onion with me that was layin' about on the window-sill at home."

"That was just what I was wantin'," said the hostess. "I gave a sigh when you spoke o' chowder, knowin' my onions was out."[11]

Generally the fish was white-fleshed—cod, haddock, sea bass—but not always, as we saw from the "boss" bluefish chowder of 1878. The salt pork added both flavor and richness to the otherwise bland and virtually fat-free dish, as did onion. The biscuit's, and later, potato's, function was to thicken it.

When chowder recipes were written down, and printed in cookbooks, they often acquired little fillips. Even a pair of manuscript recipes show a little improvement over the basic chowder. An anonymous manuscript recipe book from Newburyport (dated 1808, although some recipes may have been added later) specified brown biscuit, and suggested putting fish in first, then soaked biscuit, fried fat pork and the fat over that, then stew the whole with half a pint of red wine and a little water. "If you chose onions, cut some fine and put them in the bottom of the pot." Another manuscript recipe book, this one dating around 1823-28, was assembled for "Mrs. Dorothea Green from her affectionate cousin T.R. Green" and included "an excellent chowder" from a Mrs. Blake. This chowder also called for a glass of wine, only put in just before serving. Her recipe created many layers of the ingredients instead of the one-of-each above, and also suggested using potatoes. At the end of the chapter is another manuscript recipe, the simplest of these three. Mrs. Child's basic chowder was very similar, but she said that clams made a "pleasant addition," as did catsup, lemon, or beer. All of these recipes were for a fish chowder, and none of them required milk.[12]

Milk in chowder: A little later in the nineteenth century milk began to be added to chowder recipes, but not consistently. In 1845, Mrs. Howland's chowder recipe proceeded in the classic manner without specifying quantities of fish or potatoes, then said "add half a pint of milk, or a tea-cup of sweet cream, five minutes before you take it up." Eliza Leslie, from Philadelphia, recommended soaking the crackers in milk or water before adding them, but otherwise made no mention of milk in the 1851 edition of her *Directions for Cookery*.[13]

By the 1870s, in printed cookbooks, milk was a much more common ingredient in fish and clam chowders. (Manuscript sources from that time seem never to include chowder recipes; at least I have not yet seen one.) Into the first decade of the twentieth century, community cookbooks, assembled by various organizations and sold to raise funds, also reflect milk being used in chowder.[14] An exception is southeastern Connecticut and nearby Rhode Island, where as a regional quirk milkless chowder has continued to the present.

Thickeners: Some nineteenth-century cooks and cookbook writers, not trusting to the crackers and potatoes to do the job, recommend thickeners such as flour, cornstarch, or rice flour. This is the direction taken by many modern chowders, especially canned ones, which are quite thick. To people accustomed to a traditional chowder, the modern thick ones seemed more like a bisque—actually a different kind of soup altogether—a cream soup on a shellfish base.

No tomatoes: A genuine New England fish or clam chowder will not contain tomatoes or other common soup vegetables such as celery or carrots. Willard Sperry, writing of his boyhood summers in Maine around 1885, declared that "He [the clam] has made his name and won his deathless laurels in New England. New York and Baltimore with their thin, red, tomato juice clam chowder are *in partibus infedelium*."[15]

Some Chowder References and their Recipes

The chowder references in *Moby Dick* are famous. Ishmael and Queequeg, waiting to go on their whaling voyage, were in Nantucket boarding at the Try Pots, where the two items on the menu were clam chowder and cod chowder. When Mrs. Hussey asked them which they wanted she merely said "Clam or cod?" Ishmael gave her a bit of lip about "cold clammy reception" as he preferred to misinterpret her question to mean "do he and Queequeg want to share a clam?"

"However," wrote Melville, "a warm savory steam from the kitchen served to belie the apparently cheerless prospect before us. But when that smoking chowder came in, the mystery was delightfully explained. Oh, sweet friends, hearken to me. It was made of small juicy clams, scarcely bigger than hazel nuts, mixed with pounded ship biscuit, and salted pork cut up into little flakes; the whole enriched with butter, and being plentifully seasoned with pepper and salt."[16] When they were done with their clam chowder, they gave the cod chowder a try.

In most respects the description would serve as a recipe for traditional southern New England milkless chowder. The butter seems superfluous to me, and I wonder if Melville mistook salt pork fat for butter. Melville did not mention potatoes, and since *Moby Dick* was based on Melville's own mid-century experiences the chowder could very well have been thickened only with ship biscuit in the earlier tradition.

Chowder's distinction as a *New England* dish is underlined by Mary Lawrence's introduction of fish chowder to some British New Zealanders in 1860 when her husband's whaleship *Addison* was in Akaroa Harbor. The Lawrences had a dinner party and, as Mary reported, "Our folks had been fishing the day before, so we had a fish chowder for the first course, which was a new dish entirely to them all. I had to give them full instruction in the art of making chowders. The nicest way that they ever ate fish before, said they all. Then we had stewed pigeons with dumplings, gravy, etc. another Yankee affair, then a bread plum pudding."[17]

Two chowders, the top one made with haddock, the bottom one made with bluefish. Chowder recipes at the end of this chapter.

Mary was very fond of chowder, and recorded no fewer than four picnics ashore in Lower California, where several whaleships anchored, and captains and families visited with each other, in January and February 1859. As we have seen so often, these New Englanders in a new place continued their familiar foodways: they took ashore for their picnic bread, cake, crackers, cookies, pies, ham, fruits, beer, and coffee, made a chowder on the beach, and roasted oysters they found growing on mangrove roots.

Mary Lawrence called the chowder "quahog chowder," and to her southern New England eyes the shellfish they gathered probably looked like the familiar quahogs of home. Strictly speaking they were not, for *Mercenaria mercenaria* aren't found in the Pacific, but she could have eaten any one of the similar-sized clams that occur in Pacific waters. We know for certain that at least once the chowder had potatoes in it because, she reported, the stewards from two other vessels and the *Addison* went back to the ship to get more salt pork and potatoes for the chowders, but broke into the liquor in the stateroom instead and got drunk. Of the 24 February picnic she wrote that the cluster of ships produced "ten captains, four ladies, and seven children. We could hardly realize that we were whaling. Had a nice chowder."[18]

Portrait of Two Chowder Parties

Two wonderfully detailed accounts of September chowder parties appear in the Mystic *Pioneer*—one in 1859, another in 1861. Some of the details echo Mary Lawrence's accounts of the chowder parties in Lower California, and I think we can surmise that chowders in southern New England at mid-century followed this pattern.

A photo taken about 1896 shows the Scholfield family outside their Clift Street, Mystic, Connecticut, home with bowls on the cloth-covered table suggesting chowder. Sitting on a sawhorse could not have been the most comfortable way to enjoy the meal. Perhaps this was Fourth of July and the young fellow with the revolver planned to make some noise. [E. A. Scholfield, Albumen cabinet photograph, MSM 77.92.846]

Both parties set sail early, 8 or 9 in the morning, and stayed away all day. These were large parties—one included 72 souls. Both parties contained both men and women. The chowder-making seems to have been headed by an experienced cook—quite possibly even a chowder master, similar to the bake master of a clambake. Mystic had people at the time who were known to be chowder masters—Ebenezer Beebe was one of the best-known. The group brought additional food to round out the meal. Talking, resting, riding on swings, and going for sails in the boat, as well as making and eating chowder, seem to have been the primary amusements.

Being in good spirits was the main requirement of the day. In one account, "old and young, grave and gay—seemed in the best spirits. Our minister laid aside his

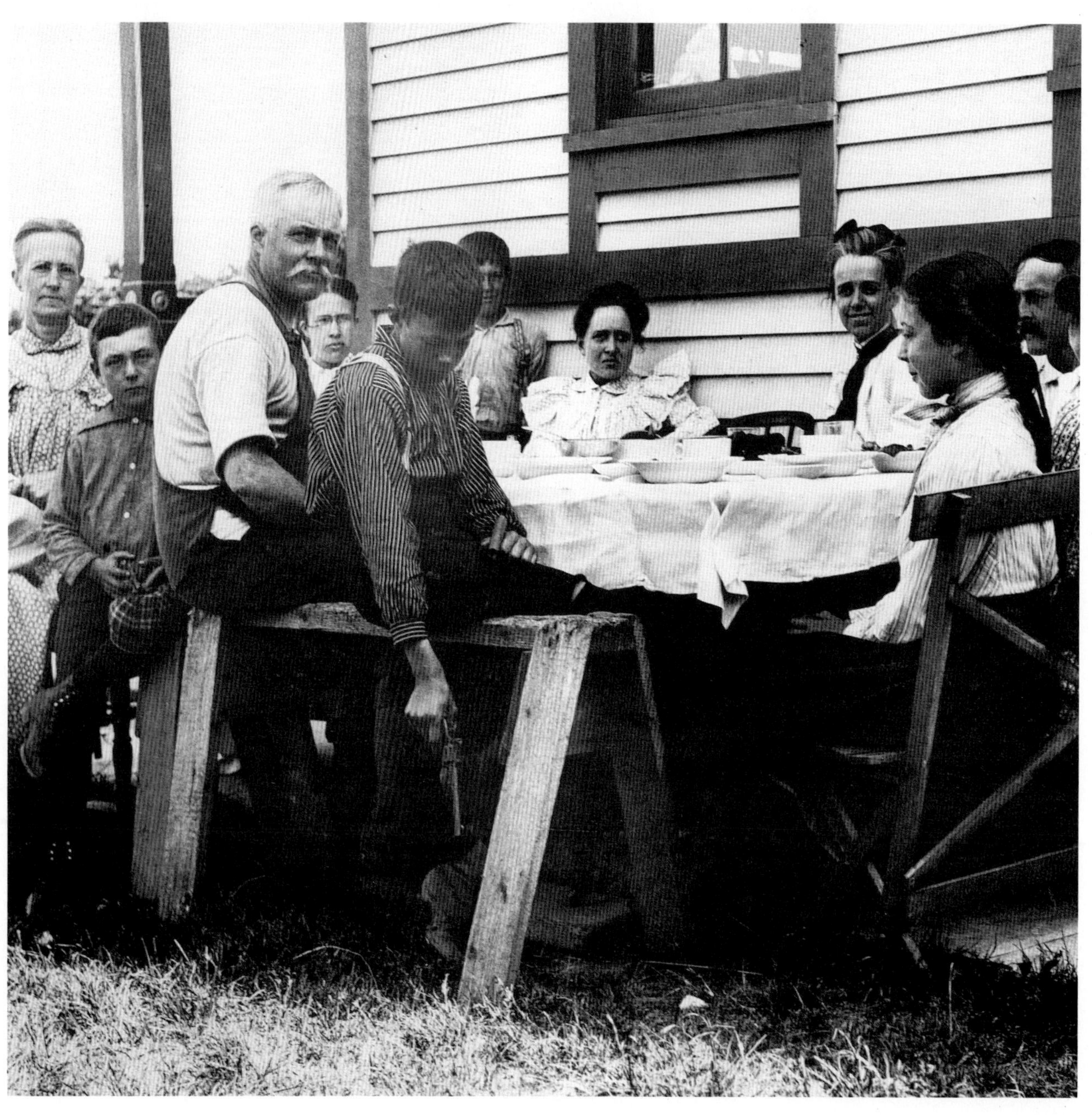

sanctimonious face, and entertained all hands to the best of his ability. Our senator laid aside his law-making and made himself agreeable to the ladies." That party was not a teetotal event, but the drinking was subdued: "The aforementioned jugs, said to contain milk, were also circulated somewhat, and milk was pronounced an excellent beverage."[19]

Both parties originated in Mystic—either Mystic Bridge or what is now called Old Mystic—and sailed downriver to picnic areas—Mason's Island and Nauyaug Cove. The trip in the boat was important to the event, providing more sociability than everyone traveling separately and meeting up for the meal. Upon arriving, the first order of business was unpacking the boat and starting the chowder: "Unloading was the next thing in order, and ladies, bundles, jugs, and baskets were soon landed upon the rocks." Among the provisions "safely stowed in the cabin...such a display of well filled baskets, boxes, and kettles we have seldom witnessed. These were followed by ten large watermelons, intended as a desert, but we can assure our readers that they were not deserted."[20]

Stashed in the baskets, boxes, and bundles were the makings for the chowder, as well as other food: "bread, pies, pickles, cheese, cold meats, &c., &c." On a third party, which ended up becalmed en route to Montauk, the group ate on board the boat, and from the menu described we can see what was intended to accompany chowder for their picnic: "While sailing home the company were treated with tea, coffee, milk, cold water, pies, melons, cakes &c, &c."[21]

The parties also brought with them suitable dishes and flatware for hot and cold food. On a "clean level grass-plot, [some of the party]...spread the cloths, arranged the dishes." One account specified knives, forks, and spoons to eat with, and the other mentioned tin-pans. Both groups brought tablecloths, and sat on the ground, although one description referred to a table that they did not literally have: "we were soon seated on the grass, making music with the knife, fork and spoon, and keeping those who kindly volunteered to wait...dancing...between the table and the chowder kettle."[22]

Making the chowder was part of the entertainment. One detailed description could be taken for a recipe: "In the first place some slices of pork were placed in the kettle, which was put over the fire and the pork thoroughly fried, when it was taken off, and a layer of sliced potatoes were put in; this was followed by a supply of fish cut up in small pieces—we had striped bass—then came hard bread or crackers, after which again came potatoes, and so on—potatoes, fish, and crackers in alternate layers until the kettle was full. These of course were interspersed with sliced onion and a proper supply of seasoning materials, such as salt, pepper, and sometimes spice with also a sprinkling of flour for each layer. A very little water being put in the kettle is again placed over the fire, and the whole thoroughly cooked."[23]

At this party two kettles of chowder were made, each with its own chief cook, but the products were so similar that the writer concluded "we could not detect the difference in quality, and came to the conclusion that [the cooks] were both proficients in the art."

At the Mystic chowder party, "Our cook captain, steward, &c., soon had all the ladies around him paring and slicing potatoes, onion, and pork."Although some ladies might object to onions, "chowder would not be chowder without onions," claimed the reporter.[24]

The first description mentioned sprinkling flour, salt, and pepper, which were commonly added to chowder earlier in the nineteenth century. While the reporter did not identify the "spice" used—possibly because he did not know or recognize it—some possibilities include cayenne, cloves, and mace. All these were mentioned in mid-century cookbooks as appropriate seasonings for chowder.[25]

The boat trip back home at the end of the day, for the 1861 party, was accompanied by "singers on board who did the patriotic songs of the day to an appreciative audience," quite possibly because the War Between the States was on the participants' minds. The two accounts close similarly: the reporter in 1859 vowed "ere these pleasant fall days are gone, to have another 'chowder party,'"[41] and in 1861 he was quite sure "your readers will all want to go on the next chowder party."[26]

The chowder-makers for the two groups we just met were not named. One sounded as though he provided boat, chowder and all, doing all the sailing, cooking, serving himself. Earlier we heard of the caterer Mrs. A.J.F. Another well-known chowder wizard in the Mystic area was sailmaker Ebenezer Beebe: "Mystic Cornet Band having a picnic at Joe Williams' Grove. They have engaged Prof. Beebe, C.M. [which means chowder maker] Uncle Neezer can beat them all on making chowder." "The Greenmans go on a chowder today. They engaged the services of Uncle 'Sneezer the celebrated chowder maker."[27]

A latter-day chowder master was Fred Hermes of Mystic, who worked for many years at Mystic Seaport Museum after his retirement. Fred learned his chowder-making from Willard Lamphere at least 60 years ago, and although Fred identified his chowder as "a real old-fashioned New England clam chowder" it is, more specifically, what is known in southeastern Connecticut as a "Stonington clam chowder." It is closer in its tradition to the chowders of nearly two hundred years ago.

Like "Uncle Neezer," Fred made chowders for large gatherings and clambakes. His chowder mastery was a part of his clambake mastery; in the early twentieth century, chowder parties were seldom identified by that name, as they had been a half-century before, but chowder continued, as it does today, to be on the menu for large parties. Fred's wife, Katie, told me that Fred used to make his chowder at home for the clambakes he put on for other people. One of the largest clambakes he did was for 300 people at an event for the Electric Boat shipyard in Groton.

Twentieth-Century Chowders and the Maxson Family Chowder

Nathan Fish and William Ellery Maxson co-owned the Maxson and Fish Shipyard in what is now called West Mystic. Nathan Fish recorded in his diary that on 8 September 1868, he, his family, and a group of friends—about two dozen altogether—went for a picnic: "Beautiful clear weather. The 'picnic' is the principle business of the day. The boat was ready and we cast off at 10....The wind was fair. We took possession of the grounds about noon and kindled fires, rambled about the island a little while the chowder was cooking. Robert and Capt. Packer made the chowders we had two and they were *good*."[28]

A descendant in the Maxson family, Silas Maxson, Jr., was busy making chowders early in this century. His daughter, Marjorie Maxson Vignot, remembers watching him "build a chowder," specifically a clam chowder, during the 1920s.[29] Even though by the time Mrs. Vignot was a girl the custom of chowder parties seems to have diminished, her father made his chowders at a small summer place the family owned at Pleasure Beach in Waterford. If he was making a big chowder he would get a group of people together to help, and make it in a big, straight-sided kettle hung over a fire in the backyard.

There are some things about this chowder that show a slightly different approach to chowder-making in this century. One is the more common use of clams. Another is that crackers were added to the chowder at the table by the person eating it.

Mrs. Vignot says that her father used no exact measurements, but worked largely by eye. The usual beginning was about a quarter of a pound of salt pork, "the fat kind,

The terrain and the life-saving station in the background indicate that this is a seaside home, an ideal setting for a chowder dinner with freshly caught fish. [MSM 84.185.3]

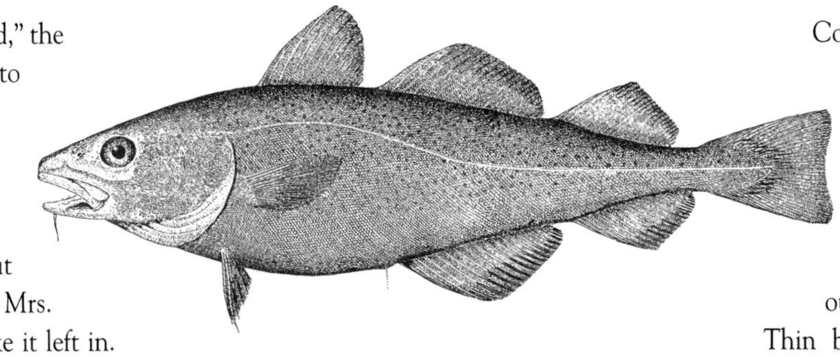

not the streaky kind," the main idea being to have enough fat to fry the onions in. The Maxsons always removed the tried-out fatback, because Mrs. Maxson did not like it left in. They ran four or five onions through the coarse blade of a meat grinder because Mr. Maxson did not like stringy onion in his chowder. These ground onions then were fried in the fat.

Mr. Maxson was particular about the potatoes: he instructed anyone slicing them to cut quarter-sized, wedge-shaped slices of potatoes, so that there was always a thick side and a thin side. As the chowder cooked, the thin side of the potato cooked through and came off, thickening the chowder. Potato was the only thickening for the chowder until it went to the table. The potatoes would be put in the pot with just enough water to cover them. When they were tender, the clams would be added.

Mr. Maxson used about a quart of clams—quahogs—and shucked them himself so he could reserve the juice, which he also added to chowder after straining it carefully to leave sediment behind. Sometimes Mrs. Maxson would snip out the black spot in the clam belly so they would have a nice clear chowder. The Maxsons also ran the clams through the meat grinder. Because they were so fine they needed to simmer only briefly, so they were added close to the end of the process. Mrs. Vignot said that her mother kept a sharp eye on Silas because he would raid the fridge at this point for butter, cream, and anything else he could spot that he thought would be a good addition. She recalled that once when he added corn no one would eat the chowder.

The chowder, Mrs. Vignot said, was "clammy enough that you could usually dilute it with milk." Accordingly, it was served with a pitcher full of room-temperature milk on the table, along with pilot crackers to break into it, which each person added to taste.

Like Mrs. Vignot, Frances Jaixen Dodge, on Block Island, recalled that clam and fish chowders were made both with and without milk, had onions and potatoes, but were never thickened with crackers during cooking. Frances's sister Mildred recalled that "the men would always load up their chowder with crackers" after it was served.[30]

Other Chowders

Among late-twentieth-century thick soups, the word "chowder" has come to describe texture more than content. The best known non-fish chowder is corn chowder, and it is a genuine chowder, with salt pork, potatoes, onions, and milk added at the end, only featuring corn instead of clams or fish. We find corn standing in occasionally for shellfish, as in corn oysters. Corn chowder did not come along until the last half of the nineteenth century, and when it did it seems to have come from outside New England. Thin broth-based corn soups certainly existed earlier in the century, as did fish and clam "soups." But these were not true chowders. One of the earliest corn chowders I could find is included among the recipes that follow.

Recipes specifying that salted or smoked fish be used to make chowder rarely appeared in nineteenth-century American cookbooks. Technically a cook could use freshened salt fish, but it seems not to have been considered generally appropriate, and fresh fish were usually preferred. Nor did New Englanders seem to use smoked fish for chowder.

In Scotland a variety of chowder called cullen skink is made from smoked haddock. Although fish was preserved in New England by smoking, I have not yet found a historical reference to using it in a chowder, even though it would work. The process of making cullen skink varies from chowder in that the potatoes are mashed before they are added, and the onions are simmered with the fish instead of being fried in fat—in this case, butter. The finished product is very chowder-like.

Hardly anyone today goes to the trouble of taking a kettle, salt pork, potatoes, onions, and all the rest to a beach in order to cook fish chowder with freshly caught fish. Chowder is often part of a clambake menu and is still considered good fare for a large crowd. Chowder mastery is still practiced and respected.

Among soups, chowder is one of the easiest to prepare, and yet it found its way into the canned food section early on. It has been embellished and varied, and its name has been given to heterodox amalgams of ingredients. But an orthodox chowder is still a fine example of a vernacular dish, largely unchanged for centuries, a simple concoction of plain ingredients that yield a rich dish with a rich history.

Edward Knapp's fisherman uncle Johnnie owned a Noank well smack named the *Amoy*. In his memoir of growing up in Noank, Knapp told how he and a young chum visited his uncle aboard the smack which had sea bass in its well that day. His uncle put the boys to work. "We set to peeling potatoes and onions, slicing salt pork and starting water to boil, while Uncle Johnnie scooped some Sea Bass from the well." The payoff? An invitation to dinner. "You can eat dinner aboard, if you can stand Sea Bass: I told your Mother you two would stay aboard for dinner; told your Pa, too, Charlie.'"

"Could we stand Sea Bass Chowder? I'd like to be condemned to eat it aboard a Noank Smack right now."[31]

The Recipes

The recipes that follow are not just for chowder, although I have included seven chowder recipes. You may not need them. It may be that now, after you've read all about chowder, you would feel comfortable building one of your own with no recipe to specify amounts or to describe each step in the process.

In addition to the chowder, Mary Lawrence served her New Zealand guests stewed pigeons with dumplings and plum bread pudding. Recipes are included for those. Mrs. Lawrence enjoyed roasted oysters, and period instructions for roasting them are included. Mrs. Lawrence also recorded that cakes and cookies were served at the whalers' chowder parties, and so we include a recipe for jumbles, a kind of cookie, this one from another whaling wife, Sallie Smith, who wrote the recipe in the back of her seagoing journal.

FISH CHOWDER

Take either a cod or a haddock, weighing about 4 lbs., skin it, cut in small pieces and wash in cold water; take a scant quarter of a pound of salt pork, cut into small pieces and fry brown in the kettle in which the chowder is to be made; for a fish weighing 4 lbs., pare and slice 5 medium sized potatoes and 1 small onion; place a layer of potato and onion in the kettle, then a layer of fish, then dredge in a little salt, pepper, and flour; keep putting in alternate layers of potatoes, fish, and the seasoning until all is used; add hot water enough to cover; cover tight and boil gently thirty minutes; add a pint of milk and 6 crackers split and dipped in cold water, and cook ten minutes longer. To sharpen the appetite take Hood's Sarsaparilla.

From *Hood's Combined Cook Books*, by C.I. Hood & Co., 1875-1885, Hood's #3, page 3

This straightforward recipe for an unpretentious fish chowder tastes very good. The recipe above is clear enough that an interpretation is not necessary. My local fish market says that a 4-pound cod dresses out to about 1 1/2 pounds of filleted fish, and in testing this recipe I found that to be a good proportion of fish to potato. I used common crackers. Yields 3-4 quarts.

STEWED PIGEONS

To Cook Pigeons. After they are well dressed, put a slice of salt pork and a little ball of stuffing into the body of each. Flour the pigeons well, and lay them close in the bottom of the pot. Just cover them with water, and throw in a piece of butter, and let them stew an hour and a quarter if young, if old longer. This is preferred to roasting, or any other way they can be prepared. They may be cooked in the same way without stuffing.

From *The Skillful Housewife's Book*, by Mrs. L.G. Abell, 1853, page 97

DUMPLINGS

Light Dumplings.—To every cup of cold water needed to make as much dough as is desired, put one teaspoonful of cream-tartar and half a teaspoonful of soda; then stir in instantly enough flour to make a little thicker than biscuit; cut out, and boil twenty minutes. If directions are strictly followed, you will have light dumplings.

From *All Around the House*, by Mrs. H.W. Beecher, 1878, page 430

Pigeons, or squab as they are called now, were certainly more common in the nineteenth century than today. Mrs. Abell's recipe is a standard one for stewing pigeons, for which she borrowed heavily from Mrs. Child, and the method would have been familiar to Mrs. Lawrence, who could have instructed the steward or cook.

The instructions above are clear enough that no interpretation is needed. Allow one squab per person. You may elect to use a commercially prepared stuffing or use the stuffing recipe on page 248.

Dumplings seem to be one of the many ordinary foods for which scant or no instruction was given in cookbooks until later in the nineteenth century. Mrs. Beecher's recipe for cut-out dumplings should be mixed half an hour before the pigeons are done, then placed on top of the stewing pigeons. Cook them for ten minutes covered, then ten minutes uncovered.

PLUM BREAD PUDDING

Quaking Plum Pudding, very nice. Take slices of light bread and spread them thin with butter, and lay in the pudding dish layers of bread and raisins, within an inch of the top; then take five eggs and beat them well, and mix them with a quart of milk, and pour it over the pudding; add salt and spice to suit your taste; you may put in a cup of sugar and eat it with butter, or you may omit the sugar, and serve it up with sweet sauce. Bake it twenty or twenty-five minutes. Before you use the raisins, boil them in a very little water, and put it all in.

From *New England Economical Housekeeper*, by Mrs. E.A. Howland, 1845, page 37

Because this lovely pudding is not baked as long as many bread puddings, the custard is not thoroughly set, and it really does quake when you take it from the oven. Mrs. Howland's suggestions about serving this pudding with butter versus a sweet sauce reminds us that nineteenth-century puddings were seldom served without sauce.

Although I recommend one cup of raisins in the interpretation that follows, there is no reason why you could not put in more if you like them.

6 slices of firm white bread
1 cup raisins soaked in 1/2 cup hot water
1/2 cup sugar, brown or white
1 quart milk
5 eggs
cinnamon, nutmeg, and salt to taste
Preheat oven to 350°

1. Butter both sides of the bread and place the whole slices in a greased two-quart baking dish with raisins sprinkled generously between the layers of bread.
2. Beat the eggs. Add the milk, sugar, salt, and spices and beat all together. Pour the mixture over the bread.
3. Bake for 25 minutes. Serve warm or cold.

Yields 6-8 servings.

JUMBLES

1/2 lb sugar
1/2 lb butter
2/4 lb flour
2 eggs

From Sallie Smith's journal of a whaling voyage aboard the bark *Ohio*, 1875-1878, Log 399, G.W. Blunt White Library, Mystic Seaport Museum

Jumbles was the name given to what most people today would identify as sugar cookies, and with some variation they have been around for centuries. This brief recipe was found among others written in pencil at the back of Sallie Smith's journal, but additional instructions for making them can be found in other period recipe collections.

Jumbles should be ring-shaped cookies. One nineteenth-century cookbook says to roll out the dough, then "cut out with a large tumbler, and cut out the middle with the top of a small canister, to leave a perfect ring."[32] The early recipes also frequently specify to roll jumbles out in sugar.

You can vary the spice in these cookies to suit your taste. In the first part of the nineteenth century lemon, nutmeg, or rosewater topped the list of preferred flavorings, and later in the century vanilla was the choice. Since Mrs. Smith doesn't specify, the choice is yours. An interpretation of the recipe above follows.

1 cup sugar
1 cup or two sticks of butter
2 1/2 cups flour
2 eggs
Preheat oven to 325°

1. Cream together sugar and butter. Add eggs.
2. Add flour. The dough will be quite stiff. If there is time, chill the dough.
3. Sprinkle your rolling surface with granulated sugar. Roll out small quantities of dough, working quickly so that the dough will not take up too much sugar. Cut in ring shapes.
4. Bake on a greased cookie sheet for 12 minutes.

Yields 6 dozen.

ROASTED OYSTERS

Select single oysters in the shell, and put them, with the rounded side down, upon a gridiron and over a sharp fire. They will roast in a very short time. Send them to the table in the shell, with coffee, cold-slaw, and fresh bread and butter.

From *The Practical Cookbook,* by Mrs. Bliss, 1864, page 34

Mrs. Lawrence roasted her oysters on a beach and accompanied them with chowder and other good things. Mrs. Bliss was suggesting a nice supper menu. In the days of fireplaces or wood stoves, roasting oysters over a fire could be easily done indoors. You may have to do this on your outdoor grill, or on a hibachi set in a fireplace.

My friend Ruth Stetson, who tried this method of cooking oysters, suggests "continuing dinner with a large stuffed fish, and corn-on-the-cob as long as your grill is hot," with French bread on the side. Cocktail sauce is good on the oysters.

Scrub the oysters well with a brush. Have a charcoal fire ready as hot as for steak. If you have a lidded grill, put the oysters on, close the lid, and roast them for only three minutes. Without a lid, you may wish to cook them a bit longer. If cooked too long, they will lose some of their liquid and be dry.

CLAM CHOWDER

The two following clam chowders, one from Fred Hermes and the other from Marjorie Vignot, seem similar but have different results. The Hermes recipe is thinner than the Vignot, with a very sturdy clammy flavor; the Vignot chowder is thicker and milder even without the milk.

Fred Hermes' CLAM CHOWDER

3 quarts quahogs—ground through meat grinder
5 pounds potatoes—sliced
2 pounds onion—ground
3/4 pound salt pork—ground

Put ground-up fat pork in a large frying pan, start cooking slowly. Then grind and add onions. In a large kettle (15-quart capacity) heat water, when boiling add potatoes, while boiling start salt pork and onions—then add them to water and potatoes. Then when having cooked awhile, add the ground quahogs and their juice. Don't cook the quahogs long. While potatoes are cooking, if you need to add water, add from a hot tea kettle full. Enough water ultimately to make 10 or 12 quarts of chowder.

From Fred Hermes, 1987

This recipe yields what is locally known as Stonington clam chowder, although Fred pointed out to me that it is really the old-fashioned New England clam chowder recipe that has survived mostly unchanged in this part of New England.

Fred's recipe makes 10 or 12 quarts. If this seems like too much, remember that Fred made chowders for large gatherings and clambakes. He said that he always bought the clams already out of the shell for his chowder.

Two important things: avoid using a food processor on the ingredients (unless you are very skilled at pulsing)—especially the clams–because it will make them too fine for an authentic chowder; be sure to slice, not cube, the potatoes. The following is an interpretation for one gallon.

1/2 pound salt pork, ground
2/3 pound onions (5-6 medium onions) ground
1 2/3 pound potatoes (4-5 medium) sliced
1 quart quahogs, ground
2 quarts water to start

1. Set chowder pot on the burner with water and potatoes and begin cooking.
2. Start frying the ground-up salt pork, and when it begins to sizzle add the onions, and cook until the onions are golden.
3. Once the onions are golden they can be added to the boiling water and potatoes. Lower the heat and cook all together for a while until the potatoes are tender.
4. About 15 minutes before serving, add the clams and their broth and simmer the whole mixture.
5. Serve with crackers.

Yields one gallon.

Marjorie Vignot's CLAM CHOWDER

Marjorie Vignot supplied the instructions in a phone conversation with me for the clam chowder she recalls her father making. While her father used no exact measurements for his chowder, Mrs. Vignot estimated the amounts you will find in the interpretation below.

The important things to remember are: slice the potatoes just as Mr. Maxson insisted, with a thin side and a thick side; avoid using a food processor (unless you are very skilled at pulsing) to grind the onions, salt pork, and clams because it will make them too fine.

1/2 pound fat salt pork ground
4-5 medium onions ground
1 1/2 pound potatoes cut thick and thin
3 cups water
1 quart shucked clams
salt and pepper to taste

1. In a large kettle, fry the salt pork until it is tried out. Remove the scraps or keep them in, as you wish.
2. Add the onions to the fat and cook until soft, then add potatoes and clam juice and enough water to cover the potatoes.

3. Cook until the potatoes disintegrate; grind clams and add them. Simmer for 15 minutes. Taste and add salt and pepper.
4. Serve very hot with a pitcher of milk on the table for each person to add to taste, and crackers.

Yields one gallon.

CORN CHOWDER

1 quart of grated corn
4 good-sized potatoes
2 medium-sized onions
1/2 pound of bacon or ham
1 large tablespoonful of butter
2 tablespoonsful of flour
1 pint of milk
6 water crackers
Yolk of one egg
1/2 pint boiling water

Pare and cut the potatoes and onions into dice. Cut the bacon or ham into small pieces and put it in a frying pan with the onions and fry until a nice brown. Put a layer of potatoes in the bottom of a saucepan, then a sprinkling of bacon or ham and onion, then a layer of corn, then a sprinkling of salt and pepper, then a layer of potatoes, and so on, until all is in, having the last layer corn. Now add the water and place over a moderate fire and simmer for twenty minutes. Then add the milk. Rub the butter and flour together and stir into the boiling chowder. Add the crackers broken; stir, and cook five minutes longer. Taste to see if properly seasoned, take it from the fire, add the beaten yolk of the egg and serve.

From Mrs. *Rorer's Cookbook,* by Mrs. S.T. Rorer, 1886, page 355

Corn chowder recipes are fairly rare until the end of the nineteenth century, and appear less frequently than corn soup recipes. What makes this a real chowder is the presence of bacon, potatoes, onions, crackers, and milk, and the characteristic layering of ingredients.

This recipe makes about a gallon of chowder. It is a very good, very thick chowder, even before you add the crackers, flour, butter, and egg yolk. You may wish to thin it out with additional milk.

If you try this recipe, keep in mind that you will probably need 12 ears of corn to give you a quart of grated corn. Otherwise, the recipe is clear enough to use without further explanation.

Yields one gallon.

FISH CHOWDER

Cut some slices of pork very thin, and fry it out in the dinner-pot; then put in a layer of fish cut in slices, on the pork and fat, then a layer of onions, and then potatoes, all cut in thin slices; then fish, onions, and potatoes again, till your materials are all in, putting some salt and pepper on each layer of onions; split some crackers, and dip them in water, and put them around the sides and over the top; put in water enough to come up in sight; boil about half an hour, till the potatoes are done; add half a pint of milk, or a tea-cup of sweet cream, five minutes before you take it up."

From *New England Economical Housekeeper,* by Mrs. E.A. Howland, 1845, page 62

This fairly standard recipe for fish chowder should sound and taste familiar to most people despite the fact that it is nearly as old as Mystic Seaport's whaleship *Charles W. Morgan*. Following is a more specific version.

2 lbs. cod or haddock, cut into bite-sized pieces
2-3 slices salt pork
1 large onion, sliced
3-4 medium potatoes, sliced
2 cups hot water
6 common crackers (optional)
salt and pepper
1 cup milk or cream

1. Fry the salt pork in the bottom of a soup kettle; when it is tried out, layer your ingredients in as the old recipe suggests—onions (with the salt and pepper sprinkled on), potatoes, and fish.
2. When everything is in the kettle, add the split common crackers, soaked in a little water, in a layer on the top.
3. Pour the hot water in until it shows through the top layer of ingredients.
4. Simmer for half an hour or until the potatoes are done.
5. Just before serving, pour in the milk or cream and mix.

Yields 4-5 servings.

Charlotte Gilbert's CHOWDER

Lay a slice or two of pork on the bottom of the pot; strew over them onions & sweet herbs; cut a cod fish in pieces about an inch thick; pepper, salt, a little flour & part of the fish on the pork & then a layer of biscuit, pour over about a pint of water & let it stew moderately—lemon if you please, sliced in.

From the manuscript recipe notebook of Charlotte T.W. Gilbert, 1829, in the collection of Old Sturbridge Village, Sturbridge, Massachusetts

This recipe comes from a manuscript recipe notebook made for Charlotte Gilbert "from her friend C.D. Waters"—apparently as a gift, which accounts in part for a main-dish recipe being included. This potato-less chowder is very thick. You may wish to add more water. If you think finding a slice of lemon in your serving is not pleasant, squeeze the juice in instead. Here is an interpretation.

1 lb. cod
2 slices salt pork
1 small onion, sliced
3-4 common crackers, pounded
parsley, thyme, tarragon, or marjoram to taste
2 cups of hot water
1 tablespoon flour

1. Fry the salt pork in a soup kettle and when it is tried out, add the onion and fry until golden.
2. Cut the fish into bite-sized pieces, and lay it on the onion, sprinkling the flour and herbs over it. Put the cracker crumbs on top of the fish layer.
3. Pour the hot water over all, and cook the chowder covered until the fish is done, and it is as thick as you like it.
4. Add the lemon or lemon juice last. Add salt and pepper to taste.

Yields 3 servings. (Increase water to four cups for 4 servings).

SMOKED FISH CHOWDER
(Cullen Skink)

Much of the "finnan haddie" available today is made from cod, but a true cullen skink would, of course, be made from only smoked haddock. A very delicious smoked-fish chowder can be made from smoked cod, haddock, or bluefish, as Mystic Seaport people found out when the Outdoor Demonstration Squad began producing "finnan bluefish" in the fish-smoking demonstration several years ago.

What follows is a interpretation of the old cullen skink recipe that can be used with almost any sort of plain smoked fish. Smoked fish vary in smokiness and saltiness, and may need to be freshened before use. The potatoes can be diced or sliced as in traditional chowders, or they can be cooked separately and mashed before adding them as in traditional cullen skink. Mashed potatoes make a creamy chowder.

2 lbs. smoked fish
2-3 slices of salt pork chopped
2 medium onions
3-4 potatoes sliced
1 cup water
1 1/2 cups milk
salt and pepper

1. If necessary, lay the fish in a pan of hot water to freshen a bit. When ready, break into bite-sized pieces.
2. Fry the salt pork in the bottom of a soup kettle until it is tried out. Add the onion and fry till golden.
3. Add the potato (unless you plan to mash it) and fish. Add water until you can see it among the potatoes. Cook until the potatoes are done.
4. Just before serving, add the milk, and bring the chowder up to a simmer. If you mashed the potatoes, add them at this point, mixing them in well. Taste for seasoning and add salt and pepper if needed.

Yields 4 servings.

And Refreshments Were Served

We have seen already how nineteenth-century New Englanders at sea and ashore observed their holidays with food, socialized around clambakes and chowder parties, and exchanged gifts of food with one another at sea and at home. Sharing food and drink is the essence of hospitality.

Food was a significant part of weddings, ship launchings, family parties, dedications, fund-raising events like ice cream and strawberry festivals, oyster suppers, and church fairs. The size and content of the meal served on these occasions varied, of course, depending upon who was expected to be present and how noteworthy an event it was. Menus ranged from full banquets to what we would call a snack. While dishes served at some events were associated with women and their preferences, others were meant to satisfy male appetites.

The highly appropriate title of the image above is "Women Enjoying a Seated Tea While Making a Strong Stand in Favor of Temperance." Tea menus set the pattern followed for refreshments at events. [Woodcut circa 1840, Albert Alden Proof Book, courtesy American Antiquarian Society]

At left, cake and ice cream were perfect for dog-day ice cream festivals. Cakes top to bottom: gold cake with chocolate frosting, coconut cake, sponge cake, silver cake. Chocolate, vanilla, and strawberry ice creams on plates with cake slices. Recipes for all cakes at end of chapter, except for sponge cake, recipe on page 77.

GRAND CENTENNIAL

TEA PARTY!

GIVEN BY THE LADIES OF MONSON,

CHRISTMAS EVE,

IN GREEN'S HALL,

FOR THE

BENEFIT OF THE MONSON HARMONY SOCIETY.

REFRESHMENTS OF ALL KINDS INCLUDING AN OLD FASHIONED FARMER'S SUPPER.

Fancy Articles IN GREAT VARIETY. A Christmas Tree

A Centennial Department, containing a great variety of relics of a Century ago.

WAITERS IN COSTUME,

And numerous other attractions.

MERRY CHRISTMAS TO ALL!

Doors open at 7 o'clock. - - Admission 10 Cents.

Eddy the Printer, Ware Mass.

Except for large fancy dinners, many refreshment menus were expanded upon or derived from the most sociable of nineteenth-century domestic meals—teas and suppers. Breakfast and the big noontime dinner were usually family meals in the 1800s, but teas and suppers were often joined by friends and relatives. Teas varied from small meals with just tea and bread and preserves to more elaborate meals with sandwiches and even hot food. Tea menus were adopted for modest social gatherings, expanded for grander occasions unless a dinner menu was required.

Social Teas Large and Small

Sarah Anna Emery gives us a glimpse of social-tea menus at the beginning of the nineteenth century: "On pleasant days fashionable ladies devoted the morning to calling or receiving visitors. Cake and wine were invariably passed to the guest." At late-afternoon teas, besides tea with cream and sugar, ladies were offered bread and butter and cake. "If the gentlemen came to tea, and this was the only refreshment, sliced ham or tongue were usually added."[1] Meat was the appropriate food to serve when men were present. Teas could turn into suppers when warm food was served.

Cold ham and tongue appear frequently in accounts of small cold meals like teas and, as we have seen, picnics. Cake and wine were then a common combination, although now it is practically unheard of.[2] These, together with bread or crackers and butter or cheese, created the basic cold meal, either formal or informal.

Later evening refreshments, not meant to satisfy as a meal would, were described by Caroline King: "The

Shortcake made in sponge-cake style, recipe on page 327.

evening treat was almost always the same. Grapes and nuts and raisins, with sometimes whips, raspberry creams, and calf's foot jelly from the genuine article, while lemonade was often handed around during the evening." Sarah Anna Emery recalled something very similar, which she described as "the choice and elegant treat" served at evening parties and balls: "Cream whipped to a froth, sweetened and flavored, was much favored. Served in glasses it looked very pretty, and whips were the one genteel thing for an evening soiree." Jellies, various cakes, fruits, wines and hot punch were the usual additional refreshments.[3]

Ship Launchings

A launching marked the culmination of large expenditures of labor and capital, and the perceived aliveness of a ship called for special celebration. A ship was usually launched when work on the hull was completed, but before she was rigged. The celebration was paid for by the vessel's owners and held at the shipyard. The magnitude of the launching paralleled the ship's importance to a community, or even region, but even small boats enjoyed some observance. In some communities, a launching meant a half-day off from school and work.[4]

The day's events included preparation of the launching ways down which the vessel rode. For large launchings, bunting and signal flags were hung on the vessel, around the yard, and on the tables from which lunch was served. A sponsor, so-called, usually a woman related to the owner or shipbuilder, was called upon to christen the ship by smashing a bottle of champagne or wine, an obvious symbol of sacrifice. During the temperance era this ancient custom was sometimes subverted in the name of reform. For example, the screw frigate *Merrimac* was sent down the ways of the Navy Yard at Boston in 1855 after Miss Mary E. Simmons broke a bottle of water from the Merrimac River over the bow; at her launch in 1897, the four-masted schooner *Frank A. Palmer* was christened with a bouquet of roses.[5]

Invited guests included both ladies and gentlemen, who sometimes rode the ship down the ways, or at least had an opportunity to tour the hull. If the vessel was important enough, politicians, businessmen, navy officials, and other distinguished guests gave speeches, offered prayers, and presented toasts. There might be music and the day might conclude with a dance.

Food was served to guests and shipyard workers, sometimes aboard the vessel, sometimes in the mold loft or joiner shop, sometimes in private homes. The menu varied from cheese and crackers to a full-scale dinner. Generally there were two separate spreads, one for shipyard workers, the other for special guests.

When the frigate *Essex* was launched in 1799, the bills submitted for the celebration showed that builder Enos Briggs purchased spirits, including rum, along with lemons, sugar, cider, beef and tongue, bread, puddings, crackers, cheese, and butter. Another bill was submitted for cooking the beef and providing four earthen platters to put it on.[6] The menu derived from this supply probably included a punch—rum, lemons, sugar—with meat and bread, crackers and cheese or butter; the puddings were probably rich, sweet confections, similar to plum pudding, which could be sliced. Everything served could have been considered finger food.

At one mid-century launching, the workers enjoyed biscuits, cheese, and rum punch outside while invited guests drank champagne in the mold loft. Shipbuilder Donald McKay apparently was in the habit of treating his guests at his home "where a sumptuous repast was prepared by Boston's leading caterer."[7]

When George Greenman and Company launched the ship *Niagara* from their yard on the present site of Mystic Seaport, on Tuesday, 18 November 1845, William Ellery Maxson recorded the day's events: "Having completed our preparations for the launching at 12 o'clock, the exciting moment arrived when she went off in good style, we then hauled her with help of spectators which were two or three hundred, into the wharf out of the mud, we then partook of an excellent dinner from roast turkey &c."[8]

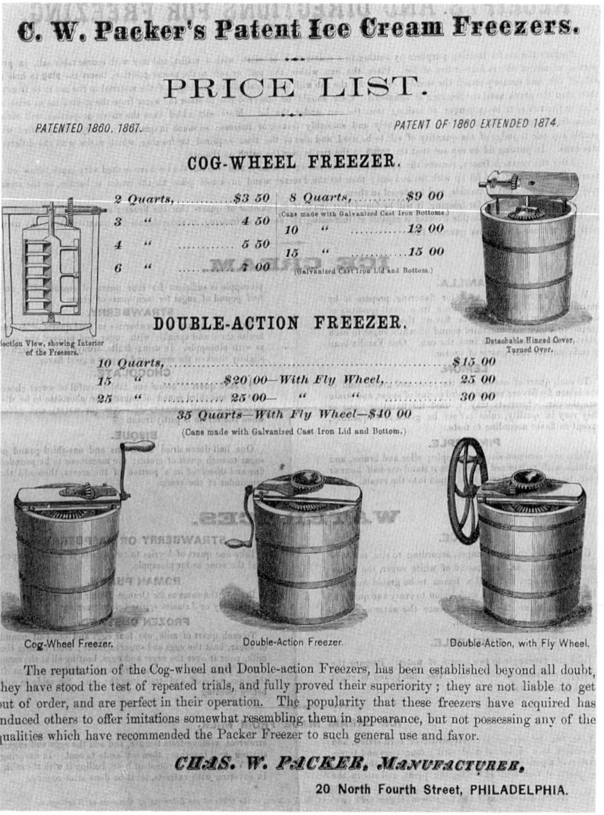

Edward Knapp cranked Packer's ice cream freezers for Noank Baptist Church ladies in the 1870s. The reward Knapp and other boys received for several hours of methodical cranking was a plate of the ice cream and a chance to lick the dashers. [Advertising card from the 1870s, MSM 81.98.17]

Small vessels were sometimes launched with at least a little ceremony. When the sloop-yacht *Bonita* was launched by Mallory and Sons at Mystic in 1859, the Mystic Cornet Band played. The Mystic *Press* pointed out that the launch in 1889 of the sloop yacht *Millie* at D.O. Richmond's yard was accompanied by "unusual interest." The owner's wife broke a bottle of wine over the bow, and "after the launching and looking over the boat, Mr. Richmond opened his house to the ladies, and they, with several of the gentlemen, partook of an excellent spread. The rest of the party fared well in the boathouse, where a table had been spread with a tempting lunch." While the interest in the *Millie* and her launch may have been unusual, the menu for the company in Mr. Richmond's house and for the group in the boathouse was probably standard for such occasions—what would have been a tea or supper spread a hundred years ago, and what we would call lunch. The "tempting lunch" in the boathouse may have paralleled one at the Franklin Post and Son boatyard early in the twentieth century, where a party table set up in the shop was spread with beer and sandwiches, possibly to celebrate a launching.[9]

Parties at the Life-Saving Station

The boatroom of the Cuttyhunk, Massachusetts, Life-Saving Station was occasionally the site of a party as it was in 1897 when this description was published: "On the last July night, just before the men go on duty a dance is usually given at the Life-Saving Station. The home of lifecars and surfboats is bare....Promptly at twelve o'clock the fiddle and the banjo, those instruments of Cuttyhunk gaiety, cease. Two guardsmen take clocks and signals and start on their four-hour watch."[10]

A few years earlier, J.H. Merryman wrote in *Scribner's Monthly*, "Now and then, when the moon is full, there is a 'surprise' party at the station. From the mainland or the neighboring settle-ments come men and women, the friends and relatives of the surfmen, bringing cakes and pastries and other good things from their homes. Then all is joy uncontained; the boatroom is cleared of carriage and cart and the merry dance goes round. But do not imagine that in these festivities the patrol is relaxed."[11]

Parties like these were continued into this century. Frances Jaixen Dodge and her sister, whose father was a cook for the Life-Saving Service, remembered dances held at the West Side Life-Saving Station at Block Island. These events, which seemed to be fairly spontaneous, not connected with any observance, were organized by the station crew. She recalled that sometimes the station provided refreshments, sometimes the visitors brought food. The parties started "after supper"—around seven—and continued to "whenever," featuring square dancing. They were temperate but not "temperance," events except for the women. The men went outside the station to drink, according to Frances, and "the women never had any."[12]

A Dedication Dinner

In 1883, Mystic's Soldier's Monument was unveiled and dedicated. The dedication is more famous for the poorly planned firing of artillery, which accidentally hurt a large group of the participants, but the menu for the day's dinner was recorded in the Mystic *Press*. This huge meal fed 1,300 participants—the governor, military companies, veterans posts, and orators. The paper described it as "the finest collation ever seen under one tent in this vicinity." While they are not credited directly with having cooked the food, the paper acknowledged the arranging of the tables by a "ladies committee led by their President Mrs. Fairbanks."

The tent was 35 feet wide and 140 feet long, "being a frame work covered by canvas." Under this were five tiers of tables running the whole length of the tent, with the distinguished guests seated in the center. On the tables "were placed over 1300 plates, each with a button hole bouquet beside it." These were certainly china plates, and because coffee was served there must have been cups or mugs on the tables, too. The menu included "a variety and profusion of food, ham, tongues, sandwiches, baked beans, lobsters, cake, etc, enough to feed all comers, altogether looking very tempting to hungry men, while the odor of the eight barrels of coffee made by steam in the barrels at the machine shop of Mr. Morgan near by, gave assurance that thirst as well as hunger was duly provided against."[13]

Weddings

In his *Travels*, Timothy Dwight reported on wedding customs in New England at the end of the eighteenth century: "Marriages were formerly festivals of considerable significance in this country. It was customary to invite even the remote relations of the parties, all their particular friends, and a great number of their neighbors. A dinner was made, in form, by the parents of the bride for the bride groom and a numerous suite. The marriage was celebrated in the evening. Cake and wine were plentifully distributed among the guests, and the festivity was concluded with dancing. At the present time the guests are usually very few."[14] Aside from a rich and ornamented cake, there seems to have been no prescribed New England menu for wedding festivities.

In a letter to Captain George Gates, Julia Gates provided a menu for a wedding she attended in 1873: "There was about 100 present and all took supper and a beautiful bill of fare. There was three roast turkeys with ham and Corned beef and Lobster salad besides every variety of bread and cake and Thomas Noyes furnished the meats." An event like this was a tremendous amount of work, as Julia told her husband, "All seemed to enjoy it but Martha was pretty well used up some hard work about it." Julia had made all the bread for the wedding, and "went early to assist with the tables." She also reported that twenty pounds of lobster had been picked from the shell for the feast.[15]

This festivity for a hundred guests would seem rich and elaborate to modern people, especially all that lobster. Still, compared to other meals for large gatherings, there was nothing unusual about the menu Julia Gates described. By this time—the 1870s—the highly favored lobster appeared often in one of the most popular ways to prepare it, a salad. By this time, salads were considered feminine fare, and a lobster salad was appropriate for an event that centered on a woman—the bride.

Another wedding-related party, which was called a "complimentary reception," was given in honor of a Stonington Borough bride-to-be in 1891. It was an evening event, with dance music, and a "collation" was served "consisting of salads, cake, coffee and ice cream."[16] Salads in this case probably included lobster and chicken, possibly salmon or ham, particularly since it was winter and a variety of salad vegetables were not available.

Wedding cakes in the 1800s usually were rich and fruited. Recipes for them are fairly common, both in manuscript sources and in standard cookbooks. In the early nineteenth century, wedding cakes—usually very rich fruit cakes—were most often leavened with eggs, although references to old-style yeasted cakes exist.[17]

For most of the century, currants, citron, and raisins were the common fruits; much spice, brandy, and wine helped flavor these cakes. In 1833, Mrs. Child called for currants and raisins in her wedding-cake recipe, saying that citron improved it but was not necessary. She specifically mentioned icing for the cake, made with egg whites and pounded loaf sugar, a standard if not particularly flavorful icing. Mrs. Abell, at mid-century, also called for raisins and currants, and instructed the cook to slice citron between layers of the cake dough,[18] as Fannie Farmer instructed forty years later.

Extraordinarily ornate cakes with sugar figures and fancy icing were the work of confectioners in the eighteenth century and early nineteenth century, but only those with means and a confectioner in the vicinity could have them.[19] When a growing middle class desired similar elegance, cookbooks provided advice for making such things at home. Nevertheless, for most of the century, cakes, whether for weddings or some other occasion, were iced with a plain, white, smooth frosting that hardened.

Mrs. Abell, for example, provided instructions for plain and ornamental icings. Two egg whites beaten till frothy with a quarter of a pound of powdered and sifted white sugar were flavored with rosewater or lemon, spread on, and allowed to get hard. For putting on ornamental icing she said "have a small syringe, draw it full of the icing and work it in any design you fancy. Wheels, Grecian borders, grapes, or flowers look well, or borders of beading. It must not be put on till the plain frosting is cold and hard."[20] By Fannie Farmer's time, the 1890s, pastry bags and tubes had been introduced and replaced the syringe.

Mrs. Gates did not say a word about any cake at the wedding she attended and helped with. But Mystic had bakeries competent to make wedding cakes if the bride's mother was inclined to purchase one instead of making it at home.

Shortcake made with biscuit-type cake, recipe on page 326.

Strawberry Festivals and Oyster Suppers: "The Public is Invited"

Church and civic groups sold food to raise money by holding fairs, festivals, lawn parties, and public suppers. In Mystic, there were seasonal cycles to the bills of fare. Winter featured chowder and oyster suppers—in those months when oysters "r" in season. In late June and early July there were strawberry festivals. Ice-cream festivals and lawn parties continued until the dog days of August. Then it seems the groups took a break until November or so when suppers began again.

These fund-raising events filled the gap between what a church could earn from its parishioners in pledges and weekly offerings and what it needed to operate or grow. Once churches were no longer supported by taxes, as they had been in early New England, and attendance and support were no longer required of citizens, other sources of revenue became very important. One elder of the Noank Baptist Church was locally renowned for eating "six or seven plates of ice cream, replying to joking remonstrators: 'I must help eat up this church debt,' and he did."[21]

Missionary societies, temperance organizations, volunteer fire companies, and social organizations followed suit, establishing a pattern that continues to this day. Food for sale accompanied the sale of needlework and craft items at church fairs and festivals, or was the sole feature of suppers. Musical entertainment and sociability made the event special. Festivals and suppers were held on church premises or in public halls; in pleasant weather, groups sometimes used church grounds or lawns of private homes to make it an outdoor event.

Strawberry festivals: Strawberries ripening gave church women an opportunity to serve their communities the first berries of the season. When, on 28 June 1883, the Mystic *Press* reported "Strawberries are at their prime and the season is fast passing," at least one batch had already been served up to the public: "Young Ladies of St. Marks Church will give a lawn party this Thursday evening at the premises of Mrs. Daniel Denison on Pearl Street with strawberries, ice cream, cake, etc. The public are invited." The paper that week announced the "Noank Brass Band's Strawberry Festival in the Baptist Church on Friday....Cake, ice cream, and strawberries will be served by fair hands." And the band, of course, would play.[22]

An effort was usually made to decorate the grounds or hall where the festival took place. In 1859, an annual strawberry festival was held at the Stonington Baptist Church where "the ladies very kindly proffered their aid in decorating the church in a style which did credit to their good taste, and contributed greatly to the pleasure of those present." In 1876, the Mystic *Press* reported that the Baptist Society of Upper Mystic [Old Mystic] held a strawberry festival on the grounds of Mr. B.F. Vanauken, and that the premises were "tastefully fitted up and made attractive delightfully."[23]

These reports do not usually say how the berries were presented. When the menu "strawberries, ice cream, and cake" is given we are left to figure out the rest. One report of a strawberry festival held at Westerly's Armory Hall in 1866 provided a little more detail: "Strawberries and cream, Oranges and pineapples, Sicilian Jam, Ice cream and ices, Lemonade and Fountain Soda, Cherries, Cakes, etc."[24]

The berries could have been served as strawberry shortcake, churned into ice cream, in bowls with cream, or on top of loaf or pound cakes—all accepted ways of serving berries in nineteenth-century New England. It is possible that these dishes were seen at festivals, along with simpler presentations of a dish of ice cream with strawberries, or a plate of cake and a dish of berries.

Ice cream and cake festivals: When strawberry season was over, the festivals went on *sans* berries. In July of 1883, "Ladies of the Methodist Episcopal Church gave a lawn ice cream party on the grounds in the rear of the church last Tuesday evening," and "A lawn party was given last evening by Mr. Simmons Bible class of the Congregational Society on the grounds of Asa Fish Esq." "Ladies of St. Mark's Episcopal church give a lawn festival on the grounds of the Hoxie House this Thursday evening." In August, "Ladies of the Road [Church] Society" sponsored a moonlight lawn festival at which the Mystic Cornet Band performed during the same week that "Young Ladies of the Mission Circle [of the Baptist Church] had an apron sale with ice cream at Mrs. Pearl Grant's cottage on Main St." This last may have been an annual event, for in 1886 the paper reported that this group held another apron sale and lawn party at Mrs. Grant's, cake and ice cream served.[25]

The making of ice cream had for a number of years been the province of confectioners, especially in larger towns and cities, and even Mystic had commercial ice-cream makers. Mrs. Newberry advertised her ice cream in the Mystic *Pioneer* in 1859 as "the best quality ice cream....Sailing Parties and Pic-Nics furnished at reasonable rates." In 1883, Randall Brown was known for his ice cream "garden" at the river's edge, "one of the pleasantest places in the state to seek cooling refreshment on a sultry summer night."[26]

But the combination of the crank freezer and the ice industry put ice cream within reach of families and church groups. For example, in the back of Westerly resident Fannie Card's manuscript recipe notebook from the later nineteenth century was a recipe for ice cream: "For the church freezer—10 qts—Take 2 gls of milk," etc. Edward Knapp described how in 1868 the Noank Baptist Church ladies "made Ice Cream and served it with or without cake," during August, September, and October. Knapp went on to tell how much work it was. Once the milk, eggs, sugar, flavorings, ice and freezers were collected together, "Pounding the ice small enough so the salt would melt it; perhaps they were fortunate enough to catch a school boy, but a Man? O never! they kept busy elsewhere....The Freezers were turned at the same slow, Long Metre time, if the motion was quickened or Long Metre was accelerated to short; they would hear Aunt Seneth hollering: 'Here! You're a-turnin that too fast—....—you'll make the cream coarse.' Back to Long Metre went the crank, till someone said: 'Don't you think that's long enough? Goodness knows it ought to be ready by this time.'" The boys' reward for cranking for a "spell" was a plate of ice cream and a chance to lick the dashes. "Caught—we went at it; with no accurate data before me, I am yet prepared to state as a *Boy-fact*: that little spell was never less than two mortal hours."[27]

When it was done, the ice cream was packed away in the C.W. Packer

A strawberry festival meant hours of picking strawberries. Benajah Davis's farm at Whitehall, a truck farm halfway between Mystic and Old Mystic, Connecticut, was one source for some of the needful for local church strawberry festivals. The festivals came in as heavily as the fruit itself in late June and early July. [Glass-plate negative by Edward H. Newbury, MSM 80.41.817]

Strawberry festival treats, left to top right, two shortcakes, pie, molded strawberry ice cream, berries to eat with cream. Recipes at the end of this chapter.

patent ice-cream freezers "with more fine pounded ice and salt and a a few lengths of old Rag Carpet over the whole, tied down with Cod, or Halibut line to keep out all heat—and small boys." Knapp recalled that in the evening at the festival ice cream was sold by the plateful, and customers could buy whatever flavor they wished, or some of each.

Cake was a prominent part of many social occasions. As we saw, it was taken along on chowder parties and picnics, was served at teas, and was even carefully packed up to go to sea. Cake recipes abound in manuscript sources at the middle of the century. Egg beaters had made beating egg whites so much easier, and for those who didn't wish to use eggs there were chemical leavenings that made cake rising practically inevitable. White flour was at last cheap enough for everyday use. White sugar similarly declined in price, and from the 1860s was sold already granulated. Cake-baking was tremendously easier, besides, in stove ovens which could be heated so much more quickly than brick ovens.

Oyster and chowder suppers: In coastal towns like Mystic, public suppers could feature seafood. "Ladies of St. Marks Episcopal Church gave a supper last evening in the vacant store next to the post office. On account of the bad weather last evening the supper is to be repeated this Thursday evening with oysters, clam chowder, clam pie, etc." The Baptist Church women apparently had a monthly supper "at their rooms" from six to seven in the evening during the winter months and into spring. To the west in Poquonnock, the Baptist Church women had a fair and festival in the church lecture rooms, and "oysters with the usual fixings were in abundance." In April of 1883 "oysters, coffee, and other good things" were served by the ladies of Stonington's Road Church at their supper and sociable.[28]

These suppers abated in favor of ice cream and fruit through the summer and early fall, then started again in November. In the fall of 1883, the Hoxie Steam Fire Engine Company raised funds with a two-day fair and festival at Central Hall in Mystic in late November. Their menu included oysters, ice cream, and other delicacies provided by "the lady friends of the company."[29]

The following February the Hoxie firefighters switched to chowders served at "elegantly spread tables, decked with flowers, and covered with all the needed adjuncts of a general supper which was rounded out and made complete by a first class clam chowder gotten up by Capt. G. M. Batty, chef de cuisine." Plenty of coffee was provided as well. They did two of these suppers in a row, with Oliver Batty doing the chowder honors at the next supper.[30]

Colonial Revival Cookery

The nation's Centenary in 1876 revived interest in "Ye Antient Times" among many Americans, perhaps especially New Englanders. Along with colonial-revival furniture, architecture, and an interest in collecting and preserving the past, came a taste for historic food. Martha Washington Teas and "New England Suppers" were offered for private and public entertainment. Participants dressed in eighteenth-century clothing or costumes representing the early days. The menu consisted of late-nineteenth-century interpretations of colonial foods.

In 1876 in Mystic the Methodist Church women and the young people of the Baptist Church both sponsored colonial-revival teas. "The young people of the Baptist Church will give a Lady Washington Tea Party at Morgan Hall, Wednesday evening, May 24th....They will appear in costumes suitable for the occasion, and tea will be served from half past seven to ten o'clock." The young people did not reveal their menu, but the Methodist Church women made this announcement in the paper: "'A Centennial Tea Party or Supper of ye Antient Times' is to be given in Morgan's Big Room, across from ye meeting house, in ye village of Mystick by ye Women who attend ye Methodist meetin', this Thursday evenin. The supper is to be Pork and Benes, Boiled Vittles, Punkin Pies, Dough Nuts, etc.; a Quire of Musick will sing appropriate melodyes. The charge for coming gin is seven-pence ha'penny (or one dime) and the supper one shilling and sixpence."[31]

The pork and beans, the "boiled vittles"—in all likelihood boiled root vegetables, or perhaps even a New England boiled dinner with corned beef or ham—the pies, and the doughnuts were certainly "ancient," dating at least to a hundred years earlier. They were also thoroughly modern in 1876. Not that much had changed. Ham and bean suppers continue in New England to this day, descendants of such "New England suppers" as the one given at the church in Poquonnock Bridge in 1883.[32]

Interest in the old foods late in the nineteenth century helps explain why an occasional anachronistic recipe appears in manuscript recipe notebooks from the time. For example, Julia Gates's notebook contains two recipes for syllabub, a whipped-cream and wine dessert that peaked in popularity in the eighteenth century. As Sarah Anna Emery explained, "Sillabub at an earlier day had been a fashionable evening beverage. There were sillibub tables...on which were placed the glass sillabub bowl and ladle, the mixture, which consisted of milk, wine or cider, sugar and spice, being dipped into tall, slender stemmed glasses. The introduction of tea brought sillibub into disuse. Ices had not then become general."[31]

In the nineteenth century, other cream desserts like Bavarians, charlottes,

In mid-to-late-nineteenth-century Mystic, and in other towns of any size, anyone disinclined to crank their own ice cream at home could saunter out to buy ice cream from a confectioner downtown. This building housed Randall Brown's ice cream parlor, on the river's edge in the 1880s, described in the Mystic *Press* as "one of the pleasantest places in the state to seek cooling refreshment on a sultry summer night." Confectioners sold other ingredients, such as coconut grated while you waited, for busy church womens' refreshment-making and for treats made at home. Some of the buildings have been replaced in a hundred years, and the bridge is different now, but downtown Mystic still looks like this. And the corner building along the river is still an ice-cream parlor. [George E. Tingley photograph, 1897, Mystic River Historical Society]

and ice cream prevailed. Temperance concerns may have helped usher syllabubs out of fashion, but such a dish would have given an eighteenth-century fillip to the meals of historically-minded Mystic people.

BANQUET MUSK MELON

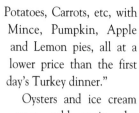

Medium size; beautifully netted; flesh deep rich salmon color; very sweet; fine grain, thick meat. Exceedingly productive, and very uniform in size and shape. lb. $1.25, ½ lb. 75, ¼ lb. 45, oz. 15, pkt. 5.

The Great Church Festival in Noank

Elements of nearly all these different kinds of food entertainments came together in a large two-day festival sponsored by the ladies of the Noank Baptist Church in December 1868. Described by Edward Knapp in his "Smacks of Noank," it was as if the church women were determined to coalesce in one event all potential smaller fund-raisers.

The second floor of the Palmer shipyard Red Shop was the scene of this event. It had been cleaned out between construction jobs and transformed with sheets tacked up inside to cover the walls, against which were strung evergreens, as well as flags and pennants borrowed from every vessel in port. To provide light, the church chandelier was brought down and suspended from the ceiling, and additional lamps were brought from homes and placed on tables. A kitchen with a stove was set up at one end, and another stove to heat the space was at the other. The usual tables for fancy needlework, candy, cake, and pie were set up, and a dining room was created by sheet partitions.

Each day there were big dinners, followed by suppers and ice cream in the evenings, with entertainment in between. The first day was Turkey Dinner. "By ten O'Clock the roasted Turkeys came in from the Homes of Neighbors; they were given a warm reception—thrust into hot ovens, basted and turned till dinner hour."

"Promptly at twelve O'Clock dinner was announced; the Waitresses passing down the aisle [of the dining room] together, the men carving and cracking jokes. Captain Fish and William Spicer took the money." This account of things by Edward Knapp described a dinner that went on until late afternoon—until everyone had had all the dinner they could hold.

From 7:30 to 10:30 the women served oyster stews, cake, and ice cream, and "If trade got a little dull, Captain Bill strolled around...shouting, 'Just ten stews left—better hurry, now's your chance to take her in for a hot Oyster stew, or you'll take her home hungry on a cold night.'"

The second day was "New England Dinner Day," with the dining room redecorated to represent an old-time kitchen and living room where a pair of Noank's older women in costume sat at spinning wheels. The menu was "Baked Beans, Brown Bread, boiled Cabbage, Turnips, Potatoes, Carrots, etc, with Mince, Pumpkin, Apple and Lemon pies, all at a lower price than the first day's Turkey dinner."

Oysters and ice cream were sold again the second evening, and the event closed with an auction of pies and cakes. Knapp described some of the cakes: "There was delicious Pound cake, weighed exactly and baked by rule: the Black Fruit cake with just so many pounds to the Loaf, and only enough flour to hold the fruit and spices together." Working at the cake and pie table "was considered a real honor...quite a responsibility to put the long knife thru the snowy white Icing and cut, without crumbling the Frosting."

Knapp recounted the scene in the temporary kitchen: "Dishes clattering; Aunt Seneth's strident voice rising above all noise: 'here dont take them plates—aint rinsed yet—Julie, hand me a dry towel. Here Ed, open that winder so I can throw this mess overboard,' for that end of the shop extended over the water." The amount of cooking, baking, and ice-cream making that an event like this represented is impressive, and the on-site effort from men and women of the church is exhausting to contemplate. But the same spirit of work-as-fun seen with clambakes seems to have prevailed here, making all the work and fuss a game and a social occasion.[34]

Substantial Fare for Gentlemen and Dainties for the Ladies

Events like ship launchings and the dedication of the soldiers' monument were open to women but were essentially celebrations of men's work. Cooks for these celebrations would prepare the substantial fare men expected: meat, bread, cheese, crackers, pastry, and cakes, and, for those who did not object to spirits, liquor punches, wines, and cider or beer. Women, of course, ate the same fare, but when an event took a more feminine turn other dishes showed up on the menu: lighter items such as salads, jellies, ices, ice cream, dainty sandwiches, and cake, and for beverages—especially under the influence of the temperance movement—tea or lemonade. Cake and ice cream was just right for apron sales. When the company was mixed, as it was at weddings, at the life-saving station parties, and in similar gatherings, so was the menu: some dainty food for the ladies and cold meat for the men. A hot supper in winter, however, called for oyster stew or pork and beans. And a strawberry or ice cream festival made dessert in warm weather.

The Recipes

The following recipes are especially replete with cake and ice cream in honor of the many cakes baked and the gallons of ice cream churned by New England women to support their favorite causes. The substantial fare preferred by men can be found elsewhere in this cookbook: roast turkey, boiled ham, oyster stews, and the like.

DELICATE CAKE

Delicate Cake
2 cups Sugar.
1/2 cup Butter.
Whites of six Eggs
3/4 cup Sweet Milk
Nearly three cups Flour.
1 teaspoonful Cream of Tartar.
1/2 " Soda.

Lemon Flavor.

From the manuscript recipe notebook of Fannie Card, 1879

"Delicate cake" is one of a handful of cake recipes that appear often in manuscript sources from southern New England in the last quarter of the nineteenth century. This recipe is a typical delicate cake; the recipes differ mainly in the number of egg whites and the amount of butter used. This recipe is identical to the one for delicate cake that appears in *Hood's Cook Book #1*, published about the same date Fannie Card commenced her receipt book. *Hood's* provides us with a frosting recipe that follows.

Delicate cake is moist, rises nicely, and makes a good white layer cake. If you like to experiment, or happen to have more egg whites than the recipe calls for, go ahead and add them. You may substitute two teaspoons of baking powder for the cream of tartar and soda.

Here is an interpretation of a delicate cake recipe:

3 cups flour
1 teaspoon cream of tartar
1/2 teaspoon baking soda
2 cups sugar
1/2 cup butter
3/4 cup milk
6 egg whites
rind of one lemon
Preheat oven to 350°

1. Grease two round 8-inch cake pans 1 1/2-inches deep, and line with waxed paper.
2. Sift together dry ingredients.
3. Cream together butter and sugar till fluffy.
4. In separate bowl, beat egg whites till stiff peaks form.
5. Adding them alternately, mix the dry ingredients and milk into the butter and sugar. Beat well.
6. Fold in the egg whites, and blend well. Pour into the greased cake pans, and bake at 350° for 30 minutes, or until a toothpick inserted comes out clean.
7. Cool inverted on a rack and then remove from the pans.

Yields two 8-inch-diameter cakes.

FROSTING

Use the white of one egg for frosting with one cup sugar, 2 tablespoonfuls cold water put the sugar and water on stove and let boil a minute, have the whites all beaten and pour the sugar in while hot, beat all together a few minutes then pour on the cake.

From the manuscript recipe notebook of Fannie Card, 1879

This is a typical nineteenth-century frosting recipe. It makes enough for two layers, and is better-tasting if you add lemon or vanilla extract. It immediately follows one of Fannie Card's gold cake recipes, but would be suitable for almost any other cake recipe in this book. A word of caution, however; nineteenth-century icings are often very disappointing to twentieth-century people. They are, to our taste, hard and flavorless. If you are interested in historical authenticity you will be using the old recipes; if you wish to make one of the cakes merely for pleasure, you may prefer one of your favorite modern frosting recipes.

The recipe is clear enough that an interpretation is not needed. Use superfine granulated sugar—or you can whirl regular granulated sugar in a blender at a high speed to make it finer.

GOLD CAKE AND SILVER CAKE

Gold Cake
The yolks of 8 eggs, 1 cup sugar, 2/3 cup butter,
2 cups flour, 1/2 cup milk, 1 teaspoon cream of tartar
1/2 teaspoon soda

Silver Cake
2 cups sugar, 2 1/2 cups flour, 1/2 cup butter, 3/4 cup milk,
white of 8 eggs, 1 teaspoon cream of tartar, 1/2 soda

From the manuscript recipe notebook of Julia Gates, 1857-1930

Gold and Silver cakes are complementary: the yolks get used in one and the whites in the other. They are often written into manuscript books one after the other, or appear written together in one recipe in cookbooks.

Mrs. Winslow's recipe in *Mrs.Winslow's Domestic Receipt Book for 1871* gives a hint of the mixing technique when she says to mix the flour and cream of tartar together and dissolve the baking soda in the milk. She also suggests to "season the silver cake with peach and the gold with lemon."[35]

Miss Parloa suggests white frosting with gold cake. You could use the frosting recipe from Fannie Card. Miss Parloa also suggests that silver cake be baked in sheet pans—"have the batter in sheets and about two inches deep." And she recommends a chocolate frosting for it.[36]

Here is an interpretation of the recipes.

GOLD CAKE

2 cups flour
1 teaspoon cream of tartar
1 cup sugar
2/3 cup butter
8 egg yolks
1/2 cup milk
1/2 teaspoon baking soda
1 teaspoon lemon extract
Preheat oven to 350°

1. Sift together flour and cream of tartar.
2. Cream together butter and sugar. Beat egg yolks till lemony and beat into the butter and sugar. Add extract.
3. Dissolve the baking soda in the milk, and add it and the dry ingredients alternately to the mixture.
4. Pour into two greased 8-inch pans, and bake for 25 minutes, or until a toothpick inserted comes out clean.
5. Cool and remove from pans.

Yields two 8-inch-diameter cakes.

SILVER CAKE

2 1/2 cups flour
1 teaspoon cream of tartar
2 cups sugar
1/2 cup butter
3/4 cup milk
1/2 teaspoon baking soda
8 egg whites
Preheat oven to 350°

1. Sift together dry ingredients. Cream together butter and sugar.
2. In a separate bowl, beat the whites till they form stiff peaks.
3. Mix together milk and baking soda, add alternately with the dry ingredients to butter and sugar mixture.
4. Fold in the whites. Pour into two greased 8-inch pans. Bake at 350° for 35 minutes, or until the top of the cake cracks slightly.
5. Cool and remove from pans.

Yields two 8-inch-diameter cakes.

PEACHES AND CREAM FROZEN

Peel and quarter the fresh peaches; mix them with sugar and cream to taste. Arrange some of the quarters of the peaches tastefully in the bottom of a basin, or charlotte mold, then fill, and freeze the mass solid, without stirring. Turn it out to serve.

From *Practical Cooking and Dinner Giving,* by Mrs. Mary F. Henderson, 1882, page 314

This is listed in Mrs. Henderson's cookbook under the heading "Ices," and is really delicious; but it is so hard when it is first turned out that it needs to be served in half-inch-thick slices so that it can thaw a bit before you try to eat it.

To fill a one-quart mold, plan on using four ripe peaches peeled and quartered, one pint of whipping cream (or one half pint each whipping and heavy cream), and two tablespoons of sugar. The recipe is clear enough that it does not require interpretation.

Yields 6-8 servings.

WEDDING CAKE

Four pounds of flour, three
pounds of Sugar, three pounds
of Butter four pounds of
currants, thirty eggs, half
a pint of molasses, one
gill of wine, one gill of
Brandy & Spice.

From the manuscript recipe notebook of Mary Miller, ca 1850-1870, in a private collection

BRIDE'S CAKE

Beat to a cream one pound of butter and one pound of fine white sugar; then add a quarter of a pound of sifted flour, and three eggs well beaten; mix this well together; then stir in another quarter of a pound of sifted flour, then three eggs well beaten; mix this well, then stir in half a gill of prime brandy, quarter of an ounce of mace, one teaspoonful of cinnamon, quarter of a pound of Muscatel raisins stoned and cut in halves, two ounces of citron, two of candied orange peel, two of candied lemon peel, all cut in slips; stir all well together, and add two eggs well beaten; mix a quarter of a pound of sifted flour with one and half pounds of Zante currants picked, washed and dried; stir the currants into the cake; mix the whole well, and bake two hours in a buttered hoop lined with double paper. If the bottom of the cake browns too fast in the oven, slip a board under it; when done, turn the cake upside down and ice it all over, according to the directions for Icing in Chap. XVIII.

TO ICE A CAKE.
Dredge that side of the cake which rested upon the tin while baking, with sifted flour, in order to remove whatever grease there may be there; then wipe off the flour carefully, put a quantity of icing in the centre, and with a broad-bladed knife spread it equally over the top and over the other sides of the cake, dipping your knife occasionally in cold water as you proceed; then put the cake in a warm oven, that the icing may harden, but not allowing it to remain in the oven long enough to discolor the icing. If you wish to ornament this icing, trail icing upon it, in whatever forms you choose, through a tin or paper tube; or adorn it with sugar plums, or other confectionary, before you harden it in the oven.

Both recipes above from *The Practical Cookbook,* by Mrs. Bliss, 1864, pages 174 and 220

Wedding cake or Bride's cake was a customary refreshment at wedding celebrations in the nineteenth century. The traditional wedding cake was a fruit cake not often seen today.

Mrs. Bliss devoted a whole chapter to "Ornaments for Cakes," providing recipes for icing and sugar trims. Most icings, as you may have noticed, are not butter frostings, but are made from varying proportions of beaten egg white and sugar. Besides icing in fancy shapes, Mrs. Bliss describes how to make colored sugar, using spinach essence, cochineal, indigo, saffron, and other sources of color. Bits of jelly could be added for decoration as well as sugar-plums, which essentially were candied fruits.

I offer this recipe for your interest, so no interpretation follows.

ORANGE CAKE

1 1/2 cups sugar
3/4 cup of butter
3 eggs
1/2 cup milk
1 teaspoon cream tartar
1/2 " soda
3 1/2 cups flour
flavor with lemon or vanilla
bake in jelly cake tins
Mixture to spread between

Beat the white of one egg to a stiff froth, then add powdered white sugar, the rind and juice of one Orange or Lemon. Beat about as thick as rich cream, spread between the cake when cold.

From the manuscript recipe notebook of Fannie Card, 1879,
courtesy of Anna North Coit, North Stongington, Connecticut

What makes this an orange cake is the orange-flavored filling, just as it is the chocolate filling that makes a chocolate cake chocolate. Fannie Card had a comparatively large selection of orange cakes in her manuscript recipe notebook. We have no way of knowing which was her favorite or who in her family liked it so well that she collected recipes for it.

In testing this cake, I found I preferred a vanilla flavoring to lemon for the cake. And I found the half-cup of milk Fannie Card suggests not nearly enough; it is necessary to double it in order to make a batter.

A word of caution about the "mixture to spread between." Made as written in the original, it is sauce-like. If you wish it more frosting-like, omit the juice and/or add confectioner's sugar to get the consistency you desire. I recommend omitting the juice. An adaptation follows.

3 1/2 cups flour
1 teaspoon cream of tartar
1/2 teaspoon baking soda
3/4 cup butter
1 1/2 cups sugar
3 eggs, separated
1 teaspoon vanilla or lemon extract
1 cup milk
Preheat oven to 350°

1. Sift together dry ingredients.
2. Cream together butter and sugar. Beat the egg yolks, and beat into the butter and sugar with the extract.
3. Beat the egg whites till stiff and set aside.
4. Alternately add the dry ingredients and the milk to the sugar and butter mixture and beat till smooth.
5. Fold the beaten egg whites into the batter. Pour into two greased and floured 8-inch pans (or three smaller-diameter jelly pans). Bake for 30-35 minutes or until a toothpick inserted comes out clean.
6. Set on racks to cool; turn out, and make the filling.

Filling
1 egg white
grated rind of one orange
(juice of half an orange)
1 1/2 cups confectioners sugar

1. Beat the egg white till very stiff, adding the sugar gradually.
2. Continue beating and add the grated orange rind (and the juice). Add more sugar to get a consistency firm enough to spread.
3. Spread over the layers of the cake. Garnish if you like with orange zest.

Yields two 8-inch-diameter layer cakes.

STRAWBERRY SHORTCAKE

330. STRAWBERRY SHORTCAKE.—
Into three pints of flour rub dry two heaping teaspoonfuls of cream of tartar, add one half cup of butter, a little salt, one teaspoonful of soda dissolved in a pint of milk and water, mix thoroughly and quickly, roll to an inch in thickness, and bake twenty minutes in a quick oven. When done divide it and cover with strawberries and sugar, to be eaten while warm.

From *The Handy Home Book,* by William M. Cornell, M.D., 1875, page 97

This strawberry shortcake is the biscuit type. Three pints of flour is six cups, so this recipe would make a large cake, several of which would be suitable for a church social. Today we usually sweeten our biscuit, but it seems that years ago the way to sweeten shortcake was to sprinkle sugar on with the strawberries. There is no mention of cream in this recipe, perhaps an oversight.

Dr. Cornell's instruction to dissolve the baking soda in "milk and water" does not specify the proportion of one to the other. In the adaptation which follows, I have called for all milk, and I have divided the recipe in thirds to produce a family-sized shortcake.

2 cups flour
3/4 teaspoon cream of tartar
1/2 teaspoon salt
1 1/3 tablespoon butter
1/2 teaspoon baking soda
2/3 cup milk
Preheat oven to 400°

1. Sift together dry ingredients.
2. Cut in butter.
3. Dissolve baking soda in the milk, and add to the mixture above, mixing thoroughly and quickly.
4. Roll or pat out to an inch thick and bake on a greased sheet for 20 minutes.
5. When baked, divide it and cover with strawberries and sugar to taste. Eat warm.

Yields 6-8 servings.

STRAWBERRY SHORTCAKE WITH CREAM

1 cup of powdered sugar, creamed with one tablespoonful of butter
3 eggs
1 cup of prepared flour, heaping.
2 tablespoonfuls of cream.

Beat the yolks into the creamed butter and sugar; the cream, then the whites, alternately with the flour. Bake in three jelly-cake tins. When cold, lay between the cakes nearly a quart of fresh, ripe strawberries. Sprinkle each layer with powdered sugar, and sift the same whitely over the top. Eat fresh with cream poured upon each slice.

From *The Dinner Year Book*, by Marion Harland, 1878, page 342

This sponge-cake type of shortcake, which tastes like lady-fingers, is one of two in Mrs. Harland's *Dinner Year Book*; her other is a biscuit-type. Both are common today. The biggest difference between Mrs. Harland's recipe and modern strawberry shortcake lies in how the cream is served—poured over, instead of whipped.

If you have "jelly tins"—small-diameter baking tins—you may want to try making a triple-layer shortcake. The interpretation of the recipe will yield two 8-inch cakes. To make powdered sugar, put granulated sugar into a blender or food processor for a few moments at a high speed; confectioners sugar is not quite the same thing. "Prepared flour" is self-rising flour; or you may use all-purpose flour and add a teaspoon of baking powder to each cup of flour.

1 cup powdered sugar
3 eggs, separated
1 cup self-rising flour
or 1 cup flour plus 1 teaspoon baking powder
2 tablespoons cream
1 quart sliced strawberries
powdered sugar
Preheat oven to 350°

1. Cream together butter and sugar. Beat yolks and add to butter and sugar.
2. Add the flour, and cream in turn.
3. Beat the whites till stiff but not dry. Add the beaten whites, folding them in gently.
4. Divide the batter between two greased and wax-paper-lined 8-inch pans or among three 6-inch pans. Bake for 20 minutes.
5. Turn cakes out of pans and cool before using.
6. Just before serving layer in the strawberries, sprinkling on sugar to taste, ending with strawberries on the top, and pouring cream over, or serving it in a pitcher at the table for each to add to taste.

Yields 4-6 servings.

CHOCOLATE ICE CREAM

CHOCOLATE ICE CREAM
is made the same way as the vanilla ice-cream, adding a flavoring of chocolate and a little vanilla powder. For instance, to make a quart and a half of cream: Make the boiled custard with the yolks of six eggs, half a pound of sugar, one pint of boiled milk, and a tea-spoonful (not heaping) of vanilla powder. Pound smooth four ounces of chocolate; add a little sugar and one or two table-spoonfuls of hot water. Stir it over the fire until it is perfectly smooth. Add this and a tablespoonful of thin, dissolved gelatin to the hot custard. When about to set in the freezer, add one pint of cream, whipped.

From *Practical Cooking and Dinner Giving*, by Mrs. Mary F. Henderson, 1882, page 308

After vanilla-and fruit-flavored ice creams and ices, chocolate appears as a popular flavor in nineteenth-century sources. Chocolate came in several forms, including "sticks," bars, and cakes that apparently varied, as they do today, in richness and sweetness. I am not certain what Mrs. Henderson means by "pounding" the chocolate in this recipe; in other recipes, cooks are advised to "scrape" chocolate, sometimes to melt it. You can find vanilla powder in some grocery stores, but not all.

In the interpretation below, I have substituted modern forms of chocolate and vanilla, and hope we will not end up with too contemporary a version of chocolate ice cream. This recipe is a personal favorite and the one I make for birthdays and special occasions.

2 cups milk
1 cup sugar
6 egg yolks
4 ounces unsweetened chocolate (2 squares)
or a scant 2/3 cups cocoa
2 teaspoons vanilla extract
1 teaspoon gelatine dissolved in 2 tablespoons hot water
2 cups cream

1. Scald the milk in a double boiler or heavy saucepan. Remove from heat.
2. Dissolve the sugar in the milk. Beat the egg yolks and add a bit of the hot milk to them, stirring to blend, then gradually add that mixture to the rest of the scalded milk.
3. Melt the chocolate or mix the cocoa with a little hot water. Stir and keep hot until the chocolate melts; add to the custard in the double boiler.
4. Add the dissolved gelatine to the hot milk, and cook over hot water until thickened as for custard. Add the vanilla.
5. Chill. (You can keep it in the refrigerator overnight and freeze it the next day; it will make a better ice cream if you do.)
6. When you are ready to freeze the ice cream, whip the cream until it holds a soft peak and fold it into the chilled custard. Pour into the freezer.
5. Churn, following the instructions for using your freezer, until the ice cream is frozen. Eat immediately or repack to freeze harder to eat later.

Yields one half-gallon.

From Sea to Table

Mystic Seaport Museum's watercraft collection is dominated by boats used in fishing. Many of the shoreside trades and businesses were dependent in the nineteenth century upon the fishing industry. Most early seafarers were fishermen. Today, with few New Englanders moving goods or passengers on deep water, fishing employs what few Yankee seafarers are left. The region's food identity is with fish and shellfish.

In the course of researching this book, I expected to find New Englanders relishing fish, and eating it more often than inlanders who did not have access to fresh seafood. I could not have been more surprised to discover the lack of interest in fish-eating among New Englanders; the evidence indicates that they were about as inclined to eat fish as inlanders were in the nineteenth century. Given other food choices, notably meat, they were likely to be content to eat fish once a week or so as a main dish, with smaller portions occasionally for breakfast or supper.

The closer I looked at the historic record the more I realized that New England's fishing industry, until fairly recent times, spent energy and effort trying, not always successfully, to overcome often-justified public prejudice against fish-eating. "Not as Nutritious as Flesh" explores the public's complaints against fish and the responses of the fishing industry.

When people did eat fish, how they chose to cook it depended largely on whether the fish were large or small, oily or white-fleshed. Fish-as-food histories of the most favored fish are found in "Cooking and Eating Seafood."

Not as Nutritious as Flesh: Fish-Eating in New England

Seafood and fishermen are terribly important to New England's identity and self-image. The region is famous for fresh fish and lobsters, clambakes, the sacred cod. Our maritime past is evoked with images of fishing vessels, the famous Gloucester fisherman at the wheel, and grizzled old characters with sou'westers on their heads and pipes in their teeth. Mainers, some of whom can't afford to eat them, drive around with the image of a boiled lobster on their car license plates.[1]

Fishermen are shown mending nets at Monhegan, Maine, a scene many New Englanders believe typifies their region. Opposite, raw oysters presented on a decorative oyster plate. [Photograph, Hudson Collection, MSM 78.228.19]

A nineteenth-century garnishing suggestion for salmon—or any other fish or shellfish salad—recipe on page 361.

For all of that, New Englanders, like many other North Americans, resisted eating fish for most of the region's history. That resistance, left from earlier times, had to be overcome before fish was more widely accepted. Fish had "problems" that needed to be solved before it became a more acceptable food.[2]

Consider the implications of the word "fishy" compared to the word "beefy." When we want to improve something we "beef it up," when we feel suspicious we think a thing is "fishy." Fish suffered from what modern people consider bad public relations—some of it deserved but most of it a matter of habit and prejudice. When people do not wish to eat a certain food, almost any set of rationalizations can be devised to excuse it. Usually, as anthropologists note, the rationalizations proceed from other issues in a culture—for example, religion or group identity—and these determine what is good or appropriate food.[3] Rationalizations or not, certain objections limited the consumption of fish in New England for 250 years.

Fish were simply not considered as substantial a food as meat. In fact, fish *is* a lighter food, especially the whiter, less oily species. When people ate fish they did not feel as satiated as they did after a meal of beef or pork.

Perishability, delicate flesh, and small bones made fish a difficult food to select, store, cook, and eat. Unless consumers were very certain of the fish supply, and knew how to judge freshness, they might end up with a tainted product. The texture of fish flesh made it difficult to handle in the kitchen. Cooked fresh fish was tender and fell apart easily. Whole fish required special poaching apparatus or had to be wrapped in cloth. Any fish less prone to these difficulties won favor: salmon, sturgeon, swordfish, and halibut, for example, were easier to work with than haddock, cod, or flounder. At table, all but the firmest-fleshed fish fell apart while, before forks were commonly used, a piece of meat stuck by a knife obligingly remained solid; forks made fish-eating easier, more graceful. But the diner still had to eat fish carefully in order to avoid the bones, sometimes even had to remove small bones from the mouth, a socially awkward activity.

For Northern Europeans and their New England descendants, fish-eating was associated with poverty and Roman Catholicism. Fish were undomesticated at a time when wild food was not preferred fare. Fish was eaten and produced by people with whom many nineteenth-century Yankees did not wish to identify.

These problems with, and objections to, fish were of less concern so long as New Englanders caught fish mostly for trade, eating relatively little of it themselves; but when fish-catching methods increased market supplies beyond the demands of distant markets it became imperative to overcome the objections and make fish a desirable food product. Convincing the public to eat fish is a case study in marketing as well as industry ingenuity in food production.

Between Meat and Vegetables

Seafood's place in the nineteenth-century dietary scheme depended on three linked ideas: nutrition, digestibility, and palatability—separate ideas that sometimes became confused with one another. To be accepted in the common diet, fish had to prove itself on all three counts.

"As a food fish ranks between meat on the one hand

and vegetables on the other. It is not so nutritious as the former...and it is thought that a diet in which fish predominates produces deficient vitality," said the author of *Goodholme's Domestic Cyclopedia* in 1885. Goodholme even cited a doctor for proof: " 'It is not desirable,' says Dr. Edward Smith, 'that fish should be the sole kind of animal food eaten by any nation; and even if milk and eggs be added thereto, the vigor of such people will not be equal to that of flesh-eating nations.' "[4]

That fish was not up to the nutritional standards of meat had been conventional wisdom for many centuries: early Christians had eaten fish when they fasted, and during the early medieval period monks ate fish in perpetual abstinence from animal flesh. Meat-eating was considered pleasurable and liable to promote carnality, and these ideas survived, with slight alteration, into the nineteenth century. On meatless days and during Lent, only the sick among religious orders or the general population were allowed meat.[5]

The pleasure in meat-eating was contrasted with the *lack* of pleasure associated with eating fish. Most species of fish were considered boring or even unpalatable. To compensate, fish was prepared with rich sauces that many people found indigestible.

The digestibility of foods, understood generally for many centuries, became an important issue for doctors and diet reformers after young Alexis St. Martin received a gunshot wound in the abdomen in 1822. The wound healed to leave an orifice to the youth's stomach through which an American army surgeon named Beaumont watched St. Martin's digestive

A fishmonger in New York's Fulton Market is shown hauling off his product. A large finfish like the one on his shoulder would be hard to find in the late twentieth century. [James E. Kelly drawing from *Scribner's Monthly*, 1877]

processes. By feeding the young man many different foods, Beaumont determined the rates of digestion and absorption and published his observations. During the nineteenth century, food writers, including Catherine Beecher and Harriet Beecher Stowe, referred to St. Martin when discussing the "digestibility" of foods.[6] The new awareness of digestibility meant that certain fish would be described as more or less digestible than other fish or meat.

For example, Sarah Josepha Hale, editor of the popular *Godey's Lady's Book*, and author of several cookbooks and household manuals, observed in 1839 that fish was easier to digest than flesh—except for salmon, which she believed should be given only sparingly to children. "It would be better for the health of those who do not labor, if they would use more fish and less flesh for food. But then fish cannot be rendered so palatable because it does not admit the variety of cooking and flavors that other animal food does." She added, "Fish is less nutritious than flesh," declaring that the white-fleshed fish like cod, haddock, flounder, and white fish were the least nutritious and more difficult to digest.[7]

Americans in the nineteenth century generally believed that fish was good food for people who wished to be economical, keep their weight down, were of nervous disposition, or who did "brain work." In the 1847 British *Encyclopedia of Domestic Economy*, Thomas Webster wrote: "Although in London fish is highly esteemed and considered rather as a luxury, yet in all countries where it is plentiful and cheap, it is reckoned somewhat inferior in its nutritive powers to what is called butcher's meat. This is *so well known* [emphasis added] that the jockeys who ride at Newmarket, and who wish to weigh as little as possible, are never allowed to eat meat if fish can be obtained."[8]

By the early twentieth century, medical experts and cookbook writers had begun to change their ideas on the comparative nutritive value of fish and meat. "Commonly we discriminate in our ideas of animal products, among fish, fowl, and flesh. From a nutritional point of view, there is, however, little difference between them." wrote Dr. Harvey W. Wiley in *The Pure Food Cookbook* in 1914. But even Dr. Wiley thought fish was boring: "Fish as a continued diet would soon pall upon every appetite. It, therefore, should not be used at every dinner," lest the cook overstep the bounds of "gustatory propriety"—a caution seldom or ever applied to beef.[9]

Fish seems to have been perceived for centuries as insubstantial food, a problem solved by sauces, cooking it in

Shown is a fish dealer's wharf at Newport, Rhode Island, in the 1890s where market fishermen, unloading great quantities of fish and gutting and processing them, created a "fishy" smell along once low-value waterfronts. This would now be unacceptable in these places that have become prime real-estate, crowded now with restaurants, bars, art galleries, yachting toggeries, and boutiques of all kinds. [Edward W. Smith Collection, MSM 69.822.105]

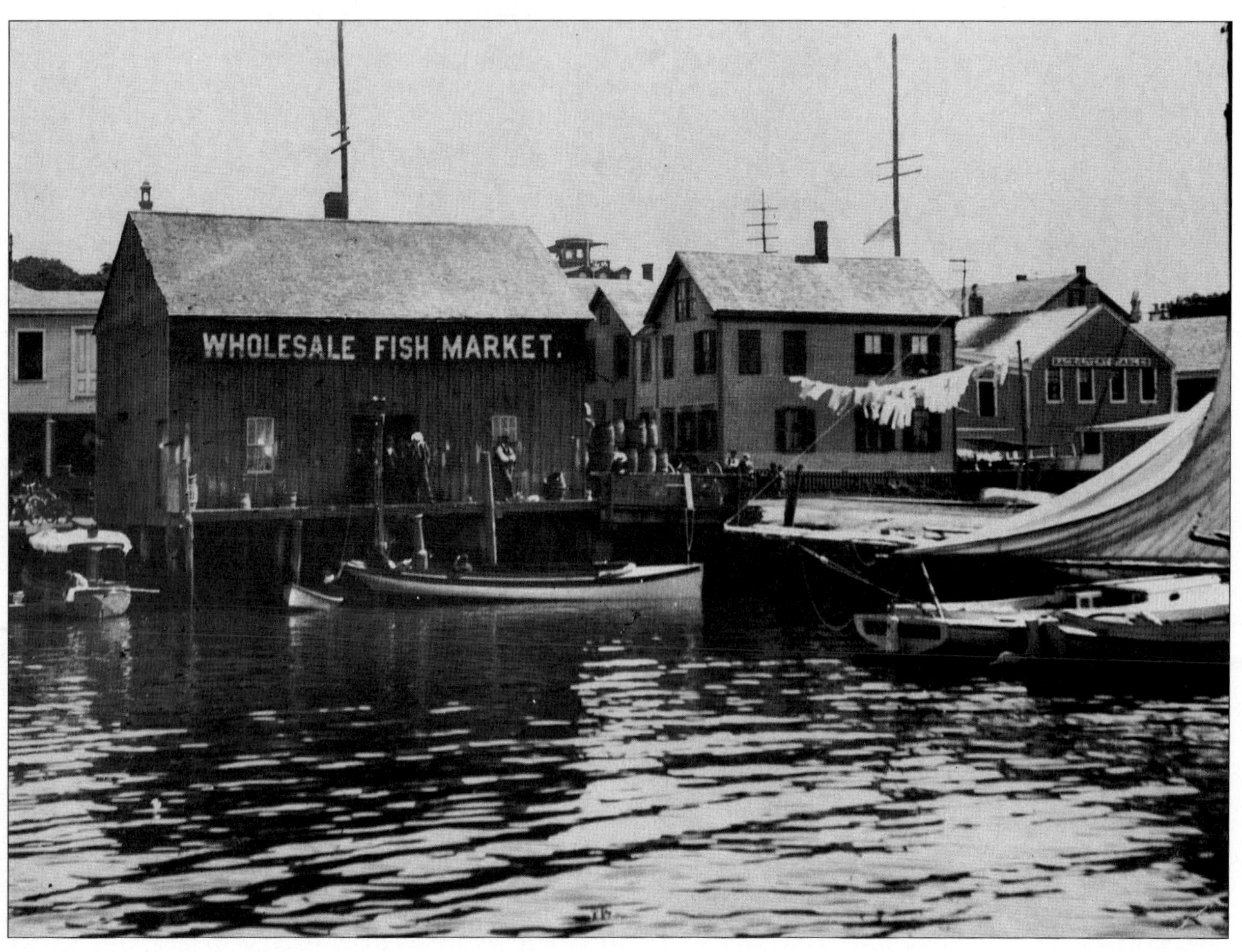

meat fat, or confining fish to one of several courses at the table. Ironically many nineteenth-century New Englanders preferred bland, white fish at the same time they desired flavor.[10] They considered the richer, more flavorful fish as cloying rather than satisfying. For this reason, Maria Parloa, in her 1894 *Young Housekeeper*, recommended lighter fish because one could serve it frequently without tiring of it. "For example," she wrote, "at the Isles of Shoals, visitors are offered broiled scrod every day in the week, yet they do not weary of the dish in a stay of months. At Nantucket broiled bluefish is served daily, and it is so delicious that its appearance three times a day would be hailed with pleasure; but after a short time the appetite would become palled." The same thing, she said, would be true of salmon and mackerel.[11]

Saucing fish was an old gambit. Backsliding monks in medieval days were weaned away from meat "by exquisitely prepared dishes of fish." Much medieval food, including fish, was richly spiced, especially for the wealthy, and the practice of serving a rich or intensely flavored sauce with fish has continued into our time. While the conventional preparation for meat was merely to roast and serve it with its own gravy, fish was not thought palatable without a complex sauce. "There seems to be no reason why stewing [fish] should be objectionable, except that it is usually accompanied by numerous additions which render it indigestible, for instance, port wine," commented *Goodholme's Domestic Cyclopedia* in 1885. "The various sauces commonly eaten with fish are probably the cause of most of the complaints made against this food." Still, the major way to vary fish was to sauce it, and a book printed in 1892 entitled *One Hundred Ways of Cooking Fish* actually contained about as many recipes for sauce as different fish and ways to cook them.[12]

New Englanders, however, had unsophisticated palates and were diffident about or even distrustful of fancy sauces. In most middle-class homes, particularly if the homemaker did her own cooking, fish—fresh and salted—was most often sauced with either cream or melted butter, thickened with flour or mashed boiled egg, and perhaps a little parsley or lemon; or with salt-pork fat and scraps. These sauces added both flavor and animal fats to fish dishes, making them seem more substantial. Most of the ways New Englanders cooked fish in the 1800s seem designed to make fish land more solidly in the stomach. Small fish were rolled in crumbs or Indian meal and fried in salt-pork fat. Fish were broiled with butter melted over them. Large whole fish were stuffed and poached—the common term was boiled—and served with one of the butter- or cream-based sauces. Leftovers were mixed with potatoes to make fish hash, cakes, or balls, then fried in lard or drippings. After being picked over to remove skin and bones, leftovers might also be warmed up in cream or milk gravy and served on toast or potatoes. Fish chowder was a very substantial meal with its salt-pork-fat base, potatoes and/or crackers, and fish simmered together.[13]

Although cookbooks were intended to broaden the public's exposure to food, they appear to have recorded the commonplace, and the more elaborate fish recipes sound strained and improbable. It was one thing for professional cooks and caterers to make elegant fish dishes that people enjoyed in hotels and restaurants; it was quite another for a housewife or untrained kitchen help to do it at home. When manufacturers produced ready-made seafood, they followed the lead of the home kitchen. The earliest products replicated the most popular dishes or, as we will see, took much of the work out of making favorite home-kitchen recipes.

The Freshness Problem

The most intimidating thing about consuming fish was knowing how to discern freshness. Fish and shellfish spoiled more quickly and dangerously than other animal food. The freshness problem had three traditional solutions: selling fish alive, selling fish promptly, and preserving fish by a number of methods. A consumer made a live purchase by selecting a fish from a tank of living fish; otherwise the customer selected from an array of recently caught dead and gutted fish, and was responsible for consuming it as quickly as possible. The customer could also purchase preserved fish or choose to buy fresh fish to preserve domestically.

The freshness problem was less acute when salt cod and salt mackerel were the prevalent New England fisheries—they were salted aboard the fishing vessels nearly as soon as they were caught; properly done, salted fish lasted a long time. Most early-nineteenth-century New Englanders (in fact, most North Americans), along the coast and in the hinterlands, were more likely to eat salt cod or salt mackerel than fresh fish.

But among the fresh-fish choices were a handful of favorites: cod, salmon, mackerel, haddock, and seasonally available fish like alewives, shad, and eels, some of which were reserved for fresh eating before the rest of the catch was salted or smoked. Among shellfish, the oyster and lobster were favorites. Inland, trout and similar local freshwater fish were eaten fresh. Sport fishing for bass or bluefish alongshore yielded fresh fish for family use. The market fisheries, which specialized in bringing fresh fish to market as quickly as possible, were the primary sources for port towns and cities. When stocks of fish were depleted alongshore, fishermen ventured farther off to catch adequate numbers; the longer the trip, the more difficult it was to keep the fish fresh.[14]

The story of market fish in the nineteenth century is dominated by efforts to solve the "freshness problem." Solutions to the freshness problem influenced fishing-vessel design, fishing technology, fish distribution, and the kinds of products made from fish. But customers lacked confidence in some of the solutions and raised new objections which fish producers had to meet and resolve.

Live Sale

How do you deliver live fish to the consumer? Fishermen tried two methods: impounding them near the marketplace, and keeping them alive in tanks or wells aboard their fishing vessels.

Impounding: For centuries, the gentry kept freshwater fish in ponds built specifically for storing them, or stocked mill ponds with favored types. Saltwater fish could be impounded in tidal ponds or in submerged wooden "cars." The successors to these efforts are the lobster pounds that can be found in many New England coastal towns today.[15]

Fish and shellfish could even be fattened to make them more marketable as they waited in captivity. Around 1900, Howard Burdick's father and uncle in Avondale, Rhode Island, built a stone-walled fish pond with an iron gate in the Pawcatuck River, and into it they threw the smaller striped bass they caught while seining in the river and in Little Narragansett Bay. They fed the little stripers with ground-up menhaden until they grew to a marketable size, then the Burdicks took them to New York. Burdick reported that the little fish doubled in size between May and November, and the effort "considerably increased the Fulton Market wholesale price, so it made all that extra work worthwhile."[16]

Well smacks: As early as the sixteenth century, Dutch fishermen had been building vessels with a "wet well"—a watertight compartment in the hold with holes bored through the bottom to allow seawater to enter—in order to bring their catch to market alive. In seventeenth-century England, as salt fish became less favored, and the market for fresh improved, some fishermen copied the Dutch method and established an English fleet of well smacks. In America, well smacks were first used in Long Island Sound, probably for the New York market. New Englanders used similar vessels to transport fish and lobsters to Boston and New York. Describing New York City fish markets in the 1740s, Peter Kalm noted that lobsters were "brought continually in great well boats from New England, where they were

"Here you are, nice fresh fish," is the caption on this magazine illustration of a fish vendor in the Bowery, New York City, in 1871. Rich and poor alike ate fish, but as a low-value food compared with meat, the urban poor ate much more of it than the urban rich. [*Scribner's Monthly*, December 1870]

An ideal way to serve salt cod for breakfast or supper. Recipe on page 359.

plentiful."[17] Southern New England smacksmen began conveying lobsters from the Maine coast to Boston in the 1820s and 1830s, and changed lobstering from a hunting and gathering activity for local subsistence into a business.

But fish wells were not the perfect solution to keeping fish alive. The sudden change in water pressure, the jostling in the well, and the depletion of oxygen in the water in the well all contributed to mortality before a catch reached market. Nor did all fish travel satisfactorily in wet wells. Cod, haddock, and halibut survived in wells, but cod and ling caught in deep water reportedly did not. Cod sounds (swim bladders) had to be punctured so that the fish did not float up in the well and perish.[18]

Well smacks—schooners, pinkies, and sloops—were used for both fishing and transporting. In the 1820s, New London smacks introduced the live well to the halibut fishery on Georges Bank.[19] Use of well smacks allowed the extension of halibut fishing from winter into the warmer months.

The Noank vessel *Emma C. Berry*, on exhibit at Mystic Seaport Museum, is an example of a well smack. Built in 1866, the *Berry* was probably involved, as other Noank smacks were, in mackerel, cod, and lobster fisheries; at least some of the time she was worked as a fish carrier rather than a fisherman, and when she was sold to Maine she worked there as a lobster well smack.[20]

Well smacks brought their cargoes into the city markets, where they were sometimes transferred from the wells into cars for live storage. The Fulton Fish Market in New York backed up to a slip chock full of fish cars, so close together that they formed a kind of floating pavement, outboard of which the vessels tied up. Fishmongers obtained fish live from the cars, killing and dressing them to order. Some references to "live fish" may not be literally true: in England in the late nineteenth and early twentieth centuries freshly killed fish were sometimes called "live" in order to distinguish them from salted or longer-preserved fresh fish.[21]

Prompt Sale

How do you get a "fresh" fish? It was one thing to catch a fish yourself or select it from a batch of live ones; it was another to buy from a fishmonger. Virtually all cookbooks printed and available to North Americans in the nineteenth century instructed housewives to determine freshness of fish by the appearance of the gills, the plumpness of the flesh, and the brightness of the eyes. Along with the advice came warnings: Amelia Simmons, in 1796, wrote concerning saltwater fish that "deceits are used to give them a freshness of appearance, such as peppering the gills, wetting the fins and tails, and even painting the gills, or wetting with animal blood...if they are soft, it's certain they are stale, but if deceits are used, your smell must approve or denounce them, and be the safest guide."[22]

During the nineteenth century people became increasingly aware of sanitation. Even before the germ theory of disease was accepted in the last part of the century, consumers understood that spoiled fish could be dangerous. As fish catches increased and were more widely distributed, the freshness issue came into higher relief. Cookbook and household manual writers cautioned buyers, and the fishing industry responded with assurances. Consumers were meanwhile uncertain and often willing to forego fish entirely.

In her 1852 *New Cook Book,* Sarah Josepha Hale wrote, "The cook should be well acquainted with the signs of freshness and good condition in fish, as many of them are most unwholesome articles of food when stale or out of season." Maria Parloa's advice to young housekeepers living inland in 1894 was to select fish peculiar to the locality, "which should have precedence over other kinds; for the first thing to be taken into account is freshness."[23]

The Bay State Fishing Company's packaging of Forty Fathom Fish solved two fish "problems." Their very fresh boneless brand-name fillets assured customers of a trustworthy product. [Photo courtesy of The Baker Library, Harvard University]

Living near the source: For fish quality and freshness nothing beat living near the source. As Sarah Josepha Hale observed, "Herrings, mackerel, and whiting lose their freshness so rapidly, that unless newly caught they are quite uneatable." Miss Parloa recommended that fresh fish be frequently substituted for meat because it was so economical a food and that "seaboard towns offer greater variety." Dr. Harvey W. Wiley reiterated that point in the *Pure Food Cookbook* in 1914: "Those who live near the source of supply can well afford economically and dietetically to increase the rations of fish." Then he cautioned that "Fish when fresh should be distinctly fresh and when cured should be well cured. The intermediate conditions are dangerous."[24]

Even some fish producers played on the public's fear of tainted fish. In a 1907 advertisement recipe book, Frank E. Davis listed reasons for buying his canned and salted fish products, one of which explained "Why it is dangerous to eat inland fish dealer's fish." Davis wrote that "The fish you see in a dealer's store has probably been dead some time, exposed to the air, to germs, to flies, and other contaminating influences," including dirty hands. He asserted that "fish, more quickly than anything else, transmits poison into your system if it is in any way tainted." He claimed that in cases of ptomaine poisoning fish had more often been implicated than any other food. This was hardly reassuring to an already dubious public. Davis obviously expected *his* customers to trust him and his product. Later, as a selling point, he circulated a picture of his plant, which he described as "a large, modern, cement structure where the most sanitary methods are employed."[25]

Buying fish on Friday: The freshness problem limited the market for fresh fish. A cook in the early 1800s bought fresh fish whenever a market fisherman had some to offer. Fishermen bringing fish to larger port cities and towns were assured of selling their catch and customers usually could find fish when they wanted it. Large cities like Boston and New York had market places designated for fish. Sarah Anna Emery, near Newburyport, Massachusetts, described the alternative for smaller ports: "No fish market had been established. Fresh fish was vended about the streets in wheelbarrows."[26] Peddlers might carry fish further inland, where it became less and less fresh.

The situation improved some, particularly inland, when larger populations of Catholic immigrants moved to New England's port cities and industrial centers. The demand for Friday fish did not quite create an-end-of-week market, but it certainly shifted the emphasis on fish to Friday. Protestant New Englanders, who had switched their fish consumption to a different day a century or more earlier, found that if they wanted fresh fish they were better off buying it on Fridays. Although they hesitated to adopt Catholic practice, those who desired fresh fish switched back to eating fish on Friday.

Many cookbooks and household manuals declared that fish was very economical food, yet fresh fish was perceived as expensive. For example, in response to a question about the high price of fresh fish, Thomas A. Rich of Boston explained in testimony to the Senate Committee on Foreign Relations in 1885: "The retail fish business is peculiar; in fact, it is all retail to the consumer for the reason that it [fish] is largely used only on certain days. That practice has come to us from Europe. With all Catholics over here Friday is fish-day, and there is always some kind of fish on the table;...For that reason, as a general thing, fish do not enter into daily consumption as many other kinds of food do." Because retailers could sell most of their fish on only a few days a week, Rich explained, the price tended to be high on those days, which made fish more expensive than other sorts of foods.[27]

By the late 1800s, and for the first few decades of the 1900s, fresh fish was transported inland by rail and distributed even to rural New England towns by Friday fish peddlers going door to door. The pattern of Friday fish sales held well into the twentieth century, with a study of New York City markets in 1939 showing that more than 75 percent of the fish sold in any week was sold on Thursday and Friday. Because the biggest sales were consistently on Friday, the author concluded, "Friday is the only fish day firmly ingrained in the minds of the

American consuming public."[28]

Young women in turn-of-the-century Gloucester are shown wrapping salt fish. The product name, "Mother of Pearl," delivered the desired image of a white, smooth product. [Lightfoot Collection, MSM 90.55.22]

Railroads and refrigeration: Railroads and refrigeration are often credited with the growth of meat-producing cities like Chicago and Omaha, allowing their fresh products to be distributed widely before they spoiled. These same systems enabled New England fishing ports to move fish to inland markets. As early as 1837, live fish brought to Boston in well smacks were shipped inland by rail, and in 1846 Gloucester was linked to Boston by rail. Railroads carried the first fish—halibut—packed in ice and shipped from Boston to New York. Boston's access to rail, in addition to effort and capital invested in cold storage, made the Hub the country's fresh-fish center in the last decade of the nineteenth century and the first three of the twentieth.[29]

Gloucester, which had dedicated itself to salted fish products and fresh halibut, competed for a while with Boston in the market for fresh fish. But Gloucester ultimately turned to value-added fish-food products, relying upon the railroad to back up direct-marketing efforts. Companies like Frank E. Davis, Crown Packing Company, and others shipped preserved-fish products directly to customers via the railroad and postal service. They often pointed out in their advertising that their products could reach consumers anywhere in the country in a matter of days: Gloucester to Buffalo, one day; Cincinnati, Chicago, Cleveland, Washington, Philadelphia, Detroit, two days; Kansas City, Milwaukee, and St. Paul, three days.[30]

Small ports benefitted from railroad connections, too. Edward Knapp noted that when the railroad came through Noank in 1858 the smack-fishermen were able to load their

A classic boiled salt-cod dinner garnished with salt pork scrunchions and boiled egg. Instructions on pages 358-359.

catch on a train that arrived in New York a few hours later, saving them a tedious trip under sail down Long Island Sound. In a hybrid of live sale and refrigeration, lobsters were, by the end of the nineteenth century, packed live in barrels with ice and seaweed. Similarly, oysters were shipped in boxes surrounded by ice in five-gallon cans, or in five- or ten-gallon wooden tubs.[31]

Fast vessels: It is well known that the first fishing vessel back to port with a catch received the highest price for it. One reason fishermen got a better price for a catch, especially of iced fish for fresh consumption, was because it satisfied the desire for the freshest possible product. The search for speed under sail while carrying fresh fish coincided with the development of other fast sailing vessels, like the clipper ships, in trades that valued speed more than carrying capacity.

In the New England fisheries, the original oceangoing vessels were small but full-hulled schooner-rigged craft well suited for carrying large loads safely at a slow pace. With the increased need to bring fresh fish from afar, the so-called sharpshooter model was developed around 1850. A shallow, wide hull and sharp wedge-shaped bow made the sharpshooter a much faster fishing vessel. The sharpshooter gave way to a more extreme model called the clipper schooner in the late 1850s. Clippers were larger, with bigger rigs but relatively less depth, making them unstable and downright dangerous in stormy weather. Yet their speed offset their hazards for more than two decades despite the loss of many vessels and hundreds of fishermen.[32]

A deeper, more stable—yet still fast—model began to emerge in the 1880s with encouragement from the Fish Commission, a government agency entrusted with the study and propagation of "American" fish species and the enhancement of the American fishing industry. A Boston fish dealer, Thomas F. McManus, designed the majority of the last New England sailing fishing schooners. McManus designs combined a graceful form with speed, seaworthiness, and capacity, allowing fishermen to speed their catch to market in almost any weather.[33]

Vessel design both reflected the desire for fresh fish, and, by supplying it, created pressure for increased markets to absorb all the fish caught and delivered. This ratcheting up of supply and demand became more pronounced when auxiliary power and the otter-trawl method of fishing were introduced in New England around 1900. Even though immigrant populations who traditionally ate more fish were growing, and meat rationing in World War One increased fresh-fish consumption substantially, coping with the tons of fresh fish caught by steam-powered trawlers in the nineteen teens continued to pose marketing challenges to the industry.

Iced Fish

The preference for fresh fish grew tremendously at the close of Protestant rule in Great Britain in the seventeenth century. The 20-year break from fast and abstinence days—and from fish, fresh or salted—between Charles I and Charles II, made many people reluctant to go back to salt fish when meatless days were reintroduced with the Restoration. The higher demand for fresh fish pushed up prices, a trend that continued into the mid-1800s.

Although New England fishermen from the start had salted their catch out of necessity, a fresh product was much preferred. In the 1820s fishermen found an alternative to the well smack—which prolonged storage of live fish—in the use of ice—which prolonged freshness in dead fish. At first they refused to let the fish touch the ice for fear of spoilage, but by the 1840s they had begun packing fresh catches in chipped ice, which might preserve the flesh for up to a week. Thereafter, a distinct "market fishery" of offshore vessels carrying ice to serve local markets developed alongside the older salt-fishing fleet.

When New England's fisheries were divided generally into market or salt fishing, there was less diversity of fish products available to consumers and in kinds of fishing trips to make. Icing fish, together with other technological improvements in catching fish, changed that. After 1840, many different fisheries flourished and the choices of fish available in markets widened. Despite all the technological changes involved in catching and processing fish, however, from 1840 to the 1880s the only substantial effect this activity had upon the appearance of fish in the kitchen was to increase slightly the housewife's choice of fish varieties and to gradually move the public taste farther away from salt fish.[34]

Frozen Fish

American iced fish were not frozen. Icing retarded spoilage but did not eliminate it, whereas freezing, which solidifies all the cellular fluids, eliminates deterioration until the flesh is thawed. This was understood by the middle of the nineteenth century, but the precise regulation of temperature necessary was beyond the technology of the time.

To the north, however, nature did the job. On the Newfoundland and Labrador coasts in the 1880s, small fish—generally herring—were spread on gravel beaches or on scaffolding and allowed to freeze in the open air. Then, frozen solid, they were scooped up and stowed in vessels' holds, between bulkheads insulated with sawdust. Taken to Gloucester, about a third were sold as bait and the rest were sold as food fish.[35]

Artificial freezing methods had been developed by 1900, but consumers resisted frozen fish just as they had resisted iced fish when *it* was introduced. Consumer concerns were justified by an 1898 government study, which found that some fish producers did not freeze fish until they observed signs of decomposition.[36]

Soon more and more fresh-fish producers began to use freezing as a way to extend the freshness of their fish, expand the territory they could serve with fresh fish, and get around natural fluctuations in the supply. This was ultimately successful enough that in the 1930s an analyst could write: "For all practical purposes fresh and frozen products are interchangeable on distant markets, and access to a freezer has become indispensable to any fillet manufacturer or wholesale fresh-fish distributor." Frozen fish were carried in refrigerated train cars into the nation's interior—by the 1880s with as little as ten days passing from the time the fish was taken from the Atlantic to when it was consumed in Kansas.[37]

"Fish, game, poultry, sweetbreads, etc., are often frozen to permit of their being transported to places where the supply of such articles is scanty," Maria Parloa wrote in her 1887 *Kitchen Companion*, but she believed the flavor of frozen food did not compare to fresh and that the homemaker should only buy it frozen "when it is impossible to obtain anything better. There should be but a short interval between the thawing and cooking."[38] Treating frozen fish as a choice of last resort did not inspire confidence in the product.

Even after another twenty-five years frozen fish was received cautiously. In 1914 the *Pure Food Cookbook* warned, "Frozen fish is perfectly wholesome but should be cooked as soon after thawing as possible, therefore the wise housewife purchases the fish while frozen and thaws it in her own home, rather than have the thawing done in the fish market. Frozen fish spoils quickly after thawing, so this is merely a safe precaution."[39] Some housewives chose not to buy it at all. Fish, fresh or frozen, seemed to be tricky stuff to deal with.

Freezing was considered by some to be only another way of "curing" fish, as salting was, and as a process was resented by fishermen engaged in fresh fishing and by dealers in fresh fish. In 1941, Edward Ackerman, describing New England fisheries in *New England's Fishing Industry*, wrote that "freezing has been developed to take the place of salting as a means of preservation."[40] Freezing eventually enabled fish sellers to hold fish for extended periods of time, much as they had done with salted fish; salting, however, produced a different food product, which we will discuss shortly.

In some respects, freezing was less a convenience to the consumer than to the producers, who used freezing to hold fish in suspension between ocean and market. "The advantages of the refrigerating process are evident. In former times, when there was a glut of fish it often had to be destroyed, because the expense of handling amounted to more than the price offered. To-day no such waste is possible...the labors of the fishermen are not lost, and the stock of food is increased," wrote a champion of industry in the 1890s. Once frozen, the fish could be sold as fresh when prices warranted, or could be salted, smoked, or canned—all at the convenience of the producer and his market.[41]

Preservation Methods

Another solution to the freshness problem was to preserve fish in some way, even though it usually meant that the fish was no longer fresh. Major fish-preservation methods are well known: chemical alteration of the fish via salting or pickling, sometimes followed by the dessication processes of smoking or drying; cooking fish, then further preserving the product by canning, or later by freezing; and freezing fish, as just discussed, for later appearance as fresh

Fish flakes like these at Provincetown, Massachusetts, covered acres of fishing communities in the last half of the 1800s. The salted and still-wet fish were laid out to dry in the air, carefully tended and covered in case of rain, and left on the flakes until dry enough to store for extended periods and perhaps be made into various dried-fish products. [Stereograph by Nickerson, Provincetown, MSM 79.176.1]

fish. Drying, salting, pickling, and cooking were ancient food-preserving techniques. In winter, people took advantage of natural freezing, and artificial freezing was developed to imitate it.

An important result of food-preservation methods is the way they create food products desirable for their own characteristics. We still enjoy the flavor of many products that originated with preservation methods, including sausage, bacon, fruit preserves, and pickles. So, too, with fish. Salt cod, smoked oysters, sardines, pickled herrings, and finnan haddie are all common in the market, although their fresh counterparts can be had virtually any time.

Fish salting and drying: The simplest preservation of fish was by air drying, which produced stockfish. Stockfish was most common in Scandinavia, where the dry, cold climate was ideal for its production. The warmer, more humid New England climate made it necessary to use a drying agent to dessicate the fish to a state in which they could safely be stored away. And the cheapest and most effective drying agent was salt, the preserving properties of which began to be exploited on a large scale in medieval times.

The effect of salt on flesh is to draw the moisture out of the muscle tissues, stabilizing them through drying and preserving them by retarding bacterial growth. Salt works best on watery-fleshed fish, such as cod. Oily-fleshed fish, such as mackerel or salmon, can be preserved but not dehydrated with salt.

As the predominant bottom-dwelling food fish of the North Atlantic, the cod has been subjected to salting for hundreds of years. In fact, the processing of codfish changed little during the 400 years from the time of the early European ventures into Newfoundland waters until the twentieth century. The idea was to remove all of the organs and sources of blood and then expose as much muscle as possible to the effects of salt. Consequently, the fish was beheaded, the belly was split open, the gills, organs, and sound bones with swim bladder attached were removed, and the carcass was then split open along the backbone to the tail. The fish were stacked skin-side down, flesh-side up, in pens in the vessel's hold, with salt applied in just the right quantity between the layers. The salt, combined with the weight of the stacked fish, began the drying process aboard ship. When the fish were landed at the end of the voyage, they were further dried in a number of different ways and then usually laid out for a final air drying. Major New England codfishing ports could be identified immediately by their vast expanses of fish flakes, wooden drying racks on which the fish were laid. Gloucester, for example, produced 53,000,000 pounds of salt cod in 1874.

Different methods of salting and drying produced several grades and categories of salt fish. The earliest New England fishermen produced two basic grades of salt cod: merchantable and refuse. Merchantable were large, prime fish intended for the demanding markets of Spain, Portugal, and the rest of Catholic Europe. The refuse fish were the poorest grade, sold to the West Indies as food for slaves. The process was refined through the nineteenth century, as will be described in the next chapter, but the most notable change was from a lightly salted product, dried well and hard, to a softer, more heavily salted, pickled product, lightly dried.

In the 1880s, more and more New England fish handlers turned to pickling fish. Even cod brought in "fresh" on ice could be treated this way if the market price of fresh fish was too low. Fish taken from the vessels were put into casks containing a heavily salted pickling brine. Here they remained until wanted for shipment, at which time they were briefly air dried. The resulting pickled fish were impregnated with brine rather than dehydrated, so they weighed more when finished than the old hard-dried fish. In testimony before the Senate Foreign Relations Committee in 1886, Edwin DeLong, a commission merchant in salt fish, asserted that pickling fish "has done more to injure the trade of New England than anything that has ever happened to it, unless it is the fresh fish trade." When DeLong was asked, "Is there any reason why our people cannot dry them dry?" he replied: "No reason whatever, only our fishermen pickle them and give them about five pounds of salt instead of three. The bulk of them cured that way become sour and stinking before a great while." Why would they process them this way? "They want to sell as many pounds as they can," claimed DeLong, and pickled fish were much heavier than dried fish.[42] The habit of pickling fish put salt fish exports at risk, and limited the market for New England's pickled fish to America. Europeans did not want them.

The consequence of this in the kitchen was that brine-salted fish needed to be kept cool and used more quickly than the old hard-dried salt cod had been. The pickled fish had softer, fatter, rounder flesh, which was actually advantageous both to domestic users and the fishery products industry. The pickled fish also tended to be whiter than the traditional hard-dried fish, which was an aesthetic advantage in the marketplace. William F. Jones, a Boston commission fish merchant, testified that pickled fish "are fish that a great many people like because they look white. They are really not so good a fish to those people who know what a good codfish is."[43]

As we observed before, and as Edwin DeLong pointed out above, the increased supply of fresh fish helped wean the public away from salted fish. In the late 1800s, the competition against salt fish came not just from the greater number of fresh fish available in New England, but from fresh fish caught in the South and on the Pacific coast as well. Importantly, New England's supply of a long-time favorite, salmon, had just about been exhausted. Halibut, which had become so popular in the mid-1800s, was less plentiful in the Atlantic than before; but New England's taste for these fish did not diminish with the supply, and Yankees turned to the Pacific fisheries for their favorites, as did the rest of the country formerly supplied by New England.[44] This helps explain the frequency of halibut and salmon in inland and western cookbooks.

Smoking: Like salt, smoke is an ancient preservation agent, although smoke alone is not as effective as salt in dessicating flesh and retarding bacterial growth. Smoke works especially well on oily-fleshed fish such as herring, mackerel, or salmon, although watery-fleshed fish, like haddock, as well as salted or pickled fish, could also be smoked. Smoking alone was rarely an adequate means of preservation—it might impart an appealing flavor, but the smoke only dried the flesh enough to retard deterioration for a few days. Consequently, smoked foods from hams to finnan haddie needed further care before and after processing. Smoked products formed only a small part of the preserved-fish trade, and demand for them was heavily dependent on the eating habits of the groups that bought them. Salmon, for example, was considered the choicest of smoked fish products, though Canadian rather than scarce American salmon was the principal supply of it at the end of the nineteenth century. The English had a long-standing taste for smoked salmon, and a preference for it was natural among English settlers and their descendants in New England. New England sold finnan haddie—smoked haddock—to the Canadian Maritime Provinces where the Scots and their descendants, who first produced finnan haddie, accounted for a substantial share of the population. Smoked sturgeon and eels apparently found a ready market where there was a sizable German population.[45]

Some people might smoke fish at home. Domestic smoking was popular enough that Mrs. Hale's *Receipts for the Millions*, published in 1857, offered instructions *"To smoke Hams and Fish on a small scale."* "Drive the ends out of an old hogshead or barrel; place this over a heap of sawdust of green hard wood, in which a bar of red hot iron is buried; or take corn cobs, which make the best smoke; place them in a clean iron kettle, the bottom of which is covered with burning coals; hang the hams, tongues, fish,

&c on sticks across the cask, and cover it, but not closely that the cobs or sawdust may smolder slowly, but not burn."[46]

We don't know how *many* people smoked fish, and how *much* fish was preserved in this way, but newspaper reference to smoked eels in Mystic, together with Howard Burdick's recollections of buckies—smoked alewives—in Westerly, Rhode Island, show that at least some coastwise families caught and preserved smaller, oilier fish for domestic use. References to the practice in narratives and journals is sparse, perhaps because it was not done frequently, or resulted in such small quantities, compared to the processing of beef or pork, which *are* described. Much of the domestic smoking may have been "hot smoking." Writing at the end of the nineteenth century, Charles Stevenson explained that, besides "hogshead smokehouses," in earlier decades "the old fashioned open kitchen chimneys were used for hot smoking by arranging the fish on sticks 3-4 feet above the fireplace." The result was a hot-smoked product with a smoky crust. Since the fish was not smoked all the way through, as was the case with more gradual cold smoking, it had to be consumed within a few days before it began to deteriorate.[47]

Cooking and canning: Cooking is one method of stabilizing food for preservation. In a sense, canning is an extension of that idea. Certainly in the kitchen, once she opened a can of fish, the cook had something comparable to leftover boiled or baked fish, ready to warm up or to make into another dish.

Canning began in the 1840s, as many new industries do, with a flurry of experimentation. Many products and variations on products were produced until the most successful emerged and the others were abandoned. In some cases, the seafood-canning industry took its direction from the domestic kitchen, performing for the cook the most tedious parts of seafood preparation. In other cases, the industry sought to solve its own problems, and the result appealed to the public.

A good example of an early success was canned lobsters. In the early 1800s, lobsters were frequently boiled before sale, and cooks were accustomed to buying them all ready to pick and put into sauces or salads. Most people in the 1800s preferred lobsters made into a dish (eating lobsters in the rough is a relatively new idea) so the canned product added convenience to established food habits.

Preserved canned seafood: Smaller fish, like sardines and herrings, succeeded as canned food. In fact, imported real sardines from Europe came with such an aura of status that by mid-century an array of serving ware was developed by silver and glass manufacturers to accommodate the little tins of fish. Popular demand for imported sardines encouraged Maine residents to make use of the great schools of herring that swam through their waters. Beginning in the 1870s, small herring were processed and canned as sardines. Variations on the fish as a relish for tea, luncheons, picnics, or snacking yielded up a wide selection of herrings packed in oil, with mustard or tomato, or other seasonings. When California and Norway began canning their local herrings as sardines, and doing it with lower production costs than the Maine canneries, the Maine industry went into decline.[48]

Canners also experimented with pickled herrings and shellfish. Pickling seafood was a very old method of preservation, but the taste for it had diminished by the end of the nineteenth century. The process worked for the canning industry, but it wasn't sustained by public demand. Salted and smoked fish were also canned "for convenience of marketing."[49]

Plain canned seafood: Canning's real utility lay in making "fresh" fish widely available in the form of plain cooked fish in cans. Canned salmon, mackerel, herring, menhaden, cod, halibut, smelt, oysters, clams, lobsters, crabs, shrimp, and green turtle were on the market by the turn of the century.[50] Among this selection, modern readers can find salmon, clams, lobster, crabs, and shrimp in their local supermarkets. Green turtle is a southern regional specialty, not so common in New England. Mackerel is still canned, but compared to tuna and salmon it is hardly noticeable.

The most popular canned cooked fish have been salmon, a perennial favorite, and tuna, which didn't even appear on the list at the end of the nineteenth century. Salmon, with its flavorful red flesh, had been sought for so long that it had just about disappeared from the New England fisheries by the middle of the nineteenth century. However, other salmon species were plentiful on the Pacific coast, where it was first canned in 1866. Mrs. Henderson in her *Practical Cooking*, 1882, was very enthusiastic: "The California canned salmon is undoubtedly one of the greatest successes in canning. By keeping a few cans in the house, one is always ready in any emergency to produce a fine dish of salmon in a few minutes."[51]

Tuna is similar in texture to salmon, but as a deep-sea rather than a coastal fish it was a late entry in the American diet. Not until southern European immigrants taught Yankees that "horse mackerel" was tasty did it find a place in the market and the cannery. With even fewer bones than salmon and an equally pleasing taste, it caught on for similar use. These two canned products, along with some of the canned shellfish, particularly lobster, appear frequently in community cookbooks and other cookbooks by the early 1900s.

Clams were the only other seafood to be canned in quantity in New England. Clams were sold fresh whenever possible, but they were canned in parts of coastal Maine that were far from major fish markets. Cookbooks indicate that canned clams were considered especially suitable for chowder. Ironically, the long-popular canned lobster, which had helped establish New England seafood canning, was no longer produced in New England by 1895. Overfishing to meet the market demand had led to legislation to protect lobster stocks even as lobster scarcity drove up prices until they were too expensive to buy for canning. In the early twentieth century, most canned lobster came from Nova Scotia and New Brunswick.[52]

Prepared canned seafoods: To provide even greater convenience for homemakers, and greater marketability for their products, canners began producing prepared products, such as codfish cakes and clam and fish chowders. Codfish cakes were an ideal blend of cannery convenience and market demand. The recipes were exceedingly simple, and the dish was commonly prepared at home in New England. One Boston canner was preparing codfish balls as early as 1878, using salt fish, potatoes, and beef tallow for fat, and onion and pepper for flavoring. Aside from the addition of saltpeter, the canned fish balls were made according to a home recipe, giving the consumer a familiar taste without the labor of mixing the ingredients. Within fifty years so many consumers depended on these prepared products that the big Gloucester fish companies had to produce them to survive. But Edward Ackerman, writing about the Gloucester prepared-food industry in 1941, had completely lost sight of the home origins of these canned foods when he said, "Emphasis is placed on ready-to-eat preparations, perhaps teaching the housewife thereby that New England fish can be good when elaborately prepared. Carloads of onions and whole trainloads of Maine potatoes come into Gloucester every year to help make the New England canned fish more appetizing to the unimaginative cook."[53]

By the 1930s, the canning industry was less important to New England than it had been before. One reason, wrote Edward Ackerman, was that New England's "most abundant fishes make very ordinary, unappealing canned food, compared with California tuna or northwestern salmon. Even the best fish flakes manufactured from cod and haddock would run a poor third choice to tuna or salmon." Additionally, western canneries were more competitive because tuna and salmon—both of them large fish containing relatively few bones—were economical to process, whereas New England groundfish like cod and haddock required "much hand labor for the separation of bones from flesh."[54]

Young women packing lobster meat at a Maine cannery in 1881 were preparing an elite product for use in Victorian salads and sauces. The picking and canning of lobster solved the lobster's external "bone problem" and mimicked the earlier whole boiled lobster that had been vended door-to-door. [*Scribner's Monthly*, June 1881]

Gloucester, according to Edward Ackerman, had developed its canning industry as a way to perpetuate economic activity, which it had to do when Boston succeeded as the major fisheries port. Gloucester specialized in the value-added market: fish cakes, fish balls, finnan haddie, which used the locally produced salt fish; fish chowder, clam chowder, even cat and dog food, among the canned products; and various frozen prepared fish products, most notably fish sticks. Ultimately, more fresh than salt fish was used in Gloucester's products.[55]

The Bone Problem

Down in Noank, Connecticut, Edward Knapp's fisherman Uncle Johnnie cautioned the boys to be sure to get "arm guards" made out of canvas if they ever went fishing down to Cape Cod. Uncle Johnnie said that Noank smacks didn't fish on Sunday, so they might come into a port on the Cape, and the boys would get all cleaned up and go ashore to spark the girls. "Pretty soon his arm would drop around her waist, just perfectly natural; now about the time he hauled taut on that arm of his he'd let out a yell; the Girl would look at him, laugh, and say: "Why, you Greenie, where's your arm guard?" "You see, Bub, down on the Cape they eat Codfish pretty much all the time; Biled Cod, Cod steak, Cod Head Chowder, Cod Jowls and Tongues rolled in cornmeal and fried. Cod someway most every day and they get sort of careless about the bones and eat so many they stick out between the Girl's ribs and if you don't wear Arm Guards you get an awful sore arm."[56]

Bones were a major disadvantage to fish-eating. Unlike the large, easy-to-find bones of mammals, or even compared to the smaller ones of poultry, bones in some fish seemed to be found in every mouthful and became all too easily wedged in one's throat. Americans were hasty cooks and hasty eaters, and as the nineteenth century progressed they responded well to anything that speeded cooking and eating. Fish required special handling in the kitchen, slowing cooks down. Fish required the diner to eat slowly and carefully to avoid bones. The most obvious response to the bone problem was to eat fish seldom or not at all.

In Newburyport, Massachusetts, early in the nineteenth century, Sarah Emery's brother had an experience with fish bones. "Joe and his crony Oliver Brown had been to the river to look at the fishing, and each had received a bunch of alewives. Highly delighted, Joe dressed his for supper. Father told him that they were so bony he would not eat them, but to gratify her son mother fried the fish. The lad sat down to the table with a keen appetite, but soon concluded that alewives were not exactly the thing for a hungry man to eat in a hurry." In 1878, the Mystic, Connecticut, *Press* reported that Captain Martin Halloway's haul of two tons of sea-shad—another notoriously bony fish—was "shipped to New York, and at least four thousand persons somewhere had employment for an hour each in sorting fish bones in the delusive hope of accomplishing a fish dinner."[57]

Fresh fish with fewer bones: Fish with large, easy-to-locate bones gained favor over the others. Sturgeon, which was highly esteemed for many centuries, has external bony plates and a cartilaginous backbone with few internal bones. This lack of pesky small bones, combined with its firm flesh, helps explain the sturgeon's position among the royal fish of earlier times. Early in the nineteenth century, halibut gained favor quickly because of its firm flesh and its few and large bones.

Of course, until this century the groundfish New England fishermen caught were considerably larger than their present-day descendants, and their bones were correspondingly larger. Still, once the big-boned halibut were more frequently fished and more widely distributed, they stayed firmly in favor. When overfishing depleted North Atlantic halibut stocks in the middle of the nineteenth century, the most accessible fish remaining were smaller-boned groundfish like cod, haddock, pollock and the multi-boned anadromous fish like mackerel, herring, alewives, and shad. When North Pacific halibut began to be fished late in the nineteenth century, New England lost much of its national business to Pacific halibut, at least in part because of the public's preference for less bony fish.

A whole unboned fish, large or small, was easier to handle in the kitchen. If the fish was small—between half a pound and four pounds—the cook would broil or fry it; if it was large—four pounds or more—she or he would bake or poach it. When a whole fish was cooked, the meat could be lifted away from the backbone as it was served or eaten. Alternatively, fish large enough to be cut in steaks—like large cod, salmon, or halibut—were favored because cooks could find and pick out the stray bones in the meaty portion of the steak, and diners could easily discern the backbone. Medium-size fish were used for chowders. In their chowder recipes, after instructing cooks to remove the skin and cut the fish into pieces, cookbook writers sometimes advised them to remove the pieces from the bones. Some cooks may not have heeded these instructions, for the author of one fish recipe booklet published in 1895 felt obliged to point out that "No fish chowder should have bones in it."[58]

The ultimate solution was a boneless cut of fish, what we call the fillet. Culinary reference to fillet is very old: a fillet was understood in the thirteenth century to be a tender cut of meat, and Hannah Glass referred to fillets of fish in 1724. The *Oxford English Dictionary* dates to 1846 its earliest citation of the verb form "to fillet" in a specific reference to fish from the French chef Soyer.[59] This is fitting, for the technique was long associated with a higher style of cooking than was found in most American homes.

Because many of the nineteenth-century American cookbooks provide neither instructions for filleting nor specific recipes for using boneless pieces of fish, we may assume most housewives did not take this extra step. While cookbook instructions for preparing fish for cooking often included the directions to remove the backbone, this step still left many bones in the fish, and was not truly filleting, which produced an entirely boneless piece of fish. References to fish fillets appear more often in the last half of the century, in such recipes as "Matelot of Codfish,"

"Fish au Gratin," "Fried Slices of Fish, with Tomato Sauce (Fish a l'Orlay)," all clearly in the French style. Occasionally stewed-fish recipes specify boneless cuts.[60]

The skill, practice, and time required for home filleting would have been most readily available in stylish kitchens with professional cooks or housekeepers. An 1895 Shute and Merchant recipe booklet assumed the cook purchased her fish in the round when describing fresh-fish cookery. In attempting to encourage sales of their fresh fish, Shute and Merchant provided instructions for scaling, cleaning out entrails, trimming fins, washing, and drying the fish. "Always split a fish on the under side and unless the fish is very small indeed remove the backbone entire," they directed.[61] The waste from this kind of operation, compared with cooking the fish whole, was substantial, unless the household used the head and backbones for stock. Later promotions of commercially prepared fillets remark that there was "no waste," suggesting that one objection to filleting was wastefulness.

Ordinary middle-class cooks and homemakers continued to prepare fish as they had for most of the century: a fresh, whole fish was served whole; its leftovers, carefully picked free of bones, went into other dishes. Cookbook fish recipes are often instructions for using these little bits of leftover fish. But even with clear instructions, sorting through flakes of cooked fish was tedious business compared to chopping a piece of leftover roast beef for hash.

Salt fish with no bones: If fish producers, including canners, had any hope of building a market for fish, either fresh or preserved, they had to cope with the bone problem. Soaked salt cod has firmer flesh than fresh fish, and cooks apparently picked over cod even before it was cooked to pull out the stray bones left when the sound bone was severed from the backbone.[62] Even after cooking, a salt cod's backbone holds together solidly and is easy to remove. Despite this, Gloucester salt-fish producers addressed the bone problem early; they understood that the easier it was to pick salt fish, the more acceptable it was in the market.

With the overseas markets for bulk salt cod drying up in the middle of the nineteenth century, the fish producers turned their efforts to making salt cod more appealing in the domestic marketplace. As they shifted more to the softer, pickle-cure process described earlier, they also attempted to address the bone problem. In 1869 they began to produce "boneless" salt fish. There were different grades of bonelessness, from "dressed"—which meant the back and nape were removed but the rib bones remained—to the best, absolutely boneless, grades.[63] By 1879 Gloucester was producing 14,000,000 pounds of boneless cod, and by 1885 part of the process had been mechanized, but the product still required manual labor.

When Gloucester celebrated its

A group of Siasconset cod fishermen at Nantucket, Massachusetts, around 1890. A kind of golden age of fishing flourished between the change from hand-lining from the sides of a vessel and the development of otter trawls deployed from powered fishboats. These fishermen set simple trawl-lines within rowing distance of shore. [Hudson Collection, MSM 78.142.385]

three-hundredth anniversary in 1924, the fish producers demonstrated the process in an exhibition tent: "In the centre of the tent was a raised platform on which were placed benches where skilled operatives demonstrate...an art that comes only by long training; it is skilled labor, especially the preliminary fish skinning. After the fish was skinned it was passed to women operatives who, with pincers, pulled out the bones, the product passing to pressmen who converted it into "bricks" or packed it into cartons and thence into the pine boxes for shipment."[64] The development of boneless fish—literally turning a wet, bony, perishable creature into an attractively packaged convenience product with some shelf life—was the most important advance in the dried-fish industry during the entire nineteenth century.

Salt-fish producers further observed how leftover salt fish was used in the kitchen. Early in the nineteenth century, cooks used leftover salt cod either by warming up the flakes in milk, cream, or cream sauce, or by mixing it with potatoes to form into balls or cakes to fry. Boneless-fish producers like Shute and Merchant, Frank E. Davis, and others offered the cook convenience by providing cod already picked apart by machine and packed in various forms. The product names described this white, boneless, easy-to-use form of fish. Shute and Merchant's line of "Absolutely Boneless Brands of Fish," packed in one- to forty-pound boxes, were named Diamond Wedge, Gold Wedge, Silver Wedge, Swan's Down Tid Bits, Barberry Brand Threaded Fish—"for Fish Balls and Cream of Fish"—"No Cooking, No Odor, No Waste"—Heliotrope Fibered Codfish, and the candidly labeled Not-a-Choke.[65] In the early 1900s, these products came with complete preparation instructions on the packages. To encourage sales, customers were invited to send for little recipe books, which contained comfortably familiar fish recipes.

We know a good deal about how producers marketed these products, but we don't know much about how consumers used them. Boneless salt fish packed in boxes, which is still available today, *was* widely accepted. But recipes calling for "shredded codfish," or "codfish picked in small pieces," or "one pint of cooked salt fish" are inconclusive evidence because the terms could describe either packaged or leftover fish. "Heliotrope Fibered Codfish" was little different from what a cook would have on her hands with leftover cooked cod. Even though the prepared fish was available, most cookbooks still described what clearly seem to be leftovers. In 1904 Mrs. Lincoln wrote, "Wash the fish, pick in half inch pieces, and free from bones...." "First boil the salt cod, after soaking, and chop it fine."[66]

Canned fish with disguised bones: Canned fish products were ultimately more practical than packaged salt fish products, but canneries had to deal with bones, too. "An objection to canning of small fish is the large number of bones," wrote Charles Stevenson in 1898. "Ordinarily the heat developed in the process of canning destroys the cohesion of the particles of the bones, so that they may be masticated and swallowed without inconvenience, but the bones of some small fish are not so easily softened."[67] Bones were a nuisance for everyone.

The Boneless, Fussless Fillet

When the fishing industry took the bones out of fresh fish, it made a big difference in the kitchen and greatly improved public acceptance of fish. It also helped the industry in some other significant ways.

The introduction of the otter trawl net into New England around 1900, which would supersede the use of hook and line for catching groundfish, made it possible for some New Englanders to catch more fish than ever before. When the Bay State Fishing Company built its fleet of steam-powered otter trawlers, it created a marketing dilemma. It was now possible to catch more fish than Americans wanted to eat. It was also possible to catch *kinds* of fish that, however well accepted they might be in Europe, were not popular in the United States. One answer to what the fishing industry perceived as its "under-consumption" problem was also a solution to the bone problem—marketing fish fillets.[68]

Bay State is credited with introducing the fillet as a commercial cut of fish in 1921. In routinely processing its fresh fish this way, the company helped make fillet a household word, and it took credit for "supplying those living inland with fish of sufficiently high quality to make it popular on menus more than a hundred or so miles from salt water." Given a brand name, Bay State's "Forty Fathom Fish" were boneless, and they were promoted to buyers—both retailers and homemakers—as wasteless. They were also described as "sweet and odorless." The fillets were wrapped in parchment paper and placed in "tin containers, which in turn are packed in wooden boxes with ice surrounding the tins." Expanding grocery chains were happy to carry such a reliable product, and consumers were delighted to discover fish in a form that was fresh, boneless, and—given all the objections to fish and fish-preparation already noted—fussless.[69]

Both consumers and fish producers benefited. "Filleting thus changed the complexion of the fresh-fish industry," wrote Edward Ackerman in 1941. Filleting lowered the transportation cost of fish because ocean fish no longer needed to be shipped inland in the round, a "factor of the utmost importance in the marketing of a low-priced article." Filleting "reduces fish to its lightest possible terms and most attractive form." Packaged fillets were a ready-to-cook product at a time when ready-to-cook was a commercially popular concept. Filleting also paved the way for other fish producers, and the simplicity of fish fillets made Clarence Birdseye's quick-freezing process—on which modern frozen food is based—easier to develop. Filleting and freezing also made possible the ultimate fish convenience food, the frozen fish stick of the 1950s.

Haddock, even more than cod, was most desirable for these products; and for most of the years since the 1920s haddock has supplanted cod as New England's principal groundfish. As usual, it is hard to tell who bought Forty Fathom fillets and just how well they penetrated the inland market. We would need considerable analysis of sales statistics, not within the scope of this book; but it seems a good guess that fish-eaters, both coastwise and inland, gratefully bought the easier-to-prepare product, and that people who didn't love fish continued to avoid them except once in a while for variety. A sample of three western community cookbooks assembled between 1924 and 1931 contain recipes for salmon, halibut, canned salmon, and canned tuna, cod, and salt cod by name; of these the only one which might have been purchased as a fillet was the cod.[70]

Perhaps as important as its boneless freshness, the fillet made fish look like competing meat products. A fish in the round looked like the creature it was. Virtually no other meat in the market looked like the animal it was derived from. As the twentieth century progressed, and Americans moved farther from farmyard and fish pier, with very few exceptions the public—New Englanders included—wanted it that way.[71]

Known by the Company It Kept

Let us leave the fish sticks of the 1950s now and return to the interesting business of attitudes toward fish and fish-eating from Puritan times up to the present. Another "problem" with fish was the company of people associated with it. Social prejudice was close to the surface in the nineteenth century; considerable evidence demonstrates that many New Englanders associated fish-eating with Catholics, immigrants, and the poor. Some people represented all three of these classifications, such as the Irish and the succeeding waves of poor Catholic Europeans who came to work in New England's industrial cities.

Roman Catholics ate fish. Before the Reformation, a great many days in the year were fast days on which only fish or dairy products could be eaten for protein; but most prominently, as we have seen, Friday was a fish day.[72] This once-a-week habit of fish-eating stayed with the Puritans even in New England, as we saw in the chapter about the Buckingham family. It was an old food habit, and it provided variety in the weekly menu. But in order to diminish identification with their Roman Catholic past and persecutors, the Puritans and their descendants merely ate fish on a different day in the week. Often it was Saturday, appropriately enough, for the Puritan Sabbath began at sunset Saturday.

In the preface to her *New Cook Book*, Sarah Josepha Hale wrote in 1857, "A greater variety of receipts, for preparing *Fish, Vegetables, and Soups*, is given here, than can be found in any other book of the kind; these preparations, having reference to the large and increasing class of persons in our country who abstain from flesh meats during Lent, will be found excellent; and useful also to all families during the hot season." An 1864 article titled "What Shall We Have for Dinner?" in the *Atlantic Monthly* told the reader, addressed as "Hero," how to plan a food budget. In a sideways reference to Irish kitchen help, the author wrote, "I do not know if you are a Catholic, Hero; but I guess your kitchen is; and so I am pretty sure that you will eat fish Fridays."[73]

Poverty fare and fish as penance: Poor people ate fish, especially salted. Since fish was poorly esteemed for its nutritional attributes, it was a low-value food affordable by poorer people. Eating fish was what you did when you couldn't do better, and in the popular mind it was associated with fasting and penance. A steady diet of fish was the food equivalent of a hair shirt.

This notion was many centuries old by the 1800s. In the fourth century the Romans had decreed fish days for economic reasons, probably to husband meat supplies. The early church merely extended this idea, placing Lent at the close of the winter months when most of the animals that weren't to be saved for breeding had been butchered. Additional fast days were scattered through the calendar on Fridays. All during the medieval period, fast days drove the early fisheries, particularly for herring and later for cod, both of which were salted. Even after the Reformation, the English calendar had 150 fast days as an encouragement for the North Atlantic cod fishery. The rich could afford to buy fresh fish and cook it with rich, spiced sauces.[74] The poor were forced to eat great quantities of salt fish.

Regarded a little more highly were "royal fish" and richer fish with firm, meat-like flesh. Salmon, swordfish, sturgeon, and a few others were at the top of the food chain—their own and that of the privileged humans who consumed them. Smaller and bonier fish lay at the bottom of the social scale. Some "royal fish" were actually not fish but mammals—whales and porpoises—conveniently confused with their finny cohabitants of the ocean for the purpose of providing hearty fare for royalty during Lent.[75] All royal fish caught or found anywhere were to be offered first to the crown.

As already noted, Protestants ended meatless days when they seized England's government in the middle of the seventeenth century. After the Restoration "people who had enjoyed freedom from obligatory fish meals during the previous years were most unwilling to go back to them," observed Anne Wilson in *Food and Drink in Britain*. Faithful Catholics still observed a fast day, but there was a discernible shift in fish preferences. The rich now included fish in their menus, but only the most favored sea and fresh fishes; the poor, given a respite from salt fish, continued to reject them along with coarse freshwater fish, but they could not afford the more expensive fish caught to supply the tables of the wealthy. When they ate fish, it was mostly salted or pickled herring and salmon.[76]

English immigrants to New England brought this history—Roman, Roman Catholic, Puritan, Anglican,

Restoration—with them when they settled here. In eighteenth-century New England, then, few people ate salt fish more often than once a week. The poorer classes ate it more often only when circumstances prevented dining on something else. Fresh fish provided variety in everyone else's menus, often paired in a meal with meat, as we have seen.

Who, then, ate the salt cod that was produced by the early New England fisheries? Salt cod was classified as "merchantable," "middling," and "refuse." The merchantable was traded to Catholic Spain and Portugal, the middling went to the Portuguese Atlantic islands and Jamaica, and the refuse was sold to sugar plantation owners in the British Caribbean islands for slave food.[72]

And who ate the easily acquired—and one would think—easily consumed and *cuisined* fish and shellfish of New England? Even certain fresh fish were, as one source described it, "disreputable," at least to those who had easy access to them. In the Connecticut River Vâlley, it was reported that shad was "despised and rejected by a large portion of the English for near one hundred years in the old towns of Connecticut, and for about seventy-five years in those Hampshire towns above the falls. It was discreditable for those who had a competency to eat shad;...Poor families ate shad, and doubtless some who were not poor," even though shad was barreled and shipped to Boston for sale. Some believed that part of the objection to shad—other than the fish's boniness—was that "they were so generally used by the Indians."[78]

Rugged, independent Yankees fishing from graceful schooners in an often dangerous job are part of fishing's folklore. But the Yankees were gradually replaced by many Atlantic Canadians and Portuguese. [Hudson Collection, MSM 78.228.8]

Some fishing people, however, ate what they caught, never thought much about it, and had some leisure time to not think about it. Describing Newport in the late 1700s and early 1800s, Timothy Dwight said, with a critical air, "The poor people catch fish for their sustenance, and lounge and saunter for their pleasure."[79]

Some fish were disdained two generations later for reasons we cannot fathom today. At the mouth of the Connecticut River in the 1870s and 1880s, Edward Chapman watched pound net fishermen sorting their catch, which sometimes included flat fish and flounder. "But the amazing thing about both flounder and flatfish in the heyday of pound fishing was the small account made of their excellent flesh," he wrote. "A few of the largest were shipped, to find a market of doubtful remuneration. Some were given

to children of poor families who waited with their baskets....But much and sometimes most of this admirable food went into the pile of waste." And quoting his Long Island correspondent Fred Mather in the 1880s, Ernest Ingersoll wrote: "We have often said that there is more good food wasted in the United States than in any other country, but as population increases this will remedy itself. At present our people are too proud to buy anything but the choicest things in market...but in a few more generations the fishermen of Long Island won't say with indignation, of a truly fine fish which graces the tables of the best in the land in Europe and some parts of New York, 'No sir; I was never poor enough to eat sturgeon.' "[80]

Clams were even less highly regarded. Sarah Anna Emery reported that around Newburyport, in the early nineteenth century, raw, whole, and cooked clams were peddled through the streets, and that they "were considered a plebeian dish, from which many persons turned in disgust."[81]

In almost every case, when it came down to basics, old-line Yankees considered fish as fit food for Catholics, whom old Yankees mistrusted; for the poor, whom many suspected of deserving their poverty; and for the enslaved, for whom New Englanders had a condescending sympathy while still providing the fish that slavemasters fed them. If New Englanders were going to eat fish, they certainly did not want to eat so much of it that they became identified with these groups they considered aliens.

Undomesticated Fish and Fishermen

Even the character of the men who caught them affected the reputation of fish. From the time of the earliest English seasonal fishing camps in New England, the men who caught fish were a "peripheral" group in society.[82] The early settlers of the Plymouth and Massachusetts Bay colonies hired itinerant fishermen, many of whom were from a large pool of maritime laborers, and few of whom embraced Puritanism, to help develop a fishing industry that would produce a commodity for trade with the mother country and with other colonies. Colony leaders first attempted to recruit fishermen among their own settlers, but only a few men knew the work or were attracted by it. Of these, some used fishing as a springboard to merchant life while others merely supplemented their farm income by fishing seasonally. More labor was needed.

The itinerants who filled the need were outsiders, often closely associated with the Anglican church, tending to prefer a loosely organized work life, and less likely to own land. They managed to evade the Puritan church, community, and a settled family life. Where the Puritan community led a life of restraint, the fishermen were perceived to lead a rough existence of drinking, carousing, and violence. They discomfited colony leaders, who endured them to populate the fishing fleet. Many of these fishermen lived, even if only temporarily, in Marblehead, which was the leading fishing port in Massachusetts in the eighteenth century. The Reverend John Barnard reported that when he arrived there he could not "find twenty families that upon the best examinations could stand upon their own legs; and they were generally as rude, swearing, drunken, fighting a crew, as they were poor."Additionally, there were strong and early connections between Newfoundland and Massachusetts via the fisheries. Similarly, the fishermen who settled in Maine, beyond the reach of Massachusetts society, were rough, irreligious people, described by one as "a dull and heavy moulded sort of people," without "either skill or courage to kill anything but fish." Even if we allow that the Reverend Barnard may have put the worst possible interpretation on Marblehead's condition before his ministry began to have positive effect, his comments are typical of early descriptions of New England fishermen, which almost always characterize them as independent, rough-mannered, and poor.[83]

The nature of fishing itself mitigated against its respectability as a Puritan calling; it was seasonal, market-oriented work, and by its nature at odds with the Puritan belief that "work was pleasing to God only when performed in a regular and disciplined manner," and that the "alternation of frantic activity and idleness [was] rooted in moral failing." Fish, like other game, was wild food, and fishing was a wild calling, not really respectable. Farming was respectable and disciplined—and a reliable source of food. Colonists turned to wild food for subsistence when there was no option, and made every effort to establish a steady supply of domesticated food such as beef or pork. Even when, by the end of the eighteenth century, fishermen settled in communities and had families, they were still largely unable to earn enough to capitalize their own voyages, so to go fishing meant chronic indebtedness to vessel owners and merchants. On the one hand this insured that fishermen remained to labor with the owner; on the other hand it kept fishermen economically marginal.[84]

By the end of the eighteenth century, fishing became more a young man's occupation, and older men stayed ashore doing land-based work. The poverty associated with fishing diminished but did not disappear. Sarah Anna Emery described the hardscrabble district of Newburyport along the river where fishing families lived around 1800: "an irregular collection of small low houses, forming the fishing hamlet of Joppa. Here in season the river bank would often be lined with wherries which had just been brought in loaded with fish, which the sun-burned, bare-footed women, in brown homespun short-gown and petticoat tucked to the knee, with the older children, aided the toil-worn fishermen to carry to the great fish-flakes on the uplands..." And even along one of New England's great rivers, where fishermen might have flourished, Timothy Dwight found at Wethersfield, Connecticut, "The fisheries of salmon, shad, and herrings in this town have always been very productive, and were it not that fishermen were prone to take little care of their earnings, could not fail of yielding considerable wealth."[85]

Whatever he may have meant by "considerable wealth," Timothy Dwight was wrong about New England's seasonal freshwater fisheries. The real wealth, if there was any, was in the coastal fisheries. By the middle of the nineteenth century, as fishing technology became more productive—and at the same time more labor-intensive and dangerous—fishing began to produce a reasonable working-class income for those willing to endure the conditions and spend an ever-larger part of their year at sea. The working conditions made fishing more of a very risky routine job rather than a brave adventure—although fishermen still received a share of the profits rather than wages, as if fishing voyages were still cooperative ventures. The old-line Yankees began to move away from the industry by mid-century, especially when they could find a routine and safer job in one of the new factories at home or else move west to work the land. Even if Yankee fishermen did not give up the sea, they discouraged their sons from following in their footsteps. To fill the void, itinerant fishermen from Newfoundland and Nova Scotia came south to work in New England fishing vessels, going home with inflated dollars in the off-season. Other immigrant groups, especially the Irish, Scandinavians, Portuguese, and Italians, entered the fisheries, often owning their own vessels and hiring men from their own communities.

George Brown Goode distinguished between the industrious fishermen of Gloucester and the fishermen of Maine in 1880. The Maine fishermen, he said, were complainers, but they submitted to difficulties, had little access to credit, were poorly educated, and generally lacked enterprise in fishing or in taking care of their homes and gardens, both of which usually showed neglect. "A larger return than common from selling fish is usually spent as fancy may first dictate or serves as a reason for deferring, as long as possible, the next fishing expedition," he reported. The families of Maine fishermen, he wrote, "subsist, for the most part, upon the products of the sea—fish, lobsters, and clams—-and upon the vegetables from their gardens."[86] In many ways these late-nineteenth-century Mainers weren't very different from Marbleheaders a century and a half before.

By contrast, Goode reported that most New England fishermen—meaning the men from Gloucester or Cape Cod that he was most familiar with—were educated, (though the women were better educated), read all the current periodicals and even dipped into Shakespeare and Dickens, and lived in neat, comfortable homes. Though fishermen were not religious, Goode testified that "a high tone of morality prevails" in most fishing towns, and while profanity was prevalent "in other respects moralists would in general find little to criticize," particularly in light of the effect of temperance reform after 1876.[87] If we can believe George Brown Goode, the fishermen had become solid citizens by the 1880s, even if their products were still somewhat suspect.

Marketing Fish

Even though the fishing industry did much to meet consumer objections to fish problems and to allay fears about its products, the American public still only halfheartedly ate fish. Consumer resistance to fish was reflected in the fishing industry's exasperation—and enterprise—in this century. During World War I, the industry geared up to produce enough fish to meet the increased wartime demand, but when the war was over and the public resumed meat-eating, fishermen found themselves over-producing fish. "But," declared the *Atlantic Fisherman* in its premier issue, "we cannot speak of over-production in a country whose people consume but 16 pounds annually against Britain's 65. Rather it is under-consumption....The solution to the problem seems obvious for it resolves itself into a fundamental of merchandising—*the creation of a market.* In a word, fish must be *sold.* It must be sold as Mr. Hoover sold it during the war—by education, publicity, advertising."[88]

The *Atlantic Fisherman* listed the industry goals: "varieties of fish that are little known could be popularized, prejudices against the freezer could be overcome, the proper methods of preparation and cooking could be explained." So the industry declared 9 March 1921 as National Fish Day, asked for cooperation among fisheries businesses, and proposed a fisheries exposition.[89]

They even sent a fish to the president. "White House Feast on Cod - A splendid specimen of cod weighing 34 pounds was shipped to President Warren G. Harding on March 5th. The fish was landed at Gloucester by one of the gill netters and carefully packed by Gorton-Pew Fisheries. Miss Viola Duclow performed the ceremony of placing the President's National Fish Day dinner in its shipping container. The young lady was very appropriately dressed in the regulation suit of oil cloths for the laying away of Mr. Cod."[90]

By 1921, several Gloucester fish businesses—and others in New England—had been learning how to market fish products. Shute and Merchant, Frank E. Davis, and Crown Packing Company had all been direct-marketing salt fish in ready-to-cook forms. Customers received fliers with information about the fish products along with prices for various-sized packages; they ordered products by mail, and the company shipped them by rail and postal service. These companies, and others like the Bay State Fishing Company, encouraged business with a blend of education, publicity, and advertising; fish producers synthesized as many solutions as they could to overcome Americans' objections to eating fish. While their solutions are not unique, they are a good example of how the industry proceeded.

Education: These companies distributed recipe booklets with all kinds of fish recipes, not just for their own products, but for fresh fish—which often represented the competition—as well. Customers received a free copy of the recipes with every order. The fliers suggested the best ways to use the product—for example, Frank E. Davis Company's Mackerel in Bordelaise Sauce—"each tin contains sufficient for a delightful lunch for three or four persons"; and "Kippered Herring—Just the Thing for Fall Breakfasts."[91]

In 1922 the American Fisheries Society heard at least one proposal for educating the public. "The public press, magazines, moving pictures, public school lectures, and the radio are some of the means by which the public could be induced to eat more and better fish." Teaching the housewife how to discern one kind of fish from another, to determine quality, and how to prepare fish beyond just one or two ways, J. H. Mathews felt, would improve the market for fish because, while most housewives could perceive the quality of vegetables and cuts of meat "at a glance; with fish, she is invariably at sea."[92]

Meeting traditional consumer concerns: The freshness problem had several ramifications: producers needed to assure consumers they had the freshest fish possible, and needed to diminish the fishy smell that confused consumers. "Few people know how delicious Salt Mackerel, Cod Fish, Halibut and Herring are, as they have been buying the usually inferior grade that is selected by the shippers for sale in the interior parts of our country where the quality of the selected fish is not truly known. By our method (direct to the consumer) you can set a new standard—you will have the best," proclaimed the Crown Packing Company in 1911. Crown's Fish Ball Codfish was shredded "ready for use, no boiling or soaking, and therefore no *odor*." Producers also played to consumers' preference for white fish products, which looked pure: "Georges Salt Cod Tongues and Sounds—These sounds are handpacked and *very white*." [93]

Fish producers also understood the value of industry standards. J.H. Mathews defined lack of standards as one problem facing commercial fisheries. "The housewife making her purchases of meat does not consider quality, knowing it is up to the standard set by the Government, or it would not be offered for sale; but in purchasing sea-food usually the first question she asks is in regard to its quality."[94]

Bad experiences with fish reinforced the public's notion that fish was not a likable food. Arthur Millett, who called for inspection and regulation of fish products, said, "on many occasions in the past the consumer has found fish absolutely unfit for food, and that has been the cause of many people not liking fish and not eating fish." Declaring that beef and canned vegetable products were subjected to stringent inspections to the benefit of health and increased consumption, he said, "If the same care were taken with the marketing of fish food as with beef and canned products, the yield of our farms of the sea, lake, and river would now be vying for supremacy with land food commodities."[95] The fact that fish products were not inspected before 1920, whereas meat products had been inspected since 1890, underlines how poorly regarded the food was. Fish was not important enough to warrant government attention.

Prejudices and fears: One observer believed fish retailers were partly to blame for "much prejudice among consumers by selling fish of poor or inferior quality and also by representing some of the cheaper and inferior grades to be more popular and expensive varieties. The unsanitary conditions of many fish markets is another factor in discouraging a more extensive use of seafoods."[96] Even at the risk of creating new prejudices and fears about fish products, some fish producers assured their customers that *their* products were pure, safe, wholesome, caught by Yankee fishermen and packed under the most reliable conditions.

In the last half of the nineteenth century the public had well-founded fears of product adulteration. In order to use fish that, strictly speaking, were in bad condition, some processors treated their fish with boric acid. In 1907, Frank E. Davis wrote in his free cookbook, *Fish Dainties and Necessities*, "Absolutely nothing is used in the way of chemicals or acids" in his fish products; he reminded them that salt could be removed, but other substances could not. Fourteen years later some fish producers were still at it, and they drew the criticism of Arthur Millett who called for government inspection of fish food.[97]

Concerns about new fishing technology were simultaneously answered and created by Davis's 1907 assurance that "every one of the cod we sell are caught on single handlines—not on trawls. When they are caught on trawls as they are on other fishing grounds, the fish are often dead when taken on board."[98] Of course, within twenty years of this statement handlining would be nearly a thing of the past and even trawl-line fishing would be in the course of replacement by the otter trawl, a method that treated the catch far more harshly than did fishhooks.

The Bay State Fishing Company may have used otter trawls to catch the haddock for its fillets, but it made a point of their clean and careful handling: "The fish are hoisted out of the [vessel] holds in easily cleaned canvas baskets, but instead of being dumped into slimy, bacteria-laden boxes, are emptied into rustless metal-lined bins on automatic scales." The company implied that whiteness in fish, increasingly valued, was jeopardized because "The practice of forking fish [to unload them] is most detrimental to quality because the tines of the forks puncture the flesh, leaving black marks and paving the way for bacteria just as a deep wound with a dirty rusty piece of metal does in any flesh."[99] If consumers were not already concerned with a little off color in their fish, they certainly would when, for example, the natural grayness of pollock or halibut could be confused with damage from careless handling.

Marketing unfamiliar species: During their inspection of the catches of the new otter trawlers in New England waters, scientists from the U. S. Fish Commission commented that many kinds of fish caught in otter trawls were discarded as unsalable in America, even though they were quite marketable in Europe. Lewis Radcliffe observed in his paper before the American Fisheries Society in 1918 that in the process of depleting stocks of popular fish, fishermen destroyed what were considered unmarketable species. He recommended that the industry develop preservation methods and a market for such fish. He presented two examples, tilefish—which had once had a brief flurry of popularity—and shark. With tilefish, he reported, a little judicious advertising plus some instruction on how to cook it stimulated consumers' curiosity enough that they gave the fish a try. With shark he was sure a similar strategy would work.[100]

Radcliffe raised three particularly interesting points about selling shark. He understood that the public would need assurance that shark was fit for consumption—its digestibility and edibility had to be established. He understood that fresh sales limited its market, so he called for development of methods for pickling, smoking, kippering, drying, dry-salting, and canning. He understood that as a new fish in the market there would be consumer resistance, so he called for an education campaign among consumers "to uproot their prejudices."[101] From our perspective, nearly eighty years later, we can see what happened. Shark was eventually widely enough accepted that it can be found today in supermarket fresh-fish displays and on restaurant menus. Neither kippered nor canned shark is found next to the canned herring or tuna. Most of the time, when shark is offered for sale it is named mako, which brings us to another aspect of marketing.

A fish by any other name: The meat of nearly all domesticated animals is given a different name than the animal itself. We do not eat cows, or steers, or calves; we eat beef or veal; pigs are pork, sheep are mutton or lamb, goats are chevon (sometimes mutton); even deer become venison. Chickens, turkeys, and geese, though known collectively as poultry, are an exception, partly because of the lower esteem in which we hold these creatures. The *name* of our food conjures up some notions of palatability, and this seems to become even more true as people are more disconnected from the sources of their food.

Most types of fish went frankly by common names, and as long as a fish was familiar and known to be edible its name did not matter very much. But introducing a new fish, or any fish in a new region or market, required thought about what to call it. For example, in the first decades of the 1900s, catfish sold better in New England under the name "whitefish," whereas the name catfish worked perfectly well in the South and in the Missouri River drainage of the Midwest. In Canada, rock-eel or marine eel-pout were sold as "mutton fish."[102]

While some argued that what a fish was called, as well as truth in claims about it, should be regulated by the industry or government, everyone understood that perceptions about palatability and edibility hinged in part on the name. Arthur Millett claimed that "Lowly pollock masquerades as 'Boston Bay Blues' even baldly and boldly as 'Bluefish.' "[103] Fish producers could explain to consumers the off-white color of pollock by the blue-toned name; with the name Boston Bay Blues no consumer expected pollock to be white. As a Boston Blue, pollock *sounded* palatable and it looked like a bluefish.

Product convenience: Deboning fish products, besides solving the bone problem, had been one step toward convenience foods, but there was more the industry could do. Crown Packing Company advertised that its salt mackerel "makes a most delicious breakfast dish. We select the finest and fattest, clean them, *cut off heads and tails and fully prepare them for cooking.*" As we saw, Crown's Fish Ball Codfish was "ready for use, no boiling or soaking." When Frank Davis introduced "Tunny" in 1917, he assured consumers "It is very dainty served cold *as taken from the can* and makes an excellent salad."[104] Thus was the world informed about tuna salad.

Trading on Gloucester's fishing fame: The fame of Georges Bank and the fishing reputation of New England, and Gloucester particularly, all seemed worth exploiting in marketing the product. Salt fish was marketed as "Prime Georges" and "Selected Bank." Frank E. Davis sold "Down East" clams and "Georges Cod," extolling the virtues of the hard bottom of Georges Bank. In his earlier promotions, Davis boasted the freshness of his products and the fact that so many thousands of people bought fish from him. By the 1930s, when he was 85, he traded heavily on his family's fishing background.

Explaining the company's origins to his customers, Davis wrote: "It all happened in the simple, most natural way in the world. As a boy, I spent a good many days aboard a fishing schooner where I learned how to catch fish and how to clean and cure them to keep. Then as a young man, I went to sea in my father's vessel, catching the wary mackerel. Once, upon the return to port, I sent a a pile of salted mackerel to inland friends. The letter that came back thanking me and telling of the difficulty of obtaining a ways from the ocean, the kind of fish that folks really like, gave me my idea....I've outgrown the little wooden building on the wharves and now have a large, modern cement structure where the most sanitary methods are employed."[105]

"Till you are afforded better fare..."

Accounts of early New England by Giovanni Caboto, Sir Ferdinando Gorges, Captain John Smith, the Reverend Francis Higginson, and others, are effusive in their descriptions of the fish and shellfish that abounded here. We can trust in the essential truth of their reports, but we really must put their enthusiasm in perspective. There *were* a great many fish and shellfish, very easily caught or gathered at the time of earliest settlement in the seventeenth century. But praising the abundance of fish had

New York's Fulton Fish Market is shown around 1868 with well-smacks in the basin. Large fish markets developed at Boston and New York, connected by rail to the hinterlands. Fresh fish were iced by mid-century and frozen by the 1880s, so fish dealers could sell fresh fish even in inland cities, or hold fish until the market improved, leveling out fluctuations in supply and price. [MSM 64.47]

more to do with promoting New England as a good place to live, or as evidence that God was providing for his people.

For example, the company backing Plymouth Plantation wrote a letter to William Bradford in 1623, saying that they had sent fishermen and salt to begin a fishing trade, adding, "If the land afford you bread, and the sea yeeld you fish, rest a while contented, God will one day afford you better fare."[106]

John Winthrop, describing in 1643 the difficulties the Massachusetts Bay Colony experienced with poor crops, wrote "Corn was very scarce all over the country, so...many families in most towns had none to eat, but were forced to live off clams, muscles, cataos, dry fish, etc." Another time, said Winthrop, "Their victuals also grew short, so as they were forced to eat muscles."[107]

In his *Wonder-Working Providence*, Edward Johnson described the patience with which the early settlers endured the poor fare they were reduced to: "in the misse of beere supplied themeselves with water, even the most honored as well as the others...as also in the absence of Bread they feasted themselves with fish." The women resorted each day at low tide to clam banks to pick mussels and clams, while "encouraging one another in Christ's careful providing for them." One day while gathering shellfish they looked up and saw two ships coming in, which proved to be from Ireland bringing provisions for the colony. Johnson claimed that the women's "poore hearts were not so much refreshed in regard of the food they saw they were like to have, as their soules rejoyced in that Christ should now manifest himself."[108] Well, maybe. Surely the prospect of beef, even if salted—and respite from mussels, clams, and fish—had something to do with it.

The descendants of these early settlers *were* afforded better fare in later years. Meanwhile, the fish that they treated so indifferently in their own diet generated capital to build New England's foreign trade and industries. It provided work for men who loved life on the sea and would never have been content farming. It provided work for many more in maritime trades and crafts, and left a legacy of lovely watercraft design.

Whatever would have happened, though, to the stocks of groundfish now depleted to the point of protection from fishing if New Englanders had taken to eating fish as much as fishermen and fish merchants so much wished they would? Perhaps we in the late twentieth century should be grateful that fish was considered "less nutritious than flesh."

Among seafood choices in the nineteenth century, oysters and salt cod were two of the favorites. What follows are several recipes for preparing oysters—fricassee, stewed oysters, oyster fritters. (The oyster-fritter recipe is also suitable for clams.) In the salt-cod department we have boiled salt cod, codfish cakes, and fish and brewis (pronounced "broose")—a Newfoundland way to prepare salt cod. There are also two robust Portuguese recipes for salt fish.

OYSTER FRICASSEE

Melt one cup of butter in a spider, put in two quarts of oysters; let them boil up once, remove from the stove; add one cup of cream, pepper to taste, and one tablespoonful of flour mixed in a little cold milk. Put back on the stove, and let it boil till the oysters are cooked. Take off, and add the yolks of three eggs well beaten; pour over a platter of hot, toasted crackers. Serve hot. "I can safely say that Hood's Sarsaparilla will drive away all impurity from the blood." G.W. HARTER, *Smithville,* O.

From *Hood's Combined Cook Books,* by C.I. Hood & Co., 1875-1885, page 11

Like all true fricassees, this is thickened with egg yolks and produces a very tasty, rich dish. The instruction to "boil" the oysters is a bit alarming because it really takes little time to cook an oyster. Since the term is used so frequently in the nineteenth century, I am inclined to believe that "boil" meant simmer, not a rolling boil. Few people today serve this sort of a dish on crackers, preferring buttered toast. The choice is yours. The following is a slightly altered interpretation.

1 cup butter
2 quarts shucked oysters
1 tablespoon flour mixed in 2 tablespoons milk
1 cup cream (or half and half)
3 beaten egg yolks

1. Melt butter in a deep, heavy pan; when butter has melted, put in the oysters and cook until the edges curl.
2. Remove oysters from the pan and whisk in flour and milk mixture. Cook for three minutes. While it is cooking, mix together cream and egg yolks.
3. Add the cream and egg yolks to the pan, and cook gently until the sauce is hot, then return the oysters to the pan and warm through.
4. Serve on top of hot pilot crackers toasted briefly under the broiler.

Yields 8 servings.

STEWED OYSTERS

Take the oysters from the liquor with a wooden fork, in order to free them from the grit that floats in the liquor, and to keep them whole; put the oysters into a stew-pan, and let the liquor stand half an hour to settle; then pour off all that runs clear, put it into the pan with the oysters, boil them over a moderate fire, and, just before they come to a boil, skim them well, braid together a table-spoonful of flour and two of butter with a pinch of pepper and mace; stir this into the oysters, give the whole one boil up, and pour it upon sippets of toast and crackers, already prepared in your dish; serve hot.

Oysters, stewed in milk

To stew oysters in milk, proceed as above, using milk and a little salt, instead of the oyster liquor.

From *The Practical Cookbook,* by Mrs. Bliss, 1864, page 34

These recipes for oyster stew are thickened with a roux, which is not commonly done today. The milkless recipe yields a stew that has a pronounced oyster flavor. The recipe is clear enough that it does not require an interpretation. Provide a half pint, more or less, of oysters for each serving. A tablespoon of flour and two of butter will thicken a pint of oysters.

OYSTER OR CLAM FRITTERS

25 oysters or clams for a full batter recipe above

1. Chop raw shucked and drained oysters coarsely; if using a food processor, be sure to leave large pieces.
2. Add to the fritter batter and mix to blend.
3. Drop about two tablespoons of batter per fritter into deep hot (350°) fat, allowing 1 1/2 minutes per side or until the fritters turn brown and float.
4. Lift out and drain on paper. Keep the fritters hot in the oven until all are fried.

Yields 40 fritters.

FRITTER BATTER

3 eggs
1 3/4 cups milk
2 cups flour
1 teaspoon baking powder
salt and pepper

1. Beat the eggs well.
2. Add 1/2 cup milk, salt and pepper, and mix well. Sift together the dry ingredients.
3. Add liquid mixture to one cup of flour, mixing it well, then the remaining milk and flour alternately till all is mixed.

OYSTER OR CLAM FRITTERS

Fritter Batter (No. 2).
Ingredients: One pint of milk, three eggs, a little salt, one pint of flour. It can be made with or without a tea-spoonful of baking-powder.
Beat the eggs well; add part of the milk and salt, then the flour and milk alternately, beating it all quickly, and cooking it immediately, dropping it by the spoonful into boiling hot lard. The fritters are improved by using prepared flour, Horsfords or Hecker's being especially good.

Oyster or Clam Fritters (No. 1).
Chop, not too fine, twenty-five of either clams or oysters (bearded or not), and mix them in the fritter batter of either of the above receipts.

From *Practical Cooking and Dinner Giving,* by Mrs. Mary F. Henderson, 1882, pages 229-30

These fritters are very good. Plan to have your oysters already chopped before adding them to the fritter batter. Save the oyster liquor and use with the milk in the fritter batter. In testing, the batter made with two cups of liquid proved to be a very loose one so in the interpretation the liquid has been reduced by a quarter cup. A friend suggests adding lemon juice to the batter as well.

As you have no doubt observed by now, lard was in the nineteenth century the universal fat for cooking. You may substitute vegetable shortening or oil. An interpretation follows.

BOILED SALT COD, OR DUN FISH

Put a salt cod, weighing seven or eight pounds into a sufficient quantity of water to cover it, and let it stand in a warm place overnight. In the morning pour off this water, wash the fish clean, put it into a kettle with cold water, add enough to cover it, and place the kettle where the water will scald. Keep the water scalding hot until within half an hour of dinner; turn off this hot water, and replace it with cold water, let it have one boil up, and the fish is ready for the table....

> **Pork scraps** *are made as follows.—Cut two slices of salt fat pork into very small bits, put these bits into a frying-pan and over a hot fire; stir them frequently until all the fat is extracted and they are a light brown crisp; serve in a sauce tureen.*
>
> From *The Practical Cookbook,* by Mrs. Bliss, 1864, page 27

As previously noted, a boiled salt-codfish dinner was usually accompanied by boiled vegetables, such as potatoes, beets, and carrots, and often was served with fried salt pork. Kiddy King's name for fried salt-pork scraps—"Essex sauce"—was a very elegant term for a plebeian item. The multiple soakings and scaldings remove every evidence that the fish has ever been salted, so the pork fat and scraps do not seem overpoweringly salty. In fact, they are needed to provide some flavor.

A seven- or eight-pound salt cod, besides being very hard to come by these days, would serve a very large group of people. One pound of salt cod will do very nicely for four, possibly with enough left over for codfish cakes or hash for breakfast.

An interpretation of this recipe is not really necessary. Follow the instructions above, but keep in mind that letting it lie in scalding water for a whole morning, or three or four hours, was easy to do in the days of open fires and cookstoves and may have been necessary depending on how dried the fish was when purchased. The salt cod available today is salted but not completely desiccated. The process Mrs. Bliss described is not required these days to cook your salt cod well. Twenty minutes of a gentle simmer will make it tender enough to flake apart.

Boil the vegetables separately, and serve all together on a platter with a sauce of your choice. Egg sauce (page 226) is a good choice.

At least once in your life, you should try boiled salt cod with salt pork fat and scraps served on it. It is perfectly delicious. The scraps when cut up should be about a quarter-inch square. Cook them till they are golden—be careful not to scorch them. Drizzle the fat over the fish and vegetables and garnish with the scraps.

CODFISH CAKES

> *Soak codfish overnight, and scald it, add to it twice its quantity of boiled potatoes, knead all well together, make in small cakes and fry in butter. If, after having boiled cod fish, you have some left, use it in the same way. It makes a nice and wholesome dish.*
>
> From *The Complete Domestic Guide,* by Mrs. L.G. Abell, 1853, page 87

Another leftovers dish, usually eaten at breakfast and known variously as fish cakes or fish balls, was usually made out of cod. In 1833, Mrs. Child wrote that "There is no way of preparing salt fish for breakfast, so nice as to roll it up in little balls, after it is mixed with mashed potatoes; dip it into an egg, and fry it brown." This New England classic appeared at breakfast all through the century, for in 1882 Mrs. Henderson wrote, "Of course they are better fried at once, but may be made the night before serving (at breakfast), if they are only properly *mixed*."[109]

If you are making the fish cakes from scratch, from salt cod, follow the instructions for boiling salt cod on the previous page. Then follow the adapted recipe below. Mrs. Henderson was right: it really does work best if the fish and potatoes are hot when you mix them.

1 cup cooked salt cod (1/2 lb. before soaking)
2 cups boiled potatoes
butter or bacon drippings

1. With a fork, finely shred the boiled cod. Mash the potatoes very smooth in a separate pan (adding, if you wish, butter, pepper, and a little milk).
2. Shape the fishcakes into the desired size and fry till golden brown on both sides.

Yields 14 two-inch fishcakes.

BOILED SALT COD, PORTUGUESE STYLE

Soak, cook, and debone the salt codfish, and serve it with boiled potatoes and cooked kale or collards. Pour olive oil over it, and pepper it.

From Rose Camacho Hirsch, Stonington, Connecticut, 1988

This way of preparing salt cod is basically like the New England style, except that kale is included and olive oil is used in place of salt-pork fat and scraps. The olive oil should be passed at the table for each to add to taste. Allow one pound of salt cod for four servings. If you buy the boneless cod, you can omit one job.

FISHERMAN'S BREWIS

Salt fish as required Hard bread as required Fat Pork as Required
To prepare Bread: Split cakes of hard bread; allow 1 cake per person. Place in large saucepan well covered with water. Soak overnight. The next day, using same water bring to near boil. (do not boil)
Drain immediately. Keep hot. To prepare fish, soak salt fish overnight, changing water once. Boil for 20 minutes until fish is flaky. Drain and remove skin and bones from fish. Combine fish and hard bread together. Serve with scrunchions (small cubes of fat pork fried to golden brown). Annie Mugford, Clarkes Beach, Newfoundland.

From *Fat Back and Molasses: A Collection of Favorite Recipes from Newfoundland and Labrador*, by Rev. Ivan Jesperson, 1974, page 130

Reading the recipe for fish and brewis ("broos") will raise for many the specters of hypertension and cholesterol problems. But it is perfectly delicious, which amazed those who tested it and thought that soaked hardbread would be all mushy (it holds its shape very well) and the whole mess either too salty or bland (it was neither). The secret is the salt pork, which you *must* use.

Traditional recipes, of course, vary the ingredients from one piece of hardtack per person to two pieces for four; from an undefined "one salt codfish" to one pound for four servings. Soaked hardtack swells considerably, and in the following recipe it outbulks the codfish by quite a bit. Adjust it to your taste; you can make a perfectly good fish and brewis with half a cake per person. Salt cod, which in some places you can buy whole, with bones in and skin on, varies in weight, but allow at least one pound for four to six servings and you will have plenty left over for hash.

A friend who lived for a while on Fogo Island, Newfoundland, reports that her neighbors cautioned her against boiling the brewis. It is to be cooked gently: "You brews the brewis."

1 lb. boned salt codfish
1/2 to 1 cake hardtack per person
1/2 to 3/4 lb. salt pork
The night before:

1. In a deep bowl put the hardtack covered well with water. In another bowl, put the cod also covered with water. Soak overnight.

Next day:
2. Change the water on the codfish and let soak until mealtime.
3. When you are ready to prepare the dish, put the hardtack (brewis) on to cook over a medium heat, allowing it to simmer only.
4. Meanwhile, cut the salt pork up into small pieces and fry over a low heat till the bits of fat are all golden brown.
5. While the salt pork is cooking, put the fish in fresh water and cook till it is flaky (about 10 minutes).
6. Drain the brewis, and break it up into smaller pieces. Flake the fish apart and mix into the brewis. Add pepper to taste. Put on a platter and drizzle all the salt pork fat over the fish and brewis and sprinkle the scrunchions on top.

Yields 4-6 very hearty servings.

BACALHAU

Flake apart salt codfish which has been soaked overnight and cooked. Get all the bones out. Cook lots of onions—3-4—with a little olive oil, garlic, paprika, salt and pepper, the onions fried till soft only. Put the fish on a plate with boiled and quartered potatoes around, and spread the onions on top, garnish with hard cooked eggs, and chickpeas.

From Rose Camacho Hirsch, Stonington, Connecticut, 1988

Mrs. Hirsch's mother, Maria Goulart Camacho of Stonington, Connecticut, prepared salt codfish this way at Christmastime, as Mrs. Hirsch's family still does. Salt cod is also made into codfish cakes and served at Christmas (a recipe can be found on page 359).

This recipe needs no interpretation. Plan on using a pound of dried salt cod to start. Follow instructions for the boiled salt codfish on page 358. Boil three to four medium potatoes separately, and have about half a cup of cooked chickpeas and two to three hard-boiled eggs for garnishing.

Yields 4-6 servings.

SALMON SALAD

Flake remnants of cold boiled salmon, mix with French, Mayonnaise, or Cream Dressing. Arrange on nests of lettuce leaves. Garnish with the yolk of a hard boiled egg forced through a potato ricer, and white of egg cut in strips.

From *The Boston Cooking-School Cookbook,* by Fannie Merritt Farmer, 1896, page 298

For her cold or shellfish salads, Miss Farmer favored French, or what we would call vinaigrette, dressing; cream dressing, a cooked dressing made with cream, vinegar, butter, and an egg flavored with mustard, salt, and sugar; and mayonnaise, for which her instructions sound very modern indeed. Though she did not say so, canned salmon substituted admirably for cold, leftover boiled—or poached—salmon. This recipe does not need interpretation.

The illustration of this salad on page 332 shows a manner of garnishing suggested in Marion Harland's *Dinner Year Book,* 1878, and is accomplished by poking the yolks out of several slices of hard boiled eggs, and laying the rings around the salad.

DEVILED LOBSTER

Deviled Lobster is made the same way as deviled crab, merely substituting the lobster for the crab, and adding a grating of nutmeg to the seasoning. In boiling lobsters and crabs, they are sufficiently cooked when they assume a bright red color. Too much boiling renders them tough.

From *Practical Cooking and Dinner Giving,* by Mrs. Henderson, 1882, page 118

To make deviled crab, Mrs. Henderson advised, take "six ounces of crab meat, mix two ounces of bread crumbs, two hard-boiled eggs chopped, the juice of half a lemon, Cayenne pepper and salt. Mix all with cream sauce, or what is still better, a Bèchamel sauce," simple enough a procedure not to require interpretation, except to note that Mrs. Henderson assumed cooked lobster or crab. The nutmeg with lobster is very good.

To make an elegant presentation, enabling the diner to eat lobster without having to crack open messy shells at table, the cook must pick the meat out of the lobster and keep the shell as intact as possible. The tail section should be made into a boat shape and the body cleaned out and laid open-side up. The deviled lobster meat is then spooned back inside, and the whole run under a broiler till golden.

Cooking and Eating Seafood

When Timothy Dwight visited Newport, Rhode Island, in 1811, he reported that Newport was acknowledged to have the best fish market in the United States. Dwight listed 112 fish and shellfish species caught in neighboring waters, of which 66 were described as fit for the table. Yet only a few dozen of these commonly appeared in comprehensive cookbooks of the period, and only another dozen or so were added in the subsequent century.[1] *As surprising as it may seem, even in maritime New England only about half the edible fish species were commonly eaten.*

Fishermen are shown dressing their catch at Biddeford Pool, Maine, circa 1884. A typical workday scene in a New England fishing community. Opposite, a pair of broiled mackerel garnished with little balls of potatoes and parsley as suggested by Mrs. Henderson in 1882. Recipe on page 400. [Baldwin Coolidge photo, MSM 79.18.1]

The culinary history of fish in America is difficult to research, even with the variety of research materials available today. Cookbooks might be considered good indicators of fish-eating in America, but until the appearance of Amelia Simmons' *American Cookery* in 1796, most cookbooks printed in this country were reprints of English cookbooks. Fish peculiar to certain regions of North America were accepted because of their similarity to a fish that settlers had known in England. The early colonists probably prepared such fish without benefit of specific recipes and ate them as they had eaten the analogous fish at home. If they needed cooking instructions they might turn to a cookbook and use one of the generic "fish" recipes that cookbooks have included since the 1600s. Consequently, cookbooks are of limited value in determining the full range and variety of fish as food. We may assume, however, that a reference to a certain fish assures us of its acceptance, sometimes indicates its status, and may even point to the frequency with which it was used compared to other fish.

Of the various kinds of cookbooks, community cookbooks assembled and sold by organizations frequently reveal trends in food popularity. They reflect at least some of a community's real food preferences; these cookbooks were not intended to be an encyclopedic source for every kind of recipe imaginable. Because recipes were included in the spirit of sharing favorites, they are one test for a recipe's prevalence. For that reason they are useful for gauging the popularity of fish and fish products. Community cookbooks are more common after the 1870s, and I have examined several from coastal New England towns. My sample of American cookbooks dates between 1796 and 1930, but it emphasizes the nineteenth century. I selected those most likely to have been used in New England. In some cases I checked subsequent editions to see which fish were added over time. In my research I included sixteen community cookbooks, eight of them from coastal towns and eight from inland communities, including the Midwest and the South. Despite the small size of this sample, some trends certainly can be observed.

Ideally, we could compare cookbook evidence with narratives, diaries, and letters to glean people's opinions of various seafoods. But all too often meals have gone unrecorded even among the literate few who most often kept written records. Given the rarity of such food references, it is difficult for us to accurately evaluate whether mentions of specific fish indicate that they were typical rather than exceptional. We do know from general sources that seafood was often food for the poor, but the written record of the poor in early America is so sparse that we can discern very little about their opinions and preferences.

Archeologists increasingly investigate seventeenth-, eighteenth-, and nineteenth-century sites, and their evidence supplements the written historical record. In archeological sites fish comprise just a small percentage of the bones remaining from long-past meals. Large bones of the biggest fish survive in such places, but the tiny bones of alewives, herring, and little panfish may have largely decayed, skewing the evidence from such sites. So only a little information on fish-eating comes to us from the archeologists.

Although we must rely on a variety of incomplete sources, it is possible to identify at least the most highly favored fish of the nineteenth century. After reviewing the general methods of serving fish, we will look at the three dozen most popular fish in nineteenth-century New England. As we have already seen, preferences for fish (in fact, for most foods) are tremendously complicated by cultural influences, regional and even local traditions, and finally by personal idiosyncrasy, all of which may change over time. The picture is full of apparent contradictions. As we go through the list of the nineteenth-century's favorites, we must bear in mind this complex of influences on anyone to accept or reject that fish as food.

General Instructions About Fish

Thomas De Voe's *Market Assistant* of 1866 distinguished among fish found in markets partly along culinary lines: large fish, preferable for roasting, boiling, or baking; and small fish, preferable for frying or broiling on the gridiron. Generally, until the late 1800s fish were sold whole, though gutted, and it was up to the cook either to section or to fillet them. Some might heed Georgiana Hill's recommendation: "Always if practicable allow the fish-dealer to prepare fish for cooking." Many recipes for fish remind the cook to remove the scales, and "clean, wash, and wipe" the fish, and often to trim the fins and tails as well. "Some kinds of small fish need to be skinned, but this is done at the market," commented Maria Parloa.[2]

Usually the size of a fish rather than its species determined how it would be cooked. Miss Parloa prefaced her instructions: "A general rule for boiling fish, which will hold for all kinds, and thus save a great deal of time and space is this: Any fish weighing between four and six pounds....a general rule, that will cover all kinds of baked fish,...A fish weighing about five pounds....Bluefish, young cod, mackerel, salmon, large trout, and all other fish, when they weigh between half a pound and four pounds are nice for broiling. When smaller or larger they are not so good." Many cookbooks instructed cooks to bake or poach larger fish and suggested ways to prepare the leftovers. Most agreed that smaller fish were best fried. "They are often called pan-fish for this reason," wrote Miss Parloa.[3] Salted fish, as well as oily fish such as mackerel, shad, and bluefish, were often split and broiled, as were other medium-sized split fish.

While these guidelines hold true in many cookbooks, a closer examination shows that, most often, the white-fleshed fish were baked or stewed, and the oilier fish were broiled. Some fish, including bluefish, shad, and mackerel,

were cooked all three ways, depending on their size.

With very large fish like salmon or halibut, consumers could buy a large piece, often weighing up to five pounds—a sort of roast of fish—or smaller cuts like steaks. Wesley Pierce described fresh cod caught in the gill-net fishery of the 1880s: "they were splendid large cod and brought a good price selling for steak-cod in the fish markets, that had the best hotel and restaurant trade." In some cases, fresh fish, especially larger ones, were cut into thick cubes or squares for cooking.[4]

Some cookbook writers declared that boiling was the least desirable method of preparation, but gave instructions for it anyway. Maria Parloa conceded that boiling produced the best leftovers, and she and others assumed that fish skin and bones would be removed before the cook made up fish cakes and balls, salads, or fish "à la crème."[5]

Serving a large fish at table meant carving it. Writing in 1869, Georgiana Hill instructed that the thickest parts were most esteemed but a bit of back and belly should be offered to each diner. She also noted that salmon should be carved lengthwise rather than across the grain. Hill and Parloa both recommended using fried smelts as a garnish for larger fish.[6]

White sauce and salt pork fat: "Our American cooks show a painful lack of ingenuity in adapting the less palatable and less expensive fish and meats by skillful cooking and the use of sauce as is done abroad," claimed Dr. Harvey W. Wiley in 1914 in the *The Pure Food Cookbook*. As we noted earlier, most people agreed that fish needed some kind of sauce to make it seem more substantial. But as Mrs. Henderson acknowledged in 1882, "The French say the English"—and by extension New Englanders—"only know how to make one kind of sauce and a poor one at that." She pointed out what Mrs. Child and others had known all along: "Notwithstanding the French understand the sauce question, it is very convenient to make the drawn butter, and, by adding different flavorings, make just so many kinds of sauce." Her drawn butter sauce recipe differed little from Mrs. Child's of fifty years earlier: "Water thickened with flour and water while boiling, with sweet butter put in to melt, is the common sauce," said Mrs. Child. She also used flour to thicken the fat from frying fish and stirred in hot water to make a gravy for fried fish. Mrs. Henderson's drawn butter sauce called for flour, butter, and water or "better, white stock," which she recommended embellishing with capers to make caper sauce, chopped pickles to make pickle sauce, hardboiled eggs to make egg sauce, and so on. Through the early twentieth century the simple white sauce made with water or milk—or sometimes cream—was used for sauce over fish. Often leftover fish was warmed over in it, or layered up with crumbs.[7]

The other popular sauce was salt-pork fat, often with the scraps included. Tried out salt-pork fat added desirable flavor and calories to chowder. Mrs. Child said that although drawn butter sauce was most common, "It is more economical to cut salt pork into small bits, and try it till the pork is brown and crispy." Caroline King called this "Essex Sauce," but in most sources it goes nameless. Salt-pork fat was poured over boiled fish, was often served over salt fish, and was also widely used to fry fish. In 1849 Mrs. Putnam recommended serving pieces of salt pork along with cod or haddock fried in the fat. Not only was salt-pork fat economical, it was downright common, so the more self-consciously stylish cookbook writers of the 1800s did not include it in their lists of sauces. However, at the turn of the century Fanny Farmer and Mary Lincoln, like the good New Englanders they were, both mentioned salt pork as an accompaniment to salt cod. Mrs. Lincoln did not advocate the salt-pork fat, but she acknowledged that if one served salt cod with boiled vegetables, an egg sauce, and "crisp salt pork scraps," they would duplicate "the old-fashioned salt fish dinner."[8]

As we saw aboard fishing schooners, the combination of salt pork, salt fish, and boiled vegetables endured into the twentieth century, sometimes with the salt-pork fat made into a milk gravy for the fish. In the Canadian Maritime Provinces, salt fish is still garnished with "scrunchions"—the crisp renderings of salt pork called "crungeons" by fisherman Barry Fisher—in fish and brewis, which is boiled salt cod and boiled hardtack.[9]

Modern dietary practices make some people hesitate to fortify fish with animal fats—butter, cream, egg, or salt pork. Yet, as we have seen, in the nineteenth century and even today such fatty sauces make fish seem more substantial and flavorful. And also, as we have seen, our more sedentary lives make such high-calorie meals less appropriate than they were a century ago.

Boning and filleting: In 1887 Maria Parloa wrote: "The word "fillet" when used in a culinary sense, means a delicate, tender piece; so when we wish for a fillet of fish, flesh, or fowl we take it from the tenderest part of the animal. All the flesh of fish can be cut into small fillets."[10]

The fillet of fish became a regular culinary feature in the middle of the nineteenth century, at least among stylish cooks. Not until later in the century, however, did the removal of fish bones become important enough to warrant consistent mention in cookbooks. Even though some fish were still being served whole, an increasing effort to diminish the natural, undomesticated appearance of the creature was accompanied by an increasing distaste for the natural, bone-filled experience of eating fish, so deboning became *de rigueur*.

In her cusk à la crème recipe, for example, Miss Parloa told the cook to use cusk, cod, or haddock, and when the fish was cooked "carefully remove all the skin and the head; then turn the fish over...and scrape the skin from the other side. Pick out all the small bones. You will find them the whole length of the back, and a few in the lower part of the fish, near the tail. They are in rows like pins in a paper, and if you start all right it will take but a few minutes to remove them. Then take out the back-bone starting at the head and working gently down toward the tail."[11] This tedious process helps explain the popularity of boneless salt fish in the 1880s and of commercially processed fillets early in the twentieth century.

Community cookbooks from the early 1900s often included salmon and halibut, usually in large sections or steaks. They occasionally gave instructions for baking or boiling whole, stuffed fish, but mostly these books contained recipes for fish already flaked apart in the form of leftovers, canned fish, or boned and processed fish.[12] This emphasis on boneless portions of fish is further evidence that having to cope with bones, either at the table or in the kitchen, suppressed fish-eating. As we saw in the last chapter, by the late nineteenth century processors understood that deboning and filleting greatly increased the acceptance of fish by consumers.

Fish fins, napes, tongues, sounds, and heads: Nineteenth-century New Englanders—in fact most North Americans—ate cuts of meat and organ meats that no longer appear in the butcher's section of modern grocery stores. So too with fish. In the processing of modern fish fillets, the heads, napes, and bones are whisked away as refuse; formerly each had a place at the table.

The elastic membrane of the swim bladder—known to fishermen as the sound—was commonly dried to produce isinglass as a clarifying agent, but it also came to the table. "The shoulder part of the codfish and mackerel, and cod-sounds are the most admired by epicures," wrote Georgiana Hill in 1869. Mrs. Beeton, in 1871, wrote: "Of (codfish) the parts about the backbone and shoulders are the firmest and most cherished by connoisseurs. The sound which lines the fish beneath the backbone is considered a delicacy, as are also the gelatinous parts about the head and neck."[13] Many other cookbooks provided recipes for preparing the head and shoulders of fish, often cod, and for dressing the sounds. As we have seen, cod sounds were occasionally salted aboard fishing vessels, as were the tongues and cheeks.

Aboard the *Fair American* off Newfoundland in 1794, William

At Monhegan Island in the late 1800s, these fishermen were dressing cod ashore in the same way fish were dressed for salting aboard ship. The man at the left with a knife in his right hand grasps the sound bone in his left, slicing it off the backbone from head to tail. [MSM 83.2.3]

Corn oysters, left, and fried oysters, right. Recipes on page 397.

Strickland observed the crew catch a halibut, which they "greedily devoured." Strickland reported that the fish was "only indifferent food being very oily, and soft in the flesh; the head and fins are equally taken by the Captain for use of the Cabin, and being baked with a little seasoning of herbs and spices, afford a good but cloying dish." To his taste, they were even less palatable when salted.[14] Of interest here is not Strickland's opinion of them, but the fact that heads and fins were appreciated highly enough to be reserved for the ship's cabin.

Commenting on the danger and relatively low profit of halibut fishing in 1852, Lorenzo Sabine urged the reader to admire the fishermen who "procure for him the luscious napes and fins which garnish his board." Another source, *The Fisheries of Gloucester*, published in 1876, confirmed fin-eating: "The fins of the [halibut] are also preserved in salt and pickle; but those who eat them in this condition know but little of the richness and delicacy of the fresh fin." And John Whidden, recalling the early days of New England fishing, said that "Great halibut were often caught, and besides furnishing a food supply, the napes were always saved by the crew, for smoking after being cured." The smoking was done in the smoky forepeaks of the old fishing vessels.[15]

Recipes for cod sounds appear in eighteenth-century cookbooks, or later ones based on them—often of English origin—and these include cod sounds in fricassee, sounds broiled and served with gravy, ragouts, and even a way to dress sounds to look like small chickens. Through the nineteenth century the eating of sounds diminished, and recipes for them are not nearly as common in later American works, although one of Frank E. Davis's early-1900s advertising cookbooks gives directions for freshening and cooking salted sounds.[16]

"We often had tongues and sounds. Sounds are like deep sea scallops," wrote Georgia Maria Blanchard, who ate them aboard the down-easter *Bangalore* when she accompanied her captain husband around Cape Horn in 1906. Cod tongues and cheeks remained in favor longer than the sounds. "I never could stand that tidbit which the captain called 'tongues and sounds.' God knows what it was but it came from a codfish. Over it the captain would smack his lips and nod his head approvingly," wrote a passenger on the coasting schooner *Alicia B. Crosby* during a trip from Maine to Virginia in 1897. Tongues and cheeks are still occasionally available in fish markets. Eighty years ago, when codfish were typically twice the size of those caught today, these pieces of fish meat were substantial. The cheeks—jaw muscles—and the tongue—not literally the tongue but rather the muscle at the base of the tongue—were dipped in beaten egg, then in flour, then in egg again, or in a batter, and fried. Judging from cookbooks, which contain few recipes for cheeks and tongues, one would think they were rarely eaten. Yet other sources tell us they were frequently consumed as a vernacular dish in rural places and among people who tended not to record their recipes.[17]

Cheeks and tongues are occasionally found in modern fish markets, and as small, boneless chunks of white flesh they appeal to modern tastes. Fish fins and sounds, however, are hardly ever seen in the market now, although they are, as some descriptions affirm, very delicate and rich. Their gelatinous quality, once praised by many, is not appreciated by modern people, most of whom do not like the "mouth feel" of such soft pieces of fish.

Fish as "relish": Salted and smoked fish were sometimes sufficiently cooked by the smoking process to be edible without much further preparation. One might simmer a bit of smoked fish in water or milk to be served, sometimes on toast; or heat a small pickled or smoked fish in the oven or on a broiler; or fry a small fresh pan fish. Each of these methods made a quick dish for breakfast, tea, or supper. Fish balls, cakes, and hash also became a relish—a small, appetizing dish. At the turn of the century, the Women's Christian Temperance Union cookbook, for example, offered "Relish for Breakfast"—salt fish soaked overnight, crackers, eggs, butter, milk, salt, and pepper, all mixed together and baked. Mrs. Lincoln wrote that salt fish, soaked, then browned over a hot fire "makes a nice relish with potatoes which have been roasted in the ashes....Smoked salmon or halibut may be prepared the same way." As Frank Davis indicated in one of his early-1900s cookbooks, many of these relishes became what we in the latter twentieth century call appetizers. "Smoked halibut is a splendid appetizer served without any preparation whatever except cut into inch cubes," commented Davis, who also offered a way of preparing it in a cream sauce to be served on toast.[18]

New England's Fish Choices

About three dozen fish, shellfish, and seafood products were sufficiently favored between the 1790s and the 1930s to appear consistently in New England's cookbooks. However, few New Englanders actually ate all three dozen, for many were only locally or seasonally available. The choices changed over time, too, as certain fish products like salt mackerel fell out of favor and others, such as canned salmon, were put on the market.

Some fish appear consistently in culinary sources from the seventeenth through the nineteenth century. Some, including cod, salt cod, mackerel, trout, haddock, salmon, sea bass, oysters, lobsters, and shrimp, were great favorites. Some appear in the early books and then disappear, either because they were overfished, like the sturgeon and terrapin, or because they fell out of favor, like eels and salt mackerel. Other fish took longer to gain popular favor, like halibut, bluefish, turbot, pollock, cusk, scallops, swordfish, and tuna. Certain fish products caught on firmly enough to be included, like finnan haddie, and canned salmon, tuna, shrimp, and crab. Mussels have the distinction of being included in very early sources and then not reappearing for nearly two centuries.[19]

The following alphabetical list of the top seafood choices includes a brief description of the fishing methods used to obtain each species, particularly as it affected the fish as food, and a discussion of how it was commonly cooked.

Alewives (Alosa pseudoharengus)

This important fish seldom exceeds a foot in length or a pound in weight, but it was a significant presence all along the Atlantic coast. Related to the herring and shad, the alewife was reportedly named for the size of its belly. Like shad, alewives swim in large numbers upstream from salt water to spawn in fresh water each spring. They were easily caught with dip nets wherever they gathered to leap over little falls.[20]

Although they were seldom named in cookbooks, alewives were important enough that communities regulated rights to fish for them, and their comings and goings were noted. The Mystic *Press* of 10 May 1877 commented: "Alewives or 'ellwhops,' as they are called on the Connecticut River—have been taken quite plentifully recently, at the outlet of Norwood Pond, Mystic Bridge. Pardon Brown took 250 in one day by sinking a piece of old net and enclosing them, and Ira Noyes took 150 with a small scoop net. These fish make their appearance yearly at this season in the rivers long this part of the coast, and are identical with the Buckies of Rhode Island which appear later in the season strung 20 on a stick, dried and smoked in our grocery stores."

Some alewives were pickled, some were smoked, and some were used as bait.[21] We assume that nineteenth-century cooks treated alewives just as they did panfish or herrings.

In Rhode Island, "buckies" were the salted and smoked version of alewives. The name perhaps was a corruption of "buckling," which was a term for hot-smoked herring, eels, mackerel, and other oily fish. Howard Burdick recalled that, once they had been smoked, buckies were strung on willow wands for storage in a manner similar to eels.[22] These fish fall into the category of "relish" for tea or breakfast.

Bluefish and Striped Bass (Pomatomus saltatrix & Roccus saxatilis)

Bluefish and striped bass are wily predators who stalk schools of mackerel and menhaden throughout the New England summers. Striped bass especially was a recreational fish in the later nineteenth century, often sought by "sports" who chartered boats to seek them during a day on the water or joined fishing clubs like those on Cuttyhunk Island, Massachusetts, to fish for them in the surf.[23] Bluefish were caught both by sports and by commercial fishermen, and both fish were favored for chowder parties.

Striped bass was similar to the European sea bass, so it was recognizable to settlers who encountered it spawning in eastern rivers. They would have prepared it in the fashion they had in Britain. As a fish with white flesh, not too oily, the striped bass was one of the species for which generic "fish" recipes were usually suitable.

Well-known as a fierce and voracious eater that follows schools of mackerel and menhaden from the South into New England waters, the bluefish has dark, oily flesh. Bluefish were caught from late spring through fall in southern New England, and less often during a shorter season in Maine. With the advent of stationary pound nets and fish traps to snare fish traveling alongshore, both bluefish and striped bass were more frequently caught and brought to market by the middle of the nineteenth century, adding an increasing commercial component to the already popular fishery for both species.[24]

Although it was eaten by coastal residents who caught it, the bluefish was not added to the list of common table fish until later in the nineteenth century. It truly was best cooked as quickly as possible. Thomas Hazard recalled that, as a boy in Narragansett, Rhode Island, bluefish—which he called "horse mackerel"—tasted best when brought to the cook "alive and flipping." In the 1870s the U.S. Fish Commission also recommended immediately bleeding the fish in order to improve the flavor, firmness, and whiteness of the flesh. "The blue-fish is, however, very sweet and savory, but does not keep very well; and the difference in taste between a fish fresh from the water and one that has been out a few days...is very great," said the Fish Commission. In his 1878 *Grocer's Manual*, Peter Felker wrote, "Its weight varies from five to ten pounds; as a fish for the table it is of superior quality."[25]

Clams (Mercenaria mercenaria, Spisula merritt & Mya arenaria)

Several different edible shellfish are called clams, and each species has numerous regional names. Three species of clam commonly appeared in New England references. First is the quahog or round clam, *Mercenaria mercenaria*, sometimes called the littleneck and hard clam. Preferences of the market have given it further names describing size—cherrystones, mediums, chowders. As their alternate names suggest, quahogs have hard, thick, cupped shells. They live in sandy bottom below the high tide level from Cape Cod south, and their habitat requires fishermen to use long-handled, curve-tined "bull rakes" to harvest them.[26]

A second species is the hen clam, *Spisula merritt*. Also called surf or bar clams, they are the largest of the New England clams. Surf clams have rather thin, shallow shells, and they live in beds off exposed beaches. In 1880, George Brown Goode dismissed quickly the sea clam and razor clam fisheries: sea clams were used for bait, and razor clams—the long, thin *Siliqua costata*—"are occasionally seen in the New York Market but have no sale as food. Their taste is sweetish and not approved."[27]

The other popular clam species was the soft-shell clam, *Mya arenaria*, also known as the steamer or long-neck clam. Steamers flourish in coarse mud between the high and low tide levels, so fishermen can harvest them with short-handled rakes at low tide. These clams are extremely prolific, inhabiting the mud and flats from Maine to the South. In 1834, the crew of the sloop *Planet* of Bridgeport, Connecticut, while fishing for cod and mackerel, found clams in astounding quantities at Martha's Vineyard: "during the night passed *Gay-Head—Tarpauline Cove* and came to anchor in *Holmes Hole* [Vineyard Haven]. lowered boats in the morning—one went a fishing, the other on shore for clams for bait—after ransacking the town found sufficient hoes & spades & commenced operations—....then steered my course for the clam flats—on arriving there found our tools were not wanted for clamming—they lay about 2 inches under the sands, so thick that it was difficult to work our fingers between them and could haul them up by the double hands full without the use of hoes in a few minutes our boats crew caught about 10 bushels and went on board pushed off and in the afternoon moored our bark in Nantucket harbor."[28]

As the *Planet*'s journal-keeper indicated, clams were highly esteemed as fish bait during the nineteenth century. For example, in Chatham, Massachusetts, in 1880, Goode reported that an estimated 35,000 bushels of soft-shell clams were dug annually, out of which just 2,600 bushels were eaten as food. In Ipswich, a town famous for fried and steamed clams in the twentieth century, the clams were dug in winter months, shucked and barreled, then "picked up by traders, who take them to storehouses where the clams are repacked, salted, and headed up for market," destined to be used for cod and haddock bait.[29]

Throughout the century, indigent clam-diggers might subsist on part of their harvest, selling the rest for bait; but, as we have seen in the chapters on clambakes and chowders, clams became increasingly valued as human food as the century progressed, particularly through the popularity of clambakes and chowders. In 1878, Felker wrote: "The common clam of the United States (Mya Arenaria) is much used for food, and is considered one of the greatest delicacies furnished us by the sea. The round clam or quahog...is also largely used for food but is much inferior to the preceding....They are, however, to some extent, put up in cans, shipped in cold weather, and sold in our markets." George Brown Goode reported in 1880 that "[clams] used for food are eaten at home by the persons catching, who are the farmers and villagers living near the shore, or who come down picnic fashion from the interior, as did the Indians of yore, to enjoy a feast of clams and seaside recreations, or they are disposed of in the markets of coast towns."[30] By 1896, clams were well enough regarded that Fannie Merritt Farmer ranked them next in value after the oyster among shellfish. This was

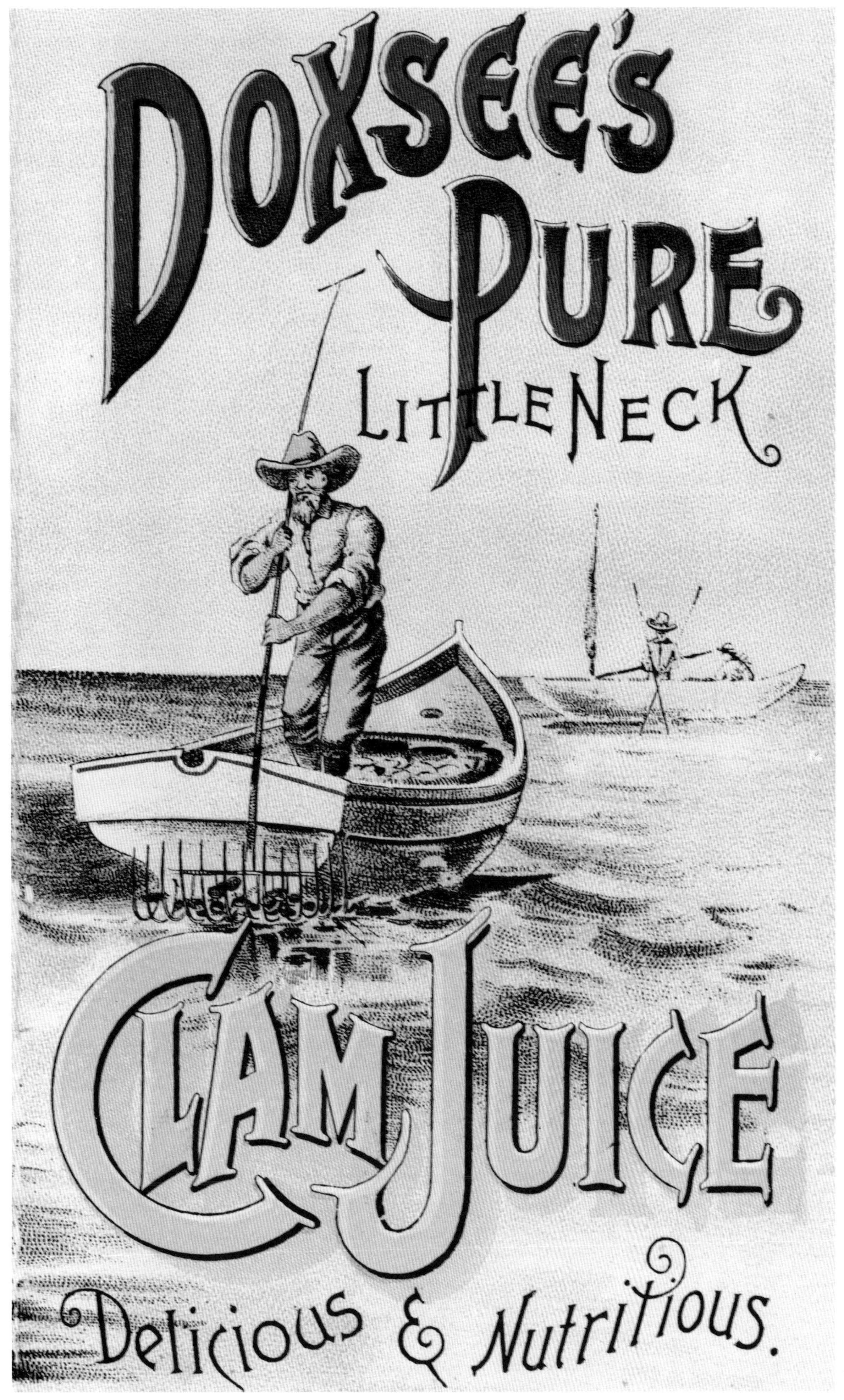
Doxsee's
Pure
Little Neck
Clam Juice
Delicious & Nutritious.

quite a promotion, as we shall see.

Cookbooks supply only sketchy information about clams consumed at home: they were made into chowder, clam soup, fritters, or were fried. Goode reported that like other shellfish, some clams were pickled. "These pickles are used primarily by ships, but in 1854 a large supply was sent to California."[31]

In the first half of the twentieth century, clams were still "so low in value, and in their fresh state offer such poor competition for oysters, that they have little sale beyond New York City," according to Edward Ackerman. There was no middleman to supply the market with clams; rather, clamming was a localized fishery, and the same person often both dug and sold clams to individuals or restaurants. Ackerman noted that Ipswich and Newburyport, Massachusetts, as well as Seabrook, New Hampshire, had large enough concentrations of clams to support shucking plants in the 1930s—as did East Greenwich, Rhode Island. All of these clam fisheries supplied New York.[32]

While both hard-shell and soft-shell clams were low in value, and the market for them not extensive beyond the summer chowder, clambake, and shore dinner circuit, still they have been locally praised and relished for the past century and a half. Throughout coastal New England, families could visit the local clam flats to dig a mess of clams to add variety to their meals. In Mystic, Connecticut, for example, "The Long Bar clam beach has been for a few days past alive with seekers after the succulent hardshells," noted the Mystic *Press* on 1 February 1877. "On Friday and Saturday probably not less than 100 different persons made drafts upon this wonderful bank each day, carrying away from a peck to a bushel each. The amount of food taken from this small

In the foreground, uncovered at low tide, is the famous Long "Bank," or bar, in the Mystic River. Here, according to the Mystic *Press*, clammers took many "drafts" of clams in the late 1800s. Clams became more popular as the nineteenth century progressed but are now gone from many of their old beds. On the east side of the river to the right is what is now Mystic Seaport. [Newbury Collection, MSM 80.41.21]

spot of ground...is simply wonderful." Edward Knapp glowingly described the clams he remembered digging on Sixpenny Island in the Mystic River during the winter of 1875-76: "the long, full 'Blue' variety, and O the sweetness of winter clams—they taste as if boiled in sugar."[33]

This appreciation for clams does not reflect their significance in the diets of most New Englanders. Clams may have been important for the subsistence of clammers, but for most others they were a recreational shellfish, ideal for consumption in clambakes, chowder parties, raw, or in shore or home dinners as fritters or fried tidbits. They were not food to offer guests at an important meal.

Cod (Gadus callarias) and Salt Cod

For most nineteenth-century New Englanders, eating fish meant eating cod, particularly salt cod. Cod is an omnivorous bottom-dwelling fish that frequents both inshore and offshore New England waters in season. It is an extremely prolific, watery, white-fleshed fish related to the haddock, hake, pollock, and cusk, but it grows far larger than any of the others, frequently exceeding six feet and 100 pounds when allowed to grow to maturity.

As we have seen in the last chapter, cod was an ideal fish to preserve with salt. Salt cod could be distributed overseas and far inland, but coastal families had the pick of the best fresh and salt cod. The weekly fish meal in New England often consisted of a boiled salt-cod dinner, as Caroline King related: "On Saturday night we always had a salt fish dinner. It must be a *dun* fish (whatever that may be) and the proper way to prepare it was to boil it encased in a cloth between two thin fishes of the same variety, which method was supposed to keep in the peculiar flavor, and render it tender. It was served with beets, carrots, potatoes, and cucumbers or lettuce; and egg sauce and Essex Sauce (made from bits of fried salt pork) were eaten with it."[34]

Salt cod: The dun fish Kiddy King referred to was one of several quality designations for salt fish. Processors divided salt fish into two general categories: merchantable and refuse. As we have already seen, the refuse grade was sent to the South and West Indies for plantation slave food. Merchantable salt fish were sold abroad, inland, and in New England, also in several grades.

During the long history of salt cod production, several terms have been used to label the fish, some of them reflecting the changes in curing methods in the nineteenth century. Two designations—stockfish and ling—commonly appeared in the British cookbooks of the sort that would have been used in early New England. As we have seen in the last chapter, stockfish was unsalted, air-dried fish—cod, pollock, or whiting—that could only be produced in a very dry climate, like Scandinavia's. Eventually, the word stockfish was generalized to include salt fish. In England, the term ling, a European relative of cod, was later used to denote salt cod. The terms stockfish and ling may also have taken on quality connotations, for in fifteenth- and sixteenth-century English records ling was far more costly than stockfish.[35] In New England, however, these terms were not commonly used, whereas dunfish and green fish were common designations.

Dunfish: Lorenzo Sabine reported that between the Revolution and 1852, when he was writing, one branch of the cod fishery was pursued in small boats at high and low slack tides by colonists of the Bay of Fundy, Isles of Shoals men, and farmer/fishermen in eastern Maine. "From the earliest, or as they are called, the spring fares of the cod-fish obtained in the Bay of Fundy, are made a considerable part of the table or dun-fish which are consumed in the New England states; and next to the Isles of Shoals fish, they are undoubtedly the best."[36]

In the 1830s, Gloucester schooner fishermen also caught cod for dunfish. According to Goode, "They were kept on flakes several weeks, and thoroughly dried until they became of a reddish color, and were highly esteemed as an article of food." In 1878, Felker described an alternative method of processing dunfish: "The Codfish are sometimes cured by being kept in a pile for two or three months, after salting, in a dark room, covered with salt grass, after which they are opened and again piled in a compact mass for about the same length of time. They are then known as dun fish, from their color, and are highly esteemed." Whether they were dried in the dark or in the light, the distinctive feature of dunfish was the light salting and relatively quick drying they received, which produced their distinctive flavor and consistency.[37]

A book called *The Husbandman and Housewife*, printed in 1820, gave instructions for preparing dunfish, comparing it to "an egg, an oyster or a clam, the more you boil the harder it grows. Let it simmer on or near the fire, in a kettle, two or three hours according as the fish is hard, and then change the water; and before dishing, put this up to near boiling heat but not higher. This management does not draw out but revives the glutinous and enlivens the nutritious substance in them, and leaves the fish tender and delicious."[38]

Kench-cured fish: Unlike dunfish, codfish split and salted aboard fishing vessels were kenched; that is, they were piled in the pens in the vessel's hold, where the combination of salt and the pressure of the stacked fish began the drying process. Brought ashore for drying at the end of the voyage, the fish were usually piled up again and even weighted down so further moisture was squeezed out. They were then laid out for air drying on the fish flakes, with canvas covers to prevent sun burn, and with doghouse-like flake boxes that were set over the stacked fish in inclement weather. Kench curing used more salt than for dunfish, but less than for pickled "green" fish. The product was sometimes called "*slack salted*" fish; it was also known variously as "*hard*" or "*dried*" salt fish.[39]

Green fish: By the 1870s, much salt cod produced in New England was "green" cured—not literally green, but undried, as in green corn—the opposite of dried corn. Green fish was literally pickled, being submerged in large casks full of brine until they had thoroughly absorbed the saline solution. British mariners fishing off Iceland in the fifteenth century had sometimes salted and barreled fish and carried them home in that state as green fish, so Gloucester fish companies preparing them in this fashion were hardly innovators.[40]

Green fish offered three advantages to fish producers. First, they could buy gutted fresh cod, haddock, or hake from the market fleet when the price was right and still process it as salt fish. Second, as was noted earlier, moist green fish were heavier, so a load of green cod meant a higher return. Third, since green fish were still fairly soft and pliable, they were ideal for skinning, boning, and packing in wooden boxes when boneless cod became a big item in the marketplace in the 1870s. Describing boneless "cod," Felker said, "Much of this form of fish is inferior in quality and consists of hake and haddock, fish closely related to the cod."[41]

Green pickled fish had several advantages for consumers as well. First, it was actually white; and, as already noted, by the middle of the nineteenth century the public preferred a white salt-fish product over reddish dunfish. And pickled fish, though dried, freshened more quickly compared to dun or kench-cured fish, which required an overnight soaking. When green fish was picked apart and sold as cod fluff it barely needed rehydrating at all; the cook could warm it up quickly in a cream sauce. By 1941, according to one report, boned and skinless salt cod constituted "from two-fifths to one half of the dried fish...consumed in the United States."[42]

Salt cod in the kitchen: As we have seen, salt cod was very often boiled and served with salt-pork scraps and fat. Mrs. Child, Mrs. Putnam, Caroline King, and many others paired salt fish and salt pork. Even salt fish carried aboard ship in the late nineteenth century was served in the cabin with salt pork. Of her voyage on board the *Bangalore* in 1906, Georgia Blanchard wrote: "On Fridays we usually had salt cod fish with pork scraps. It was delicious, in fact long after we left the sea we continued to have this for Friday dinner."[43] Contrary to what one might think, the combination of salt cod and salt pork was not necessarily too salty; when the cod is soaked properly it loses much of its saltiness—so much so that the salt from the pork seasons it.

Writing in 1849, Mrs. Putnam advised cooks to put salt fish or dunfish to soak, then put it in hot water, then remove it and wash off the fins and skin. "To make what is called scraps, cut a quarter of a pound of fat salt pork into very small square pieces; put it into a frying pan, stirring them frequently until the fat is extracted and the scraps are done light brown."[44] While it was customary to wrap fresh fish in cloth to boil it, there appears to be no reference in culinary sources to putting salt fish in cloth, as Kiddy King remembered.

Her mention of boiled vegetables, however, is consistent with cookbook recommendations to serve root vegetables along with salt fish, in a seafood version of a New England boiled dinner. Sometimes an egg sauce was substituted for the salt pork. The leftovers lent themselves nicely to fish cakes, balls, or hash, as did the leftovers of most baked or boiled fresh fish. At this stage most cookbook writers cautioned cooks to remove carefully the skin and bones.

In 1833 Mrs. Child remarked that "Salt fish mashed with potatoes, with good butter or pork scraps to moisten it, is nicer the second day than it was the first."[45] Her comment helps in part to explain why, in another fifty years, boneless flaked salt cod and ready-made codfish cakes found favor with the public. The product was consistent with a need in the kitchen.

Salt cod snacks: Salt cod was eaten for a snack much as jerked beef is today. In the 1870s, after he had moved from Mystic to New York, shipping merchant Charles Henry Mallory still ended his day with "a little raw salt codfish and some pilot bread or hardtack." And the daughter of Maine salmon fisherman Robie Ames recalled that her father hung a salt cod in his fish shack so that he and his friends could pull off a piece to chew on when so inclined.[46]

Fresh codfish: Through the nineteenth century New Englanders showed an increasing preference for fresh fish. In 1886 Captain Henry Cook of Provincetown, Massachusetts, testified before the Senate Committee on Foreign Relations that "people will use a fresh article before they will a salt one...The demand for salt fish today is not as large in proportion to our population as it was forty years ago [1846]. I was then in the fishing business and there was a demand for all our salt fish. There were very few fresh fish then. Our population has increased threefold in the last forty years, yet we do not use much more salt codfish than we did then." People had not stopped eating salt fish, but the demand for them was clearly not in proportion to increased demand for fresh fish.[47]

Cod was the white-fleshed fish that other white-fleshed fish were compared to and lumped together with in recipes for fish dishes like chowder, poached fish with sauces, stewed fish, and broiled fish. The size of these white-fleshed fishes determined how they would be prepared, as we saw in the general instructions on preparation. Titled recipes for cod did appear in cookbooks, but "cod" was often prefaced with "salt"; cookbooks offered more recipes for preparing cod tongues, sounds, or heads than the whole plain codfish. Cookbook authors commonly adorned cod with various sauces, and the recipes' names reflect it. Marion Harland listed as her cod recipes "Boiled Cod," "Boiled Cod with Sauce," "Boiled Cod with Caper Sauce," "Boiled Cod with Macaroni," and "Pâte of Salt Cod." Aside from her salt-cod recipes, Maria Parloa included only "Boiled Cod with Lobster Sauce." Catherine Beecher

These Maine shore fishermen during the 1890s are unloading a catch using a hand barrow. Shore fishermen rowed off-shore to set trawls or used small boats like these to gather fish caught in weirs. Though indistinct, this catch appears to consist of small fish, possibly herring, great quantities of which were smoked for consumption, according to some Yankees, by the Irish. Immature herrings were also packed and marketed as sardines, although strictly speaking they were not sardines. [Hudson Collection, MSM 78.228.9]

just included a recipe for "Boiled Fresh Cod," and the only fresh cod recipe in Mrs. Henderson's book is for "Codfish Crimped." A review of cookbook indices show that many, especially early or small cookbooks, do not cite fresh cod by name; rather, cod was "fish."[48]

Cutting fresh fish in pieces and placing it in cold water for a while before simmering and boiling it was called crimping, and codfish was commonly "crimped." The process made the fish firmer, and it changed slightly over time. In 1913 Mrs. Lincoln instructed the cook to put the fish in strongly salted water, followed by cooking it in water with a little vinegar.[49]

Leftover fresh cod, like other white-fleshed fish, was commonly made into dishes like croquettes, salad, or escalloped fish. Or it was "picked up"—freed of skin and bones—and warmed in cream or cream sauce.

Scrod: Scrod is generally understood to be young cod or haddock. The word appeared in cookbooks as early as 1849, but it was rarely mentioned in the nineteenth century. The *Oxford English Dictionary* credits the term with a United States origin and gives as its citation one from 1873: "made the nicest little supper ready—scrod, as brown outside and as white inside as a cocoa nut is," though the word was clearly used earlier. By 1900 to fishermen it meant a cod or haddock between one and two-and-a-half pounds in weight.[50]

Crabs (*Callinectes sapidus*)

Many species of edible crabs are found on both sides of the Atlantic, but the most prevalent on the New England coast is the blue crab, *Callinectes sapidus*, which is very common from Cape Cod south. Coastal residents might catch them for their own use, like eels, clams, smelts, and other accessible fish, but the only formal crab fishery in nineteenth-century New England was a supplier of bait.[51]

The Chesapeake Bay region is famous for its crabs, which are easier to pick than the common crabs of New England's coast. A commercial crab fishery developed in the Chesapeake in the nineteenth century, so by the twentieth century southern Atlantic and Chesapeake Bay crabs were found more often in the market; plus labor for picking out crabmeat was cheaper in the South than in New England. In the 1930s Ackerman reported that most New England crabs were disposed of near their source and in Boston.[52]

Many cookbooks did not specify which crab to use, assuming that the cook would obtain the local favorite. Their appearance in New England and inland cookbooks increased once they began to be canned near mid-century; before then they were a little less favored than clams, and came nowhere near the popularity of lobsters and oysters. "They are not used as much as the lobster, because it is a great deal of trouble to take the meat from shell," wrote Miss Parloa. But De Voe thought that crab "is certainly of a better flavor, if more troublesome to prepare," than lobster.[53]

When they appeared in northern cookbooks, crabs were often paired with lobsters, or prepared in the same manner as lobsters. Crabs were deviled and stewed, and served in sauces and salads, but lobsters were generally preferred for salads and as entrees.

Cusk (Brosme brosme)

Called torsk and tusk in England, cusk is a relative of the cod, but it has an eel-like tail with which fishermen believed it could grasp rocks and resist being hauled to the surface. Not until the increase in market fishing was cusk available in any quantity, and it did not appear by name in most cookbooks until the 1870s. Housewives may have considered it one of the generic "fish" for common use earlier in the century. Maria Parloa was one of the few who provided a named recipe for it, "cusk à la crème," but the recipe specified "a cusk, or cod or haddock," so it was presumably interchangeable with the more familiar white-fleshed fish. "In spring it is seen in the Boston markets, when it is less esteemed than cod; but in winter it brings a higher price."[54]

Eels (Anguilla rostrata)

English and other northern-European settlers brought a taste for eels when they came to New England. Eels were plentiful in estuaries along the coast, where they could be trapped in wicker or wire basket-like traps. In winter, when they burrowed into the mud, fishermen could easily spear them. "The eelers appeared on the [Mystic] river last week after a long absence, and the lovers of eel 'smudder' may now gratify their gustatory longings for that savory potpourri," announced the Mystic *Press* in the 28 December 1876 issue. Smudder was probably colloquial for "smother," a thick, rich dish. Topped with a crust, smother would pass for eel pie.

With their rather oily flesh, eels were often smoked. "Had a grand supper of broiled eels," wrote Joseph Anthony of New Bedford on 4 November 1823, suggesting a popular way of preparing fresh eels. Thomas Hazard recalled the way eels were prepared in Rhode Island, after being speared in the mud of the Pettasquamscut River in January and February during the first half of the nineteenth century: "A basket of fat, yellow breasted eels being brought fresh from the frozen river, were first saturated with a handful of live wood ashes. This loosened the coating of slime so that they were readily cleansed. Next the head was taken off, and the eels split down the entire length of the back. They were then washed in clean sea water and hung up in the kitchen chimney...for one night only. Next morning the eels were cut in short pieces and placed on a gridiron, flesh side to...coals....When sufficiently broiled on that side, they were turned on the gridiron and a thin slice of fragrant butter...put on each piece of eel."[55]

Late in the nineteenth century, the American Sardine Company of Eastport, Maine, prepared canned eels in the same ways they canned sardines: plain, or in sauce with vinegar and spices. But the demand for commercially prepared eels never really developed. In small coastal communities like Mystic, families might savor a mess of eels they had caught themselves, and ethnic demand might support a minor eel fishery to supply Boston or New York fish markets. However, Felker accurately explained the general reaction to eels in 1878: "They are fine flavored and are an excellent article of food, but from their snake-like appearance...many persons are strongly prejudiced against them."[56] A simple recipe for frying eels appeared in the 1896 edition of the *Boston Cooking School Cookbook*, but Mary Lincoln's 1913 *Boston Cook Book* did not include eels.

Flounders and Soles

European settlers in New England were accustomed to the flatfish of northern Europe called sole. Writing about flounder in 1887, Miss Parloa said: "It is very much like sole, and fashionable people always call it sole. The fact is sole has never been caught in American waters." Flounders, dabs, flukes, plaice, and soles were all names used in nineteenth-century cookbooks, in which names and recipes were used interchangeably. Sole appears earlier than the word flounder, which is more common after the 1840s. It is as if historically "sole" referred to a small, flat, white fillet, a way of dressing the fish, rather than a distinct fish with a flavor and character of its own. Since early in this century, winter flounder have been called lemon sole, but strictly speaking they're not sole.[57]

The common or winter flounder, *Pseudopleuronectes americanus*, was the most frequently caught flounder in New England's waters. It is likely that flounder were among the fish sold at dockside by New York and Boston boat fishermen, but their catch was not documented in fishery statistics so we cannot be sure. Wesley Pierce reported that some flounders were caught in the 1880s with drag nets, then iced and sent to market, but "The flounder fishery was in its infancy in those days for the general public had not then learned to eat them." As long as there were larger, meatier fish, people did not bother with flounder except as panfish. The general trend toward filleting at the turn of the century helped increase the popularity of flounders because these fish were easy to fillet, and the introduction of large-scale otter trawling after the turn of the century greatly increased the quantities of flounder coming to market.[58]

Encyclopedic cookbooks were much more likely to include flounders than were community cookbooks, perhaps because flounder could be easily used as a panfish, and, as a white, flaky fish, its fillets could be used in generic "fish" recipes.

Haddock (Melanogrammus aeglifinus) and Finnan Haddie

Haddock is a small relative of the cod that lives in similar habitat, especially on Georges Bank and the shoals east of Nantucket. It is a voracious omnivore, but it only grows to an average of four pounds, and its population can fluctuate dramatically. Some observers of the nineteenth-century fisheries claimed that the haddock was unknown, despised, or ignored until the 1860s. Haddock, in fact, was known in the eighteenth century to be a good fish for fresh eating, and we may suppose that fishermen neglected it mostly because it wasn't cod, and it did not salt and dry as well as cod. It could be salted—when split and dried haddock was produced at Provincetown. There it was called Skulljoe or Scoodled Skulljoe, according to Goode. But more often haddock was preserved by smoking, yielding the product called finnan haddie. Alan Davidson points out that haddock fare best caught by line; the condition of those caught in otter trawls is not as good. But haddock were the favored fish for filleting, and in this century they were scooped up by the ton in otter trawls for that purpose. By the 1920s haddock landings actually exceeded cod landings in New England.[59]

Early in the nineteenth century, haddock was just one of the fish landed in spring and fall by the market fleet that supplied fresh fish. The fishery expanded when fresh fishing began to edge out salt fishing after mid-century, ultimately becoming a winter fishery that was especially lucrative during Lent. As Felker pointed out, haddock "is an excellent fish when eaten fresh." Fresh haddock were merely gutted and packed in chipped ice. Haddock fishermen frequented the nearer banks, such as Georges, and they tried to get their fish back promptly, so haddock trips were rarely longer than a week to ten days and sometimes as short as three or four days.[60]

Between 1860 and 1900, the haddock fishery produced enough that some of it was pickled, dried, and smoked as finnan haddie. John R. Neal & Co., in Boston, for example, established smokehouses in the 1880s. In 1898, Charles Stevenson reported that most smoked haddock from New England was sold to the Canadian Maritime Provinces, which were largely populated by Scots and English who had developed a taste for it in the old country. Named for the Scottish product that came from the town of Findon, finnan haddie had caught on well enough between the 1880s and 1900 that early-twentieth-century cookbooks included recipes for it. Because it fell into a general category of savory smoked food, it was often cooked in cream or cream sauce, just as sausage, salt pork, and smoked dried beef were.[61]

As a white and mild-flavored fish, haddock became a favorite for chowder. According to W. H. Bishop in 1880, "the haddock has the repute of being the best chowder fish," among fishermen on Maine islands. In his *American Fishes*, Goode agreed that haddock was "especially desirable for boiling or for making chowders." Haddock, like similar fish, was sauced, fried, and stewed. In 1849, Mrs. Putnam advised the cook to "Take a haddock, split it open and take the bone wholly out; then cut the fish into square pieces about the length of your finger," before stewing it. Miss Parloa gives a recipe for "Boiled Haddock with Lobster Sauce" which begins "The same as cod. In fact, all kinds of fish can be served in this manner; but the lighter the better..."[62]

Hake (Urophycis tenuis)

Hake "is inferior to the cod," wrote the author of a fictional biography of Cape Ann fisherman Peter Gott in 1856. "It is about the size of the haddock, is somewhat coarse meated, covered with large scales. It is taken...and salted for the West Indian and South American markets, where it is consumed by negros on the plantations." A member of the cod family frequently caught from June to November on the inshore grounds of the Gulf of Maine, where it preferred muddy bottoms, hake was most valued for its large, thick sound (swim bladder). Hake sounds were preferred over cod and haddock sounds for the production of isinglass, the gelatinous material used as a clarifying agent by brewers and as an ingredient in numerous drugs and confections.[63]

As one might presume from its use as a slave food, hake was not included by name in nineteenth-century cookbooks, although it appeared in the marketplace. In 1878 Felker wrote: "It is a valuable fish when salted and is largely exported from the British Provinces. The hake, haddock, and pollock are often sold as cod to those unable to distinguish them." Because it salted so well, hake was often corned, and with the coming of processed codfish products in the 1870s hake was often substituted for cod; it constituted 25 percent of the boneless fish packed at Gloucester in 1880. So even though hake was not identified as such or frankly described by salt-fish producers, consumers frequently purchased it, knowingly

or unknowingly, and likely prepared it according to one of many generic "fish" recipes.[64]

We see again in the right foreground the two gentleman shown earlier dressing cod, but in the background is evidence of the lobstering in which these fishermen were also engaged. Traditional rounded, lath-sided lobster pots are stacked up by the building on the right, and at the center is a lobster car. In 1880, about a decade earlier than these photos were taken at Monhegan Island, Maine, a *Harper's Monthly* writer described the Monhegan fishermen as "stalwart, rawboned men in flannel shirts, well-tanned canvas jackets, and bit-boots." [Bartlett photo, MSM 83.2.2]

Halibut (Hippoglossus hippoglossus)

A NEW FISHING GROUND.—Country fish-dealer (not posted in geography): "Here's fresh cod 'n haddock 'n halib-o-a-t."

"What is the price of the halibut, Mr. Napes?"

"Twenty cents a pound, ma'am."

"Why! that is a monstrous price; what makes it so dear?"

"It is a very nice article, ma'am, the real *Georgias* halibut; comes all the way from Georgia, packed in ice; makes it come high."

Economical housekeeper concluded she would not invest.[65]

This fishermen's joke contained a bit of truth: halibut caught on New England's Georges Bank *was* "a very nice article." It *was* shipped across the country in ice, and apparently it *was* prudent to inquire of the price.

In April 1843, the Norfolk (Virginia) *Herald* announced that "Our market yesterday morning was enriched by a delicacy from the northern waters, the halibut,—*a strange fish in these parts known only to epicures and naturalists.*" An article in the April 1866 *Atlantic Monthly*, describing how a single woman should plan meals, advised: "Don't buy quails, they are all gizzard and feathers; and don't buy halibut until you have inquired of the price." Its price fluctuated along with the halibut's plenty or scarcity on the banks and in the markets.[66]

From the same *Pleuronectidae* family as flounders, halibut is the largest of the flatfish, which have both eyes on the same side of the head. Whereas flounders do not exceed a few pounds in weight, halibut can grow to 600 pounds and more than six feet in length, females usually being larger than males. They may lie on the bottom to await passing fish and crabs as other flatfish do, but they also are known to chase their prey, so they can be found throughout the water column, from the surface down to 1,500 feet. Better able to make the transition from the depths than other fish, halibut might still be fighting when fishermen hauled them to the surface. A blow on the nose with a club called a halibut killer usually served to stun them for boating.[67]

Although they were eaten in Europe, halibut were not sought by American fishermen until the nineteenth century. George Brown Goode reported that halibut were considered a nuisance in Massachusetts Bay because fishermen caught them accidentally while looking for cod. Aboard vessels fishing on Middle Bank, halibut might be strung up on ropes to keep them from bothering the fishermen. "They were never carried home except as a favor to friends on shore who wanted them," explained Goode. Lorenzo Sabine reported that Cape Ann fishermen commenced halibut fishing on Georges Bank in the early nineteenth century, and that they succeeded in developing a market for them between 1825 and 1830. Pursued in mid-winter, it was a very dangerous fishery. Proctor wrote that the halibut was not sufficiently abundant near the coast to support a fishery, but the discovery of halibut feeding grounds on Georges Bank drew fishermen to "a special prosecution of this fishery."[68]

According to Goode's informant Charles Tripland, Connecticut fishermen had begun catching halibut on handlines and conveying them live to New York in well smacks before 1858. With the introduction of long-line trawling, however, the fish were iced and the fleet was converted to tight-bottomed craft or old smacks with the wells removed and bottoms plugged up. Halibut are such large fish that a vessel could make its fare in a short amount of time if they struck on a school; Pierce reported a number of fresh halibut trips that caught a full fare in a matter of days.[69]

Care was taken to keep halibut in good, marketable condition. Once landed on deck, the halibut was flipped onto its back so the white belly was upward, "to prevent the blood settling on that side and thus making the fish look dark colored or gray. The George's fishermen frequently bleed their halibut by making a cut across the tail," explained Goode. Here again is evidence of nineteenth-century preference for white-looking fish, which we saw with salt cod; Goode reported on the phenomenon of sorting halibut into whites and grays—the grays often being larger. Goode concluded that there was little difference between them, but the purchasers made the distinction to drive down prices to the detriment of fisherman. Goode may have been right that there was little difference in the fish, but consumers were conscious of fish color—in fact of all food color—and associated white with more desirable flavor and product condition.[70]

Sabine reported that "While the fishery was confined to the coast, the consumption of the fish was very limited." But halibut was an early fish to be shipped inland on ice, and in 1852 he reported that "At present, the fish, packed in boxes with ice, is sent sound and sweet, by railroads and vessels to the most distant sections of the country."[71] This is borne out in cookbooks where halibut is frequently mentioned after 1830, both in general cookbooks and community cookbooks, inland and coastwise. It was a very popular fish.

In 1878 Felker reported that halibut flesh is "coarse and dry but much esteemed by some...In England it is but little esteemed, but in this country brings a higher price than cod." Miss Parloa wrote that only the *largest* halibut were coarse and dry, and she advised her readers to buy the ones that weighed between fifty and seventy-five pounds. "This fine fish is always good," she wrote approvingly. Felker went on to say that "Large quantities [of halibut] are dried, salted, or smoked, and largely consumed in northern countries...Our fresh water sturgeon is said to be smoked and largely sold for halibut."[72]

The salt cod fishery supplied what salted halibut it could, mainly for sale to smokehouses, but when Goode reported on it in 1889 the demand was greater than the supply, hence the substitution of sturgeon. Goode could not date the beginning of a salt halibut market, but supposed it began among the Marblehead fishermen for their own winter consumption. Because smoked halibut was so popular, there was hardly any dried salt halibut in markets. "Halibut fletching" trips were made by fishermen who cut the fish into strips with skin attached and salted it to be smoked later. Fletched halibut "when slightly broiled, find much favor as a tea table relish."[73]

The fictitious fishmonger above was named "Mr. Napes." Halibut napes were apparently prized. Mrs. Putnam said of halibut that "the nape corned is best for broiling." Proctor, describing halibut being unloaded from a fishing vessel, remarked, "Visions of nice fried or baked halibut tickle the palate." Most often halibut was sold as steaks in slices or sections, good for frying or broiling if small, or baking if large. Halibut was simply too large a fish for anyone to buy whole.[74]

Herring (Clupea harengus)

The sea herring differs from its larger relatives the alewife and shad in that it spawns at sea rather than in fresh water. Nevertheless, great schools of herring frequent the coast from Block Island to Labrador in the summer and fall. In New England the greatest concentrations are found in Maine waters.[75]

"In New England as I understand, the herring are only eaten by the Irish population; I don't think anybody else eats them," Boston fish merchant William F. Jones told the Senate Committee on Foreign Relations in 1886. "They are in the habit of buying herring by the barrel, I fancy. The very small shop-keepers buy a single barrel of herring and peddle them out by the piece."[76] Herring did appeal more to people in the British Isles than in New England. Recipes or instructions for serving them appear relatively seldom in cookbooks—almost never in community cookbooks—and casual references to them in journals or letters are rare.

Lorenzo Sabine suggested that herring were more popular during the colonial era, commenting that as long as herring came alongshore in New England they were caught for fresh eating and for curing, "and that some becoming regular fishermen caught and cured the fish for sale to their neighbors of the interior." This continued, he said, till the streams were all dammed up, and "since the peace of 1783 the herring has abandoned many of its old haunts." At mid-century, the sea fishery for herring in Maine and the Bay of Fundy was most important.

Still, herring did not catch on: "The fish is an economical one but the fishery yields low income" because the herring in this country was always subordinate to other fish. "To persons who are familiar with the character and rank of the mass of herring catchers of our day, an account of the mania [over herring] in England two centuries ago seems almost incredible," wrote Sabine in 1853.[77]

It took an influx of herring-eating immigrants to boost sales in this country. The fish was eaten fresh but was more often made into one of several herring products.

Hard herrings: Hard herrings, also known as red herrings, were whole herrings lightly pickled and then smoked for three or four weeks until they were quite dry. Consequently they kept well and long. To be considered better than refuse fish, smoked herrings had to be at least six inches long, fat, and good. The top-quality fish were called "scaled herring" and were at least seven inches long.[78]

Bloaters: The first so-called Yarmouth Bloater was produced at Boston in 1859. Like hard herrings, bloaters were also whole herrings lightly pickled. However, since they were intended for immediate use they were smoked for only a few hours in hot smoke. During the process they often puffed up; hence their name. If they didn't bloat, they were left to become hard herrings. Americans accepted bloaters very gradually, and even by the 1880s most were sold to foreigners. The smoking of bloaters became a large business in Eastport and Portland, Maine, with two-thirds sold to Boston for distribution elsewhere.[79]

Kippered herrings: According to Stevenson, kippers were eviscerated and split bloaters.[80]

Bucklings: True bucklings, which could be made with herring, mackerel, salmon, sturgeon or eels—required a lot of skill and care. The fish were lightly salted, dried slightly, then dried in two phases: the first to desiccate them further, the second to cook and hot smoke them.[81] These were very similar to buckies, a smoked alewife.

All these smoked products were made from the herring or the alewife. "Though the principle is everywhere the same," noted Goode, "In some countries the smoky products are so black and hard as to disgust a person of ordinary taste, while in others such care is taken in the preparation and such a delicate flavor is imparted to the products that they are in great favor with epicures." The variety produced by different places "command different prices, to sell under different names, and to be consumed by entirely different classes."[82] Essentially, although Goode did not mention it, tastes and preferences varied a great deal in his day. In his time, as in ours, it is difficult to define "ordinary taste," and what was sold to different classes probably had more to do with cost than taste. But herring may have been a changeable, unreliable product.

Herrings apparently received such careless treatment by Americans that they were ruined for export. Goode reported that in this country herrings waited longer for salting than did European herrings, and they were also subjected to soaking and change of pickle, which caused them "to lose much of the rich and delicate flavor for which herring are so highly prized by herring-eating nations of Europe."[83]

Fresh herrings: Frozen herrings were brought from Newfoundland and New Brunswick, partly for food, partly for bait. Caught and frozen naturally outdoors, they were packed into barrels and brought to Boston where "there was a peculiar prejudice against them." In 1877, some Irish fish-peddlers were convinced to take a few and sell them for two cents each, soon developing a market for them. Goode reported in the 1880s that "frozen herring have become a favorite article of food among the laboring classes of the larger cities...form[ing] a cheap and wholesome food" in seasons when other fresh fish were hard to find and were costly.[84]

When sardines became fashionable in the mid-1800s, immature herrings were caught and dressed as sardines by George Burnham of Portland, Maine. Mainers and others north of Boston generally were the only ones catching herring, and then only seasonally because "they are not considered sufficiently remunerative to warrant the fishermen devoting any considerable portion of their time to them." In 1880, most of the herring catch was pickled, smoked, or canned. Considerable quantities were used for fertilizer and bait.[85]

Lobsters (Homarus americanus)

The lobster has become perhaps the most recognizable symbol of New England fishing. This omnivorous crustacean lives both inshore and offshore throughout the region. With its hard shell and strong claws, the lobster has few predators other than humans, and before the nineteenth century it was not uncommon to encounter four-foot specimens perhaps 100 years old.[86]

English settlers quickly recognized American lobsters because of their similarity to the smaller English variety, and this perhaps accounts for their recorded amazement at the size of American lobsters. "The least boy in the

Lobster was most often presented at Victorian dining tables in this genteel form, neatly trimmed and garnished. The recipe is on page 361.

Plantation may both catch and eat what he will of them," wrote the Reverend Francis Higginson of Salem in 1630. "For my owne part I was soone cloyed with them, they were so great, and fat, and luscious. I have seene some my self that have weighed 16 pound, but others have divers times so great Lobsters as have weighed 25 pounds, as they assure mee."[87]

Peter Kalm saw lobsters in New York markets in the mid-eighteenth century. Kalm reported they were pickled in the same way as oysters and says that live lobsters were brought to the city by fishing smacks with wet wells in which they were carried alive, a practice that continued through much of the nineteenth century. The New York market was the earliest and strongest for most of southern New England's coast, with Connecticut smacks fishing for lobsters off Cape Cod and delivering them to the New York market as early as 1815.[88]

George Brown Goode reported that the first regular lobster dealer in Boston was a "Mr. Benjamin Simpson, who kept a restaurant in the basement of a house at the south end. He used to go out into the harbor, in a little boat, and catch them in the vicinity of Castle Fort, and then peddle them about the city." Simpson was followed by another man who fished in a smack, even hiring others to fish for him, and boiled lobsters to be sold by vendors.[89]

Lobster recipes in nineteenth-century cookbooks appeared about as often as those for cod, salt cod, and "fish." Even inland community cookbooks mentioned lobster about as frequently as cod, salmon, and crabs. Like other seafood, the introduction of canned lobster likely accounts for its widespread use, especially in the late 1800s.

Live shipment and storage was the best way to keep lobsters fresh. "If they [lobstermen] now wish to preserve them for several days, they put them into a long box or kennel, made of plank and bored full of holes, which is moored in the water at a little distance from shore," explained Dr. Reynolds in the 1850s. Otherwise, they would be cooked before being shipped to market, especially if they were to be sold for immediate consumption. "If they wish to prepare them immediately for market," continued Reynolds, "they are taken ashore in hand-barrows and carried into a sort of shed, in which is fixed a large cauldron. This is filled with water. A brisk fire is kindled under this kettle, and when the water boils, the living, crawling, squirming lobsters are thrown into it and covered with a heavy plank cover. Here they are kept boiling until their color, which when taken out of the water was a dark green, becomes a bright scarlet. They are now ready for market. In this state we see them for sale on the stalls in our cities and hawked about the streets."[90]

Cooking lobsters for market paved the way for canning. Cooks were accustomed to acquiring lobster already cooked, which had solved the freshness problem. That left only picking out the meat, which, though not as difficult as with crabs, slowed cooks down. In the early 1840s the canneries solved that problem, and after the customary initial resistance canned lobster became a very attractive product. During the 25 years between 1845 and 1870, lobster canning was a growing industry, both along the

Maine coast and eventually in Canada's Maritime Provinces. Goode reported that in the United States lobster canning was exclusively confined to Maine, where 23 lobster canneries were operating in the 1880s. Between the demands of the canneries and the increased demand fostered by efficient railroad transportation of live lobsters throughout the Northeast, Maine lobstermen found themselves in a growth industry. Before the canneries, southern New England smacksmen had begun to make regular trips to Maine, buying the catch of Maine lobstermen and transporting the live lobsters to Boston and New York in the wet wells of their vessels. With the coming of the canneries, lobstermen had a local outlet for their catch as well. Smacksmen continued their intermediary role, carrying lobsters either to the canneries or to the growing distribution center of Portland, where they could be shipped live by rail or steamboat to market.[91]

Maine's lobster production greatly exceeded that of all other New England states, but a substantial lobster fishery was conducted out of Noank, Connecticut, as the recreated Noank lobster shack at Mystic Seaport Museum illustrates. Goode wrote about Noank, "the little town of Noank, situated at the mouth of the Mystic River, about midway between Stonington and New London, is the most important lobster station in the State, the catch for that port in 1880 having been equal to about one-half the total catch for the entire state." Noank's lobstermen fished year round, unlike others in the area, setting their pots in Fisher's Island Sound, Block Island Sound, and Buzzards Bay.[92]

The popularity of lobster, particularly as a canned item, gradually led to the depletion of the local stocks. Goode wrote in the 1880s that everywhere the lobstermen acknowledged a decline in the number and size of lobsters. Some, like the Noank lobstermen, responded to the decrease in abundance with better fishing gear and more pots, managing to increase the overall catch. Like oysters, lobsters were regulated very early—in Maine by the 1870s—as they continue to be.[93]

Southeastern New England's catch was sold locally and to New York. Stonington's lobstermen sold to a home market; New London's catch was sold partly to a home market and partly to New York and interior towns; and Noank delivered its catch to New York by smack and steamer, to New London by rail, and to Norwich by wagon.[94]

Like the oyster, the lobster had a dual identity as a luxury food in cities and inland where it was not native, and as a food for all classes, including poor fishermen, along the coast. Not everyone liked lobster, despite its popularity. In 1878, Peter Felker wrote, "They are common in the markets, especially in spring and summer, and are considered a great delicacy though the meat is rather indigestible." Less diplomatically, Captain Thomas Fairfax of the Mystic smack *Mary Lane* said, "Lobsters are very good as an article of commerce, and pretty enough to look at, after they're b'iled; but as to eating them, I prefer castoff rubber shoes."[95]

In the nineteenth century, lobster was seldom served in the rough at home. Instead, cooks cracked the shell, picked out the lobster meat, and used it in a variety of dishes. It is very difficult to determine the most popular lobster dish from sources at hand. Recipes commonly called for lobster to be added to sauces, scalloped, fricasseed, stewed, deviled, used in soup or bisque, made into croquettes, in *vol au vents*, and very, very often in salad. Whole lobsters in the rough were eaten recreationally as part of shore dinners, but if a lobster shell appeared at the dining table it had been carefully opened, trimmed, and refilled with cooked lobster for neat and genteel consumption.

Howard Burdick recalled lobster meals during the time he served with the Coast Guard crew on Fisher's Island, New York, around 1920, which suggests a popular way of serving lobster in the summer at least. The crew used to get a load of lobsters from a local lobsterman. The cook "served the lobster usually as a salad and used a large white platter about four feet long and a foot or fifteen inches wide. When he got the bushel or so of lobsters cooked and picked out, he would put all the meat on the platter and garnish it with parsley and lemon slices all around the edges. To us Hooligans the whole thing looked like something from Delmonico's or the Parisian Parfait. Tom was a neat picker and he got out all the small claw meat and used that green stuff around the head too."[96]

Because so many of these dishes required only lobster meat, the canned product fit easily into most lobster recipes. Housewives who lived near the source—remember Julia Gates in Mystic, with her four pounds of lobster—as well as discerning cooks, continued to use the fresh item. In 1894, Miss Parloa advised young housekeepers, "When it is impossible to get the fresh lobster, the canned article may be used instead, though it is of the greatest importance to buy only the goods put up by the first-class houses."[97]

Mackerel (Scomber scombrus)

The mackerel is a surface-schooling fish with rich, oily flesh. Mackerel are summer visitors to New England. Great schools appear off the Virginia Capes in the spring and work their way north, finally disappearing off Nova Scotia in the fall. Mackerel are voracious feeders, even snapping at polished lures called jigs by the fishermen. Mackerel schools in turn attract predatory bluefish, striped bass, and swordfish. Although their numbers can fluctuate dramatically from year to year, mackerel are prolific. Year-old "tinker" mackerel measure up to eleven inches; they are usually two feet long by the age of two.

The first English settlers in New England brought knowledge of mackerel with them. Lorenzo Sabine noted that mackerel had been pursued since Plymouth's and

K. & S. A. FREEMAN'S FISH WHARVES.

Established in 1863.

Established in 1863.

MACKEREL.

We quote **TO-DAY'S** market:— BOSTON, July 1, 1885.

We have to note a decided advance in prices of New Mackerel. Most of the Mackerel fleet are in harbor and nearly all empty. Our latest report from Provincetown is as follows: "Seventy-five sail of the Mackerel fleet arrived to-day for a harbor from the heavy South-west wind. They report having cruised the fishing grounds from Cape Cod to Mt. Desert, and off shore to Georges, and seen but few fish. Schooner Emma Higgins has six barrels, the result of four weeks work." This is a fair sample of reports from other outports. There are no stocks of New Mackerel held by Dealers and none on the fleet. With good luck, the fleet cannot fit out and get in with fares in less than four or five weeks, and meantime we expect a very unsettled market and continued advance in prices. With a short catch and $2.00 bbl. duty going on July 1st, it is certain that much higher prices will prevail this Summer.

All orders entrusted to us will be billed at the *lowest market price* the day the order is received.

NEW MACKEREL.

	BBLS.	HALF BBLS.				QTR. BBLS.			Drums.	Pails or Kits.			
	200 lbs.	100 lbs.	90 lbs.	80 lbs.	70 lbs.	50 lbs.	40 lbs	30 lbs.	25 lbs.	20 lbs.	15 lbs.	12 lbs.	10 lbs.
New Medium No. 3, 11 to 12 inches in length,	4.50	2.57	2.34	2.12	1.80	1.42	1.20	.97	80	.63	.53	.43	.40
New Extra Fat Family, 11½ to 12 in. long,	4.75	2.69	2.45	2.22	1.98	1.47	1.24	1.00	.82	.65	.55	.44	.41
New Large No 3, 13 to 15 inches in length,	7 50	4.07	3.69	3.32	2.95	2.17	1.80	1.42	1.18	93	.75	.61	.54
New Medium No. 2, 11½ to 12½ in. long,	6 00	3.32	3.00	2.72	2.42	1.82	1.50	1.20	1.00	.78	.64	.54	.47
New Shore No. 2, 12 to 13 inches in length,	7.50	4.07	3.67	3.32	2.95	2.20	1.80	1.43	1.18	.93	.74	.61	.54
New Large No. 2, 13 to 15 " "	9.00	4.82	4.35	3.92	3.47	2.57	2.10	1.65	1.37	1.08	.85	.70	.61
Bay No. 1,	16.00	8.32	7.52	6.72	5.92	4.30	3.50	2.70	2.25	1.80	1.40	1.14	.98
Shore No. 1,	18.00	9.32	8.42	7.52	6.62	4.80	3.90	3.00	2.50	2.00	1.55	1.26	1.08
Extra Shore No. 1,	20.00	10 32	9.32	8.32	7.32	5.30	4.30	3.30	2.75	2.20	1.70	1.38	1.18
Shore Mess,	22.00	11.32	10.22	9.12	8.02	5.80	4.70	3.60	3.00	2.40	1.85	1.50	1.28
Extra Mess, OUT OF MARKET.													

We have a few NEW Extra Shore No. 2s at $12.00 bbl.

OUR NEW SPECIALTY.

The Pails which we were the first to introduce for packing Mackerel, have proved a decided success, and without doubt they will eventually take the place of kits altogether. Our pails are three-hooped and varnished, and while other firms charge from three to five cents extra. ***REMEMBER— We put them in at the same prices as kits.***

CANNED FISH.

New Block Island Mess Mackerel in 5 lb. tins, $4.00 per case, 1 doz. in C.
" Breakfast " " 3.50 " 1 " "
" Fresh " 1 lb. cans, .70 per doz., 4 " "
" Soused " 1 lb. " 1.00 " 4 " "
" " " 2 lb. " 1.35 " 2 " "
" " " 3 lb. " 2 35 " 2 " "
" " " 4 lb. " 2.85 " 1 " "
" Tomato or Mustard Sauce, " 3 lb. " 2.70 " 2 " "
" Fresh Salmon, 1 lb. " 1.25 " 4 " "
" " Lobster, 1 lb. " 1.80 " 4 " "
" Sardines, in ¼ lb. boxes, 5.00 per case, 100 boxes "
Extra New Pickled Cod, 3.75 bbl., 2.30 hlf. bbl., 1.30 qtr. bbl.
Extra New Pickled Haddock, 4.00 bbl., 2.30 hlf bbl., 1.30 qtr. bbl.
New Columbia River Salmon, 14.00 Bbl., 7.30 Hlf. Bbl.

CODFISH.

As it is impossible to give satisfaction in Codfish and Boneless during hot weather, we omit quotations and will ship them only at buyer's risk.

HERRING.

	BBLS.	HLFS.	QTRS.
New Portland Large Round Shore,	3 50	1.80	1.05
" Large Split,	4.75	2.70	1.50
" Extra Labrador Split	5.00	2.80	1.55
" Domestic Holland or Mess	40 cents per keg.		
" Strictly Medium Scaled,	14 " box.		
" Large, about 30 to 35 fish to the box,	8 " "		

We fit out vessels in the Mackerel Fishery, and save you at least 10 per cent in quality alone, and think you will find it to your advantage to purchase direct from the producers of the Mackerel. Send full shipping directions with your order.

Our 5 lb. Tins are culled from Fat, Juicy, Shore Mackerel, and we warrant them equal to any brand in the market.

K. & S. A. FREEMAN,
388, 390, 392, 394 Atlantic Avenue, Power's Wharf, Boston.

OUR TERMS. On all orders amounting to less than $ 100, draft at 30 days, or 1 per cent off for cash, on receipt of Bill Lading.
" " " to more than $ 200, " 30 " or 1 1-2 per cent off, " " "
" " " to more than $ 500, " 30 " or 2 per cent off, " " "

N.B. On sums over $200.—If Responsible Houses wish to take sixty days, they can do so by sending us note or acceptance dated 60 days from date of Invoice on receipt of Bill of Lading. If we do not receive note or acceptance, we will draw 30 days from date of Bill, on all sums if not remitted for unless notified otherwise.

Cape Cod's earliest settlement and that the mackerel fishery was part of Plymouth Colony's public property in the seventeenth century. He noted that in 1770 the town of Scituate sent out thirty-odd vessels for mackerel fishing, and in 1783 a Boston newspaper commented on the fishery's value to the economy of Massachusetts. Sabine believed that the fishery was revived during the early 1800s, although the catch fluctuated during the first two decades.[98]

The fishery grew in scale and importance during the nineteenth century. Development of the mackerel jig—a hook attached to a polished pewter lure, several of which could be handled at once by a fisherman—led to the first increase in mackerel landings. Then, in the 1850s, the purse seine net was adapted to mackerel fishing, allowing fishermen to catch tens of thousands of fish in one set of their net. Mackerel were snared in gill nets as well, both commercially and privately.

Nineteenth-century cookbooks consistently included salt and fresh mackerel; they were obviously popular. In 1833, Mrs. Child spoke matter-of-factly about them, cautioning cooks to pinch the bellies of fresh mackerel to ascertain freshness, and to cover salted mackerel (and shad) with hot water briefly before broiling to prevent "the strong oily taste, so apt to be unpleasant in preserved fish."[99] Mackerel fishermen understood the necessity of getting mackerel under salt before they had a chance to spoil; an oily fish, mackerel could go bad very quickly.

Fisherman Wesley Pierce described the manner of dressing mackerel for salting: "Beginning at the nose of the fish he [the splitter] drew the knife toward him alongside the backbone (his right thumb guiding it carefully), splitting the fish from head to tail." Unlike cod, mackerel were split down the back, which left the rib bones mostly on one side, adrift in the flesh for the cook or diner to deal with. The most desirable fat mackerel were known to show a deep split in the flesh; to improve marketability, or even make slender mackerel appear to be fat, some fishermen used a little blade called a mackerel plow to deepen the split or even create one artificially. Sabine described the salting process at mid-century. After the mackerel were split down the back, gutted, and soaked to rid them of blood, "The salter sprinkles a handful of salt in the bottom of the barrel, then takes the fish in his right hand, rolls them in salt, and places them skin down in the barrel til he comes to the top layer which he lays skin up, covering the top well with salt." Some of the more industrious men "messed" mackerel to improve quality, as described by Pierce: "first the heads were cut off, then all the settled blood around the napes, throat and backbone was scraped off with a mackerel knife, and the fish washed very clean and white." This was worth doing when crews, jigging for mackerel, fished on shares and each man put his private mark on every barrelful of his fish. Messed mackerel brought a higher price. Throughout the nineteenth century, mackerel were carefully graded by size and quality, and the first spring mackerel were awaited by an eager public.[100]

By the beginning of the twentieth century, fresh mackerel had largely supplanted salt mackerel in the market. Consequently, salt mackerel was less frequently mentioned in twentieth-century cookbooks, though it continued to be available during the first few decades. Frank Davis purveyed salt mackerel as an ideal breakfast fish, but, since the 1930s, Americans have lost their taste for mackerel and the catching of these fish has declined from a major to a minor New England fishery.

Although the mackerel is an oily fish prone to spoil quickly, its texture and flavor were highly regarded throughout the 200 years after English settlement in New England. But, because of its oiliness, Mrs. Lincoln grouped mackerel with salmon and bluefish as "nutritious for those who can digest them, but...too rich and oily for invalids."[101]

Even the largest mackerel were, by nineteenth-century standards, small fish, but they fell into the category of ideal broiling fish. Mrs. Putnam advised the cook to emulate the fishermen and split fresh mackerel down the back before broiling them. Before broiling salt mackerel, the cook had to soak it skin-side up so the salt dissolved and precipitated down without collecting on the skin. The fish was then fit for broiling, and was often served with a little butter on it.[102] Like so many other seafoods, mackerel was canned for convenience. Occasionally, late in the nineteenth century, mackerel was smoked and sent to New York, where there was a small trade in it.[103]

Mussels (Mytilus edulis)

Despite a recent surge in popularity, mussels were not among the most popular shellfish in nineteenth-century New England. With their habit of clumping together on hard surfaces, firmly attached with their strong byssal threads, mussels were available in abundance. Yet, as filter feeders they ingested great quantities of plankton and algae, including the toxic kind that causes "red tide." "Since many person who have eaten mussels have suffered severely, these fish are generally supposed to be occasionally poisonous," wrote Thomas Webster, author of *An Encyclopedia of Domestic Economy*, in 1844.[104]

A few bad experiences may have been enough to give mussels a bad name with early New Englanders. They appeared in early cookbooks, then disappeared until fairly recently. At the turn of the century, an effort to promote mussel-eating revealed the confusion about its food value. In a paper presented to the American Fisheries Society in 1911, Irving Field argued for the palatability, nutritive value, and digestibility of mussels. He reported that people in Woods Hole, Massachusetts, who ate them at home or at a large boardinghouse, found them equal to the oyster and superior to the soft-shelled clam. Field suggested that they were too common to be esteemed: "We do not appreciate the value of a thing until it is rare or beyond reach." He reported a market for them in New York City, Boston, Providence, and Philadelphia, but said the demand was small because most people did not know they were good to eat. During the discussion following the presentation, a gentleman from Rhode Island said that the English in his state had been eating mussels for 30 years. But others mentioned the mussel's poisonous reputation, even citing Native American and Eskimo avoidance of mussels. Clearly, most nineteenth-century Americans did not care for mussels.[105]

Goode related that, in the 1880s, "The men who gather mussels for [the New York] market are an inferior part of the population, as a rule since the oystermen do not care to take the trouble." He remarked that while Europeans cultivated mussels, Americans were not likely to, "since our wealth of the preferable oysters and clams is so great." However, Goode reported that, like oysters and clams in earlier years, mussels were sometimes pickled, "a troublesome and expensive matter, done by the oyster-saloon men who sell them to customers [by the quart or gallon] almost wholly in the city." The pickle consisted of mussel liquor plus vinegar and other condiments, a manner of preparing them that was centuries old.[106] Still, outside of saloons and a few localities, mussels were ignored domestically for virtually the entire nineteenth century.

As Goode predicted, we have seen mussels become accepted, even trendy, in our own time and many in the market have been cultivated. In some places mussels have filled the gap left by diminishing clam harvests, and on occasion they have even become the main shellfish in "clam" bakes.[107]

Oysters (*Cassostrea virginica*)

"I know you will often delight him with oysters, scalloped, fried, or plain, as entremets to flank his dinner table," housewives were told by the author of an *Atlantic Monthly* article titled, "What Shall We Have for Dinner?" in 1864.[108] "Oysters, Stewed, Raw, or in the Shell. Gentlemen and Ladies will find a good quiet Room where they can get Oysters, Hot Tea, Coffee and Lunch, at a few moment's notice. At Sparks Mystic Bakery," announced the Mystic *Press* on 7 September 1876. Whether at home or dining out at a "fast food" lunchroom, oysters were tremendously popular in the last half of the nineteenth century. In fact, oysters were included in more cookbooks of all sorts than any other seafood (with salt cod the next most frequently mentioned).

English settlers had arrived in New England with a well-established preference, among shellfish, for oysters. From Cape Cod south, particularly in the estuaries of what would become Connecticut, and to a lesser degree in the colder estuaries to the north, they discovered natural beds of oysters that had flourished for thousands of years. Given the right degree of brackishness and the right water temperature, oysters spawn in mid-summer (during the months without "r"), and the larvae soon "set" on a hard substrate—such as another oyster shell. Within three years they grow to an edible size, and undisturbed they survive for twenty years or so. Native Americans had made use of these natural beds long before Europeans arrived, but within a century of European settlement in Connecticut some of the beds were being overharvested.[109]

Peter Kalm, a Swedish naturalist, observed in 1748 during a visit to Long Island: "Oysters are here reckoned very wholesome, and some people assure me that they had not felt the least inconvenience after eating a considerable quantity of them. It is also a common rule here that oysters are their best in those months which have an 'r' in their names, such as September, October, etc. but that they are not so good in other months. However, there are poor people who live all the year upon nothing but oysters and a little bread."[110] As we observed with lobsters, the prized shellfish was abundant enough to be subsistence for the poor people who gathered them.

With oysters, freshness was the main concern, and because the shellfish was so favored the developing oyster industry expended considerable effort to find a way to distribute them safely. In the early 1800s, Timothy Dwight described how people gathered oysters from the extensive natural beds of the Quinnipiac River near New Haven, had them shucked from their shells by women and children, and then shipped them in the cold season "over large tracts in Connecticut, New York, Massachusetts, Vermont, and New Hampshire." In the 1830s, George Brown Goode reported, shucked oysters were packed in small wooden kegs, or in tin containers surrounded with ice, and sent well inland; by the 1880s they were sent to Chicago and other inland cities by rail.[111]

The great popularity of oysters led to overfishing, which spurred oyster cultivation. Oysters had been depleted during the eighteenth century in the Great Bay of New Hampshire and along the northern coast of Massachusetts. By the 1880s, Long Island Sound and much of Rhode Island's coast were largely depleted of their natural beds of oysters. Declining numbers of oysters had led to municipal or state regulations: gathering oysters was limited to residents; towns forbade or taxed heavy exports of oysters; and methods of gathering were controlled. For example, on natural beds tonging was permitted but dredging was prohibited. In Connecticut there had been legislation passed as early as 1750 enabling towns to enact by-laws to control the taking of shellfish. The next step was to import oysters from Long Island, New York Bay, or Chesapeake Bay to spawn and repopulate the local beds. Connecticut oystermen discovered that they could create their own beds, and by the 1850s the state was granting, later leasing, ownership of barren bottom to oystermen on which they would cultivate, or "farm," their oysters. The oystermen laid down "cultch"—old shells—on which the larvae would set, then spread "seed"—spawning—oysters when the water temperature rose. After a year, the young oysters might be dredged up and "replanted" on deeper beds to grow out for a couple of years before being brought back in to fatten before being harvested for market. It became such a highly organized process that Edward Ackerman remarked in 1941 that the oyster industry "is more a farming than an extractive operation."[112]

On 5 May 1876, the Mystic *Press* reported, "Capt. Elias Wilcox and Mr. Frank Horton visited Fire Island last week with their sloop Fanny, to get oysters to plant in Quiambog Cove. They returned on Saturday with 515 bushels, which when properly planted they expect to make marketable oysters after about a year's growth. The bivalves thrive well in those waters." This was a scene enacted all along Connecticut's coast. Among the growers was New Haven's Thomas Thomas, builder of the Thomas Oyster Company building now at Mystic Seaport Museum. Thomas's whole oyster business revolved around cultivated oysters. The Thomases sometimes procured seed oysters from as far away as the Chesapeake and used their oystering grounds—including some in Wellfleet, Massachusetts—to raise and fatten them. The Thomas Oyster Company building was also used for culling and opening.

For home consumption, people bought oysters at markets, or had them delivered: "Oysters. Every Saturday—delivered at any part of the village for 35 CENTS PER QUART, solid measure. At the old stand, Randall Browne, Jr. Exchange Block, Mystic Bridge," proclaimed the Mystic *Press* on 10 January 1878. In 1880s Boston, "Oyster men usually appeared in the evening, carrying their heavy burden, on the shell, on the shoulders in a kind of saddle-bag, crying, 'Oys! Finey Oys! Buy and Oys?' They opened their bivalves at the purchasers' doors, throwing the shells into another part of the bag. Handcarts were afterward introduced, and were found a great convenience. Many people declare that they never had such delicious oysters as those that were sold in this way."[113]

This poster with its smiling oyster faces only begins to convey the extreme popularity of oysters in the nineteenth century. It was the seafood most consistently mentioned in cookbooks both coastwise and inland in the latter 1800s. As the oyster "Express" hints, shucked and packed oysters were carried inland by rail to be enjoyed hundreds of miles from Oyster Point, in New Haven, and other places along the southern New England shore where they were tonged out of their beds. [Blockprint, 1880, courtesy New Haven Colony Historical Society]

Hotels, restaurants, and oyster saloons offered oysters on the half shell, and for this trade the most attractive oysters with regular round shells were prized. Oystermen often "freshened" their product, carrying the shellfish to fresher water and suspending them on floats in inlets or rivers near the oyster grounds, where the oysters rinsed their mantles and gills, puffed up, and became whiter, which made them more marketable.[114]

Oysters were sorted or culled at oystermen's shops. Bunches of tonged or dredged oysters were separated to produce "a clean single oyster," which was then graded and bagged for shipment. Because many people found it more convenient to buy oysters without their shells, the crooked or misshapen oysters were opened, packed, and shipped for cooking or for eating raw. Even without their shells, raw oysters could be served in style on oyster plates, china dishes with oyster shell-like indentations around the edges and a place in the center for sauce. These were enormously popular among fashionable people in the mid-1800s; for example, when maritime entrepreneur Charles Mallory of Mystic died in 1882, oyster plates were listed among the china in the estate inventory.[115]

Another elegant way to present opened oysters was on a block of ice in which indentations were made by heated bricks or sadirons. The cook decorated the ice and its platter with parsley or greenery, used lemon and flowers for garnish, and brought the oysters cold to the table. "This gives a elegant dish, and does away with the unsightly shells in which raw oysters are usually served. It is not expensive for the common oysters do as well as those of good size," explained Miss Parloa in 1880.[116]

All along the coast there were oyster-eating establishments. At some, like Sparks Bakery in Mystic, oysters were a sideline, while others were oyster houses or saloons dedicated to serving them in every style imaginable. In Boston, Peter B. Brigham opened the city's first oyster restaurant "under Concert Hall at the head of Hanover Street" and became so successful that he wound up a millionaire. Alvin Harlow described the oyster restaurants of New York City: "One of the commonest signs was the red ball—a frame work covered with red cloth, and an oil or gas lamp or even candle inside—of which Dickens said, "announce as you may see by looking up 'Oysters in Every Style.' They tempt the hungry most at night, for their dull candles glimmering inside illuminate these dainty words and make the mouths of idlers water as they read and linger. Inside you were apt to dine in a little stall, off a red or white tablecloth, usually well stained by some dozens of previous guests. In the center of each table of an eating house, must be the revolving castor, its thin silver or nickle plating rapidly disappearing, its bottle filled with mustard, vinegar, ketchup, salt, and red and black pepper, respectively."[117]

Frederick Whymper described the oyster stands in New York's Fulton Market: "Some of these retreats were like old-time coffee-houses, with their rough wooden tables, and benches with painfully straight backs. Others were not much more than cupboards or boxes. What matter? The true oyster-eater does not want—or want to pay for, perhaps—plate glass, gilding, and ostentatious display. *He* wants his oysters!"[118]

Like other shellfish, oysters were pickled. For a while in the eighteenth century there was a trade with the West Indies in pickled oysters, according to Kalm, who reported that such a product "will keep for years and may be sent to the most distant parts of the world." He described a process that included oysters being shucked, boiled, dried slightly, then "some nutmeg, allspice, and black pepper are added, and as much vinegar as thought sufficient to give a sourish taste. All this is mixed with half the liquor in which the oysters are boiled and put over the fire again....At last the whole pickling liquid is poured into a glass or earthen vessel, the oysters are put into it, and the vessel is well stopped to keep out the air."[119] Nineteenth-century cookbooks included recipes for pickled or "spiced" oysters, but the taste for them gradually diminished over the century.

Some people kept oysters at home alive in their shells.

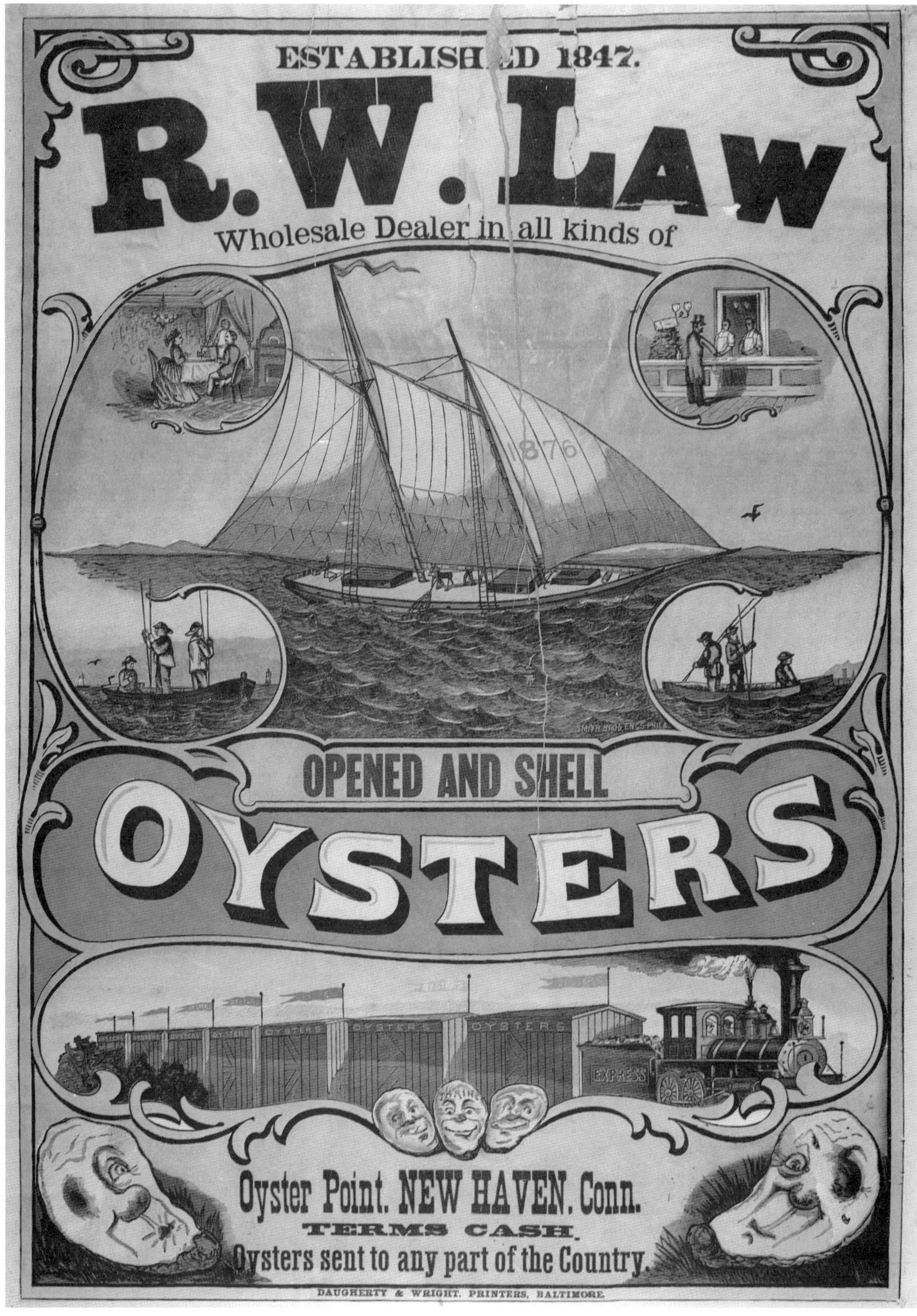

Mrs. Abell, in 1854, wrote "After washing them, lay them in a tub with the deep part of the shell undermost, sprinkle them with salt and Indian meal, or flour, fill the tub with cold water, and set it in a cool place. Change the water daily, and they will keep fresh a fortnight." In 1898, Charles Stevenson described how "Half a century ago [the 1840s] it was customary with many families in Connecticut and New York to lay in a supply of oysters every fall for use during the winter. Piled up in some cool place, usually in the cellar with the deep shell downwards and between layers of seaweed, they would live sometimes for three or four months."[120]

Perhaps the great abundance of oysters all along the American coast led cooks to develop so many ways of serving them. This is borne out by cookbooks, both coastal and inland. For instance, the *The First Texas Cookbook* of

1883 contained a chapter separate from the fish chapter devoted to oysters, which included oysters fried, scalloped, and broiled, along with oyster salad, omelet, soup, and loaf. A recipe for scalloped oysters was one of the very few entrees that Julia Gates recorded in her manuscript cookbook.[121]

At the height of oyster popularity, in 1880, Miss Parloa wrote, "No other shell fish is as highly prized as this." She offered 14 oyster recipes; Mrs. Henderson provided 10. Considering that only a few foods, including beef, apples, pork, poultry, potatoes, and eggs, were usually accorded so many variations in cookbooks, this was very flattering attention for a seafood.[122]

Given so many recipes, it is difficult to ascertain from culinary sources what the favored manner of preparing oysters may have been in the nineteenth century. In 1884, Whymper claimed that oyster " 'fry' is the *ne plus ultra* of oyster cookery, and is a national *plat*. The saloon keeper who does not conspicuously flaunt a coloured placard with some such motto as the following upon it, 'If you wish to make peace, take home a fry in a box,' would be considered behind the times." Oysters appeared frequently in the appetizer or soup course in suggested menus, but were also served raw or in a soup or stew, as we saw in the description of Christmas dinners during the nineteenth century.[123]

Early in the century, Joseph Anthony in New Bedford recorded in his diary, "Calculating on having a snug supper of oysters with Cousin Tom, but so many chaps came in during the evening that we were forced to give it up, not having enough to supply them all." A century later in Essex, Massachusetts, recalled Dana Story, "For all the 'R months' we had oyster stew at noon on Saturday after which Mother immediately prepared the [pay] envelopes for the men" in the Story shipyard.[124] No matter whether stewed, fried, scalloped, or eaten raw from the half shell, the oyster was clearly one of America's favorite seafoods in the nineteenth century.

Pollock (Pollachius virens)

The pollock is another member of the cod family, resembling the haddock in size. Pollock swim in schools and often leave the bottom in their foraging expeditions. American fishermen disliked them because, with their voracious appetites, they consumed the spawn of fish more valuable than themselves, such as cod and haddock. Most references to pollock compare it to cod: "it is about the size of a codfish—has a sharper head, and its back is of a dark blue color. Its flesh is somewhat coarser and darker than that of the cod, and contains more gluten," wrote Dr. Reynolds in the 1850s.

Pollock was similar in *use* to cod in the 1800s, but it was not named in cookbooks until the last quarter or so of the century. "When this fish is preserved with but little salt, and dried in the cool weather of autumn, it is a favorite fish for the table. It is eaten raw, stripped into small pieces.

The popularity of oysters meant that they were quickly depleted in southern New England. By the mid-1880s, one writer described oystering as more of a farming than fishing operation. Seed oysters imported from the Chesapeake were "planted" on beds of culch—old oyster shells—where the spawn settled and young oysters grew. Later the oysters might be replanted in deeper water until they were a marketable size. [Lithograph advertisement, MSM 80.107.16]

But it is generally high salted, and shipped with the hake to the south, for the use of the plantation negros," continued Reynolds. Felker wrote in 1878 that "They are valuable as food, and some of the species are cured similar to the cod, but are less valuable than the latter fish."[125]

Perhaps one reason pollock did not gain wider favor was because its flesh had a grayish tinge. Even the marketing ploy of calling it "Boston bluefish" did not eliminate public hesitation over its color. Even today, as William Warner pointed out, "American housewives and the restaurant trade tend to pass it by in favor of pure or all-white meat species. As with Wonder Bread and bleached rice, in other words, so with fish."[126]

Salmon (Salmo salar)

I've been caught in a net by a dear little pet,
and her eyes are as blue as the deep rolling sea;
She's a fisherman's daughter, she lives o'er the water,
She's going to be married next Sunday to me.
She's *as rare as the salmon*, there's really no gammon,
As sweet as shrimps, newly served up for tea;
My soul she had caught, and a place I have bought,
Where a ray of bright sunshine forever will be.[127]

"As rare as the salmon" was truly the case in the late nineteenth century. Salmon had been highly esteemed for centuries, and it was one England's royal fish. In what is now New England and the Maritime Provinces, Atlantic salmon came up most of the rivers to spawn in the summer. The "parr"—juveniles—lived in the rivers for two or three years before heading to the sea for several years, then returning to their place of birth to spawn. George Brown Goode claimed that by the 1880s extensive fishing, industrial damming of so many rivers, and increasing pollution had combined to drastically reduce the New England salmon population. Some recent research suggests that salmon may never have been as abundant as nineteenth-century New Englanders believed; yet a decline during the century cannot be denied.[128]

The esteem in which salmon was held is reflected by the consistency with which cookbooks mentioned it and the amount of mythology surrounding the fish. A common, and usually apocryphal, claim made about high-status foods—in this instance salmon—is that apprentices, the town poor, servants, workers, and the like protested against their "obligation" to eat the food more than "twice a week." For example, at Islesboro, Maine, past which the salmon ran up the Penobscot River, town historian John Farrow wrote in 1893, "Tradition informs us that the salmon were so plentiful that the first town poor protested against being served with salmon more than twice a week." Englishman Frederick Whymper, describing the American fisheries in 1884, wrote about the salmon, "We all know the traditional [English] stories of Newcastle apprentices and salmon." Whymper found the counterpart of this idea at a large sawmill on Vancouver Island on the West Coast, where salmon were even more plentiful than in New England. One day the 200 employees boarded by the firm "held an indignation meeting, and sent the managers a round-robin asking that they should not be compelled to eat salmon more than twice a week!"[129]

Salmon were caught alongshore, in or near the rivers up which they swam to spawn. In the 1830s the early fishery with hooks or Native-American brush weirs gave way to net forms of fishing, particularly stationary pound nets or floating drift nets, depending on the location of the "berths," as the fishing sites were called. In New England, by the second half of the nineteenth century, salmon had been eliminated from most rivers, and only those in Maine could support a commercial salmon fishery. The Penobscot Bay salmon fishery was the most extensive at the time Goode published his study of the fisheries. The fishery centered there on the West Bay, particularly at Camden, Lincolnville, and Northport. A number of pound-net berths were located along the eastern shore of Islesboro as well. "But they are plentiest and most productive on the north side of Duck Trap Harbor, in the town of Lincolnville, where on a single shore there are nine gangs, of which one had four traps and four others have three traps each," reported Goode. One of these gangs belonged to the Ames family, who fished the berth for 110 years between 1837 and 1947, when the salmon stocks had declined so far that it was no longer profitable for the last salmon fisherman, Robie Ames, to set the pound. His fish house with its equipment is now exhibited at Mystic Seaport Museum.[130]

Most salmon caught in mid-coast Maine were iced and sent for fresh sale to Boston. Penobscot salmon was so well known that Fannie Farmer mentioned it by name in her cookbook. Some of it was also salted and smoked, as it had been for hundreds of years in the British Isles. Goode reported: "In the early days of the Maine Salmon fishery the bulk of the catch was either salted down in barrels or smoked....Salt salmon were to some extent consumed in the local markets, but it appears that the greater portion is sent out of state." Smoked salmon was considered the choicest of fishery products, but by the end of the century Canadian salmon was used for that purpose.[131]

Salmon were smoked domestically as well; Eliza Leslie provided instructions in 1837, explaining the salting process and the method of stretching the fish open and fastening them to hang over a wood fire for five or six days. To cook them, she wrote, "cut off slices, soak them a while in lukewarm water, and broil them for breakfast."[132]

About fresh salmon, Felker wrote, "The flesh of salmon is of a reddish hue." Fannie Farmer grouped salmon with other "red-blooded" fish, generally those, she said, that have fat "distributed throughout the flesh." Salmon's richness may account for Mrs. Hale's advice to give salmon sparingly to children, and also for its popularity. As fish dealers Shute and Merchant noted, "The ordinary cookbook is full of recipes for cooking this *king of fishes*."

Richly flavored, big-boned, and with a firm meaty flesh, salmon was highly esteemed.[133]

Like halibut, salmon was cut into slices for frying or broiling. "Fried salmon cut into slices half an inch thick" said Mrs. Putnam. Large sections were good for baking; whole salmon were poached. The leftovers were used in salads or croquettes, or warmed up in cream sauce. When canned Pacific salmon came on the market in the second half of the nineteenth century they were favorably received. Felker wrote "These canned salmon will keep many years in any climate, and find a ready sale at high prices." Dozens of recipes for salmon loaf, salmon salads, and various salmon casseroles appeared in late-nineteenth- and early-twentieth-century community cookbooks, inland and coastwise. They generally began with the words, "Open a can of salmon..."[134]

Sardines

Sardinia pilchardus, the true sardine, resides in the Mediterranean, but its name was borrowed to increase the desirability of many other small fish dressed in a similar fashion for the table. At mid-century true sardines were a fancy imported item from France. For luxury use, processors dressed, scaled, and partially dried them, then scalded them in hot oil. The sardines were then hermetically sealed in tin boxes, with a sauce of hot salted oil, or oil and butter, or sometimes red wine.[135]

In New England, George Burnham of Portland, Maine, began to process immature three-to-five-inch herring as sardines in 1860, using herrings too small for his normal smoking process. An important breakthrough was a process that made the bones "so soft that they can be eaten, like the flesh of the fish, without the slightest inconvenience." By the 1870s the canneries of Eastport and Lubec on Passamaquoddy Bay on the eastern edge of Maine were processing great quantities of small herring as sardines. Since the term had come to describe a process rather than a species of fish, Felker could report in 1878 that "The menhaden, a fish abundantly caught near Long Island, and formerly used for manure and its oil, is now being preserved in oil as sardines." European herrings also came to America as sardines. In 1917 Frank E. Davis of Gloucester was importing French, Norwegian, and Portuguese sardines. He also sold domestic sardines, and in his advertising circular he wrote, "You will be surprised to see how good American Sardines can be." Customers expecting glorified menhaden might have been very surprised indeed. "The choicest of Maine coastal fish are carefully put up in pure olive oil," claimed Davis somewhat evasively.[136]

Upon their introduction in this country, sardines were so fashionable that elegant glass and ceramic containers were made to hold the little tins on the dining table. Sardines were a relish for light meals, ready to eat from the can with bread or crackers, so they did not appear in cookbooks until later in the century, when they were sometimes broiled lightly or deviled for a sandwich spread.[137]

Eventually, sardines moved from fashionable dining tables to rougher venues. According to Edward Ackerman, "The adoption of prohibition by the United States was the first blow which the Maine sardine industry suffered. Like smoked herring, the consumption of sardines fell off sharply with the closing of the saloons."[138]

Scallops (*Aequipecten irradians* and *Placopecten magellanicus*)

Like mussels, scallops ranked far below lobsters, oysters, and even clams among New England shellfish in the nineteenth century. Unlike clams, mussels, and oysters, scallops are mobile, using their strong adductor muscles to jet around the bottom. Two varieties are regarded as good for food: the bay scallop, *Aequipecten irradians*, and the larger sea scallop, *Placopecten magellanicus*. Bay scallops have short lives—usually less than two years—and they flourish south of Cape Cod in areas with abundant eelgrass, on which the larvae settle temporarily. Although the whole scallop is edible, the adductor muscle, which resembles a marshmallow, has become the preferred part.

The scallop was a relative latecomer to market. Although Catherine Beecher mentioned scallops in 1846, they did not regularly appear in New England cookbooks until the 1870s, corroborating George Brown Goode's informant of 1880: "Mr. W.A. Wilcox, who sends me notes on the subject, says it is only eighteen years ago that a fisherman of Fairhaven (opposite New Bedford) was unable to sell 5 gallons that he had caught. But the taste has been acquired, and a local market has grown up to important proportions"—but not so important that the fourteen Fairhaven fishermen employed part-time didn't have to avoid overstocking the market. Goode suggested that Connecticut oystermen first tapped the scallop resources of Long Island's Peconic Bay in the 1850s, eventually creating a demand in New York for this fall delicacy. By the time scalloping was recognized as a distinct fishery in the 1880s, commercial scallopers generally employed openers—often women—to pick out the meats and pack them for market. Yet this fishery did not take off until the 1920s and 1930s, when sea scallops were discovered on Georges Bank and improvements in transportation and marketing made it possible to get both bay and sea scallops to more people, on the coast and inland.[139]

In his role as a subtle promoter of the fisheries, Goode quoted several testimonials to scallops. They could be boiled or pickled (as we saw with mussels and oysters), but one enthusiastic writer remarked, "'Broiled and stuffed with forcemeat, and served in his own shells, he not only forms an ornament to the table, but a pleasing variety amongst the fish." And the New York *Herald* lost all objectivity when it claimed, "The unctuous morsels cannot be manductated with dispassionate pretenses...for they posses an indefinable lusciousness not possessed by any fish or fruit."[140]

That was one person's opinion; others were less sure of the scallop's flavor. The English rarely ate them, and Webster described scallops as "very palatable though of a *peculiar* flavor." Maria Parloa also commented on the flavor, "This shellfish is used about the same as the clam, but is not so popular owing to a *peculiarly sweet* flavor...and is sold shelled, as only the muscular part of the fish is used."[141]

Miss Parloa said that scallops were used as were clams; but then she had little to say about clams except that they were good for fritters. A few other cookbooks suggested scalloping or frying scallops, but most nineteenth-century cookbooks were very quiet about scallops, as if no one really knew what to do with them.

Shad (*Alosa sapidissima*)

Shad is an anadromous member of the *Clupeidae* family that includes alewives and herring. Shad travels upstream from ocean to fresh water in the spring to spawn, having spent about four years in the open sea, and they can grow up to 2 1/2 feet in length and 13 pounds. They frequented eastern rivers from Georgia to Canada, providing food for Native Americans long before Europeans arrived on these shores. Colonial settlers, who recognized the similarity of American shad to the species in Great Britain, soon established weirs to catch them. Shad fisheries developed both north and south—and in the deep South the season lasted far beyond the spring—but we will concern ourselves with shad in New England, where it was most widely sought in Connecticut.[142]

In New England, shad seem to have been victims of the adage that familiarity breeds contempt. In their early abundance they reportedly became known as food for the poor—even to the extent that an apocryphal story describes the Hadley, Massachusetts, family that hid its plate of shad when callers arrived at dinnertime. George Brown Goode reported that shad-eating became "reputable" thirty years before the American Revolution. But we must remember that these often apocryphal stories may tell us more about latter-day attitudes than those of earlier times. In some cases, perhaps including shad, people in later years had come to appreciate what they believed was a food neglected in the past, especially—as we saw with the salmon—if it was becoming rare.[143]

In the early 1800s, a great many people fished for shad in Connecticut rivers. As the state became increasingly industrialized, and more rivers were dammed to provide waterpower, the fish and the fishery were largely confined to the Connecticut River. Local people ate part of their catch fresh and salted the balance, as we saw in the chapter about the Buckingham family. Goode reported that, in the early years of shad fishing in Connecticut, haul seines were used to sweep fish out of the water as they swam near shore. In the nineteenth century fishermen began to use stationary methods: "gill-nets, then eventually, by 1849 the first pound net. The fish are packed in Lyme, Essex, and Saybrook in ice and sent to New York City." Depletion of the shad population led to prohibitions on the use of stationary nets so, like other shad fishermen, Connecticut River fishermen began to use drift nets—gill nets that float down select "shots" of the river at night—as they still do.[144]

New Englanders and people in the Middle Atlantic and Southern states particularly appreciated shad. Amelia Simmons's *American Cookery* of 1796—the earliest American cookbook—included shad, and recipes appeared consistently through the nineteenth century for both fresh and salted shad. Once icing became the accepted practice, salting was abandoned. Even as the catch declined due to overfishing in the second half of the nineteenth century, shad were "much-esteemed and cheap," according to a British observer.[145]

Connecticut River shad had an excellent reputation. In his 1866 *Market Assistant*, Thomas De Voe wrote, "Shad are found salted and also smoked, the year through, and those cured and brought from Connecticut are considered the best.[146] In its 10 January 1891 issue, the Stonington *Mirror* editorialized: "Fresh shad from the sunny south are in market. They may not taste as nice as the Connecticut River article, but they look tempting enough to passers-by," while on 28 April 1876 the Mystic *Press* announced, "Connecticut River shad from Capt. Washington's market have furnished many a nice meal in the village this week."

A decade later Goode reported that the Connecticut River shad fishery was diminishing. A limited shad fishery on the Connecticut River has continued to the present day, and the fish are still consumed locally as well as being sent to a waiting market in New York for a few weeks each spring.[147]

Bones and roe: Shad is famous for both its roe and its bones, described by one of my friends as "bones that go in *every* direction." Recipes for shad roe appeared in cookbooks nearly as often as ways to prepare the entire fish. Because of the popular demand for shad roe, at one time the males—bucks—were given away, and fish buyers took only the females.[148]

Early in the twentieth century, when filleting made so many kinds of fish more convenient and presentable, shad purveyors hired workers to pull the bones out with pliers. A method of filleting shad, the "x-y-z cut," the invention of which is variously attributed, left the fish in tatters and wasted a great deal of flesh, but is still used today. Fisheries historian John Kochiss reported that: "Even now only old timers eat unboned whole shad. They claim it is far more tasty that way. But [Connecticut River shad fisherman

This scene captured at Fulton Fish Market in New York in 1877 shows a fishmonger scooping live fish from a fish car. Live fish were "smacked" to market in vessels like Mystic Seaport's *Emma C. Berry,* and then kept alive in these cars. [James E. Kelly drawing, *Scribner's Monthly,* 1877]

Hubert] Spencer said, 'If you eat one mess of unboned shad that is enough.' "[149]

Planking shad: "The fish, fresh from the stream, is cut in twain, fastened by nails to a thick oak board, slanted towards a hot wood fire, duly basted, and finally served at table on its oak gridiron." Until recently, this description of the outdoor cooking of shad pertained to the American South and Middle Atlantic states, where it was conducted for pleasure, much as clambakes were in New England. Virtually all historic references to planking shad come from the Middle Atlantic and Southern states, and the word's etymology is supported by citations from Maryland and New Jersey. Although roasting fish or any food before a fire supported by a piece of wood is a universal method of cooking, only in recent decades has planked shad become a Connecticut tradition.[150]

Shrimp (Crangon vulgaris)

These small crustaceans related to lobsters can be found in New England waters, but they were not sought commercially there. Indeed, what was caught was often used as bait rather than food in New England. Shrimps have been mentioned in cookbooks since the 1600s—and they were eaten in Europe—but in America, like crab and turtle, they were more often included in southern cookbooks than northern ones because shrimp are larger and more abundant in southern waters. Recipes for shrimp are more common in community cookbooks after shrimp canning was established in the Gulf states in the late 1870s. Miss Parloa summed up New England's general opinion of shrimp: "These are good for sauces or stews, and, in fact, can be used, in most cases, the same as lobster. But few shrimp are found in the Eastern or Western markets. The canned goods are, however, convenient and nice for sauces."[151]

Smelts (Osmerus mordax)

Smelts, like shad, are anadromous fish, that hatch in fresh water, grow to adulthood during two years at sea, and then return to spawn in rivers between February and June. Their early arrival gave local people a pleasant diversion from their usual winter meals. These little fish, which can grow to more than a foot, were generally fried whole. Miss Parloa and others described fashionable ways to garnish with smelts: "With baked fish they are arranged around the dish in any form that the taste of the cook may dictate....When smelts are used as a garnish, serve one on each plate with the other fish. If you wish to have the smelts in rings, for a garnish, fasten the tails in the opening at the gills, with little wooden tooth picks;...When they are cooked take out the skewers, and they will retain their shape." This represented a fair amount of fussing, hardly likely in most households, but seems to have been a Boston Cooking School standard, for Fannie Farmer included an illustration for smelt garnishes in her 1896 edition and Mrs. Lincoln included instructions for it in her book.[152]

During the 1865 smelt season, on 24 March, the Mystic *Pioneer* offered an easier, more prosaic way to prepare smelts for breakfast or supper: "How to Cook Smelts.—Soak them a little while in warm water; scrape and cut the heads as far that you can gently pull them off and thus draw out the dark vein" then dip them in Indian [corn]meal and fry them in salt pork fat."

Sturgeon (Acipenser oxyrhynchus)

Sturgeon is another fish that lives in the open sea but returns to fresh water to spawn. A bottom-feeder that stirs up the mud with its blunt nose, the sturgeon can grow to 18 feet in length and nearly 200 pounds.

Sturgeon was very highly esteemed in Great Britain and Europe for centuries. It was among the fish reserved for royalty, if and when they chose to claim it; they passed it up often enough that recipes for it appeared in seventeenth- and eighteenth-century English cookbooks. The sturgeon has two outstanding characteristics: one is the flesh, which is pink like salmon, with a flavor resembling veal; the other is that cartilaginous plates help give it form, so it has many fewer bones than most fish.[153] These attributes certainly contributed to its popularity. Another reason sturgeon was esteemed is because it is the source for caviar and a high-quality isinglass. Sturgeon is now rare in the Western Atlantic, but it was quite plentiful in North America in the nineteenth century. A large fishery was dedicated to catching sturgeon until the end of the century, when the catch declined. Felker reported in the 1870s that sturgeon was caught in the Hudson River and in the streams flowing into the Great Lakes. It was also caught in the South, but had largely disappeared from New England rivers by then. Its decline was reflected in cookery books; sturgeon was seldom mentioned after the 1880s.

"The flesh is of a reddish tinge and is highly esteemed by some people," commented Felker, who also noted, "it is said large quantities are cured and smoked and sold for genuine halibut." In 1898 Stevenson wrote that practically all sturgeon was smoked and was then sold in areas with large German populations. Fresh sturgeon appeared slightly more often in southern cookbooks than northern ones. Among northern books, Mrs. Abell in 1853 referred to sturgeon cutlets, and Miss Parloa in 1887 mentioned a four-pound middle cut. Thus, in texture, consistency, and treatment, sturgeon shared a culinary tie with salmon and halibut.[154]

Swordfish (Xiphias gladius)

Another firm, oily-fleshed fish, swordfish did not catch on in New England until later in the nineteenth century. Swordfish are rather solitary deep-sea creatures that grow to nearly 1,000 pounds as they stalk schools of migratory fish like mackerel. Fishermen believed they charged into the schools with their swords flailing, then gobbled up the fish they had dismembered.

According to George Brown Goode, the earliest record of swordfish as a New England food fish dates to the 1840s on Nantucket and Martha's Vineyard. When the supply exceeded the market, they were salted and sent to the West Indies and the South. The fishery developed slowly through the 1840s and 1850s, and was fairly well-established by the 1870s, mostly in southern New England. "Its flesh is excellent food, and it is captured by harpoon, affording an exciting and even dangerous sport," commented Peter Felker. Indeed, swordfishing was a true hunt. Aboard a schooner or sloop on calm days, lookouts scanned the waters for swordfish dorsal fins. A sighting brought the crew into action, and if the vessel could be maneuvered behind the fish the harpooner took his position at the end of the bowsprit. At the right instant he darted his long-handled harpoon into the fish's back, and the removable head lodged in the fish. Attached to the dart was a line with a keg buoy on the end, which trailed after the fish, ultimately tiring it out. Then a fisherman in a dory went to lance and retrieve the fish. Here was the real sport, for angry swordfish frequently drove their bills through dories and occasionally wounded fishermen. But usually the fishermen prevailed, lancing the fish in the gills, then bringing it back to the vessel. Charles Dana Gibson reported that crews and captains looked forward to swordfishing in the summer months, considering it "a vacation when compared to line trawling and mackereling."[155]

In the fishery's first decades swordfish were sold as fresh fish in New Bedford, Fall River, and Providence. Later, in the 1880s, just about the time that swordfish began to

Salt cod was skinned, boned, and shredded to make "fluff"—the product in the center of the picture—which was packed into boxes and sold as a convenient food item. This fish needed only to be rehydrated with a little hot water, and then it could be mixed with potatoes for fish cakes or warmed up in milk sauce as codfish gravy. Fish producers discovered that processing fish to make it easy to use and to remove bones improved their sales, a principle in effect today with the prepared fish products we find in grocery-store freezers. A fishmonger friend told the author, "People want you to do everything to fish for them except eat it." The young lady boxing fish on the left is the author as a young woman. [Lightfoot Collection, MSM 90.55.23]

appear in cookbooks, the fishery was taken up in Portland, Maine, in Gloucester, and in Boston.[156]

Not until the twentieth century, however, did swordfish really catch on among consumers. George Wesley Pierce recalled a time when swordfish "brought a very small price, often as low as three cents a pound. Today [1930s], most of the time swordfish retails at thirty-five to forty cents a pound. This goes to show how people will change their minds about eating certain kinds of fresh fish in the market." Davidson pointed out that "Linnaeus compared the flesh of the swordfish to salmon, by way of compliment." He rightly comments that the compliment is deserved but not apt.[157] Even more than salmon, swordfish was sufficiently meat-like to win a place in the popular diet; a fishmonger once told me that people who don't like fish enjoy swordfish.

Swordfish appeared infrequently in later nineteenth-century cookbooks. The thorough Miss Parloa described the swordfish as "very large with dark, firm flesh. It is nutritious but not as delicate as other kinds of fish. It is cut and sold like halibut, and in season in July and August." Miss Parloa did not provide instructions for cooking it; since she compared it to halibut, we may suppose she expected it to be prepared similarly. Swordfish was more often included in twentieth-century cookbooks—swordfish steaks were recommended for broiling or frying—but we can detect a little hesitation when Mary Lincoln remarked, "This valuable seafood has many friends among those who have eaten it at its best....But tastes differ..."[158]

Tautog (Tautoga onitis)

Tautog, also known as blackfish, was a new fish to New England settlers. A dark, blunt-nosed fish that grows to about ten pounds, the tautog frequents rocky areas alongshore south of Cape Cod. Amelia Simmons mentioned it in her 1796 cookbook, and it enjoyed steady popularity. Though Goode said it was especially favored as a table fish in New York, it was highly regarded along the southern New England coast as well.

Tautog appeared in cookbooks infrequently, which suggests that it may have been considered one of the generic "fish" rather than appreciated for its individual characteristics. In 1849, Mrs. Putnam wrote that tautog was very hard to clean, cautioned the cook to scrape all the scales off, and recommended stewing it whole, sewed up with stuffing. Mrs. Abell advised that "blackfish are best broiled or fried."[159]

Terrapin and Turtles

It is necessary to mention turtles because they and mock turtle soup do appear in American cookbooks, though relatively seldom in community cookbooks. They were more popular in the South than the North.

The instructions for dealing with terrapin and turtles, which were sold alive, are horrific (see page 184). This perhaps accounts for the great numbers of mock turtle soups, which were often made from a calf's head. And even those were complicated recipes.

Green turtle appeared early among the canned seafoods, and Miss Parloa's recipe for Green Turtle Soup in 1880 begins frankly with "One can of green turtle."[160]

Trout, Sea Trout, Weakfish, Squeteague (Cynoscion regalis)

The freshwater trout was always popular in New England, as it was in old England, and it has appeared consistently in cookbooks since the 1600s, usually fried or broiled as a panfish.

Cookbook references to salmon trout or sea trout are difficult to interpret. It is possible they refer to the salmon trout or steelhead of the Pacific Northwest, which became available in canned form later in the nineteenth century. But given the mix of local and more formal names for both fresh- and saltwater species, the name is hard to pin down. Another likely candidate is the sea trout of the Atlantic, usually known as squeteague, and also called weakfish for its tender mouth. Schools of squeteague frequently visited southern New England, where they were caught both commercially and recreationally, although they were not as popular in the North as in the South.[161]

Tunny Fish (Thunnus thynnus)

Tunny or tuna fish was another late entry in the New England diet. Felker incorrectly described the tunny as "a large fish belonging to the mackerel family," and he added, "The flesh is eaten both fresh and salted, and is highly esteemed," which was true to a limited degree. Albacore and bluefin tuna were familiar to Italians and other southern European immigrants, and bluefin tuna could be found off the New England coast. It is a big fish, growing to 14 feet and up to 1,600 pounds, but it was infrequently sought until tuna fishing and canning were established in California in the 1920s.[162]

Like swordfish, tuna flesh is similar to meat—firm and dark-red—but as fresh fish it was not mentioned in nineteenth-century sources. Canned tuna appeared frequently in community cookbooks inland and coastwise after the West Coast fishery was established in the 1920s. It is hard for people today to imagine either a potluck supper without a tuna and noodle casserole or a week without at least a tuna sandwich; yet, relatively speaking, the tuna is a recent addition to the American diet.

Turbot

Turbot are European flatfish caught inshore. Accordingly, they appeared in British cookbooks reprinted in America. When they were included in American cookbooks they were apparently either confused with other white-fleshed fish or the word "turbot" became a descriptive word for a mode of preparation rather than a particular species of fish. Turbot à la crème, the recipe in which turbot appeared most frequently, usually called for cooked fish picked free of bones and baked in a flour-thickened milk sauce with butter and lemon, sometimes with crumbs on top. Miss Parloa did not give advice in her marketing guide on selecting turbot, and when she described "*turbot à la crème*" she wrote, "Boil five or six pounds of haddock," not turbot. Likewise, the Barnstable Village Improvement Society women specified for turbot à la crème to "use either haddock or halibut." In her turbot à la crème recipe Mary Witcher called for bass or cod.[163]

White Fish

While there are whitefish in some cookbooks, fish in this family, *Coregonidae*, are usually freshwater fish native to northern lakes. The Great Lakes harbored a large-scale fishery for whitefish. The fish was prized for its flavor, but it did not keep well so it did not travel far. Whitefish also may have been used for whiting, which in America is a common market name for silver hake (*Merlucccius bilinearis*).[164] Newcomers to New England who were familiar with the whiting, *Merlangius merlangus*, in Britain or elsewhere in Europe, may have applied the name to this other member of the *gadidae* family and cooked it as they did all white-fleshed fish of this sort. It is hard to tell just what cookbook authors were specifying when they used the term "white fish." In many cases they may have been using it as a generic term, emphasizing the great popularity of pure white fish both yesterday and today.

The Recipes

The recipes that follow are for some of the nineteenth century's favored fish–oysters, cod, salt cod, mackerel, shad, shad roe, halibut, lobster–all still favorites. Two oyster recipes–fried and scalloped–are followed by a mock oyster recipe for "corn" oysters. Salt fish hash and salt codfish gravy are included along with bacalhau con arroz, a Portuguese salt cod dish with rice. Baked shad and scalloped shad roes are ideal fish dishes for the Spring. Broiled mackerel and fried halibut steaks are good ways to prepare these fresh fish. And the stewed lobster is now our family's favorite Christmas Eve supper dish.

FRIED OYSTERS

Dry the oysters in a clean towel; then dip in beaten egg, and then in rolled cracker crumbs; fry about five minutes in lard or beef drippings. Butter is apt to be too oily, and lard is better for frying them in.

From *Mrs.Winslow's Domestic Receipt Book for* 1878, page 18

Next to stewing and scalloping, frying seems to have been the most popular method of preparing oysters in the nineteenth century. The earliest fried oyster recipes called for a batter that the oysters were dipped into before frying. But this simple egg and cracker batter is easy and delicious.

Despite Mrs. Winslow's caution about butter being too oily, using butter is recommended because it gives a wonderful flavor to the dish. If you want a real nineteenth-century taste, try lard or beef drippings. A more specific interpretation follows.

24 oysters
2 eggs, beaten
1 cup crushed pilot crackers
butter

1. Drain the raw shucked oysters and pat dry in a clean towel.
2. Heat enough butter to cover the bottom of a heavy deep pan over a medium heat till it bubbles but does not turn brown.
3. Dip each oyster in the beaten egg, then in the cracker crumbs, and fry for about 1 1/2 minutes on each side.
4. Drain on paper towels and keep warm in the oven before serving.

Yields 24 fried oysters.

SCALLOPED OYSTERS

Ingredients: Three dozen oysters, a large tea-cupful of bread or cracker crumbs, two ounces of fresh butter, pepper and salt, half a tea-cupful of oyster juice. Make layers of these ingredients, as described in the last article, in the top of a chafing dish, or any kind of pudding or gratin dish; bake in a quick oven about fifteen minutes; brown with a salamander.

From *Practical Cooking and Dinner Giving,* by Mrs. Mary F. Henderson, 1882, page 115

This straightforward recipe requires no interpretation. It produces a very oyster-y dish. I found the recipe worked well with crushed oyster crackers, but any cracker you like will do. Some period recipes recommend putting a few spoonfuls of milk or cream over each layer. This is good to do if you do not like a strong oyster flavor

A "salamander" was a heavy piece of iron on a long handle which could be heated in a fire and, when held over a dish, would brown the top. You will probably use your broiler.

Yields 4-6 servings.

CORN OYSTERS

Grate young sweet corn, and to a pint add one egg well beaten, small teacup of flour, half gill of cream or milk, and a teaspoonful of salt; mix well together, drop into the fat by spoonfuls about the size of an oyster. If you are all run down Hood's Sarsaparilla will build you up.

From *Hood's Combined Cook Books,* by C.I. Hood & Co., 1875-1885, *High Street,* page 12

These do indeed look like fried oysters. They are a delicious vegetable accompaniment in the fritter tradition to any meal. This recipe calls for a small teacup of flour, but you can reduce the amount as long as you make a batter thick enough to drop from the spoon.

Every year I dedicate one batch of freshly picked corn to corn oysters, which we eagerly look forward to. They are best made from fresh, uncooked corn, if you think you can bear the idea of having corn in another way besides on the cob.

2 cups grated fresh sweet corn
1 egg beaten
3/4 cup flour
1/4 cup cream or milk
1 teaspoon salt

1. Mix together corn, egg, and milk.
2. Add the flour gradually.
3. Drop by tablespoonfuls into deep fat or on a very well oiled griddle and fry quickly. Drain on paper and keep warm in oven till served.

Yields about a dozen.

SALT FISH HASH

Salt fish mashed with potatoes, with good butter or pork scraps to moisten, is nicer the second day than it was the first. The fish should be minced very fine, while it is still warm. After it has got cold and dry it is difficult to do it nicely. Salt fish needs plenty of vegetables, such as onions, beets, carrots, etc.

From *The American Frugal Housewife,* by Mrs. Child, 1833, page 60

Hash is what you made out of your leftover boiled salt-codfish dinner. The proportion of vegetables to fish depended entirely on the leftovers and personal taste, so there can be no more specific a recipe than Mrs. Child has provided. If you include beets they will, of course, turn the whole thing red. It really does taste better with salt pork or real butter.

PICKED-UP CODFISH

Pull the fish in little bits, then soak half an hour in a good deal of cold water. Pour off the water, put the fish in a saucepan, and add more cold water; simmer till tender. If too salt, pour off the water in which it is cooking, and again cover with cold water, and when it boils up drain off the water and cover with good thick cream, and add a piece of butter half the size of an egg, or larger if the cream is not rich. Set over the stove til it boils up, and thicken with flour wet with water. Stir in a beaten egg while hot, and serve.

From *All Around the House,* by Mrs. H.W. Beecher, 1878, pages 392-93

This dish is similar enough to salt pork and salt beef gravies that you could simply substitute the salted codfish for the meat in those recipes (pages 159 and 160), which is probably how it was made from time to time. Mrs. Beecher's ideas about using cream and adding an egg make this a richer dish. In southeastern Connecticut and Rhode Island, codfish gravy or creamed codfish was frequently served on jonnycakes; in other areas it was poured over potatoes or toast.

The trick to this dish is in shredding or "picking-up" the fish before soaking it. For four servings, allow a half pound of salt cod before soaking. Mrs. Beecher's recipe is clear enough that an interpretation is not needed. A piece of butter half the size of a hen's egg is about two tablespoonsful, and one tablespoon of flour should be adequate to thicken about a cup of milk or cream, especially if you use an egg.

Yields 4 servings.

BACALHAU CON ARROZ

Soak, cook, and debone the salt codfish and flake into cooked rice. Add assafroa (safflower) and cumin.

From Rose Camacho Hirsch, Stonington, Connecticut, 1988

Another way of preparing salt cod is to combine it with rice instead of potatoes, much as you would for kedgeree. The traditional Portuguese seasonings of safflower and cumin make this special.

Use any proportion of fish to rice you like, and mix the spices into the cooked rice. We enjoyed an equal proportion of rice to fish, one cup of each, and think no less than a quarter teaspoon of safflower or three-quarters teaspoon of cumin should be used. That made enough for two generous servings for a meal with a salad.

SCALLOPED ROES

The roes of the shad.
1 cup drawn butter, and the yolks of three hard-boiled eggs.
1 teaspoon anchovy paste.
Juice of half a lemon.
1 cup of bread crumbs.
Parsley, salt and pepper to taste.

Boil the roes in a water with a little vinegar stirred in. Lay in cold water five minutes and wipe dry. Break up with the back of a spoon, but do not crush the eggs. Set by, and pound the boiled yolks to a powder. Beat this into the drawn butter, then the parsley and the other seasonings, finally the roes. Strew the bottom of a bake-dish with crumbs; pour in the mixture, and cover thickly with fine crumbs. Stick dots of butter over the top, and bake, covered, until it begins to bubble, then brown upon the upper grating of the oven.

From *The Dinner Year Book,* by Marion Harland, 1878, page 298

This is a delicious way to prepare shad roe and a nice change from the fairly common roe and bacon combination. I recommend that you use white bread crumbs for authenticity. You may also wish to reduce the amount of butter by as much as half: by modern standards nineteenth-century recipes are often heavy-handed with butter.

1 1/2 pounds or 3 roe sets
4 cups water with 3 tablespoons vinegar mixed in
3 hard-boiled eggs
1 cup drawn butter
1 teaspoon anchovy paste
parsley, salt, and pepper to taste
1 cup bread crumbs
Preheat oven to 350°

1. Poach the roes in the vinegar and water for about 5 minutes. Lay in cold water for 5 minutes, then drain and pat dry.
2. Break up gently with the back of a spoon without crushing the eggs in the roe.
3. Thoroughly break up egg yolks and beat into drawn butter. Mix in parsley, salt, pepper, anchovy paste, and then the roes.
4. Grease a 9-inch baking pan and sprinkle the bread crumbs over the bottom. Spread the butter and roe mixture over the crumbs.
5. Put dots of butter on the top, if you wish. Bake covered for 15 minutes. When it begins to bubble, uncover and let brown under the broiler for another 2-3 minutes.

Yields 5-6 servings.

STEWED LOBSTER

Cut the lobster in pieces about an inch square. Place them in a stew pan, and over them pour a cup of water; put in butter the size of an egg; pepper and salt to the taste. Mix also with the green dressing of the lobster, and stir it about ten minutes over the fire. Just before taking off, add two wineglasses of port or sherry. Let it scald, but not boil. Hood's Sarsaparilla cures biliousness.

From *Hood's Combined Cook Books*, by C.I. Hood & Co., 1875-1885, *Hoods #1*, page 26

This is a straightforward recipe for a delicious luncheon soup or a small dinner appetizer dish. You could make this from prepared lobster meat, but then you would not have the tomally to use. I recommend starting with live lobsters (one per person if this is the main course), then you could save the boiling water to use when the recipe says "and over them pour a cup of water."

This recipe is clear enough that an interpretation is not needed. Don't forget that a piece of butter the size of an egg is 2 ounces or 4 tablespoonsful and that a wineglassful is about a quarter cup; for a small lobster that quarter cup will be enough. Personally, I prefer a dry sherry, but if you wanted to be adventurous you could try port.

MACKEREL

Mackerel should be broiled, and served a la maitre-d'hotel.[p.111]
Maitre-d'Hotel Butter *(for Beefsteak, Broiled Meat, or Fish).*
Mix butter the size of an egg, the juice of half a lemon, and two or three sprigs of parsley, chopped very fine; pepper and salt all together. Spread this over any fish or meat when hot; then put the dish into the oven a few moments, to allow the butter to penetrate the meat.

From *Practical Cooking and Dinner Giving*, by Mrs. Mary F. Henderson, 1882, pages 111 and 124

Mrs. Henderson was being very stylish with her French sauce for meat and fish. It is hard to tell how many cooks took her advice and made this sauce, or how many just served drawn butter and a wedge of lemon with the fish.

The recipe above is clear enough that an interpretation is not needed. Keep in mind that butter the size of an egg is about four tablespoonsful, and if you let it warm to room temperature it will be easier to mix in the lemon juice, parsley, salt, and pepper, but even so I found they do not mix willingly. Do not melt the butter. Allow half an average-sized mackerel per person.

Yields 1/4 cup butter.

FRIED HALIBUT STEAKS

Wash and wipe the steaks. Roll each in flour, and fry upon a buttered griddle, turning carefully with a spatula, or cake-turner, when the lower side is done. They should be of a nice brown, and tender throughout. Remove to a hot dish and garnish with sliced lemon; in carving see that a bit of the lemon goes to each person, as many prefer it to any other sauce for fish. Send around potatoes with the steak. Worcestershire is a good store-sauce for fish and game. Anchovy is pre-eminently a fish sauce, but many do not like it.

From *The Dinner Year Book*, by Marion Harland, 1878, page 23

So simple, so good! Halibut became a favorite fresh fish in the nineteenth century, along with cod and haddock. Halibut are large, and the steaks can be substantial cuts depending on from where in the fish they are taken; hence Mrs. Harland's comment on "carving." The steaks hold together well if you don't remove the skin.

Allow half a pound per person, and have the fishmonger cut the steaks off in inch- to inch-and-a-half-thick slices. Add salt and pepper to the flour, and grease the pan lightly with butter. The recipe above is clear enough that an interpretation is not needed.

BAKED SHAD

Put [the baked shad] into a hot dish, and keep warm while you add to the gravy a teaspoonful of anchovy sauce, the juice of a lemon, a tablespoonful of browned flour, wet up with cold water, and pepper. Boil up well, and serve in a boat.

From *The Dinner Year Book,* by Marion Harland, 1878, page 268

Mrs. Harland's recipe for baking shad, excerpted here, assumes a fresh whole fish, which she instructs you to stuff and then sew up before baking for an hour. Unless there is a fisherman in your family, you probably will not be working with a whole shad, but if you bake a fillet with the pan covered so the juices from the fish do not all evaporate then you could make this sauce, which is very good and pleasantly lemony. An interpretation follows.

Pan juices from baked shad
1 teaspoon anchovy sauce
juice of one lemon
1 tablespoon browned flour
2 tablespoons cold water
pepper

1. Put the fish, stuffed with your favorite dressing, in a pan, pour in 1/2- to 2/3-cup water. Bake till the fish flakes apart—about half an hour for a 3-4-pound whole fish.
2. Drain the pan juices into a heavy saucepan. Add the anchovy sauce, lemon juice, flour and water mixture, and pepper.
3. Boil, stirring constantly till thickened.
4. To serve, pour over the fish on a platter or serve in a gravy boat.

Yields about 2/3-cup gravy.

STEWED HADDOCK

To make stewed haddock, poach the fish lightly first, then stew it in a mixture of butter, salt, pepper, and cream. Serve over "cream lunch biscuits."

From Frances Jaixen Dodge, Block Island, Rhode Island, May 1986

Mrs. Dodge still prepares stewed haddock this way, as she remembers it being prepared when she was a girl. Her father, George Jaixen, was a cook for the West Side Life-Saving Station on Block Island, and Mrs. Dodge figures that haddock was probably prepared this way at the station early in this century.

The recipe is clear enough that an interpretation is not needed. Allow about a third of a pound of haddock fillets or steaks per person. The heavier the cream, the better the flavor. Use a heavy pan. To poach the fish, just add enough water to cover the bottom of the pan and let it simmer for just a few minutes, then add cream, butter, salt, and pepper—all to taste. To be orthodox, serve over cream lunch biscuits, which will soak up the cream. You can use crackers or toast, but it won't be the same. This is an ideal dish for people who prefer a mild-flavored fish dish.

NOTES

CHAPTER ONE

1. Susan H. Ely and Elizabeth B. Plimpton, *The Lieutenant River* (Old Lyme, Connecticut: Lyme Historical Society and Florence Griswold Museum, 1991), 20.

2. Reverend Samuel G. Buckingham, *The Life of William A. Buckingham, The War Governor of Connecticut...*(Springfield, Massachusetts: W.F. Adams Co., 1894), 7.

3. Ibid.

4. Ibid., 8. George Brown Goode's *Fisheries and Fishery Industries of the U.S.* (Washington, D.C.: Government Printing Office, 1887), however, does not name Buckingham as "the first" to develop shad fishing on the Connecticut.

5. Joanne Bowen, "A Study of Seasonality and Subsistence: Eighteenth-Century Suffield, Connecticut," (Ph.D. diss., Brown University, 1990) describes how systems of exchange networks were established and maintained at that time; Ely and Plimpton, *Lieutenant River*, 9.

6. Lucy Larcom, *A New England Girlhood* (New York: Corinth Books, 1961), 94-95.

7. Ibid., 93.

8. William N. Peterson and Peter M. Coope, *Historic Buildings at Mystic Seaport Museum* (Mystic: Mystic Seaport Museum, 1985), 62. The front was possibly built in 1758; the records are confusing.

9. Larcom, *New England Girlhood*, 21-22.

10. Amelia Simmons, *American Cookery: Or, the Art of Dressing Viands, Fish, Poultry and Vegetables* , ed. Mary Tolford Wilson, (1796; reprint, New York: Dover, 1984), 10-11.

11. Lydia Maria Child, *The American Frugal Housewife* (Boston: Carter, Hendee, and Company, 1833), 33. It is the author's experience, however, that potatoes will keep on sprouting, though less vigorously, until you eat them.

12. Child, *American Frugal Housewife*, 8-9.

13. Samuel Buckingham, Probate Inventory, 1815, Town Records, Chester, Connecticut.

14. Caroline Fuller Sloat, Old Sturbridge Village, "Dishwashing and the Domestic Landscape: Reform begins at Home," (Paper presented at the 1992 Winterthur Conference, Winterthur, Delaware).

15. Various articles in *Early American Inventories*, Proceedings of Dublin Seminar for New England Folklife, vol. 12, (Boston: Boston University Press, 1987), discuss this problem in detail.

16. Sarah Anna Emery, *Reminiscences of a Nonagenarian* (Newburyport, Massachusetts: William H. Huse & Co., 1879), 32.

17. Octagon Museum, *The Taste of Power: The Rise of Genteel Dining and Entertaining in Early Washington, Checklist for the Exhibition* (Washington, D.C.: Octagon Museum, 1990), 15; Barbara G. Carson, *Ambitious Appetites: Dining, Behavior and Patterns of Consumption in Federal Washington* (Washington, D.C.: Octagon Museum, 1990); "Knife Eating: A Cautionary Tale," *Food History News* (Summer 1990): 1.

18. Jack Larkin, *The Reshaping of Everyday Life, 1790-1840* (New York: Harper and Row, 1988), 286. Larkin writes that the estimate of per capita alcohol consumption at the time of the Revolution was 3 1/2 gallons; and since the mid-nineteenth century per capita consumption has never been much over 2 gallons a year, "a contrast that is more remarkable because the proportion of the population old enough to be serious drinkers was then much smaller." W.J. Rorabaugh, *The Alcoholic Republic* (London: Oxford University Press, 1981) also discusses the topic in depth.

19. George J. Cummings, "A Leaf From the Life of a Farmer's Boy Ninety Years Ago," *Old Time New England* (January 1929): 100.

20. Caroline Howard King, *When I Lived in Salem* (Brattleboro, Vermont: Stephen Daye Press, 1937), 43.

21. Mrs. E.A. Howland, *The New England Economical Housekeeper* (Worcester, Massachusetts: S.A. Howland, 1845), 71.

22. King, *When I Lived in Salem*, 99.

23. Fanny Merritt Farmer, *The Original Boston Cooking School Cook Book* (1896; facsimile reprint of the first edition, New York: Weathervane Books), 514.

24. Not many years ago, in the late 1970sor early 1980s, the author found this combination on the Durgin Park Restaurant lunch menu; and another time on the breakfast menu of a Rhode Island diner.

25. [Abbott Lowell Cummings], "Notes on Furnishing a Small New England Farmhouse," *Old Time New England* January-March 1958: 83.

26. Bowen, *Seasonality*, 93.

27. Ibid., 150-63.

28. Child, *American Frugal Housewife*, 40.

29. Zephaniah Pease, ed., *The Diary of Samuel Rodman 1821-1859* (New Bedford: Reynolds Printing, 1927), 10.

30. Ibid., 14.

31. Ibid., 17. This method works very well, and can be seen demonstrated at Old Bethpage Museum, in Bethpage, New York, on Long Island.

32. Ibid., 70.

33. Ibid., 71.

34. Emery, *Reminiscences of a Nonagenarian*, 275-76.

35. Mary Elizabeth Weaver Farnsworth, "Reminiscences of...," Misc. Vol. 155, G.W. Blunt White Library, Mystic Seaport Museum, hereafter cited as GWBWL.

36. Ibid.

37. Jane Nylander, *Our Own Snug Fireside: Images of the New England Home, 1760-1860* (New York: Alfred A. Knopf, 1993), 201.

38. According to William N. Peterson in *Mystic Built, Ships and Shipyards of the Mystic River, 1784-1919* (Mystic: Mystic Seaport Museum, 1989), 225, *Revenue* was one of the earliest Mystic vessels. Built in 1795 in the Eldredge Packer yard, she had been in the codfishery before she was engaged in coasting.

39. Ethan A. Denison, Diary, Misc. Vol. 566, GWBWL.

40. Zephaniah Pease, ed., *Life in New Bedford 100 Years Ago, A Chronicle of the Social, Religious, and Commercial History of the Period in a Diary Kept by Joseph R. Anthony* (New Bedford: Old Dartmouth Historical Society, 1925), 58.

41. King, *When I Lived in Salem*, 130.

42. Denison, Diary.

43. Child, *American Frugal Housewife*, 4.

44. Timothy Dwight, *Travels in New England and New York*, ed. Barbara Miller Solomon, 4 vols., (Cambridge, Massachusetts: Belknap Press of Harvard University Press, 1969), 249.

45. Emery, *Reminiscences of a Nonagenarian*, 7.

46. Dwight, *Travels in New England*, Ibid.

47. John T. Perkins, *John T. Perkins' Journal at Sea, 1845* (Mystic: Marine Historical Association, 1934), 119.

48. Cummings, "Notes on Furnishing," 84.

49. "Indian" was the name New Englanders gave to corn meal; to the earliest settlers, the word corn meant "grain," particularly wheat, and so the word Indian distinguished the Indians' maize

from English wheat.

50. Pease, *Life in New Bedford*, 19, 33, 53, 56, 78.

51. King, *When I Lived in Salem*, 99.

52. Emery, *Reminiscences of a Nonagenarian*, 7.

53. Cummings, "Notes on Furnishing," 84.

54. Ibid., 78.

55. Howland, *Economical Housekeeper*, 71.

56. Child, *AmericanFrugal Housewife*, 50.

57. Farnsworth, *Reminiscences of a Nonagenarian*.

58. Pease, *Life in New Bedford*, 19.

59. Ibid.

60. Dwight, *Travels in New England*, 249.

61. Cummings, "Notes on Furnishing," 80.

62. Mabel Cassine Holman, *Old Saybrook Stories* (Hartford: Connecticut State Library, 1949); typescript from Hartford *Daily Times*, newspaper collection, 105.

63. Cummings, "Notes on Furnishing," 84.

64. King, *When I Lived in Salem*, 99.

65. Farnsworth, "Reminiscences...."

66. Cummings, "Notes on Furnishing."

67. Charles W. Morgan, Diary, Coll. 27, vol. 1, GWBWL.

68. Farnsworth, "Reminiscences...."

69. Dwight, *Travels in New England*, 249.

70. Farnsworth, "Reminiscences...."

71. Child, *American Frugal Housewife*, 86.

72. Genevieve M. Darden, My *Dear Husband* (Taunton, Massachusetts: William S. Sullwold Publishing, Inc., for Descendants of Whaling Masters, Inc., 1980), 29.

73. Child, *American Frugal Housewife*, 82.

74. Pease, *Life in New Bedford*, 93-94.

75. E.B. Chace and L.B. Lovell, *Two Quaker Sisters* (New York: Liveright Publishing Co., 1937), 27.

76. Denison, Diary.

77. Pease, *Life in New Bedford*, 63.

78. Ibid., 84.

79. Chace, *Two Quaker Sisters*, 27.

80. Emery, *Reminiscences of a Nonagenarian*, 335.

81. Buckingham, *War Governor*, 8.

82. Ely and Plimpton, *Lieutenant River*, 10-11.

83. Emery, *Reminiscences of a Nonagenarian*, 59.

84. John Howard Redfield recalled that, in Connecticut, Election Week fell in May following the selection of the governor by the Legislature; other New England states held their elections in March, just as many towns still have annual Town Meetings with local elections in March.

85. Edmund Delaney, *Life in the Connecticut River Valley, 1800-1840 from the Recollections of John Howard Redfield* (Essex, Connecticut: Connecticut River Museum, 1988), 34.

86. Esther Alice Peck, "A Conservative Generation's Amusements: A Phase in Connecticut Social History," *Maine Bulletin* (April 1938): 17.

87. William Woys Weaver, *America Eats: Forms of Edible Folk Art* (New York: Harper and Row, 1989), 105.

88. Farnsworth, "Reminiscences...."

89.Child, *American Frugal Housewife*, 79.

90. *New Family Receipt Book*..., (Hartford: Ezra Strong, 1829), 12.

CHAPTER TWO

1. Rev. James Bailey, *History of the Seventh-Day Baptist General Conference: From its origin, September 1802 to its Fifty Third Session, Sept. 1865* (Toledo, Ohio: S. Bailey & Co., 1866), 94-105.

2. James Baughman, *The Mallorys of Mystic* (Middletown, Connecticut: Wesleyan University Press for Mystic Seaport Museum, 1972), 67.

3. Anthropologists Judith Goode, Karen Curtis, and Janet Theophano observed that "menu negotiations rely heavily on [the senior male's] preferences and activity patterns," in their study, "Meal Formats, Meal Cycles, and Menu Negotiation in the Maintenance of an Italian-American Community," in Mary Douglas, ed., *Food in the Social Order: Studies of Food and Festivities in Three American Communities* (New York: Russell Sage Foundation, 1984), 162; senior male preferences together with stage in family cycle, school and work schedules, social networks, and generational cohort of the senior female, (i.e., Charlotte Greenman) are among the most influential characteristics, besides personal and family taste, in a family's food choices. I believe this analysis would work for a family like the Greenmans whose household head was known to be a man of strong convictions, in a time when part of an ideal wife's role was to make the home a refuge suited to his needs.

4. Mid-nineteenth-century advertisements from the Mystic *Pioneer* and Mystic *Press* bear this out.

5. Only one of the three homes, George and Abby's—the oldest—has a chimney base adequate to support a cooking fireplace, but unless future architectural restoration work indicates otherwise, there never was one.

6. Mrs. L.G. Abell, *The Complete Domestic Guide Comprising the Mother's Book of Daily Duties and Skillful Housewife's Book* (New York: R.I. Young, 1853), 155.

7. Ibid, 156, 155-58.

8. Ibid, 158. The Palmer family at Pachunganuc Farm, North Stonington, in the last quarter of the nineteenth and early part of the twentieth century did hang their dried beef in the cellar way; according to family recollections, when it was needed, someone would take a knife and shave some off into a dish, according to Anna N. Coit in a statement to the author.

9. Mystic *Press*, 3 July 1879.

10. Water district map.

14. Pachunganuc Farm, North Stonington, has a room called the "woodroom" with a brick works and set kettle called the "caboose" which was used for projects unsuitable to the kitchen. The Williams family had a similar setup in the building called "the storeroom" at the Quoketaug Hill farm in Old Mystic, according to Rudy Favretti, *Once Upon Quoketaug* (Storrs, Connecticut: author, 1974), 100-102.

11. William Ellery Maxson, Diary, 1860-64, Typescript, G.W. Blunt White Library, Mystic Seaport Museum, hereafter cited as GWBWL.

12. Maria Parloa, *Miss Parloa's New Cookbook and Marketing Guide* (Boston: Estes and Lauriat, 1880), 60.

13. Clark Greenman, Probate Inventory, 11 May 1877, District of Stonington, Connecticut.

14. Refrigerators were at this time what we call "ice boxes," a designation necessary only after they became gas or electric appliances.

15. *Miss Parloa's New Cookery Book*, for instance, listed and illustrated all kinds of refinements, like bain maries, truly elaborate molds, a French vegetable scoop, and lady finger pans.

16. Typescript of Invoice from Lewis E. Spear Co., Marine and Hotel Supplies, 37 Market St., San Francisco, 6 November 1901, Mystic Seaport Museum Shipyard Research File; Accounts of Ship *Hector*, 1852, Collection 119, GWBWL; John L. Williams, "List of Stores for Fiting a vessel," 1882, VFM 1430, GWBWL; New Shoreham Life-Saving Station, Typescript from first logbook of Station #2, Mystic Seaport Museum Curatorial Department; U.S. Government, Form 9, *U.S. Life-Saving Service, Regulations for the Government of the Life-Saving Stations of the United States*; Form #1832, "Copies of Property Returns, U.S. Life-Saving Service, Dist. #2 Station #4," 1883-1887, Misc. Vol. 325, GWBWL; U.S. Life-Saving Service, Letter #12756, 24 October 1882, List of Outfits and Equipment for New Life-Saving Station at Peaked Hill Bars and Muskeget, Record Group 26, National Archives, Washington D.C.; Abell, *Complete Domestic Guide*, 159-62; Catherine E. Beecher and Harriet Beecher Stowe, *The American Woman's Home*... (New York: J.B. Ford, 1870), 373-76; Todd S. Goodholme, ed., *Goodholme's Domestic Cyclopedia of Practical Information*, new ed., (New York: C.A. Montgomery, 1887), 234.

17. Favretti, *Once Upon Quotaug*, 65; Grace Denison Wheeler, *Grace Wheeler's Memories* (Stonington, Connecticut: Pequot Press, 1947).

18. Julia Gates, Manuscript Recipe Notebook, 1857-1930, Mystic River Historical Society, Mystic, Connecticut.

19. Sara Hix Todd, transcribed letter in Log 900, GWBWL. Mrs. Todd's family lived in the New Bedford area.

20. *Scribner's Monthly* (March 1873): 643.

21. Just because they weren't listed doesn't mean there weren't any. Harriet herself may have owned one; the inventory takers may have overlooked them.

22. George Greenman & Co. Papers, Daybook, Misc. Vol. 264, GWBWL.

23. Mystic *Pioneer*, 20 August 1864. The store was not continuously in business, and this advertisement reports that there was a "New Store at Greenmanville!"

24. Mystic *Pioneer*, 17 November 1866.

25. George Greenman & Co. Papers, Misc. Vol. 510, GWBWL; This list was for taxable livestock; certain allowable numbers of poultry and animals of a certain age were not always taxed. The ordinances varied from town to town.

26. Ibid.

26. Clark Greenman, Probate Inventory; George Greenman & Co. Papers, Misc. Vol. 510.

27. Julia Gates to George Gates, 27 March 1871, April 1873, Coll. 153, GWBWL.

28. George Greenman & Co. Papers, Misc. Vol. 510.

29. Advertisement, Mystic *Press*, 28 June 1888; Julia Gates to George Gates, March 1871.

30. Photograph, Mystic Seaport Museum accession number 83.99.34, hereafter cited as Mystic Seaport Museum Photo; Mystic *Press*, 6 July 1882; Stonington *Mirror*, 15 January 1897; Mystic Seaport Museum Photo, accession number 80.26.39; Nathan Fish, Diary, 1868, Coll. 43, GWBWL.

31. Mystic *Press*, 1 October 1875, 13 August 1875.

32. George Greenman & Co., Daybook, Misc. Vol. 264. Thomas's household (three plus possibly boarders) used 20 gallons of molasses, a weekly average of about a third of a gallon *if* an extra large quantity purchased October to November is subtracted from the yearly total; otherwise the weekly average comes to a little less than half a gallon a week. Clark's similarly sized household used 19 gallons, while George, with a family of about seven (plus possible boarders), used 6 gallons. George and Abby's household consumed about 3 3/4 pounds of sugar a week to Thomas's 1 3/4, and Clark's one pound a week average.

33. *Sixth Census of the United States: 1840*, Stonington, Connecticut (microfilm of work sheets, GWBWL); *Seventh Census of the United States: 1850*, Stonington, Connecticut (microfilm of work sheets GWBWL). Clark in 1850 also had a second household, the Brown family, plus four others, who may have been boarders; *Eighth Census of the United States: 1860*, Stonington, Connecticut (microfilm of work sheets GWBWL); *Ninth Census of the United States: 1870*, Stonington, Connecticut (microfilm of work sheets GWBWL).

34. Julia Gates to George Gates, 30 March 1871, 18 April 1873, Coll. 153, GWBWL.

35. Goodholme, *Domestic Cyclopedia*, 45.

36. Dana Story, *Frame Up!* (Barre, Massachusetts: Barre Publishers, 1964), 97.

37. Mystic *Press*, 17 October 1878. The editor misspelled jonnycake, which is usually spelled without an "h" when describing the Rhode Island version. Johnnycake with an "h" was by mid-century a quick bread very similar to our modern day cornbread; Wheeler, *Memories*.

38. R.H. Dana, Jr., *The Journal of Richard Henry Dana, Jr.*, ed. Robert F. Lucid, 3 vols., (Cambridge, Massachusetts: Belknap Press of Harvard University Press, 1968), 1:112.

39. Fernand Braudel, *Capitalism and Civilization, 15th to 18th Century: Volume 1, The Structures of Everyday Life: The Limits of the Possible* (New York: Harper and Row, 1981), 190-202; A number of articles and sources reveal period attitudes about vegetarianism; among them I have found "A Ramble Through the Market," *Atlantic Monthly* (March 1866); Pauline S. Greason, ed., "Letters of Elizabeth Palmer Peabody and Others Concerning a Problem at 13 West Street," *Essex Institute Historical Collection* (January 1965): 35; Emery, *Reminiscences of a Nonagenarian* (Newburyport, Massachusetts: William H. Huse & Co., 1879), 39.

40. *High Street Cookbook* in *Hood's Combined Cook Books* (Lowell, Massachusetts.: C.I. Hood & Co., 1875-1885), 36; Mary Virginia Terhune (pseud. Marion Harland), *The Dinner Year Book* (New York: Charles Scribner's Sons, 1878), 282; Parloa, *Miss Parloa's New Cookbook*, 408-09.

41.*The Successful Housekeeper....*

42. Dana, *Journal*, 1:149; Genevieve M. Darden, *My Dear Husband* (New Bedford, Massachusetts: Descendants of Whaling Masters, Inc., 1980), 64.

43. Julia Gates to George Gates, 7 June 1873.

44. Karen Hess, *Martha Washington's Booke of Cookery* (New York: Columbia University Press, 1981), 15-16; Gervase Markham, *The English Housewife*, ed. Michael R. Best, (1615; reprint, Kingston & Montreal: McGill-Queen's University Press, 1986), 64-66; *Oxford English Dictionary*; Amelia Simmons, *American Cookery...*, ed. Mary Tolford Wilson, (1796; reprint New York: Dover, 1984); Lydia Maria Child, *The American Frugal Housewife* (Boston: Carter, Hendee, and Co., 1833) 33-36, 35, 18, 120.

45. Beecher and Stowe, *American Woman's Home*, 130; It is worth noting that even in the late-twentieth century the "five-a-day" campaign to urge Americans to eat five servings of fruit or vegetables is only two or three years old at this writing.

46. Abell, *Complete Domestic Guide*, 109; Statement of Florence Button; Statement of Anna North Coit, born 1907; Statement of Louise Curtiss Oliver, born 1917, Cornwall, Connecticut; she lived with her paternal grandparents between the ages of two and five, when she observed her grandparents' eating habits.

47. Young People's Society of Christian Endeavor of the Second Congregational Church, *The Stonington Cookbook* (reprint, Watch Hill, Rhode Island: Book and Tackle Shop, 1975); Women's Christian Temperance Union of Rhode Island, *W.C.T.U. Cook Book— Health and Comfort for the Home* (Phenix, Rhode Island: The Gleaner Print, 1905); *The Grange Cookbook* (North Stonington, Connecticut: Women of the North Stonington Grange, 1913).

48. Charles Chace, Journal, Log 146, GWBWL.

49. Nathan Fish, Diary, 1868, Fish Family Papers, Coll. 43, GWBWL.

50. Kathleen Smallzreid, *The Everlasting Pleasure: Influences on America's Kitchens, Cooks, and Cookery, from 1565 to the Year 2000* (New York: Appleton-Century-Crofts, 1956), 134.

51. Julia Gates, Recipe Notebook; Parloa, *Miss Parloa's New Cookbook*, 77; Goodholme, *Domestic Cyclopedia*, 241

52. Maxson, Diary, 14 October 1862; Julia Gates to George Gates, 31 December 1864; Statement of Anna North Coit.

53. Mrs. Mary F. Henderson, *Practical Cooking and Dinner Giving* (New York: Harper and Brothers, 1882), 138.

54. Elizabeth M. Hall, *Practical American Cookery and Domestic Economy* (New York: Saxton, Barker, and Company, 1860), 69.

55. Harland, *Dinner Year Book*, 14.

56. A very thorough discussion of the making of sweetmeats like this is found in Louise Conway Belden, *The Festive Tradition: Table Decoration and Desserts in America, 1650-1900* (New York: W.W. Norton for the Winterthur Museum, 1983).

57. Harland, *Dinner Year Book*, 214.

CHAPTER THREE

1. William N. Peterson and Peter M. Coope, *Historic Buildings at Mystic Seaport Museum* (Mystic, Connecticut: Mystic Seaport Museum, 1985,) 70-72; Ann F. Peabody, with Holly Malloy Ellis, Donna Belantone, and Mary Deveau, "The Life and Times of 'Winty' Burrows," *The Log of Mystic Seaport* (Summer 1994): 13.

2. Groton Land Records, Vol. 1AT, 37, Town Clerk's Office, Groton, Connecticut; property of Joshua Buddington attached as result of case brought against him by Burrows in assault and battery case; Groton Town Death Records, Town Clerk's Office, Groton, Connecticut.

3. New London Marriage Records, City Clerk's Office, New London, Connecticut.

4. Stonington *Mirror*, 17 December 1874. Notes from Mystic River and Vicinity included the

news that "Mystic wants the water of Long Pond brought into its streets and houses. The present intermittent supply is entirely inadequate."

5. Mystic *Pioneer*, 25 June 1868.

6. *New London City Directory*, 1878-79.

7. Stonington *Mirror*, 22 January 1870.

8. Mystic *Pioneer*, 11 December 1869.

9. Mystic *Journal*, 23 May 1870; *Ninth Census of the United States: 1870*, Groton, Connecticut (microfilm of work sheets, G.W. Blunt White Library, Mystic Seaport Museum, hereafter cited as GWBWL); R. Earl Burrows, *Robert Burrows and Descendants, 1630-1974* (Ann Arbor, Michigan: Edwards Brothers, 1975).

10. *Ninth Census of the U.S., 1870*; Mystic *Press*, 5 December 1873 to 30 January 1874; Ibid., 8 May 1874.

11. Mystic *Journal*, 25 June 1870.

12. The amounts in a great many manuscript recipes are given in coffee cups or tea cups.

13. Mystic *Pioneer*, 10 August 1861; this advertisement ran for four weeks.

14. Ibid., list of food and household goods bought in the village of Mystic in 1860 and 1861, showing inflation

15. These quotes are all taken from the Mystic *Press* except 20 October 1866 from Mystic *Pioneer* and 28 January 1875 and 6 January 1876 from the Stonington *Mirror*.

16. Richard Henry Dana, Jr., *The Journal of Richard Henry Dana, Jr.*, ed. Robert F. Lucid, 3 vols., (Cambridge, Massachusetts: Belknap Press of Harvard University Press, 1968), 1:199, 198.

17. Henry David Thoreau, *The Writings of Thoreau*, ed. Brooks Atkinson, (New York: Modern Library, 1950), 463.

18. Edward Everett Knapp, "Smacks of Noank," Typescript, Coll. 171, GWBWL, 58-59.

19. Ibid, 314. Lleywellan Palmer, a native of North Stonington, Connecticut, presently in his early eighties, once told the author, "Its a damn shame to cut a pie smaller than in quarters."

20. Knapp, "Smacks of Noank," 293.

21. Mystic *Press*, 10 March 1876; the "boiled vittles" was probably boiled ham or corned beef.

22. Samuel Samuels, *From Forecastle to Cabin* (Boston: Charles E. Lauriat, 1924), 24.

23. Catherine Beecher and Harriet Beecher Stowe, *The American Woman's Home* (New York: J.B. Ford, 1870).

24. *Godey's Lady's Book* (November 1859): 444.

25. *How to do Things Well and Cheap, for Domestic Use, by One Who Knows* (Boston: Charles Tappan, 1845); Esther A. Howland, *New England Economical Housekeeper* (Worcester: S.A. Howland, 1845).

26. Keep in mind that until wheat was no longer whole, it was not necessary to describe it as "whole" wheat.

27. *Atlantic Monthly* (April 1859): 465-68.

28. Dana, *Journal*, 3:955. Dana was not, incidentally, a vegetarian.

29. Beecher and Stowe, *American Woman's Home*, 137; Ibid., essay "Healthful Food," 119-37.

30. Ibid.

31. For more information, see Sandra L. Oliver, "The Herrick Recipes," *The Log of Mystic Seaport* (Fall 1991): 74.

32. Mrs. H.W. Beecher, *All Around the House; or; How to Make Homes Happy* (New York: D. Appleton & Co., 1878), 391.

33. Mrs. Bliss, *The Practical Cookbook....* (Philadelphia: J.B. Lippincott & Co., 1864), 75; Elizabeth M. Hall, *Practical American Cookery and Domestic Economy* (New York: Saxton, Barker, and Co., 1860), 84; Mrs. L.G. Abell, *The Complete Domestic Guide Comprising the Mother's Book of Daily Duties and Skillful Housewife's Book* (New York: R.I. Young, 1853), 93.

34. "Sauerkraut and Pickled Cabbage," *Food History News* (December 1990).

35. Lydia Maria Child, *The American Frugal Housewife* (Boston: Carter, Hendee, and Company, 1833), 85.

36. Bliss, *Practical Cook Book*, 20.

37. Mary Virginia Terhune (pseud. Marion Harland), *The Dinner Year Book* (New York: Charles Scribner's Sons, 1878), 101.

38. Fannie Card, Manuscript Recipe Notebook, 1879, owned by Anna North Coit, North Stonington, Connecticut.

CHAPTER FOUR

1. Herman Melville, *Moby Dick; or, The White Whale* (1851; New York: Mead and Co., 1942), 139.

2. R.H. Dana Jr., *Two Years Before the Mast*, World Classics Edition, (1840; New York: World Publication Co., 1946), 402.

3. Sarah G. Smith, Journal, Log 399, G.W. Blunt White Library, Mystic Seaport Museum, hereafter cited as GWBWL.

4. Felix Riesenberg, *Under Sail* (New York: Macmillan Company, 1919), 223, 37; Knut Weibust claims that improvements in food made on Scandinavian ships "was to some extent a result of the fear that the seamen would jump ship in America in order to sign on American ships, which were well known for their good food." Knut Weibust, *Deep Sea Sailors, A Study in Maritime Ethnology* (Stockholm: Nodiska Museets Handlingar 71, 1969), 316, 86.

5. Kenneth John Blume "The Hairy Ape Reconsidered: The American Merchant Seaman and the Transition from Sail to Steam in the late Nineteenth Century," *American Neptune* (Winter 1984): 43.

6. Weibust, *Deep Sea Sailors*, 20. Fear of fire apparently was not the concern of the fishing schooners whose galley was an integral part of the fo'c'sle.

7. Lloyd Briggs, *Around Cape Horn to Honolulu on the Bark Amy Turner 1880* (Boston: Charles E. Lauriat Co., 1926), 19.

8. Annie Holmes Ricketson, *The Journal of Annie Holmes Ricketson on the Whaleship A.R. Tucker, 1871-74* (New Bedford: Old Dartmouth Historical Society, 1958), 13.

9. Information Bulletin 67-1, Cost of Constructing and Outfitting the ship *Charles W. Morgan*, Mystic Seaport Museum, 9; *Compact Oxford English Dictionary*, 1:312; *Dictionary of American English on Historic Principles*, 1:381.

10. Charles Scammon, *The Marine Animals of the Northwestern Coast of North America* (San Francisco: J.H. Carmany & Co. 1874), 315; List assembled from *Outfits for a Whaling Voyage*, n.d., title page missing, GWBWL; John L. Williams, "List of Stores or fiting [*sic*] a vessel," VFM 1430, GWBWL; Bark *Globe*, Outfit, notations in chandlery order book, 1869, VFM, 425, GWBWL.

11. Typescript of Invoice from Lewis E. Spear Co., 6 November 1901, Shipyard Research File, Mystic Seaport Museum.

12. James A. Rogers, *Journal of Whaling Voyage of Ship Mentor of New London Captain William M. Baker* (New Bedford: Reynolds Printing, n.d.), 1.

13. See outfitting lists cited in note 10.

14. Accounts of Ship *Hector*, 1852, Coll. 119, GWBWL.

15. W. Jeffrey Bolster, "To Feel Like A Man: Black Seamen in the Northern States, 1800-1860," *The Journal of American History* (March 1990): 1194; George Brown Goode, *The Fisheries and Fishery Industries of the U.S.*, 5 sect., (Washington, D.C.: Government Printing Office, 1887), sect. 5, 2:291.

16. Weibust, *Deep Sea Sailors*, 313.

17. Dana, *Two Years Before the Mast*, 26, 22; Riesenberg, *Under Sail*, 90; Harpur Allen Gosnell, *Before the Mast in Clippers Composed in Large Part of the Diaries of Charles A. Abbey Kept While at Sea in the Years 1856-1860* (New York: Derrydale Press, 1937), 92.

18. Herman Melville, *Omoo, A Narrative of Adventures in the South Seas* (1847; Evanston & Chicago: Northwestern University Press and the Newberry Library, 1968), 41; Riesenberg, *Under Sail*.

19. Riesenberg, *Under Sail*, 38. Riesenberg didn't, of course, specify in the text what the "blank" is, but it doesn't take much to imagine how the cook could horribly foul the soup.

20. Stanton Garner, ed., *The Captain's Best Mate: The Journal of Mary Chipman Lawrence on the Whaler Addison, 1856-1860* (Hanover and London: University Press of New England for Brown University, 1966), 6, 34.

21. Occasionally, vessels carried a third mate, in which case the responsibility for distributing stores fell to him, according to Richard Henry Dana, Jr., *The Seaman's Friend, Containing a*

Treatise on Practical Seamanship..., 3rd ed., (Boston: Charles C. Little & James Brown, 1844), 151-52, 157.

22. John T. Perkins, *John T. Perkins' Journal at Sea, 1845* (Mystic: Marine Historical Association, 1934), 119; Goode, *Fisheries*, sect. 5, 2:291.

23. Weibust, *Deep Sea Sailors*, 319.

24. Ben Ezra Stiles Ely, *There She Blows: a Narrative of a Whaling Voyage in the Indian and South Atlantic Oceans*, ed. Curtis Dahl, (1849; Middletown, Connecticut: Wesleyn University Press for Mystic Seaport Museum, 1971), 64-65.

25. Bolster, "To Feel Like a Man," 1194.

26. Agate Brown Collord, ed., *Diary for 1870: The Diary of My Grandmother, Ann Agusta Fitch Brown, Wife of Capt. Jacob Bartlett Brown* (n.p.: privately printed, 1959), 34.

27. Dana, *Seaman's Friend*, 26.

28. Scott J. Dow, "The Story of Capt. Jonathan Dow," Typescript, 1948, Penobscot Marine Museum, Searsport, Maine, hereafter cited as PMM.

29. Richard Henry Dana, Jr., *The Journal of Richard Henry Dana*, 3 vols., ed. Robert F. Lucid, (Cambridge, Massachusetts: Belknap Press of Harvard University Press, 1968), 3:932.

30. Dow, "Capt. Jonathan Dow," 50-51.

31. Collord, *Diary of My Grandmother*, 4.

32. Mary Brewster, Journal, Log 38, GWBWL, published as Joan Druett, ed., *She Was a Sister Sailor: The Whaling Journals of Mary Brewster, 1845-1851* (Mystic: Mystic Seaport Museum, 1992); Collord, *Diary of My Grandmother*, 1.

33. Spencer Bonsall, Journal, Log 740, GWBWL; Briggs, *Around Cape Horn*, 20; Joanna Colcord, "Domestic Life on American Sailing Ships," *American Neptune* (July 1942): 195.

34. Thomas Larkin Turner, Diary, Coll. 95, vol. 14, GWBWL.

35. Dow, "Capt. Jonathan Dow."

36. Charles C. Chase, Journal, Log 146, GWBWL.

37. Garner, *Captain's Best Mate*, 22.

38. Brewster, Journal; Collord, *Diary of My Grandmother*, 35.

39. Brewster, Journal.

40. Dow, "Capt. Jonathan Dow."

41. Georgia Maria Blanchard, "Our Wedding Trip Around Cape Horn," Typescript, Blanchard Family Papers, PMM, 4.

42. Joseph Blunt, *The Shipmaster's Assistant and Commercial Digest: Containing Information Necessary for Merchants, Owners, and Masters of Ships...* (New York: Harper and Brothers, 1851), 40. This book in the collection GWBWL, apparently belonged to Captain George Wendell who wrote his name on the title page.

43. I.R. Butts, *The Rights of Seaman: The Coaster's and & Fisherman's Guide, and Master's and Mate's Manual...* (Boston: I.R. Butts, 1848), Appendix, 9.

44. Ibid, 98; Yankees ashore preferred pickled cabbage over sauerkraut, which was more common in the Middle Atlantic and Southern states where German immigrants settled, Sandra L. Oliver, "Sauerkraut and Pickled Cabbage," *Food History News* (Winter 1990): 3.

45. Butts, *Rights of Seamen*, 98.

46. Blume, "Hairy Ape," 42; Riesenberg, *Under Sail*, 37.

47. Blume, "Hairy Ape," 43.

48. Riesenberg, *Under Sail*, 384

49. Dana, *Two Years Before the Mast*, 404.

50. George H. Bishop, Diary, VFM 1050, GWBWL; Perkins, *Journal*, 129; Samuel Millet, *A Whaling Voyage in the Bark Willis* (Boston: Privately Printed, 1924), 19.

51. I have no positive proof that this is true. In the back of a good many logs, however, is a careful accounting of barrels of beef, pork, flour, bread, molasses, etc., opened. Unfortunately, these were not arranged in a countdown system which would tell us how many they started with, but if chandlers accounts showing numbers of barrels sold to a given ship could be compared against the same vessels log accounts, we could get a clear reading on how much was consumed and how much returned.

52. Perkins, *Journal*, 130; Dana, *Journal*, 3:932.

53. Perkins, *Journal*, 120.

54. Lewis William Eldredge, *Lewis William Eldredge's Whaling Voyage* (New Bedford: Reynolds Printing, 1939), 5; George S. Wasson, *Sailing Days on the Penobscot* (Salem: Marine Research Society, 1932), 5.

55. Nathan Daboll, *New England Almanac* (New London: Samuel Green, 1820), 25.

56. Sara Hix Todd, Diary, Log 900, GWBWL.

57. Gosnell, *Before the Mast in Clippers*, 49.

58. Bonsall, Journal.

59. Turner, Diary.

60. Bonsall, Journal; Turner, Diary.

61. Dana, *Seaman's Friend*, 174.

62. Perkins, *Journal*, 120.

63. Dana, *Seaman's Friend*.

64. Samuel Samuels, *From the Forecastle to the Cabin* (Boston: Charles E. Lauriat, 1924), 109-10.

65. Hiram Look, Journal, Log 409, GWBWL.

66. James C. Osborne, Journal, Log 143, GWBWL; William Griffiths, Journal, Log 158, GWBWL.

67. Ricketson, *Journal*, 14, 16.

68. Dana, *Two Years Before the Mast*, 403; Perkins, *Journal*, 122; that is, it was not customary to wash the *sailor's* utensils; the cook was responsible for keeping the kids clean.

69. Perkins, *Journal*, 129.

70. Eldredge, *Whaling Voyage*, 5; Dana, *Two Years Before the Mast*, 403; speaking of the whalemen ca. 1880, James Templeman Brown in Goode's *Fisheries* mentioned that the men had plates and bowls for soup; Lewis Eldredge, 1867, said he had a plate, but Dana and others writing in the first half of the century did not mention them.

71. Weibust, *Deep Sea Sailors*, 93.

72. Bonsall, *Journal*; Dana, *Two Years Before the Mast*, 403.

73. Colcord, "Domestic Life," 194.

74. Ship *Hector*, Outfitting List, Coll. 119, GWBWL; Genevieve M. Darden, *My Dear Husband* (Taunton, Massachusetts: William S. Sullwold Publishing for Descendants of Whaling Masters, 1980), 80.

75. Riesenberg, *Under Sail*, 278.

76. Garner, *Captain's Best Mate*, 214, 218.

77. Goode, *Fisheries*, 227; Riesenberg, *Under Sail*, 180.

78. Brewster, Journal.

79. Mess Bill, Brig *Reaper*, 1809, Isaac Hinckley Papers, Coll. 184, vol. 1, GWBWL.

80. Bonsall, Journal.

81. Perkins, *Journal*, 133.

82. Riesenberg, *Under Sail*, 36-37.

83. Eldredge, *Whaling Voyage*, 5.

84. Perkins, *Journal*, 120.

85. Hibberd, *Sixteen Times Round Cape Horn*, 9.

86. Osborne, Journal.

87. Bonsall, Journal.

88. Blume, "Hairy Ape," 42; Eldredge, *Whaling Voyage*, 5.

89. Gosnell, *Before the Mast in Clippers*, 207.

90. George S. Brewster, Journal, Log 86, GWBWL.

91. Morgan Papers, Coll. 27, vol. 26; we know they are cabin stores not only because of shipboard tradition, but also because quantities of each are limited, compared to quantities bought for the whole ship.

92. Manuscript note, "Small Stores," in back of a chandlery order book, H.S. Kirby, Dealer in Ship Chandlery & Hardware, New Bedford, VFM 1461, GWBWL; Williams, "List of Stores for Fiting a vessel"; Colcord, "Domestic Life," 197.

93. Dana, *Two Years Before the Mast*, 314; Rogers, *Journal*, 9.

94. Smith, Log 399; Darden, *My Dear Husband*, 81.

95. Garner, *Captain's Best Mate*, 170, 212, 226; Goode, *Fisheries*, sect. 5, 2:19; Dow, "Capt. Jonathan Dow," 28.

96. Colcord, "Domestic Life," 197.

97. Ibid; tongues are the soft muscle cut out between the underside of a cod's jaws. See **page TK** for illustration. Tongues, cheeks, and sounds were all salted and barreled when cod were

processed for salting and drying aboard fishing vessels; Dow, "Capt. Jonathan Dow," 55; Goode, *Fisheries*, sect. 5, 2:17.

98. Gosnell, *Before the Mast in Clippers*, 31; Riesenberg, *Under Sail*, 415.

99. Samuels, *Forecastle to Cabin*, 237.

100. George Wendell, Journal, Coll. 59, vol. 26, GWBWL.

101. Smith, Log 399; Goode, *Fisheries*, sect. 5, 2:9.

102. Garner, *Captain's Best Mate*, 173; Dow, Capt.Jonathan Dow," 86.

103. Rogers, *Journal*, 9.

104.Brewster, Journal.

105. Colcord, "Domestic Life," 201.

106. Brewster, Journal; Chace, Journal.

107. Molasses doughnuts infrequently appear in period cookbooks, but they have survived in rural Maine, a traditional form developed to make an inexpensive treat.

108. Henrietta Deblois, cited in Druett, *She Was A Sister Sailor*, 109.

109. These last terms were the ones commonly used on American ships, while terms like burgoo, loblolly, salmagundy, and skilly galee were used on English ships.

110. *Oxford English Dictionary*, 2989, 3219.

111. Consider the texture of fatback, which still has salt on the surface when you buy it, or a country style ham; by soaking them, they become moister and softer; Goode, *Fisheries*, sect. 5, 2:227; Frederick Pease Harlow, *The Making of a Sailor on a Yankee Square-Rigger* (Salem, Massachusetts: Marine Research Society, 1928), 147.

112. Harlow, *Making of a Sailor*; Dana, *Two Years Before the Mast*, 314, 315; Perkins, *Journal*, 133; the *Nautical Dictionary* defines salt junk as salt pork, but I do not find the word so specifically used in narratives and descriptions of shipboard life.

113. Biscuits intended for the British or American Navy or any branch of the military had to meet specific requirements of weight, size, etc.; Perkins, *Journal*, 122.

114. See Buckingham House, chapter 1.

115. Cognatively understanding legumes and grains as completed proteins is fairly recent, though vernacular cookery in New England and around the world have commonly combined them.

116. Gosnell, *Before the Mast in Clippers*, 207; Bonsall, Journal.

117. Morgan Papers, Coll. 27, vol. 26, GWBWL.

118. Mrs. Lydia Maria Child, *The American Frugal Housewife* (Boston: Carter, Hendee, and Company, 1833), 82.

119. Herman Melville, *Omoo*, 7; Thomas Crapo, *Strange, But True: Life and Adventures of Captain Thomas Crapo and Wife* (New Bedford: author, 1893), 15.

120. Isaac Norris Hibberd, *Sixteen Times Round Cape Horn: The Reminiscences of Captain Isaac Norris Hibberd* (Mystic: Mystic Seaport Museum, 1980), 9.

191. Gosnell, *Before the Mast in Clippers*, 31; Hibberd, *Sixteen Times Round Cape Horn*, 8-9.

122. Seafarers' manuals occasionally included instructions for preparing food, which a captain or any literate crew member could have used, for example, Capt. F.G.D. Bedford, *The Sailor's Pocket Book: A Collection of Practical Rules, Notes, and Tables; for use of the Royal Navy, The Merchant Marine, and Yacht Squadrons* (Portsmouth: Griffin & Co., 1877), which contains recipes for meat soup, Irish stew, and directions for soaking and boiling salt meat, cooking vegetables, and making tea and coffee.

123. Gervase Markham, *The English Housewife*, ed. Michael R. Best, (1615; reprint, Kingston & Montreal: McGill-Queen's University Press, 1986), 203; *Compact Oxford English Dictionary*, 2:1647; Dana, *Two Years Before the Mast*, 45; Perkins, *Journal*, 125; Eldredge, *Whaling Voyage*, 16; George Boughton, *Seafaring* (London: Faber and Gwyer, 1926), 46.

124. Goode, *Fisheries*, sect. 5, 2:228; Crapo, *Strange, But True*, 13.

125. Rev. Ivan Jesperson, *Fat Back and Molasses* (St. John's, Newfoundland: author, 1974), 11; Jane Grigson, *The Observer Guide to British Cookery* (London: Michael Joseph, 1984), 141.

126. A visitor to the Buckingham House at Mystic Seaport, when I was interpreting one day, told me how during the Great Depression his Irish immigrant family used to make something they called "Potato Bargain," which was potatoes, salt pork, and onions boiled together, which was close to, but not the same as, scouce.

128. The word dandy is defined in the *Oxford English Dictionary*, and means "fine," "dainty," etc.; in this case, I suspect dandyfunk is a corruption of a foreign word, either a whole word or part of one.

128. Gosnell, *Before the Mast in Clippers*, 98.

129. Riesenberg, *Under Sail*, 71; Crapo, *Strange, But True*, 14.

130. Perkins, *Journal*, 122.

131. Jesperson, *Fat Back*, 32, 42, 44, 45, 60, 86.

132. *Oxford English Dictionary*, 706.

133. In the early 1800s and before, "plum" was a word commonly used to denote raisins; Goode, *Fisheries*, sect. 5, 2:228.

134. Perkins, *Journal*, 122.

135. Garner, *Captain's Best Mate*, 41; Bonsall, Journal; Harlow, *Making of a Sailor*, 149.

136. Gosnell, *Before the Mast in Clippers*, 40-41.

137. Bonsall, Journal.

138. Joseph Dodderidge, in *Notes on the Settlement and Indian Wars of the Western Parts of Virginia and Pennsylvania from 1763 to 1783*...(Pittsburgh, Pennsylvania, 1912), 88; quoted in Kay Moss and Kathryn Hoffman, *The Backcountry Housewife* (Gastonia, North Carolina: Schiele Museum of Natural History & Planetarium, 1985), 37.

139. Edward Behr, "La Cuisine Quebecoise," *The Art of Eating* (Summer 1989): 2.

140. Hannah Glasse, *Art of Cookery Made Plain and Easy* (London: author, 1747), cheshire pork pie for sea; Amelia Simmons, *American Cookery*, ed. Mary Tolford Wilson, (1796; reprint, New York: Dover Publications, 1984), 23; Mary Randolph, *The Virginia Housewife*...(1824; facsimile reprint, Columbia: University of South Carolina Press, 1984), 95.

141. Bonsall, Journal.

142. Ricketson, *Journal*, 45.

143. Perkins, *Journal*, 129.

144. Walter Bechtel, interview in NBC Radio Broadcast, 30 July 1949, ME 49-1, Mystic Seaport Museum Sound Archives.

145. Riesenberg, *Under Sail*, 37; Ricketson, *Journal*, 49.

146. Millet, *A Whaling Voyage*, 12; Druett, *She Was a Sister Sailor*, 119; Briggs, *Around Cape Horn*, 83

147. Bonsall, Journal.

148. Dow, "Capt. Jonathan Dow"; Dana, *Two Years Before the Mast*, 22; Perkins, *Journal*, 130; Gosnell, *Before the Mast in Clippers*, 207.

149. Dana, *Two Years Before the Mast*, 45; Millet, *A Whaling Voyage*, 13.

150. Millett, *A Whaling Voyage*; Dana, *Two Years Before the Mast*.

151. Ricketson, *Journal*, 27.

152. Briggs, *Around Cape Horn*, 84.

153. Bonsall, Journal; Rogers, *Journal*, 9.

154. Rogers, *Journal*, 11.

155. Perkins, *Journal*, 120, 126.

156. Ibid, 137.

157. Ibid.

158. Ibid., 138.

159. Brewster, Journal.

160. Jesperson, *Fat Back*, 32, 42, 44, 45, 60, 86.

161. Mrs. L.G.Abell, *The Complete Domestic Guide Comprising the Mother's Book of Daily Duties and Skillful Housewife's Book* (New York: R.I. Young, 1853), 137.

162. Elizabeth M. Hall, *Practical American Cookery and Domestic Economy* (New York: Saxton, Barker, and Co., 1860), 190.

163. Ibid., 160.

164. Garner, *Captain's Best Mate*, 164.

CHAPTER FIVE

1. George Brown Goode, ed., *The Fisheries and Fishery Industries of The United States*, 5 sects., (Washington, D.C.: Government Printing

Office, 1887), sect. 5, 1:72; James B. Connolly, *The Book of the Gloucester Fishermen* (New York: John Day Co., 1927), 204.

2. Goode, *Fisheries*, sect. 5, 1:90.

3. W.H. Bishop, "Fish and Men in the Maine Islands," *Harper's New Monthly Magazine* (August 1880): 496.

4. Goode, *Fisheries*, sect. 5, 1:91.

5. Ibid., sect. 5, 1:140; John D. Whidden, *Old Sailing Ship Days* (Boston: Charles E. Lauriat Co., 1925), 118.

6. Wesley George Pierce, *Goin' Fishing: The Story of the Deep-Sea Fishermen of New England* (1934; reprint Camden, Maine: International Marine Publishing, 1989), 15.

7. Charles Nordhoff, *Whaling and Fishing* (New York: Dodd Mead and Company, 1855), 356-57.

8. Goode, *Fisheries*, sect. 5, 1:7; Pierce, *Goin' Fishing*, 55.

9. Thomas Norris, Typescript of Telephone Conversation, no date, Shipyard Research File, Mystic Seaport Museum, hereafter cited as SRF.

10. Winston Tibbo, Conversation with Nancy d'Estang, 1985, Shipyard Oral History File, Mystic Seaport Museum.

11. Goode, *Fisheries*, sect. 5, 1:174, 109.

12. John Francis, Typescript of Conversation with Nancy d'Estang, 13 April 1987, SRF; Harold B. Clifford, *Charlie York, Maine Coast Fisherman* (Camden, Maine: International Marine Publishing, 1979), 24.

13. Schooner *B.D. Nickerson*, Account Book, 1895-1902, Misc. Vol.175, G.W. Blunt White Library, Mystic Seaport Museum, hereafter referred to as GWBWL; Virginia Jones, Research Paper, Furnishing *L. A. Dunton* Forecastle, 1984, SRF, 26; *B.D. Nickerson*, Account Book.

14. Willard H. Boynton, "Mackerel Fishing out of Gloucester," *The Log of Mystic Seaport* (Winter 1988): 141; Francis interview, 13 April 1987, 6

15. Connolly, *Book of Gloucester Fishermen*, 127.

16. Goode, *Fisheries*, sect. 5, 1:90, 132. That is, it was "universal" in the 1880s when Goode was assembling this work. Knut Weibust bears this out in *Deep Sea Sailors*; Simon Philbrook, Diary, 1805-08, VFM 860, GWBWL.

17. Connolly, *Book of Gloucester Fishermen*, 39; Andrew German, *Down on T Wharf: The Boston Fisheries as Seen Through the Photographs of Henry D. Fisher* (Mystic: Mystic Seaport Museum, 1982), 47; Elroy Johnson, Interview, 19 March 1967, Sound Archives, G.W. Blunt White Library, Mystic Seaport Museum, hereafter cited as SA.

18. Franklin North, "Gloucester Fishers," *Century Magazine* (October 1886): 820; Goode, *Fisheries*, sect. 5, 1:23, 182.

19. Goode, *Fisheries*, sect. 5, 1:90; George H. Proctor, *Fishermen's Memorial and Record Book* (Gloucester: Proctor Brothers, 1873), 84-86, calculations by the author.

39. William Martell, Interview Transcript, 7 February 1992, SA, 6.

20. Pierce, *Goin' Fishing*, 72.

21. Goode, *Fisheries*, sect. 5, 1:22.

22. Boynton, "Mackerel Fishing," 141; J. B. Connolly, "Gloucester Fishermen, Night-seining and Winter Trawling," *Scribner's Magazine* (April 1902): 404; Barry Fisher, Interview, 1993, SA.

23. Francis, Typescript, 13 April, 6; Maxon Langworthy, Interview, January 1976, SA; Fisher, Interview.

24. Johnson, Interview; Pierce, *Goin' Fishing*, 253.

25. Schooner *Betsy*, Fishing Account Book, Misc. Vol. 414, GWBWL. Lists in this fishing account book seem to be typical of the sort; German, *Down on T Wharf*, 44.

26. *Betsy*, Account Book.

27. Pierce, *Goin' Fishing*, 30.

28. Goode, *Fisheries*, Sect. 5, part 1:90, 31.

29. Pierce, *Goin' Fishing*, 30-31.

30. Ibid., 31.

31. Goode, *Fisheries*, sect. 5, 1:174.

32. William H. Jordan, 5 October 1886, *The Report of the Committee on Foreign Relations in Relation to the Right and Interests of American Fisheries and Fishermen* (Washington, D.C.: Government Printing Office, 1887), 161.

33. Items listed in the *Fishing Gazette* in 1909 and 1912, cited in German, *Down on T Wharf*, 44.

34. Pierce, *Goin' Fishing*, 253.

35. Francis, Typescript, 13 April, 10.

36. Goode, *Fisheries*, sect. 5, 1:90, 75.

37. Ibid; 76.

38. Frederick William Wallace, *Roving Fisherman* (Gardenvale, Quebec: Canadian Fisherman, 1955), 68.

39. Ibid., 211-12.

40. Pierce, *Goin' Fishing*.

41. Goode, *Fisheries*, sect. 5, 1:90.

42. Fisher, Interview; Merchant, Interview; Francis, Typescript, 13 April.

43. Nordhoff, *Whaling and Fishing*, 374; Merchant, Interview.

44. Boynton, "Mackerel Seining," 140; Jones, Research Paper, 26; Fisher, Interview; Martell, Interview, 25, 6.

45. Connolly, *Book of Gloucester Fishermen*, 39; Merchant, Interview. One man's snack, however, may be another man's lunch; *Fishing Gazette*, 20 March 1909, cited by German, *Down on T Wharf*, 47.

46. Harry Eustis, Notes of Conversation with Glenn Gordinier, 14 February 1980, Interpretation Division Research File, Mystic Seaport Museum; Goode, *Fisheries*, sect. 5, 1:109; "Fishing Adventures on the Newfoundland Banks," *Harper's New Monthly Magazine* (March 1861): 468.

47. Wallace, *Roving Fisherman* , 70; Clifford, *Charlie York*, 23.

48. Goode, *Fisheries*, sect. 5, 1:132. The fat-cake was baked the same way bannock was made ashore, Sandra Oliver, "Bannock, Hoe-Cake, Dodgers," *Food History News* (Winter 1989): 3.

49. Goode, *Fisheries*, sect. 5, 1:90.

50. Lorenzo Sabine, *Report on The Principal Fisheries of the American Seas prepared for the Treasury Department of the U.S.* (Washington, D.C.: Robert Armstrong, 1853), 84.

51. Goode, *Fisheries*, sect. 5, 1:90.

52. Nordhoff, *Whaling and Fishing*, 374.

53. Langworthy, Interview; Francis, Typescript, 13 April, 6-7.

54. Eustis, Notes, Fisher, Interview.

55. Goode, *Fisheries*, sect. 5, l:107.

56. Ibid., 74.

57. Leslie H. Stanton, Interviews, 20 April, 6 May 1966, SA; John Francis, Interview, 19 October 1987, SRF, 15; Francis, Typescript, 13 April, 8; Stanton, Interview.

58. Francis, Interview; Eustis, Notes, Fisher, Interview.

59. Fisher, interview.

60. Merchant, Interview; Langworthy, Interview; Stanton, Interview; Johnson, Interview.

61. Francis, Interview, 14.

62. Ibid., 11; Boynton, "Mackerel Fishing," 141.

63. John Leavitt, *Wake of the Coasters* (Middletown, Connecticut: Wesleyan University Press for Mystic Seaport Museum, 1970), 28.

64. Merchant, Interview.

65. *Oxford English Dictionary*, 2:2758.

66. Goode, *Fisheries*, sect. 5, 1:75.

67. Pierce, *Goin' Fishing*, 55, 254.

68. Francis, Interview, 14; Clifford, *Charlie York*, 23.

69. Connolly, "Night-seining," 387, 402.

70. "Fishing Adventures," 459.

71. Tibbo, Interview; Fisher, Interview.

72. Merchant, Interview.

73. *Dictionary of American English*, 23.

74. Goode, *Fisheries*, sect. 5, 1:90; Amy L. Handy, *What We Cook on Cape Cod* (Sandwich, Massachusetts: Shawmee Press for the Barnstable Village Improvement Society, 1911), 17.

75. Goode, *Fisheries*, sect. 5, 1:90.

76. Whidden, *Sailing Ship Days*, 119.

77. George S. Wasson, *Sailing Days on the Penobscot* (Salem: Marine Research Society, 1932), 105-07.

78. Goode, *Fisheries*, sect. 5, 1:78.

79. Fred Hunt, describing the southern red snapper fishery between 1915 and 1919, said, "The smackmen realize that any given trip might turn out to be a 'broker,' with their net profits confined to the food stowed away," Fred Hunt, "Campeche Days," *American Neptune* (July 1942): 238.

80. Langworthy, Interview; Francis, Interview, 10.

81. Francis, Interview.

82. Richard Warren, Testimony, 4 October 1886, *Report of the Committee*, 123.

83. Goode, *Fisheries*, sect. 5, 1:8.

CHAPTER SIX

1. William N. Peterson and Peter M. Coope, *Historic Buildings at Mystic Seaport Museum* (Mystic: Mystic Seaport Museum, 1985),100-02.

2. J.H. Merryman, "The U.S. Life-Saving Service," *Scribner's Monthly* (January 1880): 322.

3. Ibid.

4. Sumner I. Kimball, *Organization and Methods of the U.S. Life-Saving Service* (Washington, D.C.: Government Printing Office, 1894), 8. Kimball wrote and spoke frequently in support of the service in the late nineteenth century.

5. Aubrey Reynolds, Interview, Sound Archives, G.W. Blunt White Library, Mystic Seaport Museum, hereafter cited as SA.

6. W.D. O'Connor, "The U.S. Life-Saving Service," *Appleton's Annual Cyclopedia* (New York: D. Appleton and Co., 1889), 759.

7. W.D. O'Connor, "The United States Life-Saving Service," *Popular Science Monthly* (June 1879): 183.

8. Form 9, *U.S. Life-Saving Service, Regulations for the Government of the Life-Saving Stations of the United States*.

9. G.G. Hallett, 12 November 1874, Bill to U.S. Life-Saving Service, 12 November 1874, Record Group 26, National Archives, Washington, D.C., hereafter cited as NA.

10. Mallory and Company, Bill to U.S. Life-Saving Service, 5 December 1874, Record Group 26, NA.

11. Nicholas Ball, Journal of the Life-Saving Station # Two, Third District, New Shoreham, Rhode Island, November 1874-April 1875, Typescript, Curatorial Files, Mystic Seaport Museum.

12. Inventory Form #1832, *Revised Regulations for the Government of Life-Saving Stations of the United States and the Laws Upon Which They Are Based* (Washington, D.C.: Government Printing Office, 1884), 149-54.

13. U.S. Life-Saving Service, Letter #12756, 24 October 1882, List of Outfits and Equipment for New Life-Saving Stations at Peaked Hill Bars and Muskeget, Record Group 26, NA.

14. Form #1832, "Copies of Property Returns, U.S. Life-Saving Service, Dist. #2 Station #4," 1883-1887, Misc. Vol. 325, G.W. Blunt White Library, Mystic Seaport Museum, hereafter referred to as GWBWL.

15. Reynolds, Interview.

16. W. W. Johnson, "The United States Life-Saving Service," *New England Monthly Magazine* (April 1890): 144.

17. Kimball, *Organization and Methods*, 29.

18. Form #1832, "Copies of Property Returns."

19. Kimball, *Organization and Methods*.

20. Johnson, *Monthly Magazine*.

21. Form #1832, "Copies of Property Returns."

22. O'Connor, *Appleton's*, 183.

23. M.J. Lamb, "The American Life-Saving Service," *Harper's New Monthly Magazine* (February 1882): 371.

24. Ellice B. Gonzales, *Storms, Ships, and Surfmen* (New York: Eastern Acorn Press, 1982), 45.

25. Frances Jaixen Dodge, Conversation with author, 29 May 1986; Mrs. Dodge's father George Jaixen was a U.S. Coast Guard life-saving station cook in the 1920s and 1930s.

26. Gonzalez, *Storms*, 48.

27. List of Provisions Destroyed by Fire at the Cahoons Hollow Life Saving Station, 25 February 1893, Photocopy, courtesy Richard Boonisar, 9.

28. Ball, Journal of Station # Two.

29. Gonzales, *Storms*, 48.

30. Reynolds, Interview.

31. *Revised Regulations*..., 49.

32. Sumner Kimball, Department Circular No. 63, "Relative to Boating, Fishing, Hunting, etc., by Life-Saving Crews," 2 May 1896, courtesy Richard Boonisar.

33. Reynolds, Interview; Gonzales, *Storms*, 49.

34. Gonzales, *Storms*, 49.

35. Howard Burdick, *Along the Shore* (Westerly, Rhode Island: Westerly Historical Society, 1988), 74; also the Keeper's Data, Plot Map for the Sandy Point Life-Saving Station at Block Island from 11 March 1916, notes that there was a henhouse on site, in poor condition, built in 1902; this station's keeper owned a cottage next to the station.

36. List of Provisions Destroyed; Louis Pearsall, Conversation with Steven Kesselman, 10 February 1978, Typescript, Curatorial Department, Mystic Seaport Museum.

37. Reynolds, Interview.

38. *Regulations for the Government of the Life-Saving Service of the United States* (Washington, D.C.: Government Printing Office, 1899).

39. In recollections from later in the twentieth century, ca. 1940s, the noon meal is sometimes called lunch.

40. Reynolds, Interview; Gonzales, *Storms*.

41. Reynolds, Interview; Gonzales, *Storms*, 45; Asa C. P. Lombard, Jr., *East of Cape Cod* (New Bedford: Reynolds, Dewalt Printing, Inc., 1976), 75; F.G. Carpenter, "Uncle Sam's Life Savers," *Popular Science Monthly* (January 1894): 438.

42. District Superintendent to Keeper, Highland Life-Saving Sation, North Truro, Massachusetts, 17 January 1889, courtesy Richard Boonisar.

43 Rebecca Davis Smith Ryder, Interview, 6 April 1978, SA, 2; Reynolds, Interview; Dodge, Conversation; Pearsall, Conversation; Gonzales, *Storms*; F.A. Doughty, "Life at a Life-Saving Station," *Catholic World* (July 1897): 523.

44. Lorenzo Littlefield Store, Ledger Books, courtesy Robert Downie, Block Island, Rhode Island.

45. Pearsall, Conversation; Captain Fred Gillikin, Interview with Dr. Scheina, 27 November 1977, Typescript, courtesy Richard Boonisar; reference from *Boston Globe* article from 1892 cited in letter, Richard Boonisar to author, 5 May 1986.

46. Dodge, Conversation.

47. Virginia Saunders, Conversation with author, May 1986.

48. Since the grocery list comes from four years after the original outfit, this station may have added a few items, such as a pitcher, which it did not originally have.

49. Benjamin F. Wilbour, *Notes on Little Compton*, ed. Carlton Brownell, (Little Compton, Rhode Island: Little Compton Historical Society, 1970).

50. Mrs. Mary F. Henderson, *Practical Cooking and Dinner Giving* (New York: Harper and Brothers, 1882). Horsford was a brand name product at that time, manufactured by the Rumford Chemical Works in nearby Providence, and is one of the earlier manufactured chemical leavenings. Additionally the company had a line of prepared flours.

51. Ball, Journal of Station # Two.

52. Littlefield Store, Ledgers.

53. Lamb, *Harper's*, 371; Doughty, *Catholic World*, 523.

54. E. G. Janes, *I Remember Cape Cod*, cited in Elinor DeWire, "Life-Saving Service," *Offshore* (February 1990): 104.

55. Ibid.

56. Anna North Coit, Conversation with author.

57. Ibid; Anna taught me how to make jonnycakes on a couple of different occasions while I lived in North Stonington, Connecticut.

58. Henderson, *Practical Cooking*, 141.

59. Ibid., 229.

60. *The Grange Cook Book* (North Stonington, Connecticut: Women of the North Stonington Grange, 1913), 47.

CHAPTER SEVEN

1. Felix Riesenberg, *Under Sail* (New York:

MacMillan Company, 1919), 82.

2. Ibid., 165.

3. Charles Chace, Journal, Log 146, G.W. Blunt White Library, Mystic Seaport Museum, hereafter cited as GWBWL.

4. Mary Brewster, Journal, 1845-49, Log 38, GWBWL, 25, published as Joan Druett, ed., *She Was a Sister Sailor: The Whaling Journals of Mary Brewster, 1845-1851* (Mystic: Mystic Seaport Museum, 1992).

5. Alan Villiers, *Cruise of the Conrad, A Journal of a Voyage*... (New York: Scribner's Sons, 1937), 288; Stanton Garner, ed., *The Captain's Best Mate: The Journal of Mary Chipman Lawrence on the Whaler Addison, 1856-1860* (Hanover and London: University Press of New England for Brown University, 1966), 44, 164; Riesenberg, *Under Sail*, 166; Richard Henry Dana, Jr., *Two Years Before the Mast*, World Classics Edition, (1840; New York: World Publishing Company, 1946), 383.

6. Brewster, Journal.

7. Samuel Samuels, *From Forecastle to Cabin* (Boston: Charles E. Lauriat Co., 1924), 124; Riesenberg, *Under Sail*, 372; Dana, *Two Years Before the Mast*, 384.

8. Sarah Smith (Mrs.Fred), Journal, Bark *Ohio*, Log 399 GWBWL;

Garner, *Captain's Best Mate*, 74.

9. Annie Holes Ricketson, *The Journal of Annie Holmes Ricketson on the Whaleship A.R. Tucker, 1871-74* (New Bedford: Old Dartmouth Historical Society, 1958), 18.

10. Ibid., 65; Garner, *Captain's Best Mate*, 69, 70.

11. Herman Melville, *Omoo, A Narrative of Adventures in the South Seas* (1847; Evanston & Chicago: Northwestern University Press and the Newberry Library, 1968), 132.

12. John T. Perkins, *John T. Perkins' Journal at Sea, 1845* (Mystic: Marine Historical Association, 1934), 141; Brewster, Journal, 24.

13. Ricketson, *Journal*, 34; Garner, *Captain's Best Mate*, 153, 170, 167.

14. Ricketson, *Journal*, 70, 38; Brewster, Journal.

15. Garner, *Captain's Best Mate*, 85.

16. Ricketson, *Journal*, 17; Garner, *Captain's Best Mate*, 219-20.

17. Ibid., 165.

18. Genevieve M. Darden, *My Dear Husband* (Taunton, Massachusetts: William S. Sullwold Publishing, Inc., for Descendants of Whaling Masters, Inc., 1980), 49; Ricketson, *Journal*, 13.

19. Riesenberg, *Under Sail*, 238.

20. Melville, *Omoo*, 40.

21. Samuels, *Forecastle to Cabin*, 234.

22. Perkins, *Journal*, 120.

23. Riesenberg, *Under Sail*, 372, 256.

24. Basil W. Bathe, *Visual Encyclopedia of Nautical Terms Under Sail* (New York: Crown, 1978), 10.

25. Riesenberg, *Under Sail*, 130.

26. Brewster, Journal.

27. Spencer Bonsall, Journal, Ship *Edward*, Log 740, GWBWL.

28. Garner, *Captain's Best Mate*, 74; Dana, *Two Years Before the Mast*, 303; Bonsall, Journal.

29. James A. Rogers, *Journal of Whaling Voyage of Ship Mentor of New London Captain William M. Baker* (New Bedford, Massachusetts: Reynolds Printing, n.d.), 2; James C. Osborne, Journal, Ship *Charles W. Morgan*, 1841-45, Log 143, GWBWL.

30. Ricketson, *Journal*, 54.

31. Francis A. Olmsted, *Incidents of a Whaling Voyage* (1841; Rutland, Vermont: Charles E. Tuttle Co., 1969), 172; Brewster, Journal.

32. Osborne, Journal.

33. Ibid; Riesenberg, *Under Sail*, 372; Garner, *Captain's Best Mate*, 63.

34. Ibid., 221, 212.

35. Brewster, Journal.

36. J. Scott Dow, "The Story of Captain Jonathan Dow," Typescript, 1948, Penobscot Marine Museum, Searsport, Maine, hereafter cited as PMM, 93, 27.

37. Sarah Smith, Journal, bark *J.P. West*, Log 78, GWBWL; Smith, Log 399; Ricketson, *Journal*, 65; Garner, *Captain's Best Mate*, 74.

38. Brewster, Journal; Garner, *Captain's Best Mate*, 126, 161.

39. Journal, ship *John Q. Adams*, 1852-53, Log 850, GWBWL.

40. Perkins, *Journal*, 141; Rogers, *Journal*, 4; Harpur Allen Gosnell, *Before the Mast in Clippers Composed in Large Part of the Diaries of Charles A. Abbey Kept While at Sea in the Years, 1856-1860* (New York: Derrydale Press, 1937), 94.

41. Ibid., 42; Brewster, Journal; Dow, "Captain Jonathan Dow," 28.

42. Knut Weibust, *Deep Sea Sailors, A Study in Maritime Ethnology* (Stockholm: Nodiska Museets Handlingar 71, 1969), 69; Perkins, *Journal*, 147.

43. C. Anne Wilson, *Foods and Drink in Britain, from the Stone Age to the 19th Century* (Chicago: Academy Chicago Publishers, 1991), 35, 44, 48, 310.

44. Margaret S. Dart, *Yankee Traders at Sea and Ashore* (New York: William Frederick Press, 1964), 81.

45. Thomas Larkin Turner, Diary, Coll. 95, vol. 14, GWBWL; Bonsall, Journal, 52; Garner, *Captain's Best Mate*, 7; Brewster, Journal; Basil Greenhill and Ann Gifford, *Women Under Sail* (London: David and Charles Ltd., n.d.), 67.

46. Smith, Journal, 3, 8, 44; Ricketson, *Journal*, 38.

47. Lloyd Briggs, *Around Cape Horn to Honolulu on the Bark Amy Turner 1880* (Boston: Charles E. Lauriat Co., 1926), 58; Georgia Maria Blanchard, "Our Wedding Trip Around Cape Horn," Family Papers, Penobscot Marine Museum, 4.

48. Samuels, *Forecastle to Cabin*, 214; Blanchard, "Our Wedding Trip," 8.

49. Garner, *Captain's Best Mate*, 5; Briggs, *Around Cape Horn*, 112, 50; Bonsall, Journal.

50. Isaac Norris Hibberd, *Sixteen Times Round Cape Horn: The Reminiscences of Captain Isaac Norris Hibberd* (Mystic: Mystic Seaport Museum, 1980), 16; George Piper Boughton, *Seafaring* (London: Faber and Gwyer, Ltd., 1926), 44; Brewster, Journal.

51. Smith, Log 399.

52. Riesenberg, *Under Sail*, 63; Dart, *Yankee Traders*, 81; Garner, *Captain's Best Mate*, 5.

53. Gosnell, *Before the Mast in Clippers*, 97.

54. Samuels, *Forecastle to Cabin*, 214.

55. Ibid.

56. Osborne, Journal; Brewster, Journal; Garner, *Captain's Best Mate*, 139.

57. Ricketson, *Journal*, 16.

58. Bonsall, Journal; Garner, *Captain's Best Mate*, 20; Brewster, Journal; Garner, *Captain's Best Mate*, 138; Smith, Log 399; Brewster Journal.

59. Brewster, Journal.

60. Dana, *Two Years Before the Mast*, 60, 106.

61. Lewis William Eldredge, *Lewis William Eldredge's Whaling Voyage* (New Bedford: Reynolds Printing, 1939), 7.

62. Garner, *Captain's Best Mate*, 123.

63. Robert Weir, Journal, Bark *Clara Bell*, 1855, Log 164, GWBWL.

64. Gosnell, *Before the Mast in Clippers*, 47; Nelson Haley, *Whale Hunt, The Narrative of a Voyage by Nelson C. Haley, Harpooneer in the Ship Charles W. Morgan, 1849-1853* (1948; Mystic: Mystic Seaport Museum, 1991), 237; Wilson, *Foods and Drink in Britain*, 127.

65. Brewster, Journal, 93; Eldredge, *Whaling Voyage*, 12, 10.

66. Dana, *Two Years Before the Mast*, 290.

67. Riesenberg, *Under Sail*, 63, 143.

68. Henry Blaney, *Journal of Voyages to China and Return 1851-1853* (Boston: privately printed, 1913), 115-16; Garner, *Captain's Best Mate*, 20-21.

69. Riesenberg, *Under Sail*, 63; Frederick Pease Harlow, *The Making of a Sailor on a Yankee Square-Rigger* (Salem, Massachusetts: Marine Research Society, 1928), 188; Blanchard, "Our Wedding Trip," 4.

70. Garner, *Captain's Best Mate*, 211, 74.

71. Briggs, *Around Cape Horn*, 149-50.

72. Olmsted, *Incidents of a Whaling Voyage*, 173.

73. Perkins, *Journal*, 145.

74. Brewster, Journal, 34; Elizabeth Schneider,

Uncommon Fruits and Vegetables: A Commonsense Guide (New York: Harper and Row, 1986), 115; Harlow, *Making of a Sailor*, 311.

75. Richard Henry Dana, Jr., *The Journal of Richard Henry Dana, Jr.*, 3 vols., ed. Robert F. Lucid, (Cambridge, Massachusetts: Belknap Press of Harvard University Press, 1968), 3:878; Briggs, *Around Cape Horn*, 136.

76. Bonsall, Journal.

77. Smith, Log 399.

78. Garner, *Captain's Best Mate*, 33.

CHAPTER EIGHT

1. Stan Hugill's *Sailortown*, and many other sailors' memoirs and narratives draw a clear picture of the predatory economic system that kept sailors at sea.

2. Frederick Marryat, *A Diary in America with Remarks on Its Institutions*, ed. Sydney Jackman, (New York: Alfred Knopf, 1962), 374.

3. Herman Melville, *Moby Dick; or, The White Whale*, (1851; New York: Mead and Company, 1942), 8.

4. Ibid., 11.

5. Ibid. 27-28; Frances Trollop, *Domestic Manners of the Americas*, ed. Donald Smalley, (New York: Random House, 1949), 390; Captain R. N. MacKinnon, *Atlantic and Transatlantic Sketches Afloat and Ashore* (New York: Harper & Brothers, 1852), 23.

6. Mystic *Pioneer*, 14 May 1859.

7. Richard Henry Dana, Jr., *The Journal of Richard Henry Dana, Jr.*, 3 vol., ed. Robert Lucid, (Cambridge, Massachusetts: Belknap Press of Harvard University Press, 1968), 2:836.

8. Mary Elizabeth Weaver Farnsworth, "Reminiscences of...," Book 1, Misc. Vol. 155, G.W. Blunt White Library, Mystic Seaport Museum, hereafter cited as GWBWL, 117.

9. Alvin F. Harlow, *Old Bowery Days* (New York: D. Appleton & Co., 1931), 118, 413.

10. "Along the Docks," *Harper's Weekly*, 11 February 1871, 998.

11. E.E. Sterns, "The Street vendors of New York," *Scribner's Monthly* (December 1870): 126.

12. *Harper's*, "Along the Docks," 998.

13. Sterns, " 123; Harlow and Sterns in *Scribner's Monthly* both provide exceptionally detailed descriptions of the vendors in New York port.

14. Marryat, *Diary in America*, 379; MacKinnon, *Sketches*, 23.

15. George Iles, "On Hotel-Keeping—Present and Future," *Century Magazine* (August 1885): 577, 583.

16. Farnsworth, "Reminiscences...," Book 1, 103.

17. Captain John D. Whidden, *Old Sailing Ship Days* (Boston: Charles E. Lauriat Co., 1925), 234.

18. Scott J. Dow, "The Story of Capt. Jonathan Dow," Typescript, 1948, Penobscot Marine Museum, Searsport, Maine, hereafter cited as PMM, 71.

19. Samuel Samuels, *From Forecastle to Cabin* (Boston: Charles E. Lauriat Co., 1924), 39.

20. Richard Henry Dana, Jr., *Two Years Before the Mast*, World Classics Edition, (1840; World Publication Co., 1946) 124, 135.

21. Ibid. 260.

22. Dana, *Journal*, 3:895, 911-12.

23. Ibid. 806.

24. Ibid. 720, 724.

25. Ibid. 711-12, 731.

26. Ibid. 803.

27. Herman Melville, *Omoo, A Narrative of Adventures in the South Seas* (1847; Evanston and Chicago: Northwestern University Press and the Newberry Library, 1968), 54-55.

28. Herman Melville, *Redburn: His First Voyage* (1849; Evanston and Chicago: Northwestern University Press and the Newberry Library, 1969), 134.

29. Whidden, *Sailing Ship Days*, 180.

30. Dana, *Journal*, 3:1116.

31. Melville, *Omoo*, 190.

32. Francis A. Olmsted, *Incidents of a Whaling Voyage* (1841; Rutland, Vermont: Charles E. Tuttle Co., 1969), 213.

33. Richard Malley, "On Shore in a Foreign Land: Mary Stark in the Kingdom of Hawaii," *The Log of Mystic Seaport* (Fall 1985): 79-92. Malley's article is an interesting look at the multitude of interconnections in the maritime and business communities of Honolulu and even in small port towns like Mystic.

34. Mary Brewster, Journal, 1845-49, Log 38, GWBWL, 51, published as Joan Druett, ed., *She Was a Sister Sailor: The Whaling Journals of Mary Brewster, 1845-1851* (Mystic: Mystic Seaport Museum, 1992); Stanton Garner, ed., *The Captain's Best Mate: The Journal of Mary Chipman Lawrence on the Whaler Addison, 1856-1860* (Providence: Brown University Press, 1966), 80, 204.

35. John T. Perkins, *John T. Perkins' Journal at Sea, 1845* (Mystic: Marine Historical Association, 1934) 145.

36. William Ellis, *The Journal of William Ellis: Narrative of a Tour of Hawaii or Owhyee with remarks on the history, traditions, manner, customs, and life of the inhabitants of the Sandwich Isles* (Rutland, Vermont: Tuttle, 1979), 147; Ellis made his trip in 1823. Dana, *Journal*, 3: 872.

37. Felix Riesenberg, *Under Sail* (New York: Macmillan Company, 1919), 188; Brewster, Journal, 137, 35.

38. I am indebted to Nancy Piianaia, a Hawaii-based food historian who explained the poi phenomenon to me in this way. She supplied me with many island references to Hawaiian food from which I quote here.

39. Mary Kawena Pukui, "Poi Making," *Polynesian Culture History*, 425-435; complete description of traditional poi making, from oral history account with Pukui; Ellis, *Narrative of Hawaii*, 147; Pukui, "Poi," 425.

40. Each part of the stone pounder, each step of the process, and the poi at each stage had its own name, according to Pukui, "Poi," 426-28.

41. Brewster, Journal, 150-51.

42. Ibid. 145-54.

43. Ibid. 83.

44. Lloyd Briggs, *Around Cape Horn to Honolulu on the Bark Amy Turner 1880* (Boston: Charles E. Lauriat Co., 1926), 138, 147-48.

45. Ibid. 142.

46. Ibid. 137; Pukui, "Poi," 429-30, 425.

47. Dana, *Journal*, 3:872.

48. Melville, *Omoo*, 257-58.

49. Ibid. 258.

50. Dana, *Journal*, 3:1069.

51. Ibid. 949.

52. Ibid. 943, 949, 954, 957.

53 Annie Holmes Ricketson, *The Journal of Annie Holmes Ricketson on the Whaleship A.R. Tucker, 1871-74* (New Bedford: Old Dartmouth Historical Society, 1958), 59.

54. Gosnell, Harpur Allen, *Before the Mast in Clippers' Composed in Large Part of the Diaries of Charles A. Abbey Kept While at Sea in the Years 1856-1860* (New York: Derrydale Press., 1937), 77.

55. Dana, *Journal*, 3: 978.

56. Lewis William Eldredge, *Lewis William Eldredge's Whaling Voyage* (New Bedford: Reynolds Printing, 1939), 13.

57. Hiram Look, Log 409, GWBWL.

58. Ibid.

59. Ricketson, *Journal*, 40.

60. "Hawaiian Meals," (Hawaiian Mission Childrens Society)*The Gospel Missionary* (1867).

61. Thomas Larkin Turner, Diary, 1832, Coll. 95, vol. 14, GWBWL.

62. Nelson Haley, *Whale Hunt, The Narrative of a Voyage by Nelson C. Haley, Harpooneer in the Ship Charles W. Morgan, 1849-1853* (1948; Mystic: Mystic Seaport Museum, 1991), 28.

63. Ricketson, *Journal*, 19.

64. Ibid. 24.

65. Frederick Pease Harlow, *The Making of a Sailor on a Yankee Square-Rigger* (Salem, Massachusetts: Marine Research Society, 1928), 234.

66. Mrs. L.G. Abell, *The Complete Domestic Guide Comprising the Mother's Book of Daily Duties and Skillful Housewife's Book* (New York: R.I. Young, 1853), 98.

67. Ibid.

CHAPTER NINE

1. William Wainwright, Journal, Log 429, G.W. Blunt White Library, Mystic Seaport Museum, hereafter cited as GWBWL.

2. Annie Holmes Ricketson, *The Journal of Annie Holmes Ricketson on the Whaleship A.R. Tucker, 1871-74* (New Bedford: Old Dartmouth Historical Society, 1958), 13.

3. Charles W. Morgan, Diary, 1854, Coll. 27, vol. 7, GWBWL; Elizabeth Dow Leonard, *A Few Reminiscences of My Exeter Life*, ed. Edwards C. Echols, (Exeter: 2x4 Press, 1972), 19; Mary J. Channing, "Sixty Year's Ago," *The Youth's Companion*, 13 December 1894, 604; Edmund Delaney, *Life in the Connecticut River Valley, 1800-1840, from the Recollections of John Howard Redfield* (Essex, Connecticut: Connecticut River Museum, 1988), 36.

4. Mystic *Journal*, 9 July 1870; Asa Fish, Diary, 1856, Coll. 43, GWBWL; Charles Q. Eldridge, *The Story of a Connecticut Life* (Troy, New York: Allen Book and Printing Co., 1919), 16-17.

5. Leonard, *A Few Reminiscences*, 19; Harriet Beecher Stowe, *Poganuc People* (1878; reprint, Hartford: Stowe-Day Foundation, 1977), 194; Stowe, "Sixty Years Ago," 193.

6. Mystic *Pioneer*, 2 July 1859; Fish, Diary, 1856.

7. Leonard, *A Few Reminiscences*; Channing, "Sixty Years Ago," 604.

8. Charles W. Morgan, Diary, 1851, Coll. 27, vol. 5, GWBWL.

9. Narragansett *Weekly*, 6 July 1865.

10.Mystic *Press*, 9 July 1865; Charles W. Morgan, Diary, 1860, Coll. 27, vol. 10, GWBWL.

11. George S. Wasson, *Sailing Days on the Penobscot* (Salem: Marine Research Society, 1932), 105; Mystic *Journal*, 6 July 1876; *Weekly Mirror-Journal*, 11 July 1872.

12. Esther Alice Peck, "A Conservative Generation's Amusements: A Phase of Connecticut's Social History" Maine Bulletin, (April 1938): 23; Zephaniah Pease, ed., *Life in New Bedford 100 Years Ago, A Chronicle of the Social, Religious, and Commercial History of the Period in a Diary Kept by Joseph R. Anthony* (New Bedford: Old Dartmouth Historical Society, 1925), 61.

13. Narragansett *Weekly*, 6 July 1865.

14. *Columbian Register*, New Haven, 5 July 1828, cited in Peck, "A Conservative Generation's Amusements," 23.

15. Stonington *Mirror*, 10 July 1873.

16. Channing, "Sixty Years Ago," 604; Delaney, *Life in the Connecticut River Valley*, 29.

17. Charles W. Morgan, Diary, 1851; Mystic *Press*, 10 July 1879.

18. *Weekly Mirror-Journal*, 11 July 1872.

19. Sallie Smith, Journal, Bark *Ohio*, Log 399, GWBWL.

20. Mystic *Journal*, 9 July 1870.

21. *Weekly Mirror-Journal*, 6 July 1871; Mystic *Press*, 11 July 1873.

22. Mystic *Pioneer*, 7 July 1866; Asa Fish, Diary, 1856.

23. Mystic *Press*, 11 July 1873.

24. Stonington *Mirror*, 9 July 1870; Mystic *Journal*, 9 July 1870.

25. Ethan Denison, Diary, 1809, Misc. Vol. 566, GWBWL; Pease, *Life in New Bedford*, 61.

26. Charles W. Morgan, Diary, 1849, 1854.

27. Stonington *Mirror*, 10 July 1873; Mystic *Press*, 9 July 1885.

28. Nathan Fish, Diary, 1868, Coll. 43, GWBWL.

29. Mystic *Press*, 9 July 1875.

30. Frederick Marryat, *A Diary in America with Remarks on Its Institutions*, ed. Sydney Jackman, (New York: Alfred Knopf, 1962), 58.

31. Maria Parloa, *Miss Parloa's Kitchen Companion* (Boston: Estes and Lauriat, 1887), 121; Mystic *Pioneer*, 10 September 1859; Edward Everett Knapp, "Smacks of Noank," Typescript, Coll. 171, GWBWL, 21.

32. Anna North Coit, Interview with author, 15 September 1986; there is a consistently high number of cake recipes using coconut in cake or in frosting in manuscript recipe books from this region in the author's collection; Mystic *Press*, 1 February 1883.

33. Mystic *Pioneer*, 10 September 1859.

34. Wainwright,Journal.

35. This and the discussion of the Fourth among seagoing forty-niners is drawn from Charles R. Schultz's ground-breaking, "A Forty-Niner Fourth of July," *The Log of Mystic Seaport* (Spring 1986): 3-4, 7-9, 10-11.

36. Log 800, GWBWL.

37. Scott J. Dow, "The Story of Capt. Jonathan Dow," Typecript, 1948, Penobscot Marine Museum, Searsport, Maine, herafter cited as PMM, 61, 64, 54.

38. Ricketson, *Journal*, 57; Harpur Allen Gosnell, *Before the Mast in Clippers Composed in Large Part of the Diaries of Charles A. Abbey Kept While at Sea in the Years, 1856-1860* (New York: Derrydale Press, 1937), 45, 56.

39. James A. Rogers, *Journal of Whaling Voyage of Ship Mentor of New London Captain William M. Baker* (New Bedford, Massachusetts: Reynolds Printing), 5; Ricketson, *Journal*, 13; Robert Weir, Journal, Bark *Clara Bell*, Log 164, GWBWL; Sarah Smith, Journal, Log 78, GWBWL.

40. Ricketson, *Journal*, 13.

41. Stanton Garner, ed., *The Captain's Best Mate: The Journal of Mary Chipman Lawrence on the Whaler Addison, 1856-1860* (Hanover and London: University Press of New England for Brown University, 1966), 40, 102.

42. Smith, Journal.

43. Schultz, "Forty-Niner," 8.

44. Weir, Journal; Felix Riesenberg, *Under Sail* (New York: Macmillan Company, 1919), 335.

45. Horatio Gray, Journal, Coll. 89, vol. 3, GWBWL.

46. Elizabeth M. Hall, *Practical American Cookery and Domestic Economy* (New York: Saxton, Barker, and Co., 1860), 65.

47. Mary Virginia Terhune [pseud. Marion Harland], *Practical Cooking and Dinner Giving* (New York: Charles Scribner's Sons, 1878), 297.

48. Mrs. S. T. Rorer, *Mrs. Rorer's Philadelphia Cook Book* (Philadelphia: Arnold and Co., 1886), 258.

49. Henderson, *Practical Cooking*, 306.

CHAPTER TEN

1. Mary J. Channing "Sixty Years Ago," *The Youth's Companion*, 13 December 1894, 604.

2. Harriet Beecher Stowe, *Oldtown Folks* (Boston: Houghton, Mifflin, and Co., 1891), 337; Edmund Delaney, *Life in the Connecticut River Valley,1800-1840, from the Recollections of John Howard Redfield* (Essex, Connecticut: Connecticut River Museum, 1988), 36.

3. W. Deloss Love, Jr., *Fast and Thanksgiving Days of New England* (Cambridge: Houghton Mifflin, 1895), 400-04.

4. Ibid. 245-46; Delaney, *Life in the Connecticut River Valley*, 36.

5. Ibid.

6. Stowe, *Oldtown Folks*, 339.

7. Richard Henry Dana, Jr., *Two Years Before the Mast* , World Classics Edition, (1840; New York: World Publishing Co., 1946), 153

8. Stanton Garner, ed., *The Captain's Best Mate: The Journal of Mary Chipman Lawrence on the Whaler Addison, 1856-1860* (Hanover and London: University Press of New England for Brown University, 1966), 58.

9. Irving Reynolds, Journal, Log 556, G.W. Blunt White Library, Mystic Seaport Museum, hereafter cited as GWBWL.

10. George W. Douglas, *The American Book of Days* (New York: H.W. Wilson Co., 1937), 587; Love, *Fast and Thanksgiving Days*, 408.

11. Delaney, *Life in the Connecticut River Valley*, 36.

12. Charles W. Morgan, Diary, 1848, Coll. 27, vol. 3, GWBWL.

13. Stowe, *Oldtown Folks*, 345-46

14. Grace Denison Wheeler, *Grace Wheeler's Memories* (Stonington: Pequot Press, 1947), 38.

15. Elinor Stearn, "A Kitchen of 1825 in a Thriving New England Town," *Old Time New England* (January 1923): 128.

16. Caroline Howard King, *When I Lived In Salem, 1822-1866* (Brattleboro, Vermont: Stephen Daye Press, 1937), 110.

17. Stowe, *Oldtown Folks*, 342.

18. Charles W. Morgan, Diary, 1860, Coll. 27,

vol. 10, GWBWL

19. "'Thanksgiving' Home and Society," *Scribner's Monthly* (December 1871): 241.

20. Delaney, *Life in the Connecticut River Valley*, 36-37.

21. Benjamin F. Fish, Diary, 1861, Coll. 43, GWBWL.

22. King, *When I Lived in Salem*, 112; Sarah Anna Emery, *Reminiscences of a Nonagenarian* (Newburyport: William H. Huse, & Co., 1879), 13; Wheeler, *Memories*, 37; Morgan, Diary, 1848.

23. Nathan Fish, Diary, 1868, Coll. 43, GWBWL; Morgan, Diary, 1860.

24. King, *When I Lived in Salem*, 114.

25. Julia Gates to George Gates, 31 November 1876, Gates Family Papers, Mystic River Historical Society, Mystic, Connecticut.

26. Channing, "Sixty Years Ago," 604.

27. Wheeler, *Memories*, 38; Benjamin Fish B., Diary.

28. King, *When I Lived in Salem*, 113.

29. Delaney, *Life in the Connecticut River Valley*, p. 37.

30. Harpur Allen Gosnell, *Before the Mast in Clippers Composed in Large Part of the Diaries of Charles A. Abbey Kept While at Sea in the Years, 1856-1860* (New York: Derrydale Press, 1937), 232.

31. Lloyd Briggs, *Around Cape Horn to Honolulu on the Bark Amy Turner 1880* (Boston: Charles E. Lauriat Co., 1926), 118.

32. *W.W. Brainard*, Log 119, GWBWL; C. W. *Morgan*, Log 149, GWBWL; Dana, *Two Years Before the Mast*, 153.

33. Annie Holmes Ricketson, *The Journal of Annie Holmes Ricketson on the Whaleship A.R. Tucker, 1871-74* (New Bedford: Old Dartmouth Historical Society, 1958), 26; Gosnell, *Before the Mast*, 233.

34. *Scribner's*, "Thanksgiving," 240-41.

35. Grace Cogswell Root, *Father and Daughter: A Collection of Cogswell Family Letters and Diaries 1772-1830* (West Hartford, Connecticut: American School for the Deaf, 1924), 17.

36. Delaney, *Life in the Connecticut River Valley*, 36; Channing, "Sixty Years Ago," 604.

37. Wheeler, *Memories*, 38.

38. Silas Fish to Mother, 24 November 1847, Coll. 43, GWBWL; Morgan, Diary, 1860; Simeon Fish, Diary, 1862, Coll. 43, GWBWL; *Good News*, Log 198, GWBWL.

39. Zephaniah Pease, ed., *Life in New Bedford 100 Years Ago, A Chronicle of the Social, Religious, and Commercial History of the Period in a Diary Kept by Joseph R. Anthony* (New Bedford: Old Dartmouth Historical Society, 1925), 84; Benjamin F. Wilbour, *Notes on Little Compton*, ed. Carlton Brownell, (Little Compton, Rhode Island: Little Compton Historical Society, 1970), 67; Genevieve M. Darden, *My Dear Husband* (Taunton, Massachusetts: William S. Sullwold Publishing, Inc., for Descendants of Whaling Masters, Inc., 1980), 65.

40. Barbara Ketcham Wheaton, *Savoring the Past: The French Kitchen and Table from 1300 to 1789* (Philadelphia: University of Pennsylvania Press, 1983), 81-82; Karen Hess, *Martha Washington's Booke of Cookery* (New York: Columbia University Press, 1981), 61.

41. Carolyn Freeman Travers, ed., *The Thanksgiving Primer* (Plymouth, Massachusetts: Plimoth Plantation, Inc., 1991), 6.

42. William Bradford, *Bradford's History of Plymouth Plantation*, *Original Narratives of Early American History* (New York: Barnes and Noble, 1908), Thanksgiving description.

43. King, *When I Lived in Salem*, 112; The *Scribner's* article "Thanksgiving," 240, describes "piglets in crisp armor of crackling"; Anna North Coit provided oral history from the North Stonington Palmer family, describing a late-nineteenth- or early-twentieth-century Thanksgiving dinner of a whole suckling pig that did not fit in the oven all the way, but was removed and the cooked portion carved off for the dinner, and the rest replaced in the oven; Notes of Conversation with author, 23 November 1982.

44. Irving Reynolds, Journal, *Mary & Helen*, Log 556, GWBWL; Ricketson, *Journal*, 26.

45. *Scribner's*, "Thanksgiving," 240.

46. King, *When I Lived in Salem*, 24.

47. A.C. Day, *Knickerbocker Life*, 213, cited in *Dictionary of American English on Historic Principles*, 66.

48. Elizabeth Dow Leonard, *A Few Reminiscences of My Exeter Life*, ed. Edwards C. Echols, (Exeter, New Hampshire: 2x4 Press, 1972), 19; John Whidden, *Old Sailing Ship Days* (Boston: Charles E. Lauriat Co., 1925), 3-4.

49. *Scribner's*, "Thanksgiving," 204.

50. Channing, "Sixty Years Ago," 604; Stowe, *Oldtown Folks*, 338.

51. Margaret S. Dart, *Yankee Traders at Sea and Ashore* (New York: William Frederich Press, 1964), 62.

52. King, *When I Lived in Salem*, 112-13.

53. Whidden, *Sailing Ship Days*, 3-6.

54. Catherine Beecher and Harriet Beecher Stowe, *The American Woman's Home* (New York: J.B. Ford and Co., 1869), 137.

55. "Letter to a Dyspeptic," *Atlantic Monthly* (April 1859): 467.

56. Emery, *Reminiscences of a Nonagenarian*, 12.

57. Asa Fish, Diary, 1811-15, Coll. 43, GWBWL.

58. Mrs. Bliss, *The Practical Cookbook....* (Philadelphia: J.B. Lippincott & Co., 1864), 78.

85. Lydia Maria Child, *The American Frugal Housewife* (Boston: Carter, Hendee, and Co., 1833), 66.

86. Mrs. L.G. Abell, *The Complete Domestic Guide Comprising the Mother's Book of Daily Duties and Skillful Housewife's Book* (New York: R.I. Young, 1853), 139.

CHAPTER ELEVEN

1. Charles W. Morgan, Diary, 1850, Coll. 27, vol. 4, G.W. Blunt White Library, Mystic Seaport Museum, hereafter cited as GWBWL.

2. Asa Fish, Diary, 1811, Coll. 43, GWBWL.

3. T.T. Waterman, *Lecture on the Christmas Festival* (Providence, Rhode Island: I. Wilcox & Co., 1835); Harriet Beecher Stowe, *Poganuc People* (1878; reprint, Hartford: Stowe-Day Foundation, 1977), 24.

4. Ibid., 26.

5. Caroline Howard King, *When I Lived in Salem* (Brattleboro, Vermont: Stephen Daye Press, 1937), 115.

6. Stowe, *Poganuc People*, 54.

7. Ibid., 115.

8. Ibid; Annie Holmes Ricketson, *The Journal of Annie Holmes Ricketson on the Whaleship A. R. Tucker, 1871-74* (New Bedford, Massachusetts: Old Dartmouth Historical Society, 1958), 68.

9. William Woys Weaver, *America Eats: Forms of Edible Folk Art* (New York: Museum of American Folk Art and Harper & Row, 1989), 115; Jack Larkin, *The Reshaping of Everyday Life, 1790-1840* (New York: Harper and Row, 1988), 273.

10. S.K. Lothrop, "The Religious Observance of Christmas," *Monthly Religious Magazine* (January 1846): 40.

11. Grace Denison Wheeler, *Grace Wheeler's Memories* (Stonington, Connecticut: Pequot Press, 1947), 39.

12. Morgan, Diaries 1849-60, Coll. 27, vols. 3, 4, 6, 10, GWBWL.

13. J.D. Fish to Mother in Mystic, Connecticut, 26 December 1864, Coll. 43, GWBWL.

14. Zephaniah W.Pease, ed., *The Diary of Samuel Rodman, A New Bedford Chronicle of Thirty Seven Years, 1821-1859* (New Bedford, Massachusetts: Reynolds Printing Co., 1927), 214.

15. B. B. Mussey, *The Book of the Seasons—A Gift for the Young* (Boston: 1842), 17-22.

16. Julia Gates to George Gates, 16 December 1864, Gates Family Papers, Mystic River Historical Society, Mystic, Connecticut.

17. Wheeler, *Memories*, 39; Stonington *Mirror*, 1 January 1874.

18. Mystic *Press*, 27 December 1877, 1 January 1880.

19. Stonington *Mirror*, 31 December 1874, 3 January 1878, 1, 8 January 1874.

20. Mystic *Press*, 27 December 1877, 1 January 1880.

21. Mystic *Press*, 31 December 1875; Stonington

Mirror, 31 December 1874.

22. F.A. Doughty, "Life at a Life-Saving Station," *Catholic World* (1897): 522.

23. Nicholas Ball, Journal of Life-Saving Station # Two, Third District, New Shoreham, Rhode Island, 30 November 1874; Francis Jaixen Dodge, Interview with author, 29 May 1986. Mrs. Dodge's father George Jaixen was a surfman at the west side station, Block Island.

24. Stonington *Mirror*, 1 January 1874.

25. Mystic *Press*, 31 December 1874.

26. Richard Henry Dana, Jr., *The Journal of Richard Henry Dana ,Jr.*, 3 vols., ed. Robert F. Lucid, (Cambridge, Massachusetts: Belknap Press of Harvard University Press, 1968), 2:476, 526.

27. James D. Fish to father, 27 December 1851, Coll. 43, GWBWL.

28. Charles W. Morgan, Diary, 1855, Coll. 27, vol. 8, GWBWL.

29. Dana, *Journal*, 2:526; Mary V. Worstell, "The Month Before Christmas," *St. Nicholas Magazine* (November 1889): 90.

30. Stonington *Mirror*, 8 January 1874.

31. Maria Stover to Captain Joseph G. Stover, 29 December 1866, Calista M. Stover Papers, Coll. 105, GWBWL.

32. C. Anne Wilson, *Foods and Drink in Britain, from the Stone Age to the 19th Century* (Chicago: Academy Chicago Publishers, 1991), 130.

33. Dana, *Journal*, 1:112.

34. T.P.W., "Auntie's Merry Christmas," *Godey's Lady's Book* (December 1861): 506.

35. Spencer Bonsall, Journal, Ship *Edward*, 1837, Log 740, GWBWL.

36. Edward Everett Knapp, "Smacks of Noank," Typescript, Coll. 171, GWBWL, 61.

37. Mrs. Mary F. Henderson, *Practical Cooking and Dinner Giving* (New York: Harper and Brothers, 1882); Mrs. H.W. Beecher, *All Around the House; or, How to Make Homes Happy* (New York: D. Appleton & Co., 1878); *Hood's Combined Cook Books* (Lowell, Massachusetts: C.I. Hood & Co., 1875-1885).

38. Susan Williams, *Savory Suppers and Fashionable Feasts* (New York: Pantheon Books, 1985), 108-09; Florence Button, "What Xmas Was to Me Long Ago," Manuscript Essay, 1979, author's possession.

39. Amelia Simmons, *American Cookery*, ed. Mary Tolford Wilson, (1796; reprint, New York: Dover Publications, 1984), xvii; some scholars attribute this to her possible residence in Albany where she was influenced by Dutch neighbors; Weaver, *America Eats*, 115.

40. Mrs. E.A. Howland, *New England Economical Housekeeper* (Worcester: S.A. Howland, 1845), 29.

41. Emma K. Parrish, "Jack's Christmas," *St. Nicholas Magazine* (December 1877): 127.

42. Wilson, *Foods and Drink*, 228, 254.

43. *Godey's Lady's Book and Magazine* (December 1856): 554-56.

44. "Twelfth Night," Home and Society Column, *Scribner's Monthly* (January 1872): 372-74; Louise Conway Belden, *The Festive Tradition: Table Decoration and Desserts in America, 1650-1900* (New York: W.W. Norton and Co., 1983), 184.

45. Michael Patrick Hearn, *The Annotated Christmas Carol: A Christmas Carol by Charles Dickens* (New York: Avon Books, 1976), 98.

46. Virginia DeForrest, "How Effie Hamilton Spent Christmas," *Godey's Lady's Book* (December 1857): 536.

47. "Home and Society Column," *Scribner's Monthly* (January 1871): 348.

48. Harpur Allen Gosnell, *Before the Mast in Clippers Composed in Large Part of the Diaries of Charles A. Abbey Kept While at Sea in the Years, 1856-1860* (New York: Derrydale Press., 1937), 102.

49. Horatio Gray, Journal, Coll. 59, vol. 3, GWBWL.

50. Mary Brewster, Journal, Log 38, GWBWL, 7 & 13, 107, published as Joan Druett, ed., *She Was a Sister Sailor: The Whaling Journals of Mary Brewster, 1845-1851* (Mystic: Mystic Seaport Museum, 1992).

51. Gray, Journal.

52. Ricketson, *Journal*, 68; Sarah Smith, Journal, Bark *Ohio*, Log 399, GWBWL.

53. Nehemiah S. Hayden, Journal, Ship *Frederick Gebhard*, Log 191, GWBWL.

54. Stanton Garner, ed., The*Captain's Best Mate: The Journal of Mary Chipman Lawrence on the Whaler Addison, 1856-1860* (Hanover and London: University Press of New England for Brown University, 1966), 6.

55. Ibid, 137, 209, 210.

56. Fred. B. Duncan, *Deepwater Family* (New York: Pantheon Books, 1969), 87.

57. Ricketson, *Journal*, 68, 45.

58. Dow, Scott J,. "The Story of Captain Jonathan Dow," Typescript, 1948, Penobscot Marine Museum, Searsport, Maine, hereafter cited as PMM.

59. Elnathan Fisher, Journal, quoted in "Christmas at Sea: A Century Ago Aboard New England Whaleships," Vineyard *Gazette*, 11 December 1980.

60. Lloyd Briggs, *Around Cape Horn to Honolulu on the Bark Amy Turner 1880* (Boston: Charles E. Lauriat Co., 1926), 165-67

61. Fisher, Journal; Brewster, Journal.

62. Smith, Journal; Garner, *Captain's Best Mate*, Bonsall, Journal.

63. Bonsall, Journal.

64. Richard Henry Dana, Jr., *Two Years Before the Mast*, World Classics Edition, (1840; New York: World Publishing Co., 1946), 64, 256.

65. Felix Riesenberg, *Under Sail* (New York: Macmillan, 1919), 55.

66. Sarah Smith, Journal, Bark *John P. West*, Log 78, GWBWL.

67. Bonsall, Journal.

68. Henry Mitchell, Journal, Log 5, GWBWL.

69. *Scribner's Monthly* (January 1871): 348; George A. Martin, *Our Homes; How to Beautify Them* (New York: O.J. Judd Co., 1888), 159.

70. Ibid.

71. Henderson, *Practical Cooking*, 93.

72. C.I. Hood and Co., *Hood's Combined Cook Books* (Lowell, Massachusetts, n.d.), in *High Street Cook Book*, 25.

CHAPTER TWELVE

1. Advertisement, Stonington *Mirror*, 17 January 1891.

2. George Brown Goode, ed., *The Fisheries and Fishery Industries of the United States*, 5 sects., (Washington, D.C.: Government Printing Office, 1887), sect 5., 2:509.

3. Kathy Neustadt, *Clambake: A History and Celebration of an American Tradition* (Amherst, Massachusetts: University of Massachusetts Press, 1992), 17, 19.

4. Ibid., 28.

5. Ibid., 32-33; Neustadt points out that shell symbolism was part of European folk culture and that the cross referencing of that with American colonial experience "can hardly be viewed as coincidental," 39, 38.

6. By "serious" I mean that certain foods convey importance; for example a large joint of meat or the presence of a high-value food at a meal signifies that the meal or the guests are important and are being honored. A hot dog is considered appropriate for children, picnics, or a fast meal whose basic purpose is to deaden hunger.

7. Elizabeth C. P. Bennet, "A Nantucketer Remembers: From the Commonplace Book of ECPB, 1843-1919," arranged by her daughter, Mrs. Florence Bennet Anderson, *Old Time New England* (July-September 1951): 9.

8. Mary Emma Weaver Farnsworth, "Reminiscences of...," Book 1, Misc. Vol. 155, G.W. Blunt White Library, Mystic Seaport Museum, hereafter cited as GWBWL, 65-66.

9. Neustadt, *Clambake*, 38; Harold Clifford, *Charlie York: Maine Coast Fisherman* (Camden, Maine: International Marine Publishing, Co., 1974), 12-13.

10. Willard L. Sperry, *Summer Yesterdays in Maine: Memories of Boyhood Vacation Days* (New York: Harper and Brothers, 1941), 65-66.

11. Ibid., 64, 72.

12. Ibid., 72.

13. Ibid., 75-76.

14. Ibid., 74, 75.

15. Ibid., 76, 80.

16. Emery Bunker to "John," in the author's possession.

17. Mr. Ingersoll just plain got this wrong; the seaweed *must* be wet to generate the steam that does the cooking.

18. Goode, *Fisheries*, sect. 5, 2:601.

19. Neustadt, *Clambake*, 55.

20. Mystic *Pioneer*, 12 August 1865.

21. Neustadt, *Clambake*, 64. Neustadt examines this phenomenon closely and identifies the connection between late nineteenth- and early twentieth-century concerns about naturalism, realism, and authenticity in art and culture.

22. Scrapbook entry, Woodburn Albums, via William N. Peterson.

23. Neustadt, *Clambake*, 55.

24. Mystic *Pioneer*, 12 August 1865.

25. Mystic *Pioneer*, 3 September 1864.

26. Neustadt, *Clambake*, 48.

27. Mystic *Pioneer*, 3 September 1864.

28. *Dictionary of American English on Historic Principles* (Chicago: University of Chicago Press, 1944), 1: 130.

CHAPTER THIRTEEN

1. *Oxford English Dictionary*, 386.

2. Mary Randolph, *The Virginia House-wife: Facsimile of 1st Edition, 1824, and Additional Materials from Editions of 1825 and 1828*, ed. Karen Hess, (Columbia: University of South Carolina Press, 1984), 265-66.

3. Ibid., 265; *Oxford English Dictionary*, 386.

4. Hannah Glasse, *The Art of Cookery Made Plain and Easy* (London: author, 1747), cited in Randolph, *Virginia House-wife*, 265.

5. Mystic *Pioneer*, 6, 20 August 1859.

6. Zephaniah Pease, ed., *Life in New Bedford 100 Years Ago, A Chronicle of the Social, Religious, and Commercial History of the Period in a Diary Kept by Joseph R. Anthony* (New Bedford: Old Dartmouth Historical Society, 1925), 63; 68.

7. Mystic *Press*, 5 September 1878, 12 July 1895.

8. Mystic *Press*, 21 January 1876; New London *People's Advocate*, 8 March 1848, via William N. Peterson.

9. Caroline Howard King, *When I Lived in Salem* (Brattleboro, Vermont: Stephen Daye Press, 1937), 99.

10. Mary Whitcher, *Mary Whitcher's Shaker House-Keeper* (1882; reprint, Pittsfield, Massachusetts: Hancock Shaker Village, n.d.); *Hood's Combined Cook Books* (Lowell, Massachusetts, C.I. Hood & Co., 1875-1885), 31.

11. Sarah Orne Jewett, *The Country of the Pointed Firs and Other Stories* (Garden City, New York: Doubleday, 1956), 39; Jewett, born in 1849, began writing in her 20s. The way of life she described in this story probably dates to the last quarter of the nineteenth century.

12. Anonymous, Manuscript Recipe Book, 1966, 118 BV, Old Sturbridge Village Library, hereafter cited as OSV; Mrs. Dorothea Green from her cousin T.R. Green, Manuscript Recipe Book, 1963, 52, OSV; Mrs. Lydia Maria Child, *The American Frugal Housewife* (Boston: Carter, Hendee, and Co., 1833), 59.

13. Mrs. E.A. Howland, *New England Economical Housekeeper* (Worcester: S.A. Howland, 1845), 62; Eliza Leslie, *Directions for Cookery in its various branches...*, 40th ed., (Philadelphia: Henry Carey Baird, 1851), 55.

14. Women's Christian Temperance Union of Rhode Island, *W.C.T.U. Cook Book—Health and Comfort for the Home* (Phenix, Rhode Island: Gleaner Print, 1905), has one fish chowder recipe that mentions no milk, but two clam chowders do, pages 29, 33, 34; Amy Handy, *What We Cook on Cape Cod* (Sandwich, Massachusetts: Shawnee Press, Inc., for Barnstable Village Improvement Society, 1911), contains no fish chowder, and the two clam chowders call for milk, as does the oyster chowder, pages 5-6; Young People's Society of Christian Endeavor of the Second Congregational Church, *The Stonington Cookbook* (reprint, Watch Hill, Rhode Island: Book and Tackle Shop, 1975) 11-12, has two clam chowder recipes; one from a Mrs. Brayton calls for tomatoes! The other, a more standard local recipe, calls for milk-soaked dry bread.

15. Willard L. Sperry, *Summer Yesterdays in Maine: Memories of Boyhood Vacation Days* (New York: Harper and Brothers, 1941), 68. The first Boston cooking school cookbook by Fannie Farmer contained a recipe called "Connecticut Chowder," which includes tomatoes; I have always wondered from whom in Connecticut Farmer obtained that recipe. My Connecticut Yankee mother from the northwestern hills always referred to tomatoey chowder as New York or Manhattan; add to that the long tradition of even milkless chowders in the southeastern part of the state. Is there a with-tomato vs. without-tomato chowder line running through Connecticut that parallels the New York Yankees vs. Boston Red Sox baseball fan lines?

16. Herman Melville, *Moby Dick* (1851; New York: Mead and Co., 1942), 59.

17. Stanton Garner, ed., *The Captain's Best Mate:: The Journal of Mary Chipman Lawrence on the Whaler Addison, 1856-1860* (Hanover and London: University Press of New England for Brown University, 1966); Elizabeth Dow Leonard, *A Few Reminiscences of My Exeter Life*, ed. Edwards C. Echols, (Exeter, New Hampshire: 2x4 Press, 1972), 222-23.

18. Ibid., 152, 151.

19. "An Excursion," Mystic *Pioneer*, 14 September 1861.

20. Ibid.; "Our Chowder Party," Mystic *Pioneer*, 10 September 1859.

21. Ibid.

34. Mystic *Pioneer*, 14 September 1861.

35. Ibid., 10 September 1859.

36. Ibid.

37. Ibid.

38. Mystic *Pioneer*, 14 September 1861.

39. Elizabeth M. Hall, *Practical American Cookery and Domestic Economy* (New York: Saxton, Barker, and Co., 1860), 120; Mary Virginia Terhune, [pseud. Marion Harland], *The Dinner Year Book* (New York: Charles Scribner's Sons, 1878), 121, 122, 52; Mrs. Bliss, *The Practical Cookbook...* (Philadelphia: J.B. Lippincott & Co., 1864), 29.

40. Mystic *Pioneer*, 14 September 1861.

41. Ibid., 10 September 1859.

42. Ibid., 14 September 1861.

43. New London *Telegram*, 25 August 1873.

44. Mystic *Press*, 27 August 1873. It was a busy week for Beebe with these two events.

45. Nathan Fish, Diary,1868, Coll. 43, G.W. Blunt White Library, Mystic Seaport Museum, hereafter cited as GWBWL.

46. Marjorie Maxson Vignot, Interview with author, 6 February 1987.

47. Frances Jaixen Dodge, Interview with author, May 1985.

48. Edward Knapp, "Smacks of Noank," Typescript, Coll. 171, GWBWL, 239.

49. Mrs. L.G. Abell, *The Complete Domestic Guide Comprising the Mother's Book of Daily Duties and Skillful Housewife's Book* (New York: R.I. Young, 1853), 132.

CHAPTER FOURTEEN

1. Sarah Anna Emery, *Reminiscences of a Nonagenarian* (Newburyport, Massachusetts: William H. Huse & Co., 1879), 245.

2. Susan I. Lesley, *Recollections of My Mother* (New York & Boston: Houghton Mifflin and Co., 1899), 421; Mary Elizabeth Weaver Farnsworth, "Reminiscences of...," Misc. Vol. 155, G.W. Blunt White Library, Mystic Seaport Museum, hereafter cited as GWBWL; Caroline Howard King, *When I Lived in Salem* (Brattleboro, Vermont: Stephen Daye Press, 1937), 105; Mystic *Press*, 14 June 1883; and others.

3. King, *When I Lived in Salem*, 64; Emery, *Reminiscences of a Nonagenarian*, 246.

4. William H. Rowe, *Shipbuilding in Casco Bay, 1727-1890* (Portland: Southworth Press, 1929), 100.

5. John H. Morris, *History of New York Shipyards* (New York: William F. Somers & Co., 1909), 31.

6. Phillip Chadwick Foster Smith, *The Frigate Essex Papers: Building the Salem Frigate 1798-1799* (Salem: Peabody Museum of Salem, 1974), 151.

7. Richard C. McKay, *Some Famous Sailing Ships*

and Their Builder, Donald McKay (Boston: G.P. Putnam, 1928), 48, 304, 318.

8. William Ellery Maxson, Diary, Log 863, GWBWL.

9. William N. Peterson *"Mystic Built": Ships and Shipyards of the Mystic River, Connecticut, 1784-1919* (Mystic: Mystic Seaport Museum, 1989), 169; Mystic *Press*, 3 May 1889; Post Collection, Mystic Seaport Museum Photo Archives, soft negative, 1987.58.2098.

10. Arthur Cleveland Hale, "Cuttyhunk," *New England Magazine* (September 1897): 51.

11. J.H. Merryman, "The United States Life-Saving Service," *Scribner's Monthly* (January 1880): 333.

12. Frances Jaixen Dodge, Conversation with author, 29 May 1986.

13. Mystic *Press*, 14 June 1883.

14. Timothy Dwight, *Travels in New England and New York*, ed. Barbara Miller Solomon, 4 vols., (Cambridge, Massachusetts: Belknap Press of Harvard University Press, 1969), 4:256.

15. Julia Gates to George Gates, 7 June, 30 May 1873, Gates Family Papers, Collection 153, GWBWL.

16. Stonington *Mirror*, 17 January 1891.

17. Elizabeth Hart, Manuscript Recipe Notebook, 1825, Old Saybrook Historical Society, Old Saybrook, Connecticut; John Howard Redfield recalled that yeasted, fruit-filled election cake was also used for weddings, Edmund Delaney, *Life in the Connecticut River Valley, 1800-1840, from the Recollections of John Howard Redfield* (Essex, Connecticut: Connecticut River Museum, 1988), 35.

18. Mrs. Lydia Maria Child, *The American Frugal Housewife* (Boston: Carter, Hendee, and Co., 1833), 72; Mrs. L.G. Abell, *The Complete Domestic Guide Comprising the Mother's Book of Daily Duties and Skillful Housewife's Book* (New York: R.I. Young, 1853), 134; Fanny Merritt Farmer, *The Original Boston Cooking School Cook Book* (1896; facsimile reprint of first edition, New York: Weathervane Books), 432.

19. Louise Conway Belden, *The Festive Tradition: Table Decoration and Desserts in America, 1650-1900* (New York: W.W. Norton and Co. for Winterthur Museum, 1983), 168, 189.

20. Abell, *Complete Domestic Guide*, 216.

21. Edward Everett Knapp "Smacks of Noank," Typescript, Coll. 171, GWBWL, 46.

22. Mystic *Press*, 21, 28 June 1883.

23. Mystic *Pioneer*, 25 June 1859; Mystic *Press*, 6 July 1876.

24. Narragansett *Weekly*, 5 July 1866.

25. Mystic *Press*, 12 July, 2, 9 August 1883, 8 July 1886.

26. Mystic *Pioneer*, 13 August 1859; Mystic *Press*, 28 July 1883.

27. Fannie Card, Manuscript Recipe Notebook, 1879, owned by Anna North Coit, North Stonington, Connecticut; Knapp, "Smacks of Noank," 47-48.

28. Mystic *Press*, 18 January, 19 April 1883, 17 February 1884.

29. Ibid., 29 November 1883.

30. Ibid., 7 February 1884.

31. Ibid., 24 May, 10 March 1876.

32. Ibid., 15 November 1883.

33. Emery, *Reminiscences of a Nonagenarian*, 246.

34. Knapp, "Smacks of Noank," 47-54; 51.

35. Mrs. Winslow, *Mrs. Winslow's Domestic Receipt Book for 1871* (Boston: Jeremiah Curtis & Sons and John I. Brown & Sons, 1871), 13.

36. Maria Parloa, *Miss Parloa's New Cookbook and Marketing Guide* (Boston: Estes and Lauriat, 1880), 317, 316.

CHAPTER FIFTEEN

1. George H. Lewis, "The Maine Lobster as Regional Icon," *Food and Foodways* (1989): 303-16.

2. Wayne M. O'Leary, in his Ph.D. dissertation for the University of Maine, Orono, 1981, "The Maine Sea Fisheries, 1830-1890: The Rise and Fall of a Native Industry," asserts the contrary. Unfortunately he was mislead by early work in food history, which has been superseded in more recent years.

3. Mary Douglas, in *Purity and Danger, An Analysis of Concepts of Pollution and Taboo* (Harmondsworth, England: Penguin Books, 1966), discusses among other things, patterns of food avoidance in various cultures.

4. Todd S. Goodholme, ed., *Goodholme's Domestic Cyclopedia of Practical Information* (New York: C.A. Montgomery, 1885), 202.

5. C. Anne Wilson, *Foods and Drink in Britain, from the Stone Age to the 19th Century* (Chicago: Academy Chicago Publishers, 1991), 30-33, 26.

6. Catherine Beecher and Harriet Beecher Stowe, *The American Woman's Home* (New York: J.B. Ford and Co., 1870), 136.

7. Sarah J. Hale, *New Cook Book, a Practical System* (Philadelphia: T.B. Peterson and Brothers, 1857), 39, 64.

8. Goodholme, *Domestic Cyclopedia*, 202; Beecher & Stowe, *American Woman's Home*, 124; Thomas Webster, *An Encyclopedia of Domestic Economy....* (London: Longman, Brown, Green, and Longmans, 1847), 407.

9. Mildred Maddocks, ed., *The Pure Food Cook Book: The Good Housekeeping Recipes; Just How to Buy; Just How to Cook* (New York: Hearst's International Library, 1914), 145.

10. The preference probably resulted from concerns about freshness, which we will discuss later.

11. Maria Parloa, *Miss Parloa's Young Housekeeper* (Boston: Estes and Lauriat, 1894), 96.

12. Wilson, *Foods and Drink*, 26; Goodholme, *Domestic Cyclopedia*, 203.

13. See Culinary Bibliography for the sources for these preparation methods; I used community cookbooks for information about how ordinary homes used fish.

14. The favored status of a fish can be determined *partly* by the frequency and consistency over time that instructions for preparing it appear. A survey of 45 cookbooks yielded part of the the evidence on which I based this assertion; extremely favorable comments in cookbooks about a given fish also point to its general acceptance and use.

15. Kenneth Martin and Nathan Lipfert, *Lobstering and the Maine Coast* (Bath, Maine: Maine Maritime Museum, 1985), describe the development of lobstering as a viable industry made possible by impounding and live transportation.

16. Howard Burdick, *Along the Shore* (Westerly, Rhode Island: Westerly Historical Society, 1988), 55.

17. Wilson, *Foods and Drink in Britain*, 48; other references to well-smack use in England include Hervey Benham, *The Codbangers* (Colchester, England: Essex County Newspapers, Ltd.,1979); Holdsworth claims that well-smacks were first tried at Harwich in England in 1712, Edmund W.H. Holdsworth, *Deep-Sea Fishing and Fishing Boats* (London: Edward Stanford, 1874), 138; Peter Kalm, *America of 1750, Travels in North America*, 2 vols., (1770 in English; reprint, New York: Dover Publications), 1:127.

18. Benham, *Codbangers*, 110-11.

19. Charles Stevenson, *Preservation of Fishery Products for Food* (Washington, D.C.: Government Printing Office, 1899), 341.

20. Willits Ansel, *Restoration of the Smack Emma C Berry at Mystic Seaport, 1969-1971*. (Mystic: Mystic Seaport Museum, 1973), 9.

21. Benham, *Codbangers*, 114.

22. Amelia Simmons, *American Cookery*, ed. Mary Tolford Wilson, (1796; reprint, New York: Dover, 1984).

23. Hale, *New Cook Book*, 28; Parloa, *Young Housekeeper*, 96.

24. Hale, *New Cook Book*, 29; Parloa, *Young Housekeeper*, 96; Maddocks, *Pure Food Cook Book*, 146.

25. Frank E. Davis Fish Co., *Fish Dainties and Necessities* (Gloucester: Frank E. Davis Fish Co., 1907); Frank E. Davis Fish Co., *Old Gloucester Seafood Recipes from Frank E.Davis the Gloucester Fisherman* (Gloucester: Frank E. Davis Fish Co., n.d. [ca. 1932]), 2.

26. Sarah Anna Emery, *Reminiscences of a Nonagenarian* (Newburyport, Massachusetts: William H. Huse & Co., 1879), 250.

27. *The Report of the Committee on Foreign Relations in Relation to the Rights and Interests of American Fisheries and Fishermen* (Washington, D.C., Government Printing Office, 1887), 22.

28. Statement of Anna North Coit, North Stonington, Connecticut; Louise Curtiss Oliver describing West Cornwall, Connecticut, in the 1930s; Edward A. Ackerman, *New England's Fishing Industry* (Chicago: University of Illinois Press, 1941), 151.

29. Harold A. Innis, *The Cod Fisheries, The History of an International Economy* (New Haven: Yale University Press, 1940), 330; Andrew German, *Down on T Wharf: The Boston Fisheries as Seen Through the Photographs of Henry D. Fisher* (Mystic: Mystic Seaport Museum, 1982), 4-5.

30. Crown Packing Co., *Gloucester Fish for You* (Gloucester: Crown Packing Co., 1911).

31. Edward Knapp, "Smacks of Noank," Typescript, Coll 171, G. W. Blunt White Library, Mystic Seaport Museum; Stevenson, *Preservation of Fishery Products*, 348; John Thomas, Interview, Sound Archives, Mystic Seaport Museum.

32. Howard I. Chapelle, *American Sailing Craft* (New York: Crown, 1936), 66.

33. Ibid., 70.

34. Testimony of Captain Henry Cook of Provincetown, before the Senate Committee on Foreign Relations, 1 October 1886, in response to a question about the effect of increased fresh fishing upon the market for salt fishing, said: "people will use a fresh article before they will a salt one. The demand for salt fish today is not as large in proportion to our population as it was forty years ago, I was then in the fishing business and there was a demand for all our salt fish. There were very few fresh fish then. Our population has increased threefold in the last forty years, yet we do not use much more salt codfish than we did then," *Report of Committee on Foreign Relations*, 48.

35. George Brown Goode, ed., *The Fisheries and Fishery Industries of The United States*, 5 sects., (Washington, D.C.: Government Printing Office, 1887), sect. 5, 1:450-53.

36. Stevenson, *Preservation of Fishery Products*, 370.

37. Ackerman, *New England's Fishing Industry*, 228; *Report of Committee on Foreign Relations*, 8.

38. Maria Parloa, *Miss Parloa's Kitchen Companion* (Boston: Estes and Lauriat, 1887), 84.

39. Maddocks, *Pure Food Cook Book*, 147.

40. Ackerman, *New England's Fishing Industry*, 151.

41. Chauncy M. DePew, ed., *One Hundred Years of American Commerce* (New York: D.O. Haynes Co., 1895), 390; *Report of Committee on Foreign Relations*, 8, 232. Testimony shows that fresh-fish and salt-fish dealers both suspected that frozen fish could easily become some other product, especially frozen fish from Canada, which came into the country duty-free because it was considered fresh, which if preserved would have been dutiable.

42. *Report of Committee on Foreign Relations*, 93.

43. Ibid.

44. Ackerman, *New England's Fishing Industry*, 150.

45. Stevenson, *Preservation of Fishery Products*, 474-506, 493; Wilson, *Foods and Drink in Britain*, 59; Stevenson, *Preservation of Fishery Products*, 501, 504.

46. Sarah Josepha Buell Hale, *Mrs. Hale's Receipts for the Millions* (Philadelphia: T.B. Peterson, 1857), 324.

47. Stevenson, *Preservation of Fishery Products*, 475.

48. Susan Williams, *Savory Suppers and Fashionable Feasts: Dining in Victorian America* (New York: Pantheon Books, in association with the Strong Museum, 1985), 111-12; Stevenson, *Preservation of Fishery Products*, 526; Ackerman, *New England's Fishing Industry*, 189-90.

49. Stevenson, *Preservation of Fishery Products*.

50. Ibid., 511.

51. Ibid.; Henderson, *Practical Cooking*, 108.

52. Ackerman, *New England's Fishing Industry*, 202; Martin and Lipfert, *Lobstering and Maine Coast*, 45.

53. Ackerman, *New England's Fishing Industry*, 186.

54. Ibid., 185, 186.

55. Ibid., 187.

56. Knapp, "Smacks of Noank," 224.

57. Emery, *Reminiscences of Nonagenarian*, 111; Mystic *Press*, 3 October 1878.

58. Maria Parloa, *Miss Parloa's New Cook Book and Marketing Guide* (Boston: Estes and Lauriat, 1880), 107; and others; Shute and Merchant, *Receipts for Cooking Fish*, 8th ed., (Gloucester: Shute and Merchant, 1895), 12.

59. *Compact Oxford English Dictionary*, 998.

60. Parloa, *New Cook Book*; Henderson, *Practical Cooking*, and others.

61. Shute & Merchant, *Receipts for Cooking Fish*, 3.

62. *Report of Committee on Foreign Relations*, 9.

63. Stevenson, *Preservation of Fishery Products*, 403.

64. James R.Pringle, comp. and ed., *The Book of the Three Hundredth Anniversary of the Foundation of the Mass Bay Colony at Cape Ann in 1623 and the Fiftieth Year of the Incorporation of Gloucester as a City* (Gloucester: Publication Board of the 300th Anniversary Executive Committee, 1924), 219-20.

65. Mrs. Lydia Maria Child, *The American Frugal Housewife* (Boston: Carter, Hendee, and Co., 1833), 60; and others; Shute and Merchant, *Receipts for Cooking Fish*.

66. Amy Handy, *What We Cook on Cape Cod* (Sandwich, Massachusetts: Shawmee Press Inc., for Barnstable Village Improvement Society, 1911), 10-11; Women's Christian Temperance Union of Rhode Island, *W.C.T.U. Cook Book— Health and Comfort for the Home* (Phenix, R.I.: Gleaner Print, 1905), 29; and others; Mrs. Mary J. Lincoln, *Mrs. Lincoln's Boston Cook Book* (Boston: Little Brown, and Co., 1913), 171; Young People's Society of Christian Endeavor of the Second Congregational Church, *The Stonington Cookbook* (reprint, Watch Hill, Rhode Island: Book and Tackle Shop, 1975), 15.

67. Stevenson, *Preservation of Fishery Products*, 509.

68. Andrew German, "Otter Trawling Comes to America: The Bay State Fishing Company, 1905-1938," *American Neptune* (Spring 1984): 114-31; *Atlantic Fisherman* (February 1921): 3.

69. German, "Otter Trawling," 127; Frank H. Wood *The Story of Forty Fathom Fish* (Boston: Bay State Fishing Co., 1931), 5, 7.

70. Ackerman, *New England's Fishing Industry*, 227; Innis, *Cod Fisheries*, 435; Louis Szathmary, ed., *Along the Northern Border: Cookery in Idaho, Minnesota, North Dakota* (New York: Arno Press, 1973); this volume contains reprints of community cookbooks from Moscow, Idaho, Presbyterian Ladies Aid, 1931; Minnesota Public Library Staff Association, 1928; and Grand Forks, North Dakota, YMCA, 1924.

71. Major exceptions were rural populations who were close to agricultural areas, or who produced their own food. The farther the growing urban and suburban population were from the source of their food, the less likely they were to eat organ meats or deal with their meat and fish whole.

72. Wilson, *Foods and Drink in Britain*, 32.

73. Hale, *New Cook Book*; E.E. Hale, "What Shall We Have for Dinner?" *Atlantic Monthly* (September 1864): 369.

74. Wilson, *Foods and Drink in Britain*, 26, 31.

75. Ibid., 35. Sealmeat was also allowed on meatless days.

76. Ibid., 46, 58.

77. Robert Albion et al, *New England and the Sea* (Mystic: Mystic Seaport Museum, 1972), 27; Bernard Bailyn, *The New England Merchants in the 17th Century* (New York: Harper and Row, 1955), 80-83.

78. Goode, *Fisheries*, sect. 5, 1:660.

79. Timothy Dwight, *Travels in New England and New York*, ed. Barbara Miller Solomon, 4 vols., (1821-22; Cambridge, Massachusetts: Belknap Press of Harvard University Press, 1969), 33; Dwight was unhappy with Newport; he wrote, "The men of wealth live by loaning their money without entering in any great degree into active, useful business"—the poor catch fish—"This state of things is unnecessary and unhappy."

80. Edward Chapman, *New England Village Life* (Cambridge, Massachusetts: Riverside Press, 1937), 39; Goode, *Fisheries*, sect. 5, 1:609.

81. Emery, *Reminiscences of Nonagenarian*, 250.

82. Daniel Vickers, "Work and Life on the Fishing Periphery," in *Seventeenth Century New England* (Boston: Colonial Society of Massachusetts, 1984), 83-117.

83. Barnard, quoted in Lorenzo Sabine, *Report on the Principal Fisheries of the American Seas prepared for the Treasury Dept. of the U.S.* (Washington, D.C.: Robert Armstrong, 1853), 129, 102, 128; quoting an account of the loss of 20 Salem fishing vessels to Indian attack, which the writer felt could have been prevented if only the fishermen had tried.

84. Vickers, "Work and Life," 99, 106-10.

85. Ibid., 115; Emery, *Reminiscences of Nonagenarian*, 228; Dwight, *Travels in New England*, 1:164.

86. Goode, *Fisheries*, sect. 5, 1:10-11.

87. Ibid., 8-9, 71.

88. "The Logical Remedy for Under-Consumption," *Atlantic Fisherman* (February 1921): 3.

89. *Atlantic Fisherman* (March 1921): 3.

90. Ibid., 9.

91. Frank E. Davis Co., Descriptive Price List, Autumn 1917, Cape Ann Historical Association, Gloucester.

92. J.H. Mathews, "Problems of the Commercial Fisheries from Producer to the Consumer," *Transactions of the American Fisheries Society*, vol. 51, (Washington, D.C.: American Fisheries Society, 1922), 200.

93. Crown Packing Co., *Gloucester Fish for You*.

94. Mathews, "Problems of Commercial Fisheries," 195.

95. Arthur L. Millett, "Adequate Fish Inspection: A Means to Better Fish for the Consumer and to Increased Fish Food Consumption," *Transactions of the American Fisheries Society*, vol. 50, (Washington, D.C.: American Fisheries Society, 1921), 160, 157.

96. Mathews, "Problems of Commerical Fisheries," 195.

97. Davis, *Fish Dainties and Necessities*; Millett, "Adequate Fish Inspection," 154.

98. Davis, *Fish Dainties and Necessities*.

99. Wood, *Forty Fathom Fish*, 22.

100. A. B. Alexander, H.F. Moore, and W.C. Kendall, "Report on the Otter-Trawl Fishery" in U.S. Fish Commission, *Report of the U.S. Commissioner of Fisheries for* the Fiscal Year Ending June 30, *1914* (Washington, D.C.: Government Printing Office, 1915), 90-93, cited in German "Otter Trawling," 123; Lewis Radcliffe, "The Development of Markets for Neglected Fishes," *Transactions of the American Fisheries Society*, vol. 47, (Columbus, Ohio: American Fisheries Society, 1918), 65-66.

101. Radcliffe, "Markets for Neglected Fishes," 67.

102. Millett, "Adequate Fish Inspection," 162.

103. Ibid., 156.

104. Davis, Price List, 1917.

105. Davis, *Old Gloucester Seafood Recipes*.

106. William Bradford, *Bradford's History of Plymouth Plantation, Original Narratives of Early American History*, (New York: Barnes and Noble, 1908), 115.

107. John Winthrop, *Journal, Original Narratives of Early American History*, 2 vols., (New York: Barnes and Noble, 1908,), 2, 91.

108. Edward Johnson, *Wonder-Working Providence, Original Narratives of Early American History*, (New York: Barnes and Noble, 1910), 77-78.

109. Child, *American Frugal Housewife*, 60; Henderson, *Practical Cooking*, 110.

CHAPTER SIXTEEN

1. Timothy Dwight, *Travels in New England and New York*, ed. Barbara Miller Solomon, 4 vols., (1821-22; Cambridge, Massachusetts: Belknap Press of Harvard University Press, 1969), 33-34.

2. Georgiana Hill, *How to Cook Potatoes, Apples, Eggs, and Fish* (New York: Dick and Fitzgerald 1869), 109; Mary Virginia Terhune, [pseud. Marion Harland], *The Dinner Year Book* (New York: Charles Scribner's Sons, 1878); and others; Maria Parloa, *Miss Parloa's Young Housekeeper* (Boston: Estes and Lauriat, 1894), 101.

3. Parloa, *Young Housekeeper*, 104, 106, 107; Maria Parloa, *Miss Parloa's New Cook Book and Marketing Guide* (Boston: Estes and Lauriat, 1880), 109.

4. Harland, *Dinner Year Book*, 193; Wesley George Pierce, *Goin' Fishing: The Story of the Deep-Sea Fishermen of New England* (1934; reprint, Camden, Maine: International Marine Publishing Co., 1989), 145. Modern cod, halibut and salmon steaks are cut traditionally, but the size of fish available in the market today is generally quite a bit smaller than were the same species in the 1800s; Parloa, *Young Housekeeper*, 101; [Elizabeth H.] Putnam, *Mrs. Putnam's Receipt Book and Young House-keepers Assistant* (Boston: Ticknor, Reed, and Fields, 1849), 16-19; and others.

5. Parloa, *Young Housekeeper*, 96; Parloa, *New Cook Book*, 106; Mary F. Henderson, *Practical Cooking and Dinner Giving* (New York: Harper and Brothers, 1882), 105.

6. Hill, *How to Cook*, 109; Parloa, *New Cook Book*, 115.

7. Mildred Maddocks, ed., *The Pure Food Cook Book: The Good Housekeeping Recipes; Just How to Buy; Just How to Cook* (New York: Hearst's International Library, 1914), 146; Henderson, *Practical Cooking*, 119, 121; Mrs. Lydia Maria Child, *The American Frugal Housewife* (Boston: Carter, Hendee, and Co., 1833), 59, 58; Fannie Merritt Farmer, *Boston Cooking School Cookbook* (1896; facsimile reprint of first edition, New York: Weathervane Books), 236-37; Parloa, *Young Housekeeper*, 96; Mary Lincoln, *Boston Cook Book* (Boston: Little Brown and Company, 1913), 187; *Good Housekeeping's Book of Menus, Recipes, and Household Discoveries* (New York: Good Housekeeping, 1922), 203; and community cookbooks like Women's Christian Temperance Union of Rhode Island, *W.C.T.U. Cook Book—Health and Comfort for the Home* (Phenix, Rhode Island: The Gleaner Print, 1905), 30; Amy Handy, *What We Cook on Cape Cod* (Sandwich, Massachusetts: Shawmee Press, for Barnstable Village Improvement Society, 1911), 34; *Penobscot View Grange Cook Book* (Glencove, Maine: Penobscot View Grange No. 388, n.d.) 7.

8. Child, *American Frugal Housewife*, 59; Putnam, *Receipt Book*, 19; Farmer, *Boston Cooking School*, 210; Lincoln, *Boston Cook Book*, 172-73.

9. Great numbers of older Mystic Seaport visitors exclaimed in recognition when they saw me cook salt pork for salt fish dinners in the Buckingham House. Anna North Coit in North Stonington, recalls the combination, and still makes creamed salt cod to put on jonnycakes; my mother similarly recalls the combination from her childhood in the 1910s and 1920s; Marjorie Standish, *Cooking Down East* (Portland, Maine: Maine Sunday Telegram, 1969), 30-31, and Willan C. Roux, *What's Cooking Down in Maine* (Orrs Island, Maine: Orr's Island Press, 1964), 47-48, also specify this manner of cooking salt cod; Rev. Ivan Jesperson, *Fat Back and Molasses* (St. John's, Newfoundland: author, 1974), 1, 2.

10. Maria Parloa, *Miss Parloa's Kitchen Companion*, 19th ed., (New York: Estes; Boston: Lauriat, 1887), 81.

11. Parloa, *New Cook Book*, 113.

12. Handy, *What We Cook on Cape Cod*; W.C.T.U. *Cook Book*; Young People's Society of Christian Endeavor of the Second Congregational Church, *The Stonington Cookbook* (reprint, Watch Hill, Rhode Island: Book and Tackle Shop, 1975); The High Street Cookbook in *Hood's Combined Cook Books* (Lowell, Massachusetts: C.I. Hood & Co., 1875-1885); and others.

13. Hill, *How to Cook*; Isabella Beeton, *Beeton's Every-day Cookery and Housekeeping Book: A Practical and Useful Guide for All Mistresses and Servants,...* (New York: D. Appleton, ca. 1875), 82. Beeton's illustration of a cod head and shoulder show the head with the head fins and a couple of inches of back.

14. William Strickland, *Journal of a Tour in the USA, 1794-1795* (Cooperstown: New York State Historical Association, 1971), 27.

15. Lorenzo Sabine, *Report on The Principal Fisheries of the American Seas prepared for the Treasury Dept. of the U.S.* (Washington, D.C.: Robert Armstrong, 1853), 197; George H. Proctor, *The Fisheries of Gloucester* (Gloucester: Proctor Brothers, 1876), 38; John D. Whidden, *Old Sailing Ship Days* (Boston: Charles E. Lauriat

Co., 1925), 118.

16. Hannah Glasse, *Art of Cookery Made Plain and Easy...* (London: author, 1747), 90, 57; [Maria Eliza Rundell], *The Experienced American Housekeeper; or, Domestic Cookery* (New York: Johnstone and VanNorden, 1823), 15; Maria Eliza Rundell, *New System of Domestic Cookery: founded upon Principles of Economy...*, 67th London ed., (Philadelphia: Carey and Hart, 1844), 35; Frank E. Davis Fish Company, *Correct Recipes for Sea Food Cookery including the Preparation of All of Davis' Fish Products* (Gloucester: Frank E. Davis Fish Co., n.d.), 4.

17. Georgia Maria Blanchard, "Our Wedding Trip Around Cape Horn," Typescript, Family Papers, Penobscot Marine Museum, Searsport, Maine, 5; Frederick Laurence Sturgis, *Coasting Passenger* (Concord, Massachusetts: Charles S. Morgan, 1968), 40; I first learned about tongues and cheeks from John Gambell and Martha Murray, who learned to cook them when they taught on the coast of Labrador; then again shortly after from Captain Francis Bowker, who occasionally got a bucket of cod's heads from the fish market from which he cut tongues and cheeks. Mystic Seaport's Special Demonstration Squad used to save tongues and cheeks for Buckingham House cooks. They are excellent eating.

18. *W.C.T.U. Cook Book*, 29; Lincoln, *Boston Cook Book*, 173; Davis, *Correct Recipes*, 7.

19. Gervase Markham, *The English Housewife*, ed. Michael R. Best, (1615; reprint, Kingston and Montreal: McGill-Queen's University Press, 1986); Karen Hess, *Martha Washington's Booke of Cookery* (New York: Columbia University Press, 1981).

20. George Brown Goode, ed., *The Fisheries and Fishery Industries of The United States*, 5 sects., (Washington, D.C.: Government Printing Office, 1887), sect. 5, 1: 667-70; sources used throughout this chapter for information on the natural history and usage of fish include Alfred Perlmutter, *Guide to Marine Fishes* (New York: New York University Press, 1961); George Brown Goode and Theodore Gill, *American Fishes: A Popular Treatise Upon the Game and Food Fishes of North America*, new ed., (1887; Boston: L.C. Page and Co., 1903); Alan Davidson, *North Atlantic Seafood* (New York: Viking Press, 1979).

21. Goode, Fisheries, sect. 5, 1:670.

22. Charles L. Cutting, *Fish Saving* (New York: Philosophical Library, 1956), 7;

Howard Burdick, *Along the Shore* (Westerly, Rhode Island: Westerly Historical Society, 1988), 21.

23. Francis Endicott, "Striped Bass," *Scribner's Monthly* 21 (March 1881): 698-708.

24. Goode and Gill, *American Fishes*, 22-29; Davidson, *North Atlantic Seafood*, 92.

25. Thomas Robinson Hazard, *The Jonnycake Papers of "Shepard Tom" together with Reminiscences of Narragansett Schools of former Days* (Boston: Subscribers, 1918), 305; U.S. Commission for Fish and Fisheries, *Report on the Sea Fisheries of the South Coast of New England in 1871 and 1872* (Washington, D.C.: Government Printing Office, 1873), 251; Goode, *Fisheries*, sect. 5, 1:604-06; Goode and Gill, *American Fishes*, 162; Peter H. Felker, *The Grocer's Manual* (Claremont, New Hampshire: Claremont Manufacturing, 1878), 23.

26. Davidson, *North Atlantic Seafood*, 232; Goode, *Fisheries*, sect. 5, 2.

27. Goode, *Fisheries*, sect. 5, 2:236, 239.

28. Ibid., sect. 5, 2:584; George Hawley, Description of a Fishing Voyage by the Sloop *Planet*, 1834, VFM 1488, G.W. Blunt White Library, Mystic Seaport Museum, hereafter cited as GWBWL.

29. Goode, *Fisheries*, sect. 5, 2:588, 585.

30. Felker, *Grocer's Manual*, 61-62; Goode, *Fisheries*, sect. 5, 2:608, 614-15.

31. Goode, *Fisheries*, sect. 5, 2:593.

32. Edward A. Ackerman, *New England's Fishing Industry* (Chicago: University of Illinois Press, 1941), 254, 258, 256.

33. Edward Everett Knapp, "Smacks of Noank," Typescript, Coll. 171, GWBWL.

34. Caroline Howard King, *When I Lived in Salem* (Brattleboro, Vermont: Stephen Daye Press, 1937), 98.

35. Davidson, *North Atlantic Seafood*, 54; C. Anne Wilson, *Foods and Drink in Britain, from the Stone Age to the 19th Century* (Chicago: Academy Chicago Publishers, 1991), 35.

36. Sabine, *Report on Principal Fisheries*, 173.

37. Goode, *Fisheries*, sect. 5, 1:214; Felker, *Grocer's Manual*, 67.

38. Thomas G. Fessenden, *The Husbandman and Housewife: A Collection of Valuable Receipts...* (Bellows Falls, Vermont: Bill Blake and Co., 1820), 33-34.

39. Charles Stevenson, *Preservation of Fishery Products for Food* (Washington, D.C.: Government Printing Office, 1899) 390-94.

40. Wilson, *Fooods and Drink*, 34.

41. *The Report of the Committee on Foreign Relations in Relation to the Rights and Interests of American Fisheries and Fishermen* (Washington, D.C.: Government Printing Office, 1887), 79; Felker, *Grocer's Manual*, 67.

42. Ackerman, *New England's Fishing Industry*, 164.

43. Child, *American Frugal Housewife*, 59; Putnam, *Receipt Book*, 23, King, *When I Lived in Salem*, 98; Blanchard, "Our Wedding Trip," 5.

44. Putnam, *Receipt Book*, 23.

45. Child, *American Frugal Housewife*, 59.

46. James Baughman, *Mallorys of Mystic* (Middletown, Connecticut: Wesleyan University Press for Mystic Seaport Museum, 1972), 169; Mrs. Leonard Norwood, quoted by Peter Coope in Memo to David Brierly, William Peterson, J. Revell Carr, and Ben Fuller, 2 October 1978, Mystic Seaport Museum.

47. *Committee on Foreign Relations*, 48.

48. By titled recipes I mean recipes with a distinctive name, not the kinds of recipe that merely instruct a cook to cook preparing a general class of foods, for example, "Cod with Lobster Sauce" versus "To prepare Salt Cod"; Harland, *Dinner Year Book*, 700; Parloa, *New Cook Book*, 105; Mrs. H.W. Beecher, *All Around the House; or, How to Make Homes Happy* (New York: D. Appleton & Co., 1878), 392; Amelia Simmons, *American Cookery*, ed. Mary Tolford Wilson, (1796; reprint New York: Dover, 1984); Child, *American Frugal Housewife*; *Hood's Combined Cook Books*; Mrs. L.G. Abell, *The Complete Domestic Guide Comprising the Mother's Book of Daily Duties and Skillful Housewife's Book* (New York: R.I. Young, 1853); Mary Whitcher, *Mary Whitcher's Shaker Housekeeper* (1882; reprint, Pittsfield, Massachusetts: Hancock Shaker Village, n.d.); and others. Simmons included a recipe "to dress Codfish," but the instructions indicate a salt fish.

49. *Compact Oxford English Dictionary*, 1:604; Lincoln, *Boston Cook Book*, 170.

50. Putnam, *Receipt Book*; *Oxford English Dictionary*, 2:2684.

51. Goode, Fisheries, sect. 5, 2:635.

52. Ackerman, *New England's Fishing Industry*, 242-43.

53. Parloa, *New Cook Book*, 45; Thomas F. De Voe, *The Market Assistant containing a brief description of every article of human food sold in the markets...* (1867; reprint, Detroit: Gale Research, Book Tower, 1975), 303.

54. Davidson, *North Atlantic Seafood*, 67; Felker, *Grocer's Manual*, 84.

55. Zephaniah Pease, ed., *Life in New Bedford 100 Years Ago, A Chronicle of the Social, Religious, and Commercial History of the Period in a Diary Kept by Joseph R. Anthony* (New Bedford: Old Dartmouth Historical Society, 1925), 82, 72, 73; Hazard, *Jonnycake Papers*, 25.

56. Goode, *Fisheries*, sect. 5, 1:496; Felker, *Grocer's Manual*, 86.

57. Parloa, *Kitchen Companion*, 81; Davidson, *North Atlantic Seafood*, 150.

58. Davidson, *North Atlantic Seafood*, 150; Pierce, *Goin' Fishing*, 219.

59. Pierce, *Goin' Fishing*, 149; Charles Stevenson, *Preservation of Fishery Products*, 363; Goode, *Fisheries*, sect. 5, 1:356-57; Goode and Gill, *American Fishes*, p. 358; Davidson, *North Atlantic Seafood*, 60.

60. Goode, *Fisheries*, sect. 5, 1:234, 239, 240; Felker, *Grocer's Manual*, 103.

61. Andrew German, *Down on T Wharf: The Boston Fisheries as Seen Through the Photographs of Henry D. Fisher* (Mystic: Mystic Seaport Museum, 1982), 144; Stevenson, *Preservation of Fishery Products*, 500.

62. W.H. Bishop, "Fish and Men in the Maine Islands," *Harpers's New Monthly Magazine* (August 1880): 336-52; 340; Putnam, *Receipt Book*, 16-19; Parloa, *New Cook Book*, 105.

63. J. Reynolds, M.D., *Peter Gott, The Cape Ann Fisherman* (Gloucester: Proctor and Brothers, 1856), 98; Goode, *Fisheries*, sect. 5, 1: 241.

64. Felker, *Grocer's Manual*, 103; Goode, *Fisheries*, sect. 5, 1:243.

65. George H. Proctor, *Fishermen's Memorial and Record Book* (Gloucester: Proctor Brothers, 1873), 130.

66. Sabine, *Report on Principal Fisheries*, 197; "A Struggle for Shelter," *Atlantic Monthly* (April 1866): 461.

67. Goode and Gill, *American Fishes*, 307-14.

68. Goode, *Fisheries*, sect. 5, 1, gives two dates: "They first came into demand about 1830," 33-34; and "Before 1825, however, a considerable demand for halibut sprang up in Boston," 29; Proctor, *Fisheries of Gloucester*, 38.

69. Goode, *Fisheries*, sect. 5, 1:9; Pierce, *Goin' Fishing*, 132-33.

70. Goode, *Fisheries*, sect. 5, 1:18, 19.

71. Sabine, *Report on Principal Fisheries*, 197.

72. Ibid., 197; Parloa, *New Cook Book*, 42; Felker, *Grocer's Manual*, 104.

73. Goode, *Fisheries*, sect. 5, 1:91; Proctor, *Fisheries of Gloucester*, 38.

74. Putnam, *Receipt Book*, 21; Proctor, *Fisherman's Own Book*, 133; Parloa, *Kitchen Companion*;. Abell, *Complete Domestic Guide*, 151; Putnam, *Receipt Book*, 20.

75. Goode and Gill, *American Fishes*, 382-83.

76. *Committee on Foreign Relations*, 79.

77. Sabine, *Report on Principal Fisheries*, 192-93, 194, 196.

78. Stevenson, *Preservation of Fishery Products*, 478-89; Goode, *Fisheries*, sect. 5, 1:480.

79. Goode, Fisheries, sect. 5, 1:486, 478, 488; Cutting, *Fish Saving*, 276; Felker, *Grocer's Manual*, 23; Stevenson, *Preservation of Fishery Products*, 486.

80. Stevenson, *Preservation of Fishery Products*, 488.

81. Cutting, *Fish Saving*, 286.

82. Goode, Fisheries, sect. 5, 1:473-75.

83. Ibid., 433.

84. Ibid., 456.

85. Ibid., 426, 432.

86. Mike Brown, *The Great Lobster Chase* (Camden, Maine: International Marine Publishing Co., 1985; Kenneth Martin and Nathan Lipfert, *Lobstering and the Maine Coast* (Bath: Maine Maritime Museum, 1985).

87. Edward Higginson, *New England's Plantation, with Sea Journal and Other Writings* (Salem: Essex Print and Book Club, 1908), 97.

88. Peter Kalm, *The America of 1750, Peter Kalm's Travels in North America*, ed. Adolph Bensen, 2 vols., (1770 in English; reprint, New York: Dover Publications, 1964), 1:127; Goode, *Fisheries*, sect. 5, 2:703.

89. Goode, *Fisheries*, sect. 5, 2:704.

90. Reynolds, *Peter Gott*, 125.

91. Martin and Lipfert, *Lobstering and the Maine Coast*, 33; Goode, *Fisheries*, sect. 5, 2:701, 681.

92. Goode, *Fisheries*, sect. 5, 2:787.

93. Martin and Lipfert, *Lobstering and the Maine Coast*, 43-45; Goode, *Fisheries*, sect. 5, 2:710-11.

94. Goode, *Fisheries*, sect. 5, 2:787-88.

95. Ibid., sect. 5, 2:659; Felker, *Grocer's Manual*, 146,147; New York *Times*, 9 April 1881, 4.

96. Burdick, *Along the Shore*, 57-58.

97. Parloa, *Young Housekeeper*, 108.

98. Sabine, *Report on Principal Fisheries*, 178-79.

99. Child, *American Frugal Housewife*, 58, 60.

100. Pierce, *Goin' Fishing*, 99, 28-29; Sabine, *Report on Principal Fisheries*.

101. Lincoln, *Boston Cook Book*, 159.

102. Putnam, *Receipt Book*, 21.

103. Goode, *Fisheries*, sect. 5, 1:496; Stevenson, *Preservation of Fishery Products*, 505.

104. Davidson, *North Atlantic Seafood*, 216; Thomas Webster, *An Encyclopedia of Domestic Economy* (London: Longman Brown, Green, Longmans, 1844), 436.

105. Irving A. Field, "Utilization of Sea Mussels for Food," *Transactions of the American Fisheries Society* (Washington, D.C.: American Fisheries Society, 1911), 159-168, 161.

106. Goode, *Fisheries*, sect. 5, 1:620, 619, 621; Hess, *Martha Washington's Booke of Cookery*, 175.

107. In my town of Islesboro, the clam flats are practically bereft of clams, and here clambakes staged in the summer largely feature mussels with the lobsters and corn; the mussels are generally accepted.

108. E.E. Hale, "What Shall We Have for Dinner?" *Atlantic Monthly* (September 1864): 369.

109. Wilson, *Foods and Drink in Britain*, 48.

110. Kalm, *America of 1750*, 126.

111. Dwight, *Travels in New England*, 2:358; Goode, *Fisheries*, sect. 5, 2:559; for a thorough treatment of oystering see John Kochiss, *Oystering from New York to Boston* (Middletown, Connecticut: Wesleyan University Press for Mystic Seaport Museum, 1974).

112. Goode, *Fisheries*, sect. 5, 2:514; Kochiss, *Oystering*, 9; Ackerman, *New England's Fishing Industry*, 243.

113. Edward G. Porter, *Rambles in Old Boston, New England* (Boston: Cupples, Upham and Co., 1887) quoted in Kochiss, *Oystering*, 275.

114. Goode, *Fisheries*, sect. 5, 2:546.

115. Kochiss, *Oystering*, 49; Charles Mallory, Probate Inventory, photocopy in Curatorial Department, Mystic Seaport Museum.

116. Henderson, *Practical Cooking*, 113; Parloa, *New Cook Book*, 118.

117. Porter in Kochiss, *Oystering*, 275; Alvin F. Harlow, *Old Bowery Days* (New York: D. Appleton and Co., 1931), 218.

118. Frederick Whymper, *The Fisheries of the World, an Illustrated and Descriptive Record of the International Fisheries Exhibition, 1883* (London: Cassel and Company, Ltd. 1884), 76-77.

119. Kalm, *America of 1750*, 1:125-26.

120. Abell, *Complete Domestic Guide*, 151; Stevenson, *Preservation of Fishery Products*, 353-54.

121. Davidson, *North Atlantic Seafood*, 225; Ladies Association of the First Presbyterian Church, Houston, Texas, *The First Texas Cookbook*, (1883; reprint, Austin, Texas: Eakin Press, 1986), 27-29; Julia Gates, Manuscript Recipe Notebook, 1857-1930, Mystic River Historical Society, Mystic, Connecticut.

122. Parloa, *New Cook Book*; Henderson, *Practical Cooking*.

123. Whymper, *Fisheries of the World*, 78.

124. Pease, *Life in New Bedford*, 91; Dana Story, *Frame Up!* (Barre, Mass.: Barre Publishers, 1964), 90.

125. Reynolds, *Peter Gott*, 120; Felker, *Grocer's Manual*, 186.

126. William Warner, *Distant Water: The Fate of the North Atlantic Fisherman* (Boston & Toronto: Little, Brown, & Co., 1977), 10.

127. Samuel Bagnall, "The Fisherman's Daughter; that lives o'er the water," in Proctor Brothers, comp., *Fishermen's Ballads, and Songs of the Sea* (Gloucester: Proctor Brothers, 1874), 11-12.

128. Wilson, *Foods and Drink in Britain*, 36-37; Goode, *Fisheries*, sect. 5, 1:663; Catherine Carlson, Paper on Salmon, delivered at 1993 Dublin Seminar for New England Folklife, Deerfield, New Hampshire.

129. John Pendleton Farrow, *History of Islesboro, Maine* (Bangor: Thomas W. Burr, 1893), 73; Whymper, *Fisheries of the World*, 75.

130. Goode, *Fisheries*, sect. 5, 1:706; William N. Peterson and Peter M. Coope, *Historic Buildings at Mystic Seaport Museum* (Mystic: Mystic Seaport Museum, 1985), 91-93.

131. Farmer, *Boston Cooking School*, 13; Goode, *Fisheries*, sect. 5, 1:683; Stevenson, *Preservation of Fishery Products*, 493.

132. Eliza Leslie, *Directions for Cookery, Being a System*... (Philadelphia: E.I. Carey and A. Hart, 1837), 46.

133. Felker, *Grocer's Manual*, 207; Farmer, *Boston Cooking School*, 136; Hale, "What Shall We Have for Dinner?" 64; Shute and Merchant Co., *Receipts for Cooking Fish*, 8th ed., (Gloucester: Shute and Merchant Co., 1895), 33.

134. Putnam, *Receipt Book*, 20; Felker, *Grocer's Manual*, 206.

135. Felker, *Grocer's Manual*, 213.

136. Davidson, *North Atlantic Seafood*, 26; Goode, *Fisheries*, sect. 5, 1:490, 491; Felker, *Grocer's Manual*, 213; Frank E. Davis Co., Descriptive Price List, 1917, Cape Ann Historical Association, Gloucester, Massachusetts.

137. Susan Williams, *Savory Suppers and Fashionable Feasts: Dining in Victorian America* (New York: Pantheon Books, in association with the Strong Museum, 1985), 111-12.

138. Ackerman, *New England's Fishing Industry*, 192.

139. U.S. Fish Commission, *Report of the Commissioner for 1879* (Washington, D.C.: Government Printing Office, 1882), 666; Goode, *Fisheries*, sect. 5, 2:575.

140. Goode, *Fisheries*, sect. 5, 2:572.

141. Webster, *Encyclopedia of Domestic Economy*, 436; Parloa, *New Cook Book*, 48; Handy, *What We Cook on Cape Cod*, 13; Lincoln, *Boston Cook Book*, 181.

142. Davidson, *North Atlantic Seafood*, 32; John Winthrop, *Journal*, *Original Narratives of Early American History*, 2 vols., (New York: Barnes and Noble, 1908), 1:76.

143. Goode, *Fisheries*, sect. 5, 1:665.

144. Ibid., 660.

145. Whymper, *Fisheries of the World*, 314.

146. De Voe, *The Market Assistant*, 202.

147. John Kochiss, "A Report on the Connecticut River Shad Fishery," August 1975, RF 299, GWBWL.

148. Ibid., 25.

149. "Shad," a brochure distributed by the Connecticut River Museum in Essex, Connecticut, says Peter Andreotti initiated the filleting of shad in 1922 in New York City, but a filleting demonstrator at the museum claimed that around 1924 "Mike" a Polish immigrant dishwasher at the Municipal Lunch, near City Hall in Hartford, learned it from watching the owner who knew how to bone shad, and *that* was the beginning of the filleting of shad; Kochiss, "Report on Shad Fishery," 3.

150. Whymper, *Fisheries of the World*, 314; *Dictionary of American English*, 1759; *Compact Oxford English Dictionary*, 2:2196.

151. Goode, *Fisheries*, sect. 5, 2:800-01; Parloa, *New Cook Book*, 46.

152. Parloa, *New Cook Book*, 115-16.

153. Wilson, *Foods and Drink in Britain*, 44; Davidson, *North Atlantic Seafood*, 178-79.

154. Felker, *Grocer's Manual*, 228; Stevenson, *Preservation of Fishery Products*, 501; Abell, *Complete Domestic Guide*, 85; Parloa, *Kitchen Companion*, 175.

155. Goode, *Fisheries*, sect. 5, 1:323; Felker, *Grocer's Manual*, 245; Charles Dana Gibson, "History of the Swordfishery of the Northwestern Atlantic," *American Neptune* (January 1981): 43.

156. Goode, *Fisheries*, sect. 5, 1:325; Gibson, "Swordfishery," 36.

157. Pierce, *Goin' Fishing*, 217; Davidson, *North Atlantic Seafood*, 134.

158. Parloa, *New Cook Book*, 44; Lincoln, *Boston Cook Book*, 492.

159. Putnam, *Receipt Book*, 22; Abell, *Complete Domestic Guide*, 151.

160. Parloa, *New Cook Book*, 88.

161. Davidson, *North Atlantic Seafood*, 45.

162. Felker, *Grocer's Manual*, 269; Davidson, *North Atlantic Seafood*, 130, says the "cooking of fresh tuna is at its best" in Italy.

163. Davidson, *North Atlantic Seafood*, 144; Parloa, *New Cook Book*, 114; Handy, *What We Cook on Cape Cod*, 11; Whitcher, *Shaker Housekeeper*, 19.

164. Davidson, *North Atlantic Seafood*, 63.

BIBLIOGRAPHY

A

Ackerman, Edward A. *New England's Fishing Industry*. Chicago: University of Illinois Press, 1941.

Albion, Robert, William A. Baker, and Benjamin W. Labaree. *New England and the Sea*. Mystic, Connecticut: Mystic Seaport Museum, 1972.

Ansel, Willits D. *Restoration of the Smack Emma C Berry at Mystic Seaport Museum, 1969-1971*. Mystic, Connecticut: Marine Historical Association, 1973.

Appleton's Annual Cyclopedia. New York: D. Appleton and Company, 1889.

Ashley, Clifford. *The Yankee Whaler*. Boston: Houghton, Mifflin Company, 1938.

B

Babson, John J. *History of the Town of Gloucester, Cape Ann, including the Town of Rockport*. 350th Anniversary Edition with Introduction and Historical Review by Joseph E. Garland. Gloucester: Peter Smith, 1972.

Bailey, Reverend James. *History of the Seventh-Day Baptist General Conference: From Its Origin, September 1802 to its Fifty Third Session, September 1865*. Toledo, Ohio: S. Bailey & Company, 1866.

Bailyn, Bernard. *The New England Merchants in the 17th Century*. New York: Harper and Row, 1955.

Bathe, Basil W., and Alan Villiers. *Visual Encyclopedia of Nautical Terms Under Sail*. New York: Crown Publishers, 1978.

Baughman, James. *The Mallorys of Mystic*. Middletown: Wesleyan University Press, 1972.

Bedford, F.G.D., R.N. *The Sailor's Pocket Book: A Collection of Practical Rules, Notes, and Tables; for use of the Royal Navy, The Merchant Marine, and Yacht Squadrons*. Portsmouth: Griffin & Company, 1877.

Beecher, Catherine, and Harriet Beecher Stowe. *The American Woman's Home*. New York: J.B. Ford and Company, 1870.

Benes, Peter, ed. *Early American Inventories*. Proceedings of the Dublin Seminar for New England Folklife, Vol. 12. Boston: Boston University, 1987.

Benham, Hervey. *The Codbangers*. Colchester, England: Essex County Newspapers, 1979.

Blaney, Henry. *Journal of Voyages to China and Return 1851-1853*. Boston: Privately Printed, 1913.

Blunt, Joseph. *The Shipmaster's Assistant and Commercial Digest: Containing information necessary for Merchants, Owners, and Masters of Ships*. New York: Harper and Brothers, 1851.

Boughton, George Piper. *Seafaring*. London: Faber and Gwyer, 1926.

Bradford, William. *Bradford's History of Plymouth Plantation*. Original Narratives of Early American History. New York: Barnes and Noble, 1908.

Braudel, Fernand. *Capitalism and Civilization, 15th to 18th Century: The Structures of Everyday Life: The Limits of the Possible*. New York: Harper and Row, English Translation, 1981.

Briggs, Lloyd. *Around Cape Horn to Honolulu on the Bark Amy Turner 1880*. Boston: Charles E. Lauriat Company, 1926.

Brown, Ann Agusta Fitch. *Diary for 1870: The Diary of My Grandmother, Ann Agusta Fitch Brown, Wife of Captain Jacob Bartlett Brown*. Ed by Agate Brown Collord. Privately printed, 1959.

Buckingham, Samuel G. *The Life of William A. Buckingham, The War Governor of Connecticut with a Review of his Public Acts, and Especially the Distinguished Services He rendered his country during the War of the Rebellion with which is incorporated a condensed Account of the more important campaigns of the War and Information from Private Sources and Family and Official Documents*. Springfield, Massachusetts: The W.F. Adams Company, 1894.

Burdick, Howard. *Along the Shore*. Westerly, Rhode Island: Westerly Historical Society, 1988.

Burrows, R. Earl. *Robert Burrows and Descendants, 1630-1974*. Ann Arbor, Michigan: Edwards Brothers, 1975.

Butts, I.R. *The Rights of Seaman: The Coaster's and & Fisherman's Guide, and Master's and Mate's Manual: including...* Boston: I.R. Butts, 1848.

C

Carr, Lois G., P.D. Morgan, and J. B. Russ, eds. *Colonial Chesapeake Society*. Chapel Hill and London: University of North Carolina Press for Institute of Early American History and Culture, Williamsburg, Virginia, 1988.

Carson, Barbara G. *Ambitious Appetites: Dining, Behavior and Patterns of Consumption in Federal Washington*. Washington, D.C.: The Octagon Museum, 1990.

Chace, E.B. and L. B. Lovell. *Two Quaker Sisters*. New York: Liveright Publishing Company, 1937.

Clifford, Harold B. *Charlie York, Maine Coast Fisherman*. Camden: International Marine Publishing Company, 1979.

Connolly, James B. *The Book of the Gloucester Fisherman*. New York: John Day Company, 1927.

Crown Packing Company. *Gloucester Fish for You*. Gloucester, Massachusetts, c1911.

Cutting, Charles L. *Fishsaving*. New York: Philosophical Library, 1956.

Crapo, Thomas. *Strange, But True; Life and Adventures of Captain Thomas Crapo and Wife*. New Bedford: by the author, 1893.

D

Daboll, Nathan. *New England Almanac*. New London: Samuel Green, 1820.

Dana, Richard Henry, Jr. *The Journal of Richard Henry Dana*. 3 vols. ed. by Robert F. Lucid. Cambridge: The Belknap Press of the Harvard University Press, 1968.

———. *The Seaman's Friend containing a treatise on Practical Seamanship*...3d ed. Boston: Charles C. Little & James Brown, 1844.

———. *Two Years Before the Mast*. World Classics Edition, World Publication Company, 1946

Darden, Genevieve M. *My Dear Husband*. Taunton, Massachusetts: William S. Sullwold Publishing, for Descendants of Whaling Masters, 1980.

Dart, Margaret S. *Yankee Traders at Sea and Ashore*. New York: William Frederick Press, 1964.

Davidson, Alan. *North Atlantic Seafood*. New York: The Viking Press, 1979.

Delaney, Edmund. *Life in the Connecticut River Valley, 1800-1840 from the Recollections of John Howard Redfield.* Essex, Connecticut: Connecticut River Museum, 1988.
DePew, Chauncy M., ed. *One Hundred Years of American Commerce.* New York: D.O. Haynes Company, 1895.
De Voe, Thomas F. *The Market Assistant containing a brief description of every article of human food sold in the markets.* (Reprint. New York: Hurd and Houghton, 1867.) Detroit: Book Tower, 1975.
Douglas, George W. *The American Book of Days.* New York: H.W. Wilson Company, 1937.
Douglas, Mary, ed. *Food in the Social Order: Studies of Food and Festivities in Three American Communities.* New York: Russell Sage Foundation, 1984.
——————, *Purity and Danger: An Analysis of Concepts of Pollution and Taboo.* Harmondsworth, England: Penguin Books, 1966.
Druett, Joan, ed. *"She Was A Sister Sailor," Mary Brewster's Whaling Journals.* Mystic, Connecticut: Mystic Seaport Museum, 1992.
Duncan, Fred B. *Deepwater Family.* New York: Pantheon Books, 1969.
Dwight, Timothy. *Travels in New England and New York.* Edited by Barbara Miller Solomon. 4 vols. Cambridge: Belknap Press of Harvard University Press, 1969.

E
Eastman, Reverend B. *The Cranberry and Its Culture.* New York: C.M. Saxton & Company, 1856.
Eldridge, Charles Q. *The Story of a Connecticut Life.* Troy, New York: Allen Book and Printing Company, 1919.
Eldridge, Lewis William. *Lewis William Eldridge's Whaling Voyage.* New Bedford: Reynolds Printing, 1939.
Ellis, William, *The Journal of William Ellis: Narrative of a Tour of Hawaii or Owhyee with remarks on the history, traditions, manner, customs, and life of the inhabitants of the Sandwich Isles.* Rutland, Vermont: Tuttle, 1979.
Ely, Ben Ezra S. *There She Blows: a Narrative of a Whaling Voyage in the Indian and South Atlantic Oceans.* Edited by Curtis Dahl. Middletown, Connecticut: Wesleyan University Press for Marine Historical Association, 1971.
Ely, Susan H. and Elizabeth B. Plimpton . *The Lieutenant River.* Old Lyme, Connecticut: Lyme Historical Society and Griswold House Museum, 1991.
Emery, Sarah Anna. *Reminiscences of a Nonegenarian.* Newburyport, Massachusetts: William H. Huse & Company, 1879.

F
Favretti, Rudy. *Once Upon Quoketaug.* Storrs, Connecticut: by the author, 1974.
Farrow, John Pendleton. *History of Islesborough, Maine.* Bangor: Thomas W. Burr Printers, 1893.
Felker, Peter H. *The Grocer's Manual, Containing the natural History and Process of Manufacture of All Grocer's Goods.* Claremont, New Hampshire: Claremont Manufacturing, 1878.
Fessenden, Thomas G. *The Husbandman and Housewife: A Collection of Valuable Receipts.* Bellows Falls: Bill Blake and Company, 1820.
Field, Irving A. "Utilization of Sea Mussels for Food." *Transactions of the American Fisheries Society.* Vol. 40. Washington, D.C.: American Fisheries Society, 1911, 159-168.

G
Garner, Stanton, ed. *The Captain's Best Mate: The Journal of Mary Chipman Lawrence on the Whaler Addison, 1856-1860.* Hanover and London: University Press of New England for Brown University, 1966.
German, Andrew W. *Down on T-Wharf: The Boston Fisheries as Seen Through the Photographs of Henry D. Fisher.* Mystic: Mystic Seaport Museum, 1982.
Gonzales, Ellice B. *Storms, Ships, and Surfmen.* New York: Eastern Acorn Press, 1982.
Goode, George Brown. *American Fisheries, a Popular treatise upon the game and food fishes of North America, with especial reference to habitats and methods of capture.* Boston: L.C. Page and Company, 1903.
—————- ed. *The Fisheries and Fishery Industries of the United States.* 5 vols., Washington, D.C.: Government Printing Office, 1887.
Goodeholme, Todd S. *Goodeholme's Domestic Encyclopedia of Practical Information.* New York: C.A. Montgomery, 1885.
Gosnell, Harpur Allen. *Before the Mast in Clippers Composed in Large Part of the Diaries of Charles A. Abbey Kept While at Sea in the Years, 1856-1860.* New York: Derrydale Press, 1937.
Greenhill, Basil, and Ann Gifford. *Women Under Sail.* David and Charles Publishers, n.d.

H
Haley, Nelson. *Whale Hunt, The Narrative of a Voyage by Nelson C. Haley, Harpooneer in the Ship Charles W. Morgan, 1849-1853.* New York: Ives Washburn, 1948.
Harlow, Alvin F. *Old Bowery Days.* New York: D. Appleton & Company, 1931.
Harlow, Frederick Pease. *The Making of a Sailor on a Yankee Square-Rigger.* Salem, Massachusetts: Marine Research Society, 1928.
Hazard, Thomas Robinson. *The Jonnycake Papers of "Shepard Tom" together with Reminiscences of Narragansett Schools of Former Days.* Boston: for the Subscribers, 1918.
Hearn, Michael Patrick. *The Annotated Christmas Carol: A Christmas Carol by Charles Dickens.* New York: Avon Books, 1976.
Hibberd, Isaac Norris. *Sixteen Times Round Cape Horn: The Reminiscences of Captain Isaac Norris Hibberd.* Mystic, Connecticut: Mystic Seaport Museum, 1980.
Higginson, Edward. *New England's Plantation, with Sea Journal and Other Writings.* Salem: The Essex Print and Book Club, 1908.
Hugill, Stan. *Sailortown.* London: Routledge and K. Paul; New York: Dutton, 1967.

I
Innis, Harold A. *The Cod Fisheries, The History of an International Economy.* New Haven: Yale University Press, 1940.

J
Jewett, Sarah Orne. *The Country of the Pointed Firs and Other Stories.* Garden City, New York: Doubleday Inc., 1956.
Johnson, Edward. *Wonder-Working Providence.* Original Narratives of Early American History. New York: Barnes and Noble, 1910.

K
Kalm, Peter. *The America of 1750, Peter Kalm's Travels in North America.* English version of 1770 revised from the original Swedish and edited by Adolph Bensen, Vol. 1 & 2; New York: Dover Publications, 1964.
Kimball, Sumner I. "Organization and Methods of the United States Life Saving Service." Read before the Committee on Life-Saving Systems and Devices, International Marine Conference, 22 November 1889. Washington, D.C.: Government Printing Office, 1894.
King, Caroline Howard. *When I Lived in Salem.* Brattleboro: Stephen Daye Press, 1937.
Kochiss, John M. *Oystering from New York*

to Boston. Middletown, Connecticut: Wesleyan University Press and Mystic Seaport Museum, 1974.

L

Larkin, Jack. *The Reshaping of Everyday Life, 1790-1840*. New York: Harper and Row, 1988.

Larcom, Lucy. *A New England Girlhood*. New York: Corinth Books, 1961.

Leavitt, John. *Wake of the Coasters*. Middletown, Connecticut: Wesleyan University Press for Marine Historical Association, 1970.

Leonard, Elizabeth Dow. *A Few Reminiscences of My Exeter Life*. Edwards C. Echols, ed. Exeter: 2x4 Press, 1972.

Lesley, Susan I. *Recollections of My Mother*. New York & Boston: Houghton Mifflin and Company, 1899.

Lombard, Asa C. P., Jr. *East of Cape Cod*. New Bedford: Reynolds, Dewalk Printing, 1976.

Love, W. Deloss, Jr. *Fast and Thanksgiving Days of New England*. Cambridge: Houghton Mifflin, 1895.

M

MacKinnon, Captain R. N. *Atlantic and Transatlantic Sketches Afloat and Ashore*. New York: Harper & Brothers, 1852.

Martin, George A. *Our Homes; How to Beautify Them*. New York: O.J. Judd Company, 1888.

Marryat, Frederick. *A Diary in America with Remarks on Its Institutions*. Sydney Jackman, ed. New York: Alfred Knopf, 1962.

Mathews, J.H. "Problems of the Commercial Fisheries from Producer to the Consumer." *Transactions of the American Fisheries Society*, 51. Washington, D.C.:American Fisheries Society, 1922, 193-200.

McKay, Richard C. *Some Famous Sailing Ships and Their Builder, Donald McKay*. Boston: G.P. Putnam, 1928.

Melville, Herman. *Moby Dick or the White Whale*. New York: Mead and Company, 1942.

————. *Omoo, A Narrative of Adventures in the South Seas*. Evanston & Chicago: Northwestern University Press and the Newberry Library, 1968.

Millett, Arthur L. "Adequate Fish Inspection: A Means to Better Fish for the Consumer and to Increased Fish Food Consumption." *Transactions of the American Fisheries Society*, Vol. 50 (Washington, D.C.: American Fisheries Society, 1920-21 153-62.

Morris, John H. *History of New York Shipyards*. New York: William F. Somers & Company, 1909.

N

Neustadt, Kathy. *Clambakes: A History and Celebration of an American Tradition*. Amherst, Massachusetts: University of Massachusetts Press, 1992.

Nordhoff, Charles. *Whaling and Fishing*. New York: Dodd Mead & Company, 1855.

Nylander, Jane. *Our Own Snug Fireside: Images of the New England Home. 1760-1860*. New York: Alfred A. Knopf, 1993.

O

O'Connor, W.D. "The United States Life-Saving Service," *Appleton's Annual Cyclopedia*. New York: D. Appleton and Company, 1889.

————. "The United States Life Saving Service," *Popular Science Monthly*. Vol. 15 # LXXXV, June 1879, extract from Articles in *Appleton's Annual Cyclopedia* for 1878.

The Octagon Museum. *The Taste of Power: The Rise of Genteel Dining and Entertaining in Early Washington; Checklist for the Exhibition*. Washington, D.C.: The Octagon Museum, 1990.

Olmsted, Francis A. *Incidents of a Whaling Voyage*. Rutland, Vermont: Charles E. Tuttle Company, 1969.

P

Pease, Zephaniah, ed. *The Diary of Samuel Rodman 1821-1859*. New Bedford: Reynolds Printing, 1927.

————. *Life in New Bedford 100 Years Ago, A Chronicle of the Social, Religious, and Commercial History of the Period in a Diary Kept by Joseph R. Anthony*. New Bedford: Old Dartmouth Historical Society, 1925.

Peck, Esther Alice. *A Conservative Generation's Amusements: A Phase of Connecticut's Social History*. Bangor: University of Maine Studies, 2nd Series, 1938.

Perkins, John T. *John T. Perkin's Journal at Sea, 1845*. Mystic: Marine Historical Association, 1934.

Peterson, William N. "Mystic Built:" *Ships and Shipyards of the Mystic River, Connecticut, 1784-1919*. Mystic: Mystic Seaport Museum, 1989.

Peterson, William N., and Peter M.Coope. *Historic Buildings at Mystic Seaport Museum*. Mystic, Connecticut: Mystic Seaport Museum, 1985.

Pierce, George Wesley. *Goin' Fishing: The Story of the Deep-Sea Fishermen of New England*. Reprint. Camden, Maine: International Marine Publishing Company, 1989.

Pringle, James R., ed. *The Book of the Three Hundredth Anniversary of the Foundation of the Massachusetts Bay Colony at Cape Ann in 1623 and the Fiftieth Year of the Incorporation of Gloucester as a City*. Gloucester, Massachusetts: Publication Board of the 300th Anniversary Executive Committee, 1924.

Proctor Brothers, comp. *Fishermen's Ballads, and Songs of the Sea*. Gloucester: Proctor Brothers Publishers, 1874.

Proctor, George H. *Fishermen's Memorial and Record Book*. Gloucester: Proctor Brothers, 1873.

————. *The Fisheries of Gloucester*. Gloucester: Proctor Brothers, 1876.

Q

R

Radcliffe, Lewis. "The Development of Markets for Neglected Fishes." *Transactions of the American Fisheries Society*, Vol.48. Columbus, Ohio: American Fisheries Society, 1918 65-66.

Ricketson, Annie Holmes. *The Journal of Annie Holmes Ricketson on the Whaleship A.R. Tucker, 1871-74*. New Bedford: The Old Dartmouth Historical Society, 1958.

Riesenberg, Felix. *Under Sail*. New York: MacMillan Company, 1919.

Rogers, James A. *Journal of the Whaling Voyage of Ship Mentor of New London, Captain William M. Baker*. New Bedford, Massachusetts: Reynolds Printing, nd.

Root, Grace Cogswell. *Father and Daughter: A Collection of Cogswell Family Letters and Diaries 1772-1830*. West Hartford, Connecticut: American School for the Deaf, 1924.

Rowe, William H. *Shipbuilding in Casco Bay 1727-1890*. Portland: Southworth Press, 1929.

S

Sabine, Lorenzo. *Report on The Principle Fisheries of the American Seas prepared for the Treasury Department of the United States*. Washington, D.C.: Robert Armstrong, 1853.

Samuels, Samuel. *From Forecastle to Cabin*, Boston: Charles E. Lauriat Company, 1924.

Scammon, Charles. *The Marine Animals of the Northwestern Coast of North America*. San Francisco: J.H. Carmany & Company, 1874.

Schneider, Elizabeth. *Uncommon Fruits and Vegetables: A Commonsense Guide*. New

York: Harper and Row, 1986.
Smith, Phillip Chadwick Foster. *The Frigate Essex Papers: Building the Salem Frigate 1798-1799*. Salem: Peabody Museum of Salem, 1974.
Sperry, Willard L. *Summer Yesterdays in Maine: Memories of Boyhood Vacation Days*. New York and London: Harper and Brothers, 1941.
Stevenson, Charles. *Preservation of Fishery Products for Food.* Washington, D.C.: Government Printing Office, 1899.
Story, Dana. *Frame Up!* Barre, Massachusetts: Barre Publishers, 1964.
————. *Hail! Columbia.* Barre, Massachusetts: Barre Publishers, 1970.
Stowe, Harriet Beecher. *Poganuc People.* Reprint. Hartford: The Stowe-Day Foundation, 1977.
————. *Oldtown Folks*. Boston: Houghton, Mifflin, and Company, 1891.
William, Strickland. *Journal of a Tour in the USA, 1794-1795*. New York State Historical Society, 1971.
Sturgis, Frederick Laurence. *Coasting Passenger.* 2nd edition. Concord, Massachusetts: Charles S. Morgan, 1968.

T

Thoreau, Henry David. *The Writings of Thoreau.* Brooks Atkinson, ed. New York: Modern Library, 1950.
Travers, Carolyn Freeman, ed. *The Thanksgiving Primer.* Plymouth, Massachusetts: Plimoth Plantation, 1991.
Trollop, Frances. *Domestic Manners of the Americas.* Edited by Donald Smalley. New York: Random House, 1949.

U,V

United States Bureau of Commerce, Bureau of the Census. *Sixth Census of the United States: 1840*, Connecticut, detail census of Stonington, Connecticut.
———. *Seventh Census of the United States: 1850*, Connecticut, detail census of Stonington, Connecticut.
———. *Eighth Census of the United States: 1860*, Connecticut, detail census of Stonington, Connecticut.
———. *Ninth Census of the United States: 1870*, Connecticut, detail census of Stonington, Connecticut.
———. *Ninth Census of the United States: 1870*, Connecticut, detail census of Groton,Connecticut.
United States Government. *The Report of the Committee on Foreign Relations in Relation to the Right and Interests of American Fisheries and Fishermen.* Washington, D.C.: Government Printing Office, 1887.
————. Form 9. *United States Life-Saving Service, Regulations for the Government of the Life Saving Stations of the United States.*
————. *Revised Regulations for the Government of Life Saving Stations of the United States and the Laws Upon Which They Are Based.* Washington, D.C.: Government Printing Office, 1884.

V

Vickers, Daniel. "Work and Life on the Fishing Periphery," in *Seventeenth Century New England*, A conference held by the Colonial Society of Massachusetts, 18 and 19 June 1982. Boston: The Colonial Society of Massachusetts, distributed by the University Press of Virginia, 1984, 83-117.
Villiers, Alan. *Cruise of the Conrad, A Journal of a Voyage*. New York: Scribner's Sons, 1937.

W

Wallace, Frederick. *Roving Fisherman.* Gardenvale, Quebec: Harpells Press, 1955.
Warner, William. *Distant Water: The Fate of the North Atlantic Fisherman.* Boston & Toronto: Little, Brown, & Company, 1977.
Wasson, George S. *Sailing Days on the Penobscot.* Salem: Marine Research Society, 1932.
Waterman, T.T. *Lecture on the Christmas Festival.* Providence, Rhode Island: I. Wilcox & Company, 1835.
Webster, Thomas, and Mrs. Parkes. *An Encyclopedia of Domestic Economy.* London: Longman Brown, Green, Longmans, 1844.
Weibust, Knut. *Deep Sea Sailors, A Study in Maritime Ethnology.* Stockholm: Nodiska museets Handlingar 71, 1969.
Wheeler, Grace Denison. *Grace Wheeler's Memories.* Stonington, Connecticut: Pequot Press, 1948.
Whidden, Captain John D. *Old Sailing Ship Days.* Boston: Charles E. Lauriat Company, 1925.
Wilbour, Benjamin Franklin. *Notes on Little Compton.* Carlton C. Brownell, ed. Little Compton, Rhode Island: Little Compton Historical Society, 1970.
Winthrop, John. *Journal, Original Narratives of Early American History.* Two volumes. New York: Barnes and Noble, 1908.
Whymper, Frederick. *The Fisheries of the World, an Illustrated and Descriptive Record of the International Fisheries Exhibition, 1883.* London: Cassel and Company, 1884.

CULINARY SOURCES

A

Abell, Mrs. L.G. *The Complete Domestic Guide Comprising the Mother's Book of Daily Duties and Skillful Housewife's Book.* New York: R.I. Young, 1853.

B

Beecher, Catherine E. *Miss Beecher's Domestic Receipt Book.* New York: Harper & Brothers, 1846.
————. *Miss Beecher's Domestic Receipt Book.* 3d. ed. New York: Harper & Brothers, 1854.
————. *Miss Beecher's Domestic Receipt Book.* 5th ed. New York: Harper & Brothers, 1871.
Beecher, Catherine E. and Harriet Beecher Stowe. *The American Woman's Home: Or, Principles of Domestic Science; Being a Guide to the Formation and Maintenance of Economical, Healthful, Beautiful, and Christian Homes.* New York: J.B. Ford, 1870.
Beecher, Mrs. H.W. *All Around the House or How to Make Homes Happy.* New York: D. Appleton & Company, 1878.
Beeton, Isabella. *Beeton's Every-day Cookery and Housekeeping Book: A Practical and Useful Guide for All Mistresses and Servants.* New York: D. Appleton, ca. 1875.
Belden, Louise Conway. *The Festive Tradition: Table Decoration and Desserts in America, 1650-1900.* A Winterthur Book, New York: W.W. Norton and Company, 1983.
Bliss, Mrs. *The Practical Cookbook: Containing Upwards of One Thousand Receipts.* Philadelphia: J.B. Lippincott & Company, 1864.
Bryan, Mrs. Lettice. *The Kentucky Housewife.* Facsimilie reprint with introduction by Bill Neal. Columbia, South Carolina: University of South Carolina Press, 1991.

C

Chase, Dr. A.W. *Dr. Chase's Recipes; or Information for Everybody: An Invaluable Collection of About Eight Hundred Practical Recipes.* Ann Arbor: R.A. Beal, 1881.
Child, Mrs. Lydia Maria. *The American Frugal Housewife.* (Reprint of 12th ed.) Boston: Carter, Hendee, and Company, 1833.) Worthington, Ohio, Historical Society, 1965.
Connecticut, North Stonington. Women of the North Stonington Grange. *The Grange Cook Book.* 1913.
Connecticut, Stonington. Young People's Society of Christian Endeavor of the

Second Congregational Church. *The Stonington Cookbook*, (Reprint) Watch Hill, Rhode Island: Book and Tackle Shop, 1975.
Cornelius, Mary Hooker. *The Young Housekeeper's Friend: Or, a Guide to Domestic Economy and Comfort*. Boston: Tappan, Whittemore, & Mason, 1850.
———. *The Young Housekeeper's Friend*, rev. ed., ca. 1871.
Cornell, William M. M.D. *The Handy Home Book of Medical and Family Receipts*. Boston: William F. Gillis, 1875.

D-E
Frank E. Davis Fish Company. *Correct Recipes for Sea Food Cookery including the Preparation of All of Davis' Fish Products*. Gloucester, Massachusetts: Frank E. Davis Fish Company, n.d.
———. *Fish Dainties and Necessities*. Gloucester: Frank E. Davis Fish Company, Fish Purveyors to the American People, 1907.
———. *Old Gloucester Seafood Recipes from Frank E.Davis the Gloucester Fisherman*. Gloucester: Frank E. Davis Fish Company, n.d., ca. 1932.

F
Farmer, Fanny Merritt. *The Original Boston Cooking School Cook Book, 1896*. (Facsimilie reprint of the first edition of the Boston Cooking-School Cook Book.) New York: Weathervane Books, n.d.
Filippini, Alexander. *One Hundred Ways of Cooking Fish*. (Handy Volume Culinary Series 2) New York: Charles L. Webster, 1892.

G
Glasse, Hannah. *Art of Cookery Made Plain and Easy Which Far Exceeds Any Thing of the Kind Ever Yet Published, by a Lady*. London: for the author, 1747.
Goodholme, Todd S., ed. *Goodholme's Domestic Cyclopedia of Practical Information*. New edition. New York: C.A. Montgomery, 1887.
Good Housekeeping's Book of Menus, Recipes, and Household Discoveries. New York: Good Housekeeping, 1922.
Grigson, Jane. *The Observer Guide to British Cookery*. London: Michael Joseph, 1984.

H
Hale, Sarah Josepha Buell. *The Good Housekeeper: Or, The Way to Live Well and to be Well While We Live*. Boston: Weeks, Jordan, 1839.
———. *Mrs. Hale's New Cook Book, a Practical System for Private Families in Town and Country*. Philadelphia: T.B. Peterson and Brothers, ca. 1857.
———. *Mrs. Hale's Receipts for the Million: Containing Four Thousand Five Hundred and Forty-five Receipts, Facts, Directions, etc*. Philadelphia: T.B. Peterson, ca. 1857.
Handy, Amy. *What We Cook on Cape Cod*. Sandwich, Massachusetts: Shawmee Press for Barnstable Village Improvement Society, 1911.
Hall, Elizabeth M. *Practical American Cookery and Domestic Economy*. New York: Saxton, Barker, and Company, 1860.
Halloway, Laura C. *The Hearthstone; or Life at Home. A Household Manual*. Chicago and Philadelphia: L.P. Miller & Company, 1887.
[Lafcadio Hearne], *La Cuisine Creole, A Collection of Culinary Recipes from Leading Chefs and Noted Creole Housewives Who Have Made New Orleans Famous for Its Cuisine*. New York: Will H. Coleman, 1885.
Henderson, Mrs. Mary F. *Practical Cooking and Dinner Giving*. New York: Harper and Brothers, 1882.
Hill, Georgiana. *How to Cook Potatoes, Apples, Eggs, and Fish*. New York: Dick and Fitzgerald, 1869.
Hood's Combined Cook Books. Lowell, Massachusetts: C.I. Hood & Company, 1875-1885.
Horry, Harriot Pinckney. *A Colonial Plantation Cookbook: The Receipt Book of Harriot Pinckney Horry, 1770*. Edited by Richard Hooker. Columbia, South Carolina: University of South Carolina Press, 1984.
Howard, Jane Grant (Gilmore). *Fifty Years in a Maryland Kitchen*. Baltimore: Turnbull Brothers, 1873.
How to Cook Fish. Boston: Massachusetts Board of Food Administration, 1917.
How to do Things Well and Cheap, for Domestic Use, by One Who Knows. Boston: Charles Tappan, 1845.
Howland, Mrs. E. A. *New England Economical Housekeeper*. Worcester: S.A. Howland, 1845.

I,J,K
Jesperson, Reverend Ivan. *Fat Back and Molasses*. St. John's, Newfoundland: Reverend Ivan Jesperson, 1974.

L
Leslie, Eliza. *Directions for Cookery Being a System of the Art in Its Various Branches*. Philadelphia: E.L. Carey and A. Hart, 1837.
———. *Directions for Cookery*. 40th ed. Philadelphia: Henry Carey Baird, 1851.
Lincoln, Mrs. Mary J. *Mrs. Lincoln's Boston Cook Book*. Boston: Little Brown, and Company, 1913.

M,N
Maddocks, Mildred, ed. *The Pure Food Cook Book: The Good Housekeeping Recipes; Just How to Buy; Just How to Cook*. New York: Hearst's International Library, 1914.
Maine, Glencove. Penobscot View Grange No. 388. *Penobscot View Grange Cook Book*. Glencove, Maine, n.d.
Maine, Portland. Ladies of State Street Parish. *Fish, Flesh, and Fowl*. Portland: J.S. Staples, 1877.
Markham, Gervase. *The English Houswife: Containing the Inward and Outward Vertues Which Ought to be in a Complete Woman*. Edited by Michael R. Best; London: Nicholas Oaks for John Harison, 1631; reprint, Kingston & Montreal: McGill-Queen's University Press, 1986.
Massachusetts, Bay View. Methodist Episcopal Church. *The Ladies Handbook and Household Assistant—A Manual of Religious and Table Etiquette*. Bay View, Massachusetts, ca. 1888.
Massachusetts. *Cape Ann Cookbook*. Picture Book Press, 1958.
Massachusetts, Fall River. *Approved Receipts, Our Third Edition, Issued in Aid of Our Harvest Festival, 1873*. Fall River: Fiske and Munroe, 1875.
Massachusetts, Gloucester. Ladies of the First Baptist Church. *Reliable Receipts for the Housewife*. 3d ed.; Gloucester, 1900.
Massachusetts, Gloucester. Trinity Congregational Church. *The Tabitha Cookbook*. 2d ed. Gloucester, Massachusetts, 1915.
Massachusetts, Haverhill. Ladies of the First Baptist Church, *The Pentucket Housewife*: A Manual for Housekeepers, and Collection of Recipes, Contributed by the Ladies of the First Baptist Church. 3d ed. Haverhill: Chace Brothers, 1888.
New Family Receipt Book, Containing all the Truly Valuable Receipts. Hartford: [Ezra Strong], 1829.
Missouri, Springfield. Calvary Presbyterian Church Ladies' Aid Society. *Cook Book*. revised ed., Springfield: Jewell, 1903.
Moss, Kay, and Kathryn Hoffman. *The Backcountry Housewife*. Gastonia, North Carolina: Schiele Museum of Natural History & Planetarium, 1985.
North Stonington, Connecticut. The Women of the North Stonington, Connecticut, Grange. *The Grange Cookbook*. 1913.

O,P,Q
Parloa, Maria. *Miss Parloa's Kitchen Companion*. 19th ed. New York: Clover, 1887.
————. *Miss Parloa's New Cookbook and Marketing Guide*. Boston: Estes and Lauriat, 1880.
————. *Miss Parloa's Young Housekeeper*. Boston: Estes and Lauriat, 1894
Putnam, [Elizabeth H.] *Mrs. Putnam's Receipt Book and Young House-keepers Assistant*. Boston: Ticknor, Reed, and Fields, 1849.
————. *Mrs. Putnam's Receipt Book*...new ed. New York: Sheldon, 1876.

R
Randolph, Mary. *The Virginia House-wife: Facsimilie of 1st ed., 1824, and Additional Material from eds. of 1825 and 1828, with Historical Notes and Commentaries by Karen Hess*. Columbia, South Carolina: University of South Carolina Press, 1984.
Rorer, Mrs. S. T. *Mrs. Rorer's Philadelphia Cook Book*. Philadelphia: Arnold and Company, 1886.
Roux, Willam C. *What's Cooking Down in Maine*. Orrs Island, Maine: Orr's Island Press, 1964.
[Rundell Maria Eliza], *Experienced American Housekeeper*. New York: Johnstone and VanNorden, 1823.
[Rutledge, Sarah.] *The Carolina Housewife by Sarah Rutledge: A Facsimilie of the 1847 with an introduction and a Preliminary Checklist of South Carolina Cookbooks Published before 1935*. (Reprint of: *The Carolina Housewife*. Charleston: W.R. Babcock, 1847.) Edited by Anna Wells Rutledge. Columbia: University of South Carolina Press, 1979.

S
Shute and Merchant Company. *Receipts for Cooking Fish*. 8th ed. Gloucester: Shute and Merchant Company, 1895.
Simmons, Amelia. *American Cookery: Or, the Art of Dressing Viands, Fish, Poultry and Vegetables*. Hartford: Hudson & Godwin for the author, 1796. Edited by Mary Tolford Wilson. Hartford: Hudson & Godwin for the author, 1796; reprint, New York: Dover, 1984.
Smallzreid, Kathleen. *The Everlasting Pleasure: Influences on America's Kitchens, Cooks, and Cookery, from 1565 to the Year 2000*. New York: Appleton-Century-Crofts, 1956.
Standish, Marjorie. *Cooking Down East*. Portland, Maine: Maine *Sunday Telegram*, 1969.
Szathmary, Louis, ed. *Along the Northern Border: Cookery in Idaho, Minnesota, North Dakota*. New York: Arno Press, 1973.

T
Terhune, Mary Virginia. [Pseudonym Marion Harland] *The Dinner Year Book*. New York: Charles Scribner's Sons, 1878.
Texas, Houston. The Ladies Association of the First Presbyterian Church. *The First Texas Cookbook*. Reprint of 1883 edition, with forewords by David Wade and Mary Faulk Koock. Austin, Texas: Eakin Press, 1986.
Tyree, Marion Cabell, ed. *Housekeeping in Old Virginia: Containing Contributions from Two Hundred and Fifty of Virginia's Noted Housewives*. Louisville: John P. Morgan, 1879.

U,V,W, X,Y,X
Washington, Martha, owner. *Martha Washington's Booke of Cookery*. Ed. by Karen Hess. New York: University of Columbia Press, 1981.
Weaver, William Woys. *America Eats: Forms of Edible Folk Art*. New York: Harper and Row, 1989.
Wheaton, Barbara Ketcham. *Savoring the Past: The French Kitchen and Table from 1300 to 1789*. Philadelphia: University of Pennsylvania Press, 1983.
Whitcher, Mary. *Mary Whitcher's Shaker Housekeeper*. (Reprint of the 1882 United Society of Believer's Publication) Pittsfield, Massachusetts: Hancock Shaker Village, n.d.
Williams, Susan. *Savory Suppers and Fashionable Feasts: Dining in Victorian America*. New York: Pantheon Books, in association with the Strong Museum, 1985.
Wilson, C. Anne. *Foods and Drink in Britain From the Stone Age to the 19th Century*. Chicago: Academy Chicago Publishers, 1991.
Winslow, Mrs. *Mrs. Winslow's Domestic Receipt Book for 1868*. Boston: Jeremiah Curtis & Sons and John I. Brown & Sons, 1868.
————. *Mrs.Winslow's Domestic Receipt Book for 1871*. Boston: Jeremiah Curtis & Sons and John I. Brown & Sons, 1871.
————. *Mrs.Winslow's Domestic Receipt Book for 1876*. Boston: Jeremiah Curtis & Sons and John I. Brown & Sons, 1876.
Rhode Island. Women's Christian Temperance Union of Rhode Island, *W.C.T.U. Cook Book—Health and Comfort for the Home*. Phenix, Rhode Island: The Gleaner Print, 1905.
Wright, Julia, et al., comp. *Food for the Hungry: A Complete Manual of Household Duties, Together with Bills of Fare for All Seasons by Marion Harland*. Philadelphia: P.W. Ziegler, 1896.

PERIODICALS

A
"The Professor at the Breakfast-Table. What He Said, What He Heard, and What He Saw." *Atlantic Monthly* (June 1859).

B
W.H. Bishop. "Fish and Men in the Maine Islands." *Harper's New Monthly Magazine* (August 1880): 336-52.
Blume, Kenneth John. "The Hairy Ape Reconsidered: The American Merchant Seaman and the Transition from Sail to Steam in the late Nineteenth Century." *American Neptune* (Winter 1984): 33-47.
Bolster, W. Jeffrey. "To Feel Like A Man: Black Seamen in the Northern States, 1800-1860." *The Journal of American History* 76 (March 1990): 1173-99.
Boynton, Dr. Willard H. "Mackerel Fishing out of Gloucester." *The Log of Mystic Seaport* (Winter 1988): 139-46.

C
Carpenter, F.G. "Uncle Sam's Life Savers." *Popular Science Monthly* 44 (January 1894).
Channing, Mary J. "Sixty Year's Ago." *The Youth's Companion* (December 1894): 603-04.
Colcord, Joanna. "Domestic Life on American Sailing Ships." *American Neptune* (July 1942): 193-202.
Connolly, J. B. "Gloucester Fisherman, Night-seining and Winter Trawling." *Scribner's Magazine* (April 1902).
[Cummings, Abbott Lowell]. "Notes on Furnishing a Small New England Farmhouse." *Old Time New England* 48 (1958): 65-84.

D
DeForrest, Virginia. "How Effie Hamilton Spent Christmas." *Godey's Lady's Book* 55 (1857): 534-38.
De Wire, Elinor. "Life Saving Service." *Offshore* (February 1990).
Doughty, F.A.. "Life at a Life Saving Station." *Catholic World* 65 (July 1897).
Gibson, Charles Dana. "History of the Swordfishery of the Northwestern Atlantic." *American Neptune* (January 1981): 36-65.
"Hawaiian Meals." *The Gospel Missionary*. 17 (1867): 177-80.
"Along the Docks." *Harper's Weekly*

(February 1871): 998.
Hale, Arthur Cleveland. "Cuttyhunk." *New England Magazine* (September 1897).
Hale, E.E. "What Shall We Have We Have for Dinner." *Atlantic Monthly* (September 1864): 364-70.
Iles, George. "On Hotel-Keeping-Present and Future." *Century Magazine* (30 August 1885): 577-83.
Johnson, W. W. "The United States Life Saving Service." *New England Monthly Magazine* (2 April 1890).
Lamb, M.J. "The American Life Saving Service." *Harper's New Monthly Magazine* 64 (February 1882).
Lewis, George H. "The Maine Lobster as Regional Icon," *Food and Foodways* 3 & 4 (1989): 303-16.
"The Logical Remedy for Under-Consumption." *Atlantic Fisherman* (1 February 1921): 3.
Malley, Richard. "On Shore in a Foreign Land: Mary Stark in the Kingdom of Hawaii." *The Log of Mystic Seaport* 37 (1985): 79-92.
Merryman, J.H. "The United States Life Saving Service." *Scribner's Monthly*. 19 (1879-1880).
North, Franklin. "Gloucester Fishers." *Century Magazine* (October 1886).
Oliver, S.L. "The Herrick Recipes." *The Log of Mystic Seaport* (Fall 1991): 74-75.
Parrish, Emma K. "Jack's Christmas." *St. Nicholas Magazine* (December 1877): 124-28.
Pukui, Mary Kawena. "Poi Making." *Polynesian Culture and History*. Schultz, Charles R. "A Forty-Niner Fourth of July." *The Log of Mystic Seaport* 38 (Spring 1986): 3-13.
"Home and Society Column." *Scribner's Monthly* 1 (1871): 347-48.
"Hyper Gentility." *Scribner's Magazine* 5 (1873): 643.
Stearn, Elinor. "A Kitchen of 1825 in a Thriving New England Town." *Old Time New England* 8 (1923): 125-30.
Sterns, E. E. *Scribner's Monthly* 1 (1870): 113-29.
"A Struggle for Shelter." *Atlantic Monthly* (April 1866): 456-62.
"Thanksgiving." Home and Society. *Scribner's Magazine* 2 (1871): 241.
"Twelfth Night." Home and Society. *Scribner's Magazine* (January 1872): 373-72.
T.P.W. "Auntie's Merry Christmas." *Godey's Lady's Book* (December 1861): 506.
Worstell, Mary V. "The Month Before Christmas." *St. Nicholas Magazine* (November 1889): 89-91.

NEWSPAPERS
Mystic *Journal* 1870-76.
Mystic *Pioneer*, 1859-69.
Mystic *Press*, 1873-88.
Narragansett *Weekly*, 6 July 1865.
Stonington *Mirror*, 1870-97.
Weekly Mirror-Journal, 1871-72

TOWN RECORDS AND PROBATE INVENTORIES
Town Records:
Groton Town Death Records
Groton Land Records, Vol. 1AT
New London Marriage Records
Probate
Chester, Connecticut: Samuel Buckingham, 1815.
Stonington, Connecticut: Clark Greenman, 11 May 1877

MANUSCRIPTS
at G. W. Blunt-White Library
Bishop, George H. Diary, bark *Edward Everett*, 1869-71. VFM 1050.
Bonsall, Spencer. Journal, ship *Edward*. Log 740.
Brewster, George S. Journal, ship *George*, 1838-41. Log 86.
Brewster, Mary. Journal, ship *Tiger*, 1845-49. Log 38.
Chace, Charles. Journal, bark *C.W. Morgan*, 1863. Log 146.
C. W. Morgan. Log, 1881-86. Log 149.
Denison, Ethan A. Diary, Mystic, 1803-1813. Misc. Vol. 566.
Farnsworth, Mary Elizabeth Weaver. "Reminiscences of Mary Elizabeth Weaver Farnsworth," Books 1 & 2, 1830-1904. Misc. Vol. 155.
Fish Family Papers. Coll 43.
Gates Family Papers. Coll 153.
Bark *Globe*, outfit notations in chandlery order book, 1869. VFM 425.
Gray, Horatio. Journal, ship *Sophia Walker*, 1851-59. Coll 89.
George Greenman & Company Records. Daybook, 1852-64. Misc. Vol. 264.
Griffiths, William. Journal, ship *Charles W. Morgan*, 1911-13. Log 158.
Good News. Abstract log for barkentine, 1896-1906. Log 198.
Hawley, George. Description of a fishing voyage by sloop *Planet* from Bridgeport, Connecticut, to Nantucket, 1834. VFM 1488.
Hayden, Nehemiah S. Journal, ship *Frederick Gebhard* 1858. Log 191.
Ship *Hector*. Accounts, New Bedford, 1852. Coll. 119.
Schooner *William B. Herrick*. Log, 1874-76. Log 713.
Kirby, H.S. Manuscript note "Small Stores," in back of H.S. Kirby, Dealer in Ship Chandlery & Hardware, New Bedford, chandlery order book for bark *Mary Frazier*, Edgartown, 1876. VFM 1461.
Knapp, Edward Everett. Typescript, "Smacks of Noank," n.d.
Kochiss, John. "A Report on the Connecticut River Shad Fishery," August 1975. RF 299.
Look, Hiram. Journal, bark *Charles W. Morgan*, 1871-74. Log 409.
Maxson, William Ellery. Typescript of diary, 1860-64. VFM 1039.
————————. Ship *Niagra*, 1845-46. Log 863.
Morgan, Charles W. Diaries, 1841-51. Coll. 27.
Mitchell, Harry B. Journal, ship *Cremorne*, 1854. Log 5.
S. Nickersons and Sons. Account Book of the schooner *B.D. Nickerson*, Boothbay Harbor, Maine, 1895-1902. Misc. Vol. 175.
Osborne, James C. Journal, *bark Charles W. Morgan*, 1841-43. Log 143.
Philbrook, Simon. Diary, 1805-08. VFM 860.
Reynolds, Irving. Journal, steamer *Acapulco*, 1881. Log 556.
Sarah Smith (Mrs.Fred). Journal, bark *Ohio*, 1875. Log 399.
Sarah Smith (Mrs.Fred). Journal, bark *John P. West*, 1882-84. Log 78.
Calista M. Stover Papers. Coll. 105.
Todd, Sara Hix. Transcribed letter in Log 900.
Turner, Thomas Larkin. Diary, brig *Palestine*, 1832. Coll. 95, vol. 14.
United States Life Saving Service. Form #1832, "Copies of Property Returns, U. S. Life-Saving Service, Dist. #2 Station #4," 1883-87. Misc. Volume 325.
U. S. Life-Saving Service, Letter 12756, 24 October 1882. List of Outfits and Equipment for New Life-Saving Station at Peaked Hill Bars and Muskegat. National Archives Collection.
W.W. Brainard. Journal on schooner, 1867-68. Log 119.
Weir, Robert. Journal, bark *Clara Bell*, 1855-58. Log 164.
Wendell, George. Journal, ship *Galatea*, 1862-63. Coll. 59.
Wainright, William. *USS Kearsarge*, 1862-64. Log 429.
Williams, John L. Manuscript "List of Stores for Fiting a vessel," New London, 1882. VFM 1430.

MANUSCRIPTS
Anonymous. Manuscript recipe notebook, Essex, Connecticut, 1848-57. Essex

Historical Society, Essex, Connecticut.
Anonymous. Manuscript recipe book, 1808. 1966.18 BV, Old Sturbridge Village Library, Sturbridge, Massachusetts, hereafter cited as OSV.
Ball, Nicholas. Typescript of journal of Life-Saving Station Number Two Third District, New Shoreham, Rhode Island, November 1874-April 1875. Curatorial Files, Mystic Seaport Museum, hereafter cited as MSM.
Bixby, Fred. Manuscript recipe notebook, 1920. Rancho Los Alamitos, Long Beach, California.
Blanchard, Georgia Maria. "Our Wedding Trip Around Cape Horn," 1906. Family Papers, Penobscot Marine Museum, Searsport, Maine, hereafter cited as PMM.
Bowen, Joanne. "A Study of Seasonality and Subsistence: Eighteenth-Century Suffield, Connecticut," Ph.D. diss., Brown University, 1990.
Button, Florence. Manuscript essay, "What Xmas Was to Me Long Ago," 1979. Author's possession.
Card, Fannie. Manuscript recipe notebook, 1879. Anna North Coit, North Stonington, Connecticut.
Frank E. Davis Company. Descriptive price list, 1917. Cape Ann Historical Association, Gloucester, Massachusetts.
Dodge, Frances Jaixen. Notes from a conversation at Block Island with the author, 29 May 1986. Author's possession.
Dow, Scott J. Typescript, "The Story of Captain Jonathan Dow," 1948. PMM.
Francis, Captain John. Typescript of conversation with Nancy d'Estang, 13 April 1987. Shipyard Documents File, MSM.
————. Typescript of conversation with Nancy d'Estang, 19 October 1987. Shipyard Documents File, MSM.
Gates, Julia. Typescript of manuscript recipe notebook, 1857-30, Mystic River Historical Society, Mystic, Connecticut.
Gilbert, Charlotte T.W. Manuscript recipe book, 1829. 1958.11, OSV.
Green, Mrs. Dorothea, from her cousin T.R. Green. Manuscript recipe book, 1823-28. 1963.52, OSV
Hallett, G.G. Bill from G.G. Hallett, New York, New York, 12 November 1874, to U.S. Life-Saving Service. National Archives, Washington, D.C.
Hastings, Caroline. Manuscript recipe notebook, 1820, near Nashua, New Hampshire. 1961.41, OSV.
Hart, Elizabeth. Manuscript recipe notebook, 1825. Old Saybrook Historical Society, Saybrook, Connecticut.
Hogan, Felix William. Notes from conversation, 22 October 1984. Shipyard Documents File, MSM.
Information Bulletin 67-1, Cost of Constructing and Outfitting the ship *Charles W. Morgan*, MSM
Jones, Virginia. Research paper on furnishing the *L. A. Dunton* fo'c'sle, 1984. Shipyard Documents File, MSM.
Littlefield, Lorenzo. Store Ledger Books, New Shoreham, Rhode Island, 1878. Property of Robert Downie, Spring Street, Block Island, Rhode Island.
Mallory and Company, New York, New York. Bill, 5 December 1874, to the U. S. Life-Saving Service. National Archives, Washington, D.C.
Miller, Mary. Manuscript recipe notebook, 1850-95. Privately owned.
New Shoreham Life-Saving Station. Typescript from first logbook of Station #2, 1874. Curatorial Department Files, MSM.
Norris, Thomas. Typed notes of a telephone conversation, no date. Shipyard Documents File, MSM.
Palmer, Julia. Manuscript recipe notebook, 1840-60. Anna North Coit, North Stonington, Connecticut.
Skinner, Louis. Record memorandum of conversation with George Emery, et al., 29 June 1984. Shipyard Documents File, MSM.
Sloat, Caroline Fuller. "Dishwashing and the Domestic Landscape: Reform begins at Home," notes from paper presented at the 1992 Winterthur Conference. Author's possession.
Lewis E. Spear Company, Typescript of Invoice from Lewis E. Spear Company, Marine and Hotel Supplies, 37 Market Street, San Francisco, California, 6 November 1901. Shipyard Documents File, MSM.
Tibbo, Winston. Notes from interview with Nancy d'Estang, 1985. Shipyard Documents File, MSM.

MYSTIC SEAPORT Sound Archives MATERIAL

Bechtel, Walter. Interview in NBC Radio Broadcast; 30 July 1949; ME 49-1.
Fisher, R. Barry. Transcript of interview with Gary Adair, 23 January 1992. OH 92-1, OH 92-2.
Elroy Johnson, Interview with Paul Stubing, 19 March 1967, OH 67-2.
Langworthy, Maxon. Interview with Thomas Parker, January 1976, 76-2.
Merchant, Robert. Interview Virginia Jones, 1 April 1978, OH 78-2.
Reynolds, Aubrey. Interview with John Kochiss 29 June 1971, OH 71-1.
Ryder, Rebecca. Interview with David Brierly, 6 April 1978, OH 78-3.
Leslie H. Stanton, Interview 20 April 1966 and 6 May 1966, Francis Bowker, OH 66-3.

COOK'S INDEX

Cook's Index
alewives, 369
ambrosia(s)
orange, **170**, 185
pineapple, 185
apple(s)
dumplings, 29-30
fried with salt pork, 24
onion stuffing, 271-272
pie, **60**, **69**, 73-74, **234**
dried, **128**, 146
in printed cookbooks, 73
varieties and uses, 29, 73
bacalhau, 361
banbury tarts, 291
bannock, 160
bass, striped, 369-370
bean(s), 107
baked, 79
frijoles, 208
refried, 208
in succotash, **67**, 76
lima in succotash, 76-77
soup, **91**, 115
beef
baked or roasted, 142
corned
boiled, **5**, **16**, 161
hash, 161-162
pressed, 228
dried, gravy, 160
hash, 161-162
mincemeat, 252
pies, 253
pot roast, 142
salt, 106
boiled, **16**
in lobscouce, **82**, 119-120
making, 120
soup, 24-25, 142-143
dumplings for, 25
steak
fried, **36**
grilled, 52
stock for soup, 51
tongue, boiled, **8**, 54
veal pie, 227
beets, pickled, **260**, 274
berry pie, 230-231
beverages
coffee, 107, 147
lemonade, 230
swanky, 137, 146-147
tea, 107-108
whiskey punch, 81
billet, 162
biscuits, **60**, **128**
hardtack, **91**, 106-107
in dandyfunk, 116-117
in lobscouce, **82**, 119-120
soda, 144-145
saleratus, 144-145
blackberry pie, 231
blueberries
canned, 188
in whortleberry pie, 120-121, **266**
bluefish, 369-370
baked, 162
billet, 162
chowder, **297**
boiled dinner, New England, **5**, 161
bread(s)
brewis, **14**
fisherman's, 360
pronunciation, 356
brown, 78-79
in brewis, 19
corn, Mississippi, **194**, 207-208
croutons, 76
gingerbread, 80-81
sugar, 228-229
graham, **36**, 56-57
and greens filling for eggs, 232
hardtack, **91**, 106-107
in dandyfunk, 116-117
in lobscouce, **82**, 119-120
and milk, **14**
pudding
gingerbread, 144
plum, 304
queen of, 58
rolls, French, **47**, 55-56, **212**
thirded, 26-27
sponge
for bread, **20**, 26-27
for rolls, 56
white, **128**, 143-144
brewis, **14**
fisherman's, 360
pronunciation, 356
brown bread, 78-79
in brewis, 19
buckwheat cakes, 159
butter
braiding, 226
drawn, 226, 366
maitre d'hotel, 400
melted, 226
sauce for salmon, 226

cabbage, 107
in cold slaw, 55
pickled, 75
red, 75
sauerkraut vs. pickled, 75
cake(s)
bride's, 325
buckwheat, 159
caraway, 28-29
coconut, **219**, 229, **310**
frosting for, 230
currant, 209
delicate, 322
election, 28, 21-22
fat, 133
frostings/icings, 186-187, 230, **310**
322-323
nineteenth century, 323
fruit, **8**, **92**, **172**, **186**, 186-187
frosting for, **186**, 186-187
gold, **310**, 323
to ice, 325
orange, 325-326
pound, 27
railroad, **148**, 163-164
shortcake, **318**
biscuit type, **316**, 326-327
sponge type, **313**, 327-328
strawberry, 326-327
with cream, 327-328
silver, **310**, 323-324
sponge, 77-78, **310**
strawberry shortcake, 326-327
with cream, 327-328
training day, 21-22
wedding, 324
candy, molasses, 278
with peanuts, 278-279
with walnuts, 279
canned fruit, **174**, 188
canning, 48, 188
capon, roasted, 118
caraway cake, 28-29
catsup, 24
celery, 273-274
cheese filling for eggs, 232
cherry pie, 231
chicken
fricasse, 250-251
gombo with oysters, 206
pie, 250-251
roasted, 118
salad, **44**, 53-54, **212**
chili sauce, 208
chocolate
forms, 328
ice cream, **310**, 328
rice, 138
chowder, **297**
clam, 305-307
corn, 307
fish, 303, 307-308
smoked fish, 309
clam(s), 370, 372-373

chowder, 305-307
fritters, **148**, 162-163, 358
clapshot, 250
cobbler, 120
coconut
cake, **219**, 229, **310**
icing, 230
cod, 373-375
crimping, 375
dunfish, 358, 373
kench-cured, 373
green, 373-374
salt, *see* cod, salt
scrod, 375
cod, salt, **266**, 373, 374, 394
bacalhau, 361
con arroz, 399
boiled, 358-359
Portuguese style, 360
codfish cakes, **337**, 359-360
dinner, **340**
dun fish, boiled, 358
fluff, **394**
picked up, 398
snacks, 374
coffee, 107, 147
cookies
ginger, 228-229
gingersnaps, 275-276
jumbles, 304-305
molasses, 147
sugar, 304-305
gingerbread, **172**
corn
bread, Mississippi, **194**, 207-208
chowder, 307
hominy, 121
hulled, **102**, 121
oysters, **368**, 397-398
popcorn balls, **259**, 279
in succotash, **67**, 76-77
corn meal, 23
Indian, 23
scalding, 26-27
in johnnycakes, 45-46, 160
corned beef,
boiled, **5**, 161
hash, 161-162
pressed, 228
cottage pudding, 145-146
crabs, 375-376
crackerhash, 109
cream and peaches, frozen, 324
cream of tartar, use of, 77
croutons, 76
crungeons, 135
cucumbers, vinegared, 47, 48
cullen skink, 309
currant(s)
cake, 209
canned, 188
jelly in floating island, 210
tart, **92**
cusk, 376
custard for snow pudding, 59

dandyfunk, 109, 116-117
doughnuts, 103-104, 117-118
dressing(s)
for cold slaw, 55
cream for salmon, 361
for lettuce, 47, 54
for sandwiches, 227
duck(s)
roasted, 273
roasting time, 273
duff, 109-110, **132**
plum, **91**, 115-116, **254**
dumplings, **190**
apple, 29-30
for beef soup, 25
light, 303
dun fish, *see* salt cod

eels, 376
egg(s)
boiled, **43**, 231
filled/stuffed, 231-232
fried, 232
fillings for
bread and greens, 232
cheese, 232
meat, 232
sauce for salmon, 226
entire wheat, 56
equivalents
entire wheat, 56
gill, 160
nutmeg, 253
rich milk, 253, 270
sherry glass, 185
sweet oil, 54
tea-cup, 253
wine-glassful, 73

figs, canned, **174**
fish, *see also* individual fish
broiled, 27-28
chowder, **297**, 303, 307-308
cullen skink, 309
smoked fish 309
cooking time, 226
grilled, 27-28
salt, *see also* salt cod
brewis, 360
hash, 398
varieties, 369-395
floating island, 209-210
Mrs. Abell's, 210
Mrs. Gates's, 210
types of, 210
flounder, 376-377
frijoles, 208
refried, 208
fricasse(s)
chicken, 250, 251
oyster, 357
fritter(s)
batter, 358
clam, **148**, 162-163, 358
oyster, 358
frostings/icings
coconut, 230
for fruit cakes, 186-187
for lemon pies, 164
fruit(s), *see* individual fruits
cakes, **8**, **92**, **172**, **186**, 186-187
frosting for, **186**, 186-187
pie, 230-231
preserved for tarts, 188

gelatine, 274-275
gingerbread
pudding, **128**, 144
soft, 80-81
sugar, **172**, 228-229, **259**
types, 80
gingersnaps, 275-276
gombo, **194**
chicken with oysters, 206
goose
roasted, 270-271, 272
roasting time, 272
sharp sauce for, 272-273
stuffings
apple and onion, 271-272
onion and sage, 271
potato, 272
gooseberries, canned, 188
graham
bread, **36**, 56
gems, 57
pans, 57
gravy, **260**
for boiled fowl, **236**, 249
dried beef, 160
uses for, 160
oyster for turkey, 248
salt pork, 159-160
uses for, 160
milk, **148**
gridiron, grilling fish on, 27-28
grunt, 120
gumbo, 194, 206

haddock, 377
stewed, **156**, 401
hake, 377-378
halibut, 378-379
steaks, fried, 400-401
ham
boiled, 74-75, **212**
curing, 74
hardtack, **91**, 106-107
in dandyfunk, 116-117
in lobscouce, **82**, 119-120
hash
corned beef, 161-162
cracker, 109
red flannel, 134-135
salt fish, 398
herring, **60**, 379-380
bloaters, 380
bucklings, 380
hard, 380
kippered, 380

ice cream, **310**
chocolate, **310**, 328
peach, 232-233
nineteenth-century favorites, 233
self-freezing, 233
strawberry, molded, **318**
ices

peaches and cream, 324
icings, *see* frostings
Indian, 23, *see also* corn meal
meal in buckwheat cakes, 159
pudding, 79-80
in thirded bread, 26-27
scalding, 26-27
isinglass, 274-275

jelly
gelatine and isinglass for, 274-275
orange, **262**, 274-275
joe-floggers, **132**, 138
jonnycake, 45-46, **148**, 160-161
meal, 23, 160

leavenings, chemical, 42, 70, 77, 104
lemon(s)
as alcohol substitute, 59
dip for steamed pudding, 59
lemonade, 230
pies, frosted, **148**, 164
sauce for cottage pudding, 145-146
lettuce salad, **43**, 47, 54, **212**
lobscouce, **82**, 108, 119-120, 137
lobster, 380-382, **381**
deviled, 361
stewed, 400

mackerel, 382-384
grilled, broiled, 27-28, **363**, 400
salt, fried, 73
maitre-d'hotel butter, 400
marmalade, quince, 187-188
meatballs, 17
meat filling for eggs, 232
meat, salt, *see* salt meat
meringue frosting for lemon pie, 164
milk gravy, **148**
mincemeat, **244**, 252
pies, **234**, 253
molasses
candy, 278
with peanuts, 278-279
with walnuts, 279
cookies, 147
in dandyfunk, 116-117
as sauce, **91**, 116
in swanky, 137, 146-147
as sweetener, 79
muffins, graham gems, 57
mussels, 384-385
mustard
made, 55, 272
mixed, 227
mutton, 52
chops
broiled, 207
fried, 207
leftover, uses for, 53
leg, boiled, 52-53

oil(s)
olive, 54
"sweet," 54
olive oil, 54
onion(s)
boiled, 251
stuffing for poultry
with apples, 271-272
with sage, 271
orange(s)
ambrosia, **170**, 185
cake, 325-326
jelly, **262**, 274-275
peel, preserved, **259**, 276-277
oyster(s), **330**, 385-388
in chicken gombo, 206
fricasse, 357
fried, **368**, 397
fritters, 358
roasted, 305
sauce for turkey, 248
scalloped, 397
soup, 270
stew, 51, **260**, 357
roux-thickened, 357

pancakes, **60**,**132**
pastry crust for pies, 252-253
pea(s) 107
soup, 76
peach(es)
brandied, 57-58
and cream, frozen, 324
ice cream, 232-233
pickled, 251
preserved, 57-58
peanut molasses candy, **259**, 278-279
pear(s)
brandied, 57-58
sauce, **30**
pickle(s)
beets, 274
cabbage, 75
peaches, 251
pie(s)
apple, **60**, **69**, 73-74, **234**
dried, **128**, 146
berry, 230-231
blackberry, 231
blueberry, **84**, 120-121, **266**
cherry, 231
chicken, 250-251
fruit, 230-231
lemon, frosted, **148**, 164
mincemeat, **234**, 253
pastry crust for, 252-253
pot, 110, **132**
seabird, 138
pumpkin, **234**, 253
sea, 110-111
types, 231
veal, 227
whortleberry, **84**, 120-121, **266**
pigeons, stewed, 303
pineapple(s)
ambrosia, 185
preserves, **174**, 189
plum(s)
bread pudding, **260**, 304
canned, 188
duff, **91**, 115-116, **254**
poi, 199
pollack, 388-389
popcorn balls, **259**, 279
pork
curried, **194**
fat fried, 360
ham
boiled, 74-75
curing, 74
roast, 184-185, **254**
salt, 106, **148**, **260**
cruncheons, 135
gravy, 159-160
uses for, 160
fried with apples, 24
fried with potatoes, 24
modern vs. early, 79
scraps, 359
scrunchions, **340**, 360
Portuguese dishes
bacalhau, 361
con arroz, 399
salt cod, 360, 361
soup, **128**, 142-143
pot roast, 142
potato(es), 107
boiled, **128**
fried with salt pork, 24, **60**
mashed, **36**
stuffing for poultry, 272
sweet, 118-119
and turnips, 250
yeast, 25-26, **47**
preserves, preserving
canning, 188
fruit for tarts, 188
orange peel, 276-277
peaches, 57-58
pineapples, **174**, 189
quince, 187
whortleberries, 188
pudding(s)
boiled, plum duff, 115-116, **254**
bread
gingerbread, **128**, 144
plum, **260**, 304
queen of, 58
chocolate, rice, 138
Christmas, 277-278
cottage, 145-146
duff, **91**, 109-110, 115-116, **132**, **254**
gingerbread, **128**, 144
Indian, 79-80
plum duff, 115-116
queen of, 58
snow, **35**, **36**, 49, 58-59
steamed, 59-60
gingerbread, 144
pumpkin pie, **234**, 253
punch, whiskey, 81

quince
marmalade, 187-188
preserves, 187

rhyming recipes, 260, 277
rice, 107
chocolate, 138
with salt cod, 399
roasting times, modern vs. early, 118
roe, shad, 391

scalloped, 399
rolls, French, **47**, 55-56, **212**
rosewater in early recipes, 28
rye
meal vs. flour, 78
in thirded bread, 26-27

sage onion stuffing for poultry, 271
salad(s)
chicken, **44**, 53-54, **212**
cold slaw, 55
combination, 47
dressing(s)
for cold slaw, 55
cream, 361
for lettuce, 54
lettuce, **43**, 47, 54, **212**
molded, **260**
salmon, **332**, 361
salamander, 397
saleratus biscuits, 144-145
salmon, 389-390
grilled or broiled, 27-28
poached, 226
salad, **332**, 361
sauces for (salmon)
butter, 226
cream, 361
egg, 226
salt cod, **266**, **337**, 373, 374, **394**
bacalhau, 361
con arroz, 399
boiled, 358-359
Portuguese style, 360
codfish cakes, **337**, 359
dinner, **340**
fluff, **394**
snacks, 374
salt meat, **91**, 106
boiled, **16**
in lobscouce, 108, 119-120, 137-138
scouse, 119-120, 137-138
stew, 137-138
salt pork, **148**, 106, **266**
cruncheons, 135,
gravy, 159-160
uses for, 160
fried with apples, 24
fried with potatoes, 24
modern vs. early, 79
scraps, 359
scrunchions, **340**, 360
sandwiches, dressing for, 227
sardines, 390
sauce(s)
butter, drawn, 226, 366
chili, 208
cream for salmon, 361
egg for salmon, 226
gravy, **260**
for boiled fowl, **236**, 249
dried beef, 160
uses for, 160
milk, **148**
oyster for turkey, 248
salt pork, 159-160
uses for, 160
lemon
for cottage pudding, 145-146
dip for pudding, 59-60
molasses, **91**, 116
oyster for turkey, 248
pear, **30**
sharp for goose, 272-273
as term for cooked vegetables, 250
sauerkraut vs. pickled cabbage, 75
scallops, 390-391
scouse, 119-120, 137-138
scrod, 375
scrunchions, **340**, 360
seabird pot pie, 138
sea pie, 110-111
shad, 391-392
baked, 401
grilled or broiled, 27-28
planking, 392
roe, 391
scalloped, 399
shrimp, 392-393
shortcake(s), **318**
biscuit type, **316**, 326-327
sponge type, **313**, 327-328
strawberry, 326-327
with cream, 327-328
smelts, 393
smother, **132**, 138
soda
in early recipes, 144
biscuits, 144-145
saleratus biscuits, 144-145
sole, 376-377
soup(s)
bean, **91**, 115
beef, 24-25, 142-143
dumplings for, 25
soup stock, 51
chicken gombo with oysters, 206
da couvas Portuguesa, **128**, 142-143
oyster, 270
pea, 76
Portuguese, **128**, 142-143
thickening, 24, 206
tomato, **36**, **51**, 51
turtle, 184
sponge
for bread, **20**, 26-27
cake, 77-78, **310**
for rolls, 56
setting, 26-27
squab, *see* pigeons
squash, **239**
steak, beef, grilled, **36**, 52
stew(s)
oyster, 51
roux-thickened, 357
stock
beef for soup, 51
strawberries
ice cream, **318**
shortcake, **316**, 326-327
with cream, **313**, 327-328
stuffing(s)
apple and onion, 271-272
onion and sage, 271
potato, 272
for turkey, 248
sturgeon, 393
succotash, 76-77
winter version, **67**, 76
sugar
cookies, jumbles, 304-305
gingerbread, **172**, 228-229, **259**
loaf, 54
clarifying, 57
yellow, 137
swanky, 137, 146-147
sweet potatoes, 118-119
swordfish, 393-394

taro, 199
tart(s)
banbury, 291
currant, **92**
tautog, 394-395
tea, 107-108
terrapin, 395
thickeners
crackers, 249
file, 206
okra, 206
roux, 357
for soup, 24, 206
tomato(es)
canning, 48
preparing, 51
soup, **36**, **51**, 51
stewing, 54-55
tongue, boiled, **8**, 54
trout, 395
fried, 206-207
tunny fish, 395
turbot, 395
turkey
boiled, **236**, 247-248
gravy sauce for, **236**, 249
oyster sauce for, 248
roast, 247, **260**
stuffing for, 248
turnip(s), 250
with potatoes, 250
swede, 250
yellow, 250
turtle, 395
soup, 184

veal
modern vs. nineteenth century, 227
pie, 227
vegetables, *see* individual vegetables
vinegar, modern vs. early, 75

walnut molasses candy, 279
weakfish, 395
whiskey punch, 81
white fish, 395
whortleberries
canned, **174**, 188
pie, **84**, 120-121, **266**

yeast
in historic recipes, 23, 143
making, 25-26
potato based, 25-26, **47**

GENERAL INDEX

A. J. Fuller, 87, 98, 99, 103, 109, 167, 168, 180, 224
A. R. Tucker,85, 97, 111, 171 202, 241
Abbey, Charles, 87, 100, 103, 108, 109, 110, 111, 113, 131, 176, 178, 180, 202, 224, 241, 265
Abell, Mrs., 33, 34, 47, 54, 79, 117, 118, 146, 159, 184, 185, 187, 207, 209, 210, 251, 253, 303, 359, 387, 393
Ackerman, Edward, 341, 345, 348, 372, 385, 390
Adams, Willie, 172
Addison, 89, 92, 98, 103, 110, 172,174, 179, 180, 182, 238, 266, 268, 269
Agate, 90, 93, 103, 103
Akbar, 110, 116, 181
Albacore, 178
Alcoholic beverages, 93, 219
Alert, 102, 174, 180, 196
Alewives, 369
Alexander Selkirk, 176
All Around the House; or How to make Homes Happy, 120, 160, 303, 398
Alicia B. Crosby, 368
Allison, Virginia Saunders, 155
American Cookery, 9, 22, 47, 110, 264, American Fisheries Society, 384
American Fishes, 377
American Frugal Housewife, 14, 20, 24, 26, 28, 47, 70, 73, 80, 107, 252, 253, 398
American Sardine Co., 376
American Woman's Home, 37, 69
Ames, Robie, 374, 389
Ames Family, 389
Amoy, 301
Amy Turner, 85, 91, 182, 200, 267
Andirons, 9, 11
Anthony, Joseph, 16, 17, 18, 41, 218, 221, 243, 295, 376, 388
Antilla, 171
Antiscorbutics, 93, 168, 169
Aqua Pura, 126
Archos,108, 178
Art of Cookery, 294
Art of Cookery Made Plain and Easy, 110
Ashley, Clifford, 115
Atlantic Fisherman, 352
Atlantic Monthly, 81, 378, 385
Ayer's Preserve Book, 189
Azores, 170, 172, 204

B. D. Nickerson, 126
Ball, Nicholas, 150, 152, 157, 260
Ballou, Norris, 91
Banbury tarts, 285
Bangalore, 177, 180, 368, 374
Barnard, Reverend John, 351
Barnstable Village Improvement Society, 395
Bates, Mrs. Henry, 56
Batty, Captain G. M., 318
Batty, Oliver, 318
Bay State Fishing Company, 348, 352, 353
Beatty, William, 220
Bechtel, Walter, 111
Beebe, Ebenezer, 298, 299
Beecher, Catherine, 37, 69, 334, 390
Beecher, H. W., 37, 69, 120, 160, 303, 334, 390, 398
See also Stowe, Harriet Beecher
Beer, 20
Belvedere, 223
Benjamin F. Packard, 84, 98
Bennet, Elizabeth C. P., 284
Betsy's, 133
Birdseye, Clarence, 348
Birthdays (sea), 103, 138
Bishop, George, 95
Bishop, W. H., 377
Bivalve, 295
Bixby, Fred, 208
Black cat, 105
Blanchard, Captain Banning, 177
Blanchard, George, 181
Blanchard, Georgia Maria, 93, 177, 368, 374
Blaney, Henry, 180
Blenheim, 177
Bliss, Mrs. 79, 118, 119, 226, 247, 250, 253, 270, 271, 305, 325, 357, 359
Block Island turkey, 155
Blue fish, 369-370
Boardman, Jettie, 160
Boat races, watching, 221
Boneless fish, 346-349
Bonita, 314
Bonito, 178
Bonsall, Spencer, 95, 96, 98, 100, 110, 111, 111, 112, 174, 177, 178, 179, 262, 268
Boston Bay Blues, 354
Boston Cook Book, 376
Boston Cooking School Cookbook, 13, 76, 361, 376
Boughton, George Piper, 108, 178
Bowhead meat, 180
Bowley, Captain Gideon, 131, 133
Boynton, Willard, 136
Bradford, William, 243, 355
Breakfast, 17, 44, 45, 68, 70, 97, 134
Bred mixin, 156, 157
Breed, Shubael, 242
Brewer, Warren family, 287
Brewis, **14**, 19, 134, 356
Brewster, Captain George, 97, 101
Brewster, Mary, 90, 92, 93, 99, 103, 113, 168, 171, 173, 176, 177, 178, 179, 183, 187, 198, 199, 200, 205 265-266, 267
Briggs, Enos, 313
Briggs, Lloyd, 85, 91, 112, 182, 200
Briggs, Vernon, 177, 178, 178, 205, 210, 267
Brigham, Peter, 386
Brown, Ann, 90, 93, 102, 103
Brown, Oliver, 346
Brown, Randall, 317
Brown's Livery Stable, photo., 62
Buckingham, Lydia Watrous, 5, 6, 7, 9, 10, 22
Buckingham, Mehetebel, 6, 22
Buckingham, Samuel, 5, 6, 9, 12, 13
Buckingham, Samuel, Jr., 6
Buckingham, William, 6
Buckingham House, **5,** 8, **19**
Buddington, Captain, house, **222**
Buel, Abel, 7
Bullocks, 180
Bull rakes, 370, **371**
Bunker, Adrianna family, 287
Bunker, Emery, 287
Bunker Hill, 135
Burdick, Howard, 336, 344, 369, 382
Burgess, Ann Hathaway, 20
Burnham, George, 380, 390
Burns, Milton, 255
Burrows, Ambrose, 62, 63
Burrows, Ann, 63
Burrows, Annie Elizabeth, 63
Burrows, Jane, 63-66, 68, 69, 71
Burrows, Lizzie, 62
Burrows, Mabel, 63
Burrows, Seth Winthrop "Winty", 61-66, 71
Burrows House, **61, 65**
Burrows Store, 41, 62, 64
Bushnell, Augustus, 9
Button, Florence, 47
Bygrave, W., 203

C. W. Packer ice cream freezers, 317-318
Cakes, 21, 22, **219, 310,** 312, 318, 320
Coconut, **219**
Shortcake, **313**
Wedding, 315
Calf's head soup, 17
Camacho, Maria Goulart 142, 361

Camboose, 85
Campbell, Jesse, 177
Canadian fishermen, 133, 135, 350
Canned food, 48-49, 85, 94, 101, 125, 344-345
Cannery, Maine, **345**
Canning, tomatoes, 48
Card, Fannie, 163, 164, 209, 317, 322, 325, 326
Card, William, 260
Carter, H. A. P., 200, 210
Cellar, 33
Ceres, 138
Chace, Charles W., 48, 91, 92, 103
Chace, Elizabeth Buffam, 21
Champlin, Horace, 43
Channing, Mary, 216, 219, 241, 242, 244
Chapman, Edward, 350
Charity
  Christmas, 264-265
  Thanksgiving, 239
Charles W. Morgan, **83**, 84, 85, 91, 92, 98, 100, 101, **104**, **105**, 111, 174, 175, 180, 241, 307
Charlie York: Maine Coast Fisherman, 147
Charmer, 176, 265
Chase, Charles, **218**
Cheese, 15, 16
Chicken salad, **44**
Child, Lydia Maria, 9, 14, 16, 20, 21, 24, 26, 47, 73, 80, 239, 252, 253, 273, 303, 359, 366, 374, 398
Chimneys, 7, 34, 63, 125
Chinese eating, 201-202
Chocolate rice, 138
Chowder, 293-301, 305, 309
  Crackers, 300
  Milk, 296
  Moby Dick, 296
  More clams, 300
  New England dish, 296-298
  Onion, 295-296
  Potatoes, 294, 301
  Tomatoes, 296
Chowder parties, 295, 298-301
Christmas, 256-268
  Cookies and candies, **259**, 262-264
  Dinner, **260**, 261-262
  At home, 260-261
  Life-saving station, 260
  Religious occasion, 256-257
  At sea, **255**, 265-268, **266**
  Sunday-school parties, 259-260
Cider, 20, 21
Cistern, 34
Clambakes, 281-289
  Family, 284-287
  "Monster" 1000 attend, 289
  Mystic, CT, photo., 281
  Rhode Island, 287-288
  Rocky Point, photo., 282
  Winslow Homer sketch, 288
Clams, 370-373
Clara Bell, 180, 224
Clarissa B. Carver, 90, 91, 93, 103, 196, 223, 267
Clifford, Harold B., 147
Clock jack, 11
Clytie 93, 103, 175
Coconut cake, **219**
Cod, 373-375
Coffee, 107, 137, 192, 192
Cogswell, Mason Fitch, 242
Coit, Anna North, 47, 74, 160, 325
Colcord, Joanna, 91, 98, 102, 103, 106
Collins, Captain J. W., 135
Colonial revival teas, 318
Comet, 39
Communal eating, 97, 113
Communal wooden kid, **110**
Complete Domestic Guide, 54, 79, 117, 118, 146, 159, 184, 187, 209, 251, 359
Connecticut River, 1783, chart, **7**
Connolly, James B., 123, 126, 133, 137
Cook
  Captains' wives, 90, 92-93
  Household, 43-44
  Life-Saving Stations, 154-155, 157
  Sea, 87-89, **88**, 108, 126-129
Cook, Captain Henry, 374
Cookbooks, 71, 364, 367, 374
Cookbook of the Young People's Society of Christian Endeavor, 291
Cookies and cakes, 22
Cooking, open hearth, 8, 11
Cooking outdoors
  Recreational beginnings 282, 284
Cooking seafood, 363-395
  Alewives, 369
  Blue fish and striped bass, 369-370
  Clams, 370-373
  Cod and salt cod, 373-375
  Crabs, 375-376
  Cusk, 376
  Eels, 376
  Fins, napes, tongues, sounds, heads, 367-369
  Flounder and Sole, 376-377
  Haddock, 377
  Hake, 377-378
  Halibut, 378-379
  Herring, 379
  Lobsters, 380-382
  Mackerel, 382-384
  Mussels, 384-385
  Oysters, 385-388
  relish, 369
  Salmon, 389-390
  Sardines, 390
  Scallops, 390-391
  Scrod, 375
  Shad, 391-392
  Shrimp, 393-393
  Smelts, 393
  Sturgeon, 393
  Swordfish, 393-394
  Tautog, 394-395
  Terrapin and turtles, 395
  Trout, Sea Trout, Weakfish, Squeteaque, 395
  Tunny fish, 395
  Turbot, 395
  White fish, 395
  White sauce and salt pork fat, 366
Cooking seafood *See also* Fish eating,
Cook stove, **65**
Coral, 102
Corinthian, **123**
Cornell, William M., 326, 327
Corn, **102**, 107
Corning, 15
Cottrell, C. B., Jr., **218**
Country of the Pointed Firs, 295
Crabs, 375-376
Crackerhash, 109
Crapo, Captain Thomas, 108, 109
Creole cookery, 196
Crown Packing Company, 339, 352, 354
Cuddy, 128
La Cuisine Creole, 206, 207
Cullen skink, 301
Cummings, George J., 12
Currant wine, 21
Cusk, 376
Custard apple, 182
Cyrus Wakefield, 178, **178**

D. O. Richmond Yard, 314
Dairy products, 15, 41
Dana, Richard Henry, 46, 68, 71, 84, 87, 90, 94, 97, 102, 106, 108, 111, 119, 168, 174, 179, 180, **180**, 194, 196, 197, 201, 205, 208, 238, 241, 256, 260, 261, 268, 269, 273
Dandyfunk, 109, 116-117
Davidson, Alan, 377
Davis, Benajah, 317
Davis, Frank E., 338, 348, 353, 359, 368, 384
Deblois, Henrietta, 104
Dedications, 314-315
DeLong, Edwin, 343
Denison, Ed, 41
Denison, Ethan, 16, 21, 221, 221
Denison, I. W., 42, 289
Denison, Lavinia, 221
Denison, Mrs. Charles H., 289
Denison, Mrs. D. W., 289
Denison, Mrs. Daniel, 316
Denison, Rev. Frederick, 216
DeVoe, Thomas, 363, 376, 391
Dewire, Elinor, 157
Diary in America, 192
Diet, 44-45, 68, 71, 84
Dining saloon, Mystic, **200**
Dinner, 16, 17, **36**, 46-48, 68, 70-71, 97, 135
  Cabin, **84**, **92**, 101-103
  Forecastle, **86**, **91**
Dinnerware, 9, 12, 35, 40, 63, 66, 86-87, 126
Dinner Year Book, 52, 53, 55, 58, 162, 185, 230, 231, 233, 248, 295, 327, 361, 399, 401
Directions for Cookery, 296
Dishwashing methods, 10, 245
Doctor (sea cook), 127, 128
Dodderidge, Joseph, 110
Dodge, Frances Jaixen, 155, 155, 314, 401
Dorado, 181
Dorothy Snow, 131
Dory-mates, **136**

Doughnut-eaters, **220**
Doughnuts, 103-104, 117-118
Dover egg beater, 58
Dow, Annie Eliza, 175
Dow, Captain Jonathan, 111, 175, 176, 223
Dow, Elizabeth, 216
Dow, Fred, 223, 224
Dow, Sara, 90, 93, 196, 267
Dow, Scott, 103, 111
Duclow, Viola, 352
Dudley, Chas., 259
Dudley, Elisha, 9
Dudleys, 6
Duff, 109-110, 115-116, **132**
Duncan, Fred, 267
Dunfish, 373
Dwight, Timothy, 17, 18, 20, 350, 351, 352, 363, 385
Dyer, Ben, 91
Dyer, Sarah, 91

Early Bird, 90
Edmondson, Catherine, 32
Edward, 90, 95, 96, 98, 99, 100, 110, 112, 173, 178, 262, 268
Edward Everett, 95
Eldredge, Lewis, 94, 100, 108, 202 180
Eldridge, Charles Q., 216
Election cake, 21
Election Day, 21
Ely, Ben, 89, 90, 91
Emerald, 125
Emerson, Ralph Waldo, 257
Emery, David, 15
Emery, Sarah Anna Smith, 11, 15, 17, 19, 21, 104, 240, 245, 312, 313, 338, 346, 351
Emigrant, 89
Emma C. Berry, 337, 392
English dining, 197
Episcopalians, 256, 257
Essex, 313
Essex Historical Society, 74
Eustis, Harry, 133, 134, 135
Experiment, 295

Fair American, 367
Fairfax, Captain Thomas, 382
"Fall Fishing,", **140**
Fanny, 385
Farmer, Fannie Merritt, 13, 76, 228, 275, 290, 361, 366, 370, 389, 393
Farmer's Inn, 194

Farnsworth, Annie, 194
Farnsworth, Mary Emma Weaver, 15, 18, 19, 20, 194, 195, 284
Farrow, John, 389
Fast-food precursor, 71, 194
Fat, 105
Fat Back and Molasses: a Collection of Old Recipes from Newfoundland and Labrador, 119, 360
Fat-cake, 133
Feast of Shells, 283
Felker, Peter, 370, 376, 377, 379, 382, 389, 389, 390, 393
Fiddles, 98, **124**
Field, Irving, 384
Fillet, fish, 346-349
Finnan Haddie, 377
Fireplaces, 7, 63, 125
Fireworks, 219-220
First Texas Cookbook, 387
Fish, Asa, 216, 221, 256, 260, 317
Fish, Benjamin F., 240, 241
Fish, James D., 258, 260
Fish, Nathan, 41, 48, 49, 221, 240, 300
Fish, Silas, 242
Fish, Simeon, 242
Fish dealers wharf, Newport, RI, **334**
Fish eating, 13-14, 46, 68, 331-335
  Bone problem, 346-349
  Freshness, 335-339
  On Friday, 338-339
  Frozen fish, 341
  Iced fish, 340-341
  Impounding, 336
  Marketing, 352-355
  Problems, 332
  Railroads and refrigeration, 339-340
  Social prejudice, 349-351
Fish flakes, **342**
Fish Hawk, 147
Fish poisoning, 181
Fish preservation methods, 341-345
  Canned, 344-345
  Cooking and canning, 344
  Salting and drying, 342-343
  Smoking, 343
Fish processing ("fluff") **394**
Fisher, Barry, 128, 129, 132, 134, 135, 137
Fisher, Captain Elnathan, 267
Fisheries, 6
Fisheries of Glouster, 368
Fishermen
  Biddeford, ME, **363**
  Dory-mates, **136**
  eating fish, 135-136, 180, 350
  Maine store, **375**
  Monhegan Island, **367, 378**
  Nantucket, **347**
  Profile, 351-352
  Yankee, **350**
Fishermen's dishes *See also* Sailor's Dishes
  Chocolate rice, 138
  Fat cake, 133
  Joe Floggers, 138
  Pea soup, 135
  Red flannel hash, 134
  Scouce, 137
  Smother, 138
  Swanky, 137
Fishing technology, 353
  Otter trawl net, 348
Fishmonger, **333**
  Fulton Fish Market, NY, **392**
Fitch, Cephas, 68
Florence, 267
Flying fish, 177
Food complaints (sea)
  Lack of variety, 112
  Quantity, 112
Food exchanges, 6, 14, 15, 18, 41, 171-173
Food for the Hungry: A Complete Manual, 76
Food storage, 8, 9, 33, 131, 151, 173-175
  Barrels, 131
  Sea, 94, 95, 111-112, 129-131
Food supply
  Buckingham house, 12-16
  Burrows House, 66-68
  Greenmans, 40-42
  Life-Saving Stations, 152-154
Foodways, XII, 49, 113, 133, 139-140, 155-157, 204
Forced meat, 17
Forecastle, 98, 102, 113, 176, 267
Forefather's Day, 283
Form 9, Inventory of Public Property, 151
Forsyth, John, 42, 67
Forty Fathom Fish, 348, 349
Fourth of July, 213-234, 287
  ashore, 213-223
  at sea, 223-224
  Traditional dinner, 221
Francis, Captain John, 126, 128, 129, 131, 134, 135, 136, 139
Frank A. Palmer, 313
Frank E. Davis Co., 339, 352, 353, 354, 390
Franklin Post and Son Boatyard, 314
Frazier, Mary, 101
Frederick Gebhard, 266
Freeman, Capt Jo., 66
French cooking, 196-197
French rolls, **47**
Fresh food, 168-173
  Nutrition, 168-169
  Sea, 177-182
  Variety, 168
Frijoles, 196
Frozen fish, 341
Fruit, 7, 16, 67, 100, 171, 182, 196
  Preserved, **174**
Fulton Fish Market, NY, **355**, 386
Furlong, Thomas, photo., 130
Furniture, kitchen, 10, 37, 65

G. W. Blunt White Library, 80, 186, 304
Galley, 85, 125
  Charles W. Morgan, **83**
Gates, Julia, 38, 41, 44, 46, 49, 50, 53, 55, 58, 209, 210, 229, 230, 240, 258, 269, 275, 315, 319, 382, 388
George, 101
George Greenman & Co., 32, 314
Gibson, Charles Dana, 393
Gilbert, Charlotte, 308
Ginger beer, 21
Glasse, Hannah, 110, 294, 346
Globe, 86
Godey's Lady's Book, 238, 262, 269, 270, 272, 277, 334
Goode, George Brown, 108, 124, 129, 283, 287, 352, 370, 377, 379, 381, 384, 385, 389, 390, 391, 393
Goodholme's Domestic Cyclopedia, 44, 333

Gorton-Pew Fisheries, 123, 352
Gott, Peter, 377
Graham, Sylvester, 32, 50
Grains, 12, 13, 15, 107
Grandy, Randall, **127**
Grant, Mrs. Pearl, 317
Gray, Captain Horatio, 224, 265, 266
Gray's, New London, CT, 193, 194, 200, 205, 207
Great generals, 129, 129
Green fish, 373-374
Greenman, Abby Chipman, 32, 33, 34, 43
Greenman, Charlotte Rogers, 6, 22, 31, **32**, 33, 34, 37, 43, 44, 49
Greenman, Clark, 32, 37
Greenman, George, 32, 34, 37, 43
Greenman, Harriet Almy, 32, 33, 48
Greenman, Mrs. Thomas S., 289
Greenman, Thomas, **31**, 32, **33**, 34, 41, 43, 49
Greenman home, **31**
Greenmanville Store, 33, 40, 41
Griffiths, William, 97
Grinnel, Eva Collins, **286**
Grocer's Manual, 370
Grocery lists, 42, 156
Grocery stores, 40-41, 64
Grub, 105

Haddock, 377
    Stewed in cream, **156**
Haines, Sally, 43
Haines, William, 43
Hake, 377-378
Hale, Sarah Josepha, 238, 334, 338, 349
Haley, Nelson, 180, 204
Hall, Miss Elizabeth M., 52, 54, 73, 75, 76, 119, 146, 188, 189, 206, 207, 227, 230, 247, 248, 251, 273, 274
Halloway, Laura C., 276
Halloway, Martin, 346
The Handy Hone Book, 326
Hardtack, 105, 106-107
Harland, Marion, 52, 53, 54, 55, 58, 162, 185, 229, 230, 231, 233, 248, 295, 327, 361, 399, 374, 400, 401
Harlow, Alvin, 386
Harlow, Frederick, 106, 110, 181
Harness cask, 106
Hart, Captain Elisha, 18
Hash, 108
Hastings, Caroline, 27
Hawaii, 168, 197-201
Hawaiian cooking, 197-201
Hayden, Nehemiah, 266
Haynes, Charles, 259
Hazard, Thomas, 370, 376
Hearthstone; or Life at Home, a Household Manual, 276
Hearne, Lafcadio, 206, 207
Hecker's flour 162
Hector, 87
Henderson, Mrs. Mary F., 51, 53, 115, 143, 144, 162, 188, 228, 230, 233, 270, 274, 324, 328, 358, 359, 361, 375, 397, 400
Herald, 180, 202
Hermes, Fred, 289, 299, 305, 306
Herring, 379-380
Hibberd, Isaac, 100, 108, 116, 178
Higgins, Reverand Francis, 381
High Street Cookbook, 274
Highland Life-Saving Station, 154

Hill, Georgiana, 364, 366, 367
Hinton, Edward, 91
Hirsch, Rose Camacho, 142, 360, 361, 399

Home brewing, 20-21
Homer, Winslow, 288
Hood, C. I. & Co., 51, 52, 54, 57, 58, 161, 227, 231, 247, 273, 303, 357, 397, 400
Hood's Combined Cook Books, 51, 52, 54, 57, 58, 161, 227, 231, 247, 273, 274, 303, 357, 397, 400
Hood's Cookbook #1, 322
Hopewell, 111, 173
Horse racing, 62, 63, 65
Horsford's flour, 162
Horton, Frank, 385
Hotel dining, 195
Howland, Mrs. E. A., 18, 27, 28, 29, 117, 187, 188, 247, 248, 249, 250, 252, 253, 264, 273, 304, 307
Hugill, Stan, 173
Hurd, Cyrus Jr., 177, 178
Hurricane house, 85
Husbandman and Housewife, 373

Ice cream and cake festivals, 317-318
Iced fish, 135, 340-341
Ice vessels, 341
Impounding fish, 336
Imu, 199
India, 202-204
Indian meal, 23, 33, 42, 110
Indian Ocean, 202-204
Ingersoll, Ernest, 287
Intrepid, 100, 241
Ishmael, 83, 192
Isinglass, 127, 367
Ivany, Netta, 119

J. M. Thurston, **203**
Jaixen, George, 155
Jane Fish, 100, 108
Janes, E. G., 157
Jarvis, Reverend Samuel, 18
Jefferson, 196
Jenckes, Amos, 89
Jennison, Frank, **130**
Jesperson, Reverend Ivan, 119, 360
Jewett, Sarah Orne, 295
Jiggs dinner, 137
Joe-floggers, 132, **132**, 138
John & Albert, 265, 266
John P. West, 175, 268, 269, 279
John Perkins's Journal at Sea, 119
John R. Neal & Co., 377
Johnson, Edward, 355
Johnson, Elroy, 129, 136
Jones, William F., 343, 379
Jonnycakes, 23, 45, 160-161
Jordan, William H., 130
Juan Fernandez, 171, 173, 176, 179
Julian, 102
July 4th *See* Fourth of July

Kalm, Peter, 336, 381, 385, 386
Kedgeree, 100
Keeper rails, 132
Kench-cured fish, 373
Kimball, Sumner, 151, 153
King, Caroline "Kiddy", 13, 16, 17, 19, 239, 240, 241, 243, 244, 257, 273, 295, 312, 359, 366, 373, 374
Kitchen Companion, 341
Kitchen furniture, 10, 37, 65
Kitchens
    Buckingham house, 7-8
    Burrows House, 63, **65**
    Greenmans, 33-34
    Life-Saving Stations, 151
Knapp, Edward, 68, 68, 222, 262, 301, 317, 320, 339, 346, 373
Knife-eating, 12, 39

L. A. Dunton, 125, 134, **134**, 137, 139
L. A. Morgan & Co., 67
Lacey, Alice, 119
Ladd, Frank, 287
Lamphere, Captain, 295
Lamphere, William, 299
Landers, Thomas C., 91, 92
Langworthy, Maxon, 129, 134, 135, 138
Larcom, Lucy, 7
Latham, William "Boss", 262
Lawrence, Mary, 89, 92, 98, 102, 110, 168, 171, 172, 174, 175, 177, 178, 179, 180, 181, 182, 183, 198, 238, **267**, 296, 297, 302
Lawrence, Minnie, 92, 103, 168, 175, 182, 267, **267**
Lawrence, Samuel, 98
Lay (share), 127
Leavitt, John F., 137
Leavitt, Virginia, 147
Lemonade vending, **196**
Leonard, Elizabeth Dow, 243
Leslie, Eliza, 296, 389
Lewer, Robert, 200
Lewis E. Spear Company, 86
Life Saving Service, 149-157
    Cook, 154-155
    Cooking and eating utensils, 151-152
    Food supplies, 152-154
    Foodway, 157
    Grocery lists, 156, 156
    Meals of the day, 154
    Parties, 314
Lincoln, Mary, 366, 375, 384
Ling, 373
Liquor sales, 64, 66
Liverpool scouce, 108, 109
Livestock, 12
    At sea, 173-175
Live Yankee, 67
Lobscouce, 108, 119-120
Long-tailed sugar, 105

Look, Hiram, 97, 202
Lothrop, Reverend S. K., 257
Lowe, J. G., 64
Loyalist, 221
Luau, 200
Lugpoles, 7
Lunches, dory, 133

Mackerel, 382-384
MacKinnon, Captain R. N., 193, 195
Macomber, Captain Benjamin, **149**
Magnolia, 227
Mallory, Charles Henry, 374
Mallory, Mrs. Charles Henry, 32, 50
Mallory and Sons, 314
Mandarin, 181
Manhattan, 173
Marion, 135
Market Assistant, 364, 391
Marr, Captain Chester, 132, 133
Marryat, Frederick, 192, 195, 221
Marshall, Jimmy, 87
Martell, William, 132
Mary & Helen, 238, 243
Mary Lane, 382
Mathews, J. H., 353
Maxon, William Ellery, 300
Maxon and Fish Shipyard, 300
Maxson, Silas Jr., 300
Maxson, William Ellery, 35, 49, 314
McKay, Donald, 314
McManus, Thomas F., 134, 340
Meals, 66, 99-100
  Cabin, 84, 98, 110, 113
  Fishing schooners, 124
  Fo'c'sle, 84, 98, 110, 113
Meals of the day
  Buckingham house, 16-20
  Burrows House, 68-71
  Fishermen, 134-137
  Greenman, 44-49
  Life-Saving Station, 154, 155
Mealtimes
  Deep water vessels, 97-99
  Fishing schooners, 131, 133
Meat, 46, 68, 95
  Beef prefered, 15, 68
  Fresh, 14-15, 102
  Pork, 15, 68
Medford, 224
Melville, Herman, 87, 108, 171, 172, 192, 197, 201
Mending nets, **331**
Mentor, 86, 102, 103, 112, 174, 176, 224
Menus, 17-18, 46
Merchant, Robert, 132, 136, 137
Merlin, 104
Merrimac, 313
Merryman J. H., 314
Mess bills, 99-100, **101**
Messroom/kitchen, 151
Messroom supper, **148**
Mexican dining, 196
Mike Lyon's restaurant, 194
Miller, Mary, 57, 78, 324
Millet, Samuel, 95, 111, 111
Millett, Arthur, 353, 354
Millie, 314
Millinery store, 61, 64
Milton, 242
Mince meat, 18
Mincemeat, **244**, 264
Miner, Capt. Thomas, 42
Miss Parola's New Cookbook and Marketing Guide, 25
Moby Dick, 83
Molde, Captain, 171
Molded desserts, 36
Mollasses barrel sugar, 68
Montauk, 242
Morgan, Bessie, 240
Morgan, Charles Waln, 19, 20, 218, 219, 221, 238, 239, 240, 242, 246, 255, 257 261
Morgan, Clara, 258
Morris, Rev. Benjamin, 238
Mother's Book of Daily Duties, 33
Mrs. Rorer's Cookbook 307
Mrs. Rorer's Philadelphia Cook Book, 121, 142, 184, 231, 278
Mrs. Winslow's Domestic Receipt Book for 1876, 57, 159, 227, 228, 250, 323, 397
Mug-ups, 137
Mulligan, 138
Mundy, Sarah, 37, 43, 46
Murphy, J. R. photo., 130
Mussels, 384-385
Mystic, dining saloon, **200**
Mystic Clam Club, 295
Mystic *Pioneer* 59
Mystic River Historical Society, 53, 229, 275
Mystic River, long bank, **372**
Mystic Seaport Museum Exhibits
  Ames Fish house etc., 389
  Buckingham Family Household, 5-22
  Burrows Family Household, 61-71
  Charles W. Morgan (whaleship), 84
  Emma C. Berry (smack), 337, 392
  Greenman Family Homes 31-49
  L. A. Dunton (fishing schooner), 134
  New Shoreman Life-Saving Station, 150, 153
  Noank lobster shack, 383
  Spouter Inn, 192
  Thomas Oyster House, 385-386

Narragansett Life-Saving Station crew, **149**
Nauss, Arthur, **130**
Neustadt, Kathy, 283
New Bedford, MA, 213
New Cook Book, 338, 349
New England boiled dinner, **4**, **16**
New England Economical Housekeeper, 13, 18, 27, 28, 29, 70, 117, 187, 188, 247, 248, 249, 250, 252, 253, 264, 273, 304, 307
New England's Fishing Industry, 341
New Family Receipt Book, 28
Newfoundlanders, 137-138,
Newport, RI, 363
New Shoreham Life-Saving Station, 150
New Shoreham Life-Saving Station, Mystic Seaport, **153**
Niagara, 314
Noank, CT, 382
Noank Baptist Church Festival, 320
Noank lobster shack, 383
Nordhoff, Charles, 125, 134
Norris, Thomas, 125
North, Franklin, 127
North America, 175, 182
Noyes, Thomas, 315

Ohio, 102, 170,175, 186, 266, 267, 304
Old Colony Club, 283
Old Harbor Station, Orleans, MA, 155
Old Sturbridge Village, 27, 307
Olmsted, Francis A., 175, 182, 197
Omoo, 87, 108, 171, 172, 201
One Hundred Ways of Cooking Fish, 335
O'Connor, Mr., 151, 152
Open-hearth cooking, 8
Orange jelly, **262**
Osborne, Henry, 123, 137
Osborne, James C., 174, 175
Otter trawl net, 348
Our Homes; How to Beautify Them, 268
Oxtail soup, 204
Oysters, **331**, 385-388
Oyster saloons, 194
Oyster stands, **193**
Oyster suppers, 316, 318

Packer, Robert, 300
Pair steelyards, 10
Palestine, 91
Palmer, Julia 74, 77
Palmer Shipyard, 320
Pamet River Life-Saving Station, 151-152
Pancho, 91
Pantry, 33, 85, 90
Parades, 216-218, **216**
Park, Ann Catherine, 63
Park Central Market, 41
Parker, Captain Abner, 7
Parloa, Maria, 25, 222, 223, 323, 335, 338, 341, 364, 366, 376, 379, 382, 388, 391, 392, 393, 394
Parties/Refreshments
  Church festival, 320
  Dedications, 314-315
  Ice cream and cake festivals, 317
  Life-Saving Station, 314
  Oyster suppers, 318
  Ship launchings, 313-314
  Social Teas, 312-313
  Strawberry festivals, 316
  Weddings, 315
Pea-coffee, 192
Peaked Hill Bars Life-Saving Station, 151-152
Pearlash, 104
Penobscot Bay Salmon Fishery, 389
Perkins, John, 17, 89, 95, 97, 99, 100, 108, 109, 111, 113, 131, 171, 172, 173, 176, 182, 198
Pewter, 10
Picnics, **212**, 222, 295, 300
Pie, New England apple, **69**
Pies, 68, **69**, **234**, 243-245
Pierce, Wesley George, 125, 128, 129,

131, 366, 376, 384, 394
Pilgrim 108, 196, 268
Pinkys, 125, 129
Place settings, table, 12, 40, 98, 132
Planet 133, 370
Plum duff, 109
Poganuc People, 256, 257
Poi, 199, 201
Pollock, 388-389
Polly & Sally, 126
Porpoise, 177
Portuguese food, 135, 136
Post, Captain Francis, 172
Post, Ruth, 172
Practical American Cookery and Domestic Economy, 52, 54, 73, 75, 76, 119, 146, 188, 189, 206, 207, 230, 247, 248, 251, 273
Practical Cookbook 79, 117, 119, 226, 247, 250, 253, 270, 271, 305, 325, 357, 359
Practical Cooking and Dinner Giving, 51, 53, 115, 142, 144, 162, 188, 228, 229, 230, 274, 324, 328, 358, 361, 397
Preservation, 175, 341-345
Processed foods, 35-36
Provisioning, 93-97, 129
Pukui, Mary Kawena, 201
Pure Food Cookbook, 334, 338, 341, 366
Putnam, Mrs., 374

Quakers, 257
Quononchontaug Life-Saving Station, 155

Radcliffe, Lewis, 354
Railroads, 339-340
Rain water, 96-97, 126
Rancho Los Alamitos, Long Beach, CA, 208
Randall Ice Cream Parlor, **319**
Reaper 99, 100
Receipts for the Millions, 343
Redfield, John, Howard, 21, 236, 216, 219, 240, 241, 242
Red flannel hash, 134
Redware, 11
Refrigeration, 94, 339-340
Refrigerator, 37
Reveley. Ida, 39
Revely, 95
Revenue, 16
Reynolds, Aubrey, 152, 153
Reynolds, Irving, 238, 243
Rhode Island clambake, 287-288
Rhode Island WCTU Recipe Book, 56
Rice, 107
Rich, Thomas A., 338
Ricketson, Annie, 85, 97, 111, 112, 170, 171, 172, 175, 177, 179, **180**, 202, 202, 203, 204, 224, 241, 243, 257, 266
Ricketson, Daniel, 266, 267
Riesenberg, Felix, 84, 87, 94, 98, 103, 109, 111, 167, 168, 169, 172, 175, 178, 180, 199, 224, 268
Roasting devices, 11
Rocky Point, RI, 282, 283, 288
Rodman, Samuel, 15, 41, 258
Rogers, Charlotte, 22
Rogers, James, 86, 102, 103, 112, 174, 176
Rorer, Mrs. S. T., 121, 142, 184, 231, 278, 279, 307
Rotch's, W. J., 258
Rowland, Captain P. E., 287
Ryder, Rebecca Smith, 155
Ryder, Richard, 155

Sabine, Lorenzo, 368, 373, 379, 380, 382
Sailor's dishes
  Crackerhash, 109
  Dandyfunk, 109
  Duff, 109-110
  Hardtack, 106-107
  Lobscouce, 108
  Peas, beans, rice, 107
  Potatoes and cabbage, 107
  salt beef, salt pork, 106
  Sea pie, 111
Salads, **43**, 47
Saleratus, 69, 104
Salmon, 389-390
Saloon, 98
Salt beef, 106
Salt cod, **337**, 373-374
Salt fish, 342-343
Salt hay, 6
Salt-haying, 21
Salt horse, 105
Salt junk, 105
Salt pork, 106
Salt pork fat, 296, 299, 366
Small generals, 129
Samuels, Samuel "Bully", 69, 97, 103, 168, 172-173, 177, 179, 180, 196, 205
San Francisco dining, 195-196
Sanitation, 337
Sardines, 390
Saunders, Captain William Franklin, 155
Saybrook, Ferry District, 6
Scallops, 390-391
Scholfield family, Mystic, **298**
Scouce, 109, 134, 137-138
Scrod, 375
Scrunchions, 366
Scudder, Newton, 135
Scurvy, 168, 169, 170, 173
Sea food cookery, *See* Cooking, seafood
Sea pie, 110-111
Sea trout, 395
Seabird pot pie, 133, 138
Seabirds, 180
Seafaring, 116
Seaman's Friend, 97
Seasickness, 87
Seawater, 126
Selkirk, Alexander, 171
Seventh Day Baptist Church, 32, 44
Shack cupboard, 125, 133, 137
Shad, 6, 14, 350, 391-392
Sharpe, Reuben, 15
Sheffield, 113
Shellfish, 179, 283
Sherman, Phebe, 242
Ship launchings, 313-314
Shrimp, 392-393
Shute and Merchant, 347, 348, 352, 389
Sicillian dining, 197
Simmons, Amelia, 9, 22, 47, 110, 264, 337, 363, 391, 395
Simmons, Mary E., 313
Simpson, Benjamin, 381
The Skillful Housewife's Book, 303
Slade, M., 216
Slave food, 350, 377, 389
Slush, 89, 105
Small generals, 129, 154
Smallzreid, Kathleen, 48, 49
Smith, Belinda, 244
Smith, Captain Fred, 170, 188, 220, **265**, 266
Smith, Dr. Edward, 333
Smith, Sallie, 102, 103, 170, 175, 177, 178, 179, 182, 183, 188, 220, 265, 266, 267, 268, 269, 302, 304
Smoke chamber, 34
Smoking fish, 343-344
Smother, **132**, 133, 138
Smotheration, 133
Snow, Captain Ansel, 131
Snow pudding, **35**
Social teas, 312-313, 312-313
Soft tack, 105
Sounds (swim bladders), 127, 367-368
South Sea Islands, 201
South Street, New York City, **191**
Spanish American dining, 196
Spark's Bakery, Mystic, 66, 229, 385, 386
Sperry, Willard, 284-286, 290, 296
Spicer, J. D., 289
Spicer, William, 320
Spoilage, 33
Spouter Inn, 192
Spuds, 105
Squantum, 283, 284
Squash, cooked, **239**
St. Martin, Alexis, 333-334
Stanton, Leslie, 135
Stanton, Maria, 289
Steamship dining, 195
Stearn, Elinor, 239
Stetson, Ruth, 305
Stevenson, Charles, 344, 348, 377, 387
Stew, 108
Stewards, 89-92
Stewart D. W., 289
Stewart, E. Agnes, 291
Stillman, Charlotte. photo., 31
Stockfish, 373
The Stonington Cookbook, 291
Storage *See* Food storage,
Storms
  Dining disasters, 112
Story, Arthur, 134, 136
Story, Dana, 45
Stove (sea), 89, 93
Stover, Maria, 261
Stove technology, 8, 37-38, 199
Stowe, Harriet Beecher, 37, 69, 216, 236, 238, 244, 256, 257, 334
Strawberry festivals, 316-317
Strawberry picking, **317**

Street vendors, 195
Strickland, William, 368
Striped bass, 369-370
Succotash, **67**
Sucking the monkey, 173
Summer Yesterdays, 284
Supper, 16, 18-19, **30**, 49, 49, 69, **128**, **190**, 312
Surprise 176, 178, 180, 224
Swanky, 137, 140
Switchel, 137, 140
Syllabub, 319
Synot, John, 126

Table manners, 39, 132
Tack, 105
Taro, 199
Tattler, 133
Taves, Joe, **130**
Taylor, A. B., 289
Tea, 107-108, 137
Tea, social, **8**, 19, 20, 312-313
Tea (supper), 18
Teal, William, 155
Temperance movement, 21, 32, 64, 93, 219
Terrapin, 395
Thanksgiving, 235-245
  Church attendance, 238-239
  Dinner, **240**, 242-245
  History, 236-241
  Pies **234**
Thomas, Captain William, 137
Thomas, Thomas, 385
Thomas Gorton, 132, 137
Thomas Oyster Company, 385
Thompson, Jane L., 63
Thoreau, Henry, 68
Thousandth barrel of oil, 103
Tibbo, Winston, 137
Tiffin, 201
Tiger, 17, 89, 94, 97, 99, 100, 110, 111, 113, 117, 168, 171, 173, 175, 176, 178, 179, 182, 183, 198
Tinkham, Captain John, 202
Tin kitchen, **10**, 11, 13
Tin oven, 11, 12
Todd, Sarah Hix, 39, 95
Tongue, 312
Tormentor, 85, 151
Training cake, 22
Training Day, 21
Trammels, 9
Tripland, Charles, 379
Trollope, Frances, 193
Trout, 395
Tunny fish, 395
Turbot, 395
Turkey, 242-243
Turner, Thomas Larkin, 91, 96, 177, 203
Turtle, 179, 395
Two Years Before the Mast, 119, 194

Under Sail, 116
United States Coast Guard, 150
USS *Kearsarge*, 213, 223
Utensils, 9, 11, 35, 36, 37, 38, 65-66, 85-86, 97, 126, 151-152, 203

Vegetable gardens, **19**, 34, **40**, 41, 42
Vegetables, 15, 16, 47, 48, 67, 100, 102, 196
Vermin, 96
Vessel, Captain Gates, 242
Victor, 123, 137
Vignot, Majorie Maxson, 300, 305, 306
Villiers, Captain Alan, 168
Vinegar, 93

W. W. Brainard, 241
Wainwright, William, 213, 223
Walkley, Mary Angelina, 17, 18
Walkley, Stephen, 14, 17, 18, 19, 100
Wallace, Frederick, 131, 133
Warner, William, 389
Wasson, George, 138
Water boat, 126
Watermelon picnic, **286**
Water storage (sea), 95, 126
Water Supply
  Buckingham house, 9-10
  Burrows House, 63
  Deep water vessels, 93, 95-97
  Fishing schooners, 126
  Greenmans, 34
  Life-Saving Stations, 151
Water tanks, 126
Waters, C. D. 308
Watrous, Joseph, 289
Weakfish, 395
Webster, Thomas, 334, 384
Weddings, 103, 315
Weevils, 111
Weibust, Knut, 176
Weir, Robert, 180, 224
Well, 34
Well smacks, 336-337
Wendell, Captain George, 103
West Side Life-Saving Station, 314
Wet well, 336
Whalemeat, 180
Wheeler, Grace Denison, 45, 160, 239, 240, 241, 246, 251, 257, 258, 259, 268
Whidden, Captain John, 125, 138, 196, 197, 205, 206, 244, 245
Whips, 313
Whitcher, Mary, 295
Whitecar, William B. Jr., 267
White Fish, 395
Whittleseys, 6
Whymper, Frederick, 386, 388, 389
Wicks, Adelaide, 102
Wife's workload, 18
Wilbur, Captain Robert, 221
Wilcox, Captain Elias, 385
Wilcox, W. A., 390
Wiley, Dr. Harvey W., 334, 338, 366
William B. Herrick, 72, 80, **81**, 141, 144, 145
William Gifford, 172
Williams, John L., 101-102
Willis, 111
Wilson, C. Anne, 261
Wine, 21, 312
Winegar, Captain, 102
Winslow, Mrs. 57, 59, 227, 228, 250, 323, 397
Winthrop, John, 355
Women's National Relief Association, 152
Wonder Working Providence, 355
Wooden ware, 11
Work as fun, 284, 320
Wright, Julia, 76

Yale University, 6
The Yankee Whaler, 115
Yellow sugar, 137
York, Charlie, 126, 133, 137, 284
York, 223
Yorke, W. F., 178

NOTES